THE WORLD IN
1972

*This volume is dedicated to
the memory of Howard C. Heyn (deceased Dec. 3, 1972),
who served as editor of the Associated Press Yearbook
from 1969 through 1971*

THE WORLD IN
1972

History as we lived it...

by the
Writers,
Photographers,
Artists and Editors
of The Associated Press

CONTENTS

Foreword

Events that seemed certain to affect U.S. security and world peace for years to come dominated the news in 1972, raising hopes for a brighter era than we have seen in a long time. But, as always, there was a dark side to the picture.

The historic U.S. summits with Red China and the Soviet Union eased tensions between Washington and the two Communist powers and raised hopes briefly for peace in Indochina.

Fighting continued in Northern Ireland, and the Middle East smoldered, flaring fitfully as Arab terrorists struck and Israel retaliated.

It was a year in which the American Presidential election was marred by the attempted assassination of a candidate, and the peaceful theme of the Summer Olympics was shattered by a bloody massacre.

But a handsome young swimmer from California left Munich with seven gold medals, and in Iceland a gangling young man from Brooklyn upgraded chess as a U.S. sport with his temperamental antics and a brilliant playing style that defeated Russia's Boris Spassky for the world championship.

On the economic home front, hopes for a boom surged as the Dow-Jones industrial average broke through the 1,000 mark for the first time. But experts warned of a possible new wave of inflation.

Whether the news was good or bad, THE WORLD IN 1972 has attempted to present a true account through the writings of the men and women who covered these events and who make up the Associated Press.

Wes Gallagher

Wes Gallagher,
President and General Manager

Jan. 1, 1973

Dallas quarterback Roger Staubach tackled by a Miami defender ⟶

January

Staubach-Thomas Combo Led Dallas to Victory

By trouncing Miami Dolphins 24–3 in Super Bowl, Cowboys proved they could win the biggest of the big football games

1966—Dallas Cowboys win Eastern title in NFL; lose to Green Bay in NFL championship game.

1967—Dallas Cowboys win Eastern title in NFL; lose to Green Bay in NFL championship game.

1968—Dallas Cowboys win Capitol title in NFL; lose to Cleveland in Eastern championship game.

1969—Dallas Cowboys win Capitol title in NFL; lose to Cleveland in Eastern championship game.

1970—Dallas Cowboys win National Conference title in NFL; lose to Baltimore in Super Bowl.

*   *   *   *

ROGER STAUBACH was a Navy ensign and Duane Thomas still was talking to people in 1966, when the Dallas Cowboys began blowing the big ones.

At the end of the 1971 season Staubach was the team's No. 1 quarterback and Thomas was the club's No. 1 problem—and together they proved that the team which people said couldn't win the big games could win the biggest one of all very big.

For it was Staubach, the acknowledged "square," and Thomas, the tight-lipped non-conformist, who ended all those years of frustration for the Cowboys by leading them to a thoroughly convincing 24–3 Super Bowl victory over the Miami Dolphins.

What it meant to the members of the Cowboys was made evident by what was said after the game. It was only then that the Cowboys acknowledged that, just 60 minutes earlier, they were keenly aware of the uncomplimentary label which the football world had tied to their tail.

"Obviously, there was more pressure on us today," said guard John Niland. "You know—people saying we could not win the big ones. It was a long road. But we made it."

"I think I'll just go home and relax now and let this victory soak in," said running back Walt Garrison. "Unless there's one that is bigger than this, I don't think anyone will ever say again that we can't win the big ones."

"I don't think I'm really very conscious of my true personal feelings yet," said Coach Tom Landry. "I do know that I'll have a very restful night, and then is when I'll probably get to feeling just how much it means. I've spent a lot of nights in the past planning to rebuild."

The Dallas Cowboys had started building in 1960, their first year in the National Football League, and had been building ever since toward the moment when they would stand on top of pro football's world.

Finally, on Jan. 16, 1972, they stood there unchallenged.

Some of the component parts of the team that ultimately achieved the goal came early, particularly on defense, where two of the key performers—tackle Bob Lilly and outside linebacker Chuck Howley—had taken their place in 1961.

But Thomas and Staubach were late starters.

In 1970, as a rookie out of West Texas State, Thomas forced his way into the Dallas line-up, gained 803 yards, was voted Rookie of the Year on Offense in the NFC and then wound up traded to the New England Patriots.

Thomas' trade came as a result of a contract dispute with the club during which he lashed out at almost every Cowboy official, including Landry. His deportment was just as disturbing when he joined the Patriots. The New England club quickly returned Thomas to the Cowboys, and there, without a word, Dallas returned to the line-up one of the best running backs in the NFL.

Staubach took a totally different route. During his Navy career he drew a term of duty in a Vietnam supply depot. When he joined the Cowboys he was four years removed from his days as a Heisman Trophy winner and the club's third quarterback, behind Don Meredith and Craig Morton.

Staubach moved up to No. 2 when Meredith retired. But he still was behind Morton until the eighth game of the 1971 regular season, when Landry, who had unsuccessfully been alternating his two passers, suddenly turned the job over to the Square.

"I don't try to be anything but myself," he explained after the Super Bowl victory. "I have three children and another on the way. I'm a Christian and I have principles to live by, like caring about other people and being faithful to my wife.

"If that's square . . . that's the life I want to lead."

When Landry tapped him to lead, the Cowboys had a 4–3 record and were second in the NFC's Eastern Division. They proceeded to rip off seven consecutive regular season victories, defeat Minnesota 20–12 in a first-round playoff game and humble San Francisco 14–3 for the NFC championship.

That placed them in the Super Bowl opposite the Miami Dolphins, a Cinderella team which in only its sixth year of existence had been performing all sorts of heroics in a manner reminiscent of baseball's New York Mets in 1969.

First they won the Eastern Division title in the American Conference with a 10–3–1 record. Then they defeated Kansas City 27–24 in a first-round playoff game that went into sudden death and took 82 minutes and 40 seconds to complete. Finally they shut out Baltimore 21–0 for the AFC championship.

Even President Nixon sensed the hand of divine guidance and jumped on the Dolphins' bandwagon, using the proximity of his Key Biscayne, Fla., White House as an excuse to become a Miami fan.

The President became so enraptured with the Dolphins, as a matter of fact, that he felt compelled to call Miami Coach Don

Dolphins' receiver Paul Warfield going high in the air as he hauled in a pass from quarterback Bob Griese

Coach Tom Landry of Dallas carried from the field by his players after they defeated Miami

Shula and offer him a play for use in the Super Bowl against the Cowboys.

The play the President told Shula to use was a down-and-in pass from quarterback Bob Griese to wide receiver Paul Warfield, a play the Dolphins had used with consistent success during the year.

The Cowboys knew about that, but were more concerned with the Dolphins' running backs, Larry Csonka and Jim Kiick, who between them had amassed close to 2,000 yards rushing and were the prime movers in a ball-control offense.

Lilly, Howley and Co., however, took care of Csonka and Kiick, holding each of them to 40 yards gained; Mel Renfro ruined the President's play by guarding Warfield so closely he couldn't get free, and Staubach and Thomas took care of the rest.

Executing perfectly the plays Landry sent in from the sidelines, Staubach looked like a veteran of 10 years rather than three as he completed 12 of 19 passes for 119 yards, including a pair of seven-yard touchdown tosses to Lance Alworth and Mike Ditka.

Thomas ran with the ball 19 times for 95 yards, scored what Shula said was the touchdown that broke the game open and led the Cowboys to a Super Bowl rushing record of 252 yards gained on the ground.

The first break in the game came the second time the Dolphins had the ball, Csonka fumbling for the first time during the year and Howley recovering for Dallas on the Cowboys' 48-yard line.

The result was a nine-yard Mike Clark field goal and a 3–0 Dallas lead.

It remained that way until just over six minutes remained in the first half, when Staubach commenced firing from his own 24. Seventy-six yards later, including a 21-yard pass to Alworth and the seven-yarder to him for the touchdown, Dallas had a 10–0 lead.

The Dolphins, however, came back at this juncture to score their first points just before half time on a 31-yard field goal by Garo Yepremian. It was enough to leave Shula hopeful as the teams went to the dressing rooms.

"We figured if we could get our hands on the ball we could turn it around," Shula said afterward.

But Dallas took the second half kickoff and didn't relinquish it until Thomas took a pitchout on the three-yard line, raced to his left, cut in and scampered standing up into the end zone for a touchdown and a 17–3 lead that all but clinched it.

Thomas ran four times during the 71-yard drive, gaining 37 yards. Staubach tried one pass during the series and completed it for an 12-yard gain.

"The touchdown drive that opened the second half wiped us out," Shula acknowledged. "That put Dallas in a commanding position."

Shula knew what everyone knew—it was all over. It was except for a final Dallas touchdown early in the fourth quarter, when Staubach found Ditka in the end zone with a seven-yard pass.

When the time came for cooling off in the dressing room, Howley summed it up for all the Cowboys:

"We've been through some hard times," he said. "It took us a long time to believe in ourselves. But Coach Landry stayed with us, we kept at it, we worked hard and we finally became a complete club.

"Now, I think we have the makings of a dynasty, if you want to call it that, because we have confidence in our abilities and we are strong at all positions."

While Howley was talking Landry was answering the telephone. It was President Nixon.

He offered congratulations. He singled out the offensive line that had opened the holes for Thomas. And he linked Landry's name with Vince Lombardi's.

He never mentioned the down-and-in to Paul Warfield.

Growing Pains Apparent in New African Nations

Many of the 41 black countries that had become independent showed advancement, but old traditions still prevailed

Left, Snake dancer performing in the Portuguese East African territory of Mozambique. Below, Kenya President Jomo Kenyatta (right) welcoming President Julius Nyere of Tanzania

Natives of Kinshasa celebrating the eighth anniversary of the former Belgian Congo's independence

Many of the old traditions endured in Africa, despite the new freedom. Witch doctors were still a way of life, and poisoned arrows often spelled a quick exit from this world. But since 1960, when the new black nations began achieving statehood, a new continent had begun to emerge, one in which senseless violence was replaced by a desire for education and economic independence.

The heady thrill of independence was gone and with it the boundless optimism that initially had engulfed the independent governments which in January 1972 numbered 41. The leaders realized that they must still conquer disease, poverty and illiteracy to attain true freedom.

Improvements were visible on all sides, but many seemed to have little point. Television stations, a symbol of status, began sprouting all over Africa, but the average peasant had little hope of amassing the $200, or roughly four weeks wages in the more backward states, that he needed to buy a set.

In the early 1960s the fledgling governments put few of their resources into development, preferring to funnel money into presidential palaces, stadiums, armies and airlines.

Mali had poured a fortune into Soviet-built jets for limited international runs that had little need for such big ships, while Madagascar set up a costly domestic air route that made a big dent in its bankroll.

Black leaders had not seemed aware of the fact that a peasant's

future would have been made far brighter by a road that enabled him to get crops to the market than by peering up at a jetliner soaring six miles above his hamlet.

Progress had been gradual because old customs were hard to shake off, and tribal feuds often took precedence over nationalist pride. Nigeria was still paying the bill for its costly civil war, and Zaire, the former Belgian Congo, was nursing wounds suffered during its blood bath. But both nations had restored a semblance of order.

More than two dozen black nations had been involved in political upheavals of varying intensity between 1960 and 1972. Many of the first generation of nationalist leaders fell by the wayside in these struggles. Among those killed were Nigeria's Sir Abukabar Balewa, Togo's Sylvanus Olympio, the Congo's Patrice Lumumba and Kenya's Tom Mboya. Some, like Ghana's flamboyant Kwame Nkrumah, were unseated but managed to flee the country.

The average black was better off, however, if for no other reason than the fact that he was governed by fellow Africans rather than some remote colonial administration with little or no interest in his welfare.

Africa's dream of development was still far from realized. Many economic experts felt that the young black nations had been trying to get ahead too fast, and in some cases had depended too much on outside help. But the dream was as bright as ever, and African leaders remained convinced that, with their vast continent's resources and potentials, there would come a day when agriculture, industry and commerce would flourish.

In many cases attainment of the goal was thwarted by too much stress on industrialization and a resulting neglect of agriculture.

During the past year the lagging economies of many of the industrialized nations, including the United States, had reduced the demand for such African exports as cocoa, coffee, palm oil, rubber, tea, copper, iron ore, diamonds and other minerals.

But still African exports were nearly double the 1960 level of $6 billion. These exports provided the chief income and a good part of the development funds of black nations.

On the other hand, African monetary reserves were being drained by higher prices for imports, quickening the inflation spiral that plagued many black states.

By 1970 overall there were signs of improvement in the economic field. The era of massive official aid showed signs of ending as the interests of the industrial powers turned elsewhere. The days when foreign firms could move into an African country and carve out an industrial empire were apparently over. Instead, a partnership was developing between foreign investors and local governments. Foreign enterprise was still encouraged, but in most black states it was more closely controlled.

A good example was Zambia, where the copper industry, responsible for 95 per cent of that nation's exports, had been entirely owned by foreign interests. In 1970 things changed when Zambian authorities moved in and took over a 51 per cent interest in all mining companies. Nigeria, Ivory Coast, Cameroon and Zaire showed some signs of progress in oil, mineral or agricultural production.

In the two years since her civil war ended, Nigeria had become one of the world's top 10 oil producers. Every day 1.7 million barrels of crude were pumped out of the lush green wetlands of eastern Nigeria and new fields were being discovered. Newly negotiated higher prices for oil boosted revenues to an estimated $912 million in 1970–71 as compared to about $535 million in 1969–70.

Ivory Coast had become one of the most prosperous countries in West Africa. Riding the crest, it had launched a $900 million development program. The project called for some 90 per cent in public or government-financed investments. But there was still plenty of room for improvement. The glittering high-rise commercial center in Ivory Coast's capital, Abidjan, stood out in marked contrast to the city's crowded native quarter. But growing numbers of apartment blocks were brightening this drab area.

In Zaire, intensive plans were under way to put this once primitive nation into a more mobile state. The plans called for a new auto assembly industry, new roads and better waterways.

Zaire's transport system, suffering from the effects of prolonged civil strife, presented a major problem. Transportation difficulties had been a major obstacle to shipment of agricultural produce to both domestic and export markets.

Cameroon, a union of the former colonies of French and British Cameroons, had taken as its official languages those of both ex-colonizers, a fact that was proving to be an important economic asset. As a local educator pointed out, French was widely used in Africa, Canada and Asia as well as in Europe. On the other hand, knowledge of English had made it possible for Cameroon to do business with the entire British Commonwealth, Japan, Scandinavia, the Low Countries, Germany and even Italy, where English was the tongue used in international trade.

Language, however, was a problem in much of Africa, where up to a thousand tongues were in use. Discussion centered on the question whether an independent nation could retain the language it had learned from the white settlers or go back to tribal idioms.

In Senegal filmmakers were showing a preference for the Wolof vernacular, rather than French. In Kenya airline stewardesses had begun to announce takeoffs and landings in Swahili instead of English.

Despite the fact that hundreds of distinct languages were spoken in Africa, any discussion of their rival merits usually touched off tribal and regional hostilities.

In Uganda, for instance, the government was anxious to do away with English, but opposed Swahili as a substitute because it was spoken in neighboring Tanzania and Kenya. By the same token, advocates of a common tongue in Nigeria, would get into a hassle whether it would be Hausa, Yoruba or Ibo, all widely used in that sprawling nation.

Since few tribal dialects were spoken by more than a million persons or so, and many by far less, linguistic scholars were convinced that the European languages were the only solution.

Black Africa was still harassed by racial issues. The Portuguese holdings of Angola, Mozambique and Portuguese Guinea and the white-ruled nations south of the Zambesi River—South Africa and Rhodesia—had become a constant irritant to black militants. When they rose to power in 1960, many nationalist leaders had predicted that these white regimes would fail within a decade. Now they knew better. Guerrilla fighters had had little success against Portuguese territories. South Africa, although on the verge of an economic recession at the outset of 1972, was still the continent's most thriving economy, and Rhodesia's white minority regime showed little sign of collapsing, despite black pressure.

Still, racism remained the No. 1 target in the minds of the nationalists. The blacks had long looked on the white man as an oppressor who treated all Africans, educated or otherwise, as inferiors who had no real culture of their own but merely reflected the background of their colonial masters.

Nationalist leaders have asserted that European colonialism and the white man's attitude of superiority were the irritants that triggered the march to independence. When the leaders of 29 emerging nations gathered in Bandung in 1955 and vowed to wipe out colonialism around the world, the tone was set. By 1957 Ghana had become the first black nation to be freed from European domination, and Nkrumah trumpeted demands for freedom for the rest of the continent. By 1960 the parade to autonomy was in full stride.

A few years later, however, one young government after another began falling to the military. By early 1972 more than half the people of black Africa were under soldier rule, the result of more than 30 coups or abrupt government switches. The military governments were spending more than half a billion dollars on their armed forces, using internal police to guard the government along with the peace. Nigeria was pumping at least $250 million a year into its 250,000-man army, the largest standing force in black Africa. Army leaders who seized power usually followed the coup with promises to return the reins to civilians as soon as the soldiers got things in order. But the promises were rarely kept.

The surge of black nationalism that had gone hand in hand with these and other developments was usually coupled with a newborn pride in the early history of the African people. Scholars were poring through musty volumes, exploring the backgrounds of the black tribes before the European settlers arrived. A keen

Ethiopia's emperor Haile Selassie

interest in African art and poetry also began to emerge. But African ambition went much further than a revival of the old cultures. At United Nations headquarters black diplomats began to bill themselves as a Third Force, a buffer between East and West. Needless to say, this proved to be more figment than fact. Failing to achieve this role, African representatives to the U.N. General Assembly shifted gears and stepped up their perennial campaign to isolate South Africa and Portugal and to eliminate the white minority government in Rhodesia.

The blacks rammed a resolution through the Assembly several years ago which ruled that South Africa no longer had the right to govern its diamond-rich mandate of South West Africa. They followed this up with a vote in the Security Council calling for mandatory economic sanctions against Rhodesia. The move was aimed at obligating all U.N. members to stop importing key commodities from the white-ruled state and to cut off all Rhodesia's oil supplies.

It did not take the United Nations long to realize that they could never enforce such drastic measures by any means short of war.

South Africa made it plain to U Thant, then the Secretary-General, that it had no intention of abdicating its responsibilities toward the mandate. And Rhodesian Prime Minister Ian Smith, prime target of the African group, soon found that he could get all the oil he wanted from both South Africa and Portugal.

The United Nations may not have gone along with the Africans' extremist ideas, but its policy as to what should come under U.N. jurisdiction on the dark continent was not as logical as it might have been.

The black Africans put through repeated calls for a military crusade against apartheid, or racial discrimination, in South Africa. But these same black statesmen managed to block any intervention by the Security Council in the "internal affairs" of Nigeria, where thousands of Biafrans were killed or starved to death in the civil conflict *(The World in 1970, 8–12)*. Then too, the United Nations accepted what really amounted to overgrown tribes as full-fledged U.N. members, but it refused to consider the right to self-determination of 8 million Ibos in Nigeria, because that would have meant supporting the secession of one part of a state from another.

In the councils of the United Nations the Africans, with the help of their Asian colleagues, had to a considerable degree managed to swing the balance on key political issues. They also learned how to use to their own advantage the rivalry between the United States and the Soviet Union. They found that, by playing off one giant against the other, they could reap handsome rewards in the form of new hospitals, highways and fertilizer plants. However, by the end of 1971 a third giant, Red China, had entered the United Nations and the game had become a little more complicated.

When the European settlers left the dark continent they usually handed over the reins to ex-aides, Africans ingrained in the ways of European rule. Thus, not only did the white man's ways survive but many young states found themselves depending heavily on the Europeans.

Of 34 African airlines several had begun in recent years to use native pilots, but only Ethiopia, which had been independent for centuries, used native captains on its major runs. The European influence was still strong in British Africa; Malawi's supreme court was staffed by whites; British experts operated Zambia's communications systems, and Britons served as advisors in many of Kenya's government ministries.

Interest in agriculture had fallen off since independence, largely because the lot of the black farmer was a hard one. Much of the land was barren because in the semi-arid savannas it baked hard during the long dry season, and when it did rain the precipitation was too brief for the land to derive any real benefit. There were rain forests but, despite their luxuriant growth and lush appearance, they provided poor nourishment for food crops. There were still vast stretches of fertile land in Africa that would yield rich crops, but only if the farmer learned more modern methods of tilling the soil. Properly cultivated, these lands could feed all of Africa with plenty of produce left to export.

A young Biafran mother breast feeding her five-months-old baby while four-year-old daughter lay dying in her arms

Scientists More Hopeful In Battle Against Five Most Crippling Diseases

ARTHRITIS—a torturing malady dreaded the world over. Cavemen suffered from it 70,000 years ago. Even dinosaurs were afflicted, 60 million years earlier. As for the Twentieth Century, scientists in 1971 estimated that 50 million Americans were, in one degree or another, plagued by this extremely painful, often deforming disease.

Of these victims some 17 million were under medical care, 3.5 million of them disabled. Their illness represented a $3.6 billion loss in wages and medical expenses.

With the arrival of 1972 no positive cure had been developed for this ancient ailment, most prevalent of the nation's five greatest cripplers. The others: Cerebral palsy, cerebral stroke, muscular dystrophy and multiple sclerosis. The best that researchers could offer was "a sense of being at long last on the trail of the answers," as one authority phrased it. The National Health Education Committee reported: "Rheumatologists concur (that) arthritis research is . . . on the right track to making good progress where until recently investigators were, in effect, flying blind."

Their studies had shown that arthritis occurred in nearly 100 forms, throughout the body. The misery of 5 million Americans was laid to rheumatoid arthritis, considered the most destructive and dangerous variation, although certain experimental drugs inspired hope that effective procedures might be expectable by 1980.

A number of factors were responsible for the encouraging attitude of researchers pursuing possible causes of rheumatoid arthritis. One sign pointed to a slow-acting virus that remained unidentified. Another was the possible disturbance of the body's normal immunity mechanism, rendering victims dangerously allergic to their own tissues. A third proposed a combination of the first two. These other findings were cited:

—Aspirin, in doses up to 16 tablets daily, and other conventional drugs were employed successfully for partial relief. This was noted in special arthritic clinics, and more such centers were recommended.

—Deeper understanding of the self-perpetuating inflammatory process typical of rheumatoid arthritis.

—Fresh information on the reaction to drugs by inflamed arthritic joints.

—The encouraging effects of histadine, cyclophosphamide and other experimental drugs at a time when they had been tested by only a few doctors. Severe side effects, however, were displayed by cyclophosphamide, which had been used earlier against leukemia and certain other kinds of cancer because of its apparent bone-protecting action.

—Surgical correction of arthritic deformities, such as twisted, clawlike fingers and thumbs. Arthritis Foundation experts said this approach had produced results "undreamed of a few years ago." Implantations of silicone rubber in finger joints were among the recent surgical techniques. On the record was a secretary with crippled fingers who regained an 80-words-a-minute typing speed following such implants. Artificial hip joints had been given thousands of arthritics, most of them in Great Britain.

Another form of the ailment, chronic inflammatory arthritis of the spine, usually showed first among teenagers and those in their early 20s. One of its peculiarities was that it occurred in men 10 times more often than it affected women. And then there was old-fashioned gout—usually inherited—which headed straight for the big toe. A pedal extremity bandaged to the size of an elephant's foot once was a favored prop in comedies, but this kind of arthritis was no joke to Sir Francis Bacon or Benjamin Franklin. Gout, oddly enough, was the first type to succumb to the scientists, who produced drugs that controlled it and traced its cause to the over-production of uric acid, which deposited needle-like crystals in joints.

* * * *

Muscular dystrophy, a combination of some 30 diseases, had been aptly described as an appalling affliction: Its effect was the wasting away of muscle tissue. Its principal victims were young boys; among females its incidence was about one-fifth as frequent.

Confined to wheelchairs for life were about 50,000 completely disabled patients whose medical bills totaled about $125 million annually. Here again there existed no preventive or controlling treatment, no proven cure. Yet here again, as in arthritis, there was the element of hope.

This faith in the future was centered in an elaborate chicken coop.

Officially it was known as the Institute for Muscle Research, sponsored by the Muscular Dystrophy Association of America and located not in the countryside but in New York. Undergoing experimentation in this very scientific $5 million henhouse were 1,000 caged chickens of a special New Hampshire breed, suffering from a disease of hereditary origin similar to MD. In this unusual laboratory scientists found that chemicals extracted from vegetable oils, including those of yellow safflower plants, were capable of reversing, with some consistency, the symptoms in the chickens that resembled MD. However, treating humans with these chemical derivatives awaited further tests, said Dr. Ade Milhorat, the institute's director.

Patients in the research institute were limited to a meat-free diet because, one investigator explained, "most meat consists of muscle, and we'd rather not have it in the bodily waste products of these research patients since we're trying to assess the condition of their own muscles." With no specific medications extant, doctors designed gentle exercises to keep the muscles of patients extended to full length, to delay development of a

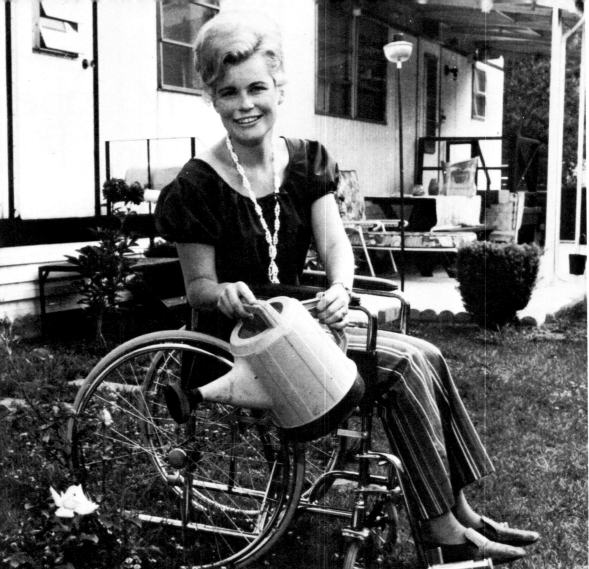
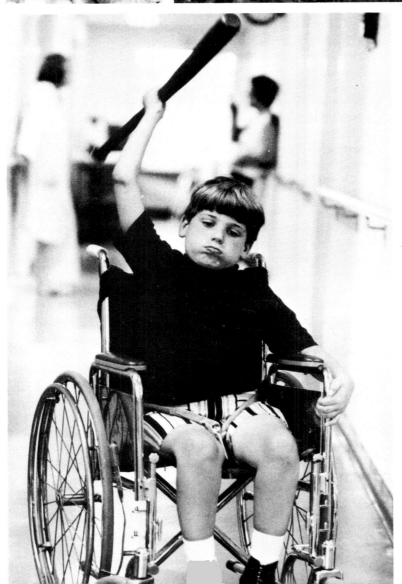

condition known as shortened joints. Encouraging results were achieved by a few physicians by tendon cutting or other surgical techniques.

The genetic aspect of MD did not bring a cure any closer but it did enable researchers to devise means for detecting up to 90 per cent of female carriers—women hereditarily doomed to produce offspring susceptible to MD. Mothers themselves rarely developed any MD symptoms. In identifying potential carriers scientists made use of a certain enzyme and conducted other tests. Dr. Carl Pearson of the Muscle Disorder Clinic, University of California at Los Angeles, said the ability to ferret out most carriers "provides a great opportunity for genetic counseling and for encouraging such women not to have children because of the risk."

Under investigation, he said, were these theories concerning the source of MD: A defect in the muscle cell membrane; faulty energy supply to the muscles; lack of the protein which normally caused muscle contraction; a primary disorder in the central nervous system or in branching nerves.

The most common—and most severe—variety of MD was Duchenne MD, named for the French physician who discovered its symptoms. Victims were boys 2 to 6, most of whom were confined to wheelchairs by age 11 and who died before reaching adulthood.

Left top, Mrs. Elizabeth Migliaro, shown (left) as Miss Connecticut of 1964, and after she was stricken with multiple sclerosis in 1968. Left bottom, a young victim of muscular dystrophy waving a plastic bat at New York's Institute for Muscle Research. Below, Dr. Louis La Borwit, left, assisted Dudley Raines, out-patient with speech therapy at Georgetown University Hospital. Raines had suffered a cerebral stroke.

* * * *

From infancy to old age, cerebral stroke was the nation's third most common cause of death, rated just behind heart disease and cancer. It was also the top killer among the crippling ailments. The battle against this often paralyzing brain disease had not been won, but medical science had determined that more had to be learned about high blood pressure and biological obstructions in the body's arteries.

Cerebral stroke, sometimes called apoplexy, took a $2 billion toll in yearly medical expenses. Aside from paralysis and numbness, strokes could cause brain damage, subsequent impairment of mental processes—and death within minutes, depending upon where, and how badly, the brain was injured.

Even so, death rates began to drop with advancement in treating hypertension and progress in identifying the first signs of an attack. Some cases wherein the stroke already had occurred were helped by surgical treatment. In the United States the most recent statistics available (1955–65) showed that stroke mortality went down 11 per cent overall and 20 per cent for persons in the 45–65 age bracket, which included most victims.

Specialists credited most of the decline in deaths to improved treatment of relatively minor attacks, thus probably forestalling a subsequent fatal stroke. This treatment included the use of anticoagulant drugs to prevent formation of clots in blood vessels and new drugs designed to dissolve clots already formed. At the same time an intensified search was launched for improved anticoagulants, clot dissolvers and drugs that would allow the brain's blood vessels to open as widely as possible.

For many years surgical treatment was confined to correcting flaws in the larger external arteries leading to the brain. Then surgeons started operating on relatively large arteries within the brain cavity itself, and a few specialists even went to work on the tiny blood vessels within the brain.

"The person known to have a greater risk of stroke," the U.S. Public Health Service reported, "probably has one or more of these problems: Overweight, a diet high in fats, high blood pressure, tobacco smoking." Dr. Fletcher McDowell, of Cornell University Medical Center in New York, maintained that World War II bolstered the argument against heavy animal fat diets. When most Europeans were reduced to Spartan diets during the war, the incidence of strokes and coronary artery disease declined acutely, he said.

Atherosclerosis was a major stroke cause because, according to the latter theory—still challenged by some researchers—its sufferers favored diets rich in animal fats and carbohydrates. Characteristic of atherosclerosis was the semi-glutinous—or porridge-like—deposit that formed on the inner linings of blood vessels, and this description no doubt explained the origin of the ailment's name: The term atherosclerosis was derivative from the Greek word for porridge (athere).

Blood vessel blockage of this nature also was known as biological rust. This sludge accumulated slowly, narrowing the vessels and slowing the blood flow. Or a clot could form and, upon breaking free, become a blood dam in such vital areas as the brain, heart or lungs. The result could be a stroke.

On the research front several defensive techniques were explored. One idea proposed was the use of a so-called fiber optics device to transmit high-intensity light through the skin to the brain cavity, thus permitting examination of the brain's circulatory system. Such light-amplification devices already had been used by the armed forces as aids in seeing in the dark.

Stroke victims who survived were not necessarily destined to lives of helplessness. The Public Health Service reported that 90 per cent of those paralyzed on one side of the body could be taught to walk again "and 30 per cent can be taught to do gainful work." However, Dr. McDowell and Dr. Margaret Kenrick, chief of Georgetown University Medical Center's physical medicine division, were not so optimistic. Dr. Kenrick said "practically any stroke victim can be taught to walk again. But restoring the functional use of an affected arm is something else."

Dr. McDowell agreed that mildly paralyzed persons "can be taught to a large degree, but patients who come to the hospital with severe paralysis in the first place don't do too well after they leave."

* * * *

Of the great cripplers multiple sclerosis apparently has been the most particular about those persons it attacked: Young adults in their prime years, most of them members of higher social and economic groups. Except in some Asian countries, residents of temperate latitudes have been more susceptible than residents of warmer climates. Most have been between 20 and 40 years old. Worldwide, victims have numbered about two million; in the United States, 250,000.

As insulation safeguards electric wires, so does a substance called myelin protect human nerve fibers. Characteristic of MS is the spotty degeneration of myelin's fatty sheath. This sclerosis—or scarring—of the sheath can lead to distortion and sometimes blockage of nerve messages controlling sight, speech, balance and walking. Symptoms can include extreme weakness, tremor, slurred speech, tingling and numbness. As the disease progresses, symptoms can appear and disappear.

Multiple sclerosis often has been difficult to diagnose. Even so, various specialists voiced new, guarded optimism that means for preventing or controlling the disease would be found ultimately. The National Institute of Neurological Diseases stated that "more and more knowledge is being gathered as investigators dig deeper into its origins and behavior."

The institute said patients live longer than was thought possible years ago. "Many people with mild or even moderately severe cases can live normal lives and work regularly for years." Some researchers have reported that up to 50 per cent of the MS cases were not invariably progressive, totally crippling or as often fatal as was once believed. Some of the hopeful signs:

—Remission from MS symptoms may last months or years, raising the possibility that, during such periods, protective treatment could be effective.

—The geographic distribution of victims had suggested that an environmental factor could be significant.

—Increasing indications that MS could be a type of disease in which the victim would become allergic to his own tissues, including nervous system tissue. In the view of some researchers, such an allergy might be set up by a virus that remained unidentified. Prominent suspects would be viruses that remained dormant in the body for perhaps 20 years before touching off degenerative reactions.

Dr. Harry Weaver, medical and research director of the National Multiple Sclerosis Society, said: "As recently as five years ago, scientists had an attitude as regards MS that this was always a progressive, devastating disease." But, he added, it is now known that, after one attack attributable to the MS process, a victim may spend the rest of his life symptom-free. Said Dr. Norman Namerov, director of the MS clinic at the University of California at Los Angeles Medical Center:

"It's true that I have some patients who become completely bed-ridden after their first illness and remain so, but a diagnosis of MS is definitely not synonymous with a wheelchair, crippled

existence." He estimated that between 40 and 50 per cent of MS patients could "go through life without major disability."

* * * *

The lack, or impairment, of control over voluntary muscles that normally move arms and legs; such symptoms as convulsive seizures, spasms, mental retardation, abnormal sensation and perception; impairment of sight, hearing and speech—all are prime indicators of cerebral palsy. By the end of 1971 no cure had been found for this disease, the cause of damage to the brain or nervous system before birth. However, as in other crippling afflictions, scientists recently uncovered signs that they may be on the trail of preventive measures in a substantial number of such cases. Additionally, they learned that much could be done to rehabilitate cerebral palsy victims.

American cerebral palsy sufferers numbered 750,000 to one million. More than 350,000 were under 21, and at least 25,000 babies were born with it annually. Known prenatal causes included prematurity of birth, complications in the mother's labor and delivery, accidents resulting from the RH factor or other metals.

At the La Jolla, Calif., campus of the University of California, Dr. Kennth J. Ryan, an obstetrician, was a leading developer of the theory that many premature births might be prevented if ways could be found to control artificially the hormonal relationship between the mother and the embryo in the womb. In his opinion this relationship could be of key importance in preserving the normal human gestation period of 257 days. To this end Dr. Ryan was studying the gestation periods of rats, monkeys, armadillos, sows and hedgehogs. Female elephants were of special interest to him because they could produce babies without special aid during gestation. Responsible for this was the male hormone progesterone, which nearly all mammals appeared to require, he said.

Dr. Eddie Wei, a scientist at the university's Berkeley, Calif., campus, was seeking to learn if prenatal or post-birth diseases of the nervous system could be caused by low doses of metals present in the environment. These would include lead, mercury and manganese. Dr. Wei, an environmental health physiologist, held that high doses could be hazardous, citing mental retardation among some slum children from lead poisoning after nibbling chips of lead-based paint that peeled from their walls.

Last fall Dr. Wei was a member of a group of California scientists who warned pregnant women not to eat any sport fish. "Lead and methylmercury are of special interest in our latest research because they are already present in food," he said, "and manganese will become a possible problem if it is accepted for use as a fuel additive to prevent smoke."

The feeling that advances in the fight against cerebral palsy had been made by government and private research was supported by these achievements:

—An effective vaccine against German measles. Normally this is a mild disease, but it can cause cerebral palsy or other congenital defects in an unborn child if the mother contracts it during the first three months—and sometimes during the second three months—of pregnancy.

—A serum which shows promise of impeding many cerebral palsy cases due to RH blood factor incompatibility between mother and fetus, if given within 72 hours of delivery or miscarriage of an RH-positive baby by an RH-negative mother.

—A technique for administering blood exchange transfusions to newborn infants threatened with cerebral palsy or certain defects attributable to other blood-type incompatibilities.

DENMARK'S KING DEAD AT 72

Standing on the first floor balcony of Copenhagen's Christianborg Palace, Premier Jens Otto Krag intoned the news three times:

"King Frederik IX is dead. Long live Her Majesty Queen Margrethe II."

Thus the people of Denmark were informed officially of the death on Jan. 14 of their popular, 72-year-old monarch and the succession of his pretty 31-year-old daughter to the throne.

Frederik had openly enjoyed many of the special privileges that went with his royal status. But he was basically a bourgeois ruler who answered the telephone himself and liked to pedal his bicycle around Copenhagen, dropping casually into bookshops and stores.

Frederik's ceremonial attire was an admiral's uniform, a sign of his lifelong interest in the Danish navy, through whose ranks he had advanced as a young man. It was as a sailor that Frederik acquired his fondness for tattoos that caused amusement among his subjects. His arms and chest were decorated with a handsome assortment of dragons and birds.

The king also had a passion for physical fitness. He patronized a professional body builder and took a correspondence course that expanded his chest measurement to 45 inches and his biceps to 15 inches. This prompted a London newspaper to describe him as the strongest monarch in history. He died of pneumonia, complemented by a heart attack.

Frederik liked to get away from affairs of state and cruise Denmark's coast and islands. He also had a fondness for trains and was often seen at the throttle of a locomotive on a test run.

Like her father, Margrethe was informal and enjoyed shopping for herself. She often arrived at places surreptitiously to avoid attracting attention.

King Frederik, Denmark's popular sailor king

Margrethe became Denmark's first reigning sovereign queen. The first Margrethe who ruled Denmark, Norway and Sweden from 1387–1412 was a regent, not a sovereign.

Known as a woman of lively views, Queen Margrethe had many talents. They ranged from archeology to ju-jitsu and from classical music to tennis, skiing and swimming. She also learned five languages.

She was married in 1967 to Count Henri de Laborde de Monpezat, a French diplomat who became Prince Henrik. They had two sons.

HAYDEN, DEAN OF SENATE, DEAD

When Carl T. Hayden attended Stanford University in the 1890s he lost a runoff contest for president of the student body. It was the only political defeat ever suffered by the noted legislator who served for 42 years in the U.S. Senate, longer than any man in the nation's history.

Hayden, who died Jan. 25 at the age of 94, had also served in the House for 14 years, making his total Congressional service 56 years. He was known by his colleagues for his political sagacity, his dedication to Senate traditions and his ability to make friends. He was also known as a prodigious worker who described himself as a workhorse.

Hayden began his national political career in 1912, going to Congress as Democratic representative of the new state of Arizona. In 1926 he was elected to the Senate, serving seven terms.

Hayden, who had been born in Tempe, Ariz., was one of his home state's most loyal boosters. President Franklin D. Roosevelt was reported to have asked the senator why he insisted on talking about the roads whenever he visited the White House. Hayden reportedly replied: "Because Arizona has two things people will drive thousands of miles to see—Grand Canyon and the Petrified Forest. They can't get there without roads."

Hayden was instrumental in establishing the modern formula for the vast Federal highway aid program. He also backed legislation in the fields of mining, public lands, reclamation and other projects affecting his Western area.

In 1957 Hayden became dean of the Senate, an honorary and unofficial title going to the legislator who had served longest in the Senate. He also became president pro tem of the Senate because the Democratic party to which he belonged was in the majority. As president pro tem, he presided in the absence of the Vice President.

In 1963, after the assassination of President John F. Kennedy, Hayden found himself second in line for the Presidency at an age when most of his political contemporaries had passed from the scene.

He became Acting Vice President and served until Sen. Hubert H. Humphrey was sworn in as Vice President in January 1965.

On Sept. 30, 1968, Hayden, then 91 years old, realized a cherished dream when President Lyndon B. Johnson signed into law the Lower Colorado River Basin Bill. Passage of the measure came just in time; he retired shortly thereafter. Hayden had already declared that he would not seek reelection to an eighth term.

Former Sen. Carl Hayden, who had served out the longest congressional term in the history of the United States

AFRICA TOURED BY MRS. NIXON

Wherever she went on the Dark Continent, America's First Lady was greeted by cheering African crowds. And she plainly enjoyed the festivities as much as did her hosts.

On Jan. 9, Mrs. Richard M. Nixon wound up an eight-day, 10,000-mile air tour of the West African nations of Liberia, Ghana and Ivory Coast. Official purpose of the journey was to represent her husband at the inauguration of William R. Tolbert Jr., as 19th president of the Republic of Liberia, formed 150 years earlier by freed American slaves.

After a gruelling nine-hour flight to Liberia followed by a 12-hour day of state activities, Mrs. Nixon told a news conference that "being First Lady is the hardest unpaid job in the world."

Greeted by a 19-gun salute usually reserved for heads of state, Mrs. Nixon was welcomed in a red carpet ceremony and proceeded to review the Liberian honor guard.

Tolbert, a 58-year-old Baptist minister, hailed Mrs. Nixon as a woman of "courage, strength of character and fortitude of spirit." He presented her with the Grand Cordon of the Most Venerable Order of Knighthood of the Pioneers of the Republic of Liberia.

The following day Mrs. Nixon was treated to a special entertainment at Monrovia's Executive Mansion. In honor of the occasion, she wore a blue lappa suit, with a bouffant head scarf, and tapped her feet to tribal drums.

In Accra, capital of Ghana, Mrs. Nixon was met at the airport by hundreds of Ghanaians singing and playing drums. At the tribal home of Chief Nana Osae Djan II, the First Lady sat next to her host while ladies brought her a garland of kente cloth and baskets of fruit.

Later she met Ghana's president, Edward Akufo-Addo, at his hilltop palace in Accra while seven heralds sounded a greeting on elephant tusk horns.

Her final stop was in a drizzling rain at the Ivory Coast capital of Abidjan. But despite the weather a crowd of 75,000 turned out to see the American visitor. They included men wearing feathers and tribal masks and women shaking gourds that rattled. This stop was climaxed by a lavish banquet at the palace of President Felix Houphouet-Boigny.

The trip brought to 74 the number of foreign nations Mrs. Nixon had visited.

Mrs. Richard M. Nixon smiling as Liberian women dressed her in their native costume

ANCIENT HISTORY VS. PROGRESS

As bulldozers and plows dug into American soil to make way for land developments, reservoirs and highways, archeologists feared that the nation's ancient history was being sacrificed.

The largely unstudied record of prehistoric man in the United States embraced thousands of sites dating back perhaps 20,000 years and including everything from entire cities to camps where bands of hunters stopped for a few nights. But some scientists contended that such sites were only partially uncovered when land developers started building, on the premise that construction was greater in value than ancient relics. Explorers cited:

—One of the most important sites of the relatively recent Adena phase of Indian culture in Delaware was destroyed by highway construction.

—A federally sponsored watershed project in Kansas dug gravel from a tract containing 30 hearths where men had kindled fires more than 2,000 years ago.

—One of the greatest archeological losses was suffered in 1969 in Washington state when a federally built dam on the Snake River flooded one of the oldest known sites of human remains in the Western Hemisphere. Along a section of the river scientists had discovered the 13,000-year-old remains of a group of humans called Marmes Man. Only 25 per cent of the site had been excavated when the dam was flooded.

"Pothunters," as some amateur archeologists were called, also destroyed numerous sites. Eager for an arrowhead or ancient bone, they often disregarded telltale signs of the site's early history. Some "pothunters" had dug huge holes and stripped them of artifacts in a single afternoon, scientists said. Strip mining and a new agricultural implement—the subsoiler that plowed three feet or more into the ground—also threatened many sites.

Numerous exploring parties reported their budgets were so low that only a fraction of the sites could be saved. Another problem they cited was the failure of the government to identify adequately historic sites and provide funds to study them.

TWO FREED IN WAR CRIMES TRIAL

Dummy showers were mounted in the ceilings of the Nazi gas chambers at the concentration camp in Auschwitz, Poland. Camp signs leading there read: "To the baths."

In reality the "showers" were baths of death, spewing deadly fumes. Within adjoining rooms, disguised as disinfection chambers, were quarters where gold teeth and hair were salvaged from bodies.

Three million Jews lost their lives in Auschwitz between the years of 1941 and 1945.

Walter Dejaco, 63, and his aide, Fritz Karl Ertl, 64, both Austrians, were brought to trial Jan. 18, charged with premeditated murder of those Jews. Dejaco was accused as the designer and builder of the gas chambers and cremation furnaces at the camp.

The indictment held that Auschwitz was not even fit for animals, that it was devoid of ventilation, and that its huts were overcrowded with bunks.

Dejaco, the indictment read, was so proud of his designs that he exhibited his construction plans in his office until the SS told him to remove them because the project was secret.

The seven-week trial, in Vienna, brought forth 60 witnesses, some of them former Auschwitz inmates who were unable to identify the defendants fully or recall their exact jobs.

Dejaco himself had stated that he did not know what he was building and that he had been.forced to make the designs. Many witnesses disputed this, however, testifying that the presence of gas chambers at Auschwitz was common knowledge.

Dejaco and Ertl were acquitted. They could have received sentences of one year to life in prison had they been convicted.

The trial, first in Austria involving Auschwitz, was inspired largely by Simon Wiesenthal of the Jewish Documentation Center in Vienna, who approached several Austrian governments before a prosecutor was assigned to the case full time.

Dejaco had been denounced in reports to the Austrian authorities in June 1961, but he remained free for another ten years before his trial and acquittal.

Twenty-four sky divers holding hands to form a "star" as they bailed out of three planes at 14,500 feet over Perris Valley airport near Riverside, Calif. They claimed a world record for such a feat

NON-RESIDENTS GIVEN WELFARE

In 1971 New York and Connecticut enacted laws barring state welfare aid to persons in residence there for less than one year. However, two Federal District Courts thereafter struck down these statutes on the ground that they were transparent efforts to circumvent the U.S. Supreme Court's 1969 ruling, 6–3, against such residential requirements.

On Jan. 24, 1972, the Supreme Court unanimously affirmed the decisions of the two lower courts in deciding against New York's appeal.

This ultimatum was greeted by Connecticut Atty. Gen. Robert Killian with the opinion that the 1972 ruling would accelerate federal assumption of welfare costs. And New York's Gov. Nelson Rockefeller commented that welfare costs were "clearly a national problem. Allocation of welfare to the federal level is essential to avoid the fiscal bankruptcy of state and local governments and to end the social and moral bankruptcy of the present welfare system."

Colorado, Rhode Island, Utah and West Virginia also had enacted "emergency" residence laws, but these likewise had been overturned by lower courts.

CONGRESSMAN OUSTED BY RUSSIA

To those who knew him the expulsion of New York Rep. James H. Scheuer from the Soviet Union did not come as a complete surprise. The energetic Democratic liberal from the Bronx had had more than one brush with authorities in the United States since he first ran successfully for the House of Representatives in 1964.

His first run-in with the law came in 1964 when he was among a dozen officials of the American Jewish Congress arrested for picketing the Jordanian Pavilion at the New York World's Fair.

Scheuer made his trip to Moscow as a member of a Congressional group to study educational institutions and stayed on in a private capacity. As a Jewish Congressman from a heavily Jewish district, he was anxious to inform himself about the lot of Jews in the Soviet Union.

On Jan. 12 Scheuer was picked up by Moscow police as he was visiting a Jewish family that had refused emigration to Israel. On Jan. 14 Scheuer was expelled from the Soviet Union on charges of "improper activities." It was believed to be the first such act involving an elected American official.

U.S. Embassy political counselor Thompson R. Buchanan expressed regret that Soviet authorities should have taken such a "grave step." He added that it would "not be helpful to relations" between the two countries.

Said Scheuer: "I did have social contacts with some (Jews) who want to leave." But the 51-year-old legislator denied that he had tried to persuade anyone to flee the Soviet Union.

"They had made up their minds long before I arrived," he declared.

FOR THE RECORD

RESIGNED. Secretary of Commerce Maurice H. Stans, to become chief fund raiser for President Nixon's reelection campaign. The day of the resignation, Jan. 27, President Nixon nominated Peter G. Peterson, the White House assistant for international economic affairs, to replace Stans. Peterson was chairman of the Bell and Howell Co. in Chicago before going to Washington in 1971.

Left, a new portrait of Britain's Queen Elizabeth II by artist Joseph Wallace King of Winston-Salem, N.C. Below, the same month the portrait of Britain's queen was unveiled the former luxury liner bearing her name burned in Hong Kong

The donkey, symbol of the Democratic party

GOP elephant with trunk aloft

U.S. Two-Party System: Was it on the Way Out?

Political professionals behind the scenes held the view that both Republican and Democratic alliances were unable to solve the problems of war, poverty and racism

FOR YEARS, Republican had battled Democrat for support from the same broad middle ground of American society, blurring distinctions between the contenders until they had begun to resemble identical twins. Now it looked as if America's two-party system might be on the way out.

"There's not a dime's worth of difference between the two," George Wallace had declared in his independent campaign for president in 1968.

Political professionals viewed the causes as rooted in the failure of both Republican and Democratic parties to solve the problems of war, poverty and racial enmity and to offer true alternatives.

The visible consequence of ignoring the political perimeter was the diminishing number of Americans who identified themselves with either major party. Another development was the growth of splinter parties on the left and right, and the first stirrings toward a coalition of these seemingly incompatible forces.

The common ground they shared was an old-fashioned populism; programs that, in effect, demanded a redistribution of wealth.

Historians and political scientists foresaw the possibility of the United States entering a situation similar to that of France after World War II and Italy in the past year, with neither major party able to command broad public support, and government turned over to shaky coalitions.

The challenge came from 25 million American voters—20 per cent of the electorate—who refused to give allegiance to either national party.

While still trailing far behind the Democrats, the number of independents rivaled the 38 million who, according to a Gallup poll taken in 1972, would register as Republicans. This independent sector had totaled only 6.2 million in 1960, and the prospect of such an increase over a long period alarmed many party politicians.

"It all goes basically to the fact people don't think too much of us so-called politicians," remarked Leonard W. Hall, long-time power in the Republican party and National Committee chairman under President Dwight D. Eisenhower.

Analysts agreed that public disgruntlement was rooted in the problems which had endured in both Republican and Democratic administrations, compounded by a weakening of the parties' structures and a blurring of distinctions between the two.

Commenting on Wallace's claim that there was little difference between Republican and Democrat, Democratic chairman Lawrence O'Brien said "I think this reflects an attitude of wonderment and concern with both parties.

"Our response to the challenge internally," O'Brien said, "is to insure that this party is totally reformed and democratized. If we do not reform, this party will perish and consequently so will the system.

"I do not envision a movement to three, four and five parties," he said. "I don't think most Americans feel this is in the best interests of the nation. But it could be the result if we don't get our jobs done."

The Republican chairman, Sen. Robert Dole of Kansas, contended that the growth in independent registration might be more due to apathy.

"What erosion we see is among registered Democrats," he said. "We see our registration as fairly stable."

This view was not borne out by a Gallup Poll showing that the Republicans had decreased from 40.4 million in 1960 to an estimated 38 million as of November 1971. But even Democratic growth did not keep pace with soaring numbers of independents.

Such studies caused Leonard Hall to wonder whether a party should at some point die, leaving its followers to regroup under a new name and structure with new ideals.

"Fifteen years ago I would have said you were nuts to think of it," said Hall. "Maybe you are not today.

"We're tending in the direction of multiple parties. Nixon won with 43 per cent of the vote. If you have four tickets in the field, I can see a president winning with less than 40 per cent of the vote. So we are on that road; how far I don't know."

Political analyst Frederick J. Dutton, deputy chairman of John F. Kennedy's 1960 presidential campaign, expressed belief that the spreading estrangement of Americans from the two traditional parties represented an important shift in the mainstream of American politics.

"This is the first time in well over a century that the independent sector has been as large as one of the two main parties," Dutton wrote in an article for the U.S. Information Service.

"The over-all drop in party loyalty is reflected not only in the polls but also in the spreading extent of ticket splitting. . . . This occurred on less than one-fifth of the ballots 20 years ago. Now it is done on over half."

Clark Clifford, longtime adviser to Democratic presidents and secretary of defense under Lyndon B. Johnson, said:

"It is entirely possible, as time goes on and erosion continues, it will reach the point where our system will operate so poorly that a drive must develop to recreate interest in the parties."

Party professionals agreed that the loss of millions of voters was partly due to structural weaknesses in party machinery.

Len Hall recalled that, when he first ran for Congress, the Republican party provided the funds.

"I notice today every candidate has to raise his own money," he said. "That makes him independent. So now we have a situation with each fellow on his own, and he does what he thinks is attractive to get money and votes.

"The fact is, there is no more party control, no caucus, from the county level on up. Now we don't have respect for the party."

Political scientist James MacGregor Burns scored the Democratic party in testimony before the party's reform commissions in November 1971. Among his complaints:

—"It lacks strong organization at the state, congressional district and local level; it has no sure foundation or structure among the great rank-and-file of the party.

—"In power it neither helps and sustains the President enough in domestic policy nor contains and stabilizes him enough in foreign policy.

—"Out of power it neither opposes the Republican party with enough vigor and consistency nor presents, clearly and creatively enough, an alternative course of action on which the party agrees."

Burns argued that, of all these failures, the most crucial was the failure to carry out its platform promises, which he termed essentially a failure to control the congressional wing of the party.

This complaint was echoed by Sen. Fred Harris, D-Okla., who appointed Democratic party reform commissions.

"We Democrats actually have a presidential party and a congressional party divided into House and Senate units," he said. "And each is independent of the other. They have been largely non-ideological. I think that's why nobody is particularly excited by the party label."

Karl Hess, who moved from chief speech writer for conservative Republican Barry Goldwater in the 1964 campaign to secretary of education of the People's party "shadow cabinet," declared that the Republicans and Democrats were trying to frighten people into thinking that the nation would crumble without a two-party system.

"But hell, we haven't had a two-party system in a long time," he said. "We just have one."

Both the Democratic and Republican parties attempted in 1971 to make their structures more responsive to public requirements through reforms intended to make sure that women, young people and blacks would be represented on national convention delegations "in reasonable relationship" to their numerical strength in the population. The Democrats tried to make these changes mandatory, the Republicans voluntary.

Marcus Raskin, of the Institute for Policy Studies, said such reforms were ridiculous.

"The notion that a Mississippi tenant farmer has a vote in the party process equal to the president of NBC is ridiculous if not stupid," he said.

"You never hear talk in the national parties of economic democracy, and people are demanding that," he said.

Joe Barrett, a precinct worker for George Wallace and a registered Republican, insisted that "there is not a damn bit of difference between Nixon and Maine Sen. Edmund Muskie.

"The so-called liberals have had the parties since 1932, and since that time nothing has been done," he said. "This kind of system doesn't work, and you and I know the average guy can't get into politics to do a damn thing about it."

Chairman of the Republican National Committee, Sen. Robert Dole, talking to newsmen in Miami about the GOP convention site

Democratic National Committee Chairman Lawrence O'Brien held a news conference in Albuquerque, N.M., before he spoke to a joint session of the state legislature

The Olympics: Discord and Drama at Sapporo

Sapporo high school boy running with the torch that opened the 11th winter games

"Yokoso."

THE JAPANESE WORD for "welcome" blared out at the visitor from everywhere—from a thousand blinking light bulbs atop miniature skyscrapers, from store fronts and from decals plastered on lamp posts, taxicabs and rubbish cans.

The Winter Olympic Games had come to Asia for the first time—the eleventh international spectacle of ice and snow—and Sapporo, a bustling metropolis of more than a million people hewn out of the stark wilderness of Japan's northernmost island of Hokkaido, was all dressed up and prepared to be the perfect host.

Bunting flapped from overhead wires. Giant ice sculpture, representing characters of fiction and fantasy, stretched out for blocks on end in the mid-town section like a frozen, unmoving Macy's parade. The city was an eye-straining cascade of neon lights. Glasses tinkled merrily in 3,000 cubbyhole bars of the honky-tonk section known as Susukino.

A sign in the fashionable Park Hotel, headquarters of the Olympic brass, reflected what was to prove an intriguing Japanese problem with English translation. The sign said:

"Please stay on with the coats."

In the distance, snowy mountain peaks—sites of the glamorous Alpine ski races, the exhausting cross-country events, the breathtaking leaps and bobsled runs—stabbed into a blue sky. Bone-chilling winds blew off the Sea of Japan from Siberia, just across the way.

On a clear day, Sapporo looked like a picture postcard.

It was to this once raw and raucous outpost that the world's greatest snow and ice performers—1,128 from 35 countries—assembled for a ten-day quest of gold, silver and bronze medals.

The Russians looked bearish in their full-length fur coats and fur hats. The East Germans, who proved the surprise of the Games, were attired in rich sealskin. The Argentines had red gaucho capes and the French were smart in dark, fitted uniforms. The American men looked uncomfortable in their wide-brimmed leather hats and boots from a mail order house.

No one needed suffer from a language barrier. Hundreds of the brightest and prettiest daughters of Nippon, multi-lingual young girls in white fur-trimmed coats and fur hats, served as interpreters.

Always smiling and overly polite, they were at every turn.

"May I help you, sir?"

"Please, sir."

"Thank you, sir."

Dedicated to international good will and peace among peoples, Olympic Games traditionally are inclined to be rent by politics, nationalism and controversy. The Sapporo Games proved no exception.

Arriving in Sapporo a week before the official opening, Avery Brundage, crusty, 84-year-old president of the International Olympic Committee and long a champion of pure amateurism, warned that he had proof that a large number of Alpine skiers had violated the amateur code and faced disqualification.

Reportedly, he had the goods on 30 or 40 of the world's best skiers, principally Austrians and French, who, he said, had lent their names and pictures for advertising purposes. He called them "trained seals" of the manufacturers.

There was apprehension among the Japanese organizers that their years of work and millions of dollars invested in the Games might be nullified.

However, on January 31, three days before the official opening, the International Olympic Committee announced that one competitor—Karl Schranz, former World Cup champion from Austria—had been declared ineligible for the Games.

The Japanese breathed a sigh of relief. Schranz, most observers agreed, was the sacrificial lamb—a price to be paid to feed Brundage's pride without completely destroying the Games.

Austrian officials objected stoutly and threatened to pull out their entire skiing team, one of the world's best. They stayed in after a dramatic staged appeal by Schranz, who returned home to a hero's welcome in Vienna.

On February 3, Emperor Hirohito declared the Games officially open before more than 53,000 in the glistening Makomanai Stadium. Wearing a fur coat and hat and sun-glasses, the Japanese ruler stood stiff-backed and without a twitch of an eyelash during the colorful parade of the athletes. The torch was lit, the flame to burn unceasingly throughout the contests.

Within less than 24 hours, the XI Winter Olympic Games had their first hero, a tall, handsome speed-skater from The Netherlands named Ard Schenk.

Schenk, 27, a bachelor, medical student and holder of numerous world records, sped around the oval track of the Makomanai Stadium to cheers of a small group of Dutch supporters to win the 5,000 meter race in 7 minutes, 23.61 seconds.

It was only one of three he was to win to establish himself as the No. 1 individual star of the Games, just as France's Jean-Claude Killy had done at Grenoble, France, with three Alpine skiing medals four years before.

Although speed skating is basically dull, with the competitors churning around the track in pairs in a race against the clock, Schenk drew sell-out crowds to the big stadium.

"He's gorgeous," one female fan was heard to remark.

"He looks like Prince Valiant," said another, of the 6-foot-2, 185-pound Dutchman with the long, ear-covering gold hair.

Schenk also won the 1,500 and 10,000 meter events and missed out only in the 500, not a specialty, when he slipped and fell at the starting line, the gold going to West Germany's Erhard Keller.

In Holland, they named a tulip for him.

It was at Makomanai that the United States enjoyed its greatest success of the Games, although surprise medals were picked up by the girls in Alpine skiing and the young, inexperienced ice hockey team won an unexpected silver after the Soviet Union had taken the gold.

Anne Henning, a tomboyish, gritty schoolgirl of 16, and Diane Holum, a 20-year-old silver medalist of the 1968 Games, took to the speed-skating oval in the wake of Schenk and kept the excitement bubbling by winning two gold medals each and four in all.

Both came from the little suburban town of Northbrook, Ill., population 20,000, outside Chicago, and Northbrook fans were out in force to cheer their heroines on.

Waving banners and flags, these vociferous supporters kept up a constant chant as the girls sped over the sparkling ice:

"Hiya, Diane, Hiya!

"Hiya, Diane, Hiya!

"Hiya, Hiya, Hiya!"

Also:

"An-nie, An-nie, An-nie,

"Hiya, Hiya, Hiya!"

Diane Holum, who waited on tables to earn money to pay for training expenses, won the 1,500 meter race in the Olympic record time of 2 minutes, 20.85 seconds.

It was America's first gold medal.

"They said I couldn't skate the 1,500—that it wasn't my distance," Diane, a pudgy 123-pounder said excitedly afterward. "I showed 'em."

Anne, streaky blonde hair falling below her shoulders, won her gold medal in the 500, skating the distance twice when a Canadian skater interfered with her in the opening race. Both times she broke the Olympic record, finishing with 43.33 seconds.

"All those Northbrook people cheering me on—I couldn't let them down," Annie said afterward. After the race, she picked up her Snoopy doll and went back to the Olympic Village where she celebrated by eating peanut butter and bananas.

Anne also won a bronze medal with a third place finish in the 1,000 meters, won by West Germany's teen-age Monika Pflug, while Diane picked up a silver, finishing second to The Netherlands' Stien Bass-Kaiser in the 3,000.

For the United States, almost every day was "Ladies' Day" at the Games. Of the eight American medals—three gold, two silver and three bronze—all but one, the ice hockey silver, were captured by women.

Whereas Misses Henning and Holum had been expected, because of their impressive international records, to do well in speed skating, little hope was breathed for Uncle Sam's female skiers on the treacherous slopes of Mt. Teine.

Alpine skiing is the specialty of the Austrians and French, for whom it is a year-around commitment.

Yet, in a wild series of upsets, a chubby, 17-year-old Swiss girl named Marie-Therese Nadig won both the ladies' downhill and giant slalom while the third main race went to Barbara Ann Cochran, 21, of Richmond, Vt., in the special slalom. Susie Corrock, a 22-year-old Ketchum, Idaho, girl who had been racing internationally for only two years, won a surprise bronze in the downhill.

Racing in a blinding snow, Miss Cochran took the lead in the first of two runs down the twisting Mount Teine slope and went for broke on the second to beat out two of the flashy French mademoiselles, Danielle Debernard and Florence Steurer.

"I didn't think about my first run," the red, white and blue spangled New England girl said afterward. "I just decided that on the second run I'd give it my darnedest."

Susie Corrock had the best time of the first ten racers in the downhill but Miss Nadig came along to finish one second faster and the pre-race favorite, Annemarie Proell of Austria, sneaked in to grab the silver.

It proved a disappointing Olympics for Miss Proell, the World Cup champion, who had to be content with second place in both the downhill and giant slalom.

In the men's Alpine events on Mount Eniwa, Americans proved a disappointment, failing to win a medal.

It was a worse travesty, however, for the French and Austrians, who were virtually shut out. Bernhard Russi of Switzerland won the downhill, Gustavo Thoeni of Italy took the giant slalom and a Spaniard, Francisco Fernandez Ochoa, made Olympic history by capturing the slalom—his country's first Winter Olympics medal.

Afterward, Brundage was asked if he thought it poetic justice that the French and Austrians, whom he had labelled as the worst offenders in the matter of commercialism, had fallen upon such bad times.

"Harumph," the IOC president said. "Perhaps so." He smiled with deep satisfaction.

If the French and Austrians were discouraged over their Alpine showing, they needed only to look toward U.S. figure skaters for companionship.

The United States had virtually dominated figure skating in the Olympic Games since World War II, both men's and women's divisions, and it remained for a figure skater, Peggy Fleming, to win America's only gold medal in the 1968 Games at Grenoble.

This time, the United States had to be content with a single bronze medal, that won by blonde and pretty Janet Lynn, 18, of Rockford, Illinois.

A dazzling free-skater, Miss Lynn brought thunderous cheers from the audience with her spectacular climactic performance but she could not overcome the large lead built up by Trixi Schuba, a tall Austrian, in the exacting compulsory figures. The 20-year-old Miss Schuba won the gold and Canadian Karen Magnussen beat out Janet for the silver.

Ondrej Nepela of Czechoslovakia won the men's individual title although the loudest applause went to John Misha Petkevich of Great Falls, Mont., and Harvard University, certainly the world's finest free skater. Russia's Irina Rodnina and Alexei Ulanov led a 1–2 Soviet finish in the pairs although the two don't speak because of a fractured romance.

The U.S. ice hockey team, a collection of scrappy youngsters plucked from various parts of the country and even from the battlefields of Viet Nam, scored a major upset early in the round robin tournament by beating Czechoslovakia 5–1. The victory was largely responsible for getting the Yanks the silver medal although the American team later was crushed by the poised and professional Russians 7–2.

Scouts from the National Hockey League said the Soviet skaters, winning their third straight Olympic crown, were good enough to play in the U.S.-Canadian pro circuit.

The Soviet Union won the unofficial team title by winning a total of 16 medals—eight gold, five silver and three bronze. East Germany was next with four golds, three silver and seven bronze, followed by Switzerland, The Netherlands and then the United States.

In addition to hockey, the Russians scored heavily in the Nordic ski events. Galina Koulacova of the Soviet Union won three gold medals, capturing the women's 5-kilometer and 10-kilometer cross country races and performing as anchor of the winning 15-kilometer relay team. Vyacheslav Vedenin won the

Right, Californians Jo Jo Starbuck and Ken Shelly figure-skated their way to fourth place. Below, Anne Henning (foreground) speeding to a new Olympic record time of 43.33 in 500-meter speed skate

30-kilometer cross country, took a bronze in the 50-kilometer and anchored the 40-kilometer cross country relay team to another Russian gold.

East Germany showed surprising all-around strength but picked up most of its medals in the luge, a strange event in which competitors slide down an icy track on sleds feet first at a speed of 80 miles an hour. In a more orthodox event, the bob sled, West Germany won the two-man race and the Swiss took the four-man, the Americans failing to place.

All events were well attended but none so well as the 70-meter ski jump at Miyanomori. Japanese by the thousands swarmed the slopes to watch their hero, Yukio Kasaya, shoot for the first gold medal ever won by the Japanese in the Winter Olympics.

Kasaya, a whisky salesman from the Sapporo outskirts, did not disappoint. Soaring like a bird in long, graceful leaps, he won the championship with two other Japanese jumpers, Akitsugu Konno and Seiji Aochi placing second and third. It was a 1-2-3 sweep.

Sapporo went wild. Women cried openly. Men danced in the streets. There was loud rejoicing throughout the night. Thousands more turned out later for the 90-meter jump, hoping for a repeat. This time they were disappointed. A young Pole, Wojeiech Fortuna, won the honors.

With all their glamour and pageantry, the Games could not shake off the discord that started with the expulsion of Karl Schranz.

Another skier, Anne Famose of France, was suspended for indulging in forbidden advertisements and broadcasts. A German hockey player was banned after a dope test. Charges of injustice were hurled at the figure skating judges. A petition was circulated to get rid of Brundage and to democratize the IOC.

"No professional will ever compete in the Olympics," Brundage bellowed.

Then the flame was extinguished and it was *sayonara* until Denver, 1976.

Above, Norwegian Paal Tyldum en route to an Olympics gold medal.
Below, Gustavo Theoni of Italy, gold medalist in men's giant slalom

$5 Million Ransom Paid to Free Hijacked Plane in International Plot

A giant jet seized by guerrillas over northwestern India. . . .
Its crew of 14 and 172 frightened passengers diverted to South
Yemen. . . . Those aboard held captive by pistol-wielding Arabs
whose orders they could not always understand. . . . Among
them, a late U.S. President's nephew. . . . Explosives wired to
the doors of the hijacked airliner. . . . Coded messages dispatched
to Aden and Frankfurt. . . . A secret letter of instructions to the
airline's headquarters in Cologne. . . . A West German courier's
race to Beirut against the deadline fixed in threats to blow up
the plane. . . . An elaborate plot, shrouded in mystery. . . . A
hairbreadth rescue for a fabulous price: $5 million.

Did this sound like a super-movie scenario? It could have been.
But these were harrowing events that actually took place.

*   *   *   *

A LUFTHANSA 747 airliner bound for Frankfurt from New Delhi via Athens had been in the air about half an hour when five Arab guerrillas commandeered the plane and diverted its course to Aden in South Yemen. Shortly thereafter air control authorities in Bombay announced that they had heard this message from the hijacked plane: "Call us Victorious Gaza. If you call us Lufthansa we won't answer you."

The five hijackers subsequently were identified by one of their number as members of the Zionist Occupation Victims Organization, with headquarters in the Israeli-occupied Gaza Strip. This evidently explained their reference to Gaza in the message.

Eight hours after leaving New Delhi the plane was landed in Aden. Women and children were allowed to leave the craft soon thereafter, but the crew and the male passengers were held on board. Eighteen hours after the seizure the rest of the 172 passengers were permitted to disembark. Among them was Joseph P. Kennedy III, 19, eldest son of the late Sen. Robert F. Kennedy. Only the crew remained captive.

Before any of the passengers were freed an Aden official said he took food to the plane and reported that "everything appeared as normal. Nobody has been harmed."

After their release some of the women said that the guerrillas had wired explosives to the doors before the landing, and that one of the passengers had been pistol-whipped. The tired and ruffled Kennedy, when he entered the Aden Airport lounge with the rest of the male passengers, commented: "This is just too much. It wasn't the worst moment of my life; I've been scared before, but it has never lasted as long as this." Later, in Frankfurt, he said he had been struck on the shoulder with the pistol held by one of the captors when he failed to raise his hands quickly enough because he had not understood the order he had been given. "It was no big thing," he added.

Most of the women passengers appeared not to have been aware that Kennedy was aboard. But one of the hijackers, walking by Kennedy in the plane Feb. 22, said: "Hello, Mr. Kennedy." Presumably he got his information from a photo and signature when the passengers' passports were collected aboard the plane.

The period of tension ended Feb. 23, when the 14 crew members were freed. Later the West German Foreign Ministry announced that this action was worked out by a senior ministry officer who had been rushed to Aden for that purpose. The passengers were taken to Frankfurt aboard special rescue flights, and Kennedy proceeded to Boston on Feb. 24. During the same day sources in Aden said the captive jet had been released after a secret code message was phoned to the Lufthansa Airlines chief in Aden and relayed to the guerrillas. It read: "Always faithful to martyr Abu Talaat." This meant, the hijackers said, that their seizure of the plane had achieved its purpose. They toasted victory with soft drinks, embraced one another and then embraced the crew members.

However, the nature of their success remained a mystery until the next day, when the West German government in Bonn disclosed the cloak-and-dagger-type ransom payoff which West Germany's transport minister, Georg Leber, described as "like a perfect thriller." His account:

The $5 million was destined for the Victims of Zionist Occupation, a branch of the Popular Front for the Liberation of Palestine. It was handed over in Beirut, but the Lebanese government disclaimed any association with the piracy.

Lufthansa Airlines was owned largely by the West German government. The ransom demand and a threat to blow up the airliner were contained in a letter mailed to Lufthansa's Cologne headquarters on Feb. 22. An emergency staff of West German officials, police and Lufthansa representatives hastily assembled the money in varied currencies, as specified in the letter. Then a Lufthansa security officer was chosen as the courier and flown to Athens, where he awaited further instructions from Bonn.

Leber said "our preparations must have been observed because the hijackers then released first the women and children and then the male passengers."

The go-ahead for payment of the ransom was given by Leber on the morning of Feb. 23. As instructed by the guerrillas, the courier wore a black jacket and light gray trousers; he carried a Newsweek magazine in his left hand and a suitcase containing the money in his right hand, when he showed up at Beirut Airport.

The deadline for paying the $5 million had passed several hours earlier. But, following directions, the courier found a Volkswagen parked outside the airport grounds. Its key had been enclosed in the Cologne letter. On the car's front seat was a message directing the courier to a spot 24 miles from the airport. Followed by another car, he passed two guerrilla check-points and reached the place where he had been told to deliver the money.

In return he received a coded communique which was relayed by phone to the hijackers in Aden. This was the "martyr Abu Talaat" message.

It was then that the plane and its crew were released at Aden. The air pirates were held for questioning, then released by South Yemen authorities.

Abu Talaat was the nom de guerre of Mohammed al Ajrami, national security chief in Jordan for the Popular Front for the Liberation of Palestine (PFLP) until he was killed in the September 1970 civil war in that nation. The Aden hijacking was named after him.

Top, the hijacked plane parked on an Aden runway awaiting takeoff. Bottom, captives relaxing in the Aden Airport lounge after their release

Above, American actress Jane Fonda joined a February rally staged in Rome by an Italian Women's Liberation organization. Below, Pope Paul VI knelt on the dais (upper left) as 14 newly appointed bishops lay prostrated during the consecration ceremony at St. Peter's Basilica in February

Demonstrators overturned a company wagon in New York during telephone strike

7-MONTH PHONE STRIKE SETTLED

The longest strike in telephone company history—seven months—took place in New York state. It caused a $300 million loss in wages and created a backlog of 200,000 phone installations, including those ordered by large business firms.

The beginning, on July 14, 1971, was a nationwide walkout called by the AFL-CIO Communications Workers of America against the Bell Telephone system *(The World in 1971, 137).* This strike was settled within a week.

However, the New York state members of the CWA refused to return to their jobs with the New York Telephone Co. They undertook to make their own settlement, which was not reached until Feb. 16, 1972, when the CWA craftsmen voted 13,769 to 9,193 to accept a three-year contract.

The New York terms were negotiated by the CWA in Washington, D.C., with the assistance of J. Curtis Counts, chief federal mediator. A 33 per cent increase in base wages, advancing top craftsmen to $259 a week base pay in the third year, was obtained. Other gains included a full agency shop, under which all employes represented by the CWA were required to join that union or pay the equivalent in union dues.

Premium pay for Saturday work performed as part of a five-day work week, with the premium starting at 10 per cent and advancing to 15 per cent by July 1972, also was provided.

Those craftsmen affected by the strike included switchmen, framemen, installers, repairmen, linemen and splicers. Pending the settlement telephone service was maintained by more than 13,000 supervisors and about 6,000 other employes of the New York company, mostly nonunion.

Approval of the negotiated pay increases was recommended March 30 by a subcommittee of the Federal Pay Board, but later the board's chairman questioned the allowance. Then, on April 25, the board approved a 15.3 per cent raise for the first year of the contract.

JOINT HEALTH PACT SIGNED BY U.S. AND SOVIET UNION

The United States and Soviet Russia both hailed it as a significant move. And it was generally agreed that the decision of the two superpowers to pool their efforts against cancer, heart disease and pollution did mark a giant step in combating these health problems.

The agreement, which had been negotiated in secret for more than a year, was made known Feb. 11 at a joint news conference in Washington by Secretary of Health, Education and Welfare Elliot L. Richardson and Soviet Ambassador Anatoly F. Dobrynin.

The accord called for a Soviet-American Committee for Health Cooperation and three subcommittees to begin work within a month on the two diseases and on environmental problems.

Washington and Moscow acted in concert on the pact. Richardson handed Dobrynin a letter announcing U.S. approval of the accord. And, in the Soviet capital, Dr. Boris V. Petrovsky, Russian minister of health, handed a similar letter to Boris H. Klosson, charge d'affaires at the U.S. Embassy.

Both Richardson and Dobrynin were plainly elated over the agreement. The U.S. health secretary hailed it as a new and significant step that should speed up progress. Dobrynin described it as a "significant event" that would not only improve health care but also promote mutual understanding between the two peoples.

The United States and Soviet Russia had actually been exchanging health delegations and individual scientists since 1956, but the new accord apparently was more far reaching. It had resulted from lengthy consultation between representatives of the United States and the Soviet Union.

Dr. Roger O. Egeberg, special consultant to President Nixon on health affairs and a special assistant to Richardson, first approached Soviet Health Minister Petrovsky on the health issue in Moscow in 1970.

Talking to Washington newsmen, Egeberg acknowledged that Soviet scientists "are ahead of us in many areas, and we hope to learn from them." He noted that the Russians had done significant work on hypertension, on the study of viruses as a possible cause of cancer and on immunology and blood diseases.

Dobrynin caused general laughter when a reporter asked him whether the Soviet Union had pollution problems. It did, the envoy said, but he added with a smile that his country was lagging behind the United States in that respect.

PACTS FOR FLORIDA FARMHANDS

For eight months the United Farm Workers Union tried to win recognition as a bargaining representative among Florida's estimated 150,000 seasonal and migrant workers. Finally, on Feb. 29, a breakthrough came when Cesar Chavez, founder of the union, and the Coca Cola Foods Division of Florida announced agreement on a three-year contract covering 1,200 citrus grove laborers.

"We are proud of the contract—the first agreement in Florida and the southern part of the United States—and we hope it will open the gates with other companies and farmers in the state," said Chavez.

But Fred Adkinson, president of Florida's Citrus Industrial Council, which represented virtually all of the growers, said of the pact: "I think it will prove very unpopular with the harvesting people in our state."

The agreement raised the top wage for full-time workers from $2.25 to $3.70 per hour. Seasonal employes would receive lesser increases in wages and piecework rates.

A month later a second Florida agreement was reached by the union with H. P. Hood and Sons, Inc., a major processor and distributor of dairy and citrus products. The company said the union would represent 300 grove workers in its citrus division.

In 1969 Chavez, a former migrant worker, gained public attention in California for himself and the Mexican-American minority group. At that time his United Farm Workers won recognition within the table grape industry after a five-year strike. He gained increased wages, better living conditions and other benefits. The following year he launched a campaign against the lettuce growers and again was successful.

His techniques were consistently non-violent although his forceful character often demanded immediate compliance from his union members.

As a child Chavez had lived in poverty, his Mexican parents earning only 50¢ a day in the California fields. The family subsisted on tortillas, beans and an occasional potato.

His resentment of discrimination was apparent at the age of 16, when he once entered a movie theater and chose a seat in a section reserved for Anglo-Americans. His confrontation thereafter with the theater manager resulted in a lecture by a police sergeant, but his belief in equality remained unshaken.

Cesar Chavez after winning a Florida citrus contract for his United Farm Workers Union

SOVIET FISHERMEN INTERCEPTED

At dawn of Jan. 17, the U.S. Coast Guard cutter *Storis* was patrolling the ice-clogged Bering Sea when it picked up an unidentified ship on its radar screen. The *Storis* fixed the stranger at 9.4 miles off Cape Upright on Saint Matthew Island.

Saint Matthew, a 22-mile long uninhabited crag rearing 1,500 feet out of the Bering Sea 200 miles west of Alaska, was the center of one of the world's richest halibut fishing grounds. It was also American territory covered by U.S. regulations which banned fishing by foreign craft within 12 miles of the Pacific shores of the United States.

The 230-foot *Storis*, rigged with an icebreaker prow, set out to investigate and found two Soviet intruders. They were the 362-foot *Lamut*, floating factory and flagship of the 80-vessel Soviet fishing fleet working the general area, and the 278-foot *Kolyvan*.

The *Kolyvan* was transferring fish to the *Lamut* and thus violated the U.S. ban on foreign fishing activity.

The *Storis* came alongside the *Lamut* and six U.S. Coast Guardsmen boarded the Soviet craft. At the same time five other guardsmen clambered aboard the *Kolyvan*. Each team was led by a guardsman armed with a pistol.

The Americans ordered the Russians to accompany the *Storis* 600 miles south to the U.S. naval base at Adak Island in the Aleutians.

Shortly after the three ships got under way, the *Lamut* veered off in the gloom and tried to flee. The *Storis* gave chase through the ice pack and her skipper, Cmdr. William P. Allen, flashed a message to the Coast Guard's 17th District Headquarters in Juneau, Alaska: "*Lamut* fleeing with custody crew aboard."

For the next hour the *Storis* and the Soviet vessel zigzagged through the ice pack. Finally Allen radioed Juneau: "*Lamut* will not stop. Request permission to fire across her bow."

The request went all the way to the Coast Guard commandant, Adm. Chester R. Bender, in his home in Chevy Chase, Md. Bender gave the okay.

"*Storis* prepared to open fire," was the message that Allen then flashed to the *Lamut*. The threat of being shot at caused the Soviet ship to heave to and permit the *Storis* to tie up alongside.

This time 10 armed U.S. Coast Guardsmen boarded the *Lamut*. The Soviet fleet commander and the master of the *Kolyvan* were arrested and placed aboard the *Storis*.

Then once again the Russians balked and refused to get their craft under way. For more than 24 hours the three vessels lay in the Bering Sea while their commanders negotiated.

Finally, after the *Storis* had chipped the *Lamut* out of the ice, she and the *Kolyvan* obediently followed the U.S. vessel on the trip to the base at Adak. The Russians were detained there until U.S. officials decided what infraction they had committed.

The two Soviet ships departed Adak Island after U.S. officials announced Feb. 18 that the Russians had paid $80,000 in fines and $170,000 in an out-of-court agreement after settling criminal and civil charges of conducting illegal fisheries' support activities in U.S. waters.

The Soviet vessels pulled out just 30 minutes after a U.S. marshal arrived at Adak in an attempt to take one of the vessels back into custody, in connection with a civil suit filed against the Soviet government by a Seattle firm.

The U.S. Coast Guard icebreaker Storis *and the Soviet factory ship* Lamut *in the North Bering Sea en route to Adak Island, Alaska, after the* Lamut *was boarded*

BLOODLESS COUP IN ECUADOR

During the past 115 years Ecuador changed its constitution 16 times. In one recent 23-year period 22 presidents were named. Political instability continued in 1972, when military leaders ousted Pres. Jose Maria Velasco Ibarra in a bloodless coup.

That was the fourth time the 78-year-old Velasco had been ousted. He had been elected five times, the latest in 1968, for a four-year term. In June 1970 he proclaimed himself dictator, with the aid of the armed forces.

He was arrested Feb. 16 in Guayaquil after he had left Quito in an effort to rally the country to his support. Subsequently he was flown to Panama.

A "nationalist revolutionary government" was set up by the commander of the army, Gen. Guillermo Rodriguez Lara, and Ecuador became the sixth South American nation to live under military rule at that time. The others were Argentina, Bolivia, Brazil, Paraguay and Peru.

In a radio and television speech Rodriguez promised that his government would "not be another dictatorship like many under which the country has suffered." Rodriguez said the coup was necessary because of "misgovernment and chaos" under Velasco. He also said that Ecuador was in strong need of social justice and suggested for the future a "political pluralism" of political parties.

Armored vehicles blocked traffic at Independence Square in Quito, Ecuador, on the first day of the cou

French couturier Paco Rabanne posed with one of his models during a February showing of his latest fashion creations in Paris, showing a fringed dress in blue, orange and white with a matching boa

UNITED NATIONS COUNCIL
CONVENED IN ADDIS ABABA

The black African nations have long swung a lot of weight in the United Nations, and they proved it by persuading the prestigious U.N. Security Council to leave its New York headquarters and hold an unprecedented meeting in the Ethiopian capital of Addis Ababa.

It all began in June 1971 when the foreign ministers of the Organization of African Unity (OAU) convened in Addis Ababa. They framed a request to the U.N. General Assembly to recommend that the council pull up stakes and convene a special session on African problems somewhere on the dark continent early in 1972.

The Assembly approved the request in December 1971, with only South Africa and Portugal, both under fire for their racial policies, voting against it.

In January 1972 the council agreed to meet in Addis Ababa from Jan. 28–Feb. 4.

The council had met in London in January 1946 in the preparatory stage of the United Nations. It had met in Paris in 1948 and again in 1951 and 1952, but only because all the delegates were there for sessions of the General Assembly. Never had it left headquarters alone.

The United States and some other member states objected to the council's spending a lot of money on the trip when the United Nations was running short of cash. But they went along with the idea when the cost was set at $139,500, including $88,000 to charter a plane to fly more than 120 U.N. employes from New York to serve the council.

The delegations, getting to Addis any way they chose, convened the first Security Council meeting of the special session in the OAU's Africa Hall in Addis the morning of Jan. 28.

Ethiopian Emperor Haile Selassie, a veteran of the League of Nations, welcomed the council and expressed hope that its first session in Africa would "usher in a new era of freedom for the peoples of Southern Africa."

During 13 meetings of the council a parade of speakers appeared, including U.N. Secretary-General Kurt Waldheim, representatives of 20 black nations, and rebel leaders from Rhodesia, South Africa and Portugal's African territories.

Each of the speakers dealt generally with all the African problems facing the council. These included such hot-potato issues as South African apartheid, or racial segregation, the status of the disputed mandate of South-West Africa, Portugal's African territories and the white minority government in Rhodesia.

Five resolutions grew out of the session and all were put to the vote on Feb. 4.

One called for abandonment of a proposed British settlement with the Rhodesian regime of Prime Minister Ian Smith. But Britain killed that resolution by using its big power veto.

The four other resolutions carried. They were
—A condemnation of South Africa for its apartheid policies.

—A call to Portugal to stop colonial wars in its African territories of Portuguese Guinea, Angola and Mozambique, and to grant independence to these territories. It also urged member states to halt the supply of arms to Portugal which might be used to repress black movements in the disputed territories.

—A demand that South Africa withdraw immediately from its mandate of South-West Africa.

—A request that Waldheim contact all parties concerned to enable the people of South-West Africa to exercise their "right to self determination and independence."

March

Cyprus Seemed Peaceful,
but Threat of Civil War
Again Followed Makarios

Archbishop Makarios acknowledging the cheers of student demonstrators outside the presidential palace in Nicosia on March 29

CYPRUS, home of Aphrodite, the legendary goddess of love, appeared peaceful and idyllic as the snows melted on mountaintops and flowers blossomed in greening fields. But civil war threatened once again, in 1972, to engulf the Mediterranean island which had been a source of intermittent strife for 5,000 years.

And once again the storm center was his Beatitude, Archbishop Makarios, bearded, 58-year-old president of Cyprus. This time Makarios was being pressured both by the Athens government and his old rival, Gen. George Grivas, 74, the former leader of the Greek Cypriot underground.

The general had returned secretly to Cyprus in September 1971 and had revived a campaign for Enosis, or union of Cyprus with Greece. Makarios and the ruling junta in Greece had finally agreed on one thing, that Enosis was unfeasible because 20 per

cent of the island population was of Turkish background and Turkey had threatened to go to war if such a union was attempted.

The minority Turks and the Greeks, who made up 80 per cent of the Cypriot population, had been unable to agree on a form of government which would acknowledge Greek power and yet protect Turkish rights. But both governments had finally indicated willingness to try to find some solution.

Makarios, however, opposed any settlement which would lessen the power of his Greek Cypriot majority. Aware of the archbishop's stand and the reasoning behind it, Athens apparently wanted to oust Makarios or turn him into a puppet. But the president, who once commented that he had survived 13 Greek premiers, was not an easy man to dislodge.

To the casual visitor Cyprus seemed little like a powder keg.

Greek Cypriot students demonstrated on March 7 in support of General Grivas and "Enosis"—the union with Greece—and for the resignation of Archbishop Makarios as president

It was a paradise of fragrant orange and lemon groves, white beaches and cool cedar forests. Business was booming, tourists thronged the shops, and nightclubs echoed to the foot-stomping "bouzouki" music.

But a closer look revealed barbed wire barricades and sandbags marking the dividing line between the rival Cypriot communities. Also visible were the scars of war: Gutted schools, factories and homes, souvenirs of the communal battles of 1964 (*The World in 1964,* 147–149).

Eight years later the biggest U.N. peace force in the world, 3,100 men, still kept the two Cypriot armed camps at bay. To head off the danger of a shooting war between the Greek and Turkish factions, the U.N. Security Council had been voting periodically to extend the life of the peace force.

It was difficult for a stranger to tell the two Cypriot factions apart. They wore the same clothes, ate the same kebab and drank the same thick, sweet coffee. But similarity ended at that point. The Turkish Cypriots saw but one solution for the island —partition, or total separation, of the two rival communities.

The Greeks, on the other hand, regarded the Turks, who had been there for nearly 400 years, as intruders. The Greek Cypriots controlled the government and economy of the island. But this imbalance was offset by other factors that would weigh heavily in the event of war.

Athens had always sworn to support its island allies in any conflict, but it probably did not relish such a prospect. After all, Greece lay 500 miles away from the island and the mountainous coast of Turkey was visible only 40 miles off. In fact, Turk-

ish jet bases were a mere four minutes flying time from Nicosia, capital of Cyprus.

The Turkish Cypriots were outnumbered four to one by their Greek counterparts, but things were different in the two mother countries. Turkey boasted half a million men under arms, while Greece had less than 120,000 men. The Turkish navy consisted of about 35,000 men and more than 70 warships. Greece had a naval manpower of about 16,000 and some 90 vessels, many of which were of the small patrol type.

The Turkish air force totaled more than 450 combat planes, while Greece had only about 260 operational aircraft.

The prospect of an outbreak had given many a western leader sleepless nights. War between Greece and Turkey could wreck the southeast bastion of NATO and leave the United States virtually alone trying to defend this strategic Mediterranean area. In recent years, the Soviet Union had been beefing up its naval strength in the area, in a bid to match the power of the U.S. 6th Fleet.

* * * *

Located at the crossroads of Europe, Asia and Africa, Cyprus had been repeatedly overrun through the years by various invaders, including Phoenicia, Egypt, Persia, Greece, Rome and the Byzantine and Ottoman empires. After the outbreak of World War I, when Turkey aligned herself with Germany, the island of Cyprus was annexed in November 1914 to Britain,

At top, contraband arms and ammo, unloaded for Greek Cypriots in Famagusta during the February 1964 hostilities. At bottom, the Old Wall of Nicosia, running three miles long and enclosing the oldest part of the Cypriot capital

Greek Cypriots waiting to be searched by their Turkish enemies after a roundup in Nicosia, Cyprus

which had actually been administering it for some years, even while it was under Ottoman control.

The Cypriots got along comparatively amiably with their British administrators until the 1950s, when Enosis became a rallying cry that shook Whitehall.

In 1955 Enosis won open acceptance from Athens, which dumped the issue in the lap of the United Nations. This inspired the Asian-African group to seize upon the case as an example of "colonial oppression."

Caught off balance, the British put out a vague manifesto which made it a punishable offense to even discuss Enosis. They thereby set off a wave of bloody rioting by Cypriots.

The demonstrations had started as harassment by teenagers, but soon contraband arms were being landed on Cypriot shores by night and bombs were being hurled into crowds from speeding cars.

The mainspring behind the agitation was an underground group called EOKA (Ethniki Organosis Kyprion Agoniston), which put out inflammatory leaflets signed Dighenis, the name of a Cypriot folk hero. Actually he was George Grivas, a retired officer of the Greek army.

As Grivas and his following of street fighters and assassins continued to step up their terror campaign, Britain put out a wanted poster on the underground chief offering a reward of $28,000 for information leading to his capture. The British also offered free passage by air or sea to any point in the world where an informer might feel beyond the reach of Eoka vengeance.

But, with the encouragement of Makarios, Grivas continued to foil repeated attempts of the 40,000-man British garrison to eliminate his band.

Also in 1955, the name Makarios meant little to the world at large, although the British were painfully aware of his presence. The son of a poor Cypriot shepherd, he had entered the priesthood at an early age and won a scholarship at Boston University. He was named a bishop while still a student and was elevated to archbishop when only 37.

As Makarios began sounding the call for Enosis at the United Nations and in various world capitals, British patience wore thin. British authorities ultimately collared the cleric as he was about to set out on an "enlightenment crusade" to Athens and elsewhere. Makarios was flown to the Seychelles, a remote clus-

Armed Greek Cypriot women entrenched near the Turkish Cypriot stronghold of St. Hilarion Castle in the Kyrenia district of Cyprus

ter of volcanic mountains in the Indian Ocean. There he was interned.

The British had little success, however, in reaching any settlement on the fate of Cyprus. Finally the United States made clear to London that four years of supporting the British cause on Cyprus was enough. So, with Turkey willing to listen to peace and Greece anxious to find some way out of the tangle, Britain agreed to discuss independence for the island.

In February 1959 the Greek and Turkish premiers met in Zurich and announced agreement on the destiny of Cyprus. A few days later a pact was signed in London by Makarios and Britain's Prime Minister Harold Macmillan.

The Greek Cypriots soon registered strong opposition to the pact, which retained British garrisons on the island and gave the Turkish minority rights that the Greeks considered all out of proportion to their numbers.

Cyprus once was a British crown colony, but when the London pact was implemented on Aug. 16, 1960, the island became an independent republic. Under the agreement, Britain retained sovereignty only over areas containing her military bases on the island.

As resentment mounted, Makarios came out with a claim that he had signed the pact under duress to head off civil war. In 1963 the archbishop submitted 13 points for revision of the constitution, but, before the Turkish Cypriots had a chance to react, there was a flat turndown from Ankara.

As tempers rose on both sides, a minor incident erupted between a Greek Cypriot patrol and a group of Turkish Cypriots. Shots were exchanged and soon the two factions were locked in combat.

Word spread that the Turkish fleet was steaming towards Cyprus, and an alarmed Makarios agreed to a plan to let an emergency force of British, Greek and Turkish troops move onto the island under British command.

Later, when the British proposed sending in a NATO force to keep order, Makarios balked and suggested putting the question before the United Nations, where he felt he could count on the support of the Third World, the so-called nonaligned nations.

Early in 1964 the issue was placed before the Security Council, and a resolution was approved calling for a U.N. peace force. The force saw action five months later when Greek Cypriots attacked a number of Turkish Cypriot villages. Ankara responded by sending over its jets and pounding Greek Cypriot hamlets.

The danger of a collision between Greece and Turkey was averted when the United States threatened to cut off military aid to Ankara. Reluctantly, Turkey backed off.

Trouble flared again in the fall of 1967 when Grivas, who had risen from guerrilla chief to commander of the Greek Cypriot army, sent two armored columns on a probing thrust into a pair of Turkish Cypriot villages. In the ensuing shoot-up, 28 Cypriots were killed on both sides. The raid had been staged against the wishes of Makarios.

Turkey, which had backed down in 1964, vowed that she would not do so again and sent an ultimatum to Greece to accede to if she wanted to avoid war. It called for:

—Removal of Grivas from his island command.

—Return of arms seized from Turkish Cypriots in the latest skirmish.

—Payment of compensation for 25 Turkish Cypriots killed in the clash.

—Withdrawal of about 10,000 Greek troops stationed on Cyprus.

Athens, fed up with Grivas, quickly recalled him to Athens but rejected the other demands.

President Lyndon B. Johnson sent Cyrus Vance, a former deputy defense secretary, to try to calm things down. NATO and the United Nations also sent in troubleshooters *(The World in 1967, 262)*.

Turkey finally agreed to cooperate with Vance, and the military junta in Athens gave grudging approval to Turkey's demands. Makarios resisted for a while, but he too came around.

An uneasy quiet prevailed on the island until last February, when Athens began putting the pressure on Makarios. The archbishop stalled by not making a formal reply to a sharp "recommendation" from Greek Premier George Papadopoulos.

The ultimatum demanded that Makarios turn over to the U.N. force some $2.5 million worth of arms he had purchased from Czechoslovakia. The archbishop's defiance posed a dilemma for the Greek government. If it tried to oust Makarios, it would provoke the thousands of Greek Cypriots who supported him.

Finally Makarios agreed to let the UN force inspect and control his cache of Czech weapons. In doing so, he removed Greece's main pretext for launching its campaign to remove the archbishop from the presidency.

Flood of Sludge, Water from Dam Collapse Left 118 Dead in Coal Camps

Some West Virginia victims failed to heed advance warnings; survivors left homeless by deluge estimated at 4,000

OVER THE YEARS, the coal mine communities of West Virginia have suffered more than one disaster, including mine roof falls, explosions and slides. But the state's mountain people long ago became inured to hardship and tragedy, carrying on with an almost fatalistic outlook.

So, when several residents of Buffalo Creek Hollow were warned early in the morning of Feb. 26 that a coal mine refuse dam at the head of the narrow valley was about to give way, many ignored the admonition. They had been warned many times before. But this was no "crying wolf." A wall of water from Elk Lick, a small tributary of Buffalo Creek, broke through the slate heap, sending the muddy flood raging through the 17-mile Logan County valley.

The torrent of sludge and water toppled everything in its wake, leaving at least 118 persons dead and virtually obliterating from the map several of the 16 coal camps strung along the hollow. Some 4,000 people were left homeless and hundreds of others suffered severe damage to their property.

Survivors who escaped to high ground told of watching from a distance as the rush of water swept away their homes. One of the first to get out of the area, Herbert Trent, 17, said, "It came too fast for us to have any warning. Suddenly it was there; water, mud and boards from houses."

The flood came shortly after 8 a.m. Saturday, just as many miners were returning home from the midnight shift. Heavy rains for three days had swollen Elk Lick, a normally placid mountain stream. Finally the earth and slate dam holding back the water could not withstand the pressure any longer; it burst, sending the flood cascading through the valley.

Officials of the Pittston Co., parent firm of Buffalo Mining Co., which maintained the dam, had inspected the site throughout the rainy periods. Steve Dasovich, a Pittston vice president, told Logan County Deputy Sheriff Otto Mutters at about 6:30 a.m. that morning that "everything was okay" at the dam. Mutters said Basovich told him a ditch had been dug to relieve the building water pressure. But at least one area resident was concerned enough about the rapidly rising water to warn his neighbors to flee to high ground. Some did not heed the warning.

The scope of the tragedy was not apparent for some time, as National Guard troops and state police moved into the area

A coal miner and his three-year-old daughter awaiting news about relatives

to begin rescue and clean-up operations. Newsmen were barred from the dam site for two days by Gov. Arch A. Moore Jr. Helicopters buzzed in and out of a makeshift landing strip at Man, a Logan County community of 1,600 at the end of the hollow, bringing the dead and injured to hospitals and a makeshift morgue at the South Man Grade School. The death toll mounted slowly and the missing list numbered in the hundreds for days.

Meanwhile, refugees gathered at Man High School, where they slept on cots in hallways and classrooms and ate hot meals prepared by volunteer workers. Nurses doled out typhoid shots and treatment for shock. The cavernous gymnasium, its "Man Hillbillies" banner proudly displayed, was the scene of many a tearful reunion as survivors found loved ones they had believed lost.

President Nixon telephoned Governor Moore from Shanghai to express his regret and to officially declare Logan County a disaster area, opening the way for federal relief funds.

Several governmental agencies set up camp in the Man area. Hundreds of mobile homes were rushed to the region and placed on sites for refugees, rent-free for one year. Clothing poured in from around the country until Salvation Army work-

ers finally said they just had more than they knew what to do with.

And commissions and counter commissions and committees began investigating the tragedy, trying to determine the cause of the dam break. Records of the Buffalo Mining Co. and the Pittston Co. were subpoenaed by a Senate subcommittee. Hearings were held in Washington, the Logan County area and the state capital of Charleston as the bureaucracy flourished. Practically every state politician and some national ones flocked to the scene for on-the-spot election-year analyses of the disaster.

In a preliminary report released March 15, the Department of the Interior concluded that the dam was not safely constructed. The study cited a number of defects in the coal-waste dam and said any number of them could have caused its collapse. Two major conclusions of the report were:

—"From an engineering point of view the dam was not designed and constructed such that it would be considered safe for the retention of large volumes of water over any lengthy period of time."

—The amount of water stored behind the dam "seems far in excess" of the amount needed to perform the dam's function as an antipollution filter.

John Chapman sitting in front of his demolished home in Man, W. Va., three days after flood waters swept the area

Meanwhile, the governor ordered the draining of all similar mine waste dams in the state.

The insurance company term "act of God" was used in some official statements about the flood, but residents of the hollow scoffed at the idea. A 35-year-old miner from Stowe, Charles Adkins, said: "I've been up there all my life, and I didn't see God driving one of them bulldozers."

The first lawsuit against the Pittston Co. was filed March 22 in U.S. District Court in Charleston. It contended that Pittston was responsible for the dam break and for the damage. It charged the corporation with "willful and wanton neglect" and negligence in not correcting a "dangerous dam."

Most residents of the coal communities down the hollow from the dam were reluctant to point to the company, since it provided their livelihood. A commonly-expressed sentiment was, "I don't care how it happened, just so long as it doesn't happen again."

A Buffalo Mining Co. official, Ben Tudor, said the state had denied permission for the company to send some of the sludge which had accumulated in the firm's lake into valley streams, relieving pressure on the dam. Tudor, general superintendent of Buffalo, said, "They were too concerned about the trout downstream. It either had to be the people or the trout and now both are gone." Tudor's comments were widely circulated, and Governor Moore called a news conference to issue an angry denial. Moore also said trout could never live in the stream. But records of the state Department of Natural Resources showed that Buffalo Creek was stocked with trout monthly during 1971.

Other questions, including ones about responsibility for inspection of the dam, were raised during Congressional hearings. Assistant Secretary of the Interior Hollis M. Dole told the House Mines and Mining subcommittee March 15 that regulation of the dam was outside his department's jurisdiction. But under questioning from subcommittee chairman Rep. Ed Edmondson, D-Okla., Dole said his department had a responsibility to enforce laws calling for active inspection and record-keeping by mine operators. And a Bureau of Mines representative said that agency had a policy of inspecting mines at least twice a year. But the mine at the site of the Buffalo Creek dam had not been inspected in 1971 or 1972, he said.

As for the flood victims themselves, many said they would move back into the hollow and try to rebuild. Typical of mountain folk's resiliency, they refused to give up. "I don't know anywhere else to go," one veteran miner said.

An aerial photograph showing, at left, where the dam broke

The Car of the Future–
Was This Still a Dream?

One of three prototypes developed by the Republic Aviation Division of the Fairchild-Hiller Corp. for a Department of Transportation experimental safety vehicle

*With pollution control a threat to gasoline-driven vehicles,
engineers were experimenting with steam and electric
engines but problems were encountered there too*

THE INTERNATIONAL AUTOMOBILE SHOW opened for the press preview on the last day of March, but the Car of the Future was not recognizable. The cars were lower, faster, shinier and more expensive. But nearly all of them ran on gasoline, and nearly all of them were threatened by the coming controls on air pollution.

True, there were some hints of what might be under the hood of the Car of the Future. There was a film of an Australian steam car in operation and there were three electric cars on display, two of them ready for sale.

But of working hardware there was none. William Lear's much-touted steam bus, despite earlier promises, was not in evidence. He told questioners at his Reno, Nev., research center that it was not there "because there was no reason for it being there." The trip, he pointed out, would have been long, the bus had not been perfected and the long drive might not have been helpful.

Another steam bus was in service on a regular route in California, but the builders thought it had had sufficient public exposure when it was shown to congressmen in Washington.

The three electric cars had all the faults of their kind. They were relatively slow, had a short range, were heavy and cost a lot. All were proof that battery systems would have to be improved markedly if electric outlets were to replace gas pumps.

As the world knew, almost no one liked the gasoline car except the builders, the oil companies and the drivers. It gave off a variety of pollutants which could build up where traffic was heavy. And the government was well down the road to insisting on low-pollution engines. The lead-free gasoline for them will cost more, a couple of cents a gallon, probably, and they would be balky and hard to start. But pollution and pollution scares were in the air, and the future car might not be able to use gasoline.

That left the steam car and the electric as possibilities. There was also talk of cars powered by sunlight, or run by the energy stored in spinning flywheels. But these were the matter of Sunday supplement science so far. Sunlight powered cars would not run at night, and spinning flywheels were only good for a few hundred feet. Anyway, if they spun fast enough to be practicable, they were likely to burst from centrifugal force.

So: steam, the original automobile propulsion system, and the electric car.

The first mechanically propelled vehicle was driven by steam. Seven years before the American revolution, in 1769, Nicholas Cugnot of the French army artillery corps built a three-wheel gun tractor powered by steam. It used the Newcomen type of engine, already about 50 years old. In that, steam in a cylinder was condensed by a jet of cold water. That left a vacuum, in which the pressure of the air pushed in a piston. The piston was hooked to the front driving wheel of the tractor. But Cugnot's tractor, on its trial trip, ran away down a hill, hit a stone wall and turned over. That was the end of automobiles for 75 years.

About the time railways came in, around 1830, there was a revival of the steam car. Coaches run by steam plied regularly between London and Bath, as well as on other routes, for several years. Business was good, but the turnpike owners—good roads were privately owned then—thought the heavy vehicles broke up the paving. And horse breeders took a dim view of the horseless carriages. They were backed by farmers who couldn't sell oats to a steam bus. Between them they had the steam coaches barred from the road and automobiles disappeared from view for another 50 years.

But the steam car had advantages to offset its manifest disadvantages. True, it took a while to get up steam pressure

after lighting the boiler, but Lear had claimed he reduced this to about 90 seconds. And it used a lot of water, even when it condensed the steam and re-used the water. Old steam cars had to re-fill their water tanks about every 60 miles.

The steam cars which came into use about 1895 and disappeared in the Great Depression had other problems. Their pipes had many joints, most of which leaked steam, water or gasoline (used for fuel) at one time or another. They were no more reliable than the gasoline engine of the time, but no less reliable, either. However, development work continued on gasoline cars during and after the Depression. Nobody continued work on the Stanley Steamer or the White or the Doble.

The advantages were what aroused new interest in steam. Because the fuel was burned with plenty of air, pollution was reported to be less than with an internal-combustion, gasoline engine. Heat was low, generally less than 1,000 degrees Fahrenheit, compared with several thousand degrees in a gasoline engine and about 1800 F. in a gas turbine. This meant that unusual (and expensive) alloys would not have to be used in the engine and boiler.

One great beauty of the steam engine was its simplicity. It needed no transmission. A gasoline engine had to be kept turning: if it stalled, it stopped. But a steam engine had even greater torque when running slowly than when running fast. The slower it ran the more usable power it produced. Steam

A gasoline-electric hybrid, one of three experimental 512 series of special purpose cars developed by the General Motors engineering staff

GM's 511 commuter vehicle, three-wheeled and gasoline powered, featured exceptional stability, fuel economy and maneuverability

engines could be connected directly to the rear wheels. They needed only one control—the same lever which let more or less steam into the cylinder could reverse the engine if moved enough.

All these considerations made the steam car the choice if gasoline engines were on their way out. Electric cars also had great advantages, but at the 1972 level of technology they couldn't match steam for the open road.

That was not to say that electricity could not be useful for a second car, for low speeds and short distances. It would be quiet, pollution-free, and as easy as steam to drive. If somebody invented a new battery which was lighter and stored more electricity, the electric car would be back in the lead.

Specifications of the electric cars at the Automobile Show demonstrated the limitations of the class. One of them would carry two passengers at speeds of as much as 26 miles per hour for as far as 60 miles. Another, also for two passengers, would go 40 miles per hour for as far as 50 miles. After that,

one of them had to halt for an overnight charge of its batteries. The other could get a recharge in 2½ minutes, but only by taking out the whole tray of batteries and putting in a tray of recharged ones.

The difficulty was that the cheapest battery still was the lead-acid type but bigger. And all drivers know what a headache they could be when they got old or the temperature dropped to zero. Cold weather took a lot of power out of them by slowing the chemical reaction which made electricity.

However, range and weight and low speeds were not insurmountable obstacles for delivery trucks or a second car used just to go to market or to drive a commuter to the station. As a second car, their batteries could be plugged into a power line (via a suitable transformer and rectifier) in the family garage. Every morning they would come out with freshly-charged batteries. For extended use during the day, an electric socket could be put into every parking meter. Parked cars could be plugged in to get a topping-up charge while waiting. The meter

Vehicles like this two-seat, plexiglass-ball, called the "Automodule," might well be a common sight by the year 2000; fitted with four wheels, it could go in all directions and turn like a top

charge then would cover both space and the electricity used.

But the great problem to any quick shift to electric cars was a shortage of electricity. Estimates in 1972—were that power stations would have to be tripled—two new stations built for every one working—if all cars were to shift to electric propulsion. And it took a minimum of two years to build a power station even after a path had been cleared through government red tape. Also, the cost of tripling the power supply would run into hundreds of billions of dollars.

So, if steam cars suffered from under-developed technology and electric cars from a shortage of electricity, what was left?

The answer: A gasoline engine, maybe of a new type, maybe the existing one cleaned up. Afterburners to burn the pollutants in the exhaust was one line of investigation, but the high heat would burn up almost any metal too quickly. Catalysts to make the pollutants burn at a low temperature was another, but most catalysts were made of platinum, 2½ times as costly as gold.

Chrysler thought of a gas turbine, but dropped it after 25 cars were built and tried. Test drivers said there was too much lag, after the accelerator was pressed, before the engine speed built up enough to move the car. However, Ford was ready with a gas turbine truck and GM reportedly was thinking about one.

Another novelty was the Wankel rotary engine, already in use in the Japanese Mazda car. Whether this caused less pollution than a piston-engined gasoline car was controversial. What did seem certain was that the Wankel was so much smaller, for the same horsepower, that it left room under the hood for more anti-pollution accessories.

The world had a lot of money invested in oilfields, pipelines, refineries and gas stations. That provided the inertia which might very well make it accept a refurbished gasoline engine, even with moderate pollution, rather than an electric or steam car. The old saying, "better the evil you know than the evil unknown," was still significant.

A massive bull elephant reaching for a marula fruit on a tree in the Kruger National Park, in South Africa. The fruit ripened at the end of March, and thousands of happy elephants began their annual spree in the vast wildlife sanctuary

A St. Louis Zoo black rhinoceros, weighing 4,000 pounds, posed with her 30-pound offspring after its birth on March 6. The zoo staff said a litter of leopard kittens was born the same day, but mother leopard, unapproachable in the seclusion of her lair in the basement of the Lion House, made the kitten count a matter of conjecture

SHARP CUT IN U.S. POPULATION INCREASE URGED BY COMMISSION

After an extensive two-year study of the population growth and its effect on life in the United States, a special commission advised the public to decrease, and ultimately stop, the rise in population. Warning that no substantial benefits would result from a continued rise and that "the plusses seem to be on the side of slowing growth and eventually stopping it all together," the Commission on Population Growth and the American Future urged the adoption of a liberalized U.S. policy. It contended that the population problem could easily be stemmed by allowing people to avoid unwanted pregnancies.

The 24-member commission, headed by John D. Rockefeller III, was created by Congress in March 1970 at President Nixon's request, and was instructed to assess the effects of the growth trend on the U.S. to the end of the 20th century. The commission also was directed to examine the impact of the population boom on government services, the economy, resources and environment and to make recommendations concerning the ways in which the country could best cope with the impact.

In a report issued on March 11, the commission warned that, if growth trends continued, social freedom in the future would be strangled by red tape and regulations. It also noted that slower population growth "can contribute to the nation's ability to solve its problems in other areas by providing an opportunity to devote resources to the quality of life rather than to its quantity."

The commission estimated that, with families averaging two children, the country's population would rise from the 1972 figure of 208 million to 271 million by the year 2000; in a three-children family, the figure in 2000 would be 322 million. In 100 years the two-child family would be responsible for 350 million people, and the three-child family would produce almost one billion.

The commission acknowledged that the distribution of the population is a factor as important as the size of the population in predicting the effects in future years. Its report held that the bulk of the population was concentrated in metropolitan areas across the country, and predicted that, by the end of the century, 85 per cent of Americans would be living in the metropolitan area, compared to the 71 per cent in 1970.

The commission encouraged people to continue what recent indicators had shown to be a sharp decline in the birth rate and the number of children women expected to have. But the commission cautioned against substitution of population policy for other policies. To address the population problem successfully, the commission noted, "requires that we also address our problems of poverty, of minority and sex discrimination, of careless exploitation of our natural resources, of environmental deterioration, and of spreading suburbs, decaying cities and wasted countrysides."

The commission urged the government to foster more liberal abortion laws, and insure people with the fullest opportunity to decide their own future. By making effective means of contraception more easily available, the commission felt that the government could advance a greater sense of freedom of personal choice in people and, consequently, promote a decrease in the population. Otherwise, "there will come a time very soon when this country, and the world, will be unable to accommodate any more people."

The chairman of the national black political convention, LeRoi Jones, addressing the delegates

AN ASSEMBLY FOR BLACK VOTERS

It marked the first countryside black political convention ever held in the United States, and it laid the groundwork for a Black National Assembly. Prime aim would be to bind America's 7.5 million non-white voters together despite philosophical and political differences and make them a force to reckon with.

The caucus, representing 43 states, was held in a sprawling high school building in Gary, Ind. It proposed that the assembly meet every four years prior to the Democratic and Republican conventions.

The 2,776 delegates passed a resolution to condemn school busing as a means of achieving school integration.

Roy Innis, executive director of the Congress of Racial Equality (CORE) which shepherded the busing resolution through the caucus, declared that blacks were "tired of being guinea pigs for social engineers and New York liberals."

"Busing is obsolete and dangerous to black people," said Innis. "We are ready for a change, ready to control our own destiny."

Demanding a louder voice in government, the delegates adopted a sweeping political agenda which called for a "minimum of 66 Congressional Representatives and 15 Senators." It also sought "proportionate black employment and control at every level of the Federal Government structure."

Authors of the agenda ran into opposition from one powerful group. The call for an independent black political movement was condemned by the National Association for the Advancement of Colored People (NAACP). Their argument: such a stand would promote racial separatism.

A key force behind the convention was Imamu Amiri Baraka, better known as LeRoi Jones, the political playwright. Baraka, who was head of the Pan-Africanist Congress of African People, appeared in a Mao suit and spoke in an impassioned manner, often switching from parliamentary language to that of the urban slums.

Dropping the stern attitude which most Americans had associated with him, Baraka worked tirelessly with blacks of every persuasion.

Many convention officials declared later that Baraka's influence predominated during the three-day convention. Continually he stressed the theme of "Unity Without Uniformity."

The agenda did not end with the U.S. political structure. It also urged that black Americans play a stronger role in framing American foreign policy, especially in regard to the nation's relations with Africa and the Caribbean.

The remains of the wrecked TWA 707 airliner in Las Vegas, Nev., after a plastic explosive enclosed in a briefcase was smuggled into the jet's cockpit and detonated

ONE JET BOMBED, 3 THREATENED

The extortion racket known as Terror in the Skies took a new twist in March 1972 when the New York office of Trans World Airlines received an anonymous phone call with an ominous message.

The male caller warned that a bomb was hidden aboard Flight 7, a 707 Boeing jet with 45 passengers and a crew of seven bound out of Kennedy Airport, New York, for Los Angeles. The male caller also told TWA to look in the 25-cent locker in the airline's Kennedy terminal.

Airline officials assessed the warning and decided to act. A radio message was flashed to Flight 7, by this time 100 miles on its way to Los Angeles, telling Capt. William Motz to turn back to Kennedy.

Meanwhile, security men opened the designated locker and found two army duffel bags and a typed note. The note warned that four TWA planes had bombs aboard, set to go off at six-hour intervals unless $2 million in cash was put in the duffels and turned over to the plotters.

Flight 7 touched down at Kennedy at 12:10 p.m. Passengers were quickly ushered off the plane. Then New York police specialists boarded

with a specially trained German shepherd named Brandy. The dog quickly sniffed out the bomb in a black box-shaped briefcase in the cockpit.

The bomb was deactivated at 12:55 p.m. by police, who said it was set to go off five minutes later. The plastic explosive was equal to about 12 sticks of dynamite.

"It would have blown that plane apart," said William F. Schmitt, a 22-year veteran of the police bomb squad.

That afternoon TWA received a second call from a man who identified himself as Gomez. He ordered the airline to put the ransom aboard a chartered executive jet and fly it to Atlanta. The airline complied, but contact was broken off although the aircraft sat in a remote corner of Atlanta airport for more than four hours.

That evening, while a Kennedy-to-Las Vegas, Nev., 707 with 12 passengers and 7 crewmen aboard, flew over Garden City, Kans., TWA got another call warning that a bomb was aboard that plane. The plane had been searched in New York. It was searched again after landing in Las Vegas without turning anything up. But at 6:55 the next morning just five minutes ahead of the schedule set in the note, a bomb did go off

inside the cockpit, blasting much of the plane's forward area.

No one was hurt.

Examination of the debris indicated that this bomb, like the first, was a plastic explosive and that it also had been smuggled aboard in a briefcase.

By this time TWA was carrying on a frantic worldwide search for the two missing bombs. Carriers across America had launched the most intensive security precautions in the history of the airlines industry. Neither was found.

Passengers were also gripped by the jitters. One New York ticketing agent estimated that TWA's business had fallen off by a third during the week of the bomb scare, while the purchase of flight insurance leaped 40 per cent.

Meanwhile, President Nixon ordered that even more stringent security measures be put into effect at once. Transportation Secretary John A. Volpe met with airline representatives to explain the new rules. Airlines were ordered to tighten airport security to keep unauthorized people away from planes and to screen passengers' baggage and cargo to prevent hiding of explosives on aircraft.

MALTA, BRITAIN PACT SIGNED

The disputed Malta military base accord was delayed for nine months by marathon bargaining, ultimatums, partial withdrawal of British troops and veiled threats by the island's prime minister, Dom Mintoff, to look elsewhere for money.

Finally, in March 1972, Britain and Malta signed a pact for continued use of British bases on the Mediterranean isle which had had military links with the United Kingdom dating back 170 years.

The seven-year accord signed in London by Mintoff and British defense secretary Lord Carrington would pay Malta approximately $37 million a year—about three times what the Maltese had been getting—for the bases used by the British and forces of the North Atlantic Treaty Organization. About two-thirds of the bill would be footed by other NATO countries.

For centuries the little teardrop-shaped island had been caught in the middle of the quarrels of other nations. It was ensnared during the Crusades, trapped in the Napoleonic wars and engulfed by the tide of conflict in World War II.

In 1964 Britain granted independence to the island, but it still served as a major naval base for the British and for NATO.

Last year, when a new round of bargaining began on payment for use of the bases, Mintoff demanded a whopping $78 million, but he soon scaled this down to $46.8 million. However, it was still too steep for Britain and her NATO partners, who had been paying about $12 million a year.

Prime Minister Edward Heath's government declared that it would withdraw its forces from Malta rather than pay what it considered an exorbitant price. Last December the British forces and their dependents began pulling out. When less than 1,000 of the 3,500-man force remained, and most of the 6,000 dependents had left, Malta was suffering from serious unemployment of

Malta's prime minister, Dom Mintoff (left), and British Defense Secretary Lord Carrington signing defense agreement at Marlborough House, London

islanders who had been working as civilians at the bases. There were laid off in droves.

Britain's desire to retain its military facilities on Malta was founded less on the island's inherent worth as a naval base than on a determination to keep it out of Russian hands. And the British threat to pull out its forces from Malta came only a few days after Mintoff's regime and the Soviet government disclosed that they had signed a trade agreement.

The turn of events raised fears in the West that Moscow might be maneuvering to make Malta a beachhead for its Mediterranean fleet.

An important provision of the accord finally accepted by Mintoff was that Malta would not permit the forces of the Soviet Union or any nation in the Warsaw Pact to be stationed on the island or to use its military facilities.

Shortly after the signing of the British-Maltese agreement, an authoritative administrative official in Washington disclosed that the United States would pay more than $9 million as its share of the $37 million package.

Britain would pay about $14 million, and most of the remaining rent would be paid out by West Germany and Italy.

TV VIOLENCE REPORT REVIEWED

It had never been determined whether or not violence depicted in American television programs actually bred an aggressive behavior pattern among some viewers, particularly the young. So, in 1969, Sen. John Pastore, D-R.I., sponsored a $1 million study of TV material and its possible relationship to "antisocial behavior among young people." The findings, released early in 1972, were followed by congressional hearings in March because of the controversy they had provoked.

The conclusions of the report had been made public on Jan. 17. Its authors, the Surgeon General's Scientific Advisory Committee on Television and Social Behavior, said that the effect of TV violence was slight when compared with such other possible causes as parental attitudes or knowledge or contact with violence in real life.

The 12 behavioral scientists said TV violence could trigger aggression by children or teenagers already prone to violence. But they cautioned against generalizing on "a very complex issue, for which there are no simple answers."

Critics called the report a whitewash and

charged that the surgeon general's panel was biased.

The surgeon general, Dr. Jesse L. Steinfeld, insisted that "the study shows for the first time a causal connection between violence shown on television and subsequent aggressive behavior by children."

One of the critics of the report, Rep. John M. Murphy, D-N.Y., accused the industry of having "bullheadedly violated its own codes in spite of a 20-year succession of congressional and Federal Communications Commission investigations." He said that the networks had a veto power over the reports of committee membership.

The New York Times said "a number of researchers who supplied the raw data and some members of the advisory committee that drew up the report reported that it understated the cause-and-effect relationship in children between watching television and aggressive behavior."

Prompted by such criticisms, the Senate's subcommittee on communications held four days of hearings on the report. The surgeon general urged "appropriate and immediate remedial action" to counter the overdose of violence television had provided for children. He added, in

response to committee sponsor Pastore's questioning, that there was "sufficient data" to establish a causal relationship. He did not spell out what action should be taken beyond parental responsibility.

Julian Goodman, president of NBC, told the subcommittee: "We have tried conscientiously to structure the children's programing so as to eliminate violence which could be harmful to children," and provide alternative programing that "will contribute to the child's education and development."

CBS president John A. Achneider presented examples of how his network was "meeting our programing responsibilities to young viewers" by changing its format.

Elton H. Rule, president of ABC, said that cartoons which depended solely on action would be eliminated from children's programing.

The report had stated that in 1969 cartoons were the most violent fare, with 97 per cent of them depicting violence and 88 per cent of the cartoon characters involved in violent acts.

During the final day of hearings Sen. Pastore suggested that the Government devise an index that could measure the amount of violence on television in the United States.

SEVEN KILLED IN BOMBER CRASH

When a burning B52 bomber crashed in a residential area adjacent to McCoy Air Force Base near Orlando, Fla., its seven crewmen were killed and eight persons were injured in houses ignited by a sheet of blazing jet fuel. One of the burned civilians died later.

"I saw the whole thing, and that pilot's action kept the plane from hitting the airport terminal," said W. M. Miller, taxi supervisor at the civilian field on the base.

Another witness, Tom Smith, 24, an ex-Marine, said: "When he broke through the cloud cover he couldn't have been more than 200 feet up. When the pilot saw what was happening he pulled it (the plane) to the right and dumped it in a field."

The pilot of the eight-engine jet, Capt. Wendell W. Campbell, 30, of Washington, D.C., had reported a fire aboard only minutes before the accident.

Smith also reported that the bomber's engines began to pop as the big plane tried to make its way back to the base after a routine training flight on March 31. He said pieces of metal were falling from the wings.

Two homes were destroyed and two others were severely damaged, sheriff's officers reported, in the fires that burned for an hour after the crash. Charred autos stood in the driveways. On one lot the burned skeleton of a child's swing remained. On another the swimming pool was covered by a thick layer of fire-fighting foam.

Smith said that at one point he heard cries behind a redwood fence. He smashed the fence bodily and rescued Mrs. Nancy Robertson and her three children, who were trapped in a space between the fence and their flaming home.

"The plane was coming out of the clouds on its final approach," commented Lt. Gen. Russell E. Dougherty, commander of the Second Air Force. "The place of impact indicated that it almost made it."

PIONEER 10 LAUNCHED ON JUPITER JOURNEY

There was an unnerving 25-minute delay because of technical problems, then at 8:50 p.m. March 10 Pioneer 10 lifted off in a brilliant flash and roared away on man's first attempt to probe the mysteries of the planet Jupiter.

Less than 12 hours after it had blasted off from Cape Kennedy, Fla., the 570-pound Pioneer streaked past the moon's orbit some 244,900 miles from earth and was off to a good start on its trail-blazing 21-month odyssey of nearly 600 million miles to the biggest planet in the solar system.

Pioneer got off to a record-breaking start, in fact. Less than 16 minutes after the launch it was traveling on course at 31,413 miles an hour.

The shoot went off when Jupiter, a roiling bulk of primordial gases and clouds 318 times the mass of earth and possible habitat of some life forms, was 525 million miles from earth.

Pioneer was designed with 11 instruments for measuring Jupiter's hydrogen-rich atmosphere, thick clouds and radiation belt. It was the first spacecraft to be aimed at one of the outer planets. It was also the first to pass through the asteroid belt, that cloud of debris ranging in size from dust specks to rocks 480 miles wide which circled the sun at distances between 170 million and 345 million miles.

When Pioneer moves to within 100,000 miles of Jupiter in December 1973, it will be close enough for observation. Hopefully the spaceship will spend four days transmitting television pictures, including some shots of the huge, mysterious red spot that astronomers have observed.

Jupiter's potential hazards included its radiation belts, said to be a million times stronger than the Van Allen Belts around earth. Instruments aboard Jupiter were expected to measure these intense radiation belts and plumb the chemical composition of the atmosphere. The plan was for the spacecraft to approach the planet on its sunlit side, swing almost completely around its dark side, then shoot out toward the fringes of the solar system.

Jupiter's strong gravitational pull was expected to step up the speed of Pioneer from about 20,000 mph to 78,000 mph.

Scientists said that, some time in 1983 or 1984, Pioneer would probably glide out of the solar system, its transmitters long since dead, and drift through the galaxy. On the remote chance that the spacecraft might encounter some form of life in its travels, scientists affixed a message to the ship. On a gold plaque measuring 6 by 9 inches were the figures of a man and a woman along with mathematical symbols indicating the time and source of Pioneer's launching.

Marie del Carmen Martinez-Bordiu and Prince Alfonso de Borbon y Dampierre taking their wedding vows during a ceremony at the Pardo Palace chapel in Madrid, Spain. At extreme left, General Francisco Franco, the bride's grandfather

Canadian John Law with his sister, Moira, before he and two British technicians were kidnaped and killed by Turkish terrorists in Kizildere, Turkey

MRS. GANDHI IN FIRM CONTROL

After she took office as India's prime minister in 1966, Indira Gandhi insisted that conservative interests in parliament and regional interests in the state governments had thwarted her efforts to achieve national stability and reduce her nation's poverty.

Then, in state elections held in March 1972, Mrs. Gandhi swept the boards as she had in parliamentary balloting a year earlier, crushing opposition parties on both right and left.

As a result of her sweeping victory at the polls, she had firm control over both the central government and the states. But even with her new political muscle, it would not be easy to improve the plight of millions of impoverished countrymen.

Even before the vote, Mrs. Gandhi had begun to overhaul her New Congress party, trying to clean out the machine politicians and bring in new, more progressive faces.

The prime minister's forces trounced the Marxist Communists in West Bengal in the March balloting. Her party won more than two-thirds of the seats in the state legislature, the largest number ever scored by a party in West Bengal.

As a result, the Congress party concentrated on restoring law and order in this state of 45 million people, packed in 80 to the square mile and beset by disease, poverty, unemployment and violence.

Disregarding objections from some members of her party, Mrs. Gandhi made an electoral alliance with the pro-Soviet Communists so that each could help the other in defeating the militant pro-Peking Marxists. The result was not only the defeat of the West Bengal Reds, but the emergence of the Moscow group as the second largest party in India. This alliance was another indication of the growing friendship between Moscow and New Delhi.

As Indian-Soviet relations became more cordial, New Delhi's association with Washington continued to deteriorate. This was reflected in Mrs. Gandhi's campaign speeches in which she repeatedly charged that the United States and China were plotting "something sinister" against India in an alliance with Pakistan. Nixon's decision to cut off aid to India after she went to war with Pakistan did not make Mrs. Gandhi any more friendly.

One Congress party official said later that "we must be thankful for Nixon."

"His Peking visit and his short sighted policy on the sub-continent helped us a lot in the election," he said.

3 HOSTAGES, 10 CAPTORS SLAIN

For eight hours on March 30, Turkish troops and police kept vigil around a small wooden house near the mountain village of Kizildere. Inside the building terrorists were holding hostage two Britons and a Canadian. The three, electronics experts for the North Atlantic Treaty Organization, had been kidnaped several days earlier from a nearby NATO base.

The 11 guerrilla captors, all members of the leftist People's Liberation Army, had snatched the trio to bargain for release of three comrades slated to be executed for abducting four U.S. airmen in Ankara in 1971.

But Turkish Premier Nihat Erim flatly rejected the kidnapers' proposal to return the hostages in exchange for safe conduct out of the country.

"You cannot escape," blared an army loudspeaker. "Do not stain your hands with blood."

Finally, the government forces moved in under a hail of grenades and bullets. When the dust had settled, 10 of the guerrillas lay dead. So did all three captives: Britons Charles Turner, 45, and Gordon Banner, 35, and Canadian John Law, 21. The three were found shot through the head, their hands tied behind their backs. They had apparently been executed before the government assault on the building.

A letter found with the bodies of the captives was addressed to "Traitors, pro-America dogs." The letter sought to justify the killings by calling the victims "British agents of the NATO forces occupying our country and . . . we consider it our basic right and honor to execute them."

FOR THE RECORD

ELECTED. Generalissimo Chiang Kai-shek, 84, to his fifth six-year term as president of the Republic of (Nationalist) China. Chiang, who was the only candidate in the March 21 balloting, received all but eight of the 1,316 ballots cast in the National Assembly on Taiwan. The eight were left blank. As soon as the official results were announced, firecrackers echoed throughout the capital of Taipei. Thousands of students marched through the streets holding aloft portraits of the president and banners reading "President Chiang is the Nation's Savior."

Workers in Mainz, West Germany, removing the cast from a glass mirror under construction for a telescope to go into use in 1980

Superfluous gases burned off as a by-product of oil production at Ahmadi, Kuwait, world's seventh biggest oil producer

Astronaut Duke collecting lunar samples ➝

April

The Craters on the Moon

The Apollo 16 astronauts boarding a transfer van before the start of their 10-day lunar voyage

*Area never before seen by man toured by exploring astronauts
of Apollo 16, who set up experiments and gathered unique
rock specimens after landing problems were solved*

THE JUBILANT Southern drawl of astronaut Charles M. Duke Jr. carried across the 240,000 miles to earth, informing Mission Control that he and John W. Young had landed safely on the moon in Apollo 16's lunar ship Orion. His first words, typical of moon visitors:

"Wow! Orion is finally here, Houston. Fantastic!"

There was reason to be happy. Just six hours earlier, Orion had been waved off on its first landing attempt after astronaut

Thomas K. Mattingly II reported a problem in the backup control system in the main engine of the command ship Casper.

"There's an oscillation in the steering system," Mattingly told the ground as he orbited the moon alone.

Mission Control immediately ordered the two spaceships to maneuver to within a few hundred feet of one another in case the command was given for a quick rendezvous, docking and return to earth.

The astronauts were in no immediate danger. But under mission rules the command ship's primary and secondary engine control systems must be working before a lunar landing can be attempted.

If both systems went out, the descent engine of the lunar lander would be needed to bring the astronauts home, just as it did on Apollo 13 in 1970 after an oxygen tank explosion wrecked the command module's engine section (*The World in 1970, 62–68*).

In Houston, and at factories, test chambers and universities in California, Massachusetts and Tennessee, a cross-country team of experts, linked by telephone, troubleshot the problem. Astronauts in spaceship trainers simulated the trouble and assessed possible effects.

After nearly four hours, it was determined that the oscillations of the engine nozzle would neither significantly alter the path of the spacecraft nor harm it structurally even if the secondary system had to be used. Exultant controllers radioed Orion: "You are go for landing."

That was the most serious of a number of problems that besieged Apollo 16 almost from the beginning of its journey, which started with the perfect launch of a Saturn 5 rocket from Cape Kennedy, Fla., at 12:54 p.m. EST Sunday, April 16.

On the three-day outward voyage, Young, Duke and Mattingly kept busy monitoring and correcting difficulties with the guidance and navigation system, a pressurization unit, a radio antenna, the drinking water and paint flaking off the lunar module.

All were overcome or were not considered serious enough to affect the mission.

The crew was commanded by the veteran Young, a 41-year-old Navy captain making his fourth space flight. He had flown previously on two Gemini earth orbit trips and on the Apollo 10 lunar orbit mission.

Air Force Lt. Col. Duke and Navy Lt. Cmdr. Mattingly, both 36, were on their first flights. Mattingly almost made it on Apollo 13 but was replaced by a backup pilot three days before launching after he became exposed to German measles.

The goal of Young and Duke was to make the first landing in the moon's ancient highlands, which comprise nearly 80 per cent of the lunar surface. Four earlier Apollo crews had landed on relatively flat plains.

Orion's target was a wide plateau in the Descartes Mountains, the highest topographical region on the moon's front side.

The delay in landing had pulled the path of the lunar ship nearly four miles south of the original Descartes approach path. But once Young and Duke fired the descent engine and started the long curving drop, the guidance system corrected for the error and the astronauts touched down just 650 feet off the bull's-eye.

The ninth and 10th men to reach the moon were logged down at 9:23 p.m., April 20.

Young commented on the roughness of the terrain.

"We don't have to walk far to pick up rocks," he said. "We're among 'em."

Exhausted from their tense ordeal, Young and Duke slept seven hours, then started their first of three outside excursions.

Young was first down the ladder, and as he planted his insulated boots in the dusty soil, he exclaimed: "Here you are, mysterious and unknown Descartes. Apollo 16 is going to change your image."

The enthusiastic Duke shouted as he stepped on the surface: "Yahoo! This is so great I can hardly believe it. We are proud to be Americans on an experience like this."

The Apollo 16 moon rocket blasting off

Above, astronauts Young, left, and Duke conferring on the moon.

Below, astronaut Young leaping up from the lunar surface to salute the U.S. flag .

Charles Duke standing before the lunar roving vehicle near Stone Mountain

They quickly set about their tasks, collecting samples, planting the American flag, assembling their four-wheel moon buggy and erecting a nuclear-powered science station to relay data long after they left on such things as the solar wind, radiation, magnetic fields, meteors and moonquakes.

The moonmen were stunned by the landscape of mountains, craters and desolate desert-like terrain.

"It's absolutely beautiful," Duke commented.

"Fantastic, super," Young added.

A television camera relayed clear pictures to earth of the two busy astronauts.

It captured Duke dropping one of the experiment packages as he loped along. And it showed Young as he accidentally tripped over a cable, tearing loose a connecting device and ruining a $1.2 million device intended to measure heat flow from the lunar interior.

"God almighty," Young apologized. "It broke right at the connector. I didn't even know it. Oh, rats. I'm sorry, Charlie."

With the rest of the experiments hooked up, Young and Duke set off on their moon car trip, a mile across the Cayley Plain to inspect two craters named Flag and Spook and to gather rocks along the way.

Like those who had explored the moon before them, the moon drivers were excited by the lunar bits and pieces they found at their feet. They reported picking up two white crystalline rocks that scientists believed might have come from volcanic flows pouring over the Descartes region during the formative years of the moon between 4 and 4.5 billion years ago—before the planet became a relatively dead body.

After 7 hours 11 minutes outside, Young and Duke returned to Orion for a night's rest.

The second excursion took them 2.6 miles south to Stone Mountain, and Young skillfully steered the moon car over a ridge and through a large boulder field before starting up the 10-degree slope.

"Here, let's stop here," Duke called out as he spotted Crown Crater about halfway up the 1,660-foot peak.

Young parked the battery-powered buggy in a shallow crater on a mountain terrace.

For the next few hours the astronauts worked at several sites on the mountain slope, struggling at times to maintain their footing and balance in the soft dust. Both took tumbles, but quickly righted themselves with a gentle push against the surface in the moon's one-sixth gravity field.

Back in the lunar module after a record 7 hours 23 minutes outside, both expressed disappointment at not having found more crystalline rocks that would be evidence of volcanic activity. Scientists on the ground theorized they had the evidence, but volcanic processes on the moon probably differed from those on earth, making it difficult to interpret the lunar rocks.

The final field trip on Sunday showed dramatically just how rugged the Descartes terrain is.

"Look at those boulders! Look at those rocks! They get bigger and bigger," Duke exclaimed as the moon car edged to the rim of North Ray Crater, 3.3 miles from the landing site.

Some of the boulders, seen on television, were as big as two-story houses, and Young and Duke eagerly chipped off samples.

They inched their way a few feet down into North Ray Crater, which is 600 feet deep and two-thirds of a mile across. As Young stuck his gloved hand into a small crater, he said: "That's one of those gopher holes."

John Young walking away from the deployment site

"You do that in west Texas and you'd get a rattlesnake," quipped Duke.

At various locations the astronauts operated a portable magnetometer and recorded the first evidence of weak but unmistakable magnetism on the moon. The finding implied that the moon once had a molten interior like earth's, and that it spun much faster on its axis than it does today.

After 5 hours 40 minutes, Young and Duke climbed back into Orion for the last time and packed away their record 213-pound haul of moon treasure.

At 8:25 p.m. that night, April 23, they launched Orion's cabin section after a stay of 71 hours, 2 minutes.

"What a ride! What a ride!" Duke shouted as they quit the moon to begin two hours of maneuvers that caught the command ship Casper in orbit 70 miles above the surface.

"Casper's captured Orion," Mattingly radioed after the linkup.

The astronauts had planned to spend an extra two days in lunar orbit to conduct photographic and scientific experiments. But, because of the remote possibility of a deterioration in the condition of the main engine's backup control system, Mission Control told them to start home a day early.

On Monday night, April 24, they triggered the engine. It worked perfectly, and they were on their way.

"Coming up like thunder," Young reported. "The burn was perfect."

The next afternoon Mattingly opened the hatch of the spacecraft and stepped outside, 199,000 miles from earth. Bundled in a white pressure suit and attached to a 25-foot lifeline, he worked his way to an equipment bay at the rear of the ship and retrieved film canisters from two cameras which had remotely mapped the moon's surface.

Before re-entering the cabin he stood in the hatch for 10 minutes and exposed 60 million microbes to determine how their growth might be affected by the harsh space environment.

On the eve of splashdown the astronauts held a news conference from space, answering questions relayed from newsmen at Mission Control.

"We've seen as much in 10 days as most people see in 10 lifetimes," Commander Young reported.

The return to earth April 27 after 11 days in space was a spectacle of beauty. A television camera for the first time captured the unfurling of the three 83-foot-diameter parachutes as Apollo 16 dropped toward the Pacific Ocean.

Hundreds of cheering, white-clad sailors lined the decks of the recovery carrier Ticonderoga to watch the dramatic sight. Casper hit the water just 3,300 feet from the ship.

During welcoming ceremonies aboard the carrier, Young called the mission one of discovery that would enable scientists to uncover basic knowledge about the moon and our solar system.

"Apollo 16 pushed back the last frontier, the frontier of the unknown," he said. "This is essential to the survival of humanity on this planet."

"By golly," he added, "you taxpayers, we taxpayers, got your money's worth."

James Byrnes' Career Covered Five Decades

As War Mobilizer, top aide to Franklin D. Roosevelt became known as 'Assistant President,' with White House offices

Byrnes displaying the American Statesman medal awarded to him by the Freedoms Foundation in 1968

A^s DIRECTOR of War Mobilization from 1943 to 1945, James Francis Byrnes had an office in the White House and held greater executive powers than any person in the United States except Franklin D. Roosevelt, who described his top aide as "assistant President."

Byrnes, who died April 9 at the age of 92 at his home in Columbia, S.C., had a career that spanned five decades. It carried him to Congress, the governor's mansion of South Carolina, the Supreme Court, to cabinet rank as Secretary of State and to the United Nations as a delegate.

Byrnes relished the authority vested in him in his wartime post. Commenting on it later, he said:

"The order establishing the Office of War Mobilization and appointing me director conferred upon me greater authority than a President had ever previously delegated.

"Essentially it gave me, under the President, power to originate policies and lay out programs that would coordinate the work of all the war agencies and federal departments in any way connected with the production, procurement, transportation and distribution of both civilian and military supplies; moreover, it gave me the power to see that these decisions were carried out." Byrnes' long career included service in county and state government and in all three branches of the Federal Government. It brought this ingratiating southerner of Irish descent close to the office of vice president at least once.

Born in Charleston, S.C., Byrnes became an international figure who met Soviet chief Josef Stalin and British Prime Minister Winston Churchill at Yalta and Potsdam. The knowledge he acquired of world affairs made Byrnes one of President Harry S. Truman's closest advisors. It was Byrnes who helped make the crucial decision to drop the atom bombs over Hiroshima and Nagasaki in August 1945. He realized the far-reaching consequences of such an act by America, then the only possessor of the A bomb. But he believed use of the awesome weapon would permit the United States to "dictate our own terms" in postwar relations with Soviet Russia.

For most of his political life, Byrnes was a staunch Democrat, but he bolted the party in 1952 to support Dwight D. Eisenhower, the GOP standard bearer for President. He backed Eisenhower again in 1956, and four years later threw his support behind Richard M. Nixon. By this time voting Republican apparently had become a habit, and he supported Barry Goldwater in 1964 and told Nixon he hoped he would win in 1968.

Byrnes' break with the national Democratic party was reported due in part to a quarrel with Truman and to Byrnes' anti-Sovietism and his opposition to Negro desegregation. He openly distrusted the Negro political and social movement. In his autobiography, *All in One Lifetime,* written in 1958, Byrnes said that he had suffered "disappointments and defeats" in his action-packed career. He especially regretted being passed over for the vice presidential nomination, first in 1940 and again in 1944.

Despite his disappointment, Byrnes kept up with his arduous job as War Mobilizer, touring the European battle fronts with Gen. George C. Marshall, the U.S. chief of staff.

Byrnes had a personal attachment to Roosevelt. Not only was he a political advisor but also he was a companion in relaxation and a confidant of the President.

His relations with Truman began on a happy note, but their ties ended in bitterness. Truman said later in his memoirs that Byrnes had developed "the illusion" that he was President and had to be put in his place and finally let go. Truman said that the parting was friendly; the two split later over civil rights.

Byrnes himself insisted that he had faithfully carried out Truman's foreign policy and that the break actually came in 1949, two years after he had stepped down as Secretary of State. The quarrel was provoked, Byrnes said, by a speech he made criticizing Truman's domestic policies and the President had accused his former colleague of conspiring against him.

Overall, however, Byrnes found his long career of public service rewarding. "It's been an exciting life," he wrote, "a terribly busy life. There haven't been many idle moments. I have not had the boredom of routine. I have no regrets."

Byrnes launched his political career in 1908 by winning election as prosecutor in South Carolina's Second Judicial Circuit. Two years later he won a seat in the House of Representatives.

"I campaigned on nothing but gall," he said, "and gall won by 57 votes."

He began his tour in the U.S. Legislature by fostering formation of the House Committee on Roads, prompting a critic to say "he was progressive on roads and regressive on almost everything else."

Later on he was appointed to the House Appropriations Committee and became one of President Woodrow Wilson's lieutenants in the House. At about that time he formed a close friendship with Assistant Secretary of the Navy Franklin D. Roosevelt.

Byrnes rarely made speeches in the House, but he was deeply involved in committee work and had a talent for reconciling the differences of various legislators and bringing them together in a working agreement.

"The art of legislating is the art of intelligent compromise," he once said. "In my experience there were really few bills in which a great principle was involved; the issues were really a matter of policy, not principle."

Byrnes made an unsuccessful bid in South Carolina for the U.S. Senate in 1924, but six years later he won. After 1932 he became a trusted legislative tactician for Roosevelt's New Deal Program. He was not an all-out New Dealer, however. He favored the Wagner National Labor Relations Act, but op-

James F. Byrnes lying in state at the State Capitol Building in Columbia, S.C.

posed sitdown strikes; he backed the Supreme Court "packing" plan of 1937, but he opposed Roosevelt's attempted party purge of 1938. He supported a ban on importation of strikebreakers, but voted against the Wages and Hours Act.

When war broke over Europe in 1939, Byrnes buried his differences with the White House and helped repeal the Neutrality Act and pass the Lend-Lease bill for aid to Britain. In recognition of his services, Byrnes was named by Roosevelt to the Supreme Court in 1941. But he soon became restless and was openly delighted when the President called on him 16 months later to step down and head the Office of Economic Stablization.

"I've got ants in my pants," he remarked after one long drawnout Supreme Court session. "I've been listening all day to some fellows here arguing about something that happened 15 years ago and, frankly, I don't give a damn about what happened then. My country's at war and I want to be in it. I don't think I can stand the abstractions of jurisprudence at a time like this." Then he added:

"I would not have left the Supreme Court if Roosevelt had not assured me he would never hear an appeal from my decisions. In all my time as Director of Economic Mobilization and War Mobilizer, he kept faith with his promise to me."

Byrnes had sweeping powers as Economic Stabilizer. He regulated prices, wages and rents and supervised the rationing of food, fuel and some clothing. He froze some men in their jobs, moved others into work directly linked to war production.

Before he left the war mobilization post in 1945, Byrnes accompanied Roosevelt to the meeting of the United States, Soviet Russia and Britain at Yalta in the Crimea.

"Why the President insisted on my going I still do not know," Byrnes wrote in his autobiography. "Perhaps it was because I had a reputation with the Congress and the public for being more conservative than other members of our delegation. . . . Or perhaps because he knew better than those close to him the state of his health."

Byrnes was deeply impressed with Stalin and later wrote: "Stalin himself was different from all other men I have known. He was direct in his conversation, and his sentences were short and emphatic. Unlike his countrymen whom I met, he had a sense of humor. At times he indulged in 'needling' Churchill, whom he seemed to admire, although it was apparent he had a deeper affection for Roosevelt. He dominated those around him. This was made evident when I saw him turn to a general and order him to bring him a cup of tea."

In July 1945, Byrnes, who had been named Secretary of State, accompanied Truman to Potsdam, where the Big Three attempted to shape the future of Europe and arranged for the Soviet Union's entry into the war against Japan.

In December 1945, Byrnes went to Moscow to negotiate an agreement to form a United Nations Atomic Energy Commission. The following month he served as the senior U.S. delegate to the first meeting of the U.N. General Assembly in London. In March 1946 he headed the U.S. delegation to the U.N. Security Council session in New York.

At about that point, Byrnes' attitude towards the Russians began to harden. He opposed Soviet attempts to thrust into Iran and clashed with Russian leaders over peace terms for Italy, Romania, Bulgaria, Hungary and Finland.

Byrnes lived in retirement in South Carolina from 1947 until 1950, when he was elected governor. He served in that post until 1955. A man of simple tastes, he once described his wants as "two-tailor-made suits a year, three meals a day and a reasonable amount of good liquor."

Secretary of State Byrnes after a meeting with President Truman in August 1945

Soledad Brothers Freed
in Three Prison Deaths

Key figures in the Soledad Brothers drama included, from left, George Jackson; convict Ruchell Magee, Angela Davis and Huey Newton, cofounder of the Black Panthers.

A<small>T SOLEDAD PRISON</small> in the lonely lettuce bowl of California's Salinas Valley, guards marched black and white prisoners together onto a new exercise field for the first time the chilly morning of Jan. 13, 1970.

Fists began to fly.

A tower guard said he feared 14 blacks were beating two white convicts to death, so he yelled a warning. He blew a whistle, then fired his rifle.

Three black convicts were shot to death. A white was wounded.

In protest, prisoners refused to eat for three days.

Then inmates in the prison TV room heard on the nightly news that the Monterey County Grand Jury ruled the black deaths "justifiable homicide."

Minutes later, rookie white guard John V. Mills, 26, lay dying on a concrete floor in Y-Wing. Someone had beaten him bloody with his own flashlight, then heaved him head first over a third-floor tier. "One down, two to go," read a note near his body.

Eight days later three black prisoners on Y-Wing were charged with first-degree murder: George Lester Jackson, 29, serving five years to life for a 1961 gas station robbery; John Wesley Clutchette, 28, and Fleeta Drumgo, 26, both serving six months to 15 years on separate second-degree burglary convictions. *(The World in 1971, 168-171).*

Through Black Panther leader Huey P. Newton and Jackson's attorney Fay Stender word of the trio's case was piped along the grapevine in California's prison system where Jackson was much respected as a black leader.

They became known as the "Soledad Brothers." After months of legal wrangling, their trial was moved to San Francisco on grounds of possible jury prejudice in the Salinas Valley. In the fall Jackson hit the best seller lists with his impassioned book, *"Soledad Brother: The Prison Letters of George Jackson."*

Among the warmest letters were those to Angela Y. Davis, a black revolutionary fired from her UCLA teaching job for being a Communist. She took up the Soledad Brothers' banner, demanded their freedom and helped raise defense money at rallies with Jackson's younger brother Jonathan, 17. On a sunny Aug. 7 afternoon about a week after his brother, Drumgo and Clutchette were moved to San Quentin Prison to await trial, Jonathan Jackson strolled into a nearby San Rafael courthouse with a flight bag filled with guns.

The State of California claimed he and Angela Davis plotted to take hostages from the courtroom to exchange later for the Soledad Brothers' freedom.

Black convicts in the courtroom helped Jackson take five hostages and, in a burst of gunfire in a yellow escape van outside, Jackson, a judge and two black kidnapers were shot to death. Miss Davis was charged with murder, kidnap and conspiracy as an accused accomplice. A year later, on Aug. 21, 1971, tower guards shot and killed George Jackson, saying he was trying to escape from San Quentin armed with a gun someone had smuggled to him.

Near his cell were found the bodies of five dead white men, three guards and two honor inmates, allegedly killed by convicts whose cells Jackson had unlocked. Drumgo was among six prisoners charged with these murders.

In hand and foot chains, the surviving Soledad Brothers were brought from prison Dec. 21, 1971 for trial under the strictest court security in San Francisco history.

A floor-to-ceiling inch-thick bullet-proof shield was erected to separate spectators from the courtroom floor. Riot-equipped tactical squad police frisked and photographed all who entered, and all women were required to drop their underpants in front of police matrons searching for weapons.

Presiding Judge S. Lee Vavuris ordered the security after two fist-swinging brawls erupted at earlier pretrial hearings—one after a bailiff got slugged for trying to take a newspaper from Jackson.

The judge also forbade attorneys from telling the all-white jury about the original killing of the three blacks by the guard.

This was despite defense contentions that many Soledad inmates were enraged enough by these deaths to kill a guard in revenge.

Key witnesses for the state were four nervous convicts who claimed they saw Clutchette and Drumgo at the death scene. One said he saw Jackson push the guard through a railing. Another said Clutchette wiped a bloody flashlight the prosecution claimed was found on the ground outside Clutchette's cell.

However, experts admitted they could find at the scene no bloodstains or fingerprints positively linking the defendants to the crime.

Both defendants proclaimed their innocence. Their lawyers sharply attacked the believability of the convict-witnesses, claiming the state promised payoffs in the form of early re-leases for those willing to testify despite fears of retaliation by other convicts.

A slender black witness, Thomas Yorke, said he feared guards would have him killed if he didn't talk and convicts would kill him if he did.

Like all three others who fingered Jackson as the principal assailant, Yorke said he saw Jackson pitch Mills over the railing but added that he loved Jackson "very much. I thought Mr. Jackson was a very beautiful example of what a black man should be."

After 13 stormy weeks, attorneys for both sides summed up arguments by telling jurors they had to decide if the four convicts were telling the truth.

Jurors deliberated 16 hours over a weekend—and said two jurors once were at a point of "physical violence"—before emerging Monday morning, Mar. 27, with a verdict: Not guilty.

Tears streaming down their faces, Drumgo and Clutchette bearhugged their attorneys and the jurors.

At that very moment in San Jose, Calif., the prosecution at the Angela Davis murder-kidnap trial was detailing its case and contending that Miss Davis plotted the San Rafael, Calif., courthouse escape attempt in order to free George Jackson because she loved him.

When she heard of the Soledad verdict, Miss Davis said: "It's beautiful."

"If George Jackson had not been struck down by San Quentin guards in August of last year," Miss Davis said, "he too would have been freed from that unjust prosecution."

Jackson's casket, draped in a Black Panther flag, being carried from funeral services in Oakland, Calif.

Town in Iran Demolished in 30 Seconds by Quake, Death toll set at 4,000

As THE SUN ROSE over the Iranian hamlet of Qeer on the morning of April 10, some men were already out working the fields and womenfolk were busy cooking rice for the next meal.

It was a rich farm region, the orange trees laden with fruit and the fields dotted with succulent Persian melons.

No one paid much attention when the earth suddenly shuddered. Tremors were felt every few days in southwestern Iran, which had been devastated by a major quake nearly four years earlier *(The World in 1968, 167)*.

Then, 10 minutes later, it happened. A 30-second shock rolled over the region in three waves that demolished Qeer and laid waste about 60 other villages. The quake killed at least 4,000 persons and left the countryside in ruins. Most of those who had gone out into the fields survived, but those still in their homes perished as the houses collapsed on them.

By week's end nearly all the 4,000 bodies had been recovered. Most of the victims were women, or children who had been playing about their yards waiting for school to open.

Rescue teams, rushed to the stricken area, saw a jumble of dust-covered rubble. And through the ruins echoed the anguished moans of old men and women and the piercing wail of children.

"I lost my wife and five children," said Ahmed Khosrovani, a 41-year-old farmer. "I lost my house and my belongings. I have only God, who is not helping me."

Others perished while seeking divine guidance. Thirty-seven Moslems attending morning prayers in the village mosque perished when the building collapsed.

"This earthquake was like throwing a pebble into a pond," said a rescue official. "The ripples spread outwards all over the province. But it was in Qeer that the stone fell."

Officials of the Red Lion and Sun (Iran's Red Cross) brought supplies to the stricken hamlets aboard helicopters, many of them flown by U.S. Air Force men who had been training pilots of the Imperial Iranian air force.

Everywhere the copters landed it was the same story, hundreds of dead, children without families. Stunned men and women whose kin had all been wiped out.

A news photographer who landed in Qeer saw a sign lying battered in a dusty road. It said "Welcome to Our Town."

Tragedy touched nearly everyone in the quake area.

"I was saying my prayers when a slight tremor shook me," said Safar Keshtar, 41-year-old farmer. "I had hardly finished when the whole roof collapsed with a shock like a bomb ex-

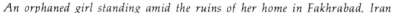

An orphaned girl standing amid the ruins of her home in Fakhrabad, Iran

A man cradling the body of his dead son while searching for a final resting place

plosion." Keshtar's wife and four children were buried beneath the wreckage of their mud-brick home.

Most of those killed in Qeer had moved from black goat-hair tents into stone houses only a few years ago. Most of those still living in the primitive tents escaped unhurt.

There were some miraculous escapes. One child was found alive under a wooden beam of a house 34 hours after the quake. A doctor taking the boy to a hospital to have a fractured skull treated jokingly asked him, "And where have you been all this time?" The boy seriously replied: "I have been in my house, uncle."

Gen. Parvis Dadsetan of the Red Lion and Sun was writing out vouchers to help survivors draw food and medicine when a tall sad-faced man confronted him.

"I am Ali Abbas," the man announced. "In my village there are 500 dead, and the only helicopter we have seen was taking pictures. I have walked down the mountain to tell you we need help."

As officials doled out rations in Qeer, an aged woman hobbled past mumbling to herself. "She has lost everyone," said a rescue worker.

There was even some grim humor in the wake of the disaster. Roghieh Salari was one of several village women who gave birth shortly after the tragedy. The name of her newborn son: Zelzelleh, meaning Earthquake.

The usual aftershocks of a big quake still shook the area of devastation two days later. The Geophysics Institute at Shiraz, about 100 miles northwest of the quake zone, said 1,000 tremors had been felt since the first big shock.

"But there is nothing left to be ruined," said a spokesman for the institute.

The Shah of Iran sent his brother, Prince Mahmoud, and Premier Amir Abass Hoveida to the stricken area to supervise rescue operations.

Dr. Simon Sahaty, who headed the medical team in Qeer, shook his head as he watched survivors clear away the rubble, ready to build once again.

"They should go," he said. "There will certainly be more earthquakes. But this is their land."

For centuries southwestern Iran had been visited by quakes of varying intensity. The reason was a geological fault extending from Shiraz to Lar, right across the province of Fars. The Zagros Mountains, which rise from the plain, are young in geological terms and are still settling. As they do so, whole villages are often destroyed.

The survivors of Qeer were offered financial assistance if they would settle elsewhere. But the villagers had a strong attachment to their barren land and nothing would induce them to leave it.

Rescue work went slowly. Flooded rivers washed away roads and bridges, making transportation all but impossible in some areas.

Meanwhile, efforts were made to avert future disasters. Research teams from the Pahlevi University in Shiraz were sent to the area to try to design a new form of simple village home which would stand up to the shocks. But this was in the future, and the surviving villagers had more urgent problems on their minds.

For one thing, the flocks had to be taken from their lowland winter pastures to the new grass appearing on the mountain slopes as the snow line receded. Usually the task went to the small boys of the village, but as a result of the disaster not enough village children were left to do the job. The men of Qeer had to lead the flocks.

Except for rescue workers and the military, everyone in Qeer was injured or in a state of shock. Many clawed through the rubble frantically, looking for relatives, friends or missing belongings, and barely noticed the rescue teams.

The scene of devastation reminded one reporter of a sentence in the account of a quake in ancient Persia written by the Arab historian Jellal As-Soyuti. "The earth vomited up the bones of the dead," the historian wrote, "and a village with its inhabitants was suspended between heaven and earth during half a day; then it was swallowed up."

HUSSEIN'S ARAB PLAN REJECTED

Among Jordan's allies, enemies and neutrals alike, no takers were in sight for King Hussein's proposal of an Arab state along that country's former West Bank, if and when Israeli troops withdrew from the area.

The Jordanian monarch disclosed his idea in March, shortly before announcing that he would discuss it with President Nixon in Washington at the end of that month.

The plan, said the king, would create two autonomous regions—Jordan and the West Bank, the latter occupied by Israel since 1967. East Jerusalem would be the capital of the West Bank region, but Amman would be the capital of the entire federation, to be known as the United Arab Kingdom, Hussein said. He added that the new state would include "any other Palestinian territories to be liberated," apparently a reference to the Gaza Strip, which Israel also occupied.

Israel's prime minister, Mrs. Golda Meir, greeted the king's West Bank suggestion with undisguised disapproval. She found fault with his omission of any reference to peace as a prelude, and contended that he was "treating as his own property territories which were not his, and are not under his control."

Her statement produced a two-hour debate in parliament, during which opposition members held that the Israeli government's reaction was too mild.

Thereafter Hussein conceded that the plan could be carried out only "after the occupation had been eliminated and our people liberated."

The Federation of Arab Republics, comprising Egypt, Syria and Libya, also denounced the Jordan king's proposal and called upon all Arab governments to reject it as a United States maneuver to block a united Arab stand against Israel.

Iraq, on March 15, termed Hussein's plan "a defeatist idea advanced by a hireling regime" and as a threat to Arab unity. On the same day a government statement in Baghdad proposed a merger of Iraq, Egypt and Syria to counteract the threat. Also on March 15 Al Fatah, the dominant Arab guerrilla group, claimed the proposal by Hussein was aimed at "stifling the guerrilla movement and at final liquidation of the Palestine cause." And, at the same time in Washington, Secretary of State William P. Rogers was reported to have issued a directive instructing Administration executives to withhold any comment, however innocuous, on Hussein's idea for fear—as one official phrased it later—that "we kill it by our embrace."

Hussein conferred with Nixon for four hours on March 28. He was given the assurance of continued American military and economic aid, but Administration sources said Jordan's king neither requested nor received any specific U.S. endorsement of his proposed Palestinian state.

In an interview in Washington on March 29, Hussein suggested that, as part of a final peace pact, Jordan and Israel should share the administration as "a unified, open city—a meeting place for the three great religions of the world." He rejected any return to the half-Arab, half-Israeli divided status that existed in Jerusalem between 1948 and 1967.

On the final day of March, military and diplomatic sources in Washington were credited with the report that the United States had agreed to supply 12 to 24 F5 jet fighter planes to Jordan over the following two years.

Alene B. Duerk chalked up another first for the fairer sex when she became the first woman admiral in the Navy's 197-year history. Her nomination for flag rank was approved by President Nixon in April. She was director of the Navy's Nurse Corps

Egypt, discreetly silent up to this point, announced on April 6 that diplomatic relations with Jordan had been terminated on the ground that Hussein's Arab federation proposal would open, for Israel, the route into the Arab world. This action was taken during a cabinet meeting a few hours before the Palestinian National Council convened in Cairo to discuss the impact of the Hussein plan. Addressing members of the council, President Anwar Sadat declared that Egypt would stand behind them.

"Egypt will not allow anyone to liquidate the rights of the Palestinian people," said Sadat. "Palestine will not be lost, and the political rights of the Palestinian people will not be a point of bargaining."

BIOLOGICAL WEAPONS OUTLAWED

Back in 1925, the Geneva protocol had outlawed use of biological weapons and poison gas, but the ban did not prevent nations from stockpiling such arms and holding them as a threat for use in some future war. In 1972 a major step was taken toward agreement that would forever ban these agents as tools of war. Seventy nations, including the United States, Britain and the Soviet Union, agreed upon a convention outlawing use or possession of biological weapons for belligerent purposes.

The historic accord was signed April 10 in separate ceremonies in Moscow, London and Washington. For the first time under a modern arms-control measure, states were required to destroy their existing stocks of such weapons. The treaty bound the signatory nations "not to develop, produce, stockpile or otherwise acquire or retain" biological agents except for peaceful purposes.

The signing prompted cautious expressions of hope from leaders of the Big Three. In Washington, President Nixon called the treaty a significant step toward the major goal, world peace. He said, however, that the world must realize that the accord, no matter how significant, was only a "means to an end," which was eliminating altogether the threat of war.

In Moscow, Soviet President Nikolai V. Podgorny was also hopeful but guarded. A ban on bacteriological weapons, he said, "to a certain degree opens up favorable new prospects" for curbing the arms race in other areas.

"By limiting the sphere of the arms race," he said, "this agreement can also serve as a good example for solving other pressing problems of disarmament."

In London, British Prime Minister Edward Heath said his government believed that the growth of destructive nuclear power was still the most serious problem facing mankind.

"But," he added, "we have to recognize that it is equally important to bring under control other forms of highly destructive weapons."

For the United States the pact represented a milestone. It formalized decisions made in 1969 by Nixon when he ordered an end to development of germ-warfare weapons. The destruction of American stockpiles of such weapons had been under way since then.

TWO ARGENTINE ASSASSINATIONS

Two rival guerrilla organizations brought Argentina to the brink of civil war in April, by executing a top army official and an Italian industrialist within a few hours.

The victims of the political slayings were Gen. Juan Carlos Sanchez, commander of the Argentine Army's 2nd Corps, and Oberdan Sallustro, president of the Fiat-Concord Company, the Argentine subsidiary of Italy's Fiat Automobile Corp.

The People's Revolutionary Army (ERP) and the Revolutionary Armed Forces (FAR), two urban guerrilla groups took responsibility for the act in a communique issued on the day of the shootings. The document said that Sanchez had been murdered in reprisal for his recent anti-guerrilla campaigns, and that Sallustro was executed for practicing unfair business ethics and for intervening in Argentine politics.

The terrorists also denounced President Alejandro Lanusse for "threatening a fascist coup" and for promoting "an electoral farce" by declaring general elections for March 1973.

Sanchez, 52, after claiming to have eliminated 85 per cent of the guerrillas in his command area, was machine-gunned while traveling to his office in the industrial city of Rosario, 150 miles north of the capital city of Buenos Aires.

The ERP, a Trotskyite faction, and the FAR, an organization created in loyalty to exiled former dictator Juan D. Peron, had kidnaped the 56-year old Sallustro on March 21. The industrialist was charged with "unfair practices against small national firms, intervention in Argentine politics, exploitation of Argentine workers and repression and imprisonment of democratically elected union leaders."

In return for Sallustro's life the terrorists demanded the release and transfer to Algeria of 50 imprisoned guerrillas, freedom for a number of jailed union leaders and $1 million worth of school supplies to be distributed, along with guerrilla propaganda, to needy children. While the Fiat corporation was willing to pay the ransom money, Lanusse refused to negotiate with the leftist revolutionaries and forbade the automobile corporation to comply with the demands. After twice extending the execution deadline, the guerrillas shot Sallustro.

The wave of terrorist action began after it was announced that Lanusse had begun negotiations with the 76-year-old ex-dictator Peron on the possibility that the powerful Peronist movement would participate as a legal party in a general election in March 1973. The election, which would end six years of military rule, was opposed by left-wing extremists, who had advocated the violent overthrow of the military and of the "capitalist system" of Argentina. By striking at the armed forces through the execution of Sanchez, the terrorists hoped to provoke a military crackdown and a cancellation of the balloting.

Fearing the onset of a civil war, Lanusse flew to Rosario after the murders, sealed the city to all traffic, and enlisted the help of private citizens in apprehending the assassins. The Argentine National Security Council convened on the day of the slayings and decreed that, thereafter, all trials for kidnaping, violating the public peace or attacking institutions would be conducted by military tribunals.

A purge of suspected subversives resulted in a number of arrests. But some of these persons could not be found later in prisons. This finding led to public accusations that some prisoners had died during tortures by the police. The charges were emphatically denied by the Argentine military.

'CRAZY JOE' GALLO KILLED BY GUNMAN IN LITTLE ITALY

"He made a mistake, Crazy Joe did," commented New York Deputy Police Commissioner Robert Daley. "He should have gone to bed last night."

If he had gone to bed, Joseph Gallo probably would have survived the night of April 7. But it was the reputed New York mobster's 43rd birthday and he decided to go out on the town.

During the evening Gallo sipped champagne in New York's Copacabana. Still in a convivial mood, he later repaired to the Little Italy sector of Manhattan. At 4 a.m. he and his bride of three weeks, her 10-year-old daughter, his sister and a bodyguard, Pete Diapioulas, were in Umberto's Clam House, a new restaurant on Mulberry Street.

The party sat around two butcher block tables, drinking wine and soda pop and munching Italian delicacies.

Just as Gallo called for a second helping of food, the side door opened. Customers dove to the floor as a man wearing a tweed coat strode through the door, took aim and drilled three shots into Gallo. Diapioulas, who returned the fire, was hit once.

After more than 20 shots were exchanged while women screamed, the intruder, firing as he went, ducked out the back door, jumped into a waiting car and sped off. Gallo, mortally wounded, staggered to the front door and fell, smashing the plate glass. But then he managed to get through the shattered entrance and tottered another 15 feet before collapsing in the middle of the intersection of Hester and Mulberry Streets.

Crazy Joe died near the big 1971 Cadillac in which he and his party rode to Little Italy. It was plastered with stickers that advertised Americans of Italian descent.

Policemen in a squad car on Mott Street heard the women screaming, picked up Gallo's body and the wounded Diapioulas, and sped to the hospital.

Diapioulas refused to give any details of the assassination while his wound was being dressed. He said: "I don't want to give you a hard time, but I'm not going to give any information."

Gallo's sister, sobbing over the dead man's body, managed to say: "He changed his image, that's why this happened."

Said New York City Chief of Detectives Albert A. Seedman: "The assassin walked in with just one thing in his mind—to get Gallo."

Ling-ling, an 18-month-old female giant panda, found life in the United States pleasant after being introduced to the public at Washington's National Zoo. She and her mate, Ching-ching, were given to the American people as a symbol of good will from the Peoples' Republic of China

DEATH ENDED UP-AND-DOWN CAREER OF ADAM CLAYTON POWELL JR.

Adam Clayton Powell Jr., a Baptist minister from Harlem, became a flamboyant spokesman for American blacks during 11 straight terms served in the U.S. House of Representatives.

During his stormy career, Powell played many roles and played them with zest. No matter what the dispute, Powell could be expected to come up with a memorable quip. Then he would present his side of the case with a blend of searching truths and claims that the opposition insisted stemmed more from figment than from fact.

Although ill health had plagued him for several years, he was still a figure to reckon with when he died in a Miami hospital April 4 at the age of 63.

Powell once summed up his legislative career with the statement: "As a member of Congress, I have done nothing more than any other member and, by the grace of God, I intend to do not one bit less."

Powell presented a complex image. He was at one and the same time the leader of what was believed to be the largest church congregation in the nation, a Congressional rebel, a civil rights leader years before other blacks took up the issue, a playboy and an acknowledged success as chairman of the House Committee on Education and Labor, despite his high absentee record in Congress.

During the Depression of the 1930s, Powell embarked on a career as a crusader. He led a series of demonstrations in Harlem against major business concerns—department stores, bus lines, the telephone company, and hospitals—forcing them to hire Negroes. As business manager and leader of the social and welfare programs at the Abyssinian Baptist Church, Powell directed a relief operation that fed, clothed and provided fuel for thousands of destitute persons in Harlem. In recognition of his relief work, Ethiopia's Emperor Haile Selassie presented Powell with a golden medallion.

In 1933 Powell married Isabel Washington, a Cotton Club dancer. The marriage ended 10 years later.

The popularity of the young man who looked more white than black grew rapidly as he taunted white institutions that had until then seemed almost invincible, and he came out on top.

Powell was elected to the New York City Council in 1941 with the third highest number of votes ever cast for a candidate in city elections. He went to Congress in 1945 from central Harlem, a district of about 300,000 persons, about 89 per cent of whom were black.

In Washington Powell quickly engaged in fiery exchanges with several Southern segregationists, sought to end racial discrimination in the military services and tried to deny federal funds to any project where discrimination existed.

As he grew in seniority, Powell fought to get Negro newsmen admitted to the Senate and House press galleries, introduced legislation that would outlaw Jim Crow transportation and forced Congress to notice discriminatory practices by certain U.S. organizations.

Although a faithful Democrat in most national elections, Powell bolted the party in 1956 to support Dwight D. Eisenhower for reelection.

Despite his rebel and maverick roles, Powell gained a high reputation as chairman of the House Committee on Education and Labor from 1960-67. Presidents John F. Kennedy and Lyndon

B. Johnson sent Powell letters of praise, and the Congressional Record reported that his committee had processed more important legislation than any other major committee.

Powell had played a key role in the development and passage of the 1961 Minimum Wage Bill, the Manpower Development and Training Act, the Anti-Poverty Bill, the Juvenile Delinquency Act, the Vocational Educational Act and the National Defense Educational Act. Under Powell, the committee helped pass 48 major pieces of social legislation involving a total outlay of more than $14 billion.

The legislator's reputation as a bon vivant also grew with his marriage in 1945 to pianist-singer Hazel Scott. The couple had a cooperative apartment in Harlem, a 10-room house in Westchester and a townhouse in Washington.

In 1960 Powell and Miss Scott were divorced and he married Mrs. Yvette Marjorie Flores Diago, a member of an influential Puerto Rican family. In March 1960, the same year that he took over the House committee, Powell appeared on a television show. During a discussion of police corruption he offhandedly referred to a Harlem widow as a "bagwoman" or collector of graft for the police. The widow, Mrs. Esther James, sued but Powell refused to make either an apology or a settlement.

During an eight-year legal battle, Mrs. James was awarded damages that ran as high as $575,000, but that was reduced on appeal to $55,787. Powell refused to pay and was finally found guilty of civil contempt. He avoided arrest by restricting his New York appearances to weekends.

In November 1966 Powell was found guilty of criminal contempt and took up fulltime residence in Bimini. His affairs were then investigated by a Select Committee of House members. It recommended public censure of Powell, and loss of seniority.

On March 1, 1967, the House went beyond the Select Committee's recommendations and voted 307-116 to exclude Powell because of alleged misuse of public funds and charges that he was in contempt of New York state courts.

During a special election to fill the seat two months later Powell, without even coming to Harlem, received 27,900 votes to 4,091 for a Republican opponent.

Damages to Mrs. James eventually were paid after Powell embarked on fund-raising ventures that included making a recording of songs by his Bimini friends and sermons by Powell. The recording was called *Keep the Faith, Baby.*

Powell returned to Harlem in March 1968 and received an ovation. In January 1969 he was seated in the 91st Congress by a vote of 251 to 160. But he was fined $25,000 for alleged misuse of payroll and travel funds and stripped of his seniority. Six months later the Supreme Court ruled that the House of Representatives had violated the Constitution in excluding him two years before.

On hearing the news, Powell told reporters in the courtyard of his Bimini Hotel: "From now on, America will know the Supreme Court is the place where you can get justice."

Powell was hospitalized in 1969 with cancer. Upon his release he said he was retiring from politics, but in January 1970 he said he had been cured by cobalt treatments and had no plans for retiring. Opposing political forces, however, mounted a full-scale campaign under the leadership of Manhattan Borough President Percy Sutton and then State Assemblyman Charles B. Rangel. Rangel defeated Powell by a slim margin in June 1970 in a six-man Democratic primary.

Powell demanded a recount, contending that 1,485 of the votes cast in the primary were illegal. He filed a suit to force a new primary election, but he lost the court fight.

Adam Clayton Powell posed for this photograph shortly before his death

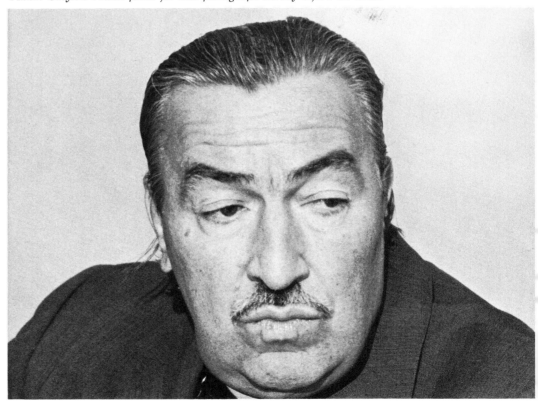

AFTER THREE MONTHS OF NEGOTIATIONS, BASEBALL'S FIRST GENERAL STRIKE LASTED 13 DAYS

There was a time when baseball players were, for the most part, not the most sophisticated group of men in the country. Their reading matter centered on the sports pages and comics.

But those days are gone forever. Now the majority of ballplayers are either high school or college graduates who read the stock market tables and Wall Street Journal.

Some six years ago the athletes founded the Major League Players Association to protect their interests. They hired Marvin Miller, a veteran labor negotiator, to handle their dealings with management.

The result of that move was a general agreement between the owners and the Players Association covering details of the players' contracts. Individual players would still bargain for themselves, but the general agreement set certain standards that management agreed to follow. Included in the agreement was a pension package that guaranteed the players an income after retirement.

It was the pension issue that caused baseball's first general strike in April and delayed the start of the sport's 103rd season for 13 days.

The Players Association had been negotiating with the owners for three months, seeking an increase in the pension and health benefits clause of their contract. When the two sides sat down for the first time in January, the owners agreed to pay the increased cost of maintaining the health package but refused to increase pension payments.

Later in the negotiations the owners took a more rigid stand, rejecting even the health benefits increase. That was when Miller started polling the players on the 24 clubs, seeking a strike authorization vote.

As Miller moved from club to club, explaining the status of negotiation and getting almost unanimous strike authorizations in each training camp, an air of tension settled on the situation. In Mid-March the owners yielded on the health-care package, agreeing to cover the $490,000 estimated to maintain the program. But they were rigid on the 17 per cent pension increase demand. "We won't give another damn cent," vowed August Busch, of the St. Louis Cardinals, one of the more militant members of management.

On March 31, one week before the scheduled start of the 1972 season, Miller met with the 24 club player representatives and their alternates in Dallas. Following a 4½-hour meeting the players voted 47–0 with one abstention to call a strike.

The decision landed like a bombshell. Reaction ranged from amazement—"I can't believe it," said Danny Cater, first baseman for the Boston Red Sox—to shock: "I'm sick," said Stu Holcomb, a vice president of the Chicago White Sox.

Quickly, training camps started shutting down and players scattered for home. There were some ironies in the situation. Ron Blomberg of the New York Yankees requested two orders of French toast for breakfast and then, reminded that because of the strike, he'd have to pay the bill himself, said, "make that a single order, please." Dick Allen, a spring training holdout throughout March, showed up at the Chicago White Sox camp and signed his contract, declaring he was ready to go to work. Unfortunately, the rest of the White Sox players were not.

Nick Mileti had just purchased the Cleveland ball club. And, the first thing he knew, it was on strike.

For two weeks Miller and John Gaherin, negotiating for the owners, met daily, trying to solve the strike. And each day a new batch of games was postponed. At first it was only exhibitions, but as the strike continued the clubs were forced to eliminate regular season games as well. "There is a possibility," said pitcher Jack Aker, the American League player rep, "that there won't be any baseball this season."

Finally, on April 12, the break came. Agreement was reached on allocating $500,000 a year from the pension plan's huge surplus for retirement benefits. This was in addition to the owners' original $490,000 health care offer and $5.4 million annual contribution to the plan. The $500,000 represented a little more than half of the 17 per cent increase the players had demanded originally.

A day later the strike officially ended with the two sides agreeing to pick up the schedule on Saturday, April 15, with no attempt at making up the 86 games which were called off because of the walkout.

"Clearly, the players have triumphed in something that few people thought they could do or would do," said Miller. "They have stood together."

"I'm delighted to have this over," declared Bowie Kuhn, commissioner of baseball. "I hope we've all learned a lesson. I will work with people in baseball for procedures to prevent this sort of thing in the future. Nobody wants it again. Neither the players, the clubs nor the fans."

HEART ATTACK AFTER 27 HOLES OF GOLF FATAL TO GIL HODGES

Gil Hodges had felt so good on that balmy Florida afternoon of April 2 that he decided to play 27 holes of golf instead of 18 on the Palm Beach Lakes course. The famed manager of the New York Mets finished the game, but less than an hour later he was dead of a heart attack. It was just two days before his 48th birthday.

There had been warning signals. Hodges suffered a mild heart seizure in September 1968 during a Mets game in Atlanta, but in a few months he had felt as good as new and bounced back to lead his team to a startling, dramatic world championship the following fall.

On a bright October afternoon in 1969, the Mets had achieved the unbelievable. And, in traditional victory fashion, they doused Hodges with champagne while they danced with Pearl Bailey in their chaotic clubhouse in New York's Shea Stadium. It was an unforgettable moment for the manager and his team.

"It was a colossal thing they did," said Hodges, rivulets of champagne coursing down his happy features. "These young men showed that you can realize the most impossible dream of all."

It was a signal tribute to the genius of Gilbert Ray Hodges, the famed first baseman of the old New York Dodgers, who had managed the Mets for two seasons and led them from last place to first in the National League. The team had lost 101 games the year before Hodges arrived in 1968. Under his leadership they had soared to the top of the heap.

A powerful 210-pounder who measured 6 feet 2 inches, Hodges had been a gentle person off the field but a formidable threat in a baseball suit. Joining the Dodgers in 1947, he soon became known as the strong, silent man with pale blue eyes who could hit balls with remarkable right-handed power.

Hodges played in seven pennant winners with the Dodgers, both in Brooklyn and Los Angeles, helping them to world championships in 1955 and 1959, before ending his playing career with the first Met teams in 1962–63. For 16 years he was one of the best first basemen in the major leagues and one of the most feared hitters. His 370 home runs were a record for a right-handed batting first baseman, and his 14 grand slams were a league career record.

Hodges appeared in seven World Series and six All-Star games before he settled into a career first as manager of the Washington Senators, then the Mets.

As manager of the Mets, Hodges laid down the law. The curfew was midnight, the hotel bar was off limits, golf was permitted in the spring, but not swimming, and every player was expected to show up in uniform by 9:30 a.m.

This regimen did not endear Hodges to his players at first, but they soon came to respect and admire him. After his first heart attack the team rallied around their pilot and surged on to win the pennant.

In the spring of 1972 Hodges had appeared healthy and relaxed. He returned to smoking cigarettes, drank coffee again and hit a few grounders. He also resumed golf.

On the afternoon of April 2 he was playing with three Met coaches, Joe Pignatano, Rube Walker and Eddie Yost. After their long day on the greens Hodges and his companions strolled casually back to their rooms. Upon crossing the parking lot next to their motel, Pignatano asked: "Gillie, what time are we meeting for dinner?"

Hodges turned and said "seven-thirty." Then he collapsed, cutting his head on the cement as he fell. That was about 5:10 p.m.

Hodges was rushed to West Palm Beach's Good Samaritan Hospital and admitted to the emergency room at 5:25 p.m. A cardiologist, Dr. William Donovan, said that an electrocardiogram showed "complete heart arrest." He was pronounced dead at 5:45 p.m.

A jubilant Gil Hodges being hugged by his wife, right, and daughter following the Mets 1969 World Series victory

CHARLIE CHAPLIN, ABROAD FOR 20 YEARS, FETED BY U.S. FANS

The era of Charlie Chaplin began back in 1914 when the London-born comic was "discovered" by producer-director Mack Sennett and presented to American moviegoers in 1916. The rest is cinema history.

Chaplin, who was touring the United States with an English comedy troupe, created the character "The Little Tramp" at the request of Sennett, who was desperately seeking a comedy sketch for an early Keystone Cops movie.

The character was catapulted to fame in such films as *The Gold Rush; The Kid; The Idle Class* and *Modern Times.*

Chaplin himself produced *The Kid* in 1920, his first great financial success, which grossed $30,000,000 and allowed him to set up an independent production company. The film also introduced Jackie Coogan to screen audiences, and made him filmdom's first child star at the age of four.

The motion picture industry grew along with, and largely because of, Chaplin's talents. From the beginning, the great mime and film fanciers across the country established a love affair that was to last for years.

But conflicts developed, and the actor soon alienated himself from some of his public's graces following certain private and political incidents. Chaplin finally chose to leave the United States for his native England, thus climaxing years of mounting tensions between himself, governmental authorities and public sentiment.

The estrangement began in the early 1940s when the silent screen comic made several speeches proclaiming the Russians, then U.S. wartime allies, as "comrades." Conservatives quickly became alarmed. Later, in June of 1943, Joan Berry, an actress and one-time protege of Chaplin, accused him of being the father of her illegitimate daughter. She first brought him to court for allegedly violating the Mann Act but, after a two-week trial in April 1944, he was acquitted. Miss Berry then filed a paternity suit and, after a series of trials and retrials, Chaplin was declared to be the father of her child despite blood test evidence that indicated he was not responsible for the birth.

In 1947 came the suggestion of the House of Representatives' Committee on Un-American Activities that the film star, long known for promoting leftist movements, was a Communist. Although the committee failed to substantiate its charge, suspicions multiplied and the entertainer became the target of right-wing conservatives during the furor of the cold war days in the early 1950s. Finally, in the spring of 1952, Chaplin returned to his native London, on vacation. Shortly thereafter James P. McGranery, then U.S. Attorney General, revoked the performer's re-entry visa. McGranery ruled that Chaplin could not return unless he consented to undergo an investigation into the never-proven charges of Communist affiliation and "gross moral turpitude." The star refused to comply with the order, relinquished his U.S. residency, and established a new home in Lusanne, Switzerland.

There Chaplin stayed for 20 years, bitterly ignoring the people who had forsaken him, until it was announced at the end of March 1972 that he would return for the week of April 4–12, at the invitation of a mellowed America. He was to be feted by friends and followers on both coasts, beginning with a salute in New York City and ending with special recognition by the Academy of Motion Picture Arts and Sciences.

And he was to see Jackie Coogan again, for the first time in over 30 years. During their reunion in New York, the comic master confided to the former film prodigy, "I wanted to see you more than anyone else."

Had he been missed? The answer was openly and lovingly revealed, first on April 4 at a celebration at New York's Lincoln Center, and again on April 10 when, before 2,900 of his revering, cheering fans at the Los Angeles Music Center, the Little Fellow was presented with an honorary Academy Award for "his incalculable effect in making motion pictures the art form of this century."

Said the 82-year- old Chaplin, amid the excitement of his triumphant comeback at a gala at Philharmonic Hall in New York, "I'm born again."

In renown he had never really died.

NOBEL WINNER A SUICIDE

In 1968, when Yasunari Kawabata became the only Japanese ever to win the Nobel Prize for Literature, he paused to reflect on the problem of suicide.

"However alienated one may be from the world, suicide is not a form of enlightenment," Kawabata had declared in his Nobel lecture delivered in Stockholm. "However admirable he may be, the man who commits suicide is far from the realm of the saint."

Nearly four years after making that appearance, Kawabata was found dead on April 17 in his studio on the outskirts of Yokohama. Police said the 72-year-old novelist had a gas hose in his mouth. They proclaimed the death a suicide.

Kawabata's death came less than two years after fellow novelist Yukio Mishima had shocked the nation by committing ritual hari kari (*The World in 1970, 232*).

Friends were at a loss to explain why Kawabata, having deplored the act of suicide, took his life. Some recalled that he had appeared in good spirits. But others said that the aging writer had been troubled with an inflamed gall bladder. Still others remembered that Kawabata had been hospitalized for toxicosis caused by habitual use of sleeping pills.

Kawabata had been a passive, solitary figure whose career was declining, but he was highly respected in the literary world. His spare prose had been described as depicting Japanese emotions often impossible to translate into English.

Kawabata had been profoundly shaken by the suicide of his 45-year-old colleague, Mishima. Presiding at the younger man's funeral in a Tokyo temple in 1970, Kawabata had said: "Quiet praying, apart from discussing wrong or right upon Mishima's death, is a traditional emotion of the Japanese people."

Charlie Chaplin gladly posed with his honorary Academy Award following ceremonies in Hollywood

FOR THE RECORD

NAMED. Tang Ming-chao, an American-educated Red Chinese diplomat, as United Nations Under Secretary General for Political Affairs and Decolonization. Tang, who spoke excellent English, had been chosen frequently by Chinese Premier Chou En-lai as a roving ambassador to conferences of the Asian and African countries.

The Nixons standing before China's Great Wall

May

President Nixon and Chairman Mao Tse-tung shaking hands in an historic meeting

The Year of the Summits: Nixon, Brezhnev and Mao

THERE WAS A TIME when Russians and Americans alike would have considered it a wildly improbably scenario. There, on the Soviet Union's Central Television, was the man Russians had been accustomed to regard as the arch-imperialist and natural enemy of the Soviet system, the man Americans had known as a leading crusader against Communism. And he was delivering a homily on peaceful coexistence, punctuated now and again by a pithy Russian proverb or the sort of earthy aphorism Russians admire.

For Richard M. Nixon this was a moment of high drama and a moment of triumph for his persistent summitry. His May 28 appearance on what the Russians call their "blue screen," along with his spectacular though less fruitful February venture

into hitherto forbidden Communist China, marked the end for policies followed by four of his immediate predecessors in the White House. The Summits of 1972 shaped up as events of enormous importance for the future of American security and of world peace. As the President said, it began to look like a new era was dawning.

Ever since World War II dissolved into the cold war between Soviet "socialism" and the West, U.S. policy had pursued a goal of "containment" of putative Soviet expansionist aims. Ever since Mao Tse-tung's Red legions overran the China mainland, America pursued a goal of isolating and quarantining the Chinese People's Republic.

Now, at the end of May 1972, those concepts lay in shreds.

The President had begun what had the look of an international-style fireside chat with the Russian words "dobry vecher," meaning "good evening," and ended it with "spasibo i do svidaniya," meaning "thank you and goodbye." For the rest, the voice of a Russian translator was imposed over the presidential baritone.

"Shortly after we arrived here on Monday afternoon," the President told his Soviet audience of many millions, "a brief rain fell on Moscow of the kind that I am told is called 'a mushroom rain'—a warm rain, with the sun breaking through, that makes the mushrooms grow and therefore is considered a good omen."

The Russians would like that reference to their folklore and its symbolic application to the situation of the world at large. Could, perhaps, a gentle mushroom rain with the sun of mutual understanding shining through now encourage the fragile seeds of peace between the two mighty superpowers? The idea would be popular with both Russians and Americans after all the years of deep and dangerous hostility. The Nixon summitry had produced a prospect of a less perilous world, a world in which the two enormously powerful dominant nations, each with enough weaponry to blast the other into oblivion many times over, could at last communicate meaningfully on the major issues.

The summitry had produced, in fact, a picture of a tripolar world in which Communist China played a balancing role between the two giants. It had produced an uncertain world, too. Russia now was unsure about Chinese-American relations; China was unsure about Soviet-American relations, and the United States could never be certain that there would not be a

reconciliation one day between Moscow and Peking. Perhaps the very uncertainty in itself would inspire caution on the part of each of the three big nations.

Against the record of his career, the Nixon diplomacy might have seemed astonishing. But the Richard Nixon who assumed the American presidency in 1969 was a man in many ways different from the one whose early career had been marked by implacable anti-Communist crusading.

In his inaugural address the new President had seen a need for an open world in which no nation, big or small, would be sequestered in angry isolation. Differences were great, but talking would be better than fighting. A short time later he let it be known that he was interested in "serious dialogue" with Red China, now a burgeoning nuclear power. For the first time he referred to it publicly by its formal name, "the People's Republic of China." Probably the message already was getting across.

The return signal came in an odd, oblique sort of way. In April 1971, a Chinese Ping Pong team in Tokyo invited an American Ping Pong team to visit Communist China and the offer was eagerly accepted. The Chinese then made it known that some American correspondents would be permitted to accompany the team. It would be the first such penetration of the mainland in two decades (The World in 1971, 62–66).

The extraordinarily cordial treatment of the Americans provided a clear indication of what was on the official Chinese Communist mind. Involved in a harsh ideological war with its enormous neighbor, the Soviet Union, Peking was extending a hand tentatively to the Americans. Premier Chou En-lai himself dispelled the guessing on that score. To AP's John Roder-

Premier Chou En-lai demonstrating the way to use chopsticks as President Nixon watched intently

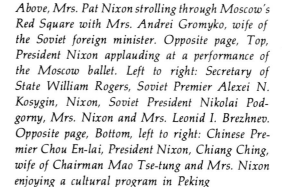

ick, one of those invited to Peking, he remarked: "You have opened the door."

The White House eyed that door with interest, as it did the door to Moscow. The interminable war in Vietnam and the chronic crisis in the Middle East loomed as barriers to an American approach to the big Communist powers, but there had, in fact, been echoes from Moscow, too. Wheels were set in motion, contacts made, possibilities probed.

In July 1971 the President startled the world and stunned Americans by announcing that he had sent his astute foreign affairs aide, Dr. Henry Kissinger, to Peking by way of Pakistan on the most hush-hush of secret missions and that the result was an invitation for a presidential visit to Communist China some time before the following spring. It would, the President said on a live TV broadcast, be a journey for peace to seek normal relations after two decades of enmity.

Above, Mrs. Pat Nixon strolling through Moscow's Red Square with Mrs. Andrei Gromyko, wife of the Soviet foreign minister. Opposite page, Top, President Nixon applauding at a performance of the Moscow ballet. Left to right: Secretary of State William Rogers, Soviet Premier Alexei N. Kosygin, Nixon, Soviet President Nikolai Podgorny, Mrs. Nixon and Mrs. Leonid I. Brezhnev. Opposite page, Bottom, left to right: Chinese Premier Chou En-lai, President Nixon, Chiang Ching, wife of Chairman Mao Tse-tung and Mrs. Nixon enjoying a cultural program in Peking

President Nixon talking with Soviet Communist party chief Leonid I. Brezhnev in the Kremlin

Kissinger, the President's special assistant for national security affairs, went back to China in October, this time with an advance White House party, to talk with Premier Chou and iron out the details. Everything but the date itself was settled when the President, that same month, announced he intended also to make an official visit to Moscow in May. He would go, he said, because he saw "a possibility of making significant progress toward settling major differences."

"I do not believe in having summit meetings simply for the purpose of having a meeting," the President said. ". . . It raises high hopes that are destroyed. . . . We are not making that mistake."

This suggested that he meant to be all business. He meant to avoid the sort of meeting that would result in an empty communique full of platitudes and little else. He meant to come home from both Red capitals with something to show Americans for his labors in a presidential election year.

The ultimate in summits would crown a Nixon record of dazzling diplomatic globe-trotting and summitry that began only a month after he was inaugurated. His travels abroad and those of foreign leaders to American shores had brought him face to face with the topmost figures of Britain, France, Italy, Germany, Belgium, Communist Romania, Pakistan, Mexico, Finland, Israel, Italy and the Vatican, Ireland, Communist Yugoslavia, Spain, India, Japan, Australia, Brazil, Canada and Austria. After Moscow, he would carry his summitry to Iran and Communist Poland as well.

The Nixon program sent shockwaves around the world. Almost immediately it meant dramatic changes for Communist China, both in her world position and her internal politics.

The autumn of 1971 brought evidence of an upheaval in Peking. Apparently there had been some strong opposition in high places to welcoming the U.S. President. Eventually it became known that Lin Piao, the defense minister and vice chairman of the Communist party who had been anointed two

years before as evident heir to Mao's power, had disappeared. One report which seemed inspired by Chinese Communist sources was that he plotted to overthrow Mao and had to be eliminated. The widespread belief was that Lin and others, including the man who had been his army chief of staff, tried to flee China in a military plane and died when the craft was shot down.

The Nixon initiative also had immense impact in the United Nations. The United States now supported the idea that Mao's government should be admitted but contended that Chiang Kai-shek's Nationalists on Taiwan should retain their seat at the same time. This was utterly unacceptable to both Chinese regimes. U.N. members who had previously followed the U.S. lead on the question of Chinese representation, acutely aware of the preparations under way for the Nixon pilgrimage, put a final end to the "two Chinas" notion. The American effort on behalf of Chiang, for what it was worth, was swamped. Mao's regime was in, Chiang's was out.

As the date of the Nixon departure neared, China's neighbors were grumpy. North Vietnam's reaction seemed to be to wonder how could a Communist regime countenance a welcome to a man so long regarded as the chief demon of imperialism. Moscow officially professed no objection so long as the visit was not aimed at Soviet interests, but the disclaimers sounded unconvincing. The Soviet press produced a torrent of anti-Mao articles, all laden with grave suspicion about what the Chinese and Americans might be up to.

On the seventh day of the Year of the Rat in the oriental year, an auspicious day in the Chinese calendar and for the Americans the birthday of George Washington, President and Mrs. Nixon with their entourage landed in Peking. The welcome was correct, formal, low key. There were no crowds. The workaday Chinese as yet had no idea they would have so unlikely a guest.

Unexpectedly, on the day of his arrival the President was

whisked off to the private study of the 78-year-old demigod Mao himself where, for a full hour, he engaged in informal but highly secret dialogue. Nobody else was present except Kissinger, Chou En-lai, a translator provided by the Chinese and a protocol officer reported to have been Mao's niece and therefore exceptionally trustworthy. The State Department was locked out. There ensued what the Chinese called a "serious and frank" discussion, meaning that Nixon and Mao were a long distance from seeing eye-to-eye.

Thereafter Nixon would have more than 20 hours of private conferences with Premier Chou, Peking's 73-year-old indispensable man. The two met every day for five days in head-to-head dialogue.

The President and First Lady Pat cheerfully endured a three-hour ceremonial state banquet, eating their way with slippery ivory chopsticks through eight courses from the bamboo shoots to the steamed chicken with cocoanut, served up by efficient white-jacketed waiters, while Chinese musicians dished up a strange melange of American folk tunes and oriental-scale singsong Chinese melodies.

The President survived innumerable "goombay," or bottoms up, toasts in fiery mao tai, the Chinese brand of bottled lightning. He probably pleased his hosts in the process by recalling the legendary trek of Mao's forces in the 1930s and proposing that now the Chinese and Americans should "start a Long March together." Mindful that the order of the day in China is familiarity with quotations from Chairman Mao, Nixon raised his glass and cited Mao's admonition that "so many deeds cry out to be done, and always urgently."

"Seize the day, seize the hour," the President advised. ". . . This is a day for our two peoples to rise to the heights of greatness which can build a new and better world."

Premier Chou responded: "The gates to friendship have been opened."

Their differences, said the premier, should not prevent China and the United States from establishing normal relations on the basis of the "five principles" he had enunciated in 1955 at the Bandung, Indonesia, conference of nonaligned nations. Those principles were mutual respect for sovereignty and territorial integrity, nonaggression, noninterference in internal affairs of others, equality and peaceful coexistence.

The Peking regime evidently warmed to Nixon. On his second day the Chinese people were permitted to know he was there. The newspapers blossomed with headlines and pictures and there was visible excitement in the streets. Also significantly, Chiang Ching, Mao's fourth wife and the erstwhile firebrand voice of the 1966-69 upheaval called "Great Proletarian Cultural Revolution," emerged as official hostess to the Nixons at a ballet performance in the Great Hall of the People. In her spectacles and drab Chinese garb she looked more a prim matron than revolutionary dragon lady. The ballet was *The Red Detachment of Women,* and it was, as Chinese Communist propaganda goes, relatively easy on the "imperialists," since it concerned itself with the sins of the landlords in the old regime. For westerners it was a heavy dose of indigestible propaganda. The President smiled his way through it.

While Nixon and Chou continued their discussions of what ailed Chinese-American relations, Mrs. Nixon assumed the role of tourist. She tasted Chinese dishes in a celebrated kitchen, visited an agricultural commune and a nursery, mingled with schoolchildren, talked with patients about acupuncture, walked bareheaded across fields and through alleys in a snowstorm and gave every indication of having a marvelous time.

Between his sessions with the Chinese leaders, the President himself did some tourist-type sightseeing. At the fabled Great Wall, built 22 centuries ago, he commented: "As we look at this wall, what is most important is that we have an open world. We don't want walls of any kind between peoples."

On the Nixons' final day in Peking, Chou and other Chinese leaders were the President's guests at yet another banquet. Again, in a toast, the President referred to the symbolism of the wall.

"In these past four days," he told his guests, "we have begun the long process of removing the wall" between the two countries in talks that recognized the great differences but aimed at achieving a way of living in peace. In response, Premier Chou also noted the breadth of the gap, but said he was convinced of a mutual desire to promote understanding, friendship and normal relations.

The next day, Saturday, Feb. 26, the President left Peking and flew to Hangchow, 710 miles to the south, in a white, Soviet-built airliner. There he spent his free time drinking in the fabled beauty of the city that Marco Polo, seven centuries ago, found the greatest in the world, where "so many pleasures may be found that one fancies himself to be in Paradise." The next day Nixon flew the 100 miles northeast to the last stop of the China visit, Shanghai, where the final communique on the talks was issued.

The communique made clear that the differences remained between the two. Each side specified its position on such major issues as, for example, Vietnam and Indochina. But each professed an intention to work for closer contacts in an atmosphere of peaceful coexistence. They agreed it was desirable to expand scientific, technical, cultural and other contacts and work for normal relations through diplomatic channels.

Said the Chinese: "All nations, big or small, should be equal; big nations should not bully the weak. China will never be a superpower and it opposes hegemony and power politics of any kind."

The Americans made it clear that they were not making these overtures at the expense of Japan.

Said the Americans: The United States "places the highest value on friendly relations with Japan; it will continue to develop the existing close bonds . . . it supports the right of South Asians to shape their own future in peace, free of military threats and without having the area become the subject of great power rivalry."

The American President seemed exultant at the results of his venture. The communique, he felt, indicated some areas of difference but also indicated areas of agreement. He described the American people as "dedicated to the principle that never again shall foreign domination, foreign occupation, be visited upon this city or any part of China or any independent country in the world." That would strike a responsive Chinese chord. Shanghai was the base of 19th century European colonialism.

The President felt he had just experienced "the week that changed the world."

"Mr. Prime Minister," he said in a final toast, "our two peoples tonight hold the future of the world in our hands."

* * * *

As the President flew off to the United States by way of Alaska, those words rankled in the official Soviet breast. Soviet suspicion of the Peking talks had been clearly indicated. The Moscow press referred darkly to China's entrance into a "dangerous plot with the ruling circles of the U.S.A." A Mandarin language propaganda broadcast to China complained that "nothing is more shameless and hypocritical" than the final American-Chinese communique. Other Soviet media suggested that collusion between Peking and Washington amounted to an alliance against Soviet interests. As New Times put it, "obviously the participants in the Peking meeting have something to conceal if they have made such a departure from their proclaimed principles."

Suspicion or not, the Russians made it abundantly clear that they wanted their own summit to take place. Leonid I. Brezhnev, general secretary of the Communist party, in a 20,000-word major speech March 20, declared the Kremlin was "approaching the forthcoming Soviet-American talks from a businesslike and realistic position."

Brezhnev did seem to find it difficult to swallow the Nixon remark in Peking that the Chinese and Americans held the world's future in their hands. Where, he seemed to be asking, did that leave the mighty Soviet Union? Nevertheless, he foresaw major areas of cooperation for the Americans and Russians, specifically mentioning anti-pollution, space research, limitation of strategic nuclear weapons, scientific and technical exchanges and trade. Brezhnev, much the boss among the equals in the Soviet "collective leadership," and clearly in charge of foreign policy, would be the man Nixon would deal with, even though the party chief held no government post.

On March 30 in Indochina, North Vietnam suddenly launched a major offensive. The Americans responded with a sharp escalation of bombing. Despite all that, the summit preparations went forward.

The President in April dispatched Kissinger on yet another secret mission, this time for four days of talks with Brezhnev and others in Moscow on Vietnam and other factors affecting the prospective summit. The White House had made no effort to hide its acute unhappiness at the extent of Soviet military aid that had made the North Vietnamese offensive possible.

Chances for the summit ever taking place seemed just about dead on May 8 when the President announced that the United States the next day would seal off North Vietnam's ports with mines and otherwise attempt to interdict the flow of supplies to the Hanoi regime. It was a direct challenge to Moscow.

"I particularly direct my comments tonight to the Soviet Union," Nixon said in a television address. "We respect the Soviet Union as a great power. We recognize the right of the Soviet Union to defend its interests when they are threatened. The Soviet Union in turn must recognize our right to defend our interests. No Soviet soldiers are threatened in Vietnam. Sixty thousand Americans are threatened. . . . Let us and let all great powers help our allies only for the purpose of their defense—not for the purpose of launching invasions against their neighbors."

In the U.S. view that was one way Russia could help wind down the war: By limiting arms aid to defensive weapons. Perhaps that was what the President would seek in return for the attractive plum Moscow wanted: Trade with the Americans along with access to American consumer technology.

Would the summit now be a casualty of that challenge? For several days the Russians said nothing officially. Then came the response, and it was astonishingly mild, full of the usual cliches about the situation being "fraught with serious consequences" but leaving the clear impression that Moscow could swallow even the mining of North Vietnamese waters in its anxiety for the summit.

There was no letup in the suspense until the President and Mrs. Nixon and their party finally boarded the "Spirit of '76" for the first leg of what would be a 13-day journey whose results would reverberate around the world. They would arrive in Moscow May 22, after a stop in Austria.

It would be Nixon's fourth visit to the Soviet Union. He had been there in 1959 officially, as Vice President, and had engaged then in what became famous as the "kitchen debate," an acrimonious argument in the kitchen of a model home of an American exhibition. He debated with Nikita S. Khrushchev on the relative merits of the Soviet and American systems. Nixon was in Moscow, too, as a private citizen in 1964 and again in 1967, when high officials of the party and government snubbed him. Now he would be there as President, the first incumbent U.S. chief executive to set foot in the Soviet capital.

The welcome was correct enough but it seemed a bit cool. President Nikolai V. Podgorny was at the airport, but not Brezhnev, whose protocol excuse could have been that he held no government position. Authorities discouraged crowds from trying to get a glimpse of the visitor.

The visit lacked the atmosphere of excitement, color, mystery, adventure and public exposure generated by the journey to China. Mrs. Nixon, again her husband's effective ambassador of goodwill, rode a subway and otherwise rubbed elbows with everyday Ivan and Sonya, but for the President, apart from some of the usual banqueting, toasting and ballet-viewing, it was all business from the moment of his arrival. For each of his seven days in Moscow he was engaged in many long hours of head-to-head conference with Brezhnev and two of his top colleagues, Premier Alexei N. Kosygin and President Podgorny.

The President evidently judged the results well worth the labor. The seven-day summit brought a series of agreements, some of them vastly important, and an unprecedented 12-point statement of principles intended to lay down ground rules of behavior for superpowers, something entirely new in relations between rival nations.

The two sides agreed to collaborate in space. A joint docking of a manned spacecraft and flight of the linked craft was set for 1975. The two nations would collaborate in space meteorology and other such research.

A joint Soviet-American commission would study problems of air, water and soil pollution and how to attack them. Another joint commission would cooperate in research on heart disease, cancer and public health.

The two sides would continue negotiating an accord intended to avoid dangerous confrontations at sea. Rules were agreed to insure safety of naval vessels and planes working in close proximity.

Most important, the two sides reached agreement on limiting strategic nuclear arms, and that had involved a cliffhanger melodrama.

There were indications of a test of wills. The President was pictured by U.S. sources as grimly holding his ground despite a chance that failure on that issue could damage a look of summit success. Each principal badly wanted some sort of arms accord for reasons of his own: Nixon's probably had to do with the impact in an election year, Brezhnev's with the state of the Soviet domestic economy.

At the last minute it was Brezhnev who made the concessions to prevent failure. Hurried instructions went to Helsinki, Finland, headquarters of SALT—the strategic arms limitation talks—where the Russian and American negotiators labored against time. The negotiators were flown to Moscow and by the time they arrived had a treaty ready for approval.

President and Mrs. Nixon gazing at a bronze statue in the Forbidden City inside Peking's imperial palace grounds. The Nixons appeared amused by the formidable visage the statue presented

Unquestionably the party chief and the President had achieved a landmark pact, the most important of any since the cold war era began in 1945. It limited deployment of antiballistic—defensive—missiles, the ABMs, to two sites each, neither side to have any more than 200 launchers. An accompanying executive agreement froze offensive missiles for five years at current levels which, incidentally, meant that each still had more than enough nuclear weaponry to wipe out the world. The agreement prevented deployment of the remaining 12 sites proposed by the President for the Safeguard ABM system and kept the Russians to their present Moscow system plus one smaller one at another place of their choosing.

Each side thus retained deterrent credibility: enough offensive wallop to respond to a first strike, enough defensive capacity to prevent being wiped out by a surprise nuclear attack. It remained a balance of terror, but it was an agreed one.

On other matters, the two sides agreed on a need for reciprocal reduction of forces in Central Europe and negotiations would continue. Also with regard to Europe, they agreed there should be a conference on European security "without undue delay." The Russians set great store by such a conference, having campaigned for it for many years. But the how and when still were subject to dickering. The declaration of principles committed the two sides to a policy of restraint in this nuclear age so that ideological differences would neither preclude normal relations nor lead to perilous tensions.

"We have laid out a road map," commented Kissinger in words that soon would be echoed by the President himself. "Will we follow this road? I don't know. It isn't automatic."

The two sides remained ready to exchange views at the summit whenever they might deem it necessary, and the President invited Brezhnev, Kosygin and Podgorny to make a return visit to the United States.

Both Brezhnev and Nixon experienced some disappointment.

For Brezhnev, a main summit objective had been to expand trade with the United States. All that was accomplished was agreement referring the matter to a commission to coordinate future talks. One snag: Dispute over the Soviet wartime Lend-Lease debt of $10.8 billion. The United States was willing to settle for $800 million, the Russians offer only $300 million.

Possibly a more important snag had to do with President Nixon's own disappointment. He had hoped for signs of willingness to use Soviet influence in helping end the Vietnam war. A trade accord might have been part of the enticement. However, the President did drop a hint that something still could happen in that respect.

As soon as he landed back in the United States after some more colorful but brief summitry in Iran and Communist Poland, the President went immediately to the Capitol to report in person to a joint session of the Congress. When he came to the discussion of Vietnam, he said he would only jeopardize the search for peace if he were to review all that was said in Moscow on the subject. But then he added these words:

"I will say simply this: Each side obviously has its own point of view and its own approach to this very difficult issue. But at the same time, both the United States and the Soviet Union share an overriding desire to achieve a more stable peace in the world."

Overall, the President sounded a note of high hope. The one series of summits, he said, would not lead to instant peace nor render an imperfect world suddenly perfect. Deep philosophical differences remained and so did a threat of war, though that threat might have been reduced. But, he noted, "we are making progress toward a world in which leaders of nations will settle their differences by negotiations, not by force." He went on:

"An unparalleled opportunity has been placed in America's hands. Never has there been a time when hope was more justified or when complacency was more dangerous. We have made a good beginning, and because we have begun history now lays upon us a special obligation to see it through. We can seize this moment or we can lose it. We can make good this opportunity to build a new structure of peace in the world or we can let it slip away.

"Together, therefore, let us seize the moment so that our children and the world's children can live free of the fears and free of the hatreds that have been the lot of mankind through the centuries."

The Rev. Daniel Berrigan with a jar of money collected for the Harrisburg Defense Fund by his supporters

Mistrial Decreed for Harrisburg 7

". . . to kidnap . . . someone like Henry Kissinger. Him because of his influence as policy maker yet sans cabinet status, he would therefore not be as much protected as one of the bigger wigs. . . . To issue a set of demands, e.g., cessation of use of B52s over N. Vietnam, Laos, Cambodia, and release of political prisoners. . . ."—SISTER ELIZABETH McALISTER.

"About the plan—the first time opens the door to murder. . . . Why not coordinate it with the one against capitol utilities?"—FATHER PHILIP BERRIGAN.

S UCH WAS the terse outline, in intercepted letters, of the sensational scheme to seize President Nixon's personal foreign affairs adviser, the man who later arranged the big 1972 presidential trips to the Summit at Peking and Moscow.

Berrigan, when he got the nun's letter and when he answered it, was an inmate of the federal penitentiary at Lewisburg, Pa., serving six years for pouring blood on and burning draft files in Maryland.

He was charged with masterminding from his cell the kidnap plot, planned for the day after Washington's Birthday, 1971.

The kidnaping never took place. Neither did the alleged antiwar plot by Berrigan's so-called Catholic radical left to blow up steam pipes under Washington, D.C., streets that carried heat to all federal buildings in the nation's capital. The allegations, did lead, however, to the trial of six Catholic peace activists—three priests, a nun, a former priest and his wife, an ex-nun—and a Pakistani Moslem on the faculty of a Chicago university. All were accused of conspiring to kidnap Kissinger, dynamite the heating tunnels, and destroy draft files in Pennsylvania, Delaware, New York and other states.

None was convicted—or acquitted. The government failed to convince all of the jurors that there was a planned conspiracy reaching into the White House, the key element in a case that had attracted international attention and brought newsmen to the guarded federal courtroom in Harrisburg, the Pennsylvania state capital, from as far away as Australia.

But before the Harrisburg 7 jury of nine women and three men was discharged as deadlocked, it did find Berrigan and Sister Elizabeth—tagged the chief plotters by the government—guilty of smuggling mail illegally in and out of a federal penitentiary, the priest on four counts and the nun on three. They were sentenced Sept. 5 to four concurrent two-year terms.

This mail included the letters about the alleged Kissinger plot which Berrigan had called "brilliant." The jury, however, was hung on two other unresolved counts—that writing about the Kissinger plan, and mailing the letters, constituted an actual threat to kidnap.

"The letters were never sent to Kissinger and we didn't feel that he personally was threatened," said one of the male jurors, Lawrence Evans, a 56-year-old supermarket owner from rural Dillsburg, York County.

The mail smuggling convictions were attacked on grounds that the prosecution was discriminatory. The defense claimed thousands of letters went in and out of prisons every day.

The jury was 10 to 2 for acquittal on conspiracy, reported Evans, one of the two who had held out for conviction. He said the other was a 60-year-old farm wife who had four conscientious objector sons.

The case required 47 court days over three months, including 15 days to pick the mostly middle-aged and white Protestant jury. Of the remaining jurors one was black and one Catholic; both were women.

The jury was out seven days, deliberating a total of 59 hours, which, the defense claimed, was a record in a federal trial.

The trial hung together on the thread of when a war was legal, and how citizens could challenge it while crying for peace. But these questions never reached the jury. Outside the courtroom they were debated constantly. Those who believed the FBI had illegally spied on anti-government protestors were pitted against those who supported the law, any law, right or wrong.

Many believed there might never have been indictments and a trial if the late director of the FBI, J. Edgar Hoover, hadn't talked in public.

Hoover blew the secrecy lid from the alleged plot in November 1970, when he asked a Senate committee for an additional $14 million to hire 1,000 new agents and 702 new clerks.

Although the hearing was closed, Hoover released his testimony, claiming the FBI had uncovered "an anarchist group on the East Coast" that was "concocting a scheme to kidnap a highly placed government official" and hold him until the United States stopped bombing in Southeast Asia. He got his $14 million.

Hoover said the "principal leaders" were two imprisoned priests, the Rev. Philip Berrigan and his brother, the Rev. Daniel Berrigan, then both incarcerated at Danbury, Conn., for destroying draft records.

The Berrigans blasted the Hoover charges as false. They demanded the right to face their accuser, and the government obliged by bringing formal charges.

When the first indictments came down, six weeks after Hoover's accusations, six defendants headed by Philip Berrigan were named. Each faced possible life imprisonment if convicted on the kidnap-bomb plot allegations.

Daniel Berrigan was named one of six co-conspirators, a legal technique by which the government could accuse while admitting it had insufficient provable evidence to convict.

Government lawyers sensed problems in the hastily-drawn, error-marked indictments which defendants insisted were rushed out solely to rescue Hoover's reputation.

So the grand jury was assembled again. William Lynch was brought in as a special prosecutor and new indictments, increasing the defendants to eight, both broadened and lightened the charges.

Added to the kidnap conspiracy was antiwar vandalism, specifically the plotting of draft board break-ins around the country. This served to reduce the penalty from life to five years and reportedly made it tougher to defend.

Daniel Berrigan was eliminated altogether, even as an accused co-conspirator. He was paroled during the trial and spent many days in the ninth floor courtroom, a familiar figure in dungarees and black sweater.

Besides the 48-year-old Philip Berrigan, self-styled "priest revolutionary," these were the other defendants who insisted they were "neither bombers nor kidnapers nor conspirators:"

—Sister Elizabeth McAlister, 31, on leave as a professor of art history at Marymount College in Tarrytown, N.Y.

—Dr. Eqbal Ahmad, 41, a Pakistani on the staff of the University of Chicago's Adlai Stevenson Institute of International Affairs.

—The Rev. Neil McLaughlin, 31, a Baltimore priest and member of a group that took public responsibility for a draft board raid in New York City.

—The Rev. Joseph Wenderoth, 36, Baltimore, who claimed to be part of a group that destroyed draft files in Philadelphia.

—Anthony Scoblick, 31, a former Josephite priest and son of an ex-congressman from Pennsylvania, and his wife, Mary Cain, 33, a former nun, both of Baltimore. They said they participated in Boston draft raids.

John Theodore Glick, 21, Lancaster, Pa., convicted of a draft break-in in Rochester, N.Y., was an eighth defendant. After insisting upon serving as his own lawyer, Glick was granted a separate trial.

Only McLaughlin wore clerical garb in court.

Prosecutor Lynch, chief of the Justice Department's organized crime unit, headed the government legal team, composed of four Roman Catholics.

The six-lawyer defense was led by former Atty. Gen. Ramsey Clark and Paul O'Dwyer, unsuccessful 1968 Democratic candidate for U.S. Senate and brother of a former New York City mayor.

Clark, a harsh critic of the prosecution, said that if he had still been boss of the Justice Department he would "never have permitted it (the case) to go to a grand jury."

It was estimated that the case cost the government more than $1 million, while defense expenses were around half that much. A big price, Clark said, to salve Hoover's ego.

U.S. Dist. Court Judge R. Dixon Herman was determined there wouldn't be the shouting, the profanities and the insults that marked the Chicago 7 conspiracy trial and resulted in contempt citations for defendants and their lawyers. Four marshals maintained strict decorum in the 80-seat spectator section, half occupied by newsmen. Passes were needed for admittance.

The case began secretly one cloudy June morning in 1970, inside the walled Lewisburg penitentiary. A guard routinely shook down the cell of Father Berrigan, while the newly-arrived militant antiwar priest was on work duty elsewhere.

A mysterious letter was found in a magazine, and the guard—considering it conspiratorial and illegal contraband—took it to the assistant warden. It read in part:

". . . the students can perhaps be led to the idea that occupying buildings, going nose to nose with the cops & N.G. (National Guard) is passe—bad politics, bad tactics. They should shut down ROTC and begin to zapp Sel. Service in college and university towns."—BERRIGAN.

Lewisburg was a university town, home of Bucknell.

The assistant warden called in the FBI, and the trail led to Boyd Douglas Jr., a fellow convict who admitted carrying mail in and out for Berrigan. Douglas, a two-time loser near the end of a sentence for bank fraud and assaulting a federal agent, was participating in a study-release program that allowed him to attend daily classes at Bucknell.

Swiftly he agreed to testify against the priest. Delmar "Molly" Mayfield, an FBI agent who monitored Douglas' activities and received his information said that the informer got paid for his tips—nearly $10,000 in about two years—but that a request for a $50,000 tax-free reward was rejected.

The Rev. Philip Berrigan, his wrists manacled, leaving the Dauphin County Prison in Harrisburg, Pa., en route to the federal building

"He was not promised one cent for his testimony," Mayfield said in court. Defendants and their lawyers laughed in unison.

There wouldn't have been any trial without Douglas, who was paroled a month before the first indictments. He was the hero of the FBI and the prosecution, the villain of the defense and their antiwar supporters.

Lawyers for the Harrisburg 7 bluntly told the jury Douglas was "a liar, a con man, a paid informer."

"I cannot conceive an honorable government agency, or an honorable human being, using a man like Douglas," said attorney Leonard Boudin, who had successfully defended baby doctor Benjamin Spock in another antiwar conspiracy case. "I am ashamed of that aspect of my government."

Fired back assistant prosecutor William Connelly: "We didn't pick the witness; Phil Berrigan picked the witness."

And, added chief prosecutor Lynch, Douglas had exhibited "sterling character" since his release. Guffaws from the defendants were silenced by the judge's gavel.

Countered Terry Lenzner, another defense lawyer: "Everybody who came in contact with him (Douglas) was in jeopardy. . . . He had larceny in his heart right from the beginning." Lenzner suggested it wasn't Berrigan who recruited Douglas but Douglas who recruited the priest.

"A fairy tale," Lynch replied, pointing to the letters Berrigan wrote and those he received from Sister Elizabeth.

"They were fantasies," said Paul O'Dwyer, referring to the letters in defending the nun. "To read these letters without understanding the people is to give them a completely different meaning."

Douglas testified he carried out 12 letters for Berrigan, brought in 16 from Sister Elizabeth. Every one was read in court, censored only for parts that were personal. Douglas dominated the courtroom action for 14 days, with time off only on Saturdays and Sundays. For seven days the prosecution questioned this chunky, cocky ex-convict—and he came off polite, respectful and well prepared. He told his story as if he had memorized both the questions and the answers.

When the defense got to him, six different lawyers trying to find a crack in his alleged tale of conspiracy, Douglas turned arrogant, mocking, surly. He avoided looking at defense counsel, or the defendants, but faced the jury with smiles.

"I don't have to look at you," he told defense lawyer Boudin.

Through it all Douglas stood firm, never wavering, insisting over and over that Berrigan was anti-government in a violent way.

The jury didn't fully believe him. "What swayed some women was that he lied to some girls (at college) when he promised to marry them, poor souls," juror Evans said.

When the government wrapped up its case after 31 days and 64 witnesses, the defendants surprised everyone by deciding, 4 to 3, not to put on any defense. Their chief counselor, Clark, put it this way:

"The defendants shall always seek peace and they proclaim their innocence of the charges. . . . I am shocked that the United States government would present such flimsy evidence following such a serious charge."

Sister Elizabeth said, "the government's case is false and they have been unable to prove it."

"I felt we ought to face squarely the violent absurdity of the indictment, insofar as we could in this suffocating court," Berrigan said in a statement.

Lynch, obviously unhappy at losing a chance to cross-examine at least Berrigan and the nun, commented stiffly, "When you don't have a defense, you don't have a defense."

Evans, speaking for the jury, said it too was shocked. "It shot me down," he said. "I feel if you didn't do something you should tell the world you didn't do it."

But after the jury deadlocked on the vital conspiracy count the defendants, laughing, mimicked Lynch:

"When you don't have a case, you don't have a case."

Defendant Sister Elizabeth McAlister leaving the Harrisburg Federal Building accompanied by the Rev. Daniel Berrigan

J. Edgar Hoover,
FBI's Veteran Director, Dead

The 77-year-old director of the FBI, who served 48 years under eight presidents

His 48-year career spanned eras of Prohibition, Depression, gang warfare, World War II, Korean and Vietnamese wars

H IS STRENGTH lay in a combination of performance, publicity and personality, and over 48 years as chief of the Federal Bureau of Investigation J. Edgar Hoover became a living legend.

Hoover's death on May 2 at the age of 77 marked the end of an era that had seen the United States emerge from World War I to become a world power. It was an era that began with Prohibition, ran through the Great Depression, the gangster days of the 1930s, World War II, the Cold War, Korea and finally Vietnam and the Civil Rights issue.

His body was found slumped by his bedside. High blood pressure was given as the cause.

Hoover's greatest achievement perhaps was his record of innovation and modernization in law enforcement. During nearly half a century the FBI under his leadership rounded up gangsters, made kidnaping a hazardous undertaking and arrested German saboteurs within days after their submarines landed them on the Atlantic Coast in World War II. In 1965 G-men seized the slayers of a civil rights worker, Mrs. Viola Gregg Liuzzo, only hours after her shotgun death in Alabama.

With his penchant for publicity, Hoover invented the "Ten Most Wanted" list and cooperated in making G-Man movies and radio programs. This not only made Hoover a household word throughout America, it made him a fixture in Washington under eight presidents.

Over the years the FBI under Hoover's guidance became a giant organization which held in its files fingerprints of more than 80 million persons. Its crime laboratory in 1971 handled 462,595 scientific tests. Its staff of 19,401 included 8,586 agents with 59 field offices and representatives in many cities. The FBI budget for the fiscal year ending June 20, 1971 was $334.5 million.

Hoover embarked on his career in 1917 when he won his

law degree and moved into a job with the Department of Justice, his only employer over a stretch that exceeded 55 years.

His first assignment in "counter-radical activities" came at the end of President Woodrow Wilson's second term; the era of the "red raids." Hoover took charge of assembling a card file on 450,000 "radicals" and built his first informer network that he used with dramatic results later against the Communist party and the Ku Klux Klan.

In 1924, during the administration of Calvin Coolidge, Hoover was named, at the age of 29, to rebuild the Bureau of Investigation. From the start he insisted that appointments to the bureau be divorced entirely from outside political influences. He also kept a personal grip on all the important strings within the organization, a hold he never relinquished.

Personal affairs were rigidly regulated at the bureau which became the Federal Bureau of Investigation in 1935. Women were not allowed to smoke on the job and no one had a coffee break.

Hoover wore custom-made shirts and suits and he instructed his agents to dress like businessmen. The unofficial uniform became a white shirt, dark suit, snap-brim hat and a handkerchief in the jacket pocket.

During the gangster era of the late 1920s the Department began to attract nationwide attention. It helped put Al Capone behind bars in 1929. In the 1930s the FBI helped solve the Lindbergh kidnaping. It also captured or killed such widely known criminals as "Baby Face" Nelson, Alvin "Kreepy" Karpis, John Dillinger and "Machinegun" Kelly. Stung by a congressman's charge that he was an "armchair detective" who never made an arrest, Hoover personally took part in the capture of Karpis in 1936.

Hoover had a genius for understanding the currents of power. When Franklin D. Roosevelt became President he dazzled him with his success against crime.

Roosevelt liked Hoover and was amused when he learned that the FBI chief had put a spy on Harry Hopkins, the President's top aide.

Roosevelt heightened Hoover's prestige in 1936 by assigning counter-espionage duties to the FBI. When the war erupted three years later, the FBI was already busy shielding the United States against espionage, sabotage and subversion. Within 72 hours after Roosevelt gave the order to the FBI to move into action following the attack on Pearl Harbor in 1941, nearly 4,000 enemy aliens were rounded up and taken into custody. The department's image was further enhanced by its capture of eight Nazi saboteurs who landed in the United States by submarine in 1942.

After the war the prime FBI targets became Red spies and Hoover until his death regarded Communists as mortal foes of America. G-men won praise for breaking up a ring stealing A-bomb secrets, but in later years, after the Cold War had begun the thaw, some legislators criticized Hoover's concern over Communism as a "witch-hunting" obsession. There were demands that the FBI boss be retired.

President Kennedy made the reappointment of Hoover the first order of business after his election in 1960, but Robert Kennedy, arriving at the Justice Department intent on wiping out organized crime, complained that the FBI scarcely admitted the existence of organized rackets.

Hoover and Robert Kennedy later became engaged in a running battle over assignment of agents to civil rights cases and organized crime. Critics of the FBI charged that Hoover concentrated on Communism not only because he viewed it as a graver threat to the nation but because, at the time, it afforded bigger

Top, FBI chief received the National Security Medal from President Dwight D. Eisenhower. Center, Hoover chatting with President Harry S. Truman. Below, FBI boss conferring with President John F. Kennedy

publicity than segregation and inspired bigger department budgets than organized crime.

Hoover became embroiled in disputes with such public figures as the Rev. Martin Luther King. A Congressman also accused the FBI of tapping his phone, a charge which Hoover denied.

Colleagues said that Hoover came to view his police work with a vision of national destiny. His men were swift in finding the bodies of three civil rights workers killed in Philadelphia and in solving the killing of Mrs. Viola Liuzzo. But they were accused of being slow in enforcing the cause of civil rights.

Demands for Hoover's retirement grew louder. But they led nowhere as lawmakers and presidents stood by him over the years. His budget appropriations continued to sail through Congress unscathed, and for millions of Americans he was "Mr. FBI," the arch foe of crime.

The period of mourning that followed Hoover's death was a measure of the man. His body lay in state in the Capitol Rotunda, an honor usually reserved for Presidents, key figures of Congress and war heroes. It was the first time a civil servant had been so honored. Flags were dropped to half staff, and in 21 hours 25,000 mourners filed past his casket.

The day after Hoover's body had lain in state Nixon did him the signal honor of delivering the funeral eulogy, in Washington National Presbyterian Church, not far from the house where Hoover had been born. Hoover and Nixon had held a mutual admiration ever since the days when Nixon had been a freshman congressman.

Hoover, said the President, "was one of the giants, a man who helped keep steel in America's backbone and the flame of freedom in America's soul."

Square-jawed FBI head posing with a boxer before a Washington dog show

Tragedy struck in Idaho

Fire swept through the nation's deepest and richest silver mine in Kellogg, Idaho, on May 2, leaving 91 miners dead

Below, Bureau of Mines Inspector Donald J. Morris boarded basket to descend into shaft of the burning mine. Right, top, Miners Tom Wilkinson (left) and Ron Flory smiling happily after their rescue from a shaft 4,800 feet below ground. Right, bottom, Idaho Gov. Cecil Andrus crouching as he talked to relatives of the trapped miners

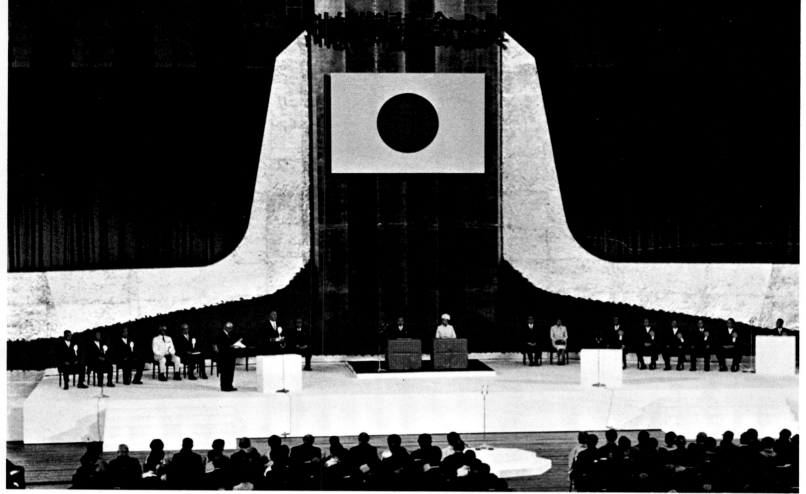

Ceremony held in Tokyo marking the return of Okinawa to Japan after 27 years of American administration

OKINAWA RETURNED TO JAPAN

Pay telephones were fitted to take yen coins instead of dimes; road signs were changed from miles to kilometers, and price tags and taximeters were readjusted to read Japanese. These and sundry other modifications on Okinawa marked the return to Japan of that 60-mile-long island in the East China Sea after 27 years of American military rule.

Japan and the United States began in November 1969 private negotiations looking toward restoration of Okinawa's prior status. Then, in San Clemente, Calif., on Jan. 7, 1972, it was announced that President Nixon and Japanese Premier Eisaku Sato had signed a treaty under which the United States relinquished control of the island. The announcement followed two days of intensive talks between the two leaders.

Terms of the treaty provided that political rule be returned to Japan. American military bases staffed with 43,000 troops were to remain on the island, but U.S. B52 bombers on Okinawa were not to strike Communist forces in Indochina, as they had done in the late 1960s. The treaty also restricted the dispatch of troops by the U.S. command directly from the island into combat in southeast Asia.

Actual reversion to Japan of Okinawa and 140 other strategic islands in the Ryukyu chain was celebrated May 15 with a ceremony attended by Sato and Vice President Agnew. The turn-over was hailed as marking a new phase in the friendly relations between America and the Far Eastern imperial empire.

As Agnew noted in a proclamation during the ceremony, "this reversion resolves the last major issue of the war between Japan and the United States and opens a new era of greater community interest between the two countries based upon full partnership."

SEVEN KILLED IN WEIRD BLAST

"They looked like mannequins. One woman looked like she was still on the telephone," said the fireman in stunned disbelief at the sight of the seven victims of a steam pipe blast in the heart of New York City's financial district.

The seven, all employes of General Utilities Corporation, had been killed, apparently in a split second, by "a combination of blast impact and 500-degree live steam," said New York's chief medical examiner, Dr. Milton Helpern.

The impact had been so swift that some of the victims were found sitting upright at their desks with paper cups of coffee before them.

"They never knew what hit them," said an ambulance attendant. He termed the blast scene "one of the worst I've seen in a long time."

The explosion, which occurred May 3 when a high pressure steam riser pipe burst, had ripped through four rooms of the 36th floor suite of offices.

One of the rooms was the carpeted private office of 30-year-old Gary Kennedy, corporate secretary of General Public Utilities, who was one of the victims. Still open on his desk was a preliminary prospectus for 3,440,000 shares of common stock of General Public Utilities which had been registered with the Securities and Exchange Commission.

The three other wrecked rooms were closer to the explosion. They were a jumble of furniture and file cabinets overturned and half buried in a pile of rubble.

Desks and walls were covered with a chalky, mudlike coating of plaster dissolved by the live steam and brick dust from blown-out wall sections.

A large room containing duplicating machines, desks and files took the brunt of the blast. Two dead women were found in that room. Two more were found in an adjoining small room. Here an electric clock remained running, but telephones had been blown off their stands and bloodstains smeared the desks.

In all the damaged rooms acoustic-tile panels and fluorescent lighting covers had been ripped from the ceilings.

A philodendron in the largest room looked like a plaster cast of a plant.

In the rain-soaked crowd milling in the street outside the lobby, a woman asked a newspaper reporter if he had any information about her cousin who worked for General Public Utilities. She gave the name of one of the dead. The reporter told a police official who silently ushered the woman into the building.

A BOMB SCARE ON OCEAN LINER

"We were 99½ per cent sure that the call was a hoax," Cunard chairman Victor Mathews said after the incident. Still, there was little the steamship company could do but cooperate with the man who had phoned its New York office and announced that six bombs had been planted on its most prestigious luxury liner, the *Queen Elizabeth* II. The passenger liner, in the mid-Atlantic at the time of the threat, was en route from New York to Cherbourg, France and Southampton, England.

On May 19 the anonymous caller warned that his two accomplices—an ex-convict bored with his life, and a terminal cancer patient—would detonate the explosives stowed on the vessel unless Cunard paid him $350,000. With 1,481 passengers, 900 crew members and a 66,000-ton ship to protect, the company could only meet the extortionist's demand.

In New York, company officials collected the ransom money. The U.S. Coast Guard alerted its cutters in the vicinity of the *Elizabeth* to the crisis, and the FBI initiated its own investigation. In London, Cunard representatives conferred with the Defense Ministry and Scotland Yard and, on the British authorities' advice, decided to parachute a team of four bomb disposal experts to the $78 million ship.

The bomb squad assembled at a Royal Air Force base in Wiltshire, England. They boarded a long-range Hercules transport jet and, by 7 p.m. on the day of the scare, they were aboard the five-year-old *Elizabeth*. Immediately they set about an almost impossible mission: Every inch of the 13-deck structure, which contained no fewer than 12,000 pieces of passenger luggage, had to be thoroughly examined. Their hours of searching through the maze of passageways and cabins failed to reveal any evidence of explosives.

Police and FBI agents in New York had left the ransom, in denominations of $10 and $20 bills, at the location specified in a letter sent by the extortionist before his call to Cunard. But he never showed up to collect the money, and he never contacted Cunard again.

Through all the commotion, the passengers remained undaunted. Orchestras played, champagne flowed and, as one passenger recalled, "people laughed and joked and placed bets on when the bomb squad would arrive."

NIGHTCLUB FIRE FATAL FOR 117

"I broke a window pane and waited for rescue. I watched several people fall to their deaths. So I decided not to climb outside, although I really wanted to." Such was the description of one survivor's escape from the fire that raged through a nightclub in Osaka, Japan. He merely waited for firemen to lead his way out. But 117 other persons died in the conflagration.

The Playtown Cabaret occupied the top floor of the seven-story Sennechi department store building in metropolitan Osaka. On Saturday night, May 14, a blaze started on the third floor and quickly spread upward. The third, fourth and fifth floors were gutted.

The fire cut off electricity, putting the cabaret's elevator out of service, and the only emergency exit in the building was locked. A total of 170 people were trapped in the nightclub.

In desperation, 20 people jumped from windows and met death on the ground. Another 96 died of asphyxiation. The 117th victim, a hostess, died later of injuries. Of the remaining few people, 42 were injured, most of them seriously.

Firemen finally contained the flames after waging a four-hour battle with what was described as Japan's worst fire since a 1951 railroad explosion that killed 107 persons.

Police blamed a 36-year-old electrician who was working on the third floor of the department store. They accused him of dropping a lighted cigarette.

115 DEAD IN SICILY JET CRASH

In Rome, Alitalia Airline officials issued a statement: "Evidence at the scene of the accident indicates that there are no survivors." The DC8 jetliner had slammed into the side of a 12,550-foot mountain bordering Palermo's Punti-Raisi Airport. On May 6, when the four-engine aircraft exploded into flames upon impact, 108 passengers and seven crew members perished.

The jetliner was carrying Sicilian-born passengers from Rome to Palermo to vote for a new parliament in Italy's May 7 elections. It was approaching Palermo when it fell, three miles away, near the town of Carini.

Officials described the crash as the worst in the Italian national airline's history.

British bomb disposal experts aboard a cutter preparing to board the Queen Elizabeth II

MICHELANGELO STATUE DAMAGED

"I am Jesus Christ!" So cried Laszlo Toth, a 33-year-old Australian geologist, as he stood in the chapel in St. Peter's Basilica. He then scaled the marble balustrade surrounding Michelangelo's masterpiece, *Pietà*, and battered at the priceless Madonna with a 12-pound hammer. Five blows cleaved the nose from her face, gouged her left eyelid, chipped her veil and severed her left arm at the elbow.

The damage done, Vatican guards belatedly apprehended the bearded, long-haired man and hauled him off to eight hours of interrogation before his internment at Rome's Queen of Heaven jail. He was charged with "damaging art work" and "offending religion by attacking an object of worship."

The mutilation, on May 21, inspired heated criticism of the Vatican for failing to protect adequately the statue of the Virgin Mary holding her dead son. The sculpture was set apart from the public only by a guardrail and a flight of stairs. At the time a shatterproof glass case was being constructed for the statue. Critics voiced concern for other similarly unprotected works of art in the Vatican.

The prospects for successful restoration of the sculpture were grim. The general director of the Pontifical museums explained that the most difficult part would be to rebuild the thin film of marble of the eyelid, while "preserving the delicate glow the sculptor gave the whole face of the Virgin." He said the restoration would take up to three years. All fragments of the sculpture had been collected and experts had an existing plaster copy of the masterpiece to help them.

The act was readily explained by the self-proclaimed savior: "Today is my 33rd birthday, the age when Christ died," he said. "For that reason I smashed *Pietà*. I did it because the mother of God does not exist. I am Christ. I am Michelangelo. I have reached the age of Christ and now I can die. If you kill me, I'll only go to heaven."

Toth, although of Australian extraction, was born in Hungary.

SUPREME COURT POLICY REMADE BY NIXON'S NEW APPOINTMENTS

For years before he became the 37th President of the United States, Richard Nixon criticized the U.S. Supreme Court for "hamstringing the peace forces and strengthening the criminal elements" in American society. During his bid for the presidency in 1968 he promised to remake the court in his own law-and-order image.

On May 21 the court fulfilled his pledge when it delivered two rulings making it easier for the prosecution in court cases to obtain indictments and convictions.

The first decision held 5 to 4 that unanimous jury verdicts are not necessary for convictions in state criminal courts. The five-justice majority consisted of Justice Byron R. White and the four Nixon had placed on the bench—Chief Justice Warren E. Burger and Justices Harry A. Blackmun, Lewis F. Powell Jr., and William H. Renquist.

At issue in the decision were three case appeals by felony suspects convicted by jury votes of 11-1 and 10-2 in Oregon and 9-3 in Louisiana. Both states allowed less than unanimous verdicts in felony trials. The judgment of the High Court held that "a state may permit convictions by an unspecified 'heavy majority' of jurors, not just by unanimous vote."

Writing for the majority, Justice White said that the framers of the Sixth Amendment, requiring only trial by jury, had deliberately omitted the unanimity requirement. Citing a 1970 Supreme Court decision that gave constitutionality to convictions by juries of less than 12 members, he said that a vote for convictions by a "heavy majority" of jurors would be the equivalent of a unanimous vote by a smaller jury. He also held that the Constitution did not give dissenting jurors "the right to block convictions" but only the right to "be heard."

The court's second ruling held that witnesses be compelled to testify before grand juries and other governmental panels, even though other evidence might later help to convict them of related crimes for which they had been indicted. The 5 to 2 decision held that to force witnesses to testify under the threat of imprisonment for contempt did not violate the Fifth Amendment's guarantee against compulsory self-incrimination, provided that the prosecution was barred from using the compelled testimony against the witness.

The decision involved appeals from a New Jersey gambler and two anti-draft conspiracy suspects, all of whom invoked the Fifth Amendment during prosecution and were convicted of contempt. The court upheld the convictions on the grounds that "the reduced protections of the Fifth Amendment are still very substantial."

In two opinions he wrote for the high court, Justice Powell said that a witness' privilege against compulsory self-incrimination was satisfied "if his testimony cannot be used against him in any way, because he is left in the same position as if he were permitted to stand on the constitutional privilege and remain mute." Powell held that if a witness was later prosecuted for crimes related to his testimony, the prosecution would have to prove "that the evidence it proposes to use is derived from a legitimate source wholly independent of the compelled testimony."

The court's two monumental decisions immediately raised several serious questions. Justice William O. Douglas, one of the four dissenting justices on the unanimous jury verdict ruling, contended that that decision made "questionable the validity of an 8-4 vote, and whether juries of less than 12 members must be unanimous." Also left uncertain, he said, was whether unanimous verdicts would be required in capital cases and how the court would justify invalidating convictions if it were confronted with votes of 3-2 or even 2-1.

FOR THE RECORD

INDEPENDENCE. Ceylon, a 25,000-square-mile island in the Bay of Bengal, proclaimed itself the independent socialist Republic of Sri Lanka on May 22, breaking a 157-year bond with the British crown. After 22 months of debate, the island's constituent assembly adopted a new constitution, making the 12,747,000 inhabitants of the former British dominion citizens of a free, democratic socialist nation. The new republic will remain a member of the British Commonwealth.

RESIGNED. For personal reasons, John B. Connally, former governor of Texas, from his post as Secretary of the Treasury, on May 16. President Nixon accepted the resignation with "the deepest regret." The President described the only Democrat in his cabinet as the "dynamic and skilled" architect of the Administration's new economic policies at home and abroad, and as a "wise and courageous counselor on matters of national security." On Aug. 9 he became national chairman of the Democrats for Nixon reelection committee.

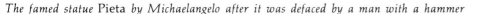

The famed statue Pieta *by Michaelangelo after it was defaced by a man with a hammer*

Silhouettes at Sunset

Left, Four fishermen trying their luck from a Clearwater pier at dusk. Below, left, a lone gull gliding over rolling sea at sunset in Clearwater, Fla. Below, right, boys searching for seashells washed up on the shore stretching along the Gulf of Mexico at Clearwater

Portrait of an assassination attempt

June

Moment before Wallace was shot

The shooting

Mrs. Wallace bending over her stricken husband

Presidential Primaries:

No primroses along the path to the Democratic nomination but Republicans had no worries

Left, an exuberant Sen. Edmund Muskie savoring the applause of his supporters at a victory party after winning in New Hampshire's March primary. Center, Sen. Hubert Humphrey tried his hand as the leader of the band while stumping through Northern California prior to the state's June 6 primary. Right, Gov. George Wallace campaigning at a rally in Laurel, Md., on May 15, just before the shooting that left him near death at a shopping center

Harry Truman once called presidential primary elections "just so much eyewash." That celebrated winner believed instead that the chips that counted were to be won or lost at the national nominating conventions. However valueless preferential primaries may have seemed to Truman 24 years previous, in the 1972 presidential year they proved to be pivotal among Democrats faced with winnowing from a regiment of contenders a single challenger to oppose President Richard M. Nixon.

Among Republicans, too, the 1972 primaries established early on that the President could safely dismiss challenges to his renomination from the left and right flanks of his own party. At last and tragically, the primary campaign produced the chilling spectacle, all the more sickening for its familiarity to Americans of the era, of a candidate—Gov. George C. Wallace of Alabama—gunned down at a political rally.

Long before the Jan. 6 filing deadline for the March 7 New Hampshire primary, Democratic hopefuls, announced and unannounced, had appeared all over the landscape. The front runners were conceded to be the party's standard bearers of 1968 in reverse order, Senators Edmund S. Muskie of Maine and Hubert H. Humphrey of Minnesota. Although Muskie had been campaigning virtually since the day the 1968 campaign ended he waited until Jan. 4 to announce his candidacy formally. Humphrey, an announced candidate for more than a year, waited until Jan. 10, conceding the first-in-the-nation primary to his rival from neighboring Maine. One early Demo-

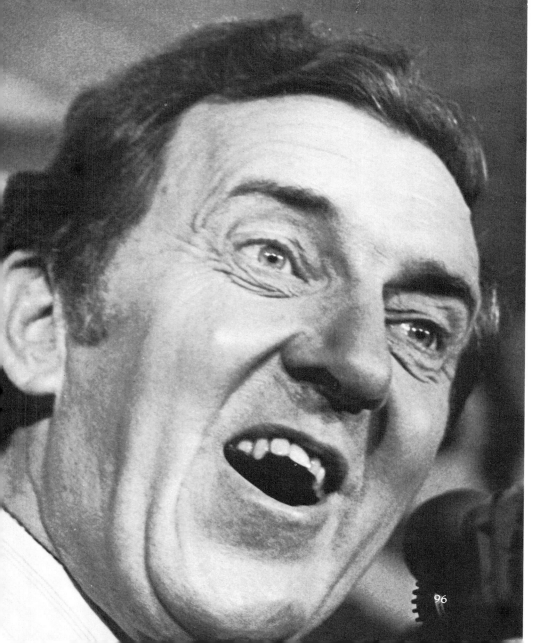

cratic contender, Sen. Fred Harris of Oklahoma, running on a "new populism" platform, had already withdrawn from competition, announcing ruefully after six weeks of campaigning, "I'm broke."

That left the favorite, Muskie, with four opponents in the New Hampshire race: Sen. George McGovern of South Dakota, Sen. Vance Hartke of Indiana, Rep. Wilbur Mills of Arkansas and Mayor Sam Yorty of Los Angeles. Another contestant, Edward T. Coll, a 32-year-old poverty worker from Connecticut, was unqualified by age to be president but did enliven the campaign by dangling a rubber rat in front of the camera during a televised debate among the serious contenders.

On the Republican side, Rep. Paul N. McCloskey Jr. of California, campaigned extensively for a program to end the fighting in Indochina and also accused the President of "deception and management of news" and of having abandoned the cause of racial equality. Against McCloskey was conservative Rep. John M. Ashbrook of Ohio, who aimed to stop the "left turn" in administration policy which he identified as budget deficits, too little defense spending and a "sellout" of Nationalist China. To combat them, the President called on political allies as well as sports and entertainment personalities plus a full-scale telephone and mail drive.

Sen. McGovern began in 1970 putting together a staff of tough, young, intelligent and politically savvy workers who recruited legions of volunteers among a vast constituency of mostly youthful Americans disenchanted with the country's established institutions yet anxious to work for changes within the political system. He, like Sen. Harris, was classified as an exponent of the "new populism." Unlike any of his opponents, however, he was put down by the political pros and pundits as a one-issue candidate; his opposition to Viet Nam involvement dated back to 1963. He was widely admired for his integrity by those who knew him, but his try for the presidential nomination was also widely considered as quixotic. In one "recognition" poll in 1971 George McGovern scored 2 per cent.

Thus, when he began his campaign in New Hampshire McGovern was in a position to work a strategy known among politicians as poor-mouthing, simply discounting his defeat in advance. His forces arbitrarily invented the criterion that if they could hold Muskie to less than 50 per cent of the vote it would constitute "victory" for McGovern.

During the campaign McGovern further advanced his reputation as a man of candor by voluntarily disclosing the amounts and donors to his campaign. McCloskey, the Republican challenger, did the same a few days later but, at least as a ploy, McGovern's forthrightness had stolen the march on all the rest. For his part, Muskie made what many interpreted as a political error when he dramatically, and tearfully, denounced publisher William Loeb from a platform outside the Manchester Union Leader. The newspaper, largest in New Hampshire, was backing Mayor Yorty and had accused Muskie of making

With the outcome of the Republican primaries a foregone conclusion, President Nixon showed no sign of worry

a slur on Americans of French-Canadian descent, which Muskie called a "lie." He also called Loeb a "gutless coward" and said, "It's fortunate for him he's not on this platform beside me." Many critics thought the outburst peevish.

Results of the election:

Democrats		
Muskie	41,235	46.4%
McGovern	33,007	37
Yorty	5,401	6
Mills	3,560	4
Hartke	2,417	3

Republicans		
Nixon	79,239	68%
McCloskey	23,190	20
Ashbrook	11,362	11

Muskie had roundly defeated McGovern by a margin verging on a landslide and had won 15 delegates to McGovern's five. Yet McGovern's forces had so successfully propagated the less-than-50 per cent tactic many political writers interpreted the election as a dark-horse McGovern victory and a front-running Muskie defeat.

McGovern used the same tactic in the Florida primary a week later. He spent little effort in the state, saying, "It was never a state where we expected to do well."

He didn't—but that was hardly the most striking fact of the Florida primary.

To begin with, no fewer than 11 Democrats entered the Flor-

ida race: Muskie; McGovern; Humphrey; Mills; Hartke; Yorty; Sen. Henry M. Jackson of Washington; New York Mayor John V. Lindsay, a recent convert to Democratic ranks; Rep. Shirley Chisholm, a black congresswoman from New York; former Sen. Eugene J. McCarthy, the peace candidate of the 1968 primaries, many of whose youthful volunteers from that campaign were now working for McGovern; and one other, Gov. George C. Wallace of Alabama.

Wallace dominated the campaign. His slogan, "Send them a message," appeared on billboards and bumpers all over the state and his flamboyant rhetoric rattled the hustings. The message he wanted the voters to send—to Washington and to the leadership of the Democratic party—was generally that people were fed up with the way things were being administered in the following areas: foreign aid, welfare, the tax structure, the courts, national defense and busing. In his fiery speeches, he always saved busing for last. "This business of busing little schoolchildren clear across town is the most callous, asinine thing I ever heard of, the whim of some social schemer in Washington . . . ." He also said, "I guarantee you that if you vote for George Wallace, President Nixon will do something to halt this busing within 30 days." (The President didn't wait 30 days; he called for a busing moratorium two days after the Florida election.)

Along with the names of 11 Democrats and three Republicans—the same three who ran in New Hampshire, although McCloskey had already withdrawn his challenge—Floridians were asked to cast a straw vote on the busing issue. By 74 per cent, they expressed their disapproval of "forced busing," and by 79 per cent their approval of "equal opportunity for quality education." What they seemed to be saying was that they believed in integration in theory but did not want to achieve it through busing.

Wallace's strong stance on the issue forced others into positions which only one, Sen. Jackson, had taken voluntarily. Jackson sought a halt to busing through constitutional amendment. Sen. Humphrey, the battle-scarred civil rights champion, waffled on the issue, calling for "more and better schools, not more buses." Muskie downgraded the issue as almost irrelevant, which at that time in history it plainly was not. McGovern, Lindsay and Chisholm unambiguously upheld the Supreme Court's position on busing and denounced Wallace's stance in equally clear terms.

Wallace's polls showed he would win about 32 per cent of the vote in the crowded field; privately he hoped for 35 per cent. When the votes were counted he had surpassed his wildest dreams, collecting 41.5 per cent of the vote and 75 of the state's 81 delegates. Humphrey, who finished second with 18 per cent, got the remaining six delegates.

The results:

Democrats		
Wallace	515,916	41.5%
Humphrey	231,219	18.6
Jackson	167,667	13.5
Muskie	109,653	8.8
Lindsay	81,322	6.5
McGovern	74,880	6.1
Chisholm	44,786	3.6
Others	. . . . . .	1.4

Republicans		
Nixon	357,356	87.1%
Ashbrook	35,983	8.8
McCloskey	16,985	4.1

Wallace, of course, was ecstatic over the outcome. "We beat the face cards of the Democratic deck," he crowed.

In a bitter election-night speech, Muskie said of Wallace: "I hate what he stands for. The man is a demagogue of the worst kind. This election result in Florida reveals to a greater extent than I had imagined some of the worst instincts of which human beings are capable." McGovern was more temperate: "No matter how we slice it, today was a setback for those who believe deeply in the cause of human rights. But I cannot accept the fact that the vote that went to George Wallace was a racist vote. Many people voted for Wallace to register their protest against the way things are."

The following Tuesday, voters in Illinois went to the polls to state their preference between Muskie and Sen. McCarthy, who had ignored the Florida primary to campaign in Illinois, and on a separate part of the ballot to apportion delegates to either Muskie or McGovern or allow them to go to the convention uncommitted to either. In the preferential race Muskie defeated McCarthy with 63 per cent of the vote, although McCarthy called his 37 per cent "a significant beginning." In the delegate race Muskie won 59 delegates to only 14 for McGovern. The largest bloc fell to Chicago Mayor Richard J. Daley, who would be in control of at least 80 of 87 uncommitted delegates.

The next primary, April 4 in Wisconsin, was even more crowded than the Florida race. Twelve candidates were in the field and it was clear that many of them would be there for the last time; Hartke, in fact, had already withdrawn his candidacy for lack of funds and announced his support of Humphrey.

Humphrey had reason to hope he might win in Wisconsin, his neighboring state with its long-standing liberal traditions. Muskie, as well, needed a solid showing to retain his fast-disappearing place near the top. As for Wallace, a victory in Wisconsin would be his first in a northern state, a nice prize which would go far toward erasing his image as a regional candidate. McGovern had a similar use for Wisconsin: to eliminate his image as a one-issue candidate. He had begun a strong organizational drive a year earlier in Wisconsin, hitting hard on economic issues—closing tax loopholes, reforming local property taxes, putting an end to inflation.

The strategy worked for McGovern. In the crowded field he polled 30 per cent of the vote and gave his candidacy a big boost.

The results:

McGovern	332,298	30%
Wallace	248,191	22
Humphrey	233,914	21
Muskie	115,512	10
Jackson	87,944	8
Lindsay	77,519	7
McCarthy	15,699	1
Chisholm	9,119	1
Others*	. . . . . .	. . .

*Yorty, Hartke, Mills and Rep. Patsy T. Mink of Hawaii received less than 1 per cent of the vote.

McGovern called his victory "a vote of protest and hope," but it was largely clouded by Wallace's strong showing. Wallace campaigned only eight days in the state, drew the largest crowds, and was convinced he could have won if he had expended more effort. In any event, he told the press, it established him as "a serious national candidate."

His next showing was even more impressive. Primaries in Massachusetts and Pennsylvania fell on the same day, April 25, and the candidates had to choose where to invest their time. Humphrey and Muskie wrote off Massachusetts and fought it out in Pennsylvania, the much larger prize in terms of delegates. Wallace made one appearance in each state. McGovern gave a scant three days to Pennsylvania and spent the bulk of his effort in Massachusetts, where his local organizers had gone all out for weeks in advance.

For McGovern, at least, the strategy paid off. He won a sweeping victory over seven candidates while his major rivals were busy elsewhere, took 52 per cent of the total vote, 30 per cent more than his nearest competitor, carried every congressional district and picked up all the state's 102 delegates.

In Pennsylvania, Humphrey won with 35 per cent of the votes. Wallace was second with 21 per cent. Muskie, who had campaigned as hard as had Humphrey, finished in fourth place just behind McGovern. It was a staggering blow to the Muskie campaign—an unexpected boost to the McGovern campaign. Indeed, in separate balloting for delegates, Humphrey won 57, McGovern 37, Muskie 29 and Wallace 2, giving McGovern the lead in committed delegates over all his rivals.

The results:

	Pennsylvania	
Humphrey	475,633	35.1%
Wallace	287,998	21.2
McGovern	277,050	20.4
Muskie	276,464	20.4
Jackson	39,507	2.9
	Massachusetts	
McGovern	255,123	52.1%
Muskie	106,551	21.8
Humphrey	38,505	7.9
Wallace	36,465	7.4
Chisholm	18,143	3.7
Mills	15,021	3.1
McCarthy	7,235	1.5

Although it was too late to claim, like Truman, that primaries were so much eyewash, the results thus far convinced Muskie that he had better spend his resources elsewhere. He announced that he would campaign in no more primaries although he would remain a candidate.

McGovern's showing in Massachusetts, on the other hand, was widely hailed as an astonishing victory and tempted the fast-moving candidate to try his luck again in the industrial Middle West. The Ohio and Indiana primaries were on the same day, May 2 (as well as primaries in Alabama and the District of Columbia, and in Tennessee on May 4). McGovern entered in Ohio. As in Illinois, however, he met defeat, this time at the hands of Humphrey. The margin was so slim, however, that—possibly as a result of McGovern's lingering underdog position—the vote was widely interpreted as a standoff. The result was Humphrey 41.5 per cent, McGovern 39.3, with Humphrey winning 77 delegates to McGovern's 63.

Humphrey also won in Indiana, by only five percentage points over Wallace (47 per cent to 42 per cent), and picked up 55 delegates to Wallace's 21. It was Wallace's strongest showing so far outside the South. As expected, Wallace won both the Alabama and Tennessee primaries where he was virtually unopposed. Meanwhile, another contender, Sen. Jackson, fell by the wayside citing "deficit financing."

It was not until the Nebraska primary, on May 9, that McGovern met Humphrey in a straight two-man race. Wallace was also in the race but did not campaign, along with eight other names on the ballot of candiates either long since withdrawn from competition or not considered serious contenders.

For the first time, McGovern was a favorite and Humphrey in his historically more familiar role as underdog. Hostile circulars and advertisements called attention to McGovern's purported liberal views on abortion and marijuana, but with solid support from farmers and students McGovern won a narrow victory, 41 per cent to 35 per cent. Wallace took 13 per cent and the rest was split among the others on the ballot.

On the same day, in West Virginia, Humphrey won a solid 2-1 victory over Wallace—67 per cent to 33 per cent—although the vote was solely a popularity contest and neither made much of a campaign effort; Wallace didn't even visit the state.

In North Carolina, however, Wallace won a singular victory over the state's popular former governor, Terry Sanford, who mounted a campaign specifically to rebuff the Alabamian. Wallace defeated Sanford 50 per cent to 37 per cent, with the rest divided among Chisholm, Muskie and Jackson.

By mid-May, then, the Democratic pecking order bore no resemblance whatever to the lineup back in March. George McGovern, once dismissed as a dreamer, and George Wallace, once regarded as a noisy nuisance, were competing with Humphrey for the lead once considered sewed up by Muskie, and the hopefuls who crowded the Florida and Wisconsin ballots now littered the wayside.

As astonishing to most observers as McGovern's surge was the meteoric rise of Wallace. The feisty Alabamian had found a ready response to his politics of discontent in all parts of the nation.

Watching him campaign in the primaries, observers thought they saw a "new" Wallace, a more polished politician than the man who very nearly threw the 1968 election into the House of Representatives with his third party effort. He had remarried since the death of Lurleen Wallace and his new wife, Cornelia, who was young and attractive, added a freshness to the Wallace entourage. The absence of hecklers in most of his crowds also contributed to his new image, considering that in previous campaigns hecklers had been an integral part of a Wallace speech, offered to the public as clear and present examples of the need for more law and order.

But when Wallace took his campaign to Maryland in anticipation of that state's May 16 primary, the hecklers—along with a foreboding atmosphere of violence and danger reminiscent of his past campaigns—returned. In Frederick he was hit in the head with a rock, in Hagerstown he was splattered with eggs, in Salisbury students flung at him, of all things, popsicles.

Wallace attracted danger like a lightning rod, and he knew it. He spoke from behind a bulletproof lectern and was constantly surrounded by policemen. A random check during the primary campaigns showed that from two to five times as many Secret Service agents were with Wallace on any given day as were with Humphrey or McGovern; 36 agents guarded Wallace at a rally in Baltimore, along with at least 150 other lawmen who frisked spectators at the door.

Wallace was well aware of the risks all right, but his compulsion to plunge into a crowd and touch the hands of his adorers was stronger perhaps than that of any other candidate on the scene. Each time he left Montgomery on an election trip his campaign manager, Charles S. Snider, said he always called to him a perfunctory farewell, "Y'all be careful!" and Wallace always muttered a perfunctory reply, "I love people too much to be careful."

Maryland was a state the Alabamian considered as true "Wallace country" despite the reappearance of violence. Indeed, on the final day of campaigning, eggs and tomatoes arched toward him from the crowd during a rally in Wheaton; Wallace was nonetheless pleased with his reception there. In fact, he was elated when he drove the short distance from Wheaton to Laurel. It had been a good campaign, and for the first time he felt confident of a victory in Maryland and a strong showing in Michigan, whose primary was on the same day and where he also had campaigned heavily. His appearance at a shopping center in Laurel would be the last rally of his Maryland campaign.

His reception at Laurel on May 15 was, once again, warm and enthusiastic despite a bit of heckling by some collegians in the rear. When he finished his speech he made his usual round of handshaking among the people at the front of the crowd, then headed for his car.

"Hey, George," a voice called. "Aren't you going to shake my hand?"

Wallace turned, hand extended, toward a young man with short, pale blond hair wearing opaque sunglasses. His name was Arthur Herman Bremer, a 21-year-old misfit from Milwaukee who, it would be learned later, had attended previous Wallace rallies in both Michigan and Maryland; who also was present at a Humphrey rally in Milwaukee and an appearance of President Nixon in Ottawa, Canada.

As Wallace approached Bremer, the young man thrust a snub-nosed revolver toward the candidate and blasted five shots about 18 inches from his target.

Wallace flipped back on the asphalt and lay there, conscious but stunned, his legs twisted crazily and blood streaming from his right arm and oozing through his shirt. Alabama state trooper Capt. E. C. Dothard fell nearby, a flesh wound in his side, and Secret Service agent Nicholas Zarvos clutched at a wound in his throat. Dora Thompson, a local Wallace worker, fell to the ground with a bullet in her right leg.

An ambulance sped Wallace to Holy Cross Hospital in nearby Silver Spring, Md., where he was treated for six wounds, in his stomach, right forearm, upper right arm, right shoulder, chest and near his left shoulder blade. A seventh wound, however, was the most damaging: a bullet in his spinal column which it would not be possible to remove until his strength returned weeks later. The bullet had severely damaged his spinal cord, paralyzing him from the waist down, and doctors had deep reservations about his ever walking again.

[A Maryland court in Upper Marlboro on Aug. 4 found Bremer guilty of the attempted assassination and sentenced him to 63 years in prison. On Sept. 28 ten years were deducted.]

Next morning Wallace heard cheering news. He had swept both the Maryland and Michigan primaries and was, at that point, in control of more delegates, 323, than any other candidate except McGovern, who led with 405. Humphrey had only 207. In Michigan, Wallace polled 51 per cent of the vote, his first majority in a northern state election in his career. McGovern got 27 per cent and Humphrey 16 per cent. In Maryland, Wallace polled 39 per cent, Humphrey 27 per cent and McGovern 22 per cent. As in previous elections, the Maryland ballot was cluttered with the names of eight other Democrats who had dropped out of the race.

McGovern and Humphrey suspended campaigning for a time after the Wallace tragedy. Both men visited him in the hospital, along with a stream of other dignitaries including President Nixon and Sen. Edward M. Kennedy. Then McGovern headed for Oregon. He was virtually unopposed there in the May 23 primary, as well as in the Rhode Island primary the same day, but he campaigned heavily in Oregon nonethe-

Mrs. George McGovern raising the hand of her husband in a sign of victory after he won the California primary in June

less looking toward the rich California primary June 6. In Oregon, for example, McGovern won the endorsement of the California migrant workers' leader Caesar Chavez. He won both primaries, taking 50 per cent of the vote in Oregon and 41 per cent in New Hampshire, and boosted his delegate total to 505, more than a third of the 1,509 needed to win his party's nomination on the first ballot at the convention.

The prize in California was 271 delegate votes. By state law it was a winner-take-all election. That system was not in accord with Democratic party reforms, which McGovern had helped write after the 1968 convention and which favored apportionment of delegates according to the percentage of the vote each candidate commanded. Nonetheless it was the state law, and that made a victory in California a rich reward indeed for the winner. On the same day, primaries would be held in New Jersey, New Mexico and in McGovern's home state of South Dakota, but California was the state on which all the candidates concentrated.

On McGovern's behalf, some 35,000 volunteers from more than 120 headquarters canvassed the electorate; McGovern estimated his people contacted personally 80 per cent of the state's potential voters. By contrast, Humphrey's campaign lacked organization; he relied primarily on labor's get-out-the-vote program and his own tireless efforts. It was a tough campaign, at times vicious, the highlights of which were three nationally televised debates between McGovern and Humphrey.

Election day June 6 proved to be a McGovern bonanza. He not only won the huge California delegation but swept the other primaries that day, picking up 71 delegates in New Jersey, 17 in South Dakota and 10 in New Mexico.

The California result:

McGovern	**1,527,392**	**47.1%**
Humphrey	**1,352,379**	**41.7**

The balance of the vote went mainly to Wallace, Chisholm and Muskie; a smattering to other candidates. The victory gave McGovern a commanding lead in delegates, 930, compared to 333 for Wallace, 319 for Humphrey and 163 for Muskie.

McGovern entered the June 20 New York primary, last of the year, as a heavy favorite. The question was not whether he would win but how many delegates would he pick up to push his total closer to the magic figure of 1,509. The efficient McGovern organization, by now the marvel of even old pro politicians, worked hard to field delegate slates in 37 of the state's 39 congressional districts and the candidate himself campaigned earnestly in the final week. On election day, only 18 of the 248 elected delegates eluded the McGovern sweep.

Five days later the process of selecting delegates ended. With McGovern agents working in every state, talking with uncommitted delegates, the candidate could claim on June 26 that he had a solid 1,492.75 delegates on whom he could count for first-ballot votes at the national convention.

From the byways of snowy New Hampshire to the teeming sidewalks of New York had been an arduous journey for George McGovern. But it was a journey that took him from virtual obscurity to virtual certainty of his party's presidential nomination. One could only wonder what that master politician, Harry Truman, weak and ailing at his home in Independence, Mo., thought of the value of primary elections in 1972.

101

Elaborate Literary Hoax
Based on Howard Hughes

Clever scheme cost McGraw-Hill publishing house $750,000 but three 'collaborators' sentenced, most of money returned

THE STORY of Howard Hughes in 1972 was, indeed, a story. A book, in fact; an "autobiography" that turned out to be one of the greatest literary hoaxes in modern times. In addition, the facts upon which this conclusion was reached presented a picture almost as bizarre as the life of secrecy billionaire Hughes had lived for two decades.

Clifford Irving's carefully constructed fake began to come to light soon after the McGraw-Hill Book Company announced, in December 1971, that it had acquired world rights to a 230,000-word book about Hughes, written in collaboration with Irving. At that time the 41-year-old Irving was the author of four remarkably undistinguished novels and lived the bohemian good life on the Spanish isle of Ibiza.

The Hughes Tool Company almost immediately denied the book's authenticity, but McGraw-Hill insisted it was genuine. "We have taken all prudent and necessary steps to verify the authenticity of the book we are going to publish," said a company statement.

The caper cost the publishers $750,000, which they thought had been passed along to Hughes. On the contrary, most of it wound up in Swiss bank deposits. The New York State Supreme Court granted McGraw-Hill's claim against Irving and his wife Edith for $776,000, including expenses, on June 9.

However, when the Hughes Tool denial was made in December, it had appeared that only Howard Hughes himself—if there was a Howard Hughes—could convince McGraw-Hill, and the world, that the book was a fraud. On Jan. 7 a most unusual news conference was arranged. Seven newsmen, all of whom had interviewed Howard Hughes in the past, sat beneath the television lights in a Los Angeles hotel to question a disembodied voice floating in over a telephone wire from the Bahamas, where they had been told that Hughes was living. The reporters sat around a semicircular table, facing a loud speaker plugged into the telephone line.

"Your question was, am I happy and content," said the incoming voice. "The answer is no."

Why do you live the life of a recluse?

"I don't really know. I will tell you one thing: I am rapidly planning to come out of it. I am not going to continue being quite as reclusive as I have been."

He said his life had attracted so much attention that he had resolved to modify it "in order not to be an oddity."

The voice branded Irving's book "a totally fantastic fiction." It added: "I only wish I were still in the movie business. This episode is just so fantastic that it taxes your imagination to believe a thing like this could happen."

Clifford Irving?

"I don't know him. I never saw him. I had never even heard of him until a matter of days ago, when this thing first came to my attention."

But McGraw-Hill says the autobiography is genuine?

"Well, I just don't see how it's possible. I don't see how in the world statements of that kind could be made by people who at least have the resources to investigate and find the truth."

How was his health?

"Well, how the hell is anybody's health at 66 years of age? I certainly don't feel like running around a track at UCLA and trying to break a record. But my health is tolerable, that's certain, and probably better than I deserve. I have no physical disabilities that would be apparent to anyone."

Is there any one thing you would like to do before you die?

"Well, for one thing, I would like to see an accurate story of my life printed because I think I have had experiences that could be helpful to others. I think, in other words, a true biography could be helpful to anyone who might read it."

The session lasted 2 hours and 40 minutes.

The answers, some incredibly detailed and lengthy, convinced the reporters that they were interviewing Hughes. Later, an expert in electronic identification of voices compared tapes of the news conference with a recording of Hughes' congressional testimony in 1947. "It is my opinion," said Lawrence Kersta, head of Voiceprint Laboratories, "that it is, indeed, the voice of Howard Hughes."

The news conference also persuaded many viewers that Irving's claim was false. For a time McGraw-Hill insisted that the book would appear, but finally the company deferred publication until the authenticity of the text was verified. It never was.

Two months later Hughes met Turner V. Shelton, U.S. ambassador to Nicaragua, at an airport in Nicaragua where Hughes had gone when Bahamian officials began questioning his aides about work permits they did not have.

"Howard Hughes appeared in good health and I found him alert, pleasant—in fact, affable," said Shelton. "I noticed no difficulty in his hearing, and his voice was firm. He was in good humor."

Hughes sported a thin beard, and his short hair "has a sort of salt-and-pepper appearance." Shelton said Hughes did not mention Irving or the purported autobiography.

* * * *

On March 9 Irving, his wife and his researcher, Richard Suskind, were indicted by state and federal grand juries in New York City. The 25-page federal indictment charged the Irvings with mail fraud and conspiracy. The state charged the Irvings and Suskind with grand larceny, conspiracy and possession of forged documents. In addition the state accused Irving and Suskind of perjury in testifying before the grand jury that they had met with Hughes.

A bearded Howard Hughes (center) being escorted by friends upon his arrival in New York in 1938 at the Floyd Bennett Field.

The Irvings, Clifford and Edith

In the federal indictment the grand jury held that Irving was convinced he could "successfully defraud McGraw-Hill based on the belief that Hughes was either deceased or not of sufficient mental or physical capacity to denounce the autobiography as a fake." In addition the indictment said Irving forged letters in Hughes' handwriting that convinced the publishing house Hughes had asked Irving to help him write an autobiography.

All three pleaded guilty to the state charges on March 13. On the same day the Irvings pleaded guilty in U.S. District Court.

The Clifford Irving who appeared in federal court for sentencing on June 16 bore little resemblance to the superbly controlled, glacially cool figure he had been months before, when publication of the book was first announced. His complexion ashen, his six-foot frame slumped, he stood before the judge and pleaded for "justice and mercy."

"As I look back, I seem to have turned my back on everything I lived for," said Irving. "I put my wife in terrible jeopardy. I know what she did and why she did it. She trusted me and I abused that trust."

Edith Irving followed him before the judge.

"Our lives have been wrecked," she said. "Don't split us up. Give us one more chance. Don't let our children pay for this. I will stay with him. He has changed in the last five months, although I know we will need years and years to work things out. We must go home to Spain. I ask for your mercy and let us go home to start again."

U.S. District Court Judge John Cannella sentenced Irving to 2½ years in prison and fined him $10,000. He sentenced Mrs. Irving, 36, to pay a $10,000 fine and serve two months in jail. He tempered the punishment by allowing Irving to delay the start of his prison term until Mrs. Irving had been released, so that Irving could care for their two children while she was in jail. Suskind, 47, was not a defendant in the federal court.

The Irvings walked from federal court to the state supreme court three blocks away. "No additional punishment will be given these defendants," said Justice Joseph Martinis. The judge did sentence Suskind to six months in jail.

On the afternoon of June 19, Mrs. Irving entered the Nassau County jail on Long Island to begin serving her sentence.

In the three months after the indictments were returned the Irvings had tried desperately to salvage their lives. They had been staying in New York's Chelsea Hotel, a residential haven for the literary and artistic set. Irving had written, reportedly, a book about his abortive book, in a last-ditch attempt to raise enough money to repay McGraw-Hill and, perhaps, to avoid jail. Mrs. Irving had painted pictures she planned to sell at auction.

On the afternoon of the day she went to jail, the auction was held in the Chelsea lobby while Irving remained upstairs with their children, Nedsky, 4, and Barnaby, 2. Although the auctioneers pleaded with the crowd to help the Irvings, only five paintings were sold, for a total of $2,400.

*   *   *   *

The guilty pleas may have been due to a series of trips Irving had taken before the book was submitted to McGraw-Hill, sometimes with Suskind, sometimes with women other than his wife. These journeys were designed to demonstrate to McGraw-Hill that he was meeting with Hughes in remote locations throughout the western hemisphere.

On one of these journeys Irving took along Baroness Nina van Pallandt, a strikingly beautiful Danish singer. But in the spring of 1972 the baroness was summoned by the federal grand jury investigating Irving's book. In 10 seconds she blew his world apart when she calmly reported that Irving had not been away from her side long enough to have met with Hughes during their trip to Mexico.

About the time of his excursions to "meet" Hughes, Irving altered his wife's passport, changing the name to Helga R. Hughes. Using the passport, Mrs. Irving had opened an account at the Swiss Credit Bank in Zurich under the name H. R. Hughes. She later deposited in the account three McGraw-Hill checks intended for Howard Robard Hughes. The checks totaled $650,000.

Suskind, meanwhile, researched the life of Howard Hughes at the New York Public Library and in the confidential files of the McGraw-Hill Book Company. Irving had gone to the Library of Congress in Washington for material on Hughes' appearance before a congressional committee investigating defense contract profiteering during World War II. He also obtained material on Hughes from the Defense Department and the Atomic Energy Commission. A then unpublished book about Hughes by a former aide, Noah Dietrich, provided additional bits and pieces on Hughes' private life.

Using all this material, Irving and Suskind sat down with a tape recorder and interviewed each other, giving answers they thought would sound like those of Howard Hughes responding to questions about the events and activities of his life. The transcript of these sessions formed the bulk of the "autobiography" Irving eventually sent to McGraw-Hill.

Finally, on Sept. 1, Swiss authorities disclosed that most of the $650,000 had been released to McGraw-Hill.

And what about Howard Hughes?

There were no photographs, no meetings with the press. At the height of the controversy over the book he had left his Bahamian retreat to which U.S. postal inspectors reportedly had been dispatched with a subpoena for him to appear before the federal grand jury investigating Irving's book.

One account had it that Bahamian authorities decided to cooperate and began hassling Hughes' aides about work permits, hoping to create a commotion during which the subpoena could be served.

What followed was a classic example of Hughes on the move. He slipped undetected from the Britannia Beach Hotel in Nassau and sailed for 23 hours on a his yacht to Miami. After his departure his aides carted personal items from his suite: a hospital bed complete with blood plasma stand, cases of bottled water, a half-dozen television sets, tennis rackets and barbells.

Custom officials never did confirm that Hughes was in Miami, but a Hughes Tool Company spokesman said later he flew from Miami to Managua, Nicaragua, on a chartered Eastern Airlines jetliner. Ambassador Shelton had arranged for Hughes' entry into Nicaragua on a VIP basis. There was no

The women in the life of Clifford Irving: from left, his wife Edith; Danish Baroness and singer Nina van Pallandt; scuba diver Ann Baxter

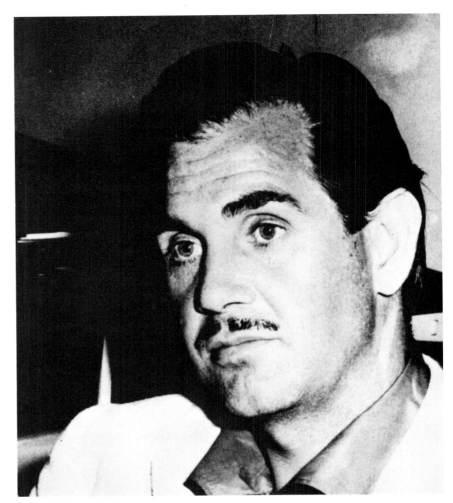

A 1955 photograph of Howard Hughes, left, and a 1954 photo of Brucks Randell, a bit actor who, a former Hughes security man said, was hired in 1957 to sidetrack reporters and process servers

customs check; he was whisked directly to the eighth floor of the Hotel Intercontinental on a bluff overlooking the city.

Hughes' stay in Nicaragua was brief. A month later he was in the air again. Hughes had said during the telephone news conference that he wanted to return to the United States. Newsmen rushed to airports around Los Angeles and Las Vegas, Nev. His plane landed in Vancouver, B.C.

"As near as we can determine, he is here," said the manager of the Bayshore Inn. Hughes' employes reportedly had taken over the top two floors of the 20-story building, implanting closed circuit television cameras to monitor all approaches and rigging the elevators so they would not go beyond the 18th floor without a special key. "We haven't been paid anything yet," said the hotel manager, "but I feel we can depend on him."

Early in June, two weeks before the sentencing of Clifford Irving, the Canadian government announced it had extended Hughes' visitor's permit to allow him to remain in Canada for another year. Canadian immigration officials said regulations required people seeking such extensions to appear in person to make their request. Hughes made no such appearance. Immigration officials said there was a "valid reason" for not requiring Hughes to appear in person.

Hughes' return to the United States could depend on a series of legal battles in which he had been embroiled. The current operators of Trans World Airlines won a $137 million damage judgment against Hughes on the basis of mismanagement dur-

ing the time he owned a controlling interest in the airline. The amount of that judgment was appealed to a federal court.

Robert Maheu, fired as head of Hughes' Nevada operations by the Hughes Tool Company, sued Hughes for $50 million and won a Nevada Supreme Court ruling that Hughes could be compelled to answer a subpoena in the case.

Hughes had said during the Jan. 7 telephone news conference that he definitely intended to return to the United States, but "I just can't give you a date. If some of these people would get off my back, I could probably come closer to it."

Howard Hughes had fascinated America and the world for decades with his various existences. His father had patented the diamond-studded drill bit still used in most oil fields. Hughes inherited the family firm, the Hughes Tool Company, and built it into a fortune estimated at $2 billion.

In his more youthful days, Hughes was a Hollywood film producer and bon vivant who squired about some of the screen's most glamorous women. His lifelong interest in aviation led first to world flying records and later to ownership of Trans World Airlines.

Writers began describing him as an industrialist at about the same time they started using the word recluse. The privacy Hughes always had cherished became almost an obsession. Only a handful of male aides had seen him since 1954.

After moving to Las Vegas, Nev., in 1966, he put together a $300 million empire that made him that state's largest land owner, employer and gambling operator.

Edward Duke of Windsor

His death closed a love story with Wallis Simpson that shook the British throne and caused his abdication in 1936

The Duke of Windsor, former King Edward VIII of England, posed in Austria for photographers in December 1936, shortly after announcing his abdication

THE LOVE STORY that shook the British throne ended on the lawns of an English garden in Windsor where Edward Duke of Windsor, "sometime most high, most mighty and most excellent monarch," went to his grave unseen by the millions who once idolized him.

His Duchess, the twice-divorced American socialite Wallis Warfield Spencer Simpson, "the woman I love" for whom he had abandoned his throne, drove straight from the graveside to return to exile in Paris. With the death of Edward at the age of 77, an affair unique in a thousand years of monarchy had come to a close.

Never before in a line of 60 monarchs had the throne been voluntarily forsaken. Edward VIII stepped down as king on Dec. 11, 1936, unswerving in his desire to marry Mrs. Simpson and certain that to do so as monarch would split the nation and a then unbroken empire covering a quarter of the earth.

Years later his biography, *A King's Story,* explained his motives: "I reject the notion that, faced with a choice of love and duty, I chose love.

"I certainly married because I chose the path of love. But I abdicated because I chose the path of duty. I did not value the crown so lightly that I gave it away hastily. I valued it so deeply that I surrendered it rather than risk any impairment of its prestige."

His reign had lasted a mere 10 months. Even on his acces-

sion, on Jan. 20, 1936, his family and the inner circle of British society had known that Mrs. Simpson stood close to the throne. The nation at large knew nothing. For two years the affair had made headlines in American newspapers. In Britain politicians and the press kept their silence, broken at last and brought to crisis point by an editorial in an obscure provincial paper.

By Dec. 3 the London newspaper barons decided that silence could hold no longer. The storm broke and as quickly passed. To the end the king believed he had the mass of the nation behind him, and that the machinery of church and political power were manipulated against him by Stanley Baldwin, a tough and hostile Conservative prime minister. Winston Churchill, then a political outcast, rallied to the king but few followed, fearful, the monarch believed, of ostracism. The abdication documents were signed, and Churchill was at hand that night to help with the script of an historic farewell broadcast.

From Windsor Castle, in the leafy countryside west of London, the ex-king spoke to a stunned nation.

The voice was clear and forthright at the outset, occasionally broken and emotional toward the end. The waiting millions heard him introduced as "His Royal Highness Prince Edward."

"A few hours ago," he said, "I discharged my last duty as king and emperor.

"You must believe me when I tell you that I have found it

impossible to carry the heavy burden of responsibility and to discharge my duties as king as I would wish to do without the help and support of the woman I love.

"And I want you to know that the decision I have made was mine and mine alone. The other person most nearly concerned has tried up to the last to persuade me to take a different course. . . .

"And now we all have a new king. I wish him, and you his people, happiness and prosperity with all my heart.

"God bless you all. God save the King."

The ex-ruler took leave of his brother, King George VI, and their mother, Queen Mary. He drove through the night to Portsmouth, boarded a destroyer and sailed into exile. The marriage that cost a realm took place in France on June 3, 1937, conducted by an Anglican clergyman who was promptly banned from the pulpit.

Queen Victoria was still on the throne when the future King Edward was born on June 23, 1894. The infant prince, first of Victoria's great grandsons, was christened Edward Albert

The Duke and his bride, the former Mrs. Wallis Warfield Simpson, for whom he relinquished the English throne, after their wedding at the Chateau de Cande near Tours, France in 1937

Christian George Andrew Patrick David. To his family and intimates he was always David. As he grew toward manhood he was known to the world as the dashing Prince of Wales, blue-eyed, fair-haired, ever on the move, the epitome of restless charm.

World War I ended his college days and he joined the Grenadier Guards as a junior officer. In France he soon won a genuine reputation for personal bravery though for dynastic reasons he was kept mainly behind the battle lines.

The war's end brought the series of journeys that earned him the nickname "the suitcase prince." He chatted with pygmy chieftains in the Congo, climbed into the snows of the Andes, swam in the Nile, danced with the daughters of Indian Princes. New York gave him a tickertape welcome in 1919. He met admirals in Japan, a president in Washington, covering thousands of miles. *I danced with a boy who'd danced with a girl who danced with the Prince of Wales,* ran the words of a popular song of the day. He was the darling of the jazz age.

Peace brought its own opportunities to demonstrate courage, this time as a steeplechase jockey. His falls were so frequent that they became an international joke and sparked fears that the heir to the throne would break his neck. He won a dozen or so races before pressure from family and friends forced him into quieter pursuits. These, according to the historian Frances Donaldson, included Mrs. Freda Dudley Ward, wife of a Liberal politician and from 1919 to 1934 the prince's mistress.

They had met in 1917 during an air raid when Mrs. Dudley Ward took refuge at a house where the prince was attending a party. The hostess was Maud Kerr-Smiley, a leader of the international set. She was the sister of Ernest Simpson, a British shipping tycoon, and at that same house on Belgrave Square in 1931 the Prince of Wales for the first time met his future wife.

He was 37, she was 35. They were introduced by Thelma Lady Furness, who in a book called *"Double Exposure"* described her own romance with the prince. There were various versions of this first meeting, including a story that the prince was captivated by the newcomer's skill at Flamenco dancing, using a pair of ice-filled cocktail shakers as castanets.

Within a year the prince and Mrs. Simpson were meeting regularly, often with her husband in attendance. By 1934 they were acknowledged lovers and Mrs. Dudley Ward and Lady Furness had been discarded. By the standards of the British aristocracy such affairs were acceptable while conducted with discretion. Edward's offense was his seeming determination first to advertise his liaison with a twice-married woman and finally to wed her.

The future duchess, born Wallis Warfield in Monterey, Pa., and reared in Baltimore, was descended from old established Southern stock. Her first marriage, at the age of 20, was in 1916 to a young U.S. naval officer, Earl Winfield Spencer. They divorced in 1927 and the next year she married shipbroker Ernest Aldrich Simpson. By 1935 she was skiing with the prince in the Alps and sailing with him in the Mediterranean while her husband was elsewhere. The headlines sprouted in the United States. Silence reigned in Britain, where the big royal news was the Silver Jubilee—25th anniversary—of the reign of George V.

As the New Year was born, the prince stayed by his father's bedside while the radio proclaimed: "The king's life is drawing peacefully towards its close."

The sailor king died, and Edward took his place. Among his titles: Defender of the Faith—temporal head of the Anglican Church and supposed personification of its teaching that Christian marriage is indissoluble.

The Duke and Duchess during their New York City visit in 1967

In May that year the court circular, formal chronicle of royal activities, listed Mr. and Mrs. Ernest Simpson among guests at a palace banquet. In July, on a similar occasion, it listed only Mrs. Simpson. That summer she joined the king for a Mediterranean cruise. In October she started a divorce action uncontested by her husband. Prime Minister Baldwin came back from vacation to find a pile of letters complaining of the American headlines.

Baldwin warned the Sovereign then, and again a month later, that in the choice of a queen the voice of the people must be heard. Edward believed, without much evidence, that the people would support him. As a last throw he suggested a morganatic marriage. Mrs. Simpson would become his wife but not his queen, and any children would have no rights of succession. Baldwin turned it down and Edward told him: "I am prepared to go."

The abdication over and the shock waves settling, the first Duke of Windsor waited five months in an Austrian castle while his future wife's divorce became final. They delayed their marriage until after the crowning of his younger brother on May 12, 1937—the same day that had originally been set for his own coronation. Baldwin's final act as prime minister was to issue a decree barring the new duchess from any right to the title "Royal Highness," a decision which the duke saw as an act of spite intended to force him and his wife into exile.

For a time after their marriage the duke and duchess shuttled between Paris and the Riviera, a progress broken by a tour of Germany, where the Duke paid a much criticized call on Adolf Hitler. Nine days after the outbreak of World War II he was called home by his brother and appointed a liaison officer with the French. In 1940, with France overrun, he went to

Spain and then Portugal until Winston Churchill appointed him to the post of governor of the Bahamas.

After the war, the duke and duchess shuttled between France and the United States. The duke kept contact with his family, but the family declined to receive the duchess. The ostracism ended only in 1967, when they were together with Queen Elizabeth II, the duke's niece, for the unveiling of a plaque in memory of Queen Mary. Many hoped that this was the signal for the duke to return to his native land. It was not to be.

The duke died in Paris on May 28, 1972. Twelve days earlier he had been briefly visited by Queen Elizabeth during a state visit to France. The coffin was brought to England and for two days lay in state in St. George's Chapel, close to the tomb of his parents. Royal mourning was perfunctory.

The duchess was for a few brief hours received on terms of equality at Buckingham Palace. At the funeral service she sat between the queen and the Duke of Edinburgh. A crowd of hundreds stood around the castle gates hoping for a glimpse of the cortege. They saw nothing. Nor was the service televised.

About 60 family and official mourners were placed in the chapel's inner sanctum under the banners of the Knights of the Garter, England's premier order of chivalry. Two hundred others were seated in the chapel's outer nave. The coffin, covered with the duke's personal standard and its embroidered imperial crown, was borne in by eight men of the Welsh Guards, preceded by dignitaries of the Anglican church.

The service lasted a scant half hour. The burial later, on the lawns of the Royal Mausoleum inside the castle grounds, was strictly private. The duchess went straight to the airport. No member of the family was there to see her go.

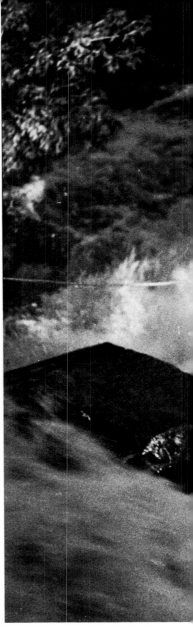

Tragic Toll of Deaths, Damage Taken by Floods

More than 300 lives lost in aftermath of torrential rainfall in six states; estimated property loss over $1.6 billion

DEATH AND DISASTER dominated the news during most of June. Highly destructive floods swept across half a dozen midwestern, southern and eastern states, leaving at least 320 dead. Many more were listed as missing. Damage estimates exceeded $1.6 billion.

These were tragic sequels to the havoc wrought by waters that burst through a West Virginia dam in March *(Pages 43–45)*.

* * * *

Rain had been falling steadily through the evening of Friday, June 9, giving citizens of Rapid City second thoughts about plans for a pleasant weekend in the South Dakota countryside.

At 9 p.m., a massive cloudburst dumped six inches of rain on the city of 43,000 people in two hours. Up to 10 inches fell in the hills above the city.

Rapid Creek, the normally serene stream that meandered through the center of town, had become a terrifying torrent. Swollen waters surged over the creek's banks, gathering up houses, automobiles and chunks of road paving and hurling them downstream.

Fears mounted in the beleaguered city as the power failed and local radio stations went dead for hours. The raging flood smashed bridges, swamped highways and tore houses from their foundations.

At 11 p.m. the dam at Canyon Lake, weakened by the rush-

Left, a rescue worker carrying a woman to safety after removing her from a flooded home for the aged in Wilkes-Barre, Pa. In the background a block-square fire burned out of control. Center, this engineer checked the lifeline around his waist before he ventured onto the base of a weakened dam holding back the fast-rising waters of Owasco Lake in Auburn, N.Y. Right, the body of a woman lay amid the debris in Rapid City's Canyon Lake Park

ing waters of the once placid lake, gave way and a wall of water charged madly towards the unprotected city. A few hours later Deerfield Dam also burst.

Gas lines were ruptured in the wreckage of houses, touching off explosions and fires. Terrified dwellers, many of whom had been asleep when the flood struck, crawled out onto the roofs of their homes. Others clambered into trees to get away from the rushing torrent of slimy water. Many were trapped in the flood and swept away.

By morning more than 240 persons had perished in devastated Rapid City. Nearly 700 were missing and about a thousand houses were destroyed. Damage passed the $100 million mark. About 80 blocks of paving had been ripped up by the flood, mud covered much of the city, second largest in the state. Drinking water was shut off for fear of typhoid. Telephones and electricity were out, and thousands of stunned survivors were in need of food, shelter and clothing.

Later, survivors recalled in disjointed sentences the night of horror. About 7:30 p.m. John Brockelsby, a 20-year-old college student and son of a former mayor, was in the family home not far below the Canyon Lake Park dam when he noticed Rapid Creek rising ominously. An hour later water had begun

seeping under the doors of the house. He tried to stem it with towels and wood, but the water kept coming.

John pulled the fuses as a precaution against fire, then went upstairs. About 8:30 p.m. Clayton Olson, manager of a local bottling plant, was gazing through a picture window at his garden when the waters of Rapid Creek surged over the yard. As the waters mounted he decided to leave, getting out just before the flood swept away his house.

At Canyon lake four firemen were inching across a bridge on a rescue mission when a floating house struck the span, snapping it. One fireman rode the house downstream to safety but the other three were killed.

S. Sgt. Steve Ringenberg, stationed at nearby Ellsworth Air Force Base, heard the muffled roar as the dam burst. He decided to flee from his home with his wife and 3½-month-old daughter. He had stopped at a gas station for fuel when the torrent reached him, knocking him unconscious and carrying away his wife and child.

Downtown, Mrs. William Medley, like her husband a major in the Salvation Army, had set out for a camp for the weekend. "But it kept raining and raining, so we turned back," she said. Mrs. Medley's husband thought he might be needed and

Hurricane Agnes spilled flood waters over a Schuylkill River dam (left) near Royersford, Pa., and inundated a water purification plant

told her "Honey, I'm going to Story Book Island to help some people." That was the last she heard from Medley, who was drowned trying to lift two people into his truck.

Farther downtown, the Rev. Francis J. Berning, 74, stood in his living room as the water rose slowly to his chin. He reached for a lamp hanging from the ceiling and clung to it.

It was much the same elsewhere. Four National Guardsmen, roped together, waded into a creek to check a flooded car, then climbed into a tree. Within 20 minutes the creek rose more than 15 feet, uprooting the tree. Two of the men were drowned.

Near Keystone a souvenir shop center below Mt. Rushmore National Memorial, six Minnesota teenagers on a graduation jaunt were trapped in a tourist cabin. They rode the building down the torrent as it was torn loose, then grabbed a mattress when the cabin was splintered. Three bodies were found.

When the waters finally subsided, Rapid City was a scene of havoc. A one-story house straddled Jackson Blvd. In Dark Canyon on the bank of Rapid Creek, only concrete slabs showed that anyone had ever lived there. Mobile homes east of the city were ripped apart and strewn all over the area. Automobile row on the edge of the business district was a jumble of cars flipped, crushed and bent double.

Bodies lay everywhere. One was pinned beneath a truck,

and the remains of a priest were found in the kitchen of the Mother Butler Center, which had been devoted to helping the Sioux Indians. Some bodies were so battered by the hurtling waters that they were scarcely recognizable as human beings. Bodies were pulled from snags, from beneath houses and from cars all over town and taken to Rapid City's three funeral homes.

People and organizations throughout the stricken area rallied to the aid of Rapid City's survivors. One Indian woman appeared at an aid station and donated clothing she said belonged to the infant she had lost in the flood.

The town of Belle Fourche, S.D., donated 20,000 pounds of beef that had been earmarked for a local barbecue celebration. At least 50 construction companies dispatched crews and heavy equipment to help clear the debris. An all-night radio marathon in Sioux Falls, S.D., raised $25,000 for the flood victims. The Boeing Airplane Co. donated $10,000; Boeing employes turned in $50,000.

Some 50 morticians who traveled up to 100 miles to the disaster scene joined in the task of preparing bodies for burial. The computer of the First National Bank of Black Hills was used to coordinate the names of the dead and missing and to eliminate duplications.

About 50 members of the Red Cross disaster task force

helped the homeless families find housing and sent food by horseback to volunteer teams working on threatened dams in the hills, where some 4,000 people had been vacationing.

The Salvation Army set up three food lines to serve more than 10,000 meals a day, and about 2,500 South Dakota National Guardsmen joined in the rescue and cleanup operations.

Airmen from Ellsworth Base directed traffic and drove emergency vehicles, Boy Scouts helped clear up the littered streets.

Personnel of the Salvation Army and Red Cross began giving typhoid and tetanus shots to long lines of mud-smeared survivors. Broadcast stations drummed out a warning: "Don't forget to boil drinking water, even if your service has been restored."

As fears of an epidemic, grew, citizens lined up at tank trucks, filling garbage containers and milk cans with drinking water.

Bulldozers and bucket loaders rumbled through the drying mud, nosing debris into splintered stacks.

Refrigerated trucks were brought in to store the bodies. Many of the dead were so caked with silt that they had to be hosed down for identification. The remains were stretched out on stone slabs while townsfolk filed by looking for relatives.

* * * *

Lashed by tropical storm Agnes, rampaging rivers of the east and northeast overflowed their banks, killing more scores of persons and leaving an estimated half a million homeless. Damage was placed at up to $1.5 billion.

Agnes started out in early June as a knot of tropical air masses forming near the island of Cozumel in the Gulf of Mexico, a few miles east of the Yucatan Peninsula.

The turbulent mass first crashed through Florida, leaving at least six dead, and veered out to sea off Virginia. Changing course, on June 22 it slammed back into the northeast mainland, already saturated by a week of nearly constant rains. The storm left nearly 50 dead in Pennsylvania, 23 in New York, 12 in Virginia and 22 in Maryland.

The impact was especially severe along the Susquehanna River in Pennsylvania. In Wilkes-Barre many of the town's 60,000 residents were ordered to move to high ground when breaks developed in the flood control dike. Three hospitals had to be evacuated and several radio stations were forced to go off the air.

Harrisburg, the capital of Pennsylvania, was virtually cut off by the rampaging waters of the Susquehanna. There the river flow was placed at 55 billion gallons a day—the highest in nearly two centuries of record keeping.

Pennsylvania Gov. Milton Shapp's $2.4 million executive mansion was flooded to its first-floor ceiling. Electric power failed, hospitals resorted to emergency generators.

With roads, railways and airports under water, President Nixon flew to the stricken area by helicopter from Camp David, Md., after an aerial survey of flood damage in Maryland, Virginia and other flooded sectors. Nixon declared five states to be disaster areas: Florida, Maryland, New York, Pennsylvania and Virginia.

In Corning and Painted Post on the Chemung River in upstate New York, hundreds of people were isolated by up to 15 feet of water. When the waters reached flood crest, all of the Corning Glass Works facilities were under water, and in nearby Elmira 20 feet of water lapped at buildings in the downtown business district.

The devastation inspired a massive volunteer effort. Thousands of persons contributed cots, blankets, clothing, food and medicine.

The disaster moved Robert M. White, head of the National Oceanic and Atmospheric Administration, to pronounce the flooding produced by Agnes as "the most extensive in the country's history."

A victim of the South Dakota floods wept on the front steps of her Rapid City home after flood waters floated the house off its foundation and smashed it

SENATE APPROVAL WON BY ATTY. GEN. KLEINDIENST

"I'm just glad it's over. If I had to do it again, I would hopefully do it the same way I did." Such was the comment of Richard G. Kleindienst on a day in June when he learned that the U.S. Senate, voting 64-19, had approved his nomination for Attorney General. Thus ended the most prolonged controversy over a Cabinet appointment so far in the Nixon Administration.

It all began at the end of March when President Nixon nominated Kleindienst, then Deputy Attorney General, to succeed former Atty. Gen. John N. Mitchell, who resigned March 31 to direct Nixon's re-election campaign.

After first being approved unanimously by the Senate Judiciary Committee, the nomination became involved in a five-week committee hearing into charges that the Justice Department had shown political favoritism in the settlement of three antitrust suits against the International Telephone and Telegraph Corporation.

The committee hearing revolved around claims by syndicated columnist Jack Anderson that Kleindienst had played a role in the out-of-court settlement of the cases against I.T.T., and that the settlement was linked to the corporation's promise of $400,000 to help underwrite the Republican National Convention in San Diego, Calif., in August.

The hearings, which included a session with I.T.T. lobbyist Mrs. Dita Beard in a Denver hospital room, were called at Kleindienst's request to "clear away any cloud" that might have hung over his nomination.

On the results of the hearings—which, according to many critics, had produced "a lot of conjecture and innuendo but no proof of wrong-doing or impropriety on the part of the nominee"—the Judiciary Committee concluded by an 11 to 4 majority that Kleindienst had not engaged in any illegal action that disqualified him as Attorney General. In addition the com-

Richard Kleindienst, left, then acting attorney general, and Felix Rohatyn, a New York director of the International Telephone and Telegraph Corp., during Senate Judiciary Committee hearings in Washington

mittee found no evidence of a direct connection between the settlement of the antitrust suits and the I.T.T. financial pledge.

The I.T.T.'s Sheraton Hotel chain had sent a check for $100,000 of the total pledge to the San Diego Convention and Visitors Bureau, but it was later withdrawn by the corporation when the GOP convention site was moved to Miami, Fla., San Diego city officials said.

By a 63 to 20 vote on June 8, the Senate as a whole rejected a motion by Democratic Sen.

Edward Kennedy to recommit the nomination to the Judiciary Committee for one more week of hearings. Kennedy, who led the fight against the nomination, argued that "substantial questions remained as to Mr. Kleindienst's fitness and competency" to serve in the post. The recommittal motion had been the last hope of Democratic liberals to defeat the Kleindienst nomination and to develop an election year issue of Republican Administration favoritism toward big business.

TWO TRAINS WRECKED BY TUNNEL COLLAPSE, 107 PERSONS KILLED

A cave-in a third of the way into the mile-long tunnel at the Vierzy train station, 60 miles north of Paris, was responsible for one of France's worst rail disasters. Two trains—one from Paris carrying 350 passengers and another traveling in the opposite direction with 20 persons aboard—entered the tunnel at almost the same time. Minutes later they were derailed by the debris.

The accident claimed the lives of 107 passengers and left more than 70 others in critical condition.

Conductors aboard said the trains sped into the 100-year-old tunnel at 60 miles an hour shortly before 9 p.m. on June 16. The six-car train from Paris first derailed after hitting a mass of rock and earth which had fallen from the tunnel's crumbling roof. The second train then struck the debris and collided head-on with the first train.

Wreckage of the diesel-powered trains was described by one of the 700 rescue workers as "what happens to an automobile after the junkyard crusher pounds it."

The rescue teams rigged supports to reinforce

the tunnel roof and used mechanical and hand saws, hydraulic jacks and cutters to enter the smashed cars in search of survivors. More powerful equipment, it was feared, would cause excessive vibrations almost certain to result in new rockfalls.

Ginette Bocquet, who lived in the Vierzy signal house 200 yards from one tunnel entrance, was the first to sense that something was amiss. The Paris-bound train had already crossed the shoe that activated the road-crossing barriers, the first indication that the train had just entered the tunnel.

"The signals kept sounding and the road barrier stayed down," Miss Bocquet said, "but the train never appeared."

464 DEAD IN MINE EXPLOSIONS

When three massive explosions rocked Rhodesia's largest coal mine, the Wankie Colliery, 464 men were entombed under innumerable layers of rock and earth. One was a tourist who had entered the mine just before the first explosion.

Another was a veteran surface worker who had gone below for the first time. A third was a teenage apprentice on his first day at work.

On the surface, mangled machinery and trolley cars blown up from the mine testified to the force of the explosions. Victims, 300 feet underground, numbered 431 Africans and 33 whites.

"Indications are that the men died instantly and were not aware of what happened," Sir Keith Acutt, chairman of the Anglo-American Company of South Africa which owned the mine, said of the country's worst mining disaster.

The June 6 explosions occurred in the second of the colliery's three operating shafts and were believed to be triggered by a coal gas leak.

Rescue teams toiled in relays in a desperate effort to reach their trapped commrades. The Rhodesian Air Force dispatched emergency flights carrying additional rescue personnel and oxygen supplies into Wankie.

All hope was abandoned by the mining company the day after the tragedy. Attempts to find survivors were hampered by additional blasts which further damaged the mine's ventilating system, and deadly methane gas and carbon monoxide filled the shaft.

TWO LANDSLIDES IN HONG KONG LEFT 100 DEAD, MANY MISSING

Three days of torrential rains that dumped 25 inches of water on Hong Kong triggered the disaster. At least 100 persons were killed, many of them poverty-stricken Chinese refugees huddled in squatter shacks, and another 69 were missing.

The driving rain that began June 16 sent hundreds of tons of earth and rock hurtling down the steep hillsides on which much of the British colony was built.

Most of the havoc was caused by two major landslides. One slide touched off a chain reaction that demolished three apartment buildings. It began when an unoccupied two-story structure on an upper level collapsed on a 10-story apartment building below. This caused an avalanche that thundered down the slope of Victoria Peak.

Locked together, the two uprooted buildings swept down upon two other apartment structures, demolishing a 12-story building and severely damaging the four top floors of an adjacent 14-story structure. Both of the latter buildings were new, and the 12-story structure had a few tenants. The 14-story one was unoccupied, or the toll probably would have been far higher.

The other landslide occurred in the Kowloon area, where a fall of rock and earth roared down upon 78 squatter shacks occupied by an estimated 400 refugees. The slide left a huge gash on the slope, in the Kwuntong district of Kowloon.

About a hundred lesser slides were recorded during the three-day deluge. These buried scores of victims under piles of dirt, rock and concrete. Thousands of victims were left without shelter.

Long after the rains stopped rescue teams, wielding high-pressure water hoses to wash away the mud, probed through damaged buildings for survivors.

One survivor, Henry Litton, 38-year-old chairman of the Hong Kong Bar Association, was dragged through a narrow escape tunnel nearly 24 hours after the 12-story apartment building in which he lived had been smashed by the sliding sea of mud and rocks. Rescuers found Litton pinned down by a heavy slab of concrete across his legs and hips and by several wooden beams across his chest.

"It is incredible that he was still alive after the building collapsed, let alone surviving the night and today," said a rescue official.

A fireman carrying an unconscious girl from one of three Hong Kong apartment buildings that collapsed in the wake of a rain-triggered avalanche

$47 MILLION GRANT TO U.S. CONFERRED BY WEST GERMANY

West German Chancellor Willy Brandt came to the United States June 5 to address a special Harvard University convocation marking the 25th anniversary of the Marshall Plan. He announced in Cambridge, Mass., that his country was establishing the German Marshall Fund of the United States and donating $47 million "in gratitude for the plan's heavy contribution to the postwar economic recovery of Western Europe."

Brandt told the Marshall Memorial Convocation that the money would be delivered in equal installments over the next 15 years. The grant was earmarked for the establishment and operation of an independent educational foundation in the United States specializing in European problems. Brandt explained that the Marshall Fund foundation would concentrate mainly on

the comparative study of international relations that pertain to the common interests of Europe and America and a study of problems confronting advanced industrial societies.

It was on June 5, 1947 that Gen. George C. Marshall, then U.S. Secretary of State, told a meeting of Harvard alumni in Cambridge that the problems of war-torn Europe were so serious that a new approach was needed to replace the United States policy of piecemeal financial aid. He proposed a plan under which European countries were to draft their own rehabilitation programs, for U.S. financing.

Under the Marshall Plan, the Organization of Economic Cooperation was created, to which the United States gave $13 billion in three-and-a-half years.

Brandt noted in his speech that the Marshall Plan was established during the cold war, but he implored the United States to maintain its interest and concern for European problems despite a reduction in cold war tensions.

"American-European partnership is indispensable," he said, "if America does not want to neglect its own interests and if Europe is to forge itself into a productive system instead of again becoming a volcanic terrain of crisis, anxiety and confusion."

Brandt stressed the need for the continued alliance between the United States and Europe. "The forms of American commitment may change," he said, "but an actual disengagement would cancel out a basic law of peace. It would be tantamount to abdication."

Police guarding the tail unit of a British Trident jet airliner that crashed after takeoff from London airport, killing all aboard

EAST-WEST GERMAN PACT SIGNED

The cold war was finally beginning to thaw in Germany. Helped in part by big power politics and in part by the tireless efforts of West German Chancellor Willy Brandt, the divided country was on its way down the long road to reconciliation.

The first major break in the political impasse came at the end of May, when the two Germanys signed their first state-to-state treaty in more than a quarter century of quarreling. The treaty served to ease surface traffic tensions between the two states.

In Berlin, West German State Secretary Egon Bahr and his East German counterpart, Michael Kohl, put their signatures on the first all-German treaty regulating traffic by road, rail and water. Included in the pact was a provision by the East German government for visiting rights to West German citizens of up to 30 days annually. For the first time since the end of World War II West Germans would be allowed to freely visit the Communist East.

The treaty-signing ceremony of May 26 ended with the announcement that the two state representatives would meet in mid-June to begin talks concerning a general treaty covering all phases of life in a reunited Germany.

BRITISH PLANE CRASH TOLL 118

Officials called it "the worst catastrophe in the history of British aviation." Minutes after leaving London's Heathrow Airport, a British European Airways jet headed for Brussels plummeted into a field and exploded. There were no survivors among the 118 passengers.

The three-engine Trident took off through fog and rain shortly after 5 p.m. on June 18 and fell near the city of Staines, just four miles from the airport.

Eyewitnesses reported that the tail section snapped on impact and the rest of the fuselage plowed onward for another 50 yards before smashing against a row of trees.

Those who perished included 34 Americans and 12 prominent Irish industrialists on their way to Brussels on Common Market business.

"The pilot got his undercarriage up, indicating he made a good take-off," a spokesman for the British Airline Pilot Association said. "But he landed with no undercarriage, and it's a complete mystery what could have gone wrong."

But the day after the crash the British Minister for Aerospace, Michael Helestine, had an answer for the House of Commons. He said the plane's flight recorder indicated that the flaps on the front edges of the wings had begun to retract when the plane had reached a height of 1,750 feet and a speed of 184 miles per hour.

"The normal speed range for raising the leading edge droop mechanism is about 250 m.p.h.," Helestine said. "The behavior of the aircraft as determined from the flight recorder and confirmed by eyewitness accounts was what would have been expected to result from retraction of the droop mechanism."

FOR THE RECORD

BANNED. By the administrator of the Environmental Protection Agency, William D. Ruckelshaus, on June 14, all uses of DDT by Dec. 31 except for such limited purposes as pest control to prevent epidemics. He said that a three-year investigation of effects from the toxic chemical pesticide established that its continued general use was "an unacceptable risk to the environment and, very likely, to the health of man."

REDUCED. The sentence of Sirhan Bishara Sirhan from death to life imprisonment, on June 16 by the California Supreme Court. The court rejected an appeal for a new trial and upheld the first-degree murder conviction of the 28-year-old Arab immigrant for the Los Angeles slaying of Sen. Robert F. Kennedy on June 5, 1968. The modification of sentence complied with the court's ruling earlier this year abolishing capital punishment in the state.

ORDERED. That no future military draftees be sent to Southeast Asia unless they volunteer, by President Nixon on June 28. The decision did not affect some 4,000 draftees en route to the war zone or those already slated for active duty there.

Algerian President Houari Boumedienne, left, and Morocco's King Hassan II signing an agreement at the African summit in Rabat

Angela Davis arriving for her trial ⟶

July

Supporters of Angela Davis massed across from the courthouse in a demonstration

Angela Davis Acquitted

*All-white jury freed her after 16 months in jail, four-month
trial on charges of murder, kidnaping and conspiracy
in 1970 California courthouse escape attempt*

A BEAMING ANGELA DAVIS stood inside a bulletproof cage at
New York's Madison Square Garden, her hand trium-
phantly raised in a clenched fist salute to thousands of the "people" she claims set her free.

It was the climax of a long journey for the 28-year-old black
Communist who had spent 16 months in jail and gone through
a four-month trial before an all-white jury acquitted her of
murder-kidnap-conspiracy charges.

Yet something was missing.

Despite the cheers of 18,000 supporters in the Garden on
June 30, Angela Davis in a sense was still a prisoner. She was
trapped behind impenetrable plexiglass because hundreds had
threatened to kill her. Those around her, remembering Martin
Luther King and Malcolm X, feared she might become the next
target of an assassin's bullet.

It was an ironic and frightening outlook for such a young

woman: Now that she was legally free to take a leadership role
in the "liberation struggle" that had become her life's goal, she
really wasn't free at all.

From the moment she was released on bail five days before
her trial started, Angela Davis was a security problem. And
after her acquittal on June 4 that problem grew to such dimensions that she was kept in virtual hiding during her nationwide
tour to thank supporters.

In three years the slim, light-skinned woman with high
cheekbones and a towering Afro hairdo had become one of the
most controversial figures in the United States—and the world.
She skyrocketed to international notoriety in 1969 while teaching philosophy at UCLA when she admitted being a member
of the Che-Lumumba Club, a black Marxist affiliate of the
Communist party, U.S.A.

The disclosure unleashed a storm of protest from California

118

Gov. Ronald Reagan, the University of California Regents and others. While the battle raged, her philosophy course at UCLA became more popular than ever. Eventually she was fired on grounds of incompetence, an act that officially launched her as a cause celebre to the New Left and large chunks of the black and Third World communities.

It was against this tumultuous background that Angela Davis was accused of purchasing four guns used in the Aug. 7, 1970 Marin County courthouse escape attempt that ended in four deaths (*The World in 1970, 153–157*). She quickly made her way to the FBI's 10 Most Wanted list and jail—first in New York where she was arrested, then in California, where she was tried in San Jose.

It had been a long and strange journey for the articulate Phi Beta Kappa graduate of Brandeis University who had steeped herself in the works of Marx and Hegel and was just a dissertation away from her doctorate. And it was a long way from the all-black middle-class area of Birmingham, Ala., where she grew up, took up piano and belonged to the Girl Scouts.

From the day of her arrest Oct. 13, 1970, Angela Davis maintained her innocence, declaring that she was the target of a "political frameup" engineered by Gov. Reagan and the State of California. A worldwide movement rallied to her defense, accusing the state of keeping her a "political prisoner" and shouting again and again: "Free Angela!"

The prosecution maintained throughout that Miss Davis' political beliefs had nothing to do with the charges against her—that it was strictly a criminal proceeding.

The heart of the case against her centered on a single question: Did Angela Davis knowingly furnish 17-year-old Jonathan Jackson with four of her guns and help him plot a courthouse escape which ended in shooting and four deaths—those of Jonathan, Superior Court Judge Harold J. Haley and convicts James McClain and William Christmas.

The prosecution contended that Miss Davis and Jonathan were inseparable during the crucial days preceding Aug. 7, and that she couldn't help but know that Jonathan planned to enter Judge Haley's courtroom and brandish her revolver, setting off the deadly escape plot.

The prosecution also maintained she had a motive for participating in the plot—her love and uncontrolled passion for Jonathan's older brother, George Jackson, one of the three Soledad Brothers then awaiting trial on charges of murdering a Soledad Prison guard (*The World in 1971, 168–171*).

The defense countered that Miss Davis was not with Jonathan very much that week, definitely not at the times the prosecution said they were together, and that she was shocked when she learned her guns might have been used in the escape. Her lawyers argued that only an "idiotic fool" could believe "a brilliant college professor," educated in the United States, France and Germany, could participate in such a haphazard, disorganized plot.

The prosecution contended that Miss Davis' disappearance after Aug. 7 was evidence of her "consciousness of guilt," noting that she traveled from Los Angeles to Chicago, Detroit, Florida and New York disguised and under assumed names.

The defense asked jurors "to be black—to think black" and try to understand why a black woman Communist like Angela Davis might make herself unavailable if she learned four guns she owned might have been used in a deadly escape.

"I say to you," exhorted defense attorney Leo A. Branton, "when you look at the situation through the eyes of a black person, you would not wonder why she fled. You would only wonder why she allowed herself to be caught."

During its seven-week presentation, the prosecution presented 95 witnesses and 201 exhibits and dwelled extensively on a replay of the events of Aug. 7—Jonathan entering the courtroom, arming three convicts and taking a judge, a prosecutor and three women jurors hostage.

Gary Thomas, deputy district attorney of Marin County, arriving to testify at the trial. Davis was wounded in the 1970 Marin escape attempt and became paralyzed from waist down

Portrait of a black revolutionary: Angela Davis on the eve of her trial in San Jose, Calif.

Miss Davis' jurors followed the path of the kidnapers and their hostages from the courtroom to a rented yellow van in the parking lot. The van took off, San Quentin guards fired, the kidnapers fired and the prosecutor fired—but there was conflicting testimony on who fired first.

Though Miss Davis was not present at the courthouse that day, three prosecution eyewitnesses placed her at a gas station across the street 24 hours earlier, with Jonathan. Prosecution eyewitnesses identified her as the woman with Jonathan at San Quentin on each of the three days preceding the escape attempt.

To illustrate Miss Davis' feelings for George Jackson, the prosecution read jurors three love letters she wrote him two months before the escape—and part of a love diary written a year later after their first face-to-face meeting while both were prisoners.

In the letters and diary, she wrote of "spontaneously" falling in love when she first saw George Jackson in a Salinas, Calif., courtroom in May 1970—the time the state contended the conspiracy to plot an escape was first hatched.

Miss Davis referred to herself as Jackson's "lifelong wife," said she was devoting "all my life-efforts" to freeing George Jackson and the Soledad Brothers—and declared she wasn't concerned about the consequences. The defense never denied Miss Davis loved George Jackson, but stressed she was active in the Soledad Brothers Defense Committee months before she laid eyes on George.

The defense disputed the testimony of every prosecution eyewitness—claiming each either "lied" or was "programmed"

by the prosecution to identify Miss Davis as the woman with Jonathan Jackson. In its three-day case, the defense put 12 witnesses on the stand—two who testified they were with Miss Davis when the state's witnesses said she was with Jonathan at San Quentin and the gas station.

A Los Angeles social worker testified Miss Davis was at a dinner party at her home the night of Aug. 7 and was so shocked she had to be given tranquilizers when she heard about the Marin County courthouse events.

Two defense witnesses also provided an explanation of how Jonathan got the four guns without Miss Davis' knowledge.

A social worker quoted Miss Davis as saying she had purchased a shotgun two days before the courthouse incident to protect the San Francisco headquarters of the Soledad Brothers Defense Committee and had turned it over to Jonathan. Miss Davis' former roommate testified that three other guns owned by Miss Davis were kept in a gun rack in her apartment for target practice by Che-Lumumba Club members—and that she had left Jonathan alone in her apartment six days before the shootings.

In his final argument, chief prosecutor Albert Harris Jr. defended the prosecution eyewitnesses, called one defense eyewitness a liar and told jurors there was a strong chain of circumstantial evidence.

"Nothing you do when you bring in a verdict will restore Judge Haley to life, to his robes, to his bench," Harris said. "But what you can do is see that justice is done in this case. . . . We think you'll be doing your duty to bring in a verdict of guilty."

In his final argument, Branton called the case a "gigantic hoax" and "a sorry stain on the history of justice in this country." He accused the prosecution of "trying to convict a woman on the weakest kind of evidence ever presented in a court of law in a case that has attracted this much attention."

"The prosecution doesn't know at all how they can connect Angela Davis with the events of Aug. 7," Branton said. "All they can prove are things that we admit that there is no doubt about—that Angela was closely related to Jonathan Jackson, that her guns were used, that she expressed a desire to free the Soledad Brothers, that Angela expressed love for George Jackson, and that on Aug. 7 Angela made herself unavailable to authorities.

"That is the totality of this case. Everything else is guess, speculation and surmise," Branton concluded.

Miss Davis, who had been given the right to be a co-attorney in the case, took a back seat in the courtroom and left arguments primarily to Branton and attorney Howard Moore Jr. She delivered the defense's opening statement but didn't testify in her own behalf.

While waiting for the verdict, she took part in a vigil by her supporters outside the heavily secured courthouse, chatting and bouncing babies on her knee in a picnic-like atmosphere, almost as if her fate were not being deliberated by seven men and five women 100 yards away.

After 13 hours, the jury sent word that a verdict had been reached. Reporters, spectators and Miss Davis' family went through a last body search and made a final trip through a metal detector.

While waiting outside the courtroom for the jury to file in, Miss Davis joined a group of supporters singing the rock spiritual: *"We've got our minds set on freedom. Hallelujah!"*

When the verdict was announced, the courtroom became a scene of pandemonium—hysterical sobs of joy intermingling with shrieks of happiness. Miss Davis wept quietly, tears streaming down her cheeks.

Superior Court Judge Richard E. Arnason praised all participants and ordered the $102,500 bail posted by a Fresno, Calif., farmer, Roger McAfee, returned.

One of the longest, costliest and most controversial criminal proceedings in California history was over. The price tag to state taxpayers: more than $1 million.

Angela Davis had said repeatedly her acquittal would be a "people's victory." As her first order of business, she went outside the courthouse to thank 300 cheering supporters.

Surrounded by a security guard of 20 men and women who linked arms around her, the beaming Miss Davis listened to the crowd shouting: "The power of the people—It set Angela free!"

Although she had been freed, Miss Davis said, there was still work to be done. "Starting from this day forward, we must work to free every political prisoner and every oppressed person in this country and the whole world."

Many had seen the trial as a testing ground for American justice. Not Angela Davis.

"The very fact of an acquittal," she said, "means that there was no fair trial because a fair trial would have been no trial at all."

After her acquittal, Miss Davis stood in a bullet-proof booth and addressed a rally in New York's Madison Square Garden

The world's first floating oil drilling rig launched at the Sasebo dockyards

Japan Still a Nation of Paradoxes, Despite Rapid Economic Growth

Japan was also a leader in the electronics field; workers at the Sony plant in Shinagana

E VERY SPRING Japanese workers, instead of taking part in traditional cherry blossom festivities, engaged in a series of labor actions known as the Spring Wage Offensive. The activities were part of postwar Japan's annual labor tactics demanding wage increases and better working conditions. The unions presented high demands and management countered with low offers. Both sides talked tough, remained poles apart at the start, but usually reached a compromise over cups of green tea minutes before the walkout was to begin.

In 1972, due to a lingering economic recession, complicated by last year's dollar shocks, management indicated it would stand firm in resisting demands by organized labor. The unions, however, refused to accept management's views on the need to hold down wage costs because of an economic slowdown, reduced production and trade concessions sponsored by the United States.

On April 27 about 1.3 million workers of 2,850 labor unions belonging to 36 major private and government industries, and spearheaded by the private and national transport workers, plunged into a scheduled 48-hour nationwide strike.

A half-day of confusion and near chaos ensued before settlement was reached—a sum slightly higher than last year but a lesser average percentage hike than in previous years.

The unions demanded an average monthly boost of 18,000 yen, or $60 and management offered 6,700 yen, or $22. The workers got 10,200 yen, or $34, an average monthly hike of 500 yen, or $1.88, over last year, bringing their monthly average wage to 109,500 yen, or $365, including bonuses and fringe benefits.

But the increase added to the difficulties of Japanese authorities trying to control spiraling prices and to curb the possibility of inflation. It also stimulated a decline in the loyalty of unions to their companies, loyalty having been part and parcel of the traditional paternalistic system of Japanese industries.

The ingenuity and energy of Japanese workers have been key factors that spurred the nation's miraculous economic growth and rocketed Japan to the position of world's third economic superpower behind the United States and Russia.

Kaoru Ota, former chairman of the left-oriented 4.5-million member Sohyo—General Council of Trade Unions—seemed pleased with this year's spring offensive. The veteran labor leader and winner of the 1965 Lenin Peace Prize said he felt that "a nationwide wage bargaining pattern, similar to those in the United States and western Europe, was taking root in Japan."

But each wage hike pushed up the cost of living, the latest sparking another round of price increases with household gas rates set to jump 32.2 per cent and train fares 23.4 per cent in the summer. The situation was likened by Japanese economists to the chipmunk furiously treading its spinning wheel inside its cage. No matter how ferociously he pumped he didn't seem to make any headway.

Japan's economic recovery from its World War II defeat had been described as one of the miracles of modern times. A nation of 110 million people, the Japanese—by sheer industriousness, determination and resourcefulness plus U.S. help and a stroke of good luck, if wars and economic crises can be called such—achieved what no one dreamed was possible.

During the first five years after the war the Japanese cleared away the debris, got their destroyed factories rebuilt and running in line with what the occupying Americans wanted. The next five years witnessed the mass introduction of fresh know-how brought on by the demands of U.S. involvement in the war in Korea. The years 1955–1960 saw the enlargement of its industries along with modernization and the application of foreign technology. A transition from light to heavy industry, from traditional to new industries, took place. There was a change to heavy mechanization requiring less manpower, to industries with greater outlets abroad at more competitive prices. The decade was highlighted by industries moving into such more advanced fields as synthetic fibers, petrochemicals, electronics, chemicals and modern shipbuilding, to be followed five years later by automobiles, computers and the like.

"Made in Japan" labels no longer represented cheap, shoddy goods. The label, on products ranging from transistor radios to automobiles, from television sets to machine tools, from mammoth ships to computers, from cameras to petrochemicals, meant top quality goods of a sophisticated industrial complex.

Japan had emerged as an economic giant and its influence had created envy and antagonism the world over. Japan's high productivity and success had become a vice rather than a virtue, particularly in the eyes of the United States, its friend and staunchest ally.

For the first time in 300 years the Japanese were enjoying a taste of an affluent society, being the best fed, best clothed and healthiest people in Asia but still lagging behind the advanced countries of the West. Its department stores and specialty shops in Tokyo, Osaka and Kyoto were stocked with consumers' goods comparable to those in New York, Paris and London.

Although there was an acute housing shortage in 1972 almost every home or apartment had a transistor radio, refrigerator, washing machine, vacuum cleaner, electric rice cooker, an iron, electric fan or air conditioning unit known as a "cooler." Many homes had bathtubs, which were bringing slow death to the traditional public bathhouses, once the nation's community centers. Gas and kerosene stoves had replaced the fire-prone hibachi or charcoal braziers. Television antennae dotted the horizon like groves of trees.

Magazines and books sold by the millions in the most literate nation of the East. Theaters and concerts were crowded. So were pleasure resorts. There was a boom in bowling, skiing and golf. Travel at home and abroad were popular. There were package deals to meet every purse—for excursions, weddings, anniversaries and year-end parties. In major department stores there was even a package deal available for funerals.

Prices apparently meant little, and the Japanese were willing to pay, for example, $35 for a shirt or a pair of shoes. Imported goods were favored.

Nevertheless, the Japanese had the highest savings rate in the world, as high as 17 per cent of personal income as compared to 8.2 per cent for the Frenchman, 5.7 per cent for the American and 5 per cent for the Englishman. The share of private savings in total national savings was also a high 30 per cent in comparison to other countries, due principally to the Japanese wage system in which families set aside much of their bi-annual bonuses. The Japanese loved postal savings. Safety deposit boxes gained popularity.

Japan, from time to time, referred to as "Japan Inc.," had no single economic control organ as such. But information gleaned from ministries and business firms at home and overseas served as guidelines and targets generally laid down by the economic experts of government. Economic policy was usually set forth by the Finance Ministry and Economic Planning Agency, and administrative guidance by the Ministry of International Trade and Industry, known as MITI. Furthermore, MITI could approve or reject joint ventures or mergers, break up or encourage cartels, discourage unfair trade practices and even set prices, production rates and export quotas.

The governor of the Bank of Japan, the central banking au-

Traditional Japanese shrine in front of a modern oil refinery

thority, was appointed by the finance minister. The Central Bank, depository of government funds, directly regulated commercial banks by setting central bank interest rates which determined interest rates charged by commercial banks.

Unlike industries in western Europe and the United States, which sought their funds from the public, Japanese industries have relied heavily on the banks for investment funds and operating capital.

Although the pre-war zaibatsu, or business combines, were broken up, Japanese industries have concentrated their power around affiliates, making it competitive among themselves but invulnerable to competition by outsiders.

Even so, experts acknowledged that Japan's economy was built on debts. Japanese industries, the multi-circulation newspaper Asahi said, besides expanding and operating their equipment and plants with borrowed money, "purchase raw materials and supplies on credit and sell finished products on credit." . . . The average industry has less than 25 per cent of its capitalization in its own equity and more than 75 per cent in bank debts, almost the opposite of what is considered acceptable in western Europe and the United States.

"In this age of relentless international economic competition," Asahi said, "the government should have liberalized capital and goods imports sooner instead of being indulgent to industry. Following the revaluation of the yen under international pressure in December 1971, Japanese industries today with less than 20 per cent net worth must compete with U.S. and European industries with a net worth of more than 50 per cent at their command."

As a result, Asahi said, "Japanese goods have glutted foreign markets and menaced industries of importer nations and export demands are down. Profits fail to increase in proportion to sales increases because industry has to pay interest on its loans for equipment financing and operating funds."

The Japanese industry had often been described as a "bicycle economy." The cyclist, to stay upright, must keep pedaling to press onward. If he slows down he is liable to topple over.

Some other factors contributing to Japan's economic success were stability, education, geographic advantage of its industries, exchange controls, value of the yen, austerity and low defense costs.

Japan, lacking raw materials, imported them. The finished products of high quality were exported at comparatively low prices, made possible by abundant manpower unafraid of hard work or working extra hours. But mounting exports and continuing prosperity had aroused resistance in various countries of the world, bringing forth charges of cheap labor and triggering demands for readjustment of Japan's trade and currency. Likewise, they had also earned such unflattering names as "economic animal" and "ugly Japanese."

Japan's economic troubles with the United States began in the mid-1970s. They reached a climax Aug. 16, 1971, when

Night view of the Idemitsu petrochemical plant in Tokuyama City

President Nixon announced sweeping economic measures to defend the dollar, impose an extra 10 per cent duty on most imports and cut the dollar loose from the yen. Japan had been jolted in July by the President's announcement of his pending visit to Peking, made without prior consultations with the Japanese government. The surtax on imports was primarily aimed at Japan, whose trade with the United States accounted for about 30 per cent of the total. Japanese exports in fiscal 1970, ended March 31, 1971, totaled $19.31 billion, its imports amounted to $18.88 billion. The United States in effect was asking Japan to revalue the yen. But Japan insisted on maintaining the 360 yen to one U.S. dollar parity rate set on April 25, 1949.

Japan kept buying up dollars in the local foreign exchange market in hope of propping up the dollar. But this failed to dispel gloomy general agreement that Japan's domestic economy and exports would suffer.

From Aug. 16 through Aug. 19 the Bank of Japan dollar purchases amounted to $2.2 billion. On Aug. 27 Japan floated the yen, letting supply and demand fix the price. The move was to help the United States by making Japanese goods more expensive in the United States and American goods cheaper in Japan. This would reduce the deficit in the U.S. balance of payments.

In two weeks the Bank of Japan's dollar purchases amounted to $3.9 billion and Japan's official reserves, which stood at $7.92 billion at the end of July 1971, were up to $12.5 billion. Japan's foreign exchange holdings had increased by $4.58 billion, more than one-fourth of the balance of payments deficit. But this merely added fuel to the fire.

Finance Minister Mikio Mizuta finally called on the Japanese people to face the yen-dollar crisis as an "honorable agony. . . . Overcome it to build a strong nation."

Meanwhile, top financial experts of the world's strongest economic countries held several meetings to try to overcome the crisis with the United States, seeking up to a 20 per cent upvaluation of the yen. Japan, however, had hoped to keep it at about five per cent.

On Oct. 13 Japan signed the 1970 extension of the international cotton textiles agreement, delayed for more than a year. On Oct. 15 MITI's Kakuei Tanaka and David Kennedy, President Nixon's special envoy for textile negotiations, initialed an agreement under which Japan was to impose item by item restrictions on exports of wool and man-made textiles for three years beginning Oct. 1, 1971.

Following a conference of U.S. and Japanese government officials in Honolulu Dec. 11–12, Japan announced it would unilaterally reduce tariffs on 31 items. Although Japan had been criticized for dragging its feet in liberalization, last August 228 industries were 100 per cent decontrolled; that is, they could be wholly owned by a foreign investor, and more than 500 were 50 per cent liberalized, while seven were off limits to foreign investment. As of April 1 trade barriers remained on 40 items of which 20 are agriculture products.

On Dec. 19, at a group of ten meeting in Washington, Japan finally agreed to realign the yen 16.88 per cent, making 308 yen equivalent to one dollar. It was a higher revaluation than what the Japanese government and business leaders had expected. But they accepted the decision.

"I believe," Prime Minister Eisaku Sato later said, "this is the beginning of a new phase in monetary development."

Finance Minister Mizuta said the settlement did not necessarily mean a "Japanese defeat in monetary diplomacy." He said government experts had spent much time and energy to close the gap between the demand—as much as 24 per cent—and the margin acceptable to Japan. "I don't have any feelings of defeat," Mizuta said.

"What made a solution to the problem . . . so difficult was that it was not a currency problem but a matter of the political, military, economic, and financial position of the United States in the world," said T.F.M. Adams and Dr. Iwao Hoshii, economic experts and co-authors of A Financial History of Japan.

Japan had been in a period of recession for a year and a half, chiefly because of the overheating of its economy. But despite the "Nixon shocks," as the Japanese referred to the President's announcements, Japan's exports held up.

On April 30 Japan's foreign exchange currency reserves totaled $16.55 billion, down for the first time since July 1970, due largely to government steps to reduce snowballing foreign currency holdings. Japan's balance of payments, however, continued firm with a record overall surplus of $8.04 billion, more than quadruple the prior fiscal year's $1.99 billion. The huge surplus made it clear that the Japanese yen was surprisingly strong.

The currency realignment, however, had hardly any effect on Japanese domestic living. Nevertheless, it implanted in the minds of the people that the nation was confronted with a dark and uncertain situation. Workers who had enjoyed big wage hikes in past booming years had to be satisfied with decreased yearend bonuses and promises of smaller margin of pay increases in the spring of 1972. There were fewer job opportunities for graduates while big and small companies had to cancel planned recruitment of large numbers of middle and high school graduates.

Accepting voluntary curbs on man-made textile imports, steel, television sets and tableware to the United States in October forced the closing down of many smaller plants. There was a cutback in production and layoff of thousands of workers.

The shift in trade winds from President Nixon's dollar defense policy encouraged Japanese businessmen to turn more and more toward mainland China. The Canton spring fair attracted 1,538 Japanese firms with 1,350 officials, compared with 815 firms with 1,408 officials the previous spring. Japan's private trade with Peking in 1971 totaled a mere $899 million, an increase of 9.4 per cent over the preceding year, according to a Feb. 21 report by the pro-Peking Association for the Promotion of International Trade. Exports increased 1.5 per cent to $577 million and imports amounted to $322 million, up 26.9 per cent over 1970.

Kiihachiro Kimura, a Socialist economic critic, called on Japanese business to shake off its heavy dependence on the United States. He said "President Nixon delivered a double punch to Japan . . . and the only way for Japan to avoid another was to cease its economic dependence on the United States. . . ."

Interest had awakened in preserving the better Japanese cul-

ture, in some cases blending the old with the new. There had been a delayed realization of the importance of careful urbanization planning, such as meeting housing needs and improving the semi-primitive sewage system, two major problems far out of line with Japan's advance in modernization. The Japanese were also slowly coming around to building, improving and expanding badly needed roads for its ever-growing motor vehicle population and to developing an efficient social welfare system which had been lower than the systems in Europe and the United States. And they were finally beginning to tackle environmental hazards, a recent evil born out of the mushrooming newer industries and widespread use of chemicals. Japan in 1972 was said to be the world's most polluted nation.

Despite its phenomenal economic growth, Japan was still a nation of paradoxes. An outsider would be surprised to learn that exchanging "meishi," or calling cards, was still indispensable, a tradition that remained in a fast changing society. The meishi and a letter of introduction would open the doors to Japanese business and industry. Without them the outsider was likely to find the door slammed in his face. Foreigners in Japan for business transactions often complained that the process was often slow and tedious because they were subjected to a round of receptions in teahouses with geisha, professional women entertainers. The result was a fabulous drinking bout, with no business transacted, and just another day of frustration.

Japan's fiscal year begins on April 1. In 1972, however, passage of the national budget was delayed almost one month by opposition parties, and it took an apology by the prime minister for many incidents disrupting legislative business. The delay didn't help the domestic economic recession or help solve monetary and trade difficulties.

The lower house approved the 11,467,680 million yen, or $37.233 million, budget on April 3, the upper house approved it on April 28. The budget included 2,104,800 million yen, or $6.908 million, for social welfare and environmental pollution measures and 5,635,000 million yen, or $18.295 million, for investments and loans.

But the earmarked amount was considered low in view of Sato's policy speech before the diet on Jan. 29. The prime minister had emphasized that "The present policy of stimulating a recovery of business activities is intended not to return to super-high economic growth led mainly by equipment investments but to pave the way . . . for reconstructing a high-level welfare state. . . .

"The time has arrived," Sato said, "to draw up development plans for the country as a whole, covering roads, railways, harbors and airports . . . and a quickening of the pace of industrial relocation. We must positively move forward with improvements on living environment such as houses, sewerage, municipal parks, rubbish. . . ."

Japan, somewhat embarrassed by its continuing economic success, was caught in a dilemma. It must conquer environmental pollution. It must find ways of lowering its excess exports without worsening its domestic recession. And, simultaneously, it must reduce the anger of its trading partners and lessen its huge hoarding of foreign currency reserves.

Some people viewed the United States as "Japan's big brother," U.S. Ambassador Robert S. Ingersoll, head of Borg-Warner Corp., told a luncheon of the American-Japan Society in Tokyo shortly after his arrival in April. But, he added, "looking at present trade statistics, I think the roles might be reversed."

Japan was making efforts to meet the economic challenges.

On May 20 the government adopted a new program designed at cutting Japan's growing balance of payments surplus and forestalling foreign pressure for another yen realignment. The program consisted of a mixture of monetary and trade policies, mapped out by Prime Minister Sato and his cabinet economic experts. It was aimed at stimulating domestic economy, promoting imports, slowing down the growth of exports, stepping up foreign aid and trimming the nation's swelling exchange reserves by increasing investments abroad. Japan had been accused of giving aid with one hand and taking it back with the other by stipulating that purchases be made in Japan.

MITI minister Tanaka said Japan hoped to "achieve and maintain equilibrium in international economic affairs" and to institute a program under which it could strive for orderly marketing of its exports.

However, Japan—whose economic growth slowed down to 4.7 per cent in 1971 after averaging about 11.1 per cent in the sixties and was expected to average 7 per cent in fiscal 1972 —would continue encountering trouble. "Unless," said an economic expert, "Japan doesn't strive harder to contribute to the prosperity and well-being of others in a world undergoing an economic revolutionary change."

Lines of new cars in the parking lot of the Toyo Kogyo auto production plant at Nagoya

Kissinger: As Nixon's Chief Advisor He Found Responsibility Was Not So Difficult to Endure

White House trouble shooter: Dr. Henry Kissinger

SOME WASHINGTON OBSERVERS insisted that Henry Albert Kissinger became the second most powerful person on earth when President Nixon placed him in control of America's foreign policy machinery. No one disputed the fact that the 49-year-old former refugee from Nazi Germany wielded vast influence in the top circles of U.S. government. The former Harvard professor dominated U.S. foreign policy more than any White House aide since John Foster Dulles had held sway as secretary of state.

Kissinger did not hold Dulles' eminent title, but he had acquired virtual control of the White House-based National Security Council, serving up options for presidential decision, whether it was a new crisis in the Indochina war or paving the way for Nixon's journey to Moscow.

This awesome image was at sharp variance with the physical appearance of Kissinger. He had a rather round, insignificant face topped by wavy brown hair, and a 5-foot-9, 175-pound frame.

Kissinger, whose blue-gray eyes were almost hidden by horn-rim glasses, looked like the accountant he once wanted to be or the college professor he once was; his features did not reflect a man of destiny. Neither did he project the picture of a swinger who was regarded as the sex symbol of an entire Administration.

A reporter asked Kissinger whether he enjoyed his job on days when grave crises confronted the Administration.

"Such days are really not that bad," he replied in a deep voice softened by the accent of the Germany from which he had fled as a teenager when Adolf Hitler was rising to power.

"You are dealing with fundamentals," he went on. "You are concerned with big issues. People think responsibility is hard to bear. It's not. I think that sometimes it is the absence of responsibility that is harder to bear. You have a great feeling of impotence."

Kissinger said that he divided his job into three parts:

"First, I try to place before the President the widest range of choices for action on foreign policy issues. Second, I see to it that, once he has made a decision, it is implemented, and implemented in the spirit the President intended. And third, I act as a sort of advisor when he asks my advice."

Kissinger felt that his most difficult role perhaps was acting as the link between the President and the many tentacles of the foreign policy establishment.

"The outsider believes that a presidential order is consistently followed out," he said. "Nonsense. I have to spend considerable time seeing that it is carried out in the spirit the President intended."

Some officials in Washington charged that Kissinger tended to push his own preferred solutions to a problem. He insisted, however, that during meetings of the National Security Council he presented recommendations from State, Defense and other government departments.

However, he added, "when the President puts his feet up at the end of the day and says 'O.K., Henry, you've presented all the options, now what do you think?', of course, I tell him what I think.

"But I try not to beat at him with my views. Anyway, he is not a man who encourages being beaten at."

There was no question that Nixon had complete confidence

128

Kissinger toasting China's Chou En-lai during the Peking summit

in Kissinger. The President picked his top aide for the secret trip to Peking to arrange for his trail-blazing China visit. The White House sent Kissinger across the Atlantic for the unsuccessful secret negotiations with the North Vietnamese in Paris. And Kissinger was at the President's side much of the time during the talks with Kremlin leaders in Moscow. This show of presidential trust vaulted Kissinger into a role as superstar of the Administration. It also plunged State Department morale to its lowest point in years.

Those who worked with Kissinger found it a difficult task. Of the original senior team on the National Security Council, hardly half remained after three years. Some quit in exhaustion from the 13-hour days and six and seven-day weeks. Others left because they did not like Kissinger.

Staff members who stayed on found Kissinger an exacting boss who squeezed the last ounce of mental effort from his aides.

"You do things for Henry you didn't think you were capable of," commented one. "He may know better than the persons themselves what they're capable of."

Kissinger, who was divorced in 1964 after 15 years of marriage, lived in a luxurious rented townhouse near Embassy Row. About 8 a.m. each day a chauffered limousine from the White House motor pool picked him up at his residence. Sometimes he lugged a bundle of soiled shirts for the laundry. He always ate breakfast in his office and sometimes lunch and dinner as well.

And yet Kissinger somehow found time to build a reputation as the only real swinger in the most staid administration that Washington had seen in many years.

His dates included Jill Saint John and other Hollywood actresses. One reported that he was a charming companion.

"I find the playboy image very amusing," Kissinger commented. But close friends described him as a devoted father to his children, Elizabeth, 12, and David, 10, who spent vacations with him.

In 1938, before Hitler's persecution of the German Jews had reached its peak, the Kissinger family managed to obtain visas and left their home town of Fuerth and emigrated first to London and then to New York.

As might have been expected, young Henry received top grades in school. In 1943 he enrolled in New York's tuition-free City College, but he received a notice from his draft board and went into the Army.

The Army brought Kissinger into contact with a new life. In the closing days of World War II he was packed off to Europe and at the age of 20 and was put in charge of reorganizing the government of Krefeld, a German textile center which had been devastated by Allied bombing raids.

When the war ended he returned to the United States. Only this time he enrolled as a student at Harvard, aided by a scholarship and the GI bill.

As an undergraduate Kissinger caught the eye of William Y. Elliott, noted professor of government, who was credited

With the hint of a halo over his head, Henry Kissinger boarded a plane for a flight to Tokyo

with encouraging the brilliant youth to set his sights higher than a teaching career.

In a letter recommending Kissinger for Phi Beta Kappa, Elliott said the young man was "more like a mature colleague than a student." But, he added, "On the other hand, his mind lacks grace and is Teutonic in its systematic thoroughness."

With the aid of other scholarships, Kissinger obtained his master's degree in 1952 and his doctorate in 1954. Then he joined the Harvard faculty as a government instructor. Later he was to become a lecturer, an associate professor and finally a full professor.

The Harvard Crimson, in an evaluation of Kissinger's Government course, said his "lectures were meaty, invariably interesting and at times witty." Students hailed his "grim description of modern policy making." One pupil commented that his discussion of Vietnam "was enough to scare the hell out of anyone."

While teaching at Harvard, Kissinger launched a project which resulted in his first book, *Nuclear Weapons and Foreign Policy,* published in 1957. It was widely praised in academic circles and established Kissinger's reputation as a foreign policy expert. The book stressed the danger of too heavy reliance on the concept of massive nuclear retaliation. He advocated instead a more flexible response.

In addition to his teaching duties, Kissinger became director of the International Seminar, associate director of the Center for International Affairs and head of the Defense Studies Program.

As a result of his growing prestige, Kissinger put in part-time hitches as foreign affairs consultant for Presidents John F. Kennedy and Lyndon B. Johnson. He also developed a close association with New York's governor, Nelson Rockefeller. When Rockefeller decided to try for the Republican presidential nomination in 1964, Kissinger signed on as his foreign affairs advisor. He served Rockefeller in the same capacity in the 1968 presidential campaign.

When Nixon won the nomination, Kissinger was not overjoyed. "I didn't think much of the President at that time," he recalled. "I had the general dislike of him. But I didn't know much about him."

Nixon and Kissinger had met only once before, in December 1967, in the Manhattan apartment of author Claire Boothe Luce.

"Neither of us likes small talk," said Kissinger, adding that the two spent several minutes in "that appalling banter people engage in" at cocktail parties.

The next time they talked was on Nov. 28, 1968. That time they spent several hours comparing views on foreign issues and found they shared many common thoughts.

A week later Nixon announced the appointment of Henry Kissinger as his assistant for National Security Affairs. Their association quickly became close, and in late afternoons it was not uncommon to see the President walking to his White House living quarters, his arm draped over Kissinger's shoulder.

A reporter once asked Kissinger whether he was sorry he had left the academic grove for the gruelling White House job.

"No," he replied quickly. Then, after a pause, "No matter how it may end."

Two Youngsters Provided Excitement at Wimbledon

Australian Evonne Goolagong defeated Christ Evert, American tennis star in semi-final; eager fans camped out all night, hoping for standing room to view the contest

I T WAS the match tennis fans had been waiting for. Evonne Goolagong and Chris Evert, the two top girls of the new generation, had never met across the net before. Wimbledon on semi-finals day had seldom seen such excitement: the Center Court sizzled with anticipation. Fans had camped out all night on the sidewalks outside the All-England Club, sleeping on blankets or curled up in deck chairs, hoping for a standing place at the match. When the girls came out on court the crowd of 15,000 was packed in like canned sardines.

The match on July 5 lived up to all expectations, and more. Evonne, the curly-headed Australian who was defending her Wimbledon title, came back from 0–3 in the second set to defeat cool little Chris, the teenage darling of America from Fort Lauderdale, Fla., 4–6, 6–3, 6–4. It was a match packed with excitement and fine strokes.

But it wasn't the result that mattered so much; it was the renewal of faith in the future of tennis. Two youngsters, Evonne 20 and Chris just 17, as different from each other as soda pop from ice cream, staged a classic semi-final in a year when many had predicted Wimbledon would be a flop.

All the stars of World Championship Tennis—John Newcombe, Rod Laver, Ken Rosewall, Arthur Ashe and the rest—were missing from the entry list. Yet it proved a memorable Wimbledon, a tournament the fans would talk about for years.

Stan Smith and Billie Jean King won the singles titles and scored the first American double since 1955. Smith overcame Ilie Nastase of Romania in a five-set thriller that was rated among the finest Wimbledon finals of all time. Yet against all this the Goolagong-Evert duel, with its effervescent freshness and the emotions it fired in the crowd, still stood out in the memory.

It was the contrasting personalities of the two girls that intrigued the fans and caused the match to be so eagerly awaited. On one side was Evonne, bubbling over with the joy of playing the game, pressing forward at the net and looking for chances to volley; on the other Chris, cool, calculating and never ruffled, firing from her baseline and winning points by sheer consistency.

Evonne had been ill early in the year and, before the semi-finals, had not looked quite the supremely confident champion of the year before. Chris, in Britain for the first time, had calmly guided an under-strength United States women's team to victory over Britain in the Wightman Cup. So she had already won immense respect from the Wimbledon fans. They called her Little Miss Iceberg.

At first it looked as if Chris' coolness would win the day against Evonne's flair. The Australian, though brimming over with talent and playing the more imaginative tennis, suffered lapses of concentration and was erratic. The little American, seldom attempting anything spectacular but steady as a rock, won the first set, went to 3–0 in the second and was in sight of reaching the final in her first Wimbledon.

At that point, however, Evonne started to fight back. She stacked up seven games in a row to level at one set all and push ahead 1–0 in the third.

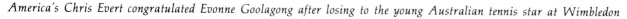

America's Chris Evert congratulated Evonne Goolagong after losing to the young Australian tennis star at Wimbledon

Stan Smith of the United States won the men's title at Wimbledon

The duel remained finely balanced but Chris, a slim little thing with a yellow ribbon in her hair, began to tire. She held on to four games all; then Evonne, playing better and better as the drama neared its climax, staged her final winning charge.

Few matches at Wimbledon have so aroused the emotions of the crowd. The only two people present who appeared unmoved were the two girls themselves. Throughout the 95-minute-duel neither disputed a line call or gave even a hint of a cross look when shots went wrong. That was partly why the fans loved it so much.

Evonne failed to reproduce the same form in the final on July 7, and Mrs. King, of Long Beach, Calif., won 6–3, 6–3 to recapture the title she had last won in 1968. That was a tame affair which never came to the boil. But the men's final between Smith and Nastase, delayed 24 hours by rain, was a match in a million.

Smith, the U.S. Army corporal from Sea Pines, Hilton Beach Island, S.C., won 4–6, 6–3, 6–3, 4–6, 7–5. Nastase, making acrobatic leaps and conjuring winning shots out of the air, was the more spectacular player, but Smith had the courage and the steadiness to outlast his rival and win the crown on July 6. The thrills never abated and the result was wide open until the very last shot. Some Wimbledon veterans said it was the greatest final since Jack Crawford toppled Ellsworth Vines in 1933.

Those were the memorable closing days of the 1972 Wimbledon. Earlier the tournament, which began on June 28, had been slow to come alive and the fans missed the WCT stars. With so many big names absent, much of the interest centered on veterans, famous in their day, who had once been Wimbledon champions—men like Neale Fraser, 38, Lew Hoad, 37, and Alex Olmedo, 36, and another majestic old-timer, Pancho Gonzales, 44, who had never won the big title.

But also there was the refreshing abundance of new talent—young stars like Chris Evert and 19-year-old Jim Connors, the left-hander from Belleville, Ill., who reached the men's quarter-finals on July 4 in his first year at Wimbledon.

JACKIE ONASSIS WON IN COURT WITH PRIVACY INVASION CLAIM

The dingy courtroom resembled a society gossip session, offering tidbit after tidbit about the glittering life of Jacqueline Onassis—former First Lady, wife of one of the richest men in the world and perennially named on the best-dressed, most-admired lists.

What's more, there was Jackie herself, elegantly coiffed and costumed, detailing day after day her shopping excursions, walks with Aristotle Onassis, her Greek tycoon husband, and Central Park bicycle rides with her son John.

What brought Mrs. Onassis to Manhattan Federal Court was a $1.3 million suit filed by free-lance photographer Ronald Galella, who for the past several years had specialized in pictures of her and her family. Galella charged that Mrs. Onassis and secret service agents were interfering with his livelihood by frustrating his shutter work.

Mrs. Onassis counter-sued, seeking a permanent injunction to keep the persistent paparazzo-style photographer away from John, daughter Caroline and herself.

After the five-week trial and several months deliberation, Federal Judge Irving Ben Cooper agreed with Mrs. Onassis.

The judge, an appointee of Mrs. Onassis' late husband, hearing the case without a jury, ruled that Galella had "relentlessly invaded" Mrs. Onassis' right to privacy and interfered with the protective duties of the secret service.

Galella was ordered to stay at least 50 yards from Mrs. Onassis, 75 yards from the children and 100 yards from the family's homes and schools.

Judge Cooper dismissed Galella's suit and said of the photographer's testimony:

"The record is studded with instance after instance where the testimony is clearly perjurious. . . . Not a single event, episode or incident, out of the scores with which the total trial record deals, was established in his favor."

The judge said he was convinced that Galella's suit had another purpose, to garner publicity for the photographer or to get Onassis or his wife to pay money to him to end the harassment.

Galella also was pronounced guilty of civil contempt of court by the judge, who became increasingly irritated as the trial dragged on.

Despite sheltered entrances and exits, newsmen scrambling outside and a courtroom daily packed with Jackie watchers, Mrs. Onassis, insisted in a soft, girlish voice that she wasn't a public figure and couldn't see why people were interested in her life style.

Galella "mortified" her on many social occasions and "terrified" her, especially when she was with her children, with his aggressive and persistent picture taking, she claimed. He dated one of her maids, interrupted one of Caroline's tennis lessons, prowled around the entrance of her Fifth Avenue apartment, and chased her and a limousine full of friends to the Twenty One Club, she said.

Galella, who had sold many of his photos to newspapers, national magazines and movie magazines, was the only photographer, Mrs. Onassis testified, "who leaps out at me, yells horrible things, and hits me with a camera strap." The photographer also "grunts" as he races about snapping pictures, she complained.

The photographer, with a fondness for mod, brightly-colored clothes, grinning and remonstrating with his hands, told the court that when

A Federal Court judge ordered photographer Ronald E. Galella to stop pursuing Mrs. Jacqueline Onassis and her children

the former first lady wore sun glasses or dark dresses the value of his pictures went down. One week, he complained, she wore the same pair of tie-dyed slacks three times.

For the mostly middle-aged spectators, carrying their lunches in brown bags, some highlights of the trial were hearing about Mrs. Onassis dining on Szechuan cuisine in New York's Chinatown, sipping iced coffee with whipped cream in Capri, and sampling chocolate mousse at Twenty One Club in mid-Manhattan.

But the seemingly fluff trial with its 4,700 pages of testimony and hundreds of exhibits brought up the issue of freedom of the press versus the right to privacy.

Addressing this issue directly, Judge Cooper said:

"We see no constitutional violence done by permitting defendant to prevent intrusion on her life which serves no useful purpose."

"We conclude," he continued, "that the First Amendment does not license Galella to trespass inside private buildings, such as the children's schools, lobbies of friends' apartment buildings, and restaurants. Nor does that amendment demand that Galella be permitted to bribe employes and maintain surveillance in order to monitor the defendant's leaving, entering and living inside her own home."

SOCIAL SECURITY INCREASED

Late in June, as President Nixon sought to raise the national debt limit to $450 billion, a lively debate erupted in the House, punctuated by cries of "Vote, vote!" The reason for this unusual interest: Attached to the bill was a rider sponsored by Senate Democrats approving a 20 per cent hike in Social Security benefits affecting 27.8 million Americans.

Thus Congress made its move to force the President to sign the bill, despite his position that such an increase would be inflationary.

When the bill with its controversial rider went before the House, spokesmen for the Administration sought to block it, warning that it would swell the already substantial budget deficit.

Republicans came up with a compromise offer of a 10 per cent increase in benefits, but when the matter came to a vote in the Senate June 30, this compromise was turned down and the 20 per cent boost was approved 82 to 4.

Returned to the House, the bill sailed through, 302 to 35, despite further Administration attempts to sidetrack it.

This confronted Nixon with the choice of endorsing a measure his supporters had assailed as faulty or vetoing it and angering millions of potential voters.

On July 1 the President signed the bill into law after issuing a statement saying he saw "some serious shortcomings" in the measure. He pointed out that it would add $3.7 billion to the budget deficit. It was the largest Social Security increase in U.S. history.

White House spokesmen said that the President's decision to sign the bill had been prompted in part by the realization that Congress might have overridden his veto.

WALDHEIM MOSCOW TRIP HOPEFUL

Secretary-General Kurt Waldheim of the United Nations expressed hope there would be a fruitful exchange of views when he arrived in Moscow July 17 for his first official visit to the Soviet Union. And when he left a week later, the Austrian statesman seemed pleased with the results.

A U.N. banner and the Soviet flag flew side by side from the terminal building of Moscow's Sheremetyevo Airport when an Aeroflot plane brought the secretary-general in from Vienna.

"I look forward to an exchange of views on the international situation, world problems and problems of the United Nations," Waldheim told newsmen. Then Soviet Foreign Minister Andrei A. Gromyko led him to a waiting limousine. At the end of the visit Waldheim spoke to newsmen again, with words of praise for his Russian hosts. He hailed Soviet efforts to improve relations with the United States during President Nixon's visit to Moscow in May and to seek an accommodation with West Germany since Willy Brandt had become chancellor.

He declared that the Soviet-sponsored move for a European conference on security and cooperation tended to "promote further positive developments."

Waldheim declined to comment, however, on an open letter addressed to him by 254 Jews charging that Soviet curbs on emigration had violated the Universal Declaration of Human Rights.

Asked if he had discussed Jewish emigration or the petition with Kremlin officials, Waldheim said "I am aware of this appeal, but you can understand I am not in a position to comment on it."

Waldheim did express concern over allegations that the United States was bombing dikes in North Vietnam.

"I firmly hope and appeal that this would be avoided," he said. U.S. officials had already denied that dikes and dams in North Vietnam had deliberately been bombed, as charged by Hanoi, but indicated that accidental strikes could not be ruled out.

Later President Nixon told a news conference that Waldheim and other "well-intentioned and naive people" had been "taken in."

"I noted with interest," he said, "that the secretary-general of the United Nations, just like his predecessor, seized upon this propaganda. . . ."

Below, U.N. Secretary-General Kurt Waldheim, stopped off in Moscow and conferred with Soviet Foreign Minister Andrei A. Gromyko. Right, pop-art decorated shelters for use in a garden or as a holiday home, being produced at a factory in Luedenscheid, Germany. Far right, jubilant Lee Trevino, who became the fourth American golfer to win the British Open, kissing the championship cup at Muirsfield, Scotland

SPACE SHUTTLE CONTRACT LET

The employees of the North American Rockwell Space Corp., in Downey, Calif., held a marathon champagne party on the last Wednesday in July. They had cause for celebration: That day the National Aeronautics and Space Administration announced that it had selected North American Rockwell, the prime contractor on the Apollo program, over three other firms to develop a space shuttle that would give the United States virtually routine access to outer space.

At stake in the bidding was a $2.6 billion contract, the opportunity to create the world's first space shuttle, and relief from a recession that had been strangling the aerospace industry in Southern California since 1969. For months prior to the decision, each of the four companies competing for the choice prize—including the Lockheed Missile and Space Co., the Grumman Aerospace Corp., and the McDonnell-Douglas Corp.—inundated the NASA headquarters in Washington, D.C., with over 7,000 pages of facts, figures and drawings designed to convince the space agency that each was the outfit best suited for handling the project.

The multibillion-dollar contract meant that North American Rockwell would construct a space shuttle large enough to accommodate a pilot, co-pilot and two passengers in a main compartment, and up to a dozen persons in a cargo compartment.

The shuttle, also known as an orbiter, would resemble a jet fighter, capable of vaulting vertically into space on rockets and landing on three wheels like a glider. When the vehicle attained an altitude of 25 miles the solid-propellant rockets that helped hurl it off its launching pad would be jettisoned, later to be recovered from the sea for re-use.

The orbiter tank and its liquid propellant tank would continue into the earth's orbit, after which the fuel tanks would be pitched into the ocean.

The shuttle and its crew and payload would be able to remain comfortably in orbit on a mission for seven days, but—if necessary—for as long as a month. Upon completion of a mission the orbiter would return to the earth and land horizontally.

The shuttle's main purpose would be to deploy and retrieve satellites, rendezvous with other spacecraft and ferry crews to orbiting space stations conducting astronomical studies and environmental surveys of the earth.

Test flights were targeted for 1976 and primary operational missions were slated for two years later. Providing there were no crippling problems during the early missions, the orbiter would be available for regular jaunts by 1980.

The awarding of the contract on July 26 was heralded by Californians, who saw it as a possible remedy for the dire financial crisis that had saddled them since 1969. NASA estimated that, during the course of the six-year building program, the shuttle would create a minimum of 50,000 new jobs and add as much as $4 billion to the state's sagging economy.

MET GIVEN 11th GOYA PAINTING

The oil portrait of the small wistful boy pausing from play with his drum and hobby-horse was the most recent addition to the European Paintings Gallery at the New Metropolitan Museum of Art. It was the 11th painting by the Spanish master, Goya, to adorn the walls of the art palace on Manhattan's upper east side. All were donated.

The canvas, 3 feet by 3½ feet, depicted a boy five years old dressed in full military costume, bedecked with glittering pantaloons, a delicately laced collar and a dark green jacket. The youngster, grasping his red-feathered military cap in his right hand and the rein of his large wooden horse in his left, stood before an ochre background highlighted with orange underpainting.

The boy was identified at the bottom of the canvas as *Pepito Costa y Bonwells*, the grandson of the physician who attended the Duchess of Alba. The duchess, a patron and confidant of Goya, who was herself the subject of many of his paintings, commissioned him in 1808 to paint Pepito for $1,000.

Beneath the name of the child was the signature "por Goya"—by Goya—in bold black lettering.

José Lopez-Rey, one of the world's foremost Goya experts, termed the painting one of the artist's masterpieces and one of his finest portraits. He placed its value at between $2 and $3 million.

The portrait was donated to the Metropolitan Museum on July 26 by Mrs. Umberto de Martini, a 75-year-old American art collector residing in Paris. The Goya was purchased in 1929 by her late fourth husband, Harrison Williams, a Long Island utilities tycoon. She inherited the painting upon his death in 1953.

The Metropolitan Museum had been hoping to obtain the priceless canvas since 1961, but legal procedures relating to Williams' estate delayed the gift.

FIDEL CASTRO'S 9-NATION TOUR

Fidel Castro's July visit to Moscow marked the climax of a two-month tour that took the Cuban prime minister to nine countries. His itinerary led from Guinea to Algeria and on to Poland and other Iron Curtain countries en route to the Soviet Union, his main stop.

The visit to Moscow, which returned Soviet Premier Alexei N. Kosygin's stopover in Havana last fall, appeared to have been dominated by economic matters.

Castro was taken to task by both the Soviet press and officials for his free-wheeling economic policies, but Cuba was made a full member of Comecon, the Soviet bloc's common market.

Cuba had been an observer-member of Comecon for several years, and about 60 per cent of its trade was with the Russians.

There had been speculation in American circles that the Russians wanted to use Comecon as a vehicle for sharing the financial burden of supporting Cuba with Eastern Europe and at the same time to bring Castro under added pressure for better economic planning.

The Kremlin also reportedly reassured Castro that the Russians were standing behind Cuba despite the accords reached during President Nixon's visit to Moscow.

In the final Moscow communique the Russians promised to continue giving Cuba economic support, which is believed to total about $500 million a year in economic aid plus about $250 million in military assistance.

Observers noted that Castro did not receive the rousing welcome accorded him when he last visited Moscow in 1964. But he was presented with the Order of Lenin, Soviet Russia's highest civilian award.

Cuba's Fidel Castro tried his skill on a basketball court in Bulgaria

35-YEAR FIGHT OVER RAILROAD FIREMEN'S JOBS ENDED BY PACT

For 35 years railroad labor and management in the United States quarreled over the role of firemen on diesel-powered locomotives. Labor argued that, for safety purposes, a second man was needed in the locomotive cab, while management contended that the modern diesel engine made the fireman's job obsolete.

Over the years the impasse led to crippling strikes, extensive talks and the drafting of five separate emergency negotiating boards and two governmental panels.

Late in July what had become perhaps the longest labor-management dispute in American history came to an end with the signing of a joint agreement aimed at eventually reducing the number of firemen on diesel freight locomotives. In return for labor's concession to management, it was agreed that the railroads would maintain firemen on passenger train crews and rehire a small number of firemen laid off by governmental rulings.

The dispute began in 1937, when the diesel engines were first put into operation. The railroads, explaining that the stoking of steam engines was no longer required, began trying to get rid of the firemen. Outraged, the firemen vowed to fight the action. Represented by the Brotherhood of Locomotive Firemen and Engineers, later merged into the United Transportation Union, they were locked in a continuing struggle to preserve their jobs.

The pact, signed in Washington, D.C., on July 20, was composed of two separate agreements concerning the latest phase of the manning dispute, which began in 1965 when the firemen's union was battling to restore nearly 20,000 jobs that had been eliminated by a federal arbitration board.

The first agreement took the form of a "manning contract" which provided for the railroads to continue the employment of the 18,000 firemen presently working "until they retire, resign, die, are dismissed for cause or are promoted to jobs as engineers."

The other agreement instituted a training program under which the railroads would train firemen to take over as locomotive engineers when vacancies occurred.

Labor was jubilant. But railroad officials predicted a gradual decrease in the number of firemen on freight train crews. For one thing, the agreement called for compulsory retirement at 65. Furthermore, the railroads were not compelled to find a replacement for a fireman who was promoted to engineer. Firemen awaiting promotion could be assigned to other railroad jobs.

A national disputes committee was established to study work rules affecting the duties of firemen and to resolve disputes as they arose. A national planning study was created to assess the effects of the pact.

Labor experts felt that the pact took a long step toward the elimination of what the industry called featherbedding—hiring more men than are needed—through collective bargaining.

Labor and management agreed that the most significant part of the pact was that "the two sides, through voluntary negotiations, had eliminated more than three decades of contention and bitterness, resolved a basic dispute and taken a step toward the modernization of the railroad industry."

A doctor in a Port Harcourt playground checks for signs of life after the execution of 14 armed robbers by a Nigerian firing squad

MITCHELL YIELDED TO MARTHA

"This is nothing but a cops and robbers game, and I'm trying to get my husband out of it." After presenting this view of politics, an angry and excited Martha Mitchell vowed to leave her husband unless he vowed to leave public life.

"There is no reason for us to be involved in politics," Mrs. Mitchell said during one of her celebrated telephone interviews. "I just can't take it any more."

John Mitchell, a Wall Street lawyer, rose to prominence and power in Washington during three years as Attorney General and then resigned on March 1, 1972 to direct President Nixon's re-election campaign. His fast talking, candid and controversial wife left their villa in Newport Beach, Calif., on June 26 after a reputed row with a security guard.

According to Mrs. Mitchell, a guard provided by the Nixon Administration yanked a telephone from her bedroom wall while she was using it, threw her down on the bed "and stuck a needle in my behind."

"Can you believe that a man can walk into your bedroom and abuse you like that?" she wailed. "It was a horrible experience."

She then took up residence at the posh Westchester Country Club in Rye, N.Y., where she promised to stay until her husband stepped out of the limelight.

The threat was effective. Less than a week later Mitchell resigned as Nixon's campaign director. He joined his wife in New York, and they both returned to Washington a few days later.

In his letter to the President, dated July 1, ad-

vising him of the resignation, Mitchell wrote of his distress upon leaving the post in which he shaped up a victory for Nixon in 1968. But, he explained, "I have found that I can no longer run the campaign on a full-time basis and still meet the one obligation which must come first: the happiness and welfare of my wife and daughter."

The President accepted the resignation with deep regret, noting that a politician's wife "must not only share the disappointments and brickbats but also must accept the frequent absence of a husband and father."

He then appointed Clark MacGregor, a former Minnesota Congressman, to fill the campaign post vacated by Mitchell, who then returned to the practice of law.

View of the July 10 total eclipse

NEW YORK AREA HIT BY POWER BLACKOUTS, RAIN, HEAT, SMOG

Not since 1965 had the residents of the New York City area been so completely in the dark. For more than a week some staggered through periods of blinding blackness, while the rest of the state pleaded for extra voltage in the wake of a suffocating heat wave.

At one stage a severe atmospheric inversion added to the dilemma in metropolitan New York and portions of Rhode Island and Massachusetts.

Six of the 10 electrical feeder cables controlled by Consolidated Edison Co., a utility monopolizing electricity throughout most of New York State, broke down in the boroughs of Brooklyn and Queens. Nearly 500,000 people were left stranded without power for 13 steamy hours in what was described by city officials as the worst blackout since the power failure seven Novembers ago that crippled the northeastern coast of the United States and ignited suspicions of sabotage *(The World in 1965, 209–213)*.

Spokesmen for Con Edison blamed the 1972 feeder cable failure on air-conditioning demands, created when temperatures zoomed into the 90s, plus the cumulative damage incurred by salt from winter snow-removal efforts—salt that promoted the corrosion of insulating material surrounding the cables—and the excessive rainfall brought by one of the wettest springs and earliest summers on record.

The lights first went out in the Bay Ridge, Gowanus and Sunset Park sections of Brooklyn at 9:53 p.m. on July 17. Service was restored at 11 o'clock the following morning, but then only partially. In the interim many hospitals had to reschedule surgical operations for lack of emergency generating equipment, race tracks were forced to close, thereby forfeiting hundreds of thousands of dollars in bets, and housewives watched as their refrigerated foodstuffs spoiled.

In addition a polluted pall of haze, created by a massive atmospheric inversion in the stifling, languid air, accelerated deaths among the chronically ill. According to Dr. Joseph A. Cimino, the city's health commissioner, countless individuals with respiratory and coronary ailments experienced increased difficulties.

To counteract the inversion and to further limit pollution, State Environmental Conservation Commissioner Henry L. Diamond ordered a ban on the open burning of refuse throughout the city's five boroughs. The ban took effect on July 19 and was lifted on July 25.

Also on July 19 four Con Edison feeder cables failed, resulting in a brownout—a reduction in power—for more than 250,000 residents of the Coney Island, Seagate and Brighton Beach sections of Brooklyn, and those of Westchester County in upstate New York. On the same day power failures in the Riverdale section of the Bronx affected some 40,000 persons, while 6,000 Queens homes also lacked power.

The brownout of July 19 came during the fourth consecutive day of 90-plus temperatures and stagnant air, and was repaired during a brief break in the humidity on July 20.

Con Edison pleaded with its customers throughout the city and the state to conserve electricity as the muggy 90-degree temperatures continued with no relief in sight. New York City Mayor John Lindsay summoned an emergency City Hall meeting of Con Edison officials and joined in the utility's appeal during the crisis.

In compliance with the entreaty for conservation, power everywhere was used sparingly: Lobby lighting at the Empire State Building was reduced; the Port Authority of New York and New Jersey announced that the cable lighting spanning the George Washington Bridge would not be in use; Yankee Stadium promised to keep off the hundreds of 1,500-watt spotlights that illuminated the baseball field during the batting practice prior to the games; the Transit Authority of New York City, which used 500,000 kilowatts at the peak of the rush hour, diminished the speed of many trains traveling through Brooklyn.

Con Edison struggled with the dire situation not only by reducing its voltage output but by purchasing more than a million kilowatts of power from outside reserves in Canada and some of the United States, including Pennsylvania and Georgia, which were not afflicted with a power shortage.

The city received a weekend respite on July 21 when a cold air mass moved down from Canada bringing with it a drop of 10 degrees in the temperature. Con Edison was able to meet the continuing high demands for electricity without a major failure.

The reprieve was short-lived; trouble returned July 24 when the temperature soared to 91 degrees, promoting a succession of cable breakdowns that blacked out southeastern Queens and northeastern Brooklyn. More than 400,000 people were left without refrigeration from 10:25 a.m. until 5:45 a.m. the following day, when most of the power was restored by repairmen who had labored around the clock.

The midsummer power failure came to an end on July 25, when both temperature and electrical resources stabilized.

FOR THE RECORD

ELECTED. As president pro tem of the U.S. Senate, James Oliver Eastland, by his colleagues on Capitol Hill on July 28. The 68-year-old veteran Mississippi Senator, who served as chairman of the Senate Judiciary Committee since 1956, was chosen to succeed his friend and fellow Democrat, Louisiana Sen. Allen J. Ellender, who died on July 27 at the age of 81.

DISMISSED. Jacques Chaban-Delmas, Premier of France, by President Georges Pompidou on July 5. The 57-year-old Chaban-Delmas had displeased many old-line members of the Union for the Defense of the Republic—the Gaullist party—with what they considered "too leftist" social and labor policies, and his relationship with Pompidou had soured during his three-year tenure because of them. The French president appointed Pierre Messmer, 56, a staunch, orthodox Gaullist, to succeed the ousted premier in the hope that Messmer could reunite the splintered ruling party before the parliamentary elections in March 1973.

Balloons filled the air in Miami's Convention Hall ——

August

National Conventions:
Their Divergent Views

*For Democrats, a unique assemblage nominated McGovern;
Nixon an obvious choice of Republicans, without fanfare*

"ONE COMES to any convention with an anticipatory sense of excitement," political historian Theodore White once wrote. "There is a game to be played, for good or bad." Rarely had the sense of excitement been as fraught with anticipation as in the days and weeks before the Democratic National Convention of 1972. The game to be played there would be one of the most intriguing experiments in the nation's political history, testing whether sweeping new rules of reform, designed to make the convention truly democratic, would work as well in selecting a nominee as smoke-filled rooms had in the past—indeed, whether they would work at all. Most predictions of how the convention would go ranged from bedlam to chaos; few anticipated the spectacle that actually happened.

The Republicans, for their part, aimed to offer the nation a study in contrast at their convention. They preferred to eliminate any suggestion of an arena atmosphere and make their formal confirmation of President Nixon for a second term more a social than a political event, a carefully orchestrated celebration of the midpoint in a triumphant Republican reign. The President himself eschewed whatever suspense there might have been by naming in advance Vice President Spiro T. Agnew as his running mate. There was a measure of anticipation as to what extent a promised horde of antiwar protesters might disrupt the festivities, but, for the convention itself, no shoes remained to be dropped. The only question was whether it would take on the aspects of a revival meeting, a coronation ceremony or simply a three-day testimonial dinner. Hardly the elements of controversy historian White had in mind.

And so in the summer of '72, to the hot and gaudy placelessness of off-season Miami Beach, descended the delegates of the nation's two political parties with their widely divergent visions of America.

For the Democrats it was the 36th time the party had met in convention since Andrew Jackson called the faithful to Baltimore in 1832. So unusual was this gathering, however, that it might as well have been the first. It became evident to the Democrats at their last convention (*The World in 1968, 143–145*) that the traditional baronies of politics—the statehouses and courthouses and local political organizations that once were the viaducts of governmental social services—had long since disappeared, their constituencies swallowed up by the welfare state. To see that the traditional barons disappeared as well, a reform commission, headed by Sen. George McGovern, instituted an entirely new system of open primaries and open caucuses in every state and precinct, with the stipulation that the chosen delegations "reasonably" reflect their constituencies by race, sex and age.

As a result, fully eight out of 10 of the delegates were attending their first convention, and the list of old pols and power brokers who *failed* to get seated read like a Democratic Who's Who. As a further result, 15 per cent of the 1972 dele-

gates were black (as compared with 5.5 per cent in 1968); 36 per cent were women (compared with 13 per cent four years previous), and 22 per cent (compared with 4 per cent) were under 30 years old. As one potential candidate cracked while driving to Convention Hall, "Don't pass up any hitchhikers, they might be delegates." Some delegates did, in fact, thumb their way to Miami Beach.

If George McGovern seemed alone among the Democratic contenders to comprehend fully the new shape of convention power, his nomination under the revitalized party still was far from certain.

By June 30 McGovern's primary victories and other commitments had left him fewer than a dozen votes short of the 1,509 he needed for nomination. But when the party's credentials committee met prior to the convention, a stop-McGovern coalition composed of his rivals succeeded in taking away 151 of the 271 delegates McGovern supposedly had won in the June 6 California primary. Their tactic had been simple and, for McGovern, ironic. Such winner-take-all primaries as California's were contrary to the party's new reform rules; McGovern had won 44 per cent of the primary votes and thus was entitled to no more than 44 per cent of the delegates. McGovern took the committee ruling to court. The Supreme Court threw it back, ruling that it was a decision the party had to make itself.

That made a dandy floor fight at the convention inevitable. If McGovern won on the California question, retaining all 271 votes, he had the nomination sewed up. If he lost, the nomination likely would turn into a free-for-all.

But wait. What would constitute a majority in a floor vote on the California question? The full convention majority of 1,509, or the 1,433 that represented a majority after the contested California delegates were subtracted? In a critical ruling that was debated at length, Convention Chairman Larry O'Brien determined that only a majority of those voting was necessary, not 1,509.

There was a further question, and none awaited its answer with greater intensity than that forlorn band of unseated political pros chewing their cigars outside the hall. Was this unlikely assemblage of 3,016 amateurs capable of deciding such niceties, long the forte of veteran wheelers and dealers, or would the whole convention collapse in a shambles of "principle?"

The convention opened Monday, July 11, with a keynote address by Florida's Gov. Reuben Askew who noted, with obvious feeling, that "It is impossible to look upon this group without feeling that one has seen the face of America." Then the delegates got down to business. The first order of business was the matter of credentials.

Before the California challenge came up, however, a dispute had to be resolved regarding South Carolina. The issue was

Old and young gathered for the conventions; this senior citizen talked to a Yippie marcher

Cuban refugees scuffled with student demonstrators outside Convention Hall

141

Sen. Thomas Eagleton listened wearily as McGovern told newsmen his running mate was stepping down

whether nine women should be added to its delegation under the reform rules. On principle, McGovern's followers would be inclined to say yes. But the question had deeper, more political implications, as far as the anti-McGovern forces were concerned. If the final vote somehow fell between 1,433 and 1,509 they could raise a point of order and bring to a vote Chairman O'Brien's ruling on what constituted a majority on challenges. In that event, all the delegates except the handful under challenge in South Carolina could vote on the question, making it far less possible for the McGovern forces to muster the votes they needed. The majority determined by the South Carolina vote would set the rule for California.

McGovern's astute floor leaders recognized those implications immediately.

As the voting began and the tally drew perilously close to 1,433 they put out the word: put aside ideological preferences and vote no. The result: South Carolina's women lost, 1,555.75 (a convention majority) to 1,429.05. There would be no point of order raised. O'Brien's ruling would stand.

As for that other question, McGovern's youthful marvels had shown themselves to be as masterfully disciplined at parliamentary infighting as any veteran pol.

Along with the other delegates in the hall they showed something else. With discipline and attentiveness, not to mention an overriding air of politeness and courtesy, they demon-

strated that they had come to Miami Beach to work, not, as in the past, to snake dance in the aisles with foolish hats and brass bands.

The California debate did not begin until just after midnight. It was the anti-McGovern forces' last chance, and they lost. A solid majority of 1,618.28 delegate votes favored giving McGovern all his 271 California delegates; only 1,238.22 against. From that moment there was no suspense as to who would get the nomination.

Other work remained to be done, however. The second night was devoted to the party platform and the serious-minded delegates were determined that every point of view would get a hearing. A touching moment occurred when the bullet-crippled George Wallace argued, from a wheelchair, for his planks. The largely hostile audience treated him with respect and compassion. Then other voices rose to be heard, and others, and others, until the business was done—at 6:21 a.m. Chairman O'Brien, at adjournment, told the delegates he had never seen anything like it. Neither had anyone else. It was the longest convention session in history, and one of the most open as well.

Wednesday, the convention's third day, was largely anticlimactic as the nominee—George Stanley McGovern—came to claim what he had already won. When the roll call reached Illinois the tally put him over the top, and before the

McGovern and his final choice for running mate, R. Sargent Shriver

vote-changing began he had 1,728.35 votes. When the band-wagon stopped rolling he had 1,864.95.

The only suspense that remained was McGovern's choice for a running mate. In a series of meetings that began Tuesday, McGovern and his advisers went through a list of two dozen possibilities. his first choice was Sen. Edward Kennedy, but Kennedy refused. The sort of man McGovern was looking for was someone with big-city appeal, friendly to labor (whose bosses were largely out in the cold with the party's new look) and with a national appeal. At length he settled on Missouri's Sen. Thomas Eagleton, 42, a border-state liberal with a good labor record and urban experience.

So many other names were put in nomination, however, and so much time spent in speeches and roll calls on parliamentary matters—prime TV time was clearly of less importance to the delegates than a legitimately open convention—that it was 2 a.m. July 13 in the East before Eagleton finally won the convention's acceptance. What was worse, it was 3 a.m.—long after most of the television audience had gone to bed—that McGovern gave his acceptance speech.

Thus did the Democratic party select its ticket for 1972: McGovern and Eagleton.

It was the shortest-lived ticket in history.

Scarcely had McGovern arrived for a rest at a retreat in the Black Hills of his native South Dakota than a political bombshell exploded. It suddenly became known that Eagleton had twice in previous years been hospitalized under psychiatric treatment, including electric shock therapy, for mental exhaustion and depression. The senator had kept his medical background such a guarded secret that it came as a surprise to close friends in Missouri, let alone McGovern.

The presidential candidate, stunned, announced immediately that Eagleton had his total support. As rumblings across the land took on earthquake proportions, however, he and Eagleton announced that the Missourian would withdraw from the ticket. It was their joint decision, they said. It was apparent, McGovern explained, that Eagleton himself had become an issue, thus distracting attention from what they both considered the substantive issues upon which the campaign ought to be waged. Eagleton stepped down on July 31.

A week later McGovern named, and the Democratic National Committee confirmed, a new running mate: R. Sargent Shriver, ambassador to France under the Lyndon B. Johnson administration, first head of the Peace Corps, and brother-in-law of the late President John F. Kennedy.

The "Eagleton affair," as it came to be called, robbed underdog McGovern of a valuable early start. He was still trying to get his campaign off the ground when the Republicans gathered in Miami Beach to begin their well-ordered convention, Monday, Aug. 21.

Down through history the Republicans always had been known to stage a much tidier quadrennial show than their brawling rivals, but at no time was the contrast at Convention Hall more striking than in 1972.

Outside the hall was a different story. As promised, some 5,000 antiwar activists had shown up to protest the President's policies, more than twice as many as were on hand during the Democratic Convention and seemingly more than twice as angry. For both conventions, Miami Beach police had set aside Flamingo Park—normally a large, green gathering place for retired persons to sit and chat under banyan trees—as a campsite for the untidy army of young people. When the Republicans arrived in town the mood at Flamingo Park changed from one of holiday abandon to purposeful militancy.

GOP leaders pretended not to notice. "Our role," said Wisconsin's Robert Knowles, the Republican convention manager, "is to attempt to display our party as a unified, businesslike party that is capable of running the country."

Unity the Republicans displayed in abundance. California Gov. Ronald Reagan, once a Nixon rival, agreed to serve as convention chairman. New York's Gov. Nelson Rockefeller, another former foe, was pleased to put the President in nomination. "The convention will be short, compact and precise," said Robert Dole, GOP national chairman. "We want a convention that will be watched, and not just by insomniacs." For the watchers, the Republicans also bussed in 3,000 young people, scrubbed and barbered, both to contrast with the masses in the streets and to counteract the youthful impression the Democrats had left.

So it went. Prior to the convention the Rules Committee even made it impossible for California's Rep. Paul McCloskey to inject a threatened note of discord. McCloskey had a single elected delegate at the convention—pledged to him by New Mexico's primary law. He therefore felt qualified to be put in nomination, which would give him a chance to air his antiwar views. The Rules Committee, however, approved a proposal which required all potential nominees to have the pledges of a majority of delegates in three states.

Instead of seeing controversy, the delegates (and TV audience) saw three films boosting the President and First Family, listened to endorsements by Hollywood stars and heard a touching speech by elder statesman Alf Landon. Then they approved the party platform, which had been tailor-made at the White House, without a single vote of dissent. A proposal to rewrite the rules for 1976 to allow the big urban states a greater convention voice was snuffed out after less than an hour of floor debate.

A report that a number of delegates were distressed over the selection of Vice President Agnew as a running mate never surfaced. Instead there was a "spontaneous" demonstration for Nixon and Agnew timed to last precisely 20 minutes on the convention agenda.

On Wednesday night the convention duly renominated President Nixon by a vote of 1,347 to 1. The single dissenting vote was cast apologetically for McCloskey by the duty-bound New Mexico delegate.

While harmony reigned inside the hall, thousands of the young activists outside roamed the streets under great clouds of police tear gas. Even as the President spoke, a cordon of policemen ringed the hall. They stood five feet apart, wore gas masks against the acrid night air and carried three-foot riot batons. Earlier in the evening, when the session opened, the demonstrators had tried to block delegates' access to the hall by slashing tires and tossing huge trash bins into the streets to snarl traffic—tactics which quickly escalated into common vandalism: broken windows, hurled rocks, shouted insults. Before the night was over 1,200 were in jail.

Even so, the Republican convention of 1972 came off as probably the most proficiently controlled and smoothly contrived in American history.

Whatever the contrasts in the machinery by which the two candidates came to their nominations, the conventions clearly defined the situation facing voters in the fall. Upon his nomination, McGovern had made it clear that the central issue of his campaign would be Richard M. Nixon. And the central issue of his campaign, the President made equally clear, would be George S. McGovern.

The campaign was on.

East Pakistani refugees returning to their homeland, the newly-formed state of Bangladesh

A Battle for Survival

Bangladesh won independence from West Pakistan but the price was high in deaths from combat, hunger, floods, typhoons

B Y THE MILLIONS the refugees poured out of India and back to their ravaged and bloodied homeland, the new state of Bangladesh. The year before they had fled in terror and despair spread by rampaging West Pakistani soldiers who had stopped at almost no atrocity in a vain attempt to keep the eastern wing of Pakistan under the heel of the West.

The ragged columns shuffled to the beat of blackened cooking pots clanking against each other. Mothers looked at crying children not with irritation but gratitude they had been spared and in time would learn the meaning of "freedom" and "long live Bangladesh."

At home they found Bengali guerrillas seeking out "traitors," or those who had cooperated with the West's soldiers. Death did not cease, and this time the Bengalis could rejoice at the cries of the dying.

Such post war excesses tempered only mildly a general enthusiasm and applause abroad for what seemed a triumph of spirit and determination over brute force and repression.

The days and weeks that followed were heady in Dacca and the new nation's countryside. Bengalis love to talk and dream. And here was the stuff to build palaces in the sky for a people almost routinely savaged more cruelly by nature's typhoons and floods than even the hated soldiers of Islamabad. Dream palaces certainly were needed in a country that suffered millions dead in the savagery of the final months of 1971.

"Did you lose anything?" a villager was asked. The reply: "What has a naked man to lose? All they could take from us were our loin cloths."

In those heady post-independence days, fellow villagers could be amused although their dwellings, too, were destroyed.

Sheik Mujibur Rahman, government chief of Bangladesh, reviewing a military honor guard with Soviet Premier Alexei N. Kosygin at Moscow airport

Much of the rural areas had been destroyed in a virtual scorched earth policy by West Pakistan. Many refugees returned to villages and towns that were not only leveled but the site of mass graves for friends and kin that could not or had not fled.

But after Indian infantry and armored columns had swept across East Pakistan, bringing independence, was not everything possible now?

Had not their beloved leader, Sheik Mujibur Rahman, returned from what had seemed almost certain death in a West Pakistan prison where he had spent the war for independence with a grave dug near his cell?

Had not the profits of the East's jute mills been forever funneled to the West, and would not this exploitation—all exploitation—end forever?

The present was perhaps a stone. Surely the future would be a raja's ruby.

But, as the months passed, no rubies appeared. Indeed, the stones became harder and developed jagged edges that tore away at the very fabric of life.

By mid-year, even Sheik Mujib was disillusioned. Unemployment soared, wages plummeted, prices galloped upward, lawlessness spread, tribal separatism flared in the Southeast, corruption ate steadily at the vitals of government and the people's faith in it. As famine became an ever greater specter, the poor—and that included nearly everyone—were divided into those who ate once a day, once every other day, once every three days and virtually not at all.

A villager staring at the nearly empty rice bowls on the family table and at the swollen bellies and reed-thin arms of his children said bitterly: "This truly is the hardest caste system of all. A man is marked not by his birth but by the thinness of his family's arms."

When Bangladesh was formed, Mujib was hailed by his people as Bangapita, or the father of Bengal. Opposition was virtually unheard of. Beatings or worse followed criticisms of the leader who had taken on an almost mystical quality in the minds of the common Bengalis.

The mood swiftly changed as things got worse instead of better. Diplomats declared, with more and more concern in their voices as time wore on, that Mujib was the only force that could hold the country together.

For by mid-year the opposition had formed. A major public demonstration was held in Dacca to demand the sheik's resignation.

"We want food; we want clothing," cried the crowd. The potential for chaos, almost inevitably present in newly independent nations with high illiteracy and empty treasuries, rose.

In the past the sheik's Awami League thrived almost unchallenged politically because the Communists and other leftist parties bled themselves white with factionalism. Now the Bhashani, who traditionally had followed Peking's Maoist line, succeeded in organizing a united front whose strength seemed to grow with each rise in rice prices and drop in employment. That the Bhashani should take the lead in the opposition was a stunning irony in the new state. Peking had backed the Western Pakistanis and China was looked upon in the early days of independence as the devil kingdom of Asia.

Recognizing the ugly temper of the times, the Awami League tried to rally the masses with a new cry to follow "Mujibism," an embodiment of the sheik's not-too-well-defined philosophy that included touches of secularism, democracy, socialism and nationalism. Such a tactic was adopted after independence in Indonesia. But neither Sukarno's mystic cult of self nor early adulation withstood the pressures of a mangled economy, and the leader was deposed by the military.

Although political stability was a critical concern among the friends of Bangladesh, the overwhelming immediate problem was in just keeping the nation fed and alive economically.

Jute had long been the kingpin of the Bengali economy as far as exports were concerned. It was widely assumed that with the profits going into the Dacca treasury now, funds would be available for reconstruction and a sounder economic development.

The nation's—and world's—largest jute mill remained shut most of the year. First it could not open because its former West Pakistani managers had fled, then because most of the workers were dismissed because they were members of a hated minority. Finally labor clashes involving Bengalis who equated independence with instant affluence blocked production.

Jute mills that did open found it difficult to get their products to world markets. Internal transportation virtually had collapsed. And Chittagong, the nation's largest port, was clogged with mines and sunken ships and could operate at only 30 per cent of capacity by August.

Also looming on the horizon was the threat of cheaper synthetics that some economists thought would drive the natural jute fibers from many markets. Food was the only other economic activity of importance in Bangladesh, and farmers even

in good times were hard pressed to raise enough for their families, let alone the entire nation. No exportable surpluses were in sight.

And so Bangladesh stumbled through its first year in the commonwealth of nations, living on little more than foreign largess, about one-third of it from the United States.

The ripping away of the more populous East also left serious wounds in West Pakistan. Gone were the dreams of one day besting India and exerting domination over the subcontinent. West Pakistanis loved their dreams, too. And seeing their country tumble perhaps forever from the level of the world's second ranked powers was a major psychic blow.

A somber President Zulfikar Ali Bhutto, who took over the West after the East was lost, faced an almost herculean task of forging his diminished nation into a viable political and economic unit. When President Gen. Agha Mohammed Yahya Khan quit in disgrace and turned power back to the civilians, Pakistan owed other countries and banks nearly $4 billion and could not pay even the yearly interest on the debt. Of 65 million people who still were ruled by Pakistan, only 10 million were literate, and national per capita income of about $64 was one of the lowest annual totals in the world.

But, foreign experts said, as sick as Bhutto's land was, it was in far better shape than Bangladesh, and in the long run would be far better off economically without the impoverished break-away eastern region.

During the war in the East, Pakistan was supported only by China among the world's great powers. However, many read into Washington's biting words for New Delhi, when Indian troops went to the aid of Bengali guerrillas, a covert backing of

Indian Prime Minister Indira Gandhi standing with Pakistani President Zulfikar Ali Bhutto in Simla, where historic meeting took place

Hung Hua, Red Chinese ambassador to the United Nations, casting veto in the U.N. Security Council to bar Bangladesh from membership in the United Nations

sorts for Pakistan by the Nixon Administration. It was another irony of the Bangladesh story that when the war was over and Bhutto had taken charge, Washington was confronted with a longtime Yankee baiter and Sinophile at the helm of what was left of Pakistan. Compounding the irony was a quickly arranged trip by Bhutto to Moscow which had backed India and Bengali insurgents. When Bhutto departed, the new Pakistani president said he had cemented relations with the Kremlin.

The United States seemed to suffer the most politically of any nation involved directly or by alliance in the war. World opinion was somewhat aroused by what was considered Washington's tacit backing of a military dictatorship engaged in a policy of massacre and against democratic India and the Bengalis who were fighting for freedom out of the same impulses that put American patriots on the path of revolt against colonial England.

India was furious and appeared in no mood to quickly better its never easy relations with Washington. And the Soviet Union picked up the job of clearing Chittagong Harbor, giving the Kremlin at least a temporary foothold in the Indian Ocean, something Russia has sought since the time of the tsars and something Washington desperately would like to head off now.

Although India emerged from the war the undisputed power on the subcontinent, it found, as had the United States and others elsewhere in the world, that big brothers cannot easily rest in their roles as saviors once the shooting stops.

Resentment broke out among the liberated once the magnitude of their problems emerged, and independence not only failed to ease their precarious livelihood but left them on a slide aimed at economic chaos. India became the scapegoat for the common Bengalis for everything from food shortages (India sent food grains to Bangladesh) to spiraling prices and the general economic gloom.

"Now we're a colony of India instead of Pakistan," said a government employe. "The Indians are exploiting us."

Some Indian businessmen indeed had taken advantage of Bangladesh's shattered economy to get a foothold in the new country. Some substandard goods were sold at high prices. Bangladesh jute and desperately needed rice were smuggled into India, depriving Dacca of foreign exchange for the former and something more to put into the rice bowls of the starving because of the latter. But the anti-Indian feeling seemed to outstrip the limited provocations.

Bangladesh's non-relations with China might add still more worries to the already overstuffed Pandora's box in Dacca. Peking cast its first U.N. veto initially barring Bangladesh from a seat at the world body and generally was hostile to the newest nation. With a pro Peking Communist party leading the growing opposition, many in Dacca were concerned about China's history of supplying the wherewithal to insurgent groups throughout Asia.

The United States moved to burnish its image in the new nation after initial hesitation following the war. It recognized the Dacca government in April and opened its treasury for about $300 million in relief. There were cries in Dacca for the sheik to reject the aid.

For Washington, the larger question was whether Pakistan and India would really end the hatreds and warfare that had marked their quarter century as independent nations. Stability on the subcontinent had always been the cornerstone of U.S. policy toward the region. India and Pakistan signed a peace treaty early in the year but months later deadlines passed without specific agreements being effected. The big stumbling block remained the 90,000 Pakistani prisoners of war still held by India in August 1972. But the biggest problem from the long-term view probably was Kashmir, the chief focal point of Indian-Pakistani feuding. Kashmir was a largely Moslem state mostly controlled by Hindu India from behind a ceasefire line set in an earlier war between the two nations.

There were some signs, however, that the ancient hatreds between Moslem and Hindu might be less dangerous in the future, if for no other reason than that weakened Pakistan no longer could logically challenge India without massive outside support, including troops. Some also saw signs that both countries had realized that their attempts to develop their backward nations had been set back many years each time the rivals hurled their field armies into battle.

In the end, governments in Asia tended to be judged by the governed as to whether there was enough food and stability to make an already hard and at times precarious life bearable. India and Pakistan appeared to realize this fact now after years of squandering resources and energies. Sheik Mujib was now faced with problems that must be resolved far more rapidly with far less margin of error if the bright promise the Bengalis saw in independence was not to disintegrate into new darkness and turmoil.

Drug Traffic Flourishes
Despite Worldwide Drive

*U.S. survey concluded that rising level of opium and heroin
seizures represented only a fraction of the illicit flow
by land and sea from Asia and Europe to North America*

FOR NINE MONTHS a study of the international drug traffic situation was conducted by the United States government. Spurred by public alarm, the Nixon Administration plunged into a full-scale investigation. When its findings were disclosed, the campaign against illicit drugs showed little to be optimistic about.

A 112-page World Opium Survey, 1972 was released by the U.S. State Department on Aug. 16. The most comprehensive report of its kind, the survey detailed the heroin story from its origins in poppy fields to its increasing popularity with every level of world society.

In essence the survey found that, despite increased and elaborate enforcement drives, the United States and other countries engaged in a battle against narcotics had succeeded in stemming only a small fraction of the total flow of the illegal drugs.

The study began in November 1971 when President Nixon commissioned the Cabinet Committee on International Narcotics Control, under the direction of Secretary of State William Rogers, to probe the drug crisis. Also involved in the inquiry were the Central Intelligence Agency, the Bureau of Narcotics and Dangerous Drugs, the Customs Bureau and the Treasury Department.

The cabinet committee noted in its report that enforcement efforts against smuggling in the last two years had resulted in an increased number of crackdowns, but that "the rising level of seizures still represents only a small fraction of the illicit flow. The international heroin market almost certainly continues to have adequate supplies to meet the demand in consuming countries."

Certain international "cartels" controlled the world's opium and heroin markets and were reaping enormous profits on

State police burning 800 pounds of marijuana at an incinerator in New Jersey

Federal narcotics agents in Miami, Fla., with heroin valued "in excess of $50 million" seized in a raid

their investment, the survey showed, along with this outline of how heroin—a derivitive of opium—was smuggled:

Three "complexes" composed the major heroin markets. The primary complex originated in Turkey, where opium was packed and shipped through Bulgaria or Greece to Yugoslavia, then to West Germany or Austria and on to France. There the opium was refined into heroin in small mobile laboratories and smuggled into the United States—usually into New York City, which functioned as the main U.S. distribution center.

Southeast Asia served as the second complex, providing opium cultivated in Burma, Thailand and Laos. The survey stated that the reduction of American military forces in Vietnam had crippled heroin production in this complex.

A third complex consisted of Iran, Pakistan and Afghanistan, providing narcotics chiefly for buyers in Iran.

The second and third complexes were "of major importance because of their potential for becoming important suppliers of opium for the international heroin market in the future, particularly as the primary complex falters." The most popular method of transporting illegal drugs, said the report, was the use of secret compartments built into passenger cars, commercial trucks and touring buses which also carried legitimate cargo and which had been sealed with a customs band.

"These sealed vehicles operating under international customs arrangements will usually be allowed to travel across various national frontiers with little or no controls. The great number of such vehicles traveling into the drug countries of the world precludes any systematic inspection."

Smuggling opium and heroin by sea, less popular than it was a few years ago, still accounted for large shipments. The main distribution ports cited by the survey were Marseilles, Barcelona, Trieste, Venice, Genoa, Naples and New York City. Smuggling by air proved to be the least popular, and the least successful, method. The opium survey held that 80 per cent of the illegal heroin entering the United States came from Turkish opium, 25 per cent from Mexican, and 5 to 15 per cent from Southeast Asian opiates.

In an appendix accompanying the opium survey, the drug situation in the following countries was reviewed:

—Turkey: "There will still be a need for vigorous law enforcement against smugglers if the flow of illegal opium is to be slowed after 1972, when production is banned by the Turkish government."

—Afghanistan: "Illicit opium sales are believed to be made almost exclusively to Iran . . . although opium production and trafficking are proscribed, there is actually little enforcement. . . ."

—Iran: "There is no evidence at present that any of Iran's legal opium production is diverted into the illicit international narcotics traffic. Nor is there evidence that Iran is a transit point for illicit narcotics not of Iranian origin destined for Europe or the United States."

—Pakistan: "The Bhutto government has expressed its willingness to cooperate with the United States to reduce opium output and traffic in Pakistan. . . ."

—India: "India's opium-control system is acknowledged to be one of the world's best. . . . Narcotics officials admit, however, that decreases in opium supplies in other foreign areas will strain the capability of their control system."

—Thailand: "The government is unable as yet to eliminate cultivation until substitute crops can be developed. . . ."

—Burma: "The government's writ is not strong enough in the Kachin and Shan states and Chin hills areas to afford rigid enforcement of opium laws. . . . Nevertheless, the government has taken action against opium traffic when possible."

—Laos: "The opium problem in Laos is essentially one of preventing opium originating in other countries, primarily Burma, from transiting Laos on the way to South Vietnam or other countries."

—France: "Most of the heroin presently entering the United States is believed to be processed from Turkish opium in southern France, primarily around Marseilles."

—Italy: "Italy is primarily a transit country for shipment of opium and morphine base en route from Turkey to southern France. . . ."

—Canada: "Canadian authorities have cooperated fully with their U.S. counterparts in attempting to stop the international traffic in illicit drugs, but Canada will probably continue to serve as one of the principal conduits for European narcotics. . . ."

—Latin America: "Of more immediate importance than the small trickle of opiates originating in Latin America is the great flow of drugs transhipped from Europe through that region to the United States. . . . One of the principal entrepots (storage houses) for European heroin in South America is Buenos Aires. . . . Much of the heroin has been shipped from Buenos Aires into Paraguay. . . ."

—China: "There is no reliable evidence that China has either engaged in or sanctioned the illicit export of opium and its derivatives."

—Soviet Union: "The Soviet Union is neither a source nor a transit point for illicit opiates."

Afghan worker in a poppy field on Pakistan's Northwest Frontier, on the border of Afghanistan, collecting opium gum after the poppy has been slashed

151

The Jesus People– a New Evangelism?

"JESUS; AM I EVER high on Jesus!"

According to some, wearing crosses as necklaces, Jesus was a 30-second cure for heroin addiction. According to most, Jesus was peace of mind. The light was seen and they were saved; a revitalized proverb for contemporary America, a proverb voiced repeatedly by hundreds of youths across the country.

Some were called Jesus People, or Street Christians; some were called Jesus Freaks. Once freaked out on drugs, mysticism, Far Eastern spiritualism, the year 1972 found them freaked out on the Lord. "The Lord," they said, "is alive and he is coming back soon."

At Long Beach, Calif., a group of longhaired, casually dressed young people were baptized in the Pacific surf. Coming out of the water they affectionately rejoiced with their brothers and sisters in a kind of family love.

From Sunset Strip in Hollywood to Telegraph Hill in San Francisco, Grand River Avenue in Detroit and Times Square in New York City, hundreds of Jesus kids spread the message of salvation. Seeking converts, they pleaded with businessmen, non-believers and pushers to come into the hands of the Lord. In major cities youths opened Christian nightclubs and Jesus coffeehouses. They held Jesus rock concerts and bought Jesus sweatshirts and silver crosses.

During the 1950s many youths snickered at Pat Boone, a pop singer and evangelist, when he refused to kiss his leading lady in a film because of his religious beliefs. Many parents nodded approval but most of the young folk labeled his atti-tude "white-buck-shoed" Christian piety. Twenty years later, however, Pat Boone was looked upon by many youths as an established member of the Jesus movement. A devoted worshiper, he frequently baptized converts in his backyard swimming pool.

Much had happened to the youth of America since Pat Boone first appeared on the screen. Many young people had renounced the establishment. College campuses were in upheaval; student demonstrations and the use of drugs were commonplace.

The Jesus movement, under these circumstances, was a peculiar development. Many of those who had taken part in the youth revolt shifted gears. They claimed that the only way to solve the problems of the world was to invoke the aid of the Lord. With His guidance, they would find the true meaning of love and peace.

The Jesus movement closely followed other revivalist techniques in the United States. Its members were basically traditional fundamentalists believing in heaven and hell and a literal interpretation of the Bible. Many observers felt that the movement was an expected and natural transition from the hippie cycle. The Jesus people discredited the established church for being, as they saw it, steeped in hypocrisy and allowing no direct communication with Christ. Most of their meetings were held in the basements of private homes or in office buildings, or wherever and whenever the opportunity presented itself. They also took with them their mode of dress

The Rev. Arthur Blessitt, left, and Jesse Wise chatted with New York City strollers as they hold the 105-pound cross they had carried across the country

An Oklahoma City girl wearing T-shirt with familiar theme while attending "The Festival of the Risen Son" held there

Members of a nomadic band calling themselves "Children of God" wore sackcloth and carried shepherd's staffs during their vigils

and the notions of love and sharing for which the counter-culture had been seeking so long.

In his book, *The Making of a Counter Culture*, Theodore Roszak stated that, in 1969, the youth movement definitely had religious overtones, beginning with Zen and gradually moving toward more exotic religions. But some theologians felt that, after years of desperation, disorder and disappointment, many youths not wholly satisfied with the traditions of Far Eastern religions veered back to Christianity, upon which they had been reared.

Their meetings were characterized by a high degree of emotionalism. As brother and sister joined hands in mutual understanding, they shed tears of joy and revelation. Some of the Jesus people spent eight hours a day reading the Bible and quoting verse to non-believers. Some, including the Children of God, renounced family ties, adopted Biblical names and preached imminent doomsday.

The life patterns of the Jesus people were fairly similar. Usually they were from middle class families, although the movement did incorporate lower and upper class youths. Some had family difficulties, others had experienced too little communication with their parents. Many had left school only to wander aimlessly, living in the streets and taking drugs. Other Jesus children had stayed in school, yet they too had become disillusioned.

"I had been to New York, then to Los Angeles," reported one Jesus youth. "I was on drugs for three years, taking pills and smoking. But I kept feeling restless, lonely and desperate. Something was missing. Then I ran into someone who gave me the gospel, and it made so much sense to me that I began to pray and pray and then, all of sudden, I understood Jesus and I was saved."

Many of the Jesus children settled in Christian communes. Communes had begun to spread throughout the country. There was Clayton House and Soul Inn, ministered in the Haight Ashbury district of San Francisco; Zion's Inn and Berachah House in Marin County, north of San Francisco; God's Love opened in Berkeley. There were communes in Texas, Colorado and New York. Visitors often found it hard to determine how these youths supported themselves. Most didn't work, but spent the day learning the Bible. When asked what they did for money, one member of a California commune responded: "Oh, we don't worry about money. Jesus in his goodness takes care of us." But in fact many commune leaders found ways of making money; among them, asking parents to donate funds or sending movement members into the streets to beg.

Public reaction to the movement was varied. It frightened many parents, for its supernatural characteristics were sometimes incomprehensible to fathers and mothers accustomed to dealing with such hard-core problems as drugs. The Jesus people usually chose to follow Christ instead of the leaders of the business world. The technological age, these youths claimed, had depersonalized their lives. Many established businessmen, on the other hand, criticized the movement for renouncing progress and production; they believed that such a trend would only bring society to a standstill.

Such evangelists as Billy Graham were pleased by the flourishing religious commitment, but many members of the established church feared the sudden awakening to Jesus among the young. And many observers insisted that Jesus people had simply found another form of escape; that, instead of dealing with their own personal problems and the problems of the world, they had isolated themselves from "reality."

Safety advocate Ralph Nader testifying in Washington

Sales of New U.S. Cars Far Exceeded by Number Called Back for Retests

Suspected defects, possibly entailing repairs, were a costly prospect for companies but millions of owners paid nothing

IN THE SEVEN MONTHS between December 1971 and June 1972, the four major automakers in the United States sold a record 5.3 million cars. But in the same period more than twice as many—11.6 million—were recalled for inspection and repair of possible defects.

The great rollback began when General Motors Corp., under growing pressure from government and consumer groups, asked owners of 6.7 million Chevrolets to return models issued in 1965 through 1969 with potentially defective engine mounts.

In the spring of 1972 Ford Motor Co. recalled more than 400,000 intermediate-sized Fords and Mercurys for correction of a defect which the company said could allow rear wheels to fall off.

In late June Ford recalled more than four million cars to replace a cheap plastic part in seatbelt assemblies.

The second half of the year promised no letup. It began with the recall of 500,000 Chevrolet Vegas to correct possible rear axle defects, the third major callback for the GM subcompact since it went on sale in the fall of 1970.

Car company officials had no explanation for the epidemic

of recalls. They pointed out that the first recalls of passenger cars were issued in 1916, and that automobiles had become steadily safer and more reliable over the years.

Recalls were a costly and complicated business for the automakers. But, contrary to widespread popular belief, the automakers were not required to make recalls or to pay for the cost of repairs. The 1965 National Highway Safety Act required automakers only to notify owners, government and the press when defects were discovered.

Why, then, did the automakers make the recalls—at an expense estimated at $30 million each in the GM engine mount and Ford rear axle reexaminations?

Some observers said automakers made and paid for the recalls because it was good business. Someone who bought a $3,000 car, then had to pay $150 out of pocket to replace the potentially dangerous rear axle, might be inclined to look at the competition next time he went car shopping. Furthermore, the companies faced the danger of liability suits for injury resulting from product defects.

A spokesman for the National Highway Traffic Safety Administration, the federal agency assigned to monitor recalls, said "the baleful glare of publicity" forced the automakers to act on defects.

The National Highway Safety Act was passed by Congress during the uproar which followed publication of Ralph Nader's book, *Unsafe at Any Speed*. Since then Nader has remained active in auto safety, publicly demanding recalls whenever

his Washington-based Center for Auto Safety received defect complaints from drivers.

The massive Chevrolet engine mount recall was largely the result of unrelenting publicity of the problem by Nader and by Detroit News automotive writer Robert Irvin. Both Irvin and Nader solicited complaints from car owners who had suffered engine mount failures and Irvin wrote a series of articles describing the mounting total of complaints.

GM originally announced plans to just send letters to car owners notifying them of a potential defect. But under public pressure from Nader and others, the industry giant relented and mounted a full-fledged recall at GM expense.

The automakers conceded that good business was one motivation in making recalls, but argued that they had a moral requirement to act. "Our wives and children ride in those cars," said John Bates, director of the GM service section. "They have to be safe."

With all the technical know-how of the auto industry, how did recall-producing mistakes occur? Very simple, said the experts: "Humans design and engineer the cars from scratch, then other humans build, maintain and operate the machines that turn out a car's 15,000 parts and put them together." Another said, "Others test the product and still other humans buy and drive it." He pointed out that a single hour's operation of one assembly line involved 900,000 parts, creating a vast number of things which could—and sometimes did—go wrong.

There were two main sources of recall-producing defects,

Worker on the body assembly line at Ford's River Rouge plant grinding off rough spots on a model way back in 1937

Plymouth cars receiving wheels and tires at Chrysler's Detroit assembly plant in 1959

these experts reported. The multi-million car recalls usually involved an engineering or design problem that simply didn't turn up in the extensive established testing programs of the automakers.

The accelerated wear tests used to judge how products would perform over the long haul, engineers held, could never be a perfect simulation of the real world, and sometimes failed to uncover what could happen when cars were driven for long periods of time under varying conditions.

Other recalls were caused when a defective lot of parts or materials came in from another plant or outside supplier. These usually involved fairly small numbers of cars.

Poor workmanship on the assembly line only rarely caused recalls and when it did very few cars were involved, company spokesmen maintained.

While the recalls kept rolling in, 1972 was not all bad news for the U.S. auto industry. On the sales front, the picture was remarkably bright. In the first six months of the year, the four major automakers sold 4.6 million cars, the best first-half performance ever. And, while small imported cars continued to sell well, the competitive edge given Detroit in the recent international currency revaluation checked the phenomenal growth the foreigners had enjoyed in recent years.

Also in those first six months, major importers sold 611,855 cars in the United States, down just under 10 per cent from the first half of 1971. In the first half, foreign cars took 11.4 per cent of the American market, down from 13.3 per cent in 1971.

Detroit's resurgence hit the economy segment of the import market hardest. Volkswagen sales, which had been sagging worldwide, were down 22 per cent in the United States during early 1972. Japanese imports, which enjoyed phenomenal success in 1971, were having trouble hanging onto their gains. Toyota sales were running slightly above 1971, while Datsun sales were down more than 10 per cent.

But things were not uniformly bleak for the importers. While the economy cars sagged, specialty autos were enjoying a boom. Luxury-oriented Mercedes-Benz, Audi and BMW enjoyed substantial increases, as did sporty Fiat and Porsche models. Ford-Europe's Capri, sold in America by Lincoln-Mercury dealers, also was a hot item.

Industry observers pointed out, however, that the most successful imports were cars without direct domestic competition. One major cloud remained on the horizon, casting uncertainty over the future of the auto industry in coming years. The carmakers were faced with a tough set of standards requiring reducing current car exhaust pollution by 90 per cent. New standards to control hydrocarbons and carbon monoxide take effect in 1975, and controls upon oxides of nitrogen are effective in 1976.

The automakers said that without a major technological breakthrough—which was not currently upon the horizon—they would be unable to meet the standards. And, even if they did, the automakers added, the required equipment would add several hundred dollars to the price of each new car.

Major car manufacturers appealed to the Environmental Protection Agency for a one-year delay in the standards, a delay authorized by the 1970 Clean Air Act. But EPA Director William Ruckelshaus refused to grant the delay, saying he was not convinced by their testimony that the automakers could not meet the deadline on time.

DEATH OF LIN PIAO CONFIRMED

Ever since he sided with Chairman Mao Tse-tung in the leader's Cultural Revolution of the mid-1960s, Red China's spindly little defense minister, Lin Piao, had been hailed as Mao's "closest comrade-in-arms." He was also named as the chief's heir designate.

Then Lin suddenly disappeared in 1971, his name last mentioned officially on June 3 of that year. The blackout touched off a rash of rumors that increased after a number of Lin's followers were reportedly ousted in a series of purges.

One report said Lin was under house arrest; another said he had died after a long illness; a third held that he had been killed in a plane crash.

Then, on July 28, 1972, after a silence of more than a year, Peking confirmed Lin's death and branded him a traitor in the same breath. The Chinese embassy in Algeria announced that the 65-year-old defense minister had perished Sept. 13, 1971, in a plane crash in Mongolia. The announcement said that Lin had plotted Mao's death and that he was trying to flee "toward the Soviet Union" when he was killed.

The announcement left a number of nagging questions. Who was with Lin in the crash? Why did the plane go down?

The statement from Algeria said:

"The Lin Piao affair is a reflection of the battle between two lines which was taking place within the party for a long time. Lin Piao committed repeated errors, and Chairman Mao Tse-tung fought many battles with him.

"Sometimes Lin Piao was obligated to tone down his arrogance and thus was able to accomplish certain useful work," the announcement said. "But he was unable to renounce his sly nature. . . ."

The Peking disclosures indicated strongly that a major factor in Lin's downfall was his opposition to a Chinese policy seeking better relations with Washington.

The Algeria announcement made plain that a drive had been launched to discredit Lin Piao and depict him as one of Communism's "nonpersons."

Gradually the campaign to downgrade Lin's memory was stepped up. On Aug. 27 the Peking theoretical journal Hung Chi proceeded to destroy his military reputation.

The Communists won a major battle in the Chinese civil war, said Hung Chi, after Mao rejected proposals by Lin. It referred to the Red capture of Shenyang, capital of Liaoning Province in 1948, which had marked the first major Communist victory against Nationalist government forces in the postwar period.

The journal's account depicted Lin Piao not only as a bad tactician but also as a coward.

The Chinese embassy in Algiers confirmed the death of Lin Piao

EAST GERMAN PLANE TOLL 156

When an East German jet crashed in a suburb of East Berlin, death claimed the second greatest aircraft toll on record to date in the history of civil aviation. All of the 156 persons aboard perished in the plane's fiery ruins.

Shortly before taking off from the Schonefeld Airport in East Berlin on Aug. 14, the four-engine, Soviet-built Ilyushin 62 underwent the routine check of equipment required of all aircraft and received flight permission from the control tower. Minutes after ascending the jet lay wrecked in a wooded area at Konigs Wusterhausen, a suburb of East Berlin six miles from the airport. The 148 passengers and eight crew members, traveling to the Bulgarian resort city of Burgas on the Black Sea, met instant death. All were citizens of East Germany.

An eyewitness to the disaster reported that the long-haul airliner, equipped with a maximum seating capacity of 150 and a cruising speed of 520 miles per hour, caught fire immediately after it had passed over his house, at an altitude he estimated to be less than 100 feet. The pilot tried in vain to raise the nose of the aircraft, the witness said, and the plane exploded into flames before crashing into a nearby field.

On July 30, 1971 an All-Nippon Airway Boeing 727 collided with a Japanese air force jet in the Japanese Alps, killing 162 persons (*The World in 1971, 134*).

REBELS FAILED A SECOND TIME TO SLAY MOROCCAN KING HASSAN

Morocco's King Hassan II was flying home from a vacation in Paris when the rebels made their bid to assassinate him. But the monarach countered with a trick that probably saved his life, his brother disclosed.

As the 727 jet carrying the 43-year-old ruler crossed the Moroccan coast over the northern city of Tetouan on Aug. 16, an F5 fighter from the group escorting him suddenly swung around and opened fire on the royal aircraft. Two other F5 escorts promptly joined in.

After two firing passes had damaged the cockpit, severed the hydraulic lines, smashed instruments and blown off a rear door, Hassan made a desparate attempt to throw off his attackers. Contacting the fighters by radio, the monarch identified himself as a mechanic, his brother, Prince Moulay Abdullah, reported later. Hassan then said into the microphone that the king had been seriously wounded, along with the pilot and co-pilot, and that he would attempt to put down at Rabat. Actually, Hassan had escaped injury.

The ruse worked, and the rebels held their fire. Hassan's pilot managed to land the plane with only one of its three engines working, and the King went into the terminal building. There he went through the protocol routine of reviewing an honor guard and greeting his ministers as though nothing had happened.

But the rebel pilots were circling the airport, keeping watch. When it became apparent there was no confusion on the ground, they peeled off and began strafing the terminal area and official parking lots. As the attacking jets screamed overhead, the king and his staff took shelter in woods near the buildings.

The fighters then swung away and moved on to attack the royal palace compound, in the heart of Rabat, sending terror-stricken citizens fleeing for cover.

The strafing attacks killed at least four persons and wounded about 25, including Tourism Minister Agderraman el Mouhen, and set dozens of parked cars afire.

Pilots loyal to the crown took to the air and engaged the rebels in a dog fight over the capital, finally driving them off.

As loyal troops took up key positions in the tense capital, three rebel airmen landed at Kenitra and were promptly arrested. Another rebel, Commandant Kouafi Kouira, ditched over the coast and parachuted into the sea. He was fished out by the coast guard and arrested.

The attack marked the second attempt against Hassan's life in 13 months. The previous attempt was made July 10, 1971, when a group of senior army oficers led 1,400 cadets in an attack on the summer palace where the king was hosting his official birthday party for a thousand guests. Hassan escaped, but nearly 100 of the guests were shot (The World in 1971, 135).

One of the accused plotters, Maj. Kouera el-Ouaffi, told police captors that the leader of the plot was Gen. Mohammed Oufkir, defense minister, who had been long regarded as a mainstay of the Moroccan monarchy, informants said. A short time later Hassan summoned Oufkir for a report on the situation.

When word reached the defense minister that he had been involved by one of the plotters, he killed himself, the minister of the interior Dr. Mohammed Ben Hima, told newsmen. Later

Damaged wing of Moroccan King Hassan's plane, strafed by Moroccan air force jets while the ruler was aboard

Hassan said in an address to the Moroccan people that Oufkir had tried to kill him and that Oufkir had later committed suicide.

AP NEWS EXCHANGE WITH CHINA

When AP correspondent John Roderick returned to China in April 1971 with the first official party of U.S. newsmen to set foot there in two decades, he was greeted by Premier Chou En-lai who had known him during The Chinese Civil War.

"Mr. Roderick," said Chou, "you have opened the door."

Fifteen months later, agreement was reached on the exchange of news and photos between The Associated Press and Hsinhua, China's news and photo agency.

The accord marked the first time in more than 22 years that a U.S. news organization had set up regular news and photo channels with the Peoples Republic. Such links ended in December 1949 with the departure of the last AP correspondent, Fred Hampson.

The agreement, providing both radio and mail exchanges, was reached in negotiations between top officials of Hsinhua and Wes Gallagher, president, and Paul Miller, chairman of The Associated Press.

During their stay in China, Gallagher, Miller and their party visited Peking and other Chinese cities in August as guests of Hsinhua.

NEW METHOD FOUND TO MEASURE AGE OF FOSSILIZED ORGANISMS

For years scientists fortunate enough to have discovered the fossilized remains of organisms older than 40,000 years could only estimate their ages by relating them to the areas where they were found and the layers of earth in which they were uncovered. A new dating method announced in August possessed the potential of helping scientists pinpoint the exact age of almost any fossil, however ancient it might be.

The new dating technique, known as racemization, was developed by Dr. Jeffrey Bada, an organic chemist and assistant professor of oceanography at the Scripps Institution of Oceanography in La Jolla, Calif. His method involved a test of the chemical change in certain amino acids, the fundamental molecules found in all living cells which make up proteins. According to Bada, the age of a fossil could be determined by measuring how great a change had occurred in the chemical structure of the acids.

Bada explained on Aug. 10 that the amino acids in all living organisms took the structural form known as L-Isomers. When an organism died the acids' structure eventually became entities referred to as D-Isomers. The structural change took place very slowly, molecule by molecule, so that by measuring the percentage of L and D isomers in a specimen its age could be determined. The older the specimen, the more D-Isomers it had.

Racemization was hailed by scientists as a major breakthrough. It was a process applicable to objects of relatively recent date as well as those dating several million years. It also offered advantages to the widely used dating process based on measuring the amount of the radio-isotope Carbon-14 in an organism. Such a process was limited because the Carbon-14 in dead matter disintegrated after 40,000 years.

Other forms of radioactive decay dating could be used to estimate the ages of only very old fossils. Hence such critical questions as to the time of the Ice Age onsets, and the steps in man's evolution, had resisted successful dating.

Bada cautioned that the rate of racemization was subject to environmental influences. The rate would occur faster at certain times under certain circumstances—as in the presence of heat. Thus racemization was particularly useful for dating fossils in sea floor sediment, which had been maintained at a uniform temperature and in a relatively constant environment throughout their history.

Bada said he had tested his dating technique on a human bone donated by the eminent anthropologist, Dr. S. B. Leakey, and found it to be 135,000 years old—the same age estimated by Leakey. A shark vertebra tested by Bada dated back 8.7 million years.

HEAVY TOLL TAKEN IN BURUNDI DURING FIERCE TRIBAL WARFARE

The tiny east African nation of Burundi had long been famous for its beautiful mountainous scenery and its tall, legendary Tutsi overlords. It had also been known for a series of bloody tribal wars between the ruling Tutsis, who represented only 14 per cent of Burundi's four million inhabitants, and the Hutu tribesmen, who represented about 80 per cent of the population.

The bloodiest clash of all erupted late in April 1972 when Hutu tribesmen rose up against the government of President Michel Micombero, a Tutsi. In the blowoff, thousands of persons were killed, including Ntare V, the nation's last Tutsi king, who had returned to his homeland in March after six years in exile.

Micombero first asserted that the uprising was a plot by Tutsi royalists bent on freeing Ntare, who had been under house arrest in his former palace. It soon became apparent, however, that the rebels were Hutu tribesmen seeking to overthrow Micombero. The uprising, whatever its cause, touched off massive retaliation, and death estimates ran as high as 200,000 persons, with another half a million reported homeless.

Burundi radio went on the air on May 30 claiming that the rebels, crazed with drugs and believing themselves immune to gunfire, had vowed to wipe out the Tutsi minority. The broadcast said the insurgents had been armed with automatic weapons, Molotov cocktails and machetes dipped in poison.

"All the bands carried out the massacres the same way," one broadcast said. "They took drugs which made them mad and stimulated them to a high state of excitment.

"They were convinced bullets would not harm them. They shouted slogans to ward them off and were covered with tattoos . . . designed to protect them from bullets."

The broadcast claimed that the rebels had mutilated children and crucified many adults.

"It quickly became clear that the massacres were not indiscriminate," the radio declared. "The number of victims indicates not only a carefully organized plot against the government but a maliciously prepared plan to exterminate the Watusi."

On June 8 an equally harrowing account of government reprisals against the rebels was issued by highly placed sources in neighboring Rwanda. They claimed that Tutsi militants had entered villages at night in Burundi, killing all Hutus who could read or write. Missionaries in the Rwandan town of Kigali said that hundreds of educated Hutus, including clergymen, teachers and medical workers, had been slain.

The violence brought a denunciation from a former ruler of Burundi who was the father of the slain Ntare. From his exile retreat in Zurich, Switzerland, ex-King Mwambutsa IV charged that Micombero was a power-hungry minority leader seemingly "determined to exterminate the entire elite of the Hutus."

The former monarch, a Tutsi like Micombero, offered to return from exile to help bring peace to his troubled land. Mwambutsa, who had been dethroned in 1966, charged that his son, Ntare, had been the victim of "cold-blooded murder" despite safe conduct guaranteed him by Micombero before his return from exile.

On July 28 the United Nations broke weeks of official silence on conditions in Burundi by calling the dimensions of the civil war "staggering."

U.N. headquarters in New York said the Burundi government itself told a mission from the world peace organization—allowed into the strife-torn country in June—that 80,000 persons had perished in the revolt. But diplomatic sources at U.N. headquarters and in Washington gave far higher estimates, ranging up to 200,000.

Jewish children parade with their "piggy banks" outside a Russian bank building in London. They were taking part in a demonstration aimed at collecting money to be used to meet the exit fees Soviet officials were demanding to permit Jewish citizens to emigrate from the U.S.S.R.

Archeologists who unearthed a tomb believed to be 2,100 years old found this body of a Chinese noblewoman near Changsha

HAN DYNASTY TOMB DISCOVERED

Historicans achieved one of their great gains when they unearthed a tomb bearing the remains of a woman who had lived 2,100 years ago, a member of the Chinese elite. The body lay amid more than a thousand burial accessories of untold value.

The woman was identified as the Marchioness Li Tsang, the wife of a nobleman who reigned over the city of Changsha during the Han dynasty. She died in middle age, having left no significant mark on her era.

The discovery was made in a tomb on the outskirts of Changsha, the capital of Hunan province, on Aug. 2. Archeologists said it was of particular importance because of the body's extraordinary state of preservation.

The tomb was 66 feet deep. Six wooden coffins had been placed one within another. A layer of charcoal a foot thick, weighing about five tons and sealed by two feet of white clay, was piled around the walls and on top of the outermost coffin.

"It is probably due to those air-tight layers and some other treatment that the corpse, coffins and many of the burial accessories are free from decay," said a spokesman for the Chinese news agency, Hsinhua, after inspecting the treasure.

"Half preserved in a reddish fluid, the well-preserved corpse was wrapped in 20 silk clothes of various types," the spokesman reported. "The fibers of the subcutaneous loose connective tissue remain distinct and elastic. The femoral artery (the artery supplying the thighs) is similar in color to that of a fresh corpse. An injection of preservatives made the soft tissue swell immediately and then the swelling spread out. It is estimated that the woman died at about the age of 50."

Most of the accessories were found between the outermost and innermost coffins. The silk fabrics, varieties commonly known to have originated during the Han dynasty, included plain silk, gauze, brocade, embroideries and damask, all spun with exquisite technique.

The funerary piece considered by experts to be the most valuable was a color painting, on silk, 77 inches long, 36 inches wide at the top and 18 inches at the bottom, with flying ribbons at the corners. The elaborate painting depicted scenes of the Chinese interpretation of life on earth. These included the legend of Yi the archer, who shot down nine of the Earth's 10 suns to make the planet inhabitable for man. Others pictured life after death. Officials said this was the only such painting dating back 2,100 years to be discovered so far in China.

Among the artifacts were 120 wooden figurines, either dressed in colored silk costumes or painted in different hues; small lacquered tables, screens, walking sticks, incense bags and dressing cases. In addition the tomb contained more than 180 pieces of lacquerware and pottery, as well as tripods, caskets, jugs and vases, some of the latter containing identifiable rice cakes, pickled vegetables, peaches, pears, melons and eggs.

CELLS FUSED TO FORM HYBRIDS

Three scientists working in a laboratory outside New York City succeeded in producing hybrid plants by fusing artificial cells and thus raised the prospect of a whole new concept of world food production.

The announcement was issued on Aug. 17 from Brookhaven Laboratory at Camp Upton, Long Island, long known for its work in atomic energy research. The scientists, Dr. Peter S. Carlson, Dr. Harold H. Smith and Miss Rosemarie D. Dearing, had succeeded in growing mature and fertile hybrid plants from artificially fused cells of two wild tobacco species.

Officials at Brookhaven said the feat completely bypassed the normal sexual reproductive process and could foreshadow a broadening of the horizons in plant hybridization.

"The new result represents the first known case where an entire organism of any higher order of life has been produced by combining two different species in this way," announced the Atomic Energy Commission, which had supported the research project.

Ordinarily a hybrid was produced by cross-pollinating mature plants. This method seldom produced live offspring, and when it did they were rarely fertile. Plants and animals have internal mechanisms that ordinarily prevent cross-species fertilization.

In principle the new method could allow cross-fertilization between widely divergent plant species. It, could cause sweeping changes in the whole concept of food production around the world, the announcement said.

Carlson indicated privately that the new method might produce hybrid species that would possess great vigor and at the same time yield such edible products as wheat. The research might also yield new methods of combating disease in food plants, he added.

The new method developed at Brookhaven involved taking cells from the leaves of two wild tobacco species, nicotiana glauca and nicotiana langsdorffi. The cells were then treated with enzymes to remove their outer walls. This step made it possible for the individual cells to fuse when placed in a solution containing sodium nitrate.

About 25 per cent of the cells fused either with their own species or with the other. From these fused cells, the scientists harvested those that combined the two species.

The inter-species cells were grown in laboratory flasks for several months until plant shoots formed. These were grafted to other tobacco roots and grown into mature plants. The plants maintained the same characteristics of the hybrids, and their seeds also grew into hybrids of the same type.

In the past the two species had been hybridized by cross-pollination. The parasexual hybrids had proved identical to those produced in the conventional way.

Detailed knowledge of the growth requirements of the hybrid species made it possible to grow the fused cells under conditions favorable to the hybrid, but not to either parental species.

FOR THE RECORD

DROPPED. By the U.S. Justice Department, on Aug. 4 a perjury indictment against Leslie Ann Bacon in connection with the bombing of the U.S. Capitol building in Washington, D.C., on March 1, 1971 *(The World in 1971, 59)*. Miss Bacon, 20, was arrested in the nation's capital on April 27, 1971 as a material witness of the bombing. Later that month she appeared before a federal grand jury and subsequently was charged with perjury in testifying that she had never visited the Capitol building. The Justice Department said it had sought dismissal of the indictment "because the decision was made not to answer the defendant's motions for disclosure of electronic surveillance" regarding the case. The department refused to specify the nature of the surveillance.

STRANDED. More than 50,000 commuters when fire in a tunnel and power failures tied up evening rush-hour traffic at New York City's Grand Central Terminal Aug. 28. Train service was out completely for more than four hours. Both Penn Central and the State Department of Transportation said "man failure" at a tunnel power station appeared to have triggered the electric failure and fire.

Death wore a ski mask ——

September

Bloody Arab Massacre Blighted Olympic Games

I T BEGAN at about 4:30 a.m. on Sept. 5 as the first rays of the sun lit up the Bavarian sky and athletes from many nations started getting ready for another day of the Summer Olympic contests in Munich, which had been dubbed the "happy games." Nineteen hours later, 17 persons had been killed in one of the most shocking displays of Arab terrorism that the world had yet witnessed. The toll: 11 Israelis, a German policeman and five of the Arab commandos.

The bloodbath came after 10 days of games that had been marked a mixed atmosphere of serenity and dissension. The XX Olympiad proved to be more of a triumph for the Russians and their East German colleagues than it did for the Americans. But the United States had a respectable total in overall medals won, and it could derive consolation from the dazzling performance of Mark Spitz, the handsome young swimmer from Carmichael, Calif., who grabbed seven gold medals, making him the most gilt-bedecked Olympian in history.

But Sept. 5 marked the start of another day, a day of death, much of which was viewed on live television by millions of horrified viewers.

As dawn broke over Munich's Olympic Village, four Arabs in track suits silently scaled the fence surrounding the compound. Seconds later they were joined by four accomplices.

The two groups melted into the shadows of an Olympic residence building. One Arab pulled out a can of blacking and smeared his face. He passed the can to another Arab, and soon they had darkened their complexions in commando style.

The leader of the group motioned to the others and they emerged from the shadows, heading for Building 31. Crouching beside the doorway, they opened plastic bags each was carrying and drew out pistols and submachine guns. Stuffing hand grenades into their pockets, they waited tensely. At a second signal from the leader, they burst into Building 31, where Moshe Weinberg, 33-year-old Israeli wrestling coach, and his teammates were housed on the second floor.

Hearing the noise outside, Weinberg, father of a three-weeks-old son, opened the door, then desperately tried to close it, shouting an alarm to his countrymen. An Arab terrorist raised his pistol and fired three times. Weinberg sank to the floor, dying.

The noise awakened Yosef Romano, 33-year-old weight lifter, who was sleeping in a room down the corridor. There was a sudden pounding on his door and he threw his weight against it. "Run, Tuvia, run!" he shouted to Israeli wrestling coach Tuvia Sokolsky.

Sokolsky ran out onto a small balcony and managed to escape from there. Then an Arab fired a submachine gun through the door, wounding Romano fatally.

By this time the noise had awakened the other occupants of the building, and most of the Israelis managed to escape through a door leading to a volleyball court. But nine Israelis didn't make it, and they were herded into a room and kept there under armed Arab guard.

At 5:03 a.m. West German police received a telephone call saying that Arab terrorists had opened fire in the Israeli building. Five minutes later there was a second call, and a voice made plain the reason for the attack. Two hundred guerrillas in Israel must be freed at once. If not, the Israeli hostages would be shot. The Arabs also demanded a plane to fly them and their hostages to Cairo.

Thus started a day of repeated, futile parleys between authorities and terrorists. It began shortly after the second call. Police cars pulled up in front of the building and an Arab lookout peering through a window signaled to his comrades inside. Finally the grim bargaining began.

In downtown Munich, Police Chief Manfred Schreiber gave orders to seal off the Olympic Village. A crisis center was set up in the village administration building, 220 yards from Building No. 31, where 22 male Israeli athletes, coaches and officials had shared five apartments in the three-story structure.

Schreiber called up 600 men, along with armored cars to cordon off the area. An ambulance crew was summoned to retrieve the body of Moshe Weinberg which had been dragged onto the steps of the Israeli compound and left there by two Arabs.

Schreiber strode up to the entrance of No. 31 and was met by an Arab in a white tennis hat and sunglasses. "It occurred to me," the police chief said later, "that I might try to take him hostage. He must have sensed what I was thinking. 'Do you want to take me?' he asked, opening his hand. I saw a hand grenade. He had his thumb on the pin."

Schreiber and Hans-Dietrich Genscher, West German interior minister, got hold of an Olympic Games stewardess who spoke fluent Arabic, and commenced the long, futile dialogue.

The commandos refused an offer of unlimited ransom for the nine hostages. No, they would not accept German hostages in exchange for the nine Israelis. And so it went all day. Offer after offer and as many rejections. Refusal of the terrorists to modify any of their demands was not surprising. The commandos were members of one of the most extremist of the Arab terror groups: the Black September organization, which took its name from the month in 1970 when King Hussein of Jordan had cracked down on guerrillas in his kingdom. The outfit first became known to the outside world when it assassinated Jordanian Prime Minister Wasfi Tell in Cairo in November 1971 (The World In 1971, 221, 238).

By now Munich authorities had a hot line operating to Bonn, where Chancellor Willy Brandt was following developments, and to Tel Aviv, where Premier Golda Meir had summoned her senior advisers. Mrs. Meir made a quick decision. Israel would not accede to the demand by the terrorists to free the 200 guerrillas. There would be no yielding to terror.

As the day dragged on, food was brought up in four boxes. Police hoped to rush four Arab captors when they came out of No. 31 to get the food. Instead one Arab made four trips.

Meanwhile, German policemen dressed as athletes took up posts on other floors of the building, and several officers put on bullet-proof vests. Across from No. 31 three policemen in civilian dress set up a machine gun.

Above, German policeman in athletic sweatsuits and bulletproof vests and armed with submachine guns on roof of building where terrorists held Israelis. Below, Arab commando talks with German policemen.

The only issue on which the Arabs gave ground was the deadline for meeting their demands for a plane to fly them to an Arab nation. First they said if the demand was not met by noon they would begin shooting the hostages.

The Germans stalled, trying to devise a plan to free the captives. At the pleading of Interior Minister Genscher, the commandos pushed back the deadline to 3 p.m., then to 5 p.m.

The bloody events of Sept. 4 provided American television networks with an unhappy first—a bloody extortion attempt

transmitted by Satellite. Because of their use of COMSAT's Atlantic "bird," millions of American viewers were able to watch live coverage of the chilling drama at Building 31.

Reaction was swift and angry. In New York the chairman of the militant Jewish Defense League, Bertram Zweiben, said retaliation for the killing of Weinberg and Romano could only be "done by the assassination of Arab diplomats all over the world."

In Munich plans to rush the Arabs inside Building 31 were

abandoned. A pitched battle in Olympic Village could cause untold harm.

Finally, around 9 p.m., the Arab commando conducting the negotiations for his side agreed to move the hostages out of the building and demanded a bus to take them and their captors to a helicopter pad. The aim was for 'copters to take Arabs and hostages to Fuerstenfeldbruck Air Base, where a Boeing 727 would fly them to an Arab capital.

At 10 p.m., the Arabs and their captors emerged from Building 31 to board an olive-drab bus that would take them and the negotiators to the airport. The terrorists and their hostages boarded two choppers parked on a strip of lawn about 300 yards outside the Olympic Village. A third chopper carrying German officials and Israeli intelligence men joined the other two craft in the 25-minute flight to Fuerstenfeldbruck airport. As the helicopters soared over the brightly lighted, empty stadium, a cheer went up from the nearby crowd of spectators.

At the air base, police sharpshooters lay in wait. Their orders were to kill the terrorists when they alighted from the helicopters. Suddenly the marksmen tensed as the muffled whir signaled the approach of the helicopters riding with their lights out.

Up in the control tower, policeman Anton Fliegerbauer watched as two choppers touched down and one Arab stepped from each ship and went over to inspect the airliner. Two more terrorists gripping submachine guns clambered out of the 'copters. Now there were four targets.

The sharpshooters opened fire, and the two Arabs who had remained by the helicopters spun and fell to the ground. The other two commandos had not been hit and one opened up with his submachine gun. He was cut down by a police sharpshooter. The fourth Arab managed to dive under a chopper.

Then the terrorists opened up. Commandos in one helicopter began gunning down their hostages, still tied and blindfolded. As Policeman Fliegerbauer watched the drama from the control tower, a bullet killed him.

The battle continued fitfully for another hour, before five guerrillas, including the leader, were killed. At midnight an Arab terrorist leaped out of one helicopter. As he hit the ground, he pulled the pin out of a grenade and tossed it inside the craft where four hostages were huddled. In seconds the craft was ablaze and the four perished.

A firetruck sped out to the flaming chopper and was met by a blast of submachine gun-fire. Then an armored car rumbled up and rolled toward the three surviving terrorists, who were slightly wounded. They offered no resistance as police hustled them away. Inside the two 'copters were the bodies of nine young Israelis.

The tragedy was heightened by the confused and conflicting reports put out by German authorities during the long, terrible day. The Germans appeared to be reluctant with bad news and quick to put out any good reports.

When news of the siege first spread, German officials were uncertain as to how many hostages were being held. And they kept changing the number of Israelis killed in the first terror attack from one to two and back to one. Only one body, that of Weinberg, had been immediately recovered, and officials apparently hoped that the second victim had somehow survived.

After the shooting climax at the airport, the German radio first announced that all the hostages were safe. About 90 minutes later a German press officer in Munich said he had word that the shooting was still going on. Thirty minutes later the press officer said one policeman and three terrorists had been killed and that the fate of the hostages was not known. Still

later he said a helicopter had been set ablaze. Finally government officials said all the hostages had been killed. This was four hours after the hostages had left the village, and three hours after the announcement that they were safe.

The grim outcome brought expressions of shock and indignation from leaders around the world. In Israel newspapers called for bloody revenge, a revenge that came on Sept. 8 when war planes from bases all over Israel roared off the runways and made simultaneous strikes at 10 different Arab guerrilla bases inside Syria and Lebanon. It was the most punishing action that Israel had yet launched against the commando movement.

King Hussein of Jordan, long a moderate in the Arab world called the killing of the 11 Israelis a "deplorable crime" committed by "sick souls working in the dark for the sole purpose of discrediting Arabs before the world . . . sick minds who are not part of humanity."

The Lebanese government expressed "deep regret" over the killing, but some Arab groups struck quite a different note.

From Cairo came a broadcast by the guerrilla radio Al Assifah. It blamed West German and Israeli authorities for the fatalities. The same theme was voiced by the Palestine Arab delegation at the United Nations in New York, which accused the Germans of "dirty and inhuman treachery" for "their assault on helicopters carrying the Palestine fedayeen and their Jewish hostages." In Cairo the semi-official newspaper Al Ahram said the terrorist attack was the desperate act of "people in a desperate condition."

President Nixon telephoned Israel's Premier Meir even before the full horror of the massacre had become known and said the terrorists were "international outlaws of the worst sort."

The U.N. Security Council was called into session and after considerable oratory came up with a resolution that mentioned only Israel's reprisal raids over Syria and Lebanon. The United States vetoed the measure because it made no mention of the Munich terror action that prompted those raids.

In Munich the big question was whether the games should continue. Finally, Avery Brundage, 84-year-old retiring president of the International Olympic Committee, declared that "the Games must go on."

One obvious reason for this was to deny the Arab terrorists the satisfaction of having halted the Olympics, but the Israeli government protested that the games should be halted while Israel mourned its dead. Many felt that the tragedy was of such magnitude that the games should have been called off.

Above, U.S. swimming star Mark Spitz surging ahead of Britain's Brian Brinkly to win fourth heat of the 200-meter butterfly. Below, Valery Borzov of the Soviet Union raising hands as he crossed the finish line to win the 100-meter dash. Right, British pentathalon star Mary Peters tossing the shotput to win her event.

Britain's John McLeod paddling through the Augsburg slalom course

The games had started on a high note of triumph for the Americans. Hardly had Spitz begun his spectacular winning streak than 16-year-old Sandra Nelson, from El Monte, Calif., beat Australia's highly touted Shane Gould, 15, in the 100-meter freestyle.

Later, the American team of Sandra and Shirley Babashof, 15, Jennifer Kemp and Jane Barkman swept to an arm's length win over a steady East German team in the 400-meter relay, in 3.55.19; a world record.

U.S. boxers under the tutelage of Coach Bobby Lewis won 10 of 11 bouts in the opening round of competition. The United States also scored well in wrestling, usually dominated by East European athletes. In one upset, Ben Peterson, 22, from Comstock, Wis., won a gold medal in the light-heavyweight class by pinning Bulgaria's Roussi Petrov.

Even before the tragedy struck at Munich, the spirit had changed. U.S. athletes bore the brunt of a number of unfavorable decisions.

The first involved Rick DeMont, 16-year-old distance swimmer from San Rafael, Calif., who had won the 400-meter freestyle by 1/100 sec. over Australia's Brad Cooper. Minutes before he was to swim in the finals of the 1,500-meter freestyle, DeMont was told he had been disqualified because an illegal medication epredrine, had been found in his urine specimen. The

ephedrine was a prescribed medication for DeMont, an asthmatic who had been taking it for years and had noted it on his Olympic form.

Another decision by Brundage's International Olympic Committee involved U.S. runners Vincent Matthews and Wayne Collett, both black. After capturing the gold and silver medals respectively in the 400-meter race, the two stood fidgeting and talking and turning away from the U.S. flag while the national anthem was being played. Both runners denied they had intended any specific protest, but the IOC labeled their behavior "disgusting" and barred them from any future Olympic competition.

But the most frustrating setback was suffered by the U.S. basketball team, which lost 51–50 to the Soviet Union, the first defeat of an American team since basketball became an Olympic sport in 1936. The Americans thought they had actually won 50–49 over the Russians, when the executive secretary of the amateur basketball federation decided that the game still had three seconds to go. He restarted it and the Soviets scored again. After bitter protests, the gold medal went to Moscow.

So ended the XX Olympiad. What was supposed to have been a sublime international event fostering the cause of peace, had been bespattered by a bloody massacre and torn by bureaucratic differences.

Bobby Fischer's Antics Put Chess on the Map

American champion attracted international interest with his brilliant performance and his outbursts of temperament

THEY POLITELY ignored the absence of Bobby Fischer at the opening ceremony of the World Chess Championship in Reykjavik, Iceland. Local dignitaries turned out in full force and speakers bowed both to Russian champion Boris Spassky and to the space beside him.

It was the first of several times the 29-year-old challenger would fail to keep a date at the "chess match of the century"—but the only time it would go unchided.

As hundreds of visitors to Iceland waited impatiently for Bobby, tempers rose and even presidential advisor Henry Kissinger urged the American chess star to get in there and fight.

When at last he did appear, Fischer's stock had plummeted, and many Westerners were rooting for Spassky.

Torn between a dislike of the media and a determination to see that "chess players aren't treated like bums," Fischer wound up with maximum publicity.

Stan Kohler

167

"For years the only ones talking were the Russians," Bobby complained, "and they weren't telling the truth. Now I realize the only way to make people understand is by making public my complaints."

But with his unfashionable singlemindedness and his unvarnished style, Fischer was a natural victim. The East-West confrontation became a good guy-bad guy tussle, with the Russian in the good role and the American in the headlines.

Fischer's insistence he was the "best around" was regarded as arrogance. Few doubted he was, but they felt he shouldn't say so. His fight to promote chess, the sporting world's poor relation, and to ensure his own future was viewed as simple greed.

"All these athletes making hundreds of thousands of dollars," he argued. "If there's room for all of them, there ought to be room for one of me."

The International Chess Federation (FIDE), the world's ruling chess body, had not expected a smooth ride. Fischer's insistence on impeccable playing conditions and his outspoken suspicion of Soviet chess masters—"a lying, cheating, hypocritical lot"—had snarled several tournaments. But no one believed the Brooklyn Star would jeopardize his career.

Trouble began months before the start of the match, with negotiations for a venue agreeable both to Spassky and Fischer, the first non-Soviet participant in the championship in 24 years of Russian monopoly of the title.

Since neither would play in the other's country, one possi-bility under FIDE rules, the match was put on the market. Fourteen bids were made, Reykjavik offering $125,000, Buenos Aires $150,000, and Belgrade $152,000.

A meeting of the principals was called for February in Amsterdam. Fischer showed, Spassky did not, and FIDE president Dr. Max Euwe ruled to split the 24 games between Reykjavik, Spassky's choice, and Belgrade, Fischer's choice.

Moscow grumbled at the decision, but accepted it. Fischer signed, but a month later scrapped the agreement. Alarmed, Belgrade withdrew its bid and Euwe relocated the match exclusively in Reykjavik. Fischer, faced with disqualification, submitted "under protest."

"There's no way to telecast the match from Iceland," he said. "That's why the Russians picked Reykjavik. They know they're going to lose the match, so they figured they might as well bury it," Fischer declared.

"But I'm not going to be psyched out of this. If I have to, I'll play somewhere I don't want to."

The Icelandic Chess Federation was faced with a task of gargantuan proportions. Reykjavik had no chess club or tournament hall, the ICF had no offices, and time was short.

Makeshift one-room headquarters were established at the back of a grocery store, a restaurant was converted to a chess club for the duration of the match, and a sports palace normally used for basketball became the playing hall, with a $17,000-dollar facelift.

A vast lighting canopy hung over the green-carpeted stage,

Fischer and Spassky met across the chess table (back in 1970) at world champsionship matches in Germany

Fischer making a point at a news conference

The first of many news conferences was called. Cramer tendered the information Bobby was having his pants pressed at that moment, but Moscow wanted written apologies.

Euwe, a tall, dignified Dutchman, apologized and promptly left Iceland. Cramer warned "Bobby never signs anything" and urged: "Let's get this show on the road. Euwe's condemnation of Bobby is going to look pretty silly to our grandchildren when they read the book of games."

The position appeared stalemated. Then, the challenger backed off. In a contrite abject apology to Spassky, "a gentleman and a sportsman," Fischer begged pardon for "my disgraceful behavior . . . my petty dispute over money."

On July 11, 10 days behind schedule, the tournament began, refereed by grandmaster Lothar Schmid, a West German.

To shore up its coffers, the ICF had sold exclusive movie and television rights to producer Chester Fox, a young New Yorker. After receiving assurances that the cameras would be out of sight and soundless, "just like candid camera," Fischer lifted a lifelong ban on filming.

For the first game, the cameras were mounted on burlap-covered towers behind the players' chairs. Schmid said Fischer turned "white as death" when he saw the setup, but nevertheless refused to eject the crew or transfer the game.

Complaining bitterly, Fischer played—and lost, after an elementary blunder. Weeks later, the head of the Icelandic film crew revealed that repairs made during the game had Fischer scowling over his shoulder.

"I knew it disturbed him," he said, "because he kept turning around. But it was inevitable."

Inevitable, too, was the rumpus that followed. Fischer refused to have any more dealings with Fox, and forfeited the second game—the first throwaway point in the history of the world championship. The situation was saved only when Schmid banned the film crew and allowed the third game to be played in a private room.

Fox filed a $1.75 million lawsuit against Fischer, "for intent to cause grave financial harm."

As the match progressed, Fischer kept up a steady stream of minor protests over noise in the cavernous 2,500-seat arena. Cramer, infuriated by Schmid's award of a forfeit point to Spassky, accused the German of "obstinacy and arrogance," and favoritism.

Schmid ordered uniformed and plainclothes police to patrol the hall for noisemakers. Guards were posted at the entrances to regulate the flow of spectators, and Schmid himself made appeals for "not a word, not even a whisper."

A new storm broke one wet Sunday, well into the second half of the match. Weekend strollers frustrated by the weather packed the hall, streaming in and out like visitors to an exhibition. Twice Fischer left the game to complain, and an aide warned: "There's going to be trouble."

In a stinging letter, Cramer argued that Schmid's efforts to silence disturbances bore witness to his "failure to ensure proper conditions." He demanded that Schmid "do something better than wave your hands from time to time."

The accusation, Schmid said, was "not nice."

"I am doing this as a favor for Bobby," he protested. "I see I need not do so. Mr. Cramer thinks I must spend all my time reading his letters. But I have other duties. This is not the normal way of doing things."

The next day, however, Schmid descended from the playing stage and anxiously scanned the rows of spectators.

"Bobby said there was someone snoring," he explained later, and sighing added: "But it is not always so easy to find the

leaving the stalls and balcony behind, like a theater, in total darkness. The seating area was as stark as a dentist's waiting room, hard-back chairs on concrete floor, and twice as cold.

Spassky arrived in Reykjavik two weeks before the scheduled start of the match, accompanied by his analyst, Efim Geller, and by Soviet grandmaster Nikolai Krogius, a psychology professor told to comb Fischer's games for flaws.

Icelanders rapidly warmed up to the champion, who was handsome and courteous.

A week later, Fischer cancelled his first plane reservation. Fred Cramer, the spokesman of the U.S. advance guard, admitted that the American player had "disappeared."

And then the word came from New York: A cut of the gate money, or no match. In a desperate bid to save the match, Euwe postponed the first game for two days. Simultaneously, London financier Jim Slater doubled the record purse.

"I gotta accept, it's stupendous," Fischer cried, and without more ado took off, accompanied by his second, The Rev. William Lombardy, a Roman Catholic priest.

On the morning of July 4, Fischer touched down at Keflavik airport, slipped past a welcoming party, ducked into his hotel room, and went to sleep.

That afternoon he failed to appear for the lot drawing ceremony, and Spassky walked out.

Cramer tried to deal with the mounting indignation. "How could Bobby be here?" he said. "We've only just put him to bed!"

Fischer was surrounded by newsmen when he arrived from Iceland at Kennedy Airport in New York

right man . . . Bobby is like a naughty child. He says 'Play it my way, or I'll take my ball away.' But he is not bad. His people should tell him to take it easy."

The champion rapidly fell behind, with errors experts said no competent club player should make. And as he eroded a two-point lead to trail three points, support for him grew, together with the conviction he had been browbeaten out of his top form.

The Russians maintained a dignified silence until the 17th game when they issued a statement suggesting that the Americans were cheating, using chemical and electronic aids to "unbalance Mr. B. Spassky and make him lose his fighting spirit."

Armed with x-ray machines, smear cloths and microscopes, a team of Icelandic scientists spent three days investigating the charges. They dismantled the players' chairs and examined the lighting and the chess table.

Two dead flies were found, and Fischer asked if there was to be an autopsy.

Not even Fischer's severest critics believed that his protests were part of a conscious campaign to unsettle the champion.

"He plays to win, to produce games that will last," said one grandmaster. "He would not stoop to win by psyching his opponent out of the game . . . Nor does he need to."

Spassky admitted that Fischer's truancy in the second game

had angered him, but he shrugged off his subsequent protests. "That's his problem, not mine," he said after the match. "I held him in my hand so many times, but I let him slip away. I did not have enough nervous strength."

However, unlike other Fischer opponents in the qualifying candidates' matches, Spassky did not crack under the strain of "Fischer-fear," but improved steadily to hold an edge in the final games, forcing a hard-fought run of seven draws.

Highpoint of the event was the 13th game—a two-day, nine-and-a-half hour, 72-move marathon, which the Russian blundered away in the final minutes.

As Fischer left the stage, Spassky sat down and dejectedly reset the pieces to the fatal 69th move. He reached out a hand and changed his play to the drawing line. Schmid helped him away.

Spassky lost the title in the 21st game and resigned by telephone. "Boris is without doubt the second finest player in the world," said Danish international master Jens Enevoldsen, sadly. "But he just hasn't got Bobby's taste for blood."

When the new champion emerged from his isolation after the match, journalists were surprised to find him affable, and talkative.

"Not such a bad chap," conceded a British interviewer. "You expect to loathe him, but then you find yourself liking him."

170

Freedom from Portuguese Domination Since 1882 Commemorated by Brazil

THE FLAG-DRAPED coffin of Emperor Pedro I, placed atop an amphibious armored troop carrier, moved slowly past the skyscrapers of Sao Paulo, Brazil's biggest city. At the national independence monument, President Emilio G. Medici and Portuguese Prime Minister Marcelo Caetano stood silently. A police band played Chopin's funeral march.

A century and a half after he freed Latin America's largest country, the emperor had been returned for final burial at the spot where, on Sept. 7, 1822, he had defied his father, the king of Portugal, by crying: "Independence or Death!"

"Just as we were benefited by the patriotism of those who won our independence, those who follow us should find a mature and powerful country, capable of contributing toward the solution of great and grave problems that affect the world," said President Medici, a 66-year-old ex-Army general, in a nationwide radio and TV address.

Only a few years ago such a statement probably would have been dismissed as typically overblown South American rhetoric. But by 1972 the world was taking a second look at the awakening of giant Brazil, where a determined effort was being made to overcome poverty and backwardness and to become a modern, respected nation.

The anniversary, celebrated in September 1972, came at a time when Brazil presented a surprise to outsiders who still were thinking of it in terms of such vague Latin stereotypes as samba dancers on the beach, coffee plantations and peasants riding burros or taking siestas. Brazil in 1972 was selling lathes to steelworks in Pittsburgh, alarm clocks to Switzerland, automobile engine blocks to South Africa, computer components to Britain and women's fashions to New York City department stores. All were products of Brazilian factories.

There still were lots of burros, coffee and samba dancers around this country of 100 million people, bigger in size than the continental United States. But more and more middle-class Brazilians matched their counterparts in the United States and Western Europe. They had new cars, color TV sets, beer in the refrigerators and shares in the stock market.

Once a nation that depended almost entirely on agriculture and had to import anything more complicated than a toothbrush, Brazil had overtaken Australia and Sweden in annual vehicle production and had drawn the attention of international financial experts by registering one of the highest sustained over-all economic growth rates in the world.

Roads, electric power lines and microwave TV channels were spiderwebbing the Brazilian interior at a record rate. The most ambitious project was the 3,350-mile Trans-Amazon Highway, designed to open up one of the world's last major frontiers. School enrollment and adult literacy had risen to record levels. The government had balanced the budget—after years of financial chaos—and encouraged citizens to pay taxes and put their money in banks.

Brazilian President Emilio G. Medici greeting Prime Minister Marcello Caetano of Portugal on his arrival for festivities in Sao Paulo

A federal congressman proposed that the line in the national anthem which described Brazil "lying eternally in its splendid cradle" be changed to something more positive.

"Today's Brazil is in a hurry," was how Brazilian journalist Murilo Melo Filho summed things up in his best seller, *The Brazilian Miracle.*

Thousands cheered during fireworks display in Sao Paulo

Despite these improvements, Brazil in 1972 remained—by world standards—an underdeveloped country. Millions of families continued to eke out livings at a subsistence level, on farms or in city slums. Because many rural Brazilians existed on barter and barely participated in the money economy, the nation's average per capita income was less than $500—about ⅛ that in the United States. Malaria, malnutrition and intestinal disease were still facts of life for large segments of the population.

Progress also was taking its toll on Brazil's 100,000 remaining primitive Indians, who were losing their traditional tribal lands to jungle highways and government-backed ranching and settlement projects.

"The economy may be doing well, but the majority of the people are doing badly," President Medici said in a speech.

Credit for trying to propel all of Brazil into the modern world went mainly to the military-led government that took over the country in 1964 from a Communist-leaning civilian administration. But the regime's economic reforms were accompanied by tough political controls.

The new government stripped thousands of its political opponents of their right to vote or hold office. More than a dozen traditional political parties were abolished in favor of two new ones: the official government party and a token opposition group. The federal Congress and several statehouses were temporarily closed. The regime purged universities of allegedly leftist professors, weakened the civilian court system, eliminated the power of labor unions and curtailed the people's basic civil rights in general.

The fanatically anticommunist armed forces and police killed, captured or exiled all the known left-wing guerrilla leaders in the country. Suspected subversives were arrested without warrants, held incommunicado and often tortured in jail.

The rough tactics were effective. As the year drew to an end, there had been no political kidnapings or successful plane hijacks in Brazil—in contrast to the terrorist activity of a few years earlier.

A powerful army general said in 1972 that attempts to soften the regime's toughness, take the military out of politics or do away with a 1968 decree that put near-dictatorial powers at the president's disposal were "useless."

Economically, Brazil won praise from many quarters, including the respected British financial publication, The Economist. U.S. Export-Import Bank President Henry Kearns took his hat off to Brazil's Finance Minister, Antonio Delfim Neto, saying: "We've got lots of confidence in a fellow who has done so many things right."

There was much worldwide criticism, however, of the Brazilian government's repressive political measures. Anti-Brazil propagandists, mostly young leftists, kept up a steady attack from Western Europe against the regime. Several U.S. senators favored giving Brazil an official cold shoulder and submitted bills seeking to cut off U.S. arms sales to the country.

Yet when Medici visited Washington in December 1971, President Nixon told him: "We know that as Brazil goes, so will go the rest of that Latin American continent." While other Latin countries were promoting Yankee-go-home demonstrations, capturing U.S. fishing boats and seizing U.S.-owned businesses, Brazil remained a close ally of the United States.

Brazil also cultivated closer economic and diplomatic ties with other areas. It gave development loans to small South American neighbors, such as Bolivia and Paraguay. It increased trade with the European Common Market and Japan. And it tried to become better friends with the emerging black countries of Africa. At the same time it expanded contacts with white supremacist South Africa and backed Portugal's efforts to keep control of its African holdings.

Brazil's outward progress and change did not much affect the traditional good nature, friendliness and tolerance of most Brazilians as individuals. The nation took pride in the fact it was a melting pot of whites, blacks, Orientals, Catholics, Protestants, voodoo cultists, Portuguese, Spaniards, Italians, Germans, Jews and Arabs.

Brazil still was a country where it was considered impolite to say "No" to someone directly. A Brazilian preferred to say: "It will be difficult."

Some Brazilian executives and government officials could still be found in 1972 playing volleyball on Copacabana Beach at 11 a.m. on a work day, while their secretaries downtown were telling callers: "I'm sorry. He's in a meeting now. Could you please phone again after lunch?"

Brazilians continued composing sambas and bossa novas for music lovers. Brazilian architecture—especially some of the ideas used in the construction of the new capital of Brasilia—provided inspiration for large-scale projects in many other countries.

Brazil had won the world soccer championship three times—a feat unequaled by any other team in the world. In 1972 a 25-year-old driver from Sao Paulo named Emerson Fittipaldi put Brazil on the automobile racing map by winning the world Formula-1 championship on difficult European grand prix circuits.

Despite the frantic boom, Brazilian officials closed the whole country down for four days every year for Carnival.

Brazil's Atlantic coast was discovered in 1500 by Portuguese

A colorful military parade was a highlight of the anniversary celebration

explorer Pedro Alvares Cabral. The colony's name derived from its abundance of brazilwood, then in demand for dye-making in Europe. The Dutch and the French tried to establish settlements in Brazil, but eventually they were overcome by Portuguese and native Brazilian forces. Adventuruous pioneers, known as "bandeirantes" or "flagbearers," then pushed westward into the new land's vast, unexplored interior in a successful quest for diamonds and gold.

Portuguese remained the country's national language—even though all the other Latin American Nations spoke Spanish. A soft, nasal language, Portuguese sounds a bit more French than Spanish.

The first serious attempt to make Brazil an independent country came in 1789. A revolutionary movement, led by a local dentist named Joaquim Jose da Silva Xavier, failed. The Portuguese government ordered Xavier—a Brazilian hero known today as Tiradentes, or "toothpuller"—executed.

Portuguese King Joao VI actually ruled the Portuguese empire from Brazil for several years, after fleeing across the Atlantic in 1808 as Napoleon's troops advanced on Lisbon. Returning to the mother country, Joao left his young son, Prince Pedro, behind as regent of Brazil.

Pressure for Brazilian independence mounted. King Joao ordered Pedro to return to Portugal. Early in 1822, Pedro, only 23 years old, cast his future with Brazil and told colonists "Fico."—"I'm staying."

After his famous "Independence or Death" proclamation, the young prince was crowned Emperor Pedro I of Brazil. Unlike its Spanish-speaking neighbors in the other half of South America, Brazil became an independent nation without bloodshed or war.

Pedro I remained only nine years on the throne. Critics said that he was temperamental and authoritarian, and that he kept too many native Portuguese in his court. The king abdicated in favor of his 5-year-old son and returned to Portugal, where he later ousted his brother Miguel from the royal palace and became King Pedro IV there.

Pedro I died and was buried in Portugal. After secret negotiations in 1971, the Portuguese government agreed to return the emperor's body to Brazil for final burial, to commemorate the 150th anniversary. Pedro's heart, however, remained in Portugal, in a glass jar in the city of Oporto.

In 1840, Brazil declared Pedro's son of age and crowned him emperor. As Pedro II he ruled for nearly 50 years.

In 1889 the emperor was overthrown without bloodshed—and a U.S.-style republican form of government was set up. In the 1930s and early 40s, popular dictator Getulio Vargas improved conditions for working people but wound up creating a neo-Fascist state in Brazil. Brazil, eventually entered World War II on the Allies' side. There were U.S. bases in Natal and Recife, and Brazil was the only South American country to actually send substantial numbers of troops to fight in Europe.

Vargas returned to power after the war, this time as a constitutionally elected president. He committed suicide in 1954. President Juscelino Kubitschek (1956–1961) started Brazil on the road to large-scale industrialization.

Kubitchek's successor, Janio Quadros, quit as president after just seven months in office. Vice President Joao Goulart took over, but on March 31, 1964, with inflation soaring, the armed forces kicked him out.

Medici became president in 1969. The top military chiefs picked him and then Congress "elected" him to a five-year term on a one-man ballot. Medici was the third military president of Brazil since the 1964 takeover.

Three U.S. Prisoners
of War Freed by Hanoi

*Overjoyed airmen, first Americans in Vietnam to be released
since 1969, escorted home by peace activists' committee*

Maj. Edward K. Elias and wife, Georgia, arriving at Maxwell Air Force Base in Montgomery, Ala.

A N AMERICAN MOTHER clasped her son and an American wife embraced her husband before glaring television lights in a simply furnished, dusty room in Hanoi. The unique ceremony, which took place Sept. 17 at the Peoples Army Headquarters, marked the release of three U.S. pilots shot down over North Vietnam.

The three fliers, plainly overjoyed on their new freedom, were neatly dressed in civilian clothing provided by their Communist captors. They were Navy Lt. Norris Charles, 27, whose wife Olga had flown from San Diego, Calif.; Navy Lt. Markham Gartley, 28, whose mother, Minnie Lee Gartley, had made the journey from Dunedin, Fla., and Air Force Maj. Edward Elias, 34, of Valdosta, Ga.

Pretty Olga Charles, who had had her hair set and washed in a Hanoi beauty shop before the ceremony, pushed impatiently through a wall of Vietnamese and European television technicians and cameramen to embrace her husband.

Minnie Lee Gartley, who had for four years picketed Congress and the White House for an end to the Indochina war, put her arms around her tall, blond son who had been a prisoner for four years. "He's even better looking than I remembered," she said. Elias' father, Barney, said in Jacksonville, Ill., that he, his wife and daughter-in-law had decided that it was "not in the best interests of all the POWs" for them to make the trip.

It was the first prisoner release by North Vietnam since 1969, and the pilots were only the fourth group of three to be freed by Hanoi. Shortly before their release the U.S. Defense Department had listed 539 Americans known to have been captured and held prisoner in Southeast Asia. However, more than 1,000 Americans were listed as missing and many of them were believed to be prisoners.

Elias, Charles and Gartley had been handed over to the custody of the Committee of Liaison, an antiwar coalition based in New York.

It began when the North Vietnamese called Mrs. Cora Weiss, a peace activist and member of the liaison committee, at her summer home in Martha's Vineyard, Mass., and said, "come to Paris."

In the French capital Mrs. Weiss and David Dellinger, her co-chairman of the committee, were told Sept. 2 the three men would be released. Upon their return to New York they began making arrangements for the trip. Tickets were booked through a friendly travel agency for Gartley's mother, Charles' wife, Mrs. Weiss, Dellinger and two other committee members, The Rev. William Sloane Coffin and Prof. Richard Falk.

It soon became apparent that the release of the prisoners was not the only thing Hanoi had in mind. When they arrived in Hanoi Sept. 16, the American party members were whisked off on a guided tour of scenes of destruction in Hanoi's suburbs, which North Vietnamese guides said were caused by U.S. bombing raids earlier in the year.

As the party stumbled over twisted courtyards and pieces of broken concrete walls and roof at one damaged site, an East European radio reporter thrust a microphone at Mrs. Gartley and said, "What do you think of all this?"

"I hate to see destruction like this, whoever might do it," she replied.

Mrs. Charles and Mrs. Gartley were told that the three POWs about to be released had been given the same tour after being brought out of their prison camps.

Finally, Mrs. Gartley protested when Hanoi officials planned

Navy Lt. Norris Charles listening to U.S. Charge d'Affaires Adolph Dubs in Moscow

a trip to the port of Haiphong, reportedly devastated by B52 strikes in April. She told her hosts she was tired.

"I came here all this way to get Mark home in good health, and by golly I'll do it," she said later.

The freed POWs adjusted quickly to their new life. After the 40-minute release ceremony at which each made a brief statement, they were driven to the Hoa Binh Hotel, where a banquet of Vietnamese sweetmeats, spring rolls, pork and cabbage and other Asian delicacies awaited them.

Mrs. Weiss proposed a toast in a sweet Vietnamese cordial provided by their hosts. Then, raising a glass of scotch provided by a newsman, Charles said: "I want to make a toast to the good people of America who brought this about."

The day after their release the three airmen and the rest of the party strolled around Hanoi, while hundreds of North Vietnamese watched in silent curiosity. The crowd did not seem antagonistic.

Later at dinner Mrs. Weiss said to the fliers, "Could you imagine Japanese pilots walking free in New York City after the bombing of Pearl Harbor?"

The pilots spoke freely to newsmen of their detention, which totaled four years for Gartley, eight months for Charles and five months for Elias. Gartley said the food was adequate, and the general policy in the camps where he had been detained was acceptable.

"We were not penalized in any way when the bombing of North Vietnam was resumed," he said.

Charles and Elias said they were well treated.

A few days later the tension began to rise and a propaganda struggle developed over the released men. As the three men became increasingly restless and anxious to return home, North Vietnamese officials continued checking health cards and preparing departure formalities. On Sept. 22 Cora Weiss cabled President Nixon her intention to take the men back to the United States in a civilian plane, declaring that this was the desire of the North Vietnam government. She insisted that, unless the release went as planned, future releases of prisoners would be jeopardized.

Back in the United States, relatives of the pilots reacted to

Navy Lt. Mark Gartley comforting his mother after military authorities told her he could not leave at once on a vacation

the delay with disappointment and resentment. When the three failed to show up in the Laotian capital of Vientiane aboard a Soviet Aeroflot airliner Sept. 23 as expected, anxiety mounted.

The handling of the release by a civilian organization also brought frowns in official Washington. Secretary of Defense Melvin R. Laird said, "I certainly would recommend these men turn themselves, as soon as possible, over to their military command." He condemned North Vietnam for "using the families of these prisoners of war as propaganda tools."

On Sunday night, Sept. 24, the three fliers messaged President Nixon that they were in good health, but said they intended to return all the way home with their civilian escorts.

On Sept. 25 the fliers finally left Hanoi for Communist China aboard a Chinese airliner on the first leg of their journey. Two days later they boarded a Soviet Aeroflot and pushed on to Moscow, where they expressed concern for the future release of other prisoners and refused an official American offer of aid. They then proceeded to Copenhagen and, on Sept. 27, embarked on the final lap after again refusing an offer of military transport.

The scene in Moscow airport had been chaotic. American Embassy officials had stood chest to chest with the antiwar organization members in what at times deteriorated into an angry confrontation. At one point U.S. Charge d'Affaires Adolph Dubs strode up to Charles and demanded: "Identify yourself." But Charles did not even hear him as the reporters closed in.

In Copenhagen it was quieter and more orderly. An American Air Force Medical evacuation plane stood on the ramp when the fliers arrived, and its use was offered to the party by U.S. Charge D'affaires Thomas Dunnegan. Gartley responded, "We appreciate your concern, but we feel that going back this way is the best thing."

The party arrived in New York Sept. 28 aboard a Scandinavian Airlines System transatlantic jetliner. The men had changed to military garb en route from Copenhagen to New York. Elias said that he felt the three had fulfilled the conditions of release laid down by Hanoi and that henceforth he intended to follow U.S. military authorities.

This prompted Cora Weiss to declare that she and other members of the party had been deceived by Elias, who she said had indicated antiwar sentiments in Hanoi but changed his attitude once they departed.

The climax of the drama came when the plane landed at New York's John F. Kennedy International Airport and about 20 Washington officials and military officers led by Dr. Roger Shields, the Pentagon's chief specialist on prisoner of war affairs, swept aboard the aircraft. The group told the three airmen that they were to be taken to military hospitals at once. This triggered an outburst from Mrs. Gartley, whose son had already asked for a two-day leave.

"We just want him to ourselves, free of the Government, free of the Navy, free of the press, free of the North Vietnamese, and now we're not going to get him."

Several days later, to the general surprise, all three airmen were released to go home to their families.

Meanwhile, more Americans were still falling into enemy hands, and Hanoi officials issued a warning: no more men would be freed until an agreement was reached on ending the war.

"It is logical," said Xuan Thuy, North Vietnam's negotiator at the Paris talks "If the war continues you cannot expect us to free more pilots who have bombed us."

DATA RETURNED BY VENUS PROBE

Lofted from Soviet soil on March 27, the 2,600-pound spacecraft Venus 8 deposited its descent capsule on Venus four months later. Then, on Sept. 9, Russian scientists announced the first fruits of the mission: a detailed description of the chemical composition of the planet's surface.

Before it disintegrated under the tremendous heat and pressure on Venus, the capsule transmitted information back to Earth for 50 minutes. Scientists interpreted the signals as showing that the surface of Venus at the point sampled resembled granite rocks of the type found on Earth.

Other data sent back indicated that sunlight does penetrate to the surface through the dense cloud cover.

Instruments aboard Venus 8 placed the temperature on the planet at a withering 880 degrees Fahrenheit and the pressure about 90 times the atmospheric pressure on the surface of the earth, which is about 14.7 pounds per square inch.

The findings, hailed in the West as an impressive technological exploit, amplified those made by the previous probe, Venus 7. Data sent back by the Soviet instrument package indicated that the extreme temperatures and pressures on the day side of Venus, where Venus 8 landed, were not significantly different from those measured by earlier Russian probes on the night side.

Above, fire which swept a fashionable restaurant on the Greek island of Rhodes killed 31 persons. Below, LOOK ALIKES—Foreign Ministers Abba Eban of Israel and Maurice Schumann of France meeting in New York.

ICE CREAM PARLOR HIT BY JET, KILLING 22, MOSTLY CHILDREN

The blue and gold jet—a relic of the Korean war—roared down the runway at Sacramento's Executive Airport. But bystanders said the vintage warplane, which had taken part in a California air show on Sunday, Sept. 24, appeared to lose power as the pilot tried to get it off the ground.

Moments later the veteran F86 Sabrejet struck an old river levee barrier beyond the end of the runway and hurtled across a four-lane highway into a shopping center parking lot. Slamming into three automobiles parked in front of an ice cream parlor, the plane burst into flames.

Alan King who had been watching the air show with his son, witnessed the disaster. "I saw the nose drop and it hit," he said. "A wing tank exploded. The plane skidded across the road, and when it hit the ice cream parlor it just exploded into the air in a ball of fire."

Dragging two of the autos with it, the blazing plane rammed through the front of the sweets shop jammed with about 100 children and their parents, many celebrating birthday parties, a speciality of the establishment.

When the holocaust was over, 22 persons lay dead, at least 10 of them youngsters. Twenty-six others, mostly children, were injured. The pilot, Richard Bingham, 36, of Novato, Calif., survived.

Seventeen kids were celebrating at a table by the big front window, wearing party hats and surrounded by favors and plates of ice cream and candy, when the plane struck.

"The plane took one wall where the 17 kids were and just pushed it," said Dave Thornton, who had rushed to the scene from a nearby bowling alley. "They were all in a big pile. It just pushed them."

Most of the casualties occurred in the front of the store, where the burning plane hit. Some of those in the rear didn't realize at first what had happened.

A 12-year-old girl said she thought it was all a "gimmick" to promote a special ice cream sundae that was being featured. "Then everyone started screaming and running."

Thornton said a fellow bowler "grabbed a pair of wire cutters, ran 300 yards to the crash site, smashed open the cockpit of the plane and pulled the pilot out."

"When the pilot went in he must have pulled his parachute cord, because he was all tangled up in the parachute. . . ." Thornton said.

Thornton said the pilot was sobbing as he was hauled from the flaming wreckage and kept saying; "I'm sorry! I'm sorry!"

Firemen reach the scene where a private plane crashed into an ice cream parlor

ARMY CLOSES MY LAI CASE

Nearly 4½ years after the so-called My Lai massacre, the Army in effect closed its books on the episode Sept. 2, after issuing administrative penalties to two officers and a sergeant.

Col. Nelson A. Parson, 51, chief of staff of the Americal Division at the time of the March 16, 1968, incident in South Vietnam, was stripped of the Legion of Merit and given a letter of censure *(The World in 1969, 257)*. Capt. Dennis H. Johnson, 36, an intelligence officer in the division,

was given a letter of reprimand. And S. Sgt. Kenneth L. Hodges, 27, a squad leader at the time, was to be discharged and barred from reenlistment. Hodges filed a Federal Court suit protesting his ouster.

The Army said the penalties, announced by Secretary of the Army Robert F. Froehlke, cleared its books on the My Lai incident, except for review of the court-martial conviction of Lt. William Calley. Calley had been sentenced to 20

years imprisonment in connection with the deaths of 22 civilians at My Lai *(The World in 1971, 67–72)*.

A total of 25 officers and enlisted men had been charged by the Army with either actual involvement in the affair or with covering it up after it happened. Of these, five were acquitted by courts martial, charges against 19 were dismissed and it was only Calley who was convicted.

A recently discovered photograph of Adolph Hitler posing with a little girl

HITLER: TWO MEN IN ONE BODY?

As if one Adolf Hitler weren't enough, a psychological study of the Nazi leader published some 29 years after it was written revealed two Hitlers "that inhabit the same body and alternate back and forth."

The deep probe into Hitler's Jekyll-and-Hyde-type mind was made in 1943 by Dr. Walter C. Langer in an effort to help the Allies understand what made their World War II enemy run.

The study, long secret but later declassified, was published in September 1972 as the main part of the book, *The Mind of Adolf Hitler.*

Langer, who read widely and interviewed many persons who had known Hitler for his study, wrote of the two Hitlers that the one "is a very soft, sentimental and indecisive individual who has very little drive and wants nothing quite so much as to be amused, liked and looked after. The other is just the opposite—a

hard, cruel and decisive person with considerable energy—who seems to know what he wants and is ready to go after it and get it regardless of cost.

"It is the first Hitler who weeps profusely at the death of his canary, and the second Hitler who cries . . . 'Heads will roll.' It is the first Hitler who cannot bring himself to discharge an assistant, and it is the second Hitler who can order the murder of hundreds, including his best friends. . . .'"

Langer, who predicted that "as Germany suffers successive defeats, Hitler will become more and more neurotic," arrived at his conclusions about the dictator by applying Freudian analytic techniques to what was known of Hitler's life and behavior and then comparing his data with clinical histories of patients with similar "behavior patterns, tendencies and sentiments."

ELDERLY JAPANESE HONORED

The Japanese have an annual national holiday called Keiro No Hi, or "Day of Respect for the Aged." Some 15,000 elderly Japanese gathered in Tokyo Sept. 15 to mark the day as well as to air their grievances—common to senior citizens in some other nations.

With a survey showing that 32 per cent of the elderly lived on a subsistence level, the senior citizens demanded larger pensions and retirement allowances, cheaper medical care, better housing—a better standard of living.

After the demands were made the crowd was entertained with folk dancing and singing. Then the 156 women and 41 men who had reached the age of 100 in the past year were given a silver cup and a letter from Premier Kakuei Tanaka.

TONSURE NO LONGER MANDATORY

About 1,400 years ago, the Roman Catholic Church began the custom of shaving the crown of an ecclesiastic to prepare his way for the priesthood. And up to modern times, monks and friars in some religious orders continued to wear only a circle of hair around their shaven pates.

Then, on Sept. 14, 1972, Pope Paul VI ordered abolition of the tonsure unless the aspirant layman wanted it that way.

In recent years many ecclesiastics had given up their tonsure and let their hair grow as soon as they had been ordained and left the seminary. In fact, churchmen suggested privately that the Pontiff and his advisors might have felt that the tonsure was keeping some young men from studying for the priesthood in an age of elaborate male hairstyles.

In the wake of the papal edict, the Vatican newspaper L'Osservatore Romano noted that the tonsure, once a symbol of "Abandonment of the world" had almost completely lost that significance and had become an empty ceremony.

It was recalled that in recent years, bishops in some dioceses had only snipped the hair of new seminarians, although in other areas future priests had still been expected to keep a full tonsure throughout their studies.

Church officials expressed belief that henceforth clergymen could continue the practice of tonsure either with a symbolic snip or a major clipping.

The Pope's reform decreed that entrance into the clerical state or membership in the ecclesiastical hierarchy took place with ordination as a deacon.

The Pontiff ruled that conferral of the first tonsure which used to mark this event was to be replaced with a new rite "by which one who aspires to the diaconate or priesthood publicly manifests his will to offer himself to God and the church."

In a second document reforming the church ministry below the priesthood Pope Paul maintained the age-old ban on women in any ministerial role.

The apostolic letter reconfirmed that married men could serve as permanent deacons—assistants to priests—and ruled that, "in accordance with the venerable tradition of the church," women remained excluded from any form of ministry.

179

MONTREAL MUSEUM ART STOLEN

"They did show quite discriminating taste . . . in terms of paintings, though as far as the objects were concerned they could do with more art and historical training."

This appraisal by Bill Bantey, public relations director of the Montreal Museum of Fine Arts, referred to three hooded robbers who broke in through a museum skylight on Sept. 4 and stole 18 paintings and 39 art objects valued at $2 million. The haul included a $1 million Rembrandt.

The burglars made interesting selections: a pair of Corots, a pair of Breughel landscapes, paintings by Courbet, Daumier and Gainsborough.

The thieves made their entry before dawn, overpowering three guards, and escaped with the loot.

The Rembrandt was a 10-by-15-inch oil on a wood panel entitled *Landscape with Cottage*. The Dutch master painted it in 1654. Since all 750 Rembrandt paintings around the world are well catalogued, museum officials said, it would be difficult to dispose of such a painting.

Officials said the thieves probably would have taken more art from the museum if one of them had not tripped the alarm as they left with the first load.

"They had stacked about 18 other paintings and left behind far more important works than they took," said Bantey.

MANY LOST IN CLUB FIRE

Some 200 persons were enjoying a night out in the upstairs room of Montreal's two-story Blue Bird Club—a popular spot offering country and Western music—when suddenly "there was lots of pitch black smoke, then a lot of heat, and then a lot of yellow light."

As the fire spread many patrons made their way to a fire escape whose railing broke under the weight, dropping some of them to the street. "By the time I reached it," George Lancia recalled, "there were several bodies lying on and draped over the fire escape, people who had fainted, I think.

"The crowds trying to get out just trampled right over the bodies. Then all of a sudden the bannister . . . gave way and people started falling. One woman smashed the side of her head on the concrete."

Mr. and Mrs. James Robson said they were waiting to get to the upper floor when they saw a ball of fire behind them and a man running down the stair. "We tried to run after him but there was a wall of fire between us that kept us from following," Mrs. Robson said. The couple went out a fire escape, she said, adding that "when we got outside the flames had spread so fast they had trapped I don't know how many girls in the women's washroom."

One policeman said the Sept. 1 blaze—which claimed 37 lives and injured more than 50 persons—engulfed the whole place within two or three minutes.

Some of the dead, a police spokesman said, were "in a corner that had no exit. They were huddled on the ground, holding on to each other like scared children."

Police said they believed the fire was started when "about a gallon" of gasoline was spread on the club's stairway and touched off. They said the flames swept through the building shortly after three men had been ejected from the club.

This giant chess board paved in the main square of the Italian town of Marostica is used by present day players to repeat the moves of noblemen competing for the hand of the daughter of the lord of the manor 500 years ago

FOR THE RECORD

AGREED. By the governments of West Germany and Poland, to open embassies in each other's capitals and to improve relations. The Sept. 14 agreement formalized a 1970 treaty of normalization signed by the two governments.

PURCHASED. By Communist China, ten American-built Boeing 707 airliners worth about $150 million. The purchase from Boeing followed closely Peking's decision to order three British-French Concorde supersonic airliners.

An Egyptian soldier manning a lookout position beside the Suez Canal near its southern end →

October

Peace Efforts Set Back in Middle East Impasse

A glimmer of hope followed expulsion from Egypt of Russia's advisors but this was canceled by guerrilla violence

WHILE LONG-TIME ADVERSARIES in other parts of the world sat down together in 1972 to try to resolve differences, the Arabs and Israel, two antagonists with a 24-year legacy of mutual fear and mistrust, remained far apart on a settlement to bring permanent peace to the Middle East. Although hopes for a settlement glimmered faintly after President Anwar Sadat's dramatic expulsion of thousands of Russian military advisers from Egypt, peace efforts suffered fresh setbacks at the hands of Palestinian guerrillas.

The U.S.-sponsored cease-fire of August 1970 endured for another year, broken only by occasional dogfights over the war-blocked Suez Canal.

But Lebanon, the only country bordering Israel that did not take part in the Six Day War of 1967, and radical Syria came under repeated ground and air attack as Israel pressed its campaign to stamp out the Arab guerrilla movement.

King Hussein of Jordan seemed increasingly inclined to become the only Arab leader to make peace with Israel. He put forth a bold plan for a Palestinian state in his kingdom that the Israelis suggested could serve as a basis for negotiation.

But peace seemed remote after the tragedy at the Munich Olympics. An angry and frustrated Israel vowed war to the bitter end against terrorists and the governments that support them.

The door to a search for peace was not closed, but Premier Golda Meir said Israel had "no choice but to strike at the terrorist organizations wherever our long arm can reach them," without waiting for an attack.

Despite this, statesmen were convinced the passions inflamed by Munich would subside and the Middle East would return to the uncertain but not unpromising state it was in before the Olympic tragedy.

"We believe the forces favoring a peaceful settlement still have the upper hand," U.S. Secretary of State William Rogers told the U.N. General Assembly.

"Our task is to do everything possible to see they are supported," he said. "The no-peace-no-war situation which prevails now does not and will not serve the interest of anyone in the area."

What gave statesmen cause for hope was President Sadat's decision in July ordering up to 15,000 Russian military advisers out of Egypt.

He charged the Soviet Union was an "overcautious" ally who would not provide Egypt with the advanced aircraft and missiles needed for another war with Israel.

The swift departure of the Russians from Egypt was the most significant development in the Middle East in 1972 because it decreased the danger of big powers being drawn into a new round of Arab-Israeli fighting.

The Russian departure also affected U.S.-Soviet rivalry in the Mediterranean, depriving the Russians of bases for aircraft that shadowed the 6th Fleet. They retained repair facilities at Egyptian ports.

It was the Kremlin's biggest setback since the 1950s when the Soviet Union first began expanding its influence in the Middle East in fulfillment of Czarist dreams. To compensate, Moscow stepped up efforts to consolidate its position at the northern end of the Arab World in Syria and Iraq.

Egypt was no match for Israel without Soviet help so, with the possibility of war substantially reduced, Israel responded quickly. In her first personal appeal to the Egyptian leader, Mrs. Meir called on Sadat to "meet as equals" to make peace.

She added in a speech to the Knesset, or parliament, "It would seem that this hour in the history of Egypt can, indeed should, be the appropriate hour for change and if it truly is the hour for change let it not be missed."

It was. Egypt repeated its long standing objection to direct talks without an Israeli commitment to withdraw from occupied territories. Israel's view is that talks without preconditions are necessary to establish recognized boundaries. Deadlock.

During a brief stop in the Middle East in July Secretary of State Rogers asked at a news conference, "Why not? Why shouldn't these talks be direct? Other parties have been obliged to meet and start a dialogue," he said referring to talks in 1972 between the two Koreas, East and West Germany and India and Pakistan.

But on the Arab side it seemed no one was listening to Rogers anymore. The peace mission of U.N. Middle East envoy Gunnar Jarring also was stalled.

After getting the two sides to agree to a cease-fire, Rogers worked to promote "proximity talks," or separate meetings between Egypt and Israel in the same hotel with an intermediary. The goal was an interim settlement that would reopen the Suez Canal and involve some Israeli withdrawal in Sinai.

Despite bellicose statements about the inevitability of war, Egypt was interested in such talks. Then as the year began, the United States let it be known it was resuming shipments of F4 Phantoms and Skyhawk jets to Israel.

The shipments had been suspended since June 1971 and relations between Washington and Jerusalem had become frosty. Arab officials saw the decision as reflecting American preoccupation with the presidential election campaign and wrote off any U.S. initiatives in the Middle East until it was over.

Israel eventually agreed to proximity talks, but by now President Sadat felt betrayed and bitterly declared he would have nothing more to do with the United States.

During a four-hour speech in which he told Egypt's only permitted political party, the Arab Socialist Union, why the

Children in Lebanese village of Kafra examining wreckage of their school building after a raid

Russians had to go, Sadat heaped scorn on U.S. officials and asserted that while Egypt and Russia were "just friends," Israel was an "instrument of American imperialism."

By removing the Russians, never much liked in Egypt, Sadat shored up his badly sagging image at home and gained more time to maneuver. His "year of decision"—1971—had produced no decisions. Early in 1972 university students in Cairo took to the streets in the first such demonstration in four years.

Their message seemed to be "make peace, make war but do something" and "tell us the truth."

Sadat had other problems. There was labor unrest. Old guard revolutionaries were grumbling. The middle class was unhappy with austerity measures instituted by the new Premier, Aziz Sidky, to get the country on a war footing.

More important, friction was building up in the army at all levels between Egyptians and their Russian advisers. One Russian general was expelled in 48 hours after he had impugned Egyptian manhood in a joke that eventually reached the ears of the popular army commander and War Minister, Lt. Gen. Mohammed Sadek.

In May, the United States and the Soviet Union carried detente between the superpowers a step farther and relegated the Middle East to a secondary level among their problems. Long promised arms did not turn up despite Sadat's three trips to Moscow. With pressure building, it was time to move, "time for a shock," as Sadat later told a friend.

With the Russians gone, Egypt was without a policy. It began planning a diplomatic campaign to get Western European countries more involved in peace efforts but the efforts foundered after Black September terrorists struck at Munich.

Named for the month in 1970 when King Hussein broke the back of the guerrilla movement in Jordan, Black September, as secret as other groups were visible in Arab capitals, had struck first late in 1971 on the steps on a Cairo hotel, assassinating Jordan Prime Minister Wasfi Tell, arch foe of the guerrillas.

Then the group hijacked a Belgian airliner on its way to Israel May 8. When the plane landed at Tel Aviv's Lod airport, they demanded release of 200 Palestinians in Israeli jails, the same demand they would make four months later in Munich.

With 100 passengers on the plane, Israeli Defense Minister Moshe Dayan decided to wait out the hijackers. The next day, Israeli troops disguised as mechanics stormed aboard, killing two men hijackers. A woman passenger later died of wounds received in the assault.

Two other skyjackers, both women, were captured and later sentenced to life in prison.

Crying foul, guerrillas vowed in statements that "next time there will be no mistakes."

In a show of solidarity, the Popular Front for the Liberation of Palestine, the airline hijack specialists, sent an assassination squad of Japanese youths to Lod airport three weeks later.

Carrying suitcases loaded with Czech-made assault rifles and

hand grenades, the three aroused little suspicion as they boarded Air France Flight 132 for Tel Aviv.

The plane touched down at Lod about 10 o'clock on a balmy spring night. The terminal was filled with other arriving passengers, including many Puerto Rican pilgrims and visitors.

After their luggage arrived, the Japanese opened their suitcases, quickly pulled out the weapons and opened point blank automatic fire and threw grenades on the floor. Twenty-six persons were killed and more than 80 wounded.

Tom Golden, who was waiting to meet his mother, said, "I cannot describe how horrible it was. I also don't know how we survived. People were killed all around us. One of the gunmen was 15 feet from us as he sprayed a group of helpless people nearby."

The surviving terrorist Kozo Okamoto ran from the terminal and threw two grenades at airliners parked on the tarmac with the idea of throwing himself in the flaming wreckage.

But he failed, was overpowered and captured by an airline employe. Okamoto's two accomplices died in the attack, apparently by their own weapons.

An army court later found Okamoto guilty and sentenced him to life in prison. He showed no emotion until he learned he had not received the desired death penalty—then he sighed deeply.

More than half the dead were Puerto Ricans arriving for a long planned tour of the Holy Land. Another victim was Israel's famed biophysicist, Professor Aharon Katzir-Katchalsky.

In Japan there was anguish and incredulity. "Could Japanese

Left, Israeli aeronautical students positioning a homebuilt rocket carrying a supersonic missile. Below, handcuffed to his guards, Japanese student Kozo Okamoto, went on trial for his role in the Lod airport massacre. Right, Israeli soldier armed with automatic weapon and bazooka leaped across a ditch in the occupied Goland Heights of Syria

really do such a thing?" asked Premier Eisaku Sato on hearing the news. Japan's foreign minister personally apologized at the Israeli embassy and promised compensation for families of the victims.

Arab reaction was different, with the exception of King Hussein, who branded the attack "a sick crime committed by sick people and planned by sick minds," almost the same words he would use to deplore the Munich tragedy.

The Arabs cited incidents of Jewish terrorism that helped create Israel and the injustices suffered by the Palestinian people, 1.5 million of them crammed into refugee camps in countries bordering what was once their homeland, dependent on international charity and the whims of Arab governments that used them as pawns. The reaction was similar after Munich.

Immoral? "Not at all," snapped a Front spokesman who said the two Sabena hijackers' deaths had been avenged. "There is a war going on in Palestine. People should realize that."

In the Knesset, Mrs. Meir blamed Lebanon, accusing it of "openly enabling centers of the terrorist organizations to reside in their midst."

This was true. The guerrillas had offices in Beirut. But as a result of increasing restrictions on their military operations from Lebanon and Syria, the radical groups and secret organizations such as the Popular Front and Black September made common cause with similar groups aboard, especially in Germany. Europe thus became a new arena of the Middle East crisis in 1972.

Lebanon, whose government had learned it could only move against the guerrillas at the risk of a political crisis that threatened the delicate Christian-Moslem balance, braced for another attack.

After a four-day Israeli incursion in February, the Lebanese army began exerting more control in the border area for the first time in three years and guerrillas for the most part moved out of villages but still maintained bases in the Arkoub, on the slopes of Mt. Hermon. The Israelis dubbed this area "Fatahland" for the name of the largest guerrilla group.

Israeli jets screamed in on June 21 hitting two villages and leaving 14 civilians and at least 30 guerrillas dead. Israeli officials later admitted that one village had been bombed by pilot error.

In one of the most spectacular intelligence coups since the 1967 war, the Israelis also captured five high-ranking Syrian intelligence officers, a brigadier general and four colonels, who were touring the border area with a Lebanese escort officer the day of the raid.

Lebanon protested to the U.N. Security Council which condemned Israel for its "repeated attacks," the United States abstaining. Israel had become accustomed to ignoring U.N. resolutions which it considered one-sided. Gen. Dayan said Israel would put more emphasis on anticommando operations.

The Lebanese and the guerrillas reached yet another face saving agreement in which attacks across the border were to be suspended. The country settled down for a quiet and it hoped profitable summer catering to tourists.

Calm was shattered July 8 when Ghassan Kanafani, the spokesman for the Popular Front for the Liberation of Palestine, and his 15-year-old niece were killed when a booby trap exploded in his car in Beirut. Later in July two Palestinian officials were blinded by letter bombs and others sent to guerrilla leaders were intercepted in Beirut.

The Israelis were blamed but officials in Jerusalem said "nonsense." There were suggestions intraguerrilla feuds may have played a part.

Then came Munich, so devastating in effect because few expected the Palestinian extremists to be so callous. But the Olympics were a logical target for a movement that had made its reputation disrupting international air traffic.

The morning after the Black September terrorists attacked the Israeli team's quarters, the Voice of Palestine Radio said from Damascus, "All glory to the men of September. We were not known in Munich before you. The gold medal you have won at Munich is for the Palestine nation."

Black September also warned West Germany it would deal "a heavy blow" if the three surviving guerrillas were not released, a promise that was made good Oct. 29 when a Lufthansa jetliner was hijacked, the second time the guerrillas had taken over a German jet in 1972.

Threatening to blow up the plane and 20 persons aboard, the skyjackers circled over Zagreb, Yugoslavia while West German officials brought the released men from Munich. The jet landed to take them aboard, then headed for Libya where they were greeted as heroes and the passengers and crew were freed.

After Munich, Israel was seething with anger. A day after the 11 slain athletes were buried, Israeli jets roared over targets in Lebanon and Syria in the heaviest raid since the 1970 cease-fire.

Lebanon reported 16 civilian dead and more than 50 wounded. Syria said casualties exceeded 150 and sought condemnation of the attack by the U.N. Security Council.

When the council met Sept. 10 to approve a resolution calling for cessation of all military operations in the Middle East without mentioning the violence that provoked them, the United States cast its second veto in the history of the council.

Arab commentators said the veto gave Israel the green light to strike again. On Sept. 16 an armored brigade rumbled into Lebanon, advancing deeper than ever before on a 32-hour search and destroy raid. For the first time the Lebanese army put up resistance. The government in Beirut declared a state of emergency.

Once again guerrilla and government leaders met, this time under pressure of an army ultimatum to the commandos. Yet another agreement was reached to get the guerrillas out of the south but dissident groups again said they would not abide by it.

A month later the Israelis were back, this time flying in from the Mediterranean without apparent provocation to hit suspected guerrilla bases in four areas, including a garage 24 miles from Beirut.

The aftermath of Munich also produced an epidemic of letter bombs in September and October and the deaths of an Israeli embassy official in Brussels and a Palestinian working at the Libyan embassy in Rome.

The first wave of letter bombs, mailed from Amsterdam, were aimed at Israelis and one took the life of an agricultural attache in London. In late October bombs mailed from Belgrade and addressed to Palestinian officials blew up in three Arab countries, injuring six persons.

There were other developments in 1972 that had a direct or indirect bearing on the Middle East crisis.

After nine months of negotiations in the Middle East, Europe and New York five Arab oil-producing countries reached an historic agreement Oct. 5 with Western, mostly American-owned, oil companies on an eventual 51 per cent share in their operations by 1983.

Saudi Arabian Petroleum Minister Ahmed Zaki Yamani, who represented the Arab side, proposed in a speech that oil from his country be given "a special place" in American markets by being allowed in duty free. He also proposed that Saudi Arabia be allowed to invest in the U.S. oil industry down to the operating of gasoline stations across the nation.

The participation agreement—an alternative to nationalization—and Yamani's proposal came amid increasing talk of an "energy crisis" in the United States in the next decade. Studies show that by 1980 at least one-third of U.S. fuel needs will have to be met with oil from Arab countries.

Some analysts suggested that the United States might have to temper its domestic electoral interests to its long term fuel interests. This suggestion implied that there should be less support for Israel and therefore greater pressure to reach a settlement.

In March, King Hussein proposed establishing a new autonomous region of Palestine under his throne, comprising the Israeli-held West Bank and "any other Palestinian territories to be liberated," a reference to the Gaza Strip which Egypt administered until 1967.

During the summer a record number of Arabs crossed the Jordan River into Israeli-held areas to visit relatives in the continuing process of detente. Hussein pressed his case with Arab notables from the West Bank and the strip who visited him in Amman.

Israel at first scorned the proposals, charging they were based on unreal assumptions. Any other reaction would have unleashed Arab fury against the monarch and lent credence to recurring reports of secret meetings between Hussein and Israeli leaders.

But the Israelis were interested and there was discussion in the cabinet about which Arab state, Jordan or Egypt, to concentrate on in efforts to reach peace.

Other Arab leaders were outraged at Hussein's plan. Assembled in Cairo in April, the guerrilla-dominated Palestine National Council roared approval as President Sadat announced Egypt was retaliating by breaking diplomatic relations with Jordan, the third Arab state to do so.

Later, after the Munich massacre had embarrassed Egypt and soured European-Arab relations, Sadat tried to get the Palestinians in line by proposing that they form a government in exile. But the idea was rejected by the disarrayed guerrilla movement.

Egypt also embarked on another experiment in Arab unity, a merger with Libya to be completed within a year. But even if the new state comes into being, it will have little effect on the strategic balance with Israel. With unhappy memories of the three-year union with Syria, many Egyptians are skeptical of the Libya merger. And there was the possibility present leaders of both countries might not be around to consummate the unification.

Two other Arab states, North and South Yemen, located on the southwest corner of the Arabian peninsula, also agreed to unite after reaching agreement in October to end two months of border fighting.

Influenced by its oil wealthy neighbor Saudi Arabia, North Yemen had adopted a more conservative line in recent years. It became the first Arab state to restore diplomatic relations with the United States, broken during the 1967 war. Secretary of State Rogers visited the capital, Sanaa, July 2 to mark the event.

A week later another Arab state, Sudan, restored ties with Washington. President Gaafar Numeiry had reached a peace settlement in February with rebels in the south, ending 16 years of fighting that left an estimated half million persons dead.

Now he was embarked on a restoration program and adopted a more moderate policy, turning away from his Arab neighbors to the north who wanted him to join a federation. Relations with the Soviet Union remained sour as a result of the failure of a Communist-inspired coup against him in 1971.

As the year drew to a close, President Sadat again was on the spot. The expulsion of the Russians had failed to produce any breakthrough in the diplomatic logjam. In October he sought to make up with the Kremlin and sent Premier Sidky to Moscow.

Sidky returned with promises of Soviet help. Although it was denied, the price of reconciliation apparently included the resignation of army commander and War Minister, Gen. Sadek, whose anti-Soviet views had played a major role in Sadat's decision to oust the Russians. The commander of the navy also was removed.

The Egyptians maintained that Sadek was dismissed because he had failed to carry out orders.

For their part, the Russians, burned once, were unlikely to backtrack and supply Egypt all the weapons it wanted. Communist Party chief Leonid Brezhnev after all was scheduled to visit the United States in 1973.

One thing was clear. The stalemate with Israel had increased the political role of the army, and President Sadat appeared headed for another phase in the struggle to stay in the drivers' seat.

A's catcher Gene Tenace connected with a pitch by Jim McGlothin of the Cincinnati Reds for his fourth homer of the World Series

Gene Tenace Starred as Athletics Topped Reds in 69th World Series

THE UNLIKELIEST OF HEROES for the 1972 World Series had to be Fury Gene Tenace, a light-hitting catcher of little note for Oakland's mustachioed Athletics. But when the seven-game showdown between Charley Finley's American League champions and Cincinnati's redesigned Big Red Machine was over, it was Tenace the Menace who decided the issue.

There certainly was no hint before the Series began that Tenace would be anything more than a peripheral character in the drama of the 69th World Series. He had batted an undistinguished .225 during the regular season and had managed only one hit in 17 at bats during the A's five-game playoff victory over Detroit.

But that one hit, a single that barely made it through the

Detroit infield, drove home the A's deciding run in the final playoff game that clinched the American League pennant for Oakland. It was an omen of things to come for the light-hitting catcher.

That meant the colorful A's, featuring long hair, mustaches and garish gold and green uniforms, would face the Reds for baseball's World Championship. It would be hard to imagine any more exciting baseball than the kind these two teams had just been through in the playoffs. But they produced it in the World Series.

The tempo was set in Game 1. On his very first World Series at bat, Tenace hit a home run. He liked the feeling so much, that on his very next World Series swing, he hit another

187

Oakland's John "Blue Moon" Odom was tagged out at the plate

one. No player in the history of the World Series had ever done that before.

Tenace's two homers provided the A's with three runs and a trio of Oakland pitchers anchored by Vida Blue allowed the Reds just two. Blue came out of the bullpen for the fifth time in six post-season games and shut the Reds out for the final 2⅓ innings to clinch the victory.

In Game 2, the A's needed a glove equal to the situation in left field in the ninth inning and Joe Rudi qualified there.

Rudi had smashed an early homer and Jim "Catfish" Hunter carried a 2–0 lead into the ninth inning. Tony Perez opened with a single and then Denis Menke rocketed a Hunter fast ball towards the left field wall.

Rudi raced to the wall, leaped and caught the ball at the edge of the web of his glove, "I couldn't believe it when he caught it," said Hunter. "I thought the game was tied."

So did Rudi.

"I thought the ball was out," the left fielder said. "Four to six inches higher, and I miss it. My stretch might have been the limit. It was right at the end of my glove."

The Reds nicked Hunter for a run later in the inning, but Rollie Fingers came out of the bullpen to get the final out in the 2–1 victory and the A's headed home leading the Series 2–0.

A torrential rain and hail storm pelted the Oakland Coliseum minutes before Game 3 was to start and forced postponement. The next day, heliocopters hovered over the outfield, trying to dry the drenched turf. That night, the Reds and A's went at each other and this time, Oakland wished it had rained again.

Faced with a must-win situation, Cincinnati manager Sparky Anderson handed the baseball to Jack Billingham, a journeyman

right-handed pitcher who had a mediocre career record of 44–44. It didn't figure, but Billingham responded with brilliant three-hit pitching for eight innings and bullpen ace Clay Carroll hurled the scoreless ninth as the Reds won, 1–0.

"I don't think," said Billingham, "that I threw any bad pitches." The A's had to agree with that assessment.

It was Tenace's turn to swing back into action in Game 4 and the catcher connected with his third homer of the Series.

"I don't consider myself a power hitter," said Tenace. "I'm a line drive hitter, but in this Series, the man upstairs has been good to me."

Tenace's friend upstairs wasn't bad to the rest of the A's either. Oakland rallied for two runs in the bottom of the ninth inning on four singles, three of them by successful pinch hitters, to win the game 3–2. The deciding hit was delivered by Angel Mangual after singles by Tenace (of course), Gonzalo Marquez and Don Mincher had tied the score. The Reds pulled their infield in and Mangual punched the ball into right field for the victory. The A's led the Series 3–1.

Staring at elimination, the Reds turned stubborn. Pete Rose opened Game 5 with a home run. Then, after Tenace poled a record-tying, three-run homer, the Reds battled back, tied the score and eventually won it 5–4 on Rose's ninth inning single.

Tenace's fourth homer of the series moved him into the record book alongside Babe Ruth, Lou Gehrig, Duke Snider and Hank Bauer. But it wasn't enough to hold off the Reds, who were determined to send the Series back to Cincinnati.

After Tenace's blast and another RBI-pinch single by Marquez had put the Reds in a hole, they climbed out. Menke got one run back with a homer and Bobby Tolan drilled a pair of key hits, scoring Joe Morgan twice. That sent the game tied into the ninth inning.

Cesar Geronimo opened with a single, and pitcher Ross Grimsley popped his bunt in the air. Oakland reliever Fingers tried to turn the bad bunt into a double play, but bobbled the ball and had to settle for the sacrifice that sent Geronimo to second. Rose followed with the single that chased home the deciding run and sent the Series back to Cincinnati.

The first five games of the Series had all been tight, one-run affairs. Game 6 broke that mold. Blue started for the A's and Manager Dick Williams ran through three other arms, but none of them could handle the hot Reds' bats.

Johnny Bench drove in his first run of the series with a huge home run off Blue, and Cincinnati broke the game wide open with five runs in the seventh inning as Tolan and Geronimo each drilled a pair of two-run singles.

The victory tied the series and forced a seventh game, winner-take-all showdown. The Series would go seven, just as Reds' Manager Anderson had predicted it would right along.

Williams had a wrinkle up his sleeve for the final game. Facing a right-handed pitcher, third game winner Billingham, Williams defied strategy and packed his lineup with right-handed hitters. He benched lefty-swinging Mike Epstein, who had been mired in an 0-for-16 slump, shifted Tenace to first base, and put Dave Duncan behind the plate. Tenace, who usually swung seventh, was elevated to fourth in the batting order.

The shakeup worked. Batting cleanup, Tenace drove in a pair of runs with a single and a double, giving him nine RBIs in a seven-game Series in which his team only scored 16 runs.

After Tolan misplayed Mangual's first inning drive for a three-base error, Tenace bounced a bad-hop single off the seam of the Astro-turf infield for a 1–0 Oakland lead. The Reds tied the score in the fifth on a long sacrifice fly by pinch hitter Hal McRae that missed being a grand slam homer by no more than 10 feet. An inning later, the A's were ahead for keeps and again, it was Tenace who did the damage.

Bert Campaneris opened with a single, ending an 0-for-21 slump. Two infield outs moved him to third and Tenace delivered a double to left center, breaking the tie. With his hottest batter on second base, Williams pulled another wrinkle, lifting Tenace for a pinch runner. Even Tenace hesitated, not sure Williams wanted to get his bat out of the lineup. But a moment later, Sal Bando doubled for a 3–1 Oakland lead.

In the eighth, the Reds tried to come back. Rose opened with a single and Morgan doubled him to third. Fingers, the reliever with the handlebar mustache, came in and got pinch hitter Joe Hague on a popup. Now the problem was what to do with cleanup hitter Bench. Williams, whose unorthodox strategy had worked so far, ordered the Cincinnati slugger walked, defying the unwritten baseball law that said you never put the potential winning run on base intentionally.

That brought up Tony Perez, only a shade less dangerous than Bench. But Fingers got him on a sacrifice fly and then retired Menke, keeping Oakland ahead, 3–2.

The first two Reds' batters in the ninth went down easily but then Fingers faltered, hitting pinch batter Darrel Chaney with a pitch. Quickly Manager Williams hustled to the mound to talk to his pitcher.

"I had decided to take him out," said Williams. But catcher Duncan wouldn't let that happen. He convinced Williams to stay with Fingers and a moment later, the move paid off when Rose lined to Rudi for the final out.

For Williams, it was vindication. He had managed Boston to a seventh game showdown against St. Louis in the 1967 Series, only to lose that one.

"I saw one of those five years ago," he said, admiring the World Championship trophy. "It's a beautiful thing and it belongs right here."

The only thing missing on the award was a miniature statue of Gene Tenace swinging a bat.

Oakland celebrated winning world series

Accord Limiting Atomic
Weapons Put In Effect
By United States, USSR

U.S. Negotiator Gerard Smith, left, Finnish Foreign Minister Vaino Leskinen center and Soviet Vladimir Semyonov right in Helsinki during talks

O N OCT. 3, 1972, President Nixon assembled his cabinet and key members of Congress in the festive East Room of the White House. There, the President and Soviet Foreign Minister Andrei A. Gromyko exchanged formal documents putting into effect the first agreements between two great nuclear powers for limitation of atomic weapons.

The scene paralleled a meeting nearly five months earlier in Moscow. There on May 26 President Nixon and Soviet General Secretary Leonid I. Brezhnev signed a treaty limiting the number of anti-ballistic missiles (ABM) in the United States and the Union of Soviet Socialist Republics and agreed on a five-year curtailment of nuclear attack weapons.

In the interval between the two meetings, the ABM treaty had been ratified by Soviet officials and by the U. S. Senate by an 88–2 vote on Aug. 3, and the interim agreement on offensive arms had survived a Senate filibuster and won overwhelming approval of both branches of Congress.

The product of two and a half years of strategic arms limitation talks (SALT), the agreements were widely acclaimed in the United States as the outstanding achievement of President Nixon's first four-year term in office.

President Nixon himself viewed them as a first step toward "a world that is much safer" and "possibly free from the danger of nuclear disaster."

The Nixon Administration opened SALT negotiations with the Soviet Union on Nov. 17, 1969, in Helsinki, Finland. For more than a year the talks shifted back and forth between Helsinki and Vienna, Austria, with little visible progress. The Russians pressed for an initial agreement limiting only ABM systems. America held out for limitations on offensive weapons.

A breakthrough occurred on May 20, 1971. The two governments agreed to concentrate on an agreement to limit ABM defensive systems, while at the same time striving for whatever accords might be possible on strategic offensive arms.

Negotiations were still underway when President Nixon went to Moscow in May 1972 for a summit meeting with Soviet leaders. The climax came on May 26 with the signing of two copies of the agreements—one in English and the other in Russian.

The ABM treaty:

—Limits the United States and the Soviet Union to two ABM complexes each, one in an intercontinental ballistic missile (ICBM) deployment area and one in the national capital area. (The U.S. Defense Department had proposed a 12-site ABM system; Congress had authorized construction of two and planning of two more, all to protect ICBM silos. Russia had one in the vicinity of Moscow.)

—Limits each ABM site to no more than 100 ABM launchers and 100 associated interceptors.

—Limits the number and power of ABM radars at each ABM complex and limits deployment of certain types of non-ABM radars.

—Forbids development, testing or deployment of ABM systems of components which are sea-based, air-based, space-based or mobile land-based.

—Bans development or deployment of ABM launchers for launching more than one ABM interceptor missile at a time from each launcher.

—Forbids development, testing and deployment of automatic or semi-automatic rapid reload systems for ABM launchers, and deployment of ABM missiles with more than one independently guided warhead.

—Bans qualitative improvement of future ABM systems, such as systems depending on such devices as laser beams, even in permitted areas.

—Prohibits upgrading of anti-aircraft systems or their conversion to perform an ABM role.

—Forbids each nation from interfering with the other's national technical means of verifying compliance with terms of the treaty or the interim agreement on offensive weapons.

—Provides for a bi-lateral Standing Consultative Commission to monitor operations of the treaty and consider questions of compliance.

The duration of the treaty is unlimited, but it contains a withdrawal clause. Each party can withdraw upon six months notice if it decides that "extraordinary events" have jeopardized its supreme national interests.

The importance attached by the United States to the withdrawal clause as it relates to continuing negotiation for a more comprehensive agreement on offensive weapons limitation was emphasized in a formal statement to the Russian negotiators on May 9, 1972, by Gerard C. Smith, director of the U.S. Arms Control and Disarmament Agency and chief U.S. SALT negotiator:

"If an agreement providing for more complete strategic offensive arms limitations were not achieved within five years, U.S. supreme interests could be jeopardized. Should that occur, it would constitute a basis for withdrawal from the ABM treaty."

The five-year interim agreement:

—Freezes at current levels the aggregate number of ICBM and submarine launched ballistic missile (SLBM) launchers in operation or under construction on each side. Although not stated in the treaty, the United States relies on intelligence estimates that the Soviet Union had 1,618 ICBM's operational or under active construction on May 26, 1972; the stated (U.S.) total was 1,054 operational land-based ICBM launchers, with none under construction.

—Commits both sides not to convert launchers for light or older ICBM's into launchers for modern heavy ICBM's.

—Sets a ceiling of 62 modern nuclear powered submarines for the Soviet Union and 44 for the United States.

—Sets a ceiling of 950 SLBM launchers for the USSR and 710 for the United States.

—Permits both sides to improve their missile forces through modernization and replacement. Multiple warhead development and deployment may continue.

—Commits both sides to continue active negotiations for more complete limitations on strategic offensive arms.

—Imposes no limitation on intercontinental strategic bombers.

Returning from his 13-day, 16,000-mile trip to Russia, Austria, Iran and Poland, President Nixon hastened to the Capitol to address a special night joint session of Congress, his Marine Corps helicopter from Andrews Air Force Base in Maryland silhouetting in darkness against the Capitol dome as it landed on the cleared parking plaza.

"The foundation has been laid for a new relationship between the most powerful nations on earth," the President said in his June 1 speech urging prompt action by Congress on the SALT accords.

"We took the first step toward a new era of mutually agreed restraint and arms limitation between the two principal nuclear powers.

"With this step we have enhanced the security of both nations. We have begun to check the wasteful and dangerous spiral of nuclear arms which has dominated relations between our two countries for a generation. We have begun to reduce the level of fear by reducing the causes of fear, for our two peoples and for all peoples."

When the treaty and executive agreement and accompanying documents were submitted formally on June 13, Congress began its review promptly.

Hearings were conducted by the Senate Foreign Relations Committee and the House Foreign Affairs Committee. The Senate Armed Services Committee conducted a review of the military implications of the agreements, with Sen. Henry M. Jackson, D-Wash., alone at first in questioning the wisdom of an offensive weapon agreement giving numerical advantage to Russia in quantity and size of missiles.

The Senate, with sole Congressional jurisdiction over the treaty, ratified it on Aug. 3 with only two dissenting votes.

"I have strong misgivings," said Sen. James L. Buckley, New York Conservative, "as to both the prudence and the ultimate morality of denying ourselves for all time—or denying the Russians for that matter—the right to protect our civilian populations from nuclear devastation."

"I consider it immoral," said Sen. James B. Allen, D-Ala., "and an invitation to nuclear blackmail not to develop defenses against nuclear attack."

The prompt Senate action on the ABM treaty was not duplicated, however, on the resolution authorizing the President to accept the five-year interim agreement on offensive weapons.

An amendment by Senator Jackson, introduced with administration support and with Republican Senate Leader Hugh Scott of Pennsylvania as a co-sponsor, caught the Senate Foreign Relations Committee by surprise.

The Jackson amendment, ultimately adopted, was intended in his words to set "guidelines for future negotiations."

"Congress recognizes," the amendment stated, "the principle of United States-Soviet Union equality reflected in the antiballistic missile treaty, and urges and requests the President to

President Nixon shaking hands with Soviet Foreign Minister Gromyko in the White House East Room after SALT instruments of ratification were signed. Below, U.S. negotiator Gerard Smith, right, clenched fist as he and Russia's Vladimir Semyonov bottom center, talked with Finnish President Urho Kekkonen top left

seek a future treaty that, inter alia, would not limit the United States to levels of intercontinental strategic forces inferior to the limits provided for the Soviet Union."

Viewing the amendment as an unwarranted declaration that the interim agreement gave advantage to the Soviet Union, Foreign Relations Chairman J. W. Fulbright, D-Ark., prevented any Senate voting on the issue until after a mid-August Congressional recess for the Republican National Convention.

The month-long Senate struggle continued until Sept. 13, when the Senate voted 76–15 to shut off debate, adopted the Jackson amendment 56–35, and approved the interim agreement 88–2. The House accepted the amended resolution of approval 306–4 on Sept. 25.

The Oct. 3 White House ceremony putting the agreements into effect was punctuated with references to future negotiations to reach a more comprehensive agreement on offensive nuclear arms.

The goal, President Nixon said, is to "lift the burden of fear of war from all the people of the world."

Russia's Gromyko said the agreements reached in Moscow in May are "based on the recognition of the principle of equal security of the parties and offer no one nation unilateral military advantage."

"We are confident," Gromyko added, "that the interests of the Soviet and American peoples and the interests of the peoples of all countries of the world demand that efforts to limit the arms race should continue unabated."

Jack Roosevelt Robinson Broke the Black Barrier

The first man of his color to win his way into major league baseball, despite racial slurs, succumbed at age 53

Robinson completed a double play against the Philadelphia Phillies in 1950

P LAY BALL! April 15, 1947. Out at Ebbets Field in Brooklyn the Dodgers were tangling with Boston. Just another baseball game? Not quite. Prominent in the Dodger lineup that day was a black player at first base. His name was Jackie Robinson, and he was making sports history by becoming the first black baseball player in the major leagues.

It wasn't easy. There were racial slurs. Some players signed a petition refusing to play on the same team as a black. Runners slid into Robinson—hard. Pitchers threw at his head. But Robinson—the grandson of a slave—made it.

That first season—fresh up from the Montreal Royals of the International League—Robinson batted .297, led the National

League with 29 stolen bases, was named Rookie of the Year, and helped the Dodgers get into the World Series.

Jack Roosevelt Robinson, who suffered a heart attack at his Stamford, Conn., home Oct. 24, 1972, and died at the age of 53, wasn't just a one-season flash in the pan.

During his 10-season tenure with the Dodgers, he proved a versatile ballplayer as clutch hitter, daring base runner, first, second and third baseman and left fielder, as well as compiling a career batting average of .311. In 1949 he was voted the league's Most Valuable Player Award, batting .342 and driving in 124 runs. The Dodgers won six National League pennants while he was among their ranks. He was elected to baseball's

Jackie Robinson

Hall of Fame in 1962, and, most of all, he opened the door for black ball players.

Monte Irvin, who played for the New York Giants, recalled that: "Robinson opened the door of baseball to all men. He was the first to get the opportunity, but if he had not done such a great job, the path would have been so much more difficult.

"Bill Russell says if it hadn't been for Jackie, he might not ever have become a professional basketball player. Jack was the trail-blazer, and we are all deeply grateful. We say, thank you, Jackie; it was a job well done."

And Elston Howard, first black member of the New York Yankees, noted, "Jack said he hoped some day to see a black manager in baseball. Now I hope some of the owners will see how important that would be as the next step.

"He meant everything to a black ballplayer. I don't think the young players would go through what he did. He did it for all of us, for Willie Mays, Henry Aaron, Maury Wills, myself."

Or, as Robinson himself was to write, "I had to fight hard against loneliness, abuse and the knowledge that any mistake I made would be magnified because I was the only black man out there. Many people resented my impatience and honesty, but I never cared about acceptance as much as I cared about respect."

Robinson, who earned the distinction of "Best All-Around Athlete" from President Nixon in a bylined article written in 1972 for The Associated Press, grew up in Pasadena, Calif. As a young man he got a scholarship to the University of California at Lost Angeles and at the school proved an all-round athlete, starring in football, track and field, basketball and baseball.

After World War II service in the U.S. Army—he went in a private and came out a lieutenant in 1945—Robinson coached baseball at Sam Houston College, then joined the Kansas City Monarchs of the Negro National League.

It was during this period that Robinson was approached by Branch Rickey, general manager of the Dodgers.

"Do you want a man who doesn't have the courage to fight back?" Robinson asked.

"I want a man with courage enough not to fight back," Rickey said.

Rickey signed Robinson for the 1946 season—a period the young player spent with the Montreal Royals, leading Dodger farm team. The next season he went to the big league.

"If Mr. Rickey hadn't signed me, I wouldn't have played another year in the black league," Robinson said later. "It was too difficult. The travel was brutal. Financially, there was no reward. It took everything you made to live off.

"I more than likely would have gone to coach baseball at Sam Houston College. My minister had gone down there to

Texas as president of the college. That was about the only thing a black athlete had left then, a chance to coach somewhere at a small black college."

Rickey warned Robinson of the insults and slurs that would come his way that first season in the majors and urged the player to hold his temper. Robinson did. But the following season, he was an established player and Rickey released him from his commitment. Robinson fought back then and became a fierce competitor.

"I was told that it would cost me some awards," Robinson recalled in later years. "But if I had to keep quiet to get an award, it wasn't worth it. Awards are great, but if I got one for being a nice kid, what good is it?"

He also was to recall that "the Rickey Experiment, as I call it, would not have come about as successfully with anybody other than Mr. Rickey. The most important results of it are that it produced understanding among whites and it gave black people the idea that if I could do it, they could do it, too, that blackness wasn't subservient to anything."

But Robinson also kept his part in baseball in perspective. When Ebbets Field—the site of his debut in the majors—was razed and replaced with apartment houses, Robinson was to say, "I don't feel anything. They need those apartments more than they need a monument to the memory of baseball. I've had my thrills."

Robinson's baseball career ended in 1956, when, at season's end, the Dodgers announced the pioneering black player had been traded to the New York Giants. Robinson, instead, chose to retire from the game and accepted a vice presidency with a restaurant chain.

In 1972, Robinson was presented a plaque commemorating the 25th anniversary of his entrance into baseball, after throwing out the first ball for the second game of the World Series in Cincinnati Oct. 15.

After accepting the plaque, Robinson said, "I am extremely proud and pleased, but I will be more pleased the day I can look over at third base and see a black man as a manager." Although he suffered a heart attack in 1968 and then lost the sight of one eye and the partial sight of the other as a result of diabetes, Robinson continued active in campaigns against drug addiction—from which his son, Jackie Jr., had been recovering before he was killed in a 1971 auto accident.

Robinson, in fact, had been planning to attend a drug symposium in Washington the day he died.

Said President Nixon, in a tribute to the dead ballplayer:

"His courage, his sense of brotherhood and his brilliance on the playing field brought a new human dimension not only to the game of baseball but to every area of American life where black and white people work side by side.

"This nation, to which he gave so much in his lifetime, will miss Jackie Robinson, but his example will continue to inspire us for years to come."

Some of Robinson's former Brooklyn Dodger teammates carried his casket from New York's Riverside Church

TRAIN WRECK LEFT 214 DEAD

Returning from an annual religious pilgrimage to pray to St. Francis at Real de Catorce, Mexico, more than 1,500 adults and an unknown number of children were riding to Saltillo when, as one passenger later recalled, their train began "moving like a wild animal."

As the 24-car train raced along at more than 70 miles an hour—twice the permitted speed—it came to a downhill curve some six miles from Saltillo and derailed, piling some of the crowded cars atop one another and trapping many in the wreckage. Fire broke out and spread through four of the battered cars.

Leovigildo Rivera, a passenger, recalled that "the train was moving like a wild animal. I felt the danger and told my wife to hold her seat tightly. She started to cry." He added:

"Later I heard screams. The people went crazy—and then I felt the impact. I did not know anything else. I lost consciousness. When I awoke I saw that many people were dead. I heard crying and screams. . . ."

The Oct. 5 wreck claimed at least 214 lives. More than 1,000 persons were injured. Some of these lost limbs when doctors were forced to amputate to free them from the twisted wreckage.

"Don't cut my mother, please, she's my mother," a 10-year-old boy wept as a doctor amputated the arm of his mother to free her. Another doctor sighed, looked at another woman, and said, "To free that poor woman we will have to amputate both her legs." Many of the bodies pulled from the wreckage by rescuers could not be identified because they were mutilated or burned beyond recognition.

In the investigation that followed, rail officials said a study by experts disproved the crew's claim that the brakes on the train failed. They also said blood tests showed there was alcohol in the blood of the engineer and his assistant. A federal district judge later declared the "formal imprisonment" on homicide and other charges of five crew members.

Victims of train derailment buried in a cemetery in Saltillo, Mexico

44 KILLED IN TRAIN COLLISION

"Help! Help! Help!"

The pleading cry was always the same. But the voices were different. They came from the luckless men and women trapped in the tangled mass of steel and broken glass that was the wreckage of two Illinois Central Gulf Railroad trains which had crashed in Chicago.

The crowded trains—with an estimated 1,000 aboard—were taking commuters from the outer reaches of Chicago and its suburbs to the city's downtown area Oct. 30.

At the 27th Street station on the city's south side, the lead train—a four-car, double-decker—overshot by some 300 feet. It began to back up. As it was doing so, a train of six cars of old one-level equipment rammed into its rear with the lead car of the second train telescoping through the last half of the rear car of the lead train. Most of the 44 persons killed and 350 injured were riding in these cars.

Record books list the Feb. 6, 1951, crash of a Pennsylvania Railroad commuter train at Woodbridge, N.J., as the worst recent domestic rail accident. That train plunged off a temporary trestle, claiming 84 lives. A train wreck in September 1958 in Elizabethport, N.J., claimed 48 lives.

Laureice Browning, 33, a survivor of the Chicago wreck, said "People were flying all over the place. I just screamed and screamed, and somehow I was able to find my way off that thing."

A crowd of some 1,000 gathered quickly in an effort to give aid. As they ripped at the twisted steel, the screams of pinned victims tore at their ears. When they could, doctors and medical teams crawled through the debris to give morphine and other aid.

"Some of the passengers just sat there in their seats," one rescuer said. "They were in shock. They couldn't believe what had happened."

The National Transportation Safety Board initiated an investigation of the crash. It said the study would require several months.

INTERNATIONAL "THINK TANK"

The idea was first hatched in 1966 by a White House planning group. The aim: to have the scientific minds of a number of nations form a "think tank" to seek solutions to the problems created by increasing industralization of Society today.

The idea intrigued the leadership of the Soviet Union, and finally in October Moscow and Washington led a move to set up such a think tank composed of scientific academies of a dozen nations.

It was believed to be the first time the Russians had given official sanction and funds to an East-West project that was not linked directly to either the Soviet government or to the United Nations.

In fact, the Kremlin thought so well of the idea that it enlisted the services of Premier Alexei N. Kosygin's son-in-law, Djhermen M. Gvishiani, a member of the Soviet Academy of Sciences. Gvishiani was appointed to a three-year term as chairman of the council of the group, to be known as the International Institute of Applied Systems Analysis.

The Institute was regarded as another step in the bridge-building effort that the United States hoped would eventually bring about a liberalization of the Communist systems of the Soviet Union and the nations of Eastern Europe. Associated with the United States and Soviet Russia in the institute were the leading scientific organizations of Canada, Czechoslovakia, Bulgaria, France, East Germany, Japan, West Germany, Italy, Poland and Britain.

Pollution control, urban growth, public health and over-population were among the problems to be examined by the institute, based in the Laxenburg Palace, near Vienna.

GEN. ABRAMS CHIEF OF STAFF

The Senate on Oct. 12 confirmed promotion of Gen. Creighton William Abrams to Army Chief of Staff, replacing Gen. William C. Westmoreland, who retired June 30 after serving the full four-year tour of duty. Abrams, commander of U.S. Forces in South Vietnam since mid-1968, was nominated for the promotion by President Nixon on June 20. This nomination had been endorsed Oct. 6 by the Senate Armed Services Committee.

Also on Oct. 6 the Senate committee rejected a token promotion for former four-star Gen. John D. Lavelle, erstwhile commander of the U.S. 7th Air Force in South Vietnam. Lavelle acknowledged on June 12 that he had been relieved of his post following assertions that he had ordered unauthorized bombing strikes in North Vietnam.

He retired April 7, the Defense Department announced, "because of irregularities in the conduct of his responsibilities" after some reports had said that "his pilots flew too low and took too many risks," and others that "they flew too high and did not take enough."

Secretary Melvin R. Laird of the Department of Defense announced in May that Lavelle had been relieved "because the Chief of Staff of the Air Force had lost confidence" in his leadership. When he was relieved Lavelle's rank was reduced to two stars. Restoration of one star had been unsuccessfully considered by the Senate committee on Oct. 6.

However, later in October the U.S. Air Force ruled that no further disciplinary action against Lavelle would be taken, holding that his removal as a commander was punishment enough for the 28 unauthorized bombing strikes in North Vietnam by his planes between November 1971 and last March.

Above, Gen. Creighton W. Abrams, named U.S. army chief of staff, was decorated by Vietnamese President Nguyen Van Thieu upon leaving his Vietnam command. Left, Chinese doctors visiting the United States strolling in Wall Street, heart of New York's financial district

SOVIET JET CRASH CONFIRMED

It was raining. Visibility was bad. It was the night of Friday the 13th of October.

Cruising through the unfriendly sky was an Ilyushin-62, the Soviet Union's most advanced civil transport aircraft. Three times the big plane— on an unscheduled flight from Leningrad—made passes over Moscow's Sheremetyevo Airport, apparently checking landing possibilities.

Then, as it attempted to land on its fourth turn, the ship fell from the sky, crashing and exploding on the outskirts of a small village three miles from the airport.

Secrecy immediately surrounded the disaster. The government reported the day after it happened that all aboard the plane were killed, but refused to release any other information, including the number aboard.

However, a reliable Soviet source later reported that 176 persons died in the crash, making it the worst disaster in commercial aviation history. The previous record was set in 1971 when a Japanese airliner and fighter plane collided, killing all 162 persons on the liner. The fighter pilot escaped, (*The World in 1971, 134*).

The Russian plane had flown from Paris to Leningrad. It then took off on its unscheduled flight to Moscow. The source said that the plane was full when it left Leningrad and that five persons had to be removed because of overbooking.

"BILLIONAIRES" IN YUGOSLAVIA

President Tito stood before a cheering audience of Yugoslav shipworkers in the Adriatic port of Rijeka and denounced an "amassing of wealth" by some Yugoslavs since his government had adopted economic reforms seven years earlier.

Tito complained that even some members of the League of Communists had accumulated riches totaling "hundreds of millions and even billions of old dinars."

Actually it took a million of the old dinars to equal 600 American dollars, but even at this ratio a billionaire would have a healthy nest egg of $600,000 or more. Yugoslavia's currency had been revalued at the rate of one new dinar for 100 of the old ones.

Tito's disclosure did not come to light until October, although his Rijeka address had been delivered Sept. 4. He seemed perturbed by what he described as a tendency of this new billionaire class to squander their dinars on one or more posh homes in the mountains or along the Adriatic coast.

Tito's remarks had a snowballing effect. Less than a month later, demands were raised for curbs on the so-called socialist rich, touching off fears of a run on savings accounts by nervous depositors.

Simeon Zatezalo, chairman of the Belgrade Economic Chamber, warned that the campaign against the affluent could have a negative effect on the nation's banks.

The campaign against the well-to-do also influenced the middle income group that had savings accounts. They apparently were unnerved by reports that authorities would launch a drive to find out just who the "billionaires" really were.

Bank officials sought to allay anxieties by noting that any probe into the origin of savings deposits and other forms of wealth would be illegal, unless the persons being investigated had been accused of a crime. It had been estimated that more than 150 Yugoslavs did possess wealth in excess of $600,000, but the identity of these "billionaires" remained vague.

The average Yugoslav worker earned about $100 a month, but some commercial representatives and factory directors made up to $1,000 a month. The best chance of amassing real wealth, however, was in private business, as in most countries.

In recent years private business had been encouraged in Yugoslavia, but the law restricted such firms to a maximum of five employes.

A news weekly in Belgrade cited the case of a Yugoslav who had allegedly amassed a tidy fortune with a private bus line, a trucking business, taxis and two restaurants. One eatery had been registered in the name of the man's wife, the paper said, and the other in the name of a daughter.

The paper declared that the enterprising businessman took off for West Germany after tax authorities questioned his claim that he had made an annual profit of only $1,300.

CLAMMERS BESET BY "RED TIDE"

The rugged New Englanders who dig clams for a living have a tough life, even when times are good. Clamming was one of the most arduous forms of stoop labor, and exposing the digger to the fury of the "Down East" winter. Being self-employed, these men received no welfare or unemployment benefits when they were out of work. Unable to save much money for lean times, most of them lived from day to day.

But despite these hazards and discomforts, the men were a hardy, independent breed, willing to pull on their boots in darkness and freezing weather and "dig the tide down," wading through half frozen mud while they groped for clams with a hoe.

Last fall, the diggers faced a new hazard when the "Red Tide," a dreaded infestation of poisonous algae, invaded the New England coast and left thousands of clam seekers idle.

Alarmed authorities in Maine and Massachusetts closed their flats to the harvesting of shellfish affected by the potentially toxic rust-red waters. New Hampshire has no commercial beds, but it also came under the embargo since it packages shellfish from the other two states.

But the worst was yet to come. The U.S. Food and Drug Administration (FDA) issued orders to recall clams and mussels distributed throughout the affected area. The agency warned that the toxic algae had infected seafood and that the toxin could not be destroyed, even by cooking.

More than 30 persons had been affected by the shellfish poisoning, officials said. They described the "Red Tide" as a minute marine organism whose toxic symptoms included numbness and tingling with vomiting. They added, however, that the poisoning was rarely fatal.

The embargoes meant unemployment for thousands of clam diggers and independent smalltime harvesters of shellfish. In Maine alone the loss was placed at $1 million a week.

Finally President Nixon, prompted by appeals from the Governors of Maine and Massachusetts, agreed to call the "Red Tide" a national disaster and the diggers became eligible for relief payments of about $47 a week.

Meanwhile scientists attempted to find out why the invasion had struck. Toxic varieties of the "Red Tide" had plagued coastal waters around the world for centuries, but the normally cold waters off New England's coast generally resisted the pest.

Biologists expressed belief that the New England plague had been brought on by a high degree of sunlight, low salinity and unusually warm water.

On Oct. 4, the FDA announced that the worst of the emergency was over and that shellfish being harvested and shipped from New England were safe for consumers. Parts of the New England coast was kept under a harvesting ban for some time after that, however, until the contamination had been eliminated.

EIGHT VIRGIN ISLANDS GOLFERS MURDERED BY JUNGLE GUNMEN

Lying some 100 miles southeast of Puerto Rico, St. Croix—the tip of an underwater mountain that spears up from the clear, blue Caribbean waters—is a tiny, tourist island in the U.S. Virgin Islands chain. A normally placid vacation spot; a place to sunbathe, swim, loaf.

And to play golf, at places such as the manicured, 350-acre grounds of the Fountain Valley Golf Course.

The usual sunny calm at the course was shattered Sept. 6 when a group of fatigue-clad men armed with automatic weapons burst from the heavy foliage bordering the course and began shooting.

Sweden's King Gustaf VI Adolf spending vacation in Italy to carry on archeological excavations near Viterbo

"I heard a sound—pop, pop, pop," recalled Justin Herman, 26, a pro shop delivery man. "I turned to look, and then I saw two men running from the big bush around the end of the clubhouse. They both had what looked like rifles, and one of them pointed at me and fired without saying anything." The bullet struck Herman in the face. He was one of four persons wounded. Eight others were shot to death.

After gunning down their victims, the raiders scooped $731 from the clubhouse's cash drawers, took the wallets of the dead, and retreated into the nearby jungle. Slain in the brief, violent attack were Charles Meisinger, 47, of Miami, and his wife, Joan, 45; Richard Griffin, 55, of Miami, and his wife, Mattie Ruth, 49; John Gulliver, 23, of Lunnenburg, Mass.; Mrs. Pat Tarbet, 45; Nick Beale, 50, and Aliston Lowery, 24. The Griffins and Meisingers were tourists; the other four course employes.

Some 150 lawmen fanned out into the jungle where the raiders had fled to comb a 15-square mile area. Some were FBI sharpshooters armed with telescopic rifles. Others were shotgun-carrying policemen. The hunters, aided by helicopters and machete-wielding officers, found nothing.

Then, acting on an anonymous tip Sept. 12, the police raided a house in the town of Frederiksted and arrested three men. It was revealed that two other suspects had been arrested earlier. All were from the Virgin Islands. The five were charged with eight counts of first-degree murder.

The victor in his White House office ➡

November

PRESIDENTIAL ELECTION:

*Nixon landslide was marred by the fact that only
55 per cent of the registered voters cast ballots*

In Minneapolis, McGovern campaigned with Sen. Edward Kennedy

IN THE UNITED STATES, a presidential campaign is traditionally a celebration of sorts, a festive confirmation of the democratic process and the two-party system. Beneath the hoopla real issues are joined, debated on the hustings, and as the first Tuesday after the first Monday in November approaches, tension builds steadily. At last, in quadrenially increasing numbers, Americans make their choice.

The election of 1972, however, bore little resemblance to that noble tradition. It was a desultory episode. Many could agree with columnist Marquis Childs when, toward its end, he called it "one of the most unhappy campaigns in American history." For all the claims by both President Richard M. Nixon and his Democratic opponent, Sen. George S. McGovern, that it would be "the clearest choice in this century," there was no real debate involved. Instead of growing in presence and stature as the campaign progressed, both the candidates and the issues seemed to blur and fade. Indeed, the President scarcely campaigned at all and his opponent, enmeshed in early mistakes and misunderstandings and unable to lure Nixon into debating his chosen issues, never seemed to get his campaign off the ground.

As the pollsters had predicted weekly throughout the campaign, Nixon and his running mate, Vice President Spiro T. Agnew, won in a landslide over McGovern and his running mate, Sargent Shriver Jr. The Nixon-Agnew ticket captured 49 of the 50 states, losing only Massachusetts and the District

Appearing in New York, President Nixon spoke with the Statue of Liberty as a backdrop

George McGovern shaking hands with Ohio voters on Labor Day

of Columbia. Such a clear-cut mandate for a second term, however, was marred by the fact that only 55 per cent of the 139.6 million registered voters chose to vote, the lowest percentage turnout in 24 years. The popular vote totals were 47,168,963 for Nixon; 29,169,342 for McGovern. Even so, for Nixon it was a sweet victory, coming a decade to the day after his loss in a bid for the governorship of California after which he announced his retirement from politics. No matter that it seemed to many analysts, after it was over, that it was a victory built less on affection for Nixon than an antipathy toward McGovern and his New Democrats. The clearest evidence of that was the runaway ticket-splitting that prevailed throughout the country: Democrats actually gained two seats in the Senate, increasing their majority to 57-43, and held the Republicans to a net gain of 12 seats in the House, far short of the 41 they needed to gain control.

From the outset of the campaign McGovern committed errors which he admitted later cost him the confidence of the electorate. The first, he said, was making his acceptance speech at the Democratic National Convention, with the display of party unity attending it, at 2 a.m., long after a potentially large television audience had gone to bed. Also, he said, "the Eagleton affair was definitely harmful" to his campaign, referring to his replacement of Sen. Thomas Eagleton as a running mate after Eagleton's medical history was disclosed. McGovern also refined his views throughout the campaign on a number of issues, most notably welfare, and gave the impression of indecision. Finally, the issue of war in Vietnam, the issue that propelled him to national prominence and which he clearly

thought would lead him to victory, became muted and Nixon emerged in the minds of many as the peace candidate. Indeed, on Oct. 26, in a news conference in Washington, Nixon's foreign affairs adviser Henry A. Kissinger announced that "peace is at hand" in all of Indochina and thus removed the war as an issue.

Another issue that McGovern apparently failed to excite the electorate about was what came to be known as "the Watergate affair."

At 2 a.m. on June 17, five men were seized at gunpoint in the headquarters of the Democratic National Committee in Washington's Watergate Hotel. They were caught with cameras and electronic "bugging" equipment in their possession. The police who nabbed them said file drawers had been opened and ceiling panels removed near the office of Democratic National Chairman Lawrence F. O'Brien. One of the men captured, James W. McCord, a former CIA agent, was employed as a security agent by both the Republican National Committee and the Committee for the Re-Election of the President. Another, Bernard L. Barker, who was apparently the leader of the raid and also a former CIA agent, was discovered to have met in Miami in early June with E. Howard Hunt, a former White House consultant. Later disclosures traced the money that financed the raid to the Committee for the Re-Election of the President.

In a news conference June 22 the President disavowed any knowledge of the raid. "This kind of activity has no place whatever in our electoral process," he said, "and the White House had no involvement whatever in this particular incident."

But that didn't make the "incident" die. A month before the

election, the Washington Post reported that it had discovered, from information allegedly in Justice Department files, that the Committee for the Re-Election of the President had financed a vast network of political saboteurs bent on disrupting Democratic campaigns as far back as the primaries. Again, White House spokesmen denied that the President had any knowledge of such activities and McGovern, though he tried hard—calling the Nixon administration "the most corrupt in history"—failed to have much success with it as a campaign issue.

Throughout, McGovern leaped on other charges of scandal in the administration; charges that huge financial donors to the Republican Party had received favors in return. McGovern cherished a forlorn hope that he could draw the President out into open combat. But given the reassurance of the polls, the President had no reason to climb down from his posture of statesmanship. As far back as July, pollster Louis Harris had McGovern trailing Nixon by 20 points. In August, both Harris and George Gallup showed McGovern dropping even farther behind, with the impact of Eagleton's departure from the ticket. Both pollsters showed a slight gain for McGovern in October, and in their last polls before election day, both opinion samplers were right on the money, predicting that Nixon would win by 61 per cent to 39 per cent.

During the entire campaign the President did not once identify his opponent by name. He rarely appeared on the stump and delivered only one set campaign speech on television, although he used the radio extensively. For the most part he left his campaigning to "surrogates," including his wife and daughters, and to Agnew, as well as to massive direct-mail appeals. Although McGovern never let up, logging 65,000 miles criss-crossing the country and appearing frequently on television,

the Republicans outspent the Democrats by about $50 million to about $25 million.

Nothing about the "noncampaign" as it came to be called in the press, however, could diminish the sheer outsize arithmetic of the Nixon victory. He ran close to Lyndon Johnson's share of the popular vote in 1964, took more states than Franklin D. Roosevelt in 1936 (though Alf M. Landon got the eight electoral votes of Maine and Vermont in that year; McGovern got 17 from Massachusetts and the District of Columbia), and even took McGovern's home state of South Dakota.

The President received his honors graciously. In a subdued speech from the Oval Office his tone was conciliatory and his theme was national unity in the interests of peace and good works. McGovern, too, was gentle in defeat. At 9 p.m., before the polls had even closed in some western states, he sat down at a motel in Sioux Falls, S.D., exhausted and somehow tranquil, and drafted a concession statement, pausing only now and then to comfort his tearful wife and children. He delivered it two hours later to a wildly cheering audience at the Sioux Falls Coliseum. He combined a pledge of "full support" to President Nixon's efforts toward "peace abroad and justice at home" with a moving testimonial to "the great joy this campaign has brought us." For him it was the end of a campaign that had lasted two years, beginning as a candidate whose overriding issue was simply an end of the war in Vietnam.

"I want every one of you to remember and never forget it," he told his workers, "that if we pushed the day of peace just one day closer, then every minute and every hour and every bone-crushing effort in this campaign was worth the entire effort."

The awesome scope of the McGovern debacle appeared to

The GOP standard bearer and his wife stumping in Atlanta, Ga.

rate of 16 per cent for the previous five elections. The President seemingly lacked support only among the blacks and the very poor—he even captured about half of the youth vote, those 18 to 25, who were voting in their first presidential election.

For one who had won the presidency by a plurality of less than one per cent of the vote in 1968, it was a victory Nixon could relish. After delivering his acceptance message from the White House, he drove to Washington's Shoreham Hotel and found the ballroom awash with his faithful whose shouts of "four more years" nearly drowned out the band's "Hail to the Chief." The President looked relaxed and remarked contentedly, "I've never known a national election when I could go to bed earlier."

Left, McGovern's running mate, Sargent Shriver. Below, Spiro Agnew hitting the campaign trail.

have brought an era in Democratic politics to an end. His defeat left in splinters the historic coalition forged by Roosevelt: an amalgam of Southern whites, Jews, "ethnic" and mostly Catholic blue-collar workers, blacks and campus-oriented intellectuals. Surveys showed that more than a third of all Democrats voted for Nixon, compared with an average defection

At Least 38 Commercial Jets Hijacked in 1972

But unsuccessful air piracy attempts boosted the total of such incidents to 57 by early November

THE TWIN-ENGINE DC9 Southern Airways jet—its main tires badly bullet-damaged—wheeled for some time in the Cuban sky burning off excess fuel. Then the bone-weary pilot eased the ship down to Havana's Jose Marti Airport, its bare wheels kicking up a huge shower of sparks as it touched on the foam-covered runway.

The Nov. 12 landing ended a 28-hour aerial hijack nightmare—later described as seeming "like a million years"—for 31 exhausted passengers and crew members. They had been held captive by three heavily armed gunmen who took over the plane the evening of Nov. 10 after it took off from Birmingham, Ala., and in the tense hours that followed forced Pilot William R. Haas to take them on a journey that hopscotched across three countries, with landings at Cleveland, Ohio; Toronto; Lexington, Ky.; Chattanooga, Tenn., and then Havana.

The plane stayed at Havana about two hours the first time. Then the hijackers apparently grew nervous, and ordered the aircraft aloft again. This time it landed at Key West, Fla., then hopped to Orlando, where, as it began rolling for takeoff to Havana again, its tires were shot by FBI agents in hope of preventing its leaving.

The ship took off, however, and Copilot Billy Johnson said the gunmen responded to the shooting by using him as a shield to keep the pilot from being shot, then shot him in the shoulder to show the other captives "they meant business."

The hijackers had demanded $10 million, and at one point the air pirates vowed to send the plane crashing into the giant nuclear research facility at Oak Ridge, Tenn., unless the ransom was paid. The threat led to the shutdown of three nuclear reactors and evacuation of the Oak Ridge plant, but authorities later said only a minimal amount of radioactivity would have leaked out if the jetliner actually had crashed. However, after the threat, the plane landed at Chattanooga and money was put aboard—a reported $2 million.

After the second Havana landing, the three air pirates identified as Lewis K. Moore, 27, Melvin Cale, 21, and Henry D. Jackson, 25, were taken into custody by Cuban officials, who also confiscated the ransom money. Air piracy warrants for the trio were issued in the United States.

At least 38 commercial jetliners were commandeered around the world in 1972, and unsuccessful attempts at hijacking raised the total of such incidents to 57 by early November.

In preceding years the over-all world figures were 60 in 1971, 83 in 1970, 87 in 1969, and 35 in 1968. These figures included both successful and unsuccessful attempts.

The Federal Aviation Administration recognized three categories of hijacking attempts: those that were successful, with the hijacker controlling the flight and reaching his destination or objective (24 in 1972); incomplete hijackings, in which the hijacker was apprehended or killed during the attempt or as a result of hot pursuit (14 in 1972), and those that were wholly unsuccessful, in which the hijacker tried to take control of the flight but failed (19 in 1972).

The plight of the Southern Airways flight led Cuba to call for a broad agreement with the United States to cover all forms of hijacking and violence affecting the two countries. Following the call, the United States moved to arrange negotiations with Cuba to curb airline hijacks.

The move came after a Nov. 15 appeal by Air Line Pilots Assn. President John J. O'Connell that negotiations with Cuba "must be reached if we are ever to see an end to this skyjacking menace."

O'Donnell also wrote President Nixon that U.S. airports should have federal police to supervise passenger screening and boarding in an effort to curb skyjacks.

"Due to the magnitude of the problem and the apparent inability of local, state and federal officials or the industry to achieve effective results, we must request that you immediately provide airports with federal officers to be utilized during the boarding of all commercial airlines," he wrote.

The ALPA, which represented some 31,000 pilots of 38 U.S. airlines, also threatened to call another worldwide air service strike in protest of government inaction against hijackers. Earlier in the year airline pilots had put into effect a partially-successful 24-hour shutdown of air service in many parts of the world as a protest against hijacks.

In September, the International Civil Aviation Organization's legal subcommittee sent its parent organization a proposal for sanctions against nations that violate anti-hijack treaties.

The U.S. Senate and House passed stiff legislation to suspend air service to countries that harbored skyjackers and terrorists, and to permit juries to recommend death sentences for air piracy.

Of the 31 U.S. hijacking attempts by early November, only 10 were successful. Seven were frustrated, and in the other 14 instances the hijacker was overcome, captured, or surrendered after gaining temporary control of the plane.

Two of the air pirate teams hijacked planes to Algiers after collecting $1.5 million in ransom, only to see the money taken away and returned to its owners, along with the commandeered jet airliners and the crews that had been held hostage.

In the first of those incidents Willie Roger Holder, 23, a member of the Black Panther Party, and a 20-year-old white woman took command of a Western Air Lines Boeing 727 on a flight from Los Angeles to Seattle June 2, transferred to a longer range 707, collected $500,000 and flew to Algiers by way of San Francisco and New York. They won political asylum of sorts, but had to give up the ransom.

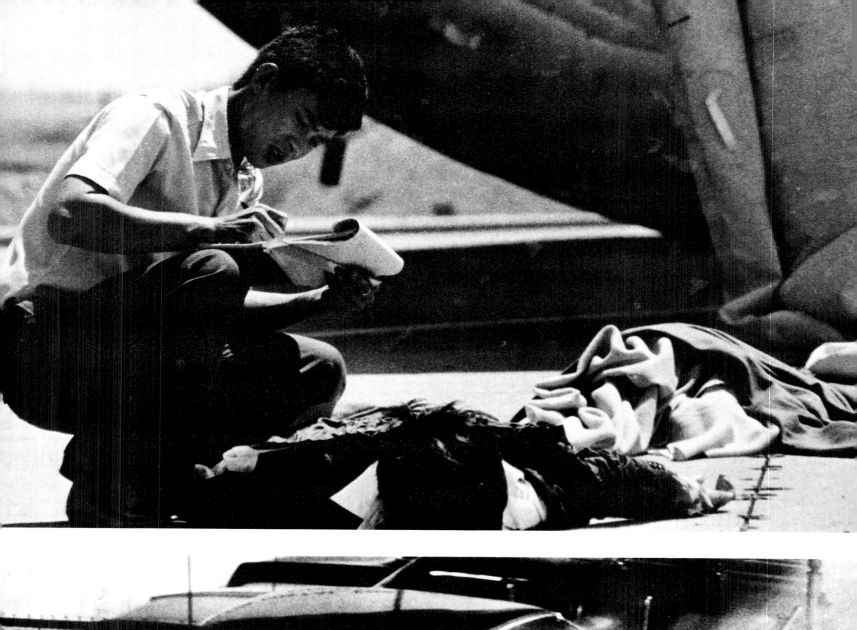

Opposite, top, a plainclothes policeman kneeling beside the body of a young Asian man killed when he attempted to hijack a Pan American 747 from Saigon to Hanoi. Opposite, bottom, a man identified by FBI as David J. Hanley of Florissant, Mo., drove his car through a fence at St. Louis Airport before ramming a hijacked American jetliner. Above, Turkish hijacker, left, with pistol and grenade stood guard as a Bulgarian airline official helped an injured passenger from a hijacked Turkish airliner in Sofia

Also on the same June 2 date, Ross D. Heady, 22, wearing a yellow pillow case over his head, commandeered a United Air Lines 727 at Reno, Nev., held the crew of five at gunpoint for several hours until $200,000 in ransom had been collected, and then bailed out over a remote valley. He was arrested several hours later, and the ransom was found hidden in sagebrush. In August Heady was sentenced to 30 years in prison.

As if to emulate the Western hijacking to Algeria, three black men and two women, accompanied by three children, took over a Delta Air Lines jet en route from Detroit to Miami July 31, collected $1 million in ransom, and ordered the plane to Algiers. Two of the hijackers were escapees from prison where one had been serving a sentence for murder and the other for armed robbery.

They attempted to smuggle $300,000 of their loot into Algiers, but were foiled by thorough search of their persons. Algerian officials handed the $1 million over to two Delta officials and ignored protests by the hijackers and by Black Panther spokesmen. In granting the two hijack teams sanctuary, however, Algeria faced possible future retaliatory action by other governments or by airline flight crews.

The Reno airport was the scene of its second hijacking on Aug. 18 when Frank Markoe Sibley, 43, pedaled a bicycle through a hole in the airport fence and, wearing a ski mask and holding a rifle, barged onto a United 727 and forced the crew to fly him first to Vancouver, B.C., and then to Seattle. At Vancouver he demanded $15,000 in gold bars, a submachine gun and other weapons, a flashlight, pep pills and radio, and ordered that $2 million be ready for pickup at Seattle. While the plane circled Vancouver he broadcast to a radio station there a protest against the war in Vietnam and said his ransom would be used to aid crippled children. In a shootout with FBI officers at Seattle-Tacoma airport he was wounded and captured. He faced a minimum penalty of 20 years.

Another who tried to use a hijacked plane as a platform for protest was Ricardo Chavez-Ortiz, 36, a Mexican national. He flourished an unloaded gun to commandeer a Frontier Airlines twin-engine 737 over New Mexico April 12, ordered it flown to Los Angeles and then surrendered after a rambling two-hour interview with newsmen he had summoned to the plane. In July he was sentenced to life imprisonment.

Melvin Martin Fisher, 49, took over an American Airlines 727 between Oklahoma City and Dallas July 12, forced it to return to Oklahoma City, demanded $550,000 and a parachute, and finally released the 57 passengers and three of the stewardesses on payment of $200,000. However, Fisher thereafter ordered the plane back into the air, and demanded that the rear stairway be lowered in preparation for a bail-out. Then, rather than make the jump, he handed his pistol to a stewardess who had remained hostage along with the pilot and flight engineer.

On the same date two blacks, Michael Stanley Green, 34, and Ethiopian student Lulseged Tesfa, 22, hijacked a National Airlines jet nearing Miami from New York City, ordered it to fly to Philadelphia, and held the 111 passengers prisoners for more than eight hours. The hijackers and hostage crew changed to a longer-range jet and took off with $600,000 and 20,000 Mexican pesos in ransom. The plane landed virtually out of fuel at a small field 50 miles south of Houston, Tex. After two injured crew members jumped out and one stewardess escaped, an FBI agent talked the men into surrendering.

Richard Floyd McCoy, 29, parachuted with $500,000 from a United Air Lines plane near Provo, Utah, April 7. The FBI arrested him at his Salt Lake City home two days later, and recovered all but $30 of the ransom. McCoy received a 45-year sentence.

Most modest of the extortion demands was the $50,000 with which Richard LaPoint parachuted from a Hughes Airwest DC9 over Colorado Jan. 20. He and the ransom were recaptured within hours, and before long he was serving a 40-year prison term.

Some of the hijackings involved assistance from accomplices on the ground. At St. Louis, Mo., Martin J. McNally, 28, wearing a shaggy wig and carrying a gun in a trombone case, seized an American Airlines jet en route to Tulsa, Okla., June 23, ordered it back to St. Louis, and demanded $502,500.

As the plane was about to take off again, a speeding automobile crashed into it. McNally and the crew he held hostage switched to another plane, and he parachuted out with the money near Peru, Ind. Five days later police arrested him with the cooperation of Walter J. Petlikowsky, 31, who had driven McNally to St. Louis from their home in Michigan and later had picked him up in Indiana. Petlikowsky was charged with aiding and abetting an air piracy.

Dimitr Alexiev and Michael Azmanoff, Bulgarian immigrants, hijacked a Pacific Southwest jet July 5 en route from Sacramento to San Francisco and demanded $800,000, parachutes, and charts for a flight by way of Canada and Alaska to Siberia and held the 79 passengers and 5 crew members captive on a runway at San Francisco for six hours. They were killed by FBI agents storming the plane at the airport, and an elderly passenger from Quebec also was injured fatally. Arrested as an accomplice was Lubert Peichev, 29, who had been waiting for the two hijackers at a remote airstrip in British Columbia.

Hijacking attempts also were fatal for Heinrich Merlyn St. George, 45, killed by FBI agents at Poughkeepsie, N.Y., Jan. 27 after seizing a Mohawk Airlines flight in upstate New York and collecting $200,000 ransom, and for Nguyen Thai Binh, 24, who tried to order a Pan American World Airways 747 chartered military flight with 153 persons aboard to Hanoi July 2 but was shot dead by a passenger after the huge plane landed at Saigon.

Hijacking abroad was an especially dangerous venture. In May Israeli paratroops disguised as mechanics burst into a Belgian jetliner that had been forced to land at Tel Aviv and killed the two Arab guerrilla hijackers. Three of the 97 passengers were injured.

Two weeks later Ecuadorian soldiers burst into a hijacked airliner at Quito and killed a skyjacker who had demanded $40,000 ransom and a parachute. Seven days afterward a gunman shot himself to death at Sao Paulo as Brazilian troops rushed the Varig airliner he had seized. He died moments after having released 80 passengers on payment of $250,000 ransom.

In October police at Ronchi dei Legionari, Italy, after an all-night vigil at the airport stormed a domestic airliner from which the three crew members and six passengers had escaped, and found the bullet-riddled body of the youthful hijacker who had demanded $344,000 and a flight to Cairo.

Oddity of the year among the hijackers was Frederick W. Hahneman, 50, an Easton, Pa., electronics engineer who took command of a Miami-bound American Airlines 727 May 5 after takeoff from Allentown, Pa., with 49 passengers aboard. Hahneman forced a landing at Dulles International Airport near Washington, collected $303,000 and six parachutes, ordered the plane flown south, and bailed out over his native Honduras.

A month later he surrendered to the U.S. Embassy at Tegucigalpa, apparently out of fear guerrillas might kill him for the hidden money. He was said to have told an FBI agent he placed the $303,000 in a secret bank account in Hong Kong, to be used for "humanitarian purposes." He pleaded guilty at Alexandria, Va., to air piracy, and was sentenced to life in prison. In court he asked the judge not to question him as to his motives. And when a reporter asked about the missing money as he was being led away by marshals, Hahneman replied, "none of your bloody business."

The only other failure to recover ransom money was in the first extortion of this type, in which a man identified only as D. Cooper bailed out of a Northwest Airlines plane Nov. 24, 1971 *(The World in 1971, 259),* somewhere between Seattle and Reno.

Since no trace of the man had been found and the ransom bills apparently had not entered circulation, most authorities believed the hijacker was killed in the night-time jump.

The first successful hijacking of 1972, on Jan. 7, was that of a Pacific Southwest 727 carrying 138 passengers, seized by an armed man and a woman with a 5-month old baby. After leaving San Francisco, the plane was flown to Havana by way of Los Angeles and Tampa, Fla.

A gunman duplicated the crime May 6 by taking control of a Western Air Lines jet over Salt Lake City and forcing it, with 61 other passengers, to fly to Cuba by way of refueling stops at Los Angeles and Dallas.

During March two small chartered planes were forcibly detoured from Florida to Cuba. The pilot, a mechanic and a bystander were wounded in gunplay during one of the incidents en route.

Other hijacking episodes of 1972:

Jan. 12—Billy E. Hurst, 22, hijacked a Braniff 727 en route from Houston to Minneapolis, forced it to land at Dallas, demanded $1 million and 10 parachutes, but surrendered after the hostages escaped. He was placed under mental examination.

Jan. 29—Garrett Trapnell, 33, took command of a Trans World Airlines 707 over Iowa, demanded $303,000, and forced a landing at New York's Kennedy International Airport, where an FBI agent wounded and arrested him. He also was held for mental examination.

Feb. 22—Three Arabs seized a Lufthansa jetliner carrying 175 passengers, including Joseph Kennedy III, on its way from New Delhi to Athens, and forced it to land at Aden. The plane and passengers were released after the Bonn government paid $5 million, the largest air piracy ransom on record (Pages 31–32).

March 11—Attillia Lazzeri, 55, hijacked an Alitalia jetliner from Italy to Munich but surrendered after freeing 31 passengers and five crewmen.

March 14—New York Mario V. Maimone commandeered a Swiss jetliner from Geneva to Rome. He demanded an audience with the Pope and the U.S. ambassador, but surrendered after releasing the passengers.

April 9—Stanley Speck, 31, took over a Pacific Southwest jet carrying 92 persons out of Oakland, Calif., demanded $500,000 and four parachutes. He was captured by the FBI at San Diego after being tricked by the pilot into leaving the plane. Held for mental examination.

April 17—William H. Greene III, 31, seized a Delta Air Lines jet shortly after takeoff from West Palm Beach, Fla., for Chicago, demanded $500,000 and a flight to Nassau, Bahamas. He was arrested by FBI men at Chicago's O'Hare Airport, and was sentenced to 20 years.

May 4—Four Turkish terrorists hijacked a Turkish Airlines DC9 jet from Ankara to Bulgaria, demanded freedom for six imprisoned compatriots, and after threatening to blow up the plane and crew were granted asylum.

May 30—Three Japanese terrorists left a plane at Tel Aviv airport and machinegunned the crowd, killing 27 and wounding more than 70. Two gunmen were killed, the other arrested.

June 8—Seven men and three women, one carrying a small child, took over a Czechoslovak airliner, killing the pilot in the process, and forced the plane into West Germany where they requested political asylum.

July 5—Charles E. Smith, 23, seized an unoccupied 707 at Buffalo, N.Y., airport, and threatened to kill his 18-month-old daughter unless he was flown out of the United States. The FBI

Michael Stanley Green, above, and Lulseyd Tesfa, below, in custody of FBI agents after a hijack attempt in Lake Jackson, Texas

refused, and he surrendered after three hours and was indicted for air piracy.

July 6—Francis Michael Goodell, 21, an AWOL soldier, hijacked a Pacific Southwest plane at San Diego, collected $450,000 in ransom, but surrendered at Oakland International airport. He was held for mental examination.

Sept. 9—Yugoslav separatists hijacked a Swedish airliner at Malmö, extorted $105,000 from the Swedish government before freeing 83 passengers, and then ordered the plane to Madrid. There they were detained, and Spain indicated that ultimately they would be extradited.

Oct. 22—The May 4 hijacking to Bulgaria was duplicated when another four Turkish hijackers took over a Boeing 707 plane in Turkey with 81 persons aboard and forced the crew to fly to Sofia. There they threatened to blow up the jet unless 13 leftist prisoners in Turkey were released.

The Turkish government refused, but agreed not to oppose asylum in Bulgaria. The next day the hijackers surrendered.

They told Bulgarian authorities their purpose had been to "tear down the Turkish regime and set up a Marxist-Leninist system."

Oct. 29—Stanley E. Hubbard, 34, an Eastern Airlines gate agent, was checking in passengers for a flight from Houston to Atlanta when four men armed with pistols and a shotgun shot and killed him and rushed aboard the plane. Once aboard, they forced the jet to take off for Havana. On landing, the four hijackers were taken into custody by Cuban authorities and the plane with its 42 passengers and crew members were allowed to return to the United States.

Indicted in the hijack were Charles A. Tuller, 49, his sons, Bryce, 19, and Jonathan, 18, and William Graham, 18. Tuller, who had resigned a $26,000 a year job with the Department of Commerce just days before the skyjack, his sons, and Graham also were charged in Alexandria, Va., with murder, attempted murder and attempted robbery of a bank Oct. 25 during which a policeman and a bank manager were shot to death.

U.N. Secretary-General Kurt Waldheim meeting at United Nations headquarters in New York with international representatives of pilots and transport workers on the hijack situation

Joint session of Congress heard President Nixon report on his summit meeting with Soviet leaders in Moscow

Congress Battled Nixon On a Variety of Issues Throughout 1972 Session

THE DEMOCRATIC-CONTROLLED Congress battled President Nixon on foreign and domestic issues throughout the 1972 session and ended up killing about as many major bills as it passed.

Nixon charged the legislators with reckless spending and with ignoring major initiatives advanced in his "New American Revolution" address at the opening of the 92nd Congress in 1971.

Democrats replied that the President killed with vetoes funds needed for education, health and other programs and blunted their efforts to develop new plans to deal with social ills.

The lawmakers did send to the White House just before final adjournment a landmark bill to share $30.2 billion of federal revenues with state and local governments over the next five years—the only major new Nixon domestic recommendation to pass.

It also cleared during the year a 20 per cent boost in Social Security along with higher payroll taxes to finance it, far more than the 5 per cent the President recommended; an equal rights for women constitutional amendment; an historic $19.5 billion higher education bill; and a $24.6 billion water pollution control measure on which Congress overrode a Nixon veto.

But it rejected or failed to act on a welfare reform plan which Nixon repeatedly called his most important domestic proposal, anti-busing legislation, all of the President's broad government reorganization proposals, all of the various national health care plans including Nixon's, an increase in the minimum wage, and a bill to set up a potent consumer protection agency.

Congress fought the President on foreign policy and military issues as it did in 1971, but Nixon emerged victorious in all these encounters.

End-the-Vietnam war amendments cleared the Senate twice in 1972, but they failed in the House.

Senate Democratic Leader Mike Mansfield failed to get Congress to accept his proposal for a reduction of the 300,000 American troops in Europe.

On overwhelming votes, Congress ratified the agreements worked out by the President with Russia on arms limitations.

Many members objected to the new weapons projects he said were necessary despite the agreements, but they generally failed in attempts to deny funds for these.

It was in the domestic field that Congress balked at several key Nixon proposals, and that it tried to insist on others which he rejected. Some of these, such as a broad new child development program, he killed with vetoes.

Congress claimed that it cut the President's record-high appropriations requests in 1972 by more than $5 billion.

But the administration insisted it took other actions on Social Security increases, miners' black lung benefits, revenue sharing and other measures, which would have the effect of increasing spending by $9.5 billion over the Nixon budget.

For this reason, the President demanded that the legislators give him power to make unlimited cuts in any program in order to hold spending to $250 billion for fiscal 1973.

The House agreed but the Senate declined to go along with what it called a complete abdication of Congressional responsibility, and the ceiling was killed on the final day of the session.

The President retaliated by pocket vetoing a dozen bills after the lawmakers had left.

He rejected for the second time a $30.5 billion appropriations measure for the Labor and Health, Education and Welfare Departments.

Also killed were bills to benefit the elderly, veterans, the chronically handicapped and the unemployed, and measures involving spending for airports and other public works projects.

Democrats vowed they would try to revive these early in the 93rd Congress.

House Speaker Carl Albert, speaking for the Democrats, declared the 92nd had been a "do-something Congress" which "responded to the urgent needs of the American people" in the fields of Social Security, veterans benefits, education, environment, health, human rights and consumer programs.

But liberal groups such as Americans for Democratic Action, declared the 92nd had "a shameful record."

ADA said the Congress was regressive on civil rights, and cited the failure of welfare reform, a national health plan, child development, no-fault insurance and legislation to control hand guns.

These were the major measures cleared in the 1972 session:

An equal rights amendment to the constitution barring discrimination because of sex. It was not ratified by the states in 1972, however.

An $8 billion, 20 per cent increase in Social Security benefits for 28 million Americans, together with the taxes to pay for it. This measure also provides for automatic future increases tied to the cost-of-living index.

A $30.2 billion revenue sharing bill providing grants to states, cities, counties and townships over the next five years with few strings attached.

A $19.5 billion higher education bill establishing a program of general federal financial aid for all colleges and universities and a system of basic grants for all needy college students. A provision in this measure held up all school busing orders until Dec. 31, 1973, unless court appeals had been exhausted.

The $24.6 billion water pollution control measure designed to clear up the nation's streams and lakes by 1985.

A $6 billion Social Security-welfare bill increasing benefits for widows, all male Social Security recipients, the disabled, persons who work after reaching retirement age, sufferers from chronic kidney disease, and other groups, and establishing a new federally-financed national level of benefits for the aged, blind and disabled on welfare. It also raised Social Security taxes for a second time during the year.

Legislation qualifying thousands of additional coal miners for black lung benefits and increasing the federal cost $4.2 billion over the next decade.

Authority for the Equal Employment Opportunity Commission to file its own suits against job discrimination based on color, sex or national origin, together with an extension of the agency's coverage to millions of additional workers.

An election reform bill requiring much broader disclosure of political contributions and expenditures, and putting tighter limits on contributions.

Approval of the U.S.-Soviet interim agreement to limit offensive nuclear weapons, but with a request to the President to seek equality for U.S. arms in future agreements.

In addition, the Senate ratified the treaty with Russia to limit antiballistic missile sites to two each and to limit the number of missiles at each site to 100.

These were major proposals rejected or not acted on:

Nixon's Family Assistance Plan to reform the welfare program by establishing a guaranteed annual income of $2,400 for a family of four, providing aid for the first time to the working poor, and tightening work requirements. Passed the House, rejected by the Senate.

All proposals for a national health care plan.

A bill to impose strict limits on school busing orders and to reopen previous cases under the new guidelines. Passed the House, failed in the Senate.

Nixon's broad government reorganization plan involving four big new omnibus cabinet departments.

Legislation to create permanent machinery to settle national emergency transportation strikes.

A bill to ban commercial sales of easily concealable hand guns. Passed the Senate, not considered in the House.

All of the President's proposals for special revenue sharing plans in such fields as education, housing and transportation.

Legislation designed to assure that 30 million workers in private pension plans actually receive some benefits in retirement.

A bill to create a Consumer Protection Agency to serve as an advocate for consumer interests, compiling complaints, intervening in cases before federal regulatory agencies, and appealing decisions in the courts.

Legislation to set up a national no-fault insurance system.

A bill to regulate strip mining. Passed the House, not considered in the Senate.

A bill to allow tax credits for parents who send children to parochial schools.

Legislation to provide compensation for victims of crime. Passed the Senate, died in the House.

Legislation raising the $1.60 an hour minimum wage to $2, as voted by the House, or $2.20, as favored by the Senate, and extending coverage to millions of additional employes. The House refused to send the bill to conference.

A $9 billion omnibus housing bill seeking to reduce closing costs on home mortgages, providing subsidies for operating costs of mass transit, requiring suburbs of big cities to provide some homes for low and middle-income families, and providing more subsidized housing for the elderly. Passed the Senate, died in the House.

After the Senate voted passage of a constitutional amendment giving women equal rights, Sen. Birch Bayh, D-Ind., left, met with opponent Sen. Sam Ervin, D-N.C., second from right, and two supporters, Rep. Martha Griffiths, D-Mich., and Sen. Marlow Cook, R-Ky.

An $18 billion measure extending major highway programs and providing some additional mass transit funds. Passed both branches, compromise version failed.

A war powers bill to limit the President, without approval of Congress, to not more than a 30-day use of American armed forces in an emergency situation. Passed the Senate but died in the House.

A $2.8 billion bill extending the Hill-Burton hospital construction grant program and seven other health programs and changing the grant formula for some of them to give greater help to urban areas. Passed the Senate, not considered in the House.

A bill to require honest disclosure of warranties on consumer products and to give the Federal Trade Commission power to move against deceptive market practices. Passed the Senate, died in the House.

The Senate again failed to act on ratification of the international treaty on prevention and punishment of genocide.

Other bills passed in 1972:

A $250 million federal grant program, that would assist states in providing meals for needy persons who are 60 years of age or older.

A $322.5 million bill extending federal programs to combat communicable diseases including tuberculosis and venereal diseases and to encourage family planning.

A $400 million rural development program to improve living conditions in small towns and to lure job-creating industries there.

A $1.38 billion measure to mount a greatly stepped-up attack on heart, stroke and lung diseases.

Legislation authorizing $800 million for drug education, treatment and rehabilitation programs and seeking to fix a long-term strategy for all federal drug abuse programs.

A $115 million program to help screen, counsel and treat victims of sickle cell anemia and to conduct research into prevention and control of the disease.

A bill making available $225 million to pay Amtrak's losses on passenger train service.

A $260 million, 10 per cent increase in compensation to 2,177,000 service-connected disabled veterans.

A $4.7 billion, two-year, anti-poverty measure dropping efforts to put the Legal Services for the poor program under an independent corporation.

Legislation to help victims of Hurricane Agnes and of other floods by providing forgiveness of up to $5,000 on Small Business Administration loans and farm loans, grants to stricken colleges, and loan interest subsidies.

A two-year $65 million extension of the National Health Service Corps designed to provide health personnel to rural and other shortage areas.

Legislation to give the Environmental Protection Agency greater powers to ban insecticides and herbicides found dangerous to the environment.

A measure to protect whales, seals, sea otters, polar bears, porpoises and other marine mammals by placing a moratorium against killing, capture or importation of many species.

A measure increasing veterans education benefits from $175 to $220 a month for a single veteran, $205 to $261 for a married veteran.

A ban on dumping at sea of radiological, chemical and biological agents, and a requirement for permits for dumping of other materials.

Creation of an independent consumer product safety agency to protect against unreasonable hazards.

Britain Joining World's Biggest Free Trade Area

Nine-nation European economic partnership may rival the United States and Russia as a superpower

Opening session of the enlarged Common Market in Paris

THROUGHOUT THE LONG SWEEP of European history, beginning with the Roman conquests centuries before the birth of Christ, 25 years has often proved little more than a breathing space between wars. In the last 25 years alone, however, the nations of Western Europe may have changed that pattern for all time. They have worked closer together than ever before in peacetime. As a result, a New Europe will come into being Jan. 1, 1973, changing the world power structure without spilling a drop of blood. Some 250 million people from nine West European countries will form the expanded Common Market, the largest free trade area in the world, richer in gold reserves and annual exports than the United States. Over the next decade, as these nine nations move toward political union, they are likely to rival America, the Soviet Union, China and Japan as a new world superpower.

Rarely has more fundamental change been dramatized in one lifetime than it was on November 20, 1972, the silver anniversary of Britain's Queen Elizabeth II and Prince Philip.

Britain's Queen and her consort returned to Westminster Abbey for a silver anniversary service in a different world from 1947. Western Europe enjoyed unparalleled prosperity. The U.S. dollar was no longer almighty. The six founding members of the Common Market—France, West Germany, Italy, Belgium, the Netherlands and Luxembourg—had produced an enviable record of economic growth Britain could no longer ignore. The Empire was dead and the Commonwealth that replaced it could not match Europe either as a natural market or as a political power base for Britain. Europe and Britain, finally, were ready for each other.

But it was a vastly weakened Britain which was ready for the Common Market. Years of conflict between labor and capital, between managers and workers, had reduced the country almost to the have-not class. The fact that bright young men from the lower class could climb into managerial ranks only occasionally had shifted many good brains into labor union leadership. The way to the top for these sharp men from poorer families could not lead them into management so they turned to leadership in unions.

Strikes, always bad in Britain, were finally attacked by the Heath government. Although the measures he introduced were mild by American standards—a labor court, secret union elections, cooling-off periods—British labor refused to accept them.

Many unions refused to register with the government, thereby losing their privileged status under the law. Some refused to recognize the labor court's decrees, and even to defend themselves before the court. As a result, fines of hundreds of thousands of dollars were assessed against the unions and collected from their bank accounts.

But the strikes continued, with appeals from the labor court preventing any quick court action. A seven-week strike of coal miners reduced the country's desperately-needed industry to half-time working. Rail workers struck for three months, port workers for a month. Both straitened the flow of export goods which Britain must have to live.

The strike record for 1972 was the worse since the 1926 General Strike.

The British had agreed to exchange 900 years of independent power status for a role in a united Europe, bringing in Ireland and Denmark as well. Only Norway, among the four nations applying for Common Market membership, decided in a referendum to stay out. Western Europe was ready to begin the biggest exercise in peaceful cooperation in its history.

The year 1973 would show how far and how fast the impetus given by the new members would carry the Common Market forward to west European unity. All nine would try to work together in the big international negotiations scheduled; on the world's monetary system, on new rules for international trade, on security and cooperation in Europe, on mutual force reductions with the Soviet Union and its allies.

The year would also show how well they could get together internally:

—to form international corporations that could rival the giants based in the United States.

—to supply British industry with a badly needed stimulus by the prospect of broader markets and tougher competition.

—to give the Common Market more meaning for the ordinary European by attacking problems of immediate concern to him: high prices, the gulf between rich and poor, the threat and reality of unemployment, the growing pollution of his air, rivers, beaches and high seas.

That was for the short term. Prime Minister Edward Heath and others who fought for British membership had the long term more in mind. They have argued that even if wages fail to rise or business earnings to improve, unity offered a last chance to regain some of the global influence that the European countries wielded individually before the advent of World War II.

If this chance is successfully taken, the New European superpower would draw its influence more from economic than from military might. The nine made this clear at a summit meeting in Paris in October, pledging to work toward economic union by 1980. They deliberately left the details vague, to be worked out in future political negotiations.

With inflation mounting and currencies unstable, with some governments leaning left and some right, any leader trying to predict the shape of eventual unity was like an aspiring fortune teller wondering if he could afford a crystal ball. The United States of Europe might come some day. At the moment the price of steak was shooting right off the graph paper. These were the kind of problems to be tackled first.

A few days before the summit, however, Lord Carrington, Britain's secretary for defense, had suggested that the members would some day have to consider building a joint nuclear defense. This was not officially discussed at the summit, but the idea was certainly not forgotten.

Many west Europeans were eager to develop a separate "identity", independent of the United States. It was not Heath but Chancellor Willy Brandt of West Germany who proposed a link between the new Common Market and the United States. Heath joined French President Georges Pompidou against him and Brandt lost out.

President Nixon came out with a warm endorsement of the summit's work, despite misgivings in the United States about one direction the Common Market was taking. Jan. 1 will not only mark the accession of the three new members. On the same date free trade treaties were to take effect with Austria, Sweden, Switzerland, Finland, Portugal and Iceland. A series of special agreements will link them all with nearly all the other Mediterranean countries, most of Africa and probably much of the British Commonwealth. All these countries will be agreed on one article of foreign policy: trade preferences for one another. That is another way of saying trade discrimination against outsiders such as the United States and Japan. This

Evening News

Lloyds put interest rates up again

Ulster o

brink aga

Cabinet i

BRAKE SLAMMED
ON EASY MONEY

crisis tal

Evening Standard

CITY PRICES

Lloyds move as £ hits new low

BANK PUTS UP
COST OF LOANS

Walker acts to

theatres

British newspapers headlined the boosting of interest rates on loans by British banks in response to the pound crisis

takes the form of tariff reductions for the favored nations, standard high tariffs for the others.

The west Europeans, including the new members, have been working on this problem for more than two years, with only modest success. They have acted together on some matters of Middle East policy in the United Nations and their diplomats have been coordinating their activities in many capitals. But the member governments were still a long way from being able to shout in chorus what ought to be done about southeast Asia or how to improve the lot of the southern hemisphere.

The old Common Market had already surveyed another path toward a united western Europe and the summit agreed that it was a good one: economic and monetary union. The goal is to create a single currency by about 1980. This is more ambitious

than it sounds. In order for francs, pounds, lire and other moneys to become part of a single currency—that is, to have a fixed relationship with one another—the countries concerned would have to adopt uniform policies on wages, prices, government spending and most of the other controversial issues that make up the main business of politicians.

In over 22 years of hard, unspectacular work the six countries of the old Common Market had made a start. First they welded together their coal and steel industries. The idea was to prevent France and Germany from ever again fighting another war such as had swept over western Europe three times in the preceding two generations.

Then they tore down the tariff walls among them, so far as manufactured goods were concerned, and set up a new one of

216

uniform height around the whole area. For farm products they worked out a single policy: to support high prices and to subsidize the export of the resulting surpluses by levies on imports from outside the area.

The member governments also made a beginning on joint anti-trust action and agreed on thousands of trade regulations from the height of auto bumpers (uniform) to taxes on internal trade in works of art (forbidden).

To lay this basis required hundreds of interminable night sessions by cabinet ministers over such dreary subjects as the tariff on benzenoid chemicals and the permissable ingredients for mayonnaise. Thousands more such meetings were in prospect. To impatient critics, European officials like to point out that building the United Nations required not only the debates of the Constitutional Convention, but the armed conquest of a continent and a civil war. Europeans hope to do it differently.

One measure of the distance already traveled: the Common Market governments planned to spend something over $5 billion jointly in 1973 and about $100 billion separately.

Expanding the Common Market just to include Britain had been a political nightmare in itself. This one major accomplishment alone could ease the way past future obstacles.

Opinion polls in Britain consistently showed more than 60 per cent of the population against joining Europe, largely from fears of higher food prices and a loss of sovereignty. Heath's Conservative government argued that removal of Europe's tariff walls would boost British trade by $700 million a year, more than enough to absorb entry costs. With opinion polls running against them, however, Heath's government refused either a referendum or an election on the Common Market question. After a yearlong battle, they finally beat down the opposition Labor Party's delaying tactics and ratified entry terms in the Conservative-controlled parliament in October.

The once mighty British nation stood on the threshold of Common Market membership as a weak man of Europe. Its inflation rate was higher than any on the continent, approaching 10 per cent a year. Unemployment stood at a 30-year high. Business investment was critically low, despite generous tax concessions. A record number of strikes virtually halted economic growth. In June, the weakened pound sterling was forced to float down outside fixed exchange rates and by November it had lost 10 per cent of its purchasing power. On Nov. 6, Heath had to impose a 90-day freeze on wages and prices in an attempt to curb inflation.

For the prime minister, a convinced European all his political life, the longer term answer to the nation's many economic problems was a share in the more prosperous European trading community five times the size of Britain's home market of 50 million people. His countrymen were not so sure.

Many had grown cynical over the inability of successive British governments to solve the country's post World War II difficulties. A 1972 survey showed that despite the massive welfare state benefits in the past quarter century, working class children were still slower readers, likely to leave school earlier and take jobs that would keep them trapped at lower income levels.

For Britain, Common Market membership would be a double-edged sword. British industry would at last be able to compete freely for larger sales on the continent. But at the same time, continental firms would be equally free to try to take the British market away from them. Only time would tell whether entry into Europe would reverse or accelerate Britain's long postwar economic decline.

Many Norwegian farmers were opposed to joining. They got even higher prices than the Common Market offers, under their national support system. Fishermen, fearing for their exclusive rights in offshore waters, were also opposed.

But it was probably more important that Norway's dominant Labor Party has strong Socialist leanings. Its members apparently saw little in the Common Market for the ordinary workingman. This might have been shortsighted on their part but it focused the attention of some Common Market leaders on a major failure: their inability to give the organization much meaning to the ordinary European-in-the-street. The Common Market's benefits for the common man tend to be of the "filter down" variety, based on the conservative assumption that what is good for business is good for labor.

Recent west European history seemed to justify that view. Unemployment in the six countries of the old Common Market was lower than in Britain and much lower than in Canada or the United States. Real wages had risen much faster among the six than in Britain or the United States—though not so fast as in Japan.

But little had been done to give western Europe's variety of private enterprise the "human face" that Alexander Dubcek tried and failed to give Communism in Czechoslovakia.

A dockworker was hauled off by police at wharf in Keadby, England, where authorities and pickets clashed

Higher Education Forces Competing for Increased Allotments of Tax Funds

OUTWARDLY A STRANGE quietness had settled over the entire educational community, but was it largely illusionary? Many would say yes. Admittedly, disruptive and destructive student activism had diminished rapidly since the major upheavals that plagued campuses immediately following the Cambodia invasion.

Although not as visible as rampaging students, a variety of issues was causing turmoil and division within the educational community. Unionization of teachers at all levels and personnel practices in higher education was creating a gap between former allies and, in some instances, setting teacher against teacher.

Private and public higher education was waging a silent but nevertheless fierce behind-the-scene battle for state tax dollars, and the huge Roman Catholic parochial school systems continued its attack on a wide front to win court approval of some type of public financial support.

Meantime, the educational community was faced with the hard fact that the job market for both educators and the college students they train was shrinking and not likely to improve in the next decade. The Department of Labor estimated that by 1980 less than 20 per cent of the jobs would require more than a high school education, yet 50 per cent of that age group enrolled in college.

Against a backdrop of public apathy, if not outright antagonism, the large state universities were finding state legislatures tight-fisted, and the voters were expressing their displeasure by turning down school bond elections in record numbers.

The National Association of State Universities and Land Grant Colleges' 1972–73 Chambers report on state appropriations to the major state universities showed 57 of 98 institutions received less than 10 per cent increases a year, the amount educators said was needed to keep pace with growth and inflation. Eleven schools reported decreased allotments. The state appropriation represents about half the revenue available to state universities.

The U.S. Office of Education said public schools were faring badly at the polls on bond elections. Latest OE figures showed that, in 1970–71, voters approved only 46.7 per cent of the 1,086 bond issues as compared with a 72.4 per cent approval in 1961–62. Dollarwise it was even worse. Only 41 per cent of $3.3 billion was approved, as compared with a 68.9 per cent approval 10 years earlier.

Public elementary and secondary classrooms for the past 10 years had been steadily moving toward more labor union-like relations with school boards and administrators. About three years ago organizing efforts began on college and university campuses.

A pensive New Jersey college student during a protest demonstration

The climate organizers from the National Education Association and the American Federation of Teachers, AFL-CIO, should find this aim epitomized by a statement on the University of California Berkeley campus by Neil Smelser, sociology professor and chairman of the academic senate policy committee.

"Most faculty feel picked out for excessive punishment by state officials," he said, "through lack of pay increases and staff reductions. Motions are afoot to organize teachers."

Higher education had an estimated 335,000 professionals, but also included 500,000 administrative, nonteaching professionals and nonprofessionals.

The NEA already had 40,000 higher education personnel under 73 agreements, the AFT 19,000 under 26 agreements and the American Association of University Professors 4,000 under nine agreements. In the decade ahead, the fight to represent the professionals in higher education was likely to bring about major changes in two of the organizations.

The AFT, whose membership was expected to skyrocket to 400,000 early in 1972, always had been union-oriented. The NEA, on the other hand, was not. It was less than a decade ago that it was largely guided by administrators rather than classroom teachers, who numbered about 900,000 of the NEA's 1.2 million members.

The classroom teachers by 1972 were the power, and they exhibited it at the NEA's annual convention when they approved by a landslide vote a proposed new constitution and bylaws. Dr. Sam Lambert, executive director of the organization, said the proposals "are one more step in NEA's gradual drift toward unionism. You will stop this drift this summer or not at all."

Two months later Lambert arranged an early retirement from the $65,000 a year job.

NEA began its drift toward unionism 10 years ago when the AFT won the bargaining rights for New York City teachers. The prestigous AAUP took a step in that direction when delegates at the annual convention in New Orleans voted to authorize collective bargaining "as a major additional way of realizing the association's goals in higher education."

A third fight swirled in the complicated labor field. The AFT, as a national policy, favored merger of AFT and NEA. The NEA opposed formal affiliation with any union belonging to the AFL-CIO and had a new policy to disaffiliate any unit that joined in the future with an AFL-CIO union formally.

It was adopted over stiff opposition at the NEA's annual convention and was largely prompted by the merger of the New York Teachers Association and the AFT's New York City United Federation of Teachers. Under the merger, to be finalized in 1973, New York teachers would pay dues to both national organizations.

Despite the threat of disaffiliation, Dave Selden, president of AFT, announced that NEA affiliates in Baltimore, Md., Springfield, Mass., Portland, Ore., and Kenosha, Wisc., were talking merger with their AFT counterparts.

Whether the NEA and AFT ever would get together formally, they did face one common enemy: mass unemployment. For the third straight year, the nation's colleges and universities produced a surplus of teacher graduates. An NEA survey showed that 110,000 potential teacher graduates were unable to find teaching posts when school opened in the fall of 1972. The year before 100,700 teacher graduates had to look elsewhere for employment.

Higher education, plagued by financial problems and only just recovering from the years of student disorder, found itself under sharp criticism for hiring and personnel practices. It was an unexpected attack, since the colleges and universities had provided a great deal of the leadership in the fight for equal opportunity.

The turmoil began when the Office of Civil Rights in the Department of Health, Education and Welfare began demanding strict compliance with Executive Order 11246 or give up badly needed federal dollars. The order, originally issued in 1964 and later amended to include sex, demanded that any institution receiving federal funds "not discriminate against any employe or applicant for employment because of race, color, religion, sex or national origin."

Historically, college and university faculties had been dominated by white males who had supported the order as applied to the nonprofessional staffs of the institutions.

"When it was amended and women began screaming, like a turtle, the men pulled back their heads," said one official at the American Association of University Professors.

Trying to force his way through antiwar pickets at Columbia University, a student took matters into his own hands

Above, left, gown flying, this happy youth drove to his high school commencement in Las Vegas. Above, right, an unidentified coed dragged to a police bus after being arrested for taking part in "an unlawful assembly" during an antiwar protest.

J. Stanley Pottinger, 32-year-old Harvard law graduate and director of OCR, let it be known that he expected compliance when he temporarily held up $23 million in federal funds until several blue ribbon schools developed "affirmative action plans" for eliminating discrimination, especially against women.

Opponents immediately charged that enforcement would result in a quota system and force schools to hire less qualified personnel. President Nixon, in accepting the nomination for a second term, said "dividing Americans into quotas is totally alien to the American tradition."

Agreeing, Pottinger said, "The overall thrust (of affirmative action) is to remove artificial barriers against minorities and women and not to create reverse discrimination against white males."

Dr. Sidney Hook, distinguished New York University professor and an outspoken foe of OCR, said in an article, "The effect of the ultimata to universities to hire blacks and women under threat of losing crucial financial support is to compel them to hire unqualified Negroes and women to discriminate against qualified non-blacks and men . . ."

HEW Secretary Elliot L. Richardson replied to these comments in a speech delivered at Princeton University. He said:

"Affirmative action does not mean that any institution is called upon to dilute non-discriminatory employment standards. Nor does the executive order call for termination or demotion of an incumbent employe to make room for women or minority group members."

"My own personal fear," said Margaret Rumbarger of the AAUP, "is that through sheer laziness schools will grab the first woman or black body regardless of qualification, to fill self-imposed quotas."

Pottinger believed the program was bearing fruit, and cited these Texas cases: "A woman whose salary was inequitable at a larger school had her salary increased from $18,000 to $28,000 per year; at the same school another woman was promoted and given an increase from $15,000 to $28,000 per year after both had filed complaints with HEW."

As the fall term began, OCR produced a new set of guidelines for affirmative action for developing goals and timetables,

Most states were permitting students to vote where they attended school, Carbone said, but it still was a question of whether students will use their voting status to seek reclassification as resident students. Thus far most schools had denied reclassification on the ground that the university's criteria for residency were not based on being a registered voter of the state.

Already there were a number of cases in the courts, and Carbone foresaw that the question of residency undoubtedly would have to be settled there. So he advised public schools to commence searching for more realistic alternatives to the nonresident tuition.

"If nonresident tuition is declared illegal," he said, "it is likely that the institutional response will be to increase the fees of all students to cover lost income. Clearly, this expediency would strike a telling blow to the low tuition principle upon which public higher education in America has been built."

The pressure on the public institutions to win more generous appropriations from state legislatures was getting greater as more and more states adopted programs providing financial assistance to private colleges and universities.

A background paper prepared by the office of research and information of the National Association of State Universities and Land Grant Colleges showed that 11 states enacted new laws in 1972 to provide financial aid to colleges or to students attending private schools.

As an example, the Georgia state legislature voted a $2.8 million appropriation to provide grants of $400 each to every Georgia student attending a private college in the state. Connecticut's legislature passed a bill allowing $500 per year for each Connecticut student enrolled in a private college.

Only 18 of the 50 states had no program for assisting private higher education or the students who enrolled in them. The most popular method of help was in the form of student aid, and 30 states had such programs. Thirteen states had programs identified as direct institutional aid.

The Roman Catholic parochial school system, second in size only to the public school system, again in 1972 took its lumps in the U.S. Supreme Court. By an 8 to 1 decision, the court declared unconstitutional an Ohio law that would have granted $90 to parents who send their children to private schools. A year earlier the court had knocked down a variety of plans to assist parochial schools.

The Catholic system now was pinning its hopes for assistance on state tax credit proposals. They had won favorable decisions in cases in New York and Minnesota, but the issue probably would go to the Supreme Court for a final decision.

Edward R. D'Alessio, director of Catholic elementary and secondary education, said in a press statement that the most recent Supreme Court decision was not directed at the 1972 tax credit law passed in Ohio. However, Theodore Mann of Philadelphia, co-chairman of the American Jewish Congress, which opposed parochiaid (aid to parochial schools), said the tuition grant arrangement condemned in the Ohio case "differs in no significant way from the tax credit plan for aid to sectarian schools now being given wide publicity."

The going was rough also for the campus radicals. They couldn't find broad support for any of their movements and, complained Don Lee, self-styled Marxist-Mao communist and presently suspended from Stanford University, the Madison avenue approach was killing "signs of rebellion."

"Even the pigs have long hair," he said. "The system is so perverted it sells its own destruction. They say 'don't fight it: buy it and sell it back'."

and Mary Jo Small, assistant vice president at the University of Iowa, seemed to sum up the consensus of a poll of large state universities when she wrote:

"The new guidelines are ones we can live with. Their basic thrust seems to us reasonable and not oppressive."

Even if the public state colleges and universities solved the affirmative action problem, the institutions could see on the horizon a potential $300 million annual headache. It was riding toward them on the 26th amendment to the U.S. Constitution extending voting rights to 18-year-olds.

Dr. Robert F. Carbone, dean of the school of education at the University of Maryland, uncovered this fact in a survey of the impact of the amendment on nearly 400 public four-year colleges and universities holding membership in the National Association of State Universities and Land Grant Colleges and the American Association of State Colleges and Universities:

"If adult status and voting rights for college-age citizens eliminate nonresident tuition charges in the public colleges and universities," Carbone said, "the effect on higher education budgets would be staggering."

The schools surveyed by Carbone enrolled 465,357 nonresident students in the fall of 1972. The potential tuition differential paid by these students who migrate to another state for their college education was $329,090,406.

PERON RETURNED TO ARGENTINA
AFTER 17 YEARS IN EXILE

Jamming more than 12 normally quiet, tree-lined blocks in the Buenos Aires suburb of Vincent Lopez were thousands of cheering, chanting, drum-beating people.

Street vendors hawked baseball caps and photographs in the milling crowd which filled some streets so tightly that area residents were unable to get out of their doors. One home owner even feared that his house would collapse under the weight of nearly 100 leaping and cheering persons on his terrace and roof. "If they keep this up," he fretted, "we may all be killed."

The reason for all the adulation was a man who had just moved into a $96,000 Tudor-style house in the neighborhood. He was Juan D. Peron, former Argentine dictator, returned to his native land Nov. 17, 1972, after 17 years in exile, but still tall and erect at 77.

Despite his long absence, the crowd outside the house had not forgotten Peron nor what he had done for them—lowered rents, increased salaries, enforced collective bargaining—during the 10 years of his rule which ended Sept. 21, 1955, when he was ousted by his generals.

Many in the crowd—chanting slogans such as "Our life for Peron"—were Peronists, and, as such, members of Argentina's largest political movement. They also controlled most of the nation's labor unions.

Since Peron's ouster there had been 17 years of instability in Argentina. Seven governments, most of them military, did much to restore Peron's political status by convincing many Argentinians he represented a hope for a viable civilian government. When it was decided to hold elections in March 1973 to return Argentina to civilian rule, the head of the ruling junta, President Alejandro Lanusse, in an effort to gain Peronist participation in the election, reversed policies of earlier juntas that barred Peron from Argentina, provided the former dictator would support the scheduled election.

Former Argentine dictator Juan Peron returned from exile

U.N. EDUCATION REPORT GLOOMY

If the authors of the United Nations study had looked for signs of progress in the world education picture, they were doomed to disappointment. In fact in some areas the opposite had occurred.

"In the education race, as in the march to economic progress," efforts to narrow the gap between the have and have-not nations "have all failed," said the bleak report issued Oct. 1 by the U.N. Educational, Scientific and Cultural Organization (UNESCO).

The 313-page report said that the "enormous difference" in expenditures for education between the industrialized and developing countries was getting ever wider despite "large scale efforts, financial sacrifices and considerable results" in the 1960s.

The study, prepared for UNESCO by an international commission, was supervised by Edgar Faure, French minister of social affairs.

"The ever-growing gap between industrialized and developing countries has produced the fundamental drama of the contemporary world," said the report.

A basis for narrowing this gap, it said, was elimination of "the disparate availability of the right to education for people in different parts of the world."

"But once again," the panel declared, "exactly the opposite is happening."

Most of the material in the report that dealt with industrialized nations referred to North America, Europe and the Soviet Union. Material dealing with the have-not countries concentrated on Asian countries, Africa and Latin America.

The panel said that, in 1968, the affluent nations spent more than $120 billion on education, while the developing nations spent less than $12 billion. It noted that this disparity occurred despite the fact that the industrialized countries have only one-third of the world's population and one-fourth of its young people.

"The most serious aspect of this enormous difference is that it is growing larger," the commission said.

The report noted that in 1968 more than 95 per cent of the children of primary school age

were attending school in North America, Europe and the U.S.S.R. In Latin America, the proportion dropped to 75 per cent, in Asia it was 55 per cent and in Africa 40 per cent.

The panel cited "unequal distribution of resources in out-of-school information and communications media, which are increasingly essential instruments for educational action."

It disclosed for example that there were only 45 radio receivers per 1,000 persons in Africa and 33 in Asia, while in North America there were 1,339 sets per 1,000 persons. Of the more than 250 million television receivers in the world, the report went on, less than 5 million were in Africa, South Asia and the Arab states.

In its report, the commission proposed a number of reforms designed to improve education from the pre-school level into adult life.

"Every individual must be in a position to keep learning throughout his life," the panel said. "We propose lifelong education as the master concept for educational policies in the years to come for both developed and developing countries."

UGANDA'S PRESIDENT EXPELLED
AN ESTIMATED 40,000 ASIANS

Claiming that God had directed him in a dream to expel the Asians from his East African nation, Uganda's President Idi Amin did just that. He forced an estimated 40,000 persons of mostly Indian and Pakistani origin to leave the country by midnight Nov. 8.

Adding that the dream revealed to him the Asian situation was becoming "explosive" and that "God was directing me to act immediately to save the situation," Amin ordered the ouster of the noncitizen Asians on grounds they had been dominating Uganda's economy.

And they went, in ever-growing streams, leaving their worldly goods behind them in the place they had looked on as home. Many held British citizenship—Uganda gained independence from England in 1962—and some 24,000 went there to receive a mixed reception since Britain at the time had almost a million unemployed. Another 7,500 went to India and Pakistan, 6,000 to Canada, 800 to the United States and smaller numbers to countries around the world—Australia, Switzerland, Denmark, Malawi.

As to their feelings, Ramesh Patel summed it up, perhaps, on arriving in London with his wife and five children, by saying, "We are homeless and uprooted, and we have lost most of our worldly possessions, but we are thankful to be together."

The forced migration followed by less than two years Amin's seizure of power in Uganda, a nation of 10 million. Amin, a longtime soldier and former heavyweight boxing champion, was serving as Ugandan army commander in early 1971 when President Milton Obote left the country for a conference. Amin led a coup which ousted the president, and Obote was given sanctuary in neighboring Tanzania.

During the Asian ouster, Amin, 47, claimed during September that some 1,000 troops—described as Ugandan exiles who were followers of Obote—invaded his country from Tanzania.

There was fighting in southwest Uganda, but Amin later claimed his troops successfully turned the invaders back. A peace agreement between Uganda and Tanzania then was worked out.

As the Asian exodus continued, Ugandan sources said hundreds of shops had been closed, producing shortages in consumer items from salt and sugar to shoes and toothpaste. They said the departure of the Asians, who ran most of Uganda's small businesses, had thrown some 75,000 Africans out of work and that many schools had closed because the Asian teachers had left.

For those Asians with Ugandan citizenship and non-citizen Asians exempted from the ouster, Amin promised that, "They will be dealt with humanely. We are human beings and we must not mistreat them."

He added, however, that those citizen Asians who elected to stay on must leave the cities and go and live among the Africans in the rural areas of Uganda.

Members of an Asian family forced to move out offer their household goods for sale

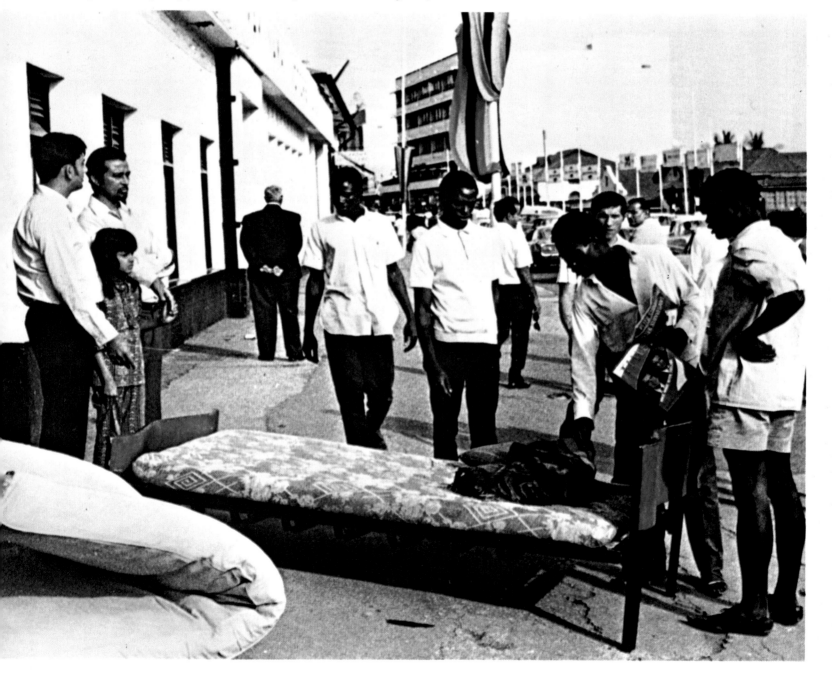

SECRETS OF THE OCEAN BOTTOM DRILLED UP BY RESEARCH SHIPS

For centuries man had been fascinated by the secrets of the ocean floor. Geologists realized many years ago that the sediment-covered ocean bottoms might resolve mysteries of earth's evolution if only a device to tap this treasure trove of information could be developed.

A handful of research vessels had plied the oceans for several decades studying the seabeds. But their instruments often were crude and the data frustratingly insufficient. Then in 1968, the research vessel *Glomar Challenger*, operated by the Scripps Institution of Oceanography at La Jolla, Calif., began service as part of the National Science Foundation's Deep Sea Drilling Project.

In just four years the *Glomar Challenger* and the Deep Sea Drilling Project had a profound impact on geology and man's concept of how the earth evolved and was continuing to evolve.

The *Glomar Challenger* provided the long-sought evidence that earth's continents were sliding about upon the globe like chips of wood on a pond—an idea that had riddled geology with controversy since nearly the turn of the century. But now, most geologists agreed that continental drift was real. The data from hundreds of holes bored into the ocean bottoms around the world left little doubt.

As it left port on another leg of the continuing Deep Sea Drilling Project, the *Glomar Challenger* might have reminded a beachcomber of the brush-covered flatlands of oil-rich Texas. Rising out of the vessel amidships was a giant derrick, incorporating the best in oil well drilling technology.

A visitor to the ship would be suprised by some of the *Glomar Challenger's* facilities in addition to the usual ocean-going essentials. There were laboratories for scientists and technicians to use during each cruise, performing preliminary analysis on ocean bottom sediments. A sophisticated electronic navigation system used signals from satellites far out in space to precisely pinpoint *Glomar Challenger* anywhere on

earth. A complex propulsion system not only moved the ship forward or back, but could move the entire vessel right or left when exact placement of the drill stem on the ocean floor hundreds of feet below was required.

Once a drill site was selected and the *Glomar Challenger* positioned, the drill stem was lowered from the derrick and drilling into the sediment was begun. Samples of the material that piled up on the ocean floor for millions of years were retrieved. Scientists studied the rocks, the skeletons of marine organisms and other data to reconstruct the area's past. To the skilled researcher, the corings were like the open pages of a history book.

From such studies, both in the *Glomar Challenger* laboratories and later in the respective scientists' institutions, came a growing body of knowledge that made the Deep Sea Drilling Project one of the most successful oceanographic expeditions undertaken.

On May 28, 1972, Drs. William A. Nierenberg, head of Scripps Institution, and Melvin Peterson, co-director of the Deep Sea Drilling Project, released a summary of the project's first four years. The *Glomar Challenger* data showed:

—That the sea floors in several areas were spreading apart at the summit of underwater mountain ranges when molten material from deep inside the earth welled up. The Atlantic Ocean was growing several inches wider each year as the Mid-Atlantic Ridge was pushed apart.

—The record of the most ancient oceans—the oceans that existed 180 million years ago when mammals first began evolving—had disappeared. The oldest oceans found so far were much, much younger, geologically speaking, than life on the continents.

—A land mass larger than New Jersey, Connecticut and Massachusetts combined, which flourished in the days of early mammals, sank nearly a mile below sea level between Ireland and Iceland.

—Great salt beds, pushed up into telltale dome formations, were found beneath the floors of the Gulf of Mexico and the Mediterranean Sea, promising immense new oil resources.

—A layer rich in iron and manganese ores formed by volcanic activity as new sea floor was generated underlies much of the Atlantic and Pacific oceans. At the bottom of 800 feet of sediment on the continental shelf bordering New York state was a large deposit of iron, zinc and copper.

—On the floor of the Bering Sea gravel was deposited millions of years ago by melting glaciers.

—Several times during the earth's history the Strait of Gibralter closed and the Mediterranean Sea dried up only to be flooded again by the Atlantic Ocean when the Strait opened. Drill sites in the Mediterranean revealed anhydrite salt deposits, formations that would have resulted only if the ocean bottom once had been exposed to sunlight.

Combined with other geological studies on land, the *Glomar Challenger* data became the core of a strong argument for continental drift. It seemed certain, geologists said, that the earth's land masses were sliding about upon the planet's rigid mantle underneath. This movement of a few inches a year was intimately related to sea floor spreading and was responsible for earthquakes, volcanoes and other geological events that puzzled scientists.

On the western coast of North America, for example, the land mass of Baja California and coastal Southern California was moving steadily northward a few inches each year. At some point millions of years hence, Los Angeles would be opposite San Francisco.

The Deep Sea Drilling Project was expected to last until 1975. After surveying data from the first four years, scientists eagerly awaited the continued probing of the ocean sediments for more secrets to earth's past.

TWO GUILLOTINED IN FRANCE

For more than 3½ years the deadly guillotine gathered dust in France. Then, in the cold pre-dawn hours of Nov. 28, 1972, the machine invented by the 18th century Dr. Guillotin briefly was revived to behead two men.

The first to die was Roger Bontems, 36. Seven minutes later, Claude Buffet, 38, was beheaded. Both had been condemned to death in the slaying of two hostages during a prison riot. They were the first men to be executed in France since March 11, 1969.

President Georges Pompidou, previously had not allowed anyone to be executed in France since he took office in June, 1969. He gave no reasons for his action.

REP. HALE BOGGS AMONG THOSE ABOARD MISSING ALASKA PLANE

It was a light plane. A Cessna 310, bound from Anchorage, Alaska, to Juneau, some 560 miles to the southeast.

Aboard were House Democratic Leader Hale Boggs, 58; Alaska Congressman Nick Begich, 40;

Russell L. Brown, 37, a Begich aide, and Don E. Jonz, 38, the pilot.

Boggs was in Alaska on a fund-raising campaign for Begich, who was seeking election to his second consecutive term as Alaska's lone congressman. After speaking at a banquet Oct. 16, Boggs and the others left on what was normally a 3½ hour flight.

Some 10 minutes after flying off, the pilot radioed Anchorage with his flight plan and asked about the weather conditions around Sitka, an alternative landing site. Then there was only silence. The plane was not heard from again.

Numerous planes, among them Phantom jets equipped with cloud-piercing electronic equipment, fanned out on a massive wilderness search in the days that followed, covering some 102,000 square miles of land and sea. They did not find the missing plane or its passengers.

Boggs first was elected to Congress in 1941, but was defeated two years later. He served with the Navy until 1946, when he won re-election to the House. He became Democratic whip in 1962 and took over as majority leader in 1971.

On Nov. 7, some 20 days after his disappearance, Boggs was re-elected without opposition to Congress by his Louisiana constituents.

Missing Congressman Hale Boggs

BRITAIN'S QUEEN HAILED ON 25TH WEDDING ANNIVERSARY

The main theme of the celebration was the pride and joy a people took in the durable marriage of their sovereign: a union that had lasted for 25 years.

Britain's Queen Elizabeth II and her husband, Prince Philip, shared that spirit with their subjects as they celebrated their silver wedding anniversary Nov. 20.

Thousands of flag-waving British cheered as they watched the queen and her husband stroll among them. It marked the first time a reigning monarch had walked the streets of London since World War II.

"God love us, ma'am! I never thought I'd shake hands with you," exclaimed an elderly Cockney woman as the queen stopped to chat.

The celebration began with a colorful service of thanksgiving at Westminster Abbey where Princess Elizabeth had married Lt. Philip Mountbatten of the Royal Navy Nov. 20, 1947.

After the queen, dressed in pale blue, and Prince Philip, in a cutaway, had taken their places in the Abbey, the Dean stepped forward and gave thanks "for the blessings which have come to each and all of us through their marriage and their lives of service."

At the Guildhall, the Lord Mayor and the Corporation of the City of London hosted an anniversary lunch for the royal couple. The queen responded to a toast from the lord mayor by saying: "I think everybody will coincide that on this day, of all days, I should begin my speech with the words "My husband and I." It was a form opening that has often been parodied, and the audience laughed appreciatively.

After the luncheon, Elizabeth, Philip and the two oldest of their four children, Prince Charles and Princess Anne, set out on a royal procession into a housing development near St. Paul's Cathedral. Leaving their carriages, they walked nearly a mile chatting with spectators lining police barricades.

At one point, the royal couple mingled with a group of students from Indiana.

"They were so nice," said one of the American girls later. "We wouldn't be so excited about talking to President Nixon."

Britain's royal couple marked silver wedding anniversary

CHICAGO SEVEN CONVICTIONS VOIDED

From the start, the trial of the Chicago Seven had produced one of the most unlikely scenes in the history of American jurisprudence.

During the proceedings in Chicago's Federal District Court in 1969–70, Judge Julius J. Hoffman had aimed sarcastic remarks at the defendants. They had responded by munching jelly-beans in the courtroom and hurling insults at the judge and prosecutors.

At one point, a defendant was bound and gagged. Spectators who raised clenched fists were ejected by marshals.

On Nov. 20, nearly three years after the trial had ended, *(The World in 1970, 34–37)* the U.S. Court of Appeals for the Seventh Circuit reversed the five convictions handed down in the conspiracy case.

In its ruling, the appeals court referred to Judge Hoffman's "antagonistic" courtroom behavior. The opinions of the three-judge panel said Hoffman's "deprecatory and often antagonistic attitude toward the defense is evident in the record from the very beginning."

The panel's decision freed Rennard C. Davis, David T. Dellinger, Thomas E. Hayden, Abbie Hoffman and Jerry C. Rubin. All five had been convicted of crossing state lines with the intent of inciting a riot at the 1968 Democratic National Convention. The two remaining defendants, John R. Froines and Lee Weiner, had been acquitted at the trial which ended in February 1970.

By a vote of 2 to 1, the appeals court upheld the constitutionality of the controversial antiriot statute—the so-called "Rap Brown Act" under which the defendants had been prosecuted. That law forbids the use of mail, telephone, radio, television or other means of interstate commerce with the intent to incite or organize acts or threats of violence.

British anthropologist Richard Leakey, showing the cast of a 2.5 million-year-old skull unearthed in Kenya

TWO STUDENTS DIE IN CAMPUS
TURMOIL AT SOUTHERN UNIVERSITY

His press secretary recalled that when Louisiana Gov. Edwin W. Edwards first heard the news, "He just kind of looked off into nowhere and said, 'Why did somebody have to get killed?'"

It was not an easy question to answer. Some said it was a terrible accident, a panicky deputy sheriff mistakenly firing buckshot instead of teargas.

But many blacks cited the fatal shooting Nov. 16 of two Southern University students as one more case of racism and oppression.

It was ironic that the outburst of racial temper came in the early months of Edwards' term.

A graying 45-year-old, Edwards was regarded as the most racially liberal governor in Louisiana history. He had polled 70 per cent of the black vote in the Democratic primary, and virtually all of it in the general election.

In his inaugural address, he had promised black people "the old barriers are gone and a new spirit is with us."

Evidently many students at predominantly black Southern University didn't believe it. Comparing their drab little campus with the shady lawns and sumptuous accommodations of Louisiana State University across town, they felt shortchanged.

LSU's main campus at Baton Rouge has been the state's educational showcase. The main campus of Southern, on the other hand, was north of town in the polluted, high-crime suburb of Scotlandville. So, in mid-October, Southern students began protesting alleged substandard conditions.

Complaining of no satisfaction from the university president, Dr. G. Leon Netterville, 65, students composed a 15-page outline of demands and grievances, marched 10 miles into Baton Rouge and presented it to the State Board of Education.

The students wanted Netterville fired, as well as department and executive councils with majority student representation to hire and fire faculty members, and otherwise run the university.

They also complained of incompetent teachers, lack of a qualified doctor in the dispensary, and obsolete hand-me-down books in the library.

The all-white board of education promised to appoint a study committee. Discouraged, students returned to campus and organized a boycott of classes.

On Oct. 31 a bomb exploded in the basement of a classroom building, and Netterville closed the school for a week.

Sympathy protests broke out at Southern's branch campus in New Orleans, where students seized the administration building and camped there nine days and nights.

With the situation deteriorating, Edwards decided to step into what had now become a tangled problem, not just racially and educationally, but also politically.

The state board, which had legal jurisdiction, was inclined to take a hard line. But most of the state's eight black legislators sympathized with the students' claim that Netterville and Dean Emmett Bashful of the New Orleans campus ought to resign.

Edwards tried to steer a middle course. He offered to negotiate with the protesters but set a noon Thursday, Nov. 9 deadline for evacuation of the building at New Orleans.

The deadline came and went, with students

still lodged in the building. Around 2 p.m. New Orleans Mayor Moon Landrieu telephoned the governor's mansion at Baton Rouge. His police wanted to move on campus and get it over with before nightfall.

An aide said, "I walked in and said, 'Governor, the police are getting itchy,' and he said, 'Well, tell them to go on in.'"

As the police moved toward campus in riot gear, Bashful sent word: he would resign.

Students volunteered to leave the building, and possible violence had been averted.

Now, the building vacated and a precedent for compromise established, Edwards went to New Orleans hoping for a permanent truce.

He told students most of their grievances could be resolved, but that it was impossible to fire Netterville in the present atmosphere, and that the state board would never agree to student majority control of university administration.

They jeered and shouted him down. He left the meeting feeling the protest leaders "were looking for trouble. They wanted a confrontation."

Boycotts continued in New Orleans and Baton Rouge, and on Nov. 16, Netterville had four protest leaders rousted out of bed at 4:30 a.m. on arrest warrants. A band of students marched to Netterville's office demanding an explanation.

Netterville told them he had a meeting to attend and he left the campus. Sheriff Al Amiss was notified to send in deputies to clear the administration building.

The deputies, plus a state police riot squad, rolled onto campus with a show of force—armored vehicles by land, a helicopter by air.

They surprised an estimated 2,000 students standing in the vicinity of the administration building. Most retreated, but some 100 stood at the front steps, answering police ultimatums with shouted insults and black power salutes.

As a line of deputies advanced, someone—officers say a student, students say an officer—threw a teargas grenade into the grassy no-man's-land between police and students.

State troopers then pelted the crowd with smoking canisters, deputies' shotguns spewed teargas cartridges, students scurried coughing and gagging in the gas clouds. When the smoke lifted, two young men lay dead on the sidewalk, heads and shoulders splattered with buckshot. They were identified as Denver A. Smith and Leonard Douglas Brown.

National Guard troops occupied the campus that day, to quell student arson and vandalism. Classes were suspended until after the first of the year.

Initially, Sheriff Amiss contended his men had fired nothing more lethal than teargas. The buckshot must have come from the students themselves he said.

Edwards refused to draw any firm public conclusions. The buckshot could have come from a deputy's shotgun or from some other source, he said. He would await an official investigation.

But speaking privately with Justice Department investigators, he said, "I have no doubt it was a deputy sheriff who fired."

By one popular theory, a deputy had loaded and fired a live round by mistake. Officers had carried both teargas and buckshot cartridges, of the same general size and appearance. A state-appointed commission investigating the deaths said later both men were killed by a single shotgun blast "from an area where sheriff's deputies were deployed."

Students at Louisiana's Southern University gav black power salutes as they ran up the black lib eration flag

POET EZRA POUND, THE MAN OF MANY FACES

Ezra Pound: A man of many faces.

To some, Pound was a stellar poet who served as teacher and guide for other major poets and was regarded as one of this century's most important figures in English literature.

To others, he was an eccentric, an anti-Semite, a supporter of Hitler and Mussolini, and a traitor to his native United States.

The complexity of Pound as poet and man touched off a storm in 1972—before his death Nov. 1 of an intestinal blockage in Venice, Italy, at the age of 87—when a panel of writers and critics, agreeing that his political views had been despicable but that he was a great poet, proposed he be awarded the annual Emerson-Thoreau Medal of the American Academy of Arts and Sciences. The academy council, however, voted against granting the award, 13 to 9.

As the critic M. L. Rosenthal wrote:

"His intelligence indeed has been a flowering of Western self-awareness, with life-bestowing and poisonous blossoms intermingled, as if all the beautiful vitality and all the brilliant rottenness of our heritage in its luxuriant variety were both at once made manifest in it."

Whatever role history decided to assign Pound, the fact remained that he—along with such other major literary figures as D. H. Lawrence and James Joyce—was to change the path of English and American literature from Victorian to modern.

Pound, born Oct. 30, 1885, in Hailey, Idaho, showed an early aptitude for languages and because of his knowledge of Latin was admitted to the University of Pennsylvania at the age of 15.

He was to later recall that "I knew at 15 pretty much what I wanted to do . . . I resolved that at 30 I would know more about poetry than any man living, that I would know the dynamic content from the shell, that I would know what was accounted poetry everywhere . . . .

"In this search I learned more or less nine foreign languages, I read Oriental stuff in translations, I fought every university regulation and every professor who tried to make me learn anything except this, or who bothered me with requirements for degrees.' "

After taking an M.A. at Penn and serving as an instructor, Pound left for Europe in 1908, working as a deckhand on a cattle boat.

His first book *With Tapers Quenched* was published in Italy. But it was the publication in 1908 in London of *Personae*, his third volume, that was to propel him into the midst of the literary world and into the company of such writers as Henry James, Joseph Conrad, H. G. Wells, Ford Madox Ford, and William Butler Yeats.

The poet was to write later that "I came to London with three pounds knowing no one. I had been hungry all my life for 'interesting people.' I wanted to meet certain men whose work I admired. I have done this . . . ."

It was during these years that Pound formulated his method of poetry—which he called Imagism, the use of specifics rather than abstractions to create images. An example of his method was the poem *In a Station of the Metro*, which read in its entirety:

"The apparition of these faces in the crowd;
"Petals on a wet, black bough."

While doing his own work, Pound also served as European editor of Poetry magazine and later for The Little Review. While at Poetry, Pound recommended the work of T. S. Eliot and the magazine printed *Portrait of a Lady*—the first publication of an Eliot work. But it was Pound's help to Eliot on *The Waste Land* that was, perhaps, to be most important since the poem later became one of the most famous of modern times.

Pound also befriended James Joyce, and when the Irish writer finished *Ulysses* in 1918, Pound persuaded The Little Review to print the manuscript serially.

Pound published *Homage to Sextus Propertius* in 1917 and *Hugh Selwyn Mauberley* in 1920—the two cycles of poems that are considered among his best—then moved from London to Paris in 1921 to devote much of his time to writing *The Cantos*—a huge work that was to be modeled on Dante's *Divine Comedy*.

After moving to Italy in 1925, Pound turned his attention to odd economic theories, became an anti-Semite and also a Fascist. In 1941, he began to make broadcasts in English for the Italian government, holding in one that "for the United States to be making war on Italy and Europe is just plain damn nonsense, and every native-born American of American stock knows that it is plain downright damn nonsense."

Pound was captured after the fall of Italy and returned to the United States in 1945 to face 19 counts on a treason indictment. But he was ruled mentally incompetent to stand trial and was kept instead, for 12 years at St. Elizabeth's Hospital in Washington.

Poet Robert Frost presented a petition for Pound's release in 1958, writing "I feel authorized to speak very specially for my friends, Archibald MacLeish, Ernest Hemingway and T. S. Eliot. None of us can bear the disgrace of letting Ezra Pound come to an end where he is."

After the hospital superintendent declared in court that Pound was "permanently and incurably insane" but "not a dangerous person" the poet was released and returned to Italy. He spent his remaining years working on the earlier conceived *Cantos*.

Shortly after World War I, Pound wrote a poem called *Ode on Choosing His Tomb*. It was his own epitaph. And in it he wrote: "He strove to resuscitate the dead art of poetry. . . ."

Expatriate American poet Ezra Pound praised for his esoteric verse

Leaning too far?

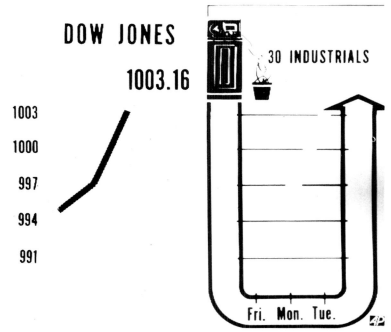

On Nov. 14, the Dow Jones industrial average closed above 1,000 for the first time in history

PISA'S LEANING TOWER NEARED THE POINT OF NO RETURN

The trouble with the Leaning Tower of Pisa was that it leaned.

Or, as Ubaldo Lumini, Italy's superintendent for Pisa monuments, put it: "The tower is ill, very ill."

Actually the tower had been "ill" since the Pisans started building the belltower for their cathedral 800 years earlier. They found that the foundations on the south side sank by as much as 11 inches a year, so the architects tried to correct the list by slanting the tower to the north.

The 179-foot-high tower, however, remained leaning and by 1972 it was canting 14 feet out of the perpendicular, its stability apparently affected by a sinking of the water table in the subsoil.

Plans to use a harness of steel cables to keep the tower from falling down were announced in November. This was to be followed by an international contest that aimed at coming up with a plan to consolidate the soil on which the tower stands so that the steel harness eventually could be removed.

FOR THE RECORD

ELECTED. West German Chancellor Willy Brandt's coalition government won a strong vote of confidence Nov. 19 as it took 54 per cent of the total in federal elections. Brandt's Social Democratic party polled 45.9 per cent of the vote while the Free Democrats, his partners in the governing coalition, received 8.4 per cent.

Americans lost another helicopter as the war went on

December

A B52 unleashing a cluster of bombs over North Vietnam

Peace In Vietnam, An Elusive Target

Hopes rose high for a settlement of the conflict in 1972,
but before the year was out, peace seemed uncertain

S OUTH VIETNAM's 3rd Infantry Division could perhaps be for-
given its complacency in 1972's opening months when monsoon rains clawed away at its earthen and sandbagged bunkers
just south of the Demilitarized Zone. Washington, Saigon, the
world were in a similar mood about the war which had become America's longest and most frustrating.

The fighting had ebbed, and President Nixon in January
reported that his national security adviser, Henry Kissinger,
had held 12 secret meetings in Paris with high North Vietnamese diplomats and officials. While results at that point
were still unacceptable to Washington, the talks would continue, and this alone buoyed hopes for peace. The President also

announced a new, more conciliatory eight-point peace plan supported by the Allies. He then settled down to wait, as Washington was forced to do in the Korean War, for shifts in Communist negotiating strategy and packages that might eventually lead to peace.

Peace was a big word in early 1972 for other reasons. Nixon went to Peking in February and opened lines of communication between the formerly antagonistic capitals. Moscow was on the presidential agenda later in the year, and diplomats said logic virtually precluded moves in Vietnam that would jeopardize such crucial moves for detente between Washington and the two great communist powers.

Such was the news on the world's radios and television sets. Such was the news on the small Japanese transisters carried by members of the 3rd Division, who were guarding the bloodiest battleground of the Vietnam War.

Who could blame the soldiers of the 3rd if they could not foresee in advance their key role in one of the most explosive years in the entire war? Who could see their failure as a fighting unit as a major reason for Washington's decisions to launch history's most violent bombing campaign both in North and South Vietnam? Or that Haiphong and other North Vietnamese harbors would be mined for the first time?

Had the 3rd Division not collapsed and run, the awesome bombing campaign might never have been launched against the North. Without the vastly expanded bombing, Hanoi's combat casualties would not have been so staggering. And without this, Kissinger said, the much sought after negotiating breakthroughs might not have come in Paris, thus giving the world its first solid hope for peace in Vietnam.

And the survivors of the 3rd Division felt more acutely than many the year's grim twist in the Vietnam War—the collapse of the Paris talks and a renewal of bombing against the Hanoi and Haiphong regions on a yet bigger scale.

Then, on Dec. 30 came the White House disclosure that Nixon had ordered a halt to the bombing of the North above the 20th parallel. It was coupled with an announcement that Kissinger would resume the Paris peace talks with North Vietnam's Le Duc Tho.

As the Christian world closed the year with prayers for peace on earth and goodwill toward men, historians were presented with the bloodiest year in the sad history of the Indochinese Peninsula.

In 1972's opening months such visions were lost far above to rolling, ash-grey clouds of the northeast winter monsoon which drenched the 3rd Division and the 17th Parallel dividing the two Vietnams.

As the monsoon rained itself to a close there were scattered warnings from Allied intelligence of a new North Vietnamese build-up, but hard reports were rare and command officials did not consider the threat dangerous enough to bother reinforcing border units. When shellings picked up against the 3rd Division's forward posts, established and defended at the cost of so many thousands of U.S. Marine casualties, few thought there was any real cause for alarm. Had the 3rd Division patrolled more aggressively and spent less time in bunkers against the cold and rain, military men said, the surprise would not have been so nearly total that Easter weekend. Nor, perhaps, so disastrous for the Allies.

Led by tanks, waves of North Vietnamese infantrymen from the 304th Division smashed across the border and rolled over the defenders' combat bases with the ease of ocean rollers oblit-

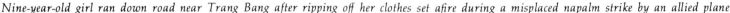

Nine-year-old girl ran down road near Trang Bang after ripping off her clothes set afire during a misplaced napalm strike by an allied plane

231

erating sand castles on a beach. Within days, much of the South Vietnamese division was destroyed and half of Quang Tri Province was lost. Washington warned that it considered the attack an all-out invasion and in "flagrant" violation of the 1954 Geneva Peace Treaty. Washington, spokesmen were at pains to point out, considered all retaliatory options open. This was a clear warning to the North to call off its most sophisticated offensive or face an aerial pounding.

The warning went unheeded in Hanoi, where such attacks no doubt had previously been discounted by the Politburo and Hanoi's defense minister, Gen. Ve Nguyen Giap, who drove the French from Indochina 18 years earlier. As defeat followed defeat for the 3rd Division and intelligence pinpointed huge buildups just north of Saigon and in the Central Highlands, Nixon ordered the resumption of regular bombing in the North. Targets were quickly expanded to include those in the Hanoi-Haiphong heartland with not only military but industrial targets being hit.

The loss to Hanoi's troops was staggering, some 100,000 were said to have died during the offensive. The destruction in both North and South was unprecedented.

Despite such losses, Hanoi pressed the offensive. Two district capitals just across from the Communists' Cambodian border bases were quickly overrun by tanks and infantry which swept on to encircle the provincial capital of An Loc, 60 miles north of Saigon. Inside An Loc was nearly the entire South Vietnamese 5th Division, a unit charged with a key role in defending Saigon. At the same time increasing pressure was applied in the Highlands and just to the east on the central coast in Binh Dinh Province. These two last attacks threatened to cut the country in two. Allied hopes for dictating a tough peace dwindled daily and plummeted with the final collapse of the 3rd Division, turning over to the North Vietnamese the provincial capital of Quang Tri, thus handing the enemy its biggest psychological success of the war.

But oddly enough, French papers quoting Communist sources said intensive peace efforts were going on even at this time behind the scenes in Paris. With battlefield successes in hand and more expected, however, the Communists were never tougher at the peace talks.

Meanwhile Nixon ordered the mining of Haiphong and other North Vietnamese harbors and intensive aerial strikes against rail lines leading out of southern China. With the Peking trip only recently concluded on a note of friendship and talks between the President and leaders of the Kremlin in the near future, the world held its breath awaiting the reaction of Hanoi's two biggest allies. The reaction was relatively mild and Washington claimed a potential flash point in international relations had been bypassed.

May saw the high point of the North's offensive. Saigon's

Henry A. Kissinger meeting in Paris suburb with North Vietnam's chief negotiator Le Duc Tho

232

Battered figure of Chinese household god in An Loc

5th Division was under withering attack daily and suffered huge casualties, but its defenders held. The enemy rolled up border outpost after border outpost north of Kontum in the Central Highlands and ravaged three-quarters of Binh Dinh Province on the coast. Then the threat passed under wave after wave of U.S. bombing raids. An expected major push against the old imperial capital of Hue failed to materialize. The Kontum front stabilized although the Saigon division in the region was virtually destroyed as an effective fighting unit.

Although by year's end the enemy still controlled wide areas captured during the spring offensive, Hanoi's "last throw of the dice" had to be reckoned a military failure. The enemy had committed all but two training divisions to the push, apparently confident that with virtually all American ground combat units out of Vietnam, it could triumph militarily at last. It either misjudged American willingness to launch huge aerial onslaughts in the face of world opinion, or miscalculated the stunning losses air power was to inflict on its finest infantry divisions and armored units.

It was now the chance for the adversaries to try to wage peace. Talks had broken off in November, 1971, the President revealed in January. By April, just when the American aerial offensive against the north was being unleashed, Le Duc Tho, a member of the North Vietnamese politburo, sent word to Washington via a delegation of U.S. labor leaders saying he would like to resume his secret talks with Kissinger. Late in April, perhaps as the North's generals realized the fate of their offensive, Le Duc Tho seemed to ease his hard stand on peace terms. Moscow, at the same time it was funneling war material to Hanoi, reportedly exerted its influence on the Communist regime to get responsible peace talks under way.

To no one's surprise, the maneuvering for peace was difficult and filled with frustration and reiteration. Kissinger's talks with Tho went on behind a cloak of secrecy as to any progress. But privately U.S. officials and diplomats said nothing could be done because of Hanoi's insistence that South Vietnamese President Nguyen Van Thieu had to go in any peace deal. Comparatively fruitless sessions continued until October with many wondering whether any solution short of major new fighting could be achieved.

Then, just as it had in Korea, the break came. Or, so it seemed at the time. On Oct. 8, Kissinger reported to the world that Hanoi dropped its demand for a coalition government in Saigon and gave up its most strident demand—the ouster of Thieu.

In declaring peace at hand, Kissinger told newsmen in Washington Oct. 26, that final agreement with the communist side could be reached in one more negotiating session lasting

A South Vietnamese marine carrying dead comrade near Quang Tri

Would it be a de facto government, as Saigon feared, or merely an administrative body to set the stage for election of a new political regime as the United States believed? Tensions mounted between Washington and Saigon on an almost unprecedented scale. Thieu said the Kissinger-Tho accords would mean "a surrender of the South Vietnamese people to the Communists" and pledged to fight on alone if necessary.

Nixon, with his landslide reelection less than a week away, promised Washington would sign no truce pact until he considered the terms right and the document's language free of any possible ambiguity. The next day the Pentagon leaked word that reconnaissance had spotted 100 enemy tanks and large bodies of troops moving across the DMZ into the South. The United States itself had mounted a massive airlift flooding new equipment into the South in anticipation of a cease-fire, thus making good on President Nixon's pledge that the South Vietnamese would have the means to defend themselves, once the United States abandoned the battlefield.

As Kissinger began the year's final round of talks with Le Duc Tho, straws in the wind were scattering in all directions. Details of the final sessions were kept secret both by Hanoi and Washington until Dec. 16 when Kissinger, fresh from Paris, told Washington newsmen that the talks had failed for the moment. Washington accused Hanoi of "frivolity" and going back on deals made in earlier sessions. Officials said privately that Thieu's demands also had received more of a hearing in the final talks, especially one that his regime be recognized as the sole legitimate political force in the South. Hanoi said Washington had broken faith by reopening areas of the cease-fire pact already agreed to. It said it was prepared to sign the October accords as previously negotiated. Washington refused.

At the White House, Nixon was reported furious at both Vietnams, the South for being so obdurate and the North for what the President considered bad faith.

The White House dashed, at least momentarily, world hopes for peace in Indochina with an even greater bombing campaign against North Vietnam and especially the Hanoi-Haiphong heartland. For the first time giant B52s, each carrying 40 tons of bombs, were sent in wave after wave against the heartland area and its dense rocket and antiaircraft artillery defenses. The Pentagon reported little more about the aerial offensive than the fact that it was going on and to give the number of U.S. aircraft shot down. The latest figures announced by the Pentagon were 15 B52s and 10 other fighter-bombers lost since Dec. 18 and the loss of 82 airmen, killed, captured or missing.

Even a bombing pause for Christmas did nothing to cool international passions stirred by the renewal of violence in a land many had hoped, perhaps unrealistically, was on the verge of peace. Although the United States insisted that its targets were only military, the world got other reports of the campaign through foreign newsmen and diplomats stationed in Hanoi, together with statements issued by the North Vietnamese government. Non-Communist reports also said Hanoi was struggling on despite the rain of bombs. In Washington experts noted privately that such bombing historically had not broken the will of the attacked but had stiffened their determination to fight on.

Then came the Dec. 30 announcement of another halt in the bombing and the rescheduling of the Paris peace talks. The sudden turn of events caused some observers to speculate whether the move toward a new round of negotiations had been initiated by North Vietnam battered by the B52 raids, or by Washington possibly deciding to suspend the raids which had touched off such an international furor.

"not more than three or four days." American bombing was restricted to areas south of the 20th parallel, well away from the Hanoi-Haiphong heartland.

With the U.S. presidential election only a week and a half away, Republicans were jubilant over the report. Democrats, although hopeful, often were cynical. Could it be that the violence was so near an end? Had the President made good his pledge to end the war with honor, a war that had cost 20,000 dead Americans during the Nixon Administration alone? Both hope and fear were high.

Storm clouds were not long in coming. South Vietnamese Foreign Minister Tran Van Lam quickly denounced the proposed settlement as "unacceptable" and amounting to a "surrender" for his country. Saigon had not been a party to the Kissinger-Tho talks.

President Thieu's most immediate concerns centered on two issues. Would North Vietnam pledge itself to withdraw its 145,000 troops from the South? The issue was not even addressed in the preliminary cease-fire agreement worked out in Paris. And second, just what would be the exact role of the communist-government-neutralist body agreed to in Paris?

One consequence of the latest bombing offensive had been to deal Hanoi more trump cards in the form of POWs. Hanoi released three earlier in the year. Freedom for Lts. Norris A. Charles and Mark L. Gartley of the Navy and Maj. Edward Elias of the Air Force spotlighted for Americans the fact that more than 1,000 Americans were prisoners or missing in action. And in the first phase of the bombing campaign some two score more airmen went onto the POW and missing lists. Hanoi long had recognized the highly emotional impact of the prisoner issue in America and had constantly dangled their freedom as a price for major American bargaining concessions. Speculation mounted toward the end of the year that a simple cease-fire might not be enough to win release for these men, some of whom had been held for nearly 10 years. It was recalled that French prisoners were forced to work in North Vietnam after peace was restored there on the grounds that they had a responsibility to repair the damage they had helped cause.

Above, South Vietnamese troops fighting a blaze set off by enemy artillery in the village of Luong May. Below, wreckage of a B52 which crashed in Thailand after being hit over North Vietnam.

The nation's 33rd President, Harry S Truman, shown at his White House desk in 1948

Harry S Truman, President, 1945-53
"The Buck Stops Here"

THE DAY AFTER Harry S Truman was sworn in as 33rd President of the United States he said it seemed as if "the whole weight of the moon and stars and all the planets fell on me."

"I feel a tremendous responsibility. Please pray for me, I mean that."

Truman, who picked up the reins of government after President Franklin D. Roosevelt died in office April 12, 1945, indeed inherited a heavy load of responsibility. But, as he was to recall when he left the Presidency nearly eight years later, "the work was mine to do, and I had to do it. I . . . tried to give it everything that was in me."

Determined to be President "in my own right," Truman recalled that he had made clear at the first session with his cabinet "that I would assume full responsibility for such decisions as had to be made."

This thought was expressed in a plaque on his White House desk which read: "The buck stops here."

The decisions that Truman had to make were awesome. They sent atomic bombs crashing down on two Japanese cities in World War II; set in motion work on the hydrogen bomb, and—even at the risk of touching off World War III—sent American troops into what was to become known as the Korean War.

It was this last decision that Truman, who died Dec. 26 at the age of 88, was to regard as the hardest he ever had to make. Just before leaving the Presidency in January of 1953, Truman said that because he felt his sending American forces into Korea involved the risk of a third World War, he found it even more difficult than his decision to drop the atomic bomb on the cities of Hiroshima and Nagasaki.

He said he had been told the bombing would shorten the war and save the lives of possibly a quarter of a million American fighting men.

"In that case," he said, "there was no question of the course to take."

But as for the Korean venture, he said he was convinced that even though there was a risk of another global war he was also convinced his decision was right in that it halted communism in its drive to engulf the world. In fact, he believed the dispatch of American troops to Korea under a United Nations mandate may have saved the world from World War III.

Truman, who once described himself as a "home-grown American farm product" that was "a little of everything—Scotch, Irish, Dutch. If you shook the family tree, anything might fall out," was born May 8, 1884, the oldest of three children of a farmer and livestock dealer. After finishing high school and failing to get into West Point because of weak eyes, he held a variety of jobs until World War I when he went overseas with his Missouri National Guard unit. As a captain of artillery he saw some of the heaviest fighting of that conflict, including the St. Mihiel and Meuse-Argonne offensives.

Discharged as a major in 1919, Truman and an Army buddy opened a men's clothing store in Kansas City but the enterprise failed in the farm depression of 1921. "I know some of the troubles of small business," Truman told a Small Business

Advisory Committee when he was President. "I was in one of them myself. It took me 20 years to get out from under that experience. . . ." Friends said he was prouder of having paid all the debts of that unsuccessful venture—around $20,000—than of anything else he had done.

It was at this difficult time that Truman turned to politics and in 1922 was elected to one of the three positions on the county court, governing body of Jackson (Mo.) County. After a two-year term, he was defeated for re-election, but in 1926 he was elected presiding judge and served in that position until 1934, overseeing public works construction projects.

Truman ran for the U.S. Senate in 1934 and won. When he came up for another term in 1940, he won again. Truman went to the Senate promising to do "lots of listening and mighty little talking," becoming one of the "silent senators" who rarely took the floor and made few public speeches outside his home state.

Unable to get active duty in the Army after Pearl Harbor because of his age, Truman decided the next best thing he could do was keep a close eye on government spending in the war effort to be sure money was not wasted. "It doesn't do any good to go around digging up dead horses after the war is over," he said. "The thing to do is to dig this stuff up now and correct it."

Truman became a symbol for honesty in the carrying out of

Truman at the Potsdam Conference in 1945 flanked by British Prime Minister Clement Attlee, left, and Soviet Premier Joseph Stalin

Truman beamed at a cheering crowd at St. Louis' Union Station on Nov. 4, 1948 as he held an early copy of the Chicago Tribune with its erroneous headline: "Dewey Defeats Truman"

war contracts and his committee—"The Truman Committee" as it was known—a watchdog over war spending.

Truman's work as chairman of the committee boosted him to national prominence and, when he went to the Democratic National Convention in 1944, he was picked as a compromise choice for President Roosevelt's running mate. Within less than three months, Roosevelt died and Truman moved into the nation's highest office at a critical moment in history.

The new president had been in office barely two weeks when statesmen from 50 nations met at San Francisco to form the United Nations, and Truman told the group: "Let us not fail to grasp this supreme chance to establish a worldwide rule of reason—to create an enduring peace under the guidance of God."

He had been President for less than a month when Germany's military machine collapsed, and three months later Japan gave up and World War II ended after Truman warned that nation it would suffer utter desolation from atomic attacks.

It was on Aug. 5, 1945, that a statement from the White House told of the existence of the atomic bomb and that it had been dropped on Hiroshima by American bombers. That city of 400,000 lost 80,000 dead. On Aug. 9, the second atomic

bomb was dropped, this time on Nagasaki and that city of 250,000 suffered 40,000 dead.

Some 12 years after the bombs were dropped on Japan, Truman defended his decision in reply to criticisms by the Hiroshima City Council. The President said, "When Japan surrendered, the military estimated at least a quarter of a million of the invasion forces against Japan and a like number of Japanese had been spared destruction and that twice that many on each side would otherwise have been maimed for life." He also pointed out he would not have had to make the bombing decision if "we had not been shot in the back by Japan at Pearl Harbor."

The unconditional surrender terms which Japan accepted were dictated at Potsdam by a "Big Three" conference of Truman, Joseph Stalin of the Soviet Union and Winston Churchill of Britain. The conference also occupied itself with the peace that was to come after the end of the global conflict.

But with the end of the hot war, the world now was to enter an uneasy state marked by Communism's thrusts at Democracy. This clash of ideologies was to become known as "the cold war." It was marked by Russian expansion into a number of Eastern European countries and by numerous clashes between the United States and the Soviet Union. One of these was over the European Recovery Program, which Moscow tried to wreck. The program, or Marshall Plan as it was called in honor of Gen. George C. Marshall, poured out more than $12 billion in an effort to save Europe from bankruptcy and Communism.

There also was the Truman Doctrine which consisted of American aid to nations that resisted direct or indirect communist aggression. Under it, both military and economic aid was given to Greece and Turkey. The aid checked a communist-supported civil war in Greece and bolstered Turkey's military strength. In 1948, the Soviet Union tried to squeeze the other three occupying powers out of Berlin—the city was surrounded by the Russian zone. The Russians banned rail traffic between the city and the Western zones, then said they would not feed the Germans in the U.S., French, and British sections. A massive airlift of supplies into the city was launched by the West and lasted 327 days. Its success marked a diplomatic defeat for Russia. Then, in 1949, 12 nations joined in the North Atlantic Treaty in which the United States and the others agreed that an attack on one member was an attack on all. Later three other nations joined the North Atlantic Treaty Orga-

nization, which, for the first time in history, put America into a peacetime military alliance with European nations.

After the war, Truman called for a sweeping program, "The Fair Deal," which was an extension of President Roosevelt's "New Deal." Among Truman's proposals were expanded Social Security, a higher minimum wage, and a permanent fair employment practices commission to protect minority rights. Few of his proposals were enacted, his chief success being legislation for public housing and a plan to unify the armed forces by creating the U.S. Department of Defense. His administration also was beset by intra-party troubles. Southern Democratic members of Congress bitterly fought his recommended civil rights program and some, along with dissatisfied Northerners, joined in a move to "stop Truman" at the 1948 National Convention. But the anti-Truman drive fell apart when Gen. Dwight D. Eisenhower said he would not accept the nomination and Truman got the nomination on the first ballot.

With Truman assailed both within and without the party, most political experts looked on Thomas E. Dewey, the Republican standard bearer, as a sure winner for President. But Truman, proclaiming, "I'm going to fight hard. And I'm going to

Truman met on Wake Island in October 1950 with Gen. Douglas MacArthur whom he later relieved of his command

give 'em hell," hit the campaign trail, telling the people that the Republican-controlled 80th Congress was a "do-nothing Congress" and that he was on a great "crusade" for their interests against the special interests. In the upset election, Truman took 24,105,812 popular votes to Dewey's 21,970,065 and 303 electoral votes to Dewey's 189. He also racked up a comfortable majority in both Senate and House.

The cold war became hot in Truman's new term when Russian-trained troops from Soviet-backed North Korea invaded the western-recognized Republic of South Korea June 25, 1950. The U.N. Security Council issued a cease-fire order and called for a rollback by the North Koreans which they ignored. Truman then sent American forces, assisted by a number of other U.N. member nations, into action against the aggressors.

Truman, who immediately left his Missouri home for Washington at news of the invasion, said, "Flying over the flatlands of the Middle West and over the Appalachians that summer afternoon, I had a lot of time to think. I turned the problems over in my mind in many ways, but my thoughts kept coming back to the 1930s—to Manchuria—Ethiopia—the Rhineland—Austria—and finally to Munich. Here was history repeating itself. Here was another probing action, another testing action. If we let the Republic of Korea go under, some other country would be next, and then another. And all the time, the courage and confidence of the free world would be ebbing away, just as it did in the 1930s. And the United Nations would go the way of the League of Nations."

Commanded by Gen. Douglas MacArthur, the U.N. forces had all but smashed the North Korean army when Chinese communists suddenly came to its help with a great number of troops. That action made the struggle, in effect, a new war. MacArthur then proposed bombing China and Manchuria and attacking the Chinese mainland with Chinese Nationalist troops. Truman, not wishing to extend the war, rejected the plan. When MacArthur criticized the administration, Truman removed him from his command, touching off a huge emotional and political outburst. Despite the uproar, Truman held to his action, concluding that MacArthur was "unable to give his wholehearted support to the policies" of the administration and of the United Nations. If MacArthur's policy were followed, the President added, "we would be running a very grave risk" of touching off World War III. The Korean War came to a close under President Eisenhower in 1953.

Truman also faced serious problems on the domestic scene. Much of his domestic program had hard sledding. Faced with charges of corruption in the Bureau of Internal Revenue, the President devised a plan to revamp the bureau and this was written into law. He also ordered a government clean-up under which the Justice Department—a target of criticism—was almost completely reorganized. Truman, who had traded verbal punches with Sen. Joseph McCarthy, R-Wis., over the latter's charges that the Truman Administration harbored communists, also set up a federal loyalty board to deal with the problem.

On March 29, 1952, Truman announced that he would not seek re-election. He said he'd like for the "epitaph" on his administration the same inscription he said appeared on a grave marker in Tombstone, Ariz.:

"Here lies Jack Williams,

"He done his damndest."

As Truman prepared to leave the Presidency in 1953, he said that if he had it all to do over again his major decisions would be the same. Pointing to a globe he kept in his office, he said, "During these eight years, we've kept that old globe out of disaster."

TRUMAN ADMINISTRATION HIGHLIGHTS

The Truman Administration encompassed many important events. These included:

End of World War II.

Launching of the United Nations.

Dawn of the atomic age with dropping of atomic bombs on Japan.

Envelopment of a number of countries by communism.

The cold war of ideologies between the western powers and Russia.

Hot war in Korea, where United Nations forces, mainly those of the United States, fought the invasion of the Republic of Korea by North Korean Communists and Chinese Reds.

Formation of the North Atlantic Treaty Organization (NATO), the first peacetime military alliance between the United States and European nations.

Establishment of a multi-billion dollar program of the United States to help post-war Europe get back on its feet. This was called the European Recovery Program or Marshall Plan. It was succeeded by the Mutual Security Agency.

Promulgation of the Truman Doctrine—the granting of military as well as economic aid to countries fighting the march of communism.

Launching of a U.S. program to give technical aid to under-developed countries.

Operation in 1948–49 of a $250 million airlift to supply Russian-blockaded Berlin with food and fuel. Its success was a diplomatic setback for Russia which had sought to force the western powers out of Berlin.

Industrial unrest including critical strikes in coal, steel and rails.

A peacetime draft of men between 18½ and 26 to serve for 24 months.

Unification of the armed services under a single Secretary of Defense, with the Army, Navy and Air Force made co-equal branches.

A complete overhaul of the nation's immigration and naturalization laws.

A labor-management law that hardened the federal policy toward organized labor. This Taft-Hartley Act was enacted over President Truman's strongly-worded veto.

Adoption of the 22nd Amendment to the Constitution that bars future Presidents from serving more than two elective terms, or more than 10 years in the White House if a Chief Executive served part of a predecessor's term.

British troops stood guard as families tried to relax on a beach near Belfast

In Ireland, Another Year of Slaughter and Destruction

The toll for 1972 was nearly 500 dead and thousands maimed

Pretty, 19-year-old Kathleen Dolan walked across the street to mail her wedding invitations. She was blown to bits by a bomb in a car parked near her home in Killetter Village on Northern Ireland's war-torn border with the Irish Republic.

That was in December, climaxing a year of slaughter and destruction. Bombs tore at the heart of Belfast and Londonderry. Then, as urban security tightened, attacks were launched against unprotected villages. By New Year's Eve the toll in more than three years was 680 dead, of which 1972 contributed 469. Thousands had been injured.

At the core of the violence were the urban guerrillas of the Irish Republican Army, battling to wrest Northern Ireland from the British Crown. Against them were ranged more than 20,000 British troops, plus a variety of private Protestant armies sworn to resist any move to submerge the province into a Catholic-dominated republic.

The violence had mounted steadily since August 1969 when British troops were called out to head off Protestant-Catholic clashes that came close to civil war (*The World in 1969, 164*).

The first big bombing of 1972 erupted early in January injuring 62 civilians on Belfast's Callender Street. By the end of the month the bombings were averaging 40 a day.

On Jan. 30, the Civil Rights Assn., now heavily laced with the Marxist "official" wing of the IRA, called a demonstration march and rally in Londonderry, Northern Ireland's second city. About 5,000 marchers turned out to protest Prime Minister Brian Faulkner's use of internment without trial of IRA suspects.

Troops and police ringed the city center to try to keep the marchers inside the Roman Catholic strongholds of Bogside and Creggan. But some demonstrators left the marching columns and began hurling rocks and bottles at the troops.

Above, left, a relative wept at the funeral of a man killed when his car exploded in Belfast. Above, right, police held back demonstrators in front of the British embassy in Dublin. Building was set afire by bomb-throwing mob protesting Londonderry shootings. Below, rioters fleeing after attacking British armored cars in Londonderry with nail bombs and gelignite explosives

The British countered by sending in 600 paratroops to move among the rock throwers and arrest as many as they could. The paratroops charged, and the army asserted that they came under fire. Thirteen civilian men were shot dead and 16 civillians wounded. The IRA swore vengeance.

As Londonderry buried its dead, angry crowds in Dublin marched on the British embassy behind 13 symbolic coffins containing gasoline bombs. The embassy was burned to the ground.

The Republic's prime minister, Jack Lynch, order the recall of the Irish ambassador from London. As pressure mounted, Britain instructed its top judge, Lord Chief Justice Widgery, to inquire into the killings. After hearing 750,000 words of evidence, the Justice said, "I am entirely satisfied that the first firing was directed at the soldiers."

Widgery also found that the British operation commander had underestimated the dangers involved and that some soldiers "bordered on the reckless" in directing their fire. However, the Catholic oppositionists denounced the report.

February added 22 dead to the January toll of 26. Gun battles and bombings continued nightly.

The 18th century town hall at Stabane on County Londonderry's border with the republic was reduced to rubble by a bomb. John Taylor, 34-year-old home affairs minister, took six bullets from an assassination gang in Armagh, the ecclesiastical capital, and survived.

Still in February, a car bomb wrecked an officers' mess at the paratroops' headquarters at Aldershot, England. Of the seven who died, five were women cleaners, one a gardener and the seventh a Roman Catholic chaplain.

In March the Abercorn restaurant in Belfast was bombed costing two girls their lives and a third her legs.

Mrs. Anita Currie sat with her children as she reported that two terrorists burst into her home near Belfast and beat and branded her

Amid the carnage a political row erupted between Britain's Prime Minister Edward Heath and Northern Ireland's Faulkner. Heath wanted all control of Northern Ireland security in British hands. As it was, responsibility was blurred. The province had always held a wide measure of domestic autonomy, and that included control of police and paramilitary reserves. Faulkner argued that a government without control of its own police was no government at all and quit, along with all his ministers. Heath then suspended the provincial parliament and appointed William Whitelaw, a 53-year-old farmer and former soldier, as administrator.

Disbandment of the Stormont Parliament had long been the prime objective of the IRA provisionals, and the Northern Protestant majority reacted angrily. They closed down the province in a two-day strike, and swarmed in thousands onto the trim lawns of Stormont as the 51-year-old parliament voted itself into the icebox for at least a year. Stormont had been born in the partition of Ireland. The idea then was that two parliaments, one for the north and one for the south, would eventually come together through a Council of Ireland, and form one government closely linked to Britain.

Protestant anger and fears of a British sellout to a united Ireland brought the emergence of paramilitary organizations to line up alongside the Ulster volunteer force, a longstanding Protestant counterpart to the IRA. The largest and apparently best organized was the Ulster Defense Association, which claimed it could field more than 40,000 uniformed and disciplined men. Another was Ulster Vanguard, led by former home affairs minister Bill Craig. Together they prepared to fight if Stormont were not revived in 1973.

Whitelaw had two objectives. One was to win peace by assuring the Catholic portion of the population a fair deal. The other was to persuade the Protestants that Britain stood by its 1949 pledge that they would never be forced into unity with Dublin against their will. He began to dismantle Faulkner's internment apparatus and to bring judges into the internment process rather than make it a simple administrative act. The aim, aides declared, was to defeat guerrilla violence by methods acceptable to the standards of western Democracy. Truce feelers went out and on June 26, the provisionals announced a cease-fire. It came, said Faulkner, "328 lives, 1,682 explosions and 7,258 injuries too late." And it lasted just 13 days.

Suffolk, a housing development on the Belfast outskirts, is far removed from the decaying rows of houses where the troubles first erupted. It is a modern development of smart white houses around trim lawns. Catholics and Protestants had for the most part lived peacefully alongside each other. But in midsummer IRA snipers opened up on an army post. Bullets penetrated Protestant houses and 16 families moved out. Sixteen Catholic families, themselves homeless from former troubles, were given permission to move in, then were hastily offered alternatives when the UDA threatened trouble.

For a week the military and civil authorities negotiated with the two communities. Then a crowd of several hundred Catholics tried to force the issue, marching on the empty houses with two truckloads of furniture. Bricks and bottles began their routine flight toward the army barricades and shooting started. Again came the question: Who fired first? Shooting continued through the July 10 weekend and the truce was over.

The next 10 days saw fierce gun battles and bombings. Londonderry was devastated by a rash of bombs. Sectarian murder spread, with nightly killings by rival assassination squads. July 21 brought Belfast its worst devastation since World War II.

Within 30 minutes, 20 bombs exploded in and around the city center, ripping through bus stations, railroad stations, shopping centers and a bridge over the Lagan River. Clouds of black smoke climbed up over the city. Eleven people died and scores were injured. Six died at the busy Oxford Street bus station next to the city's fire headquarters.

Soon an argument broke out between the police and the IRA, who admitted planting the bombs. IRA leaders accused the police of ignoring warnings with the aim of causing civilian casualties. Police replied that Belfast got a bomb scare every few minutes but that when 20 real bombs arrived in half an hour it was impossible to cope. Whitelaw, who had been attacked for talking with provisional leaders during the truce, told the House of Commons in London they had "degraded the human race" and he and his aides would never talk with them again.

It had long been British policy that to invade the IRA strongholds—Bogside and Creggan in Londonderry; Andersonstown and Ballymurphy in Belfast—would risk unacceptable civilian casualties. Now, that risk had to be faced. The assault came at dawn on July 31. Centurion tanks equipped with bulldozer blades smashed into the barricades and met only token resistance.

Two young IRA men were shot dead in Londonderry and two others wounded. Six people died the same day in Claudy, were a bomb shattered a village street.

The army reported massive hauls of arms and explosives from the former forbidden areas and Whitelaw began to plan his blueprint for the future, calling feuding politicians into talks.

IRA bosses, forced out of Belfast and Londonderry, began to regroup. They began to look for help from abroad.

A year earlier a top provisional leader, David O'Connell, had taken off for Europe with a trim Dublin student, Maria Maguire, and negotiated a purchase of three tons of sophisticated weaponry originating from Czechoslovakia. The arms were intercepted at Amsterdam Airport. In 1972 Miss Maguire defected, charging in a series of newspaper interviews that top provisional leaders were feuding to the point of assassination. Miss Maguire—"Writing her memoirs before she's even dead," as one IRA man commented—promptly vanished to avoid IRA vengeance.

As the killing went on—95 dead in July, 55 in August, 40 in September—the British developed anti-guerrilla tactics of their own, each in turn countered by some new technique of the IRA.

A first priority was to establish control of gelignite, a cheap industrial explosive which was the base of most early IRA bombs. This done, the IRA switched to farm chemicals laced with diesel oil, producing bombs of 50 to 150 pounds and in one case a blockbuster of 600 pounds. Bigger bombs meant a change in the IRA's planting system. Instead of the small gelignite package planted furtively or dumped by armed men, the car bomb became the main danger. Hence traffic control became a vital security weapon. Belfast banned unattended parking in the city center; main streets were gated and barred to traffic. The bombs still got through, though in deceasing numbers as the year wore on.

Squads of undercover agents were formed to combat the nightly sectarian killings, the work of assassination squads who roamed town in bogus taxis looking for victims of the opposite faith. Catholics made up most of the 120 who died this way, though some of their deaths were put down to IRA action against informers. A cut price dry cleaning firm did

Youths carried the flag of the Irish Republic as they marched through Belfast in a protest demonstration against the British

good business in the trouble spots until its driver was identified as a British soldier and gunned down. All the clothing he collected went for forensic tests to show whether the wearer had been in contact with explosives or ammunition. Then it was returned, impeccably cleaned. "The ploy lasted four months, and we expected a mere four weeks," a British officer said.

In the Republic, Prime Minister Lynch won two votes of confidence in national referenda and set up the machinery for a major crackdown on the IRA. The votes approved Ireland's entry to the European Common Market—something the IRA opposed—and gave power to delete from the 1937 constitution the "special position" of the Roman Catholic Church.

Special courts sitting without juries jailed some 70 IRA activists who responded by wrecking Mountjoy Jail. In December more sweeping powers for detention of subversives won reluctant approval in the Irish parliament while Dublin was rocked by two bombings, one at Liberty Hall, headquarters of the labor unions, and another near a downtown department store. Two people died and more than 100 were injured.

Sean Macstiofain, IRA Chief of Staff, had been arrested in November and jailed for six months as a member of the organization, which had long been illegal though often tolerated in the Republic. On arrest he announced a hunger strike, vowing to fast and thirst until death. Gunmen disguised as priests and physicians tried to free him from police guard in Dublin's Mater Hospital and were beaten off in a gunfight in which four were captured. Macstiofain, was moved to a military hospital at the Curragh camp west of Dublin and in mid-December was reported surviving on a diet of orange juice, glucose and tea.

By this time the IRA was deploying Soviet-made rockets in the North. The British were convinced that both sides in the sectarian struggle .there had become infiltrated by Soviet agents. The British asked the Russians for help in tracing the source of the rockets. As a result, Britain was accused of anti-Soviet slander.

At midnight on Dec. 31 the Irish Republic and Northern Ireland moved along with Britain into the European Economic Community, but with no guarantee that this could smooth the path to peace.

245

After the Victory
Nixon Shook Up His
Official Family

I T WAS AFTER MIDNIGHT when Richard Nixon entered the hot, crowded and noisy ballroom of Washington's Shoreham Hotel to receive the acclaim of his partisans for a landslide victory. As the reelected President walked into the room, press secretary Ronald L. Ziegler tossed out a casual business-as-usual announcement to newsmen trailing behind: Nixon would hold separate post-election meetings, with his cabinet, members of the White House staff and heads of federal bureaus and agencies.

Many of the administration stalwarts assembled at the Shoreham knew they were to meet with Nixon a few hours hence. As they basked in the champagne glow of success after laboring for weeks in the campaign cause, most anticipated an orgy of self-congratulation. They knew nothing about a then-unpublished interview in which Nixon had told the Washington *Star and Daily News*:

"Now, let me say, as far as presidential appointees are concerned, and all of those subject to appointments by the departments, as far as they are concerned, they have had their four years, and I will expect all of them to submit their resignations. If it is found that any of them no longer are needed or that their jobs are no longer needed, then their resignations will be accepted."

The President personally conveyed this startling word to top members of his official family on Nov. 8, the morning after the election, then flew to his Florida home to ponder plans, long gestating in secret, for a major shakeup and reorganization of the federal bureaucracy. Left behind in Washington were nearly 2,000 uncertain political appointees.

After a brief working sojourn in the sun, Nixon was airborne again, bound this time for Camp David, his Marine-guarded hideaway in Maryland's Catoctin Mountains. There, as expectant officials shuttled in and out by helicopter, the President summoned reporters and philosophized aloud about his second-term thoughts and plans:

". . . the tendency is for an administration to run out of steam after the first four years, and then to coast, and usually coast downhill. That is particularly true when there is what you call a landside victory . . .

"What I am trying to do is to change that historical pattern. The only way that historical pattern can be changed is to change not only some of the players, but also some of the plays . . .

"What I am suggesting here is that when a new administration comes in, it comes in with new ideas, new people, new programs . . . A second administration usually lacks that vitality. It lacks it not because the men and the women in the administration are any less dedicated, but because it is inevitable when an individual has been in a cabinet position or, for that matter, holds any position in government, after a certain length of time he becomes an advocate of the status quo; rather than running the bureaucracy, the bureaucracy runs him."

Nixon went on to say he did not regard the election outcome as an endorsement of the status quo.

"We feel that we have a mandate," he said, " a mandate not simply for approval of what we have done in the past, but a mandate to continue to provide change that will work in our foreign policy and in our domestic policy . . ."

By early December, Nixon had selected his second-term cabinet, and it was different. Of all the department heads who took office with him in 1969, only Secretary of State William P. Rogers remained in his original post.

In contrast to the original Nixon cabinet, the second-term model contained fewer professional politicians and more recruits from special interest groups in the private sector. Some observers also suspected the reshuffled team would be more receptive to White House directives, permitting the President to get a firmer grip on the sprawling bureaucracy.

Besides Rogers, the only cabinet holdovers in first-term slots were economist George P. Shultz as secretary of the treasury, lawyer-politician Richard G. Kleindienst as attorney general, former GOP congressman Rogers C. B. Morton as secretary of the interior and former educator Earl L. Butz as secretary of agriculture.

Three survivors of the first term were given new cabinet assignments. Elliott L. Richardson moved to the Defense Department, replacing Melvin R. Laird who was leaving government. Taking Richardson's old job at the Department of Health, Education and Welfare was Casper W. Weinberger, who had been director of the Office of Management and Budget. Moving up from the under secretaryship at the Commerce Department to succeed resigning George W. Romney as secretary of housing and urban development was James T. Lynn.

Nixon also added three new faces to his first string lineup. The biggest surprise came when he nominated Peter J. Brennan, leader of "hardhat" construction trades unionists in New York, and an enthusiastic Nixon cheerleader, to replace James D. Hodgson as secretary of labor. Brennan was the first union official in 20 years to be tagged for the post.

The final two cabinet assignments went to businessmen: Frederick B. Dent, a South Carolina textile executive, to replace departing Peter G. Peterson as secretary of commerce, and Claude S. Brineger, a California oilman, to take over the Department of Transportation from John A. Volpe who was becoming ambassador to Italy.

Wholesale changes were made in the sub-cabinet with some key spots going to graduates of Nixon's personal staff—further evidence of presidential intent to keep a tight rein on the various departments and agencies. These moves also served to pare the swollen White House payroll.

"I felt from the beginning," said Nixon at Camp David, "that it was important that the White House establish the example for the balance of the government in terms of cutting down on personnel, doing a better job with fewer people. Consequently, while there will be cuts in personnel across the government, throughout the department, the biggest cuts will be made in the White House staff itself."

Nixon made no move, however, to disturb the status of the White House "big three": chief of staff H. R. Haldeman, domestic policy advisor John D. Ehrlichman and foreign policy aide Henry A. Kissinger, the Vietnam peace negotiator and co-architect of summit trips to Peking and Moscow that did much to assure the President's reelection. But there were resignations; from Robert Finch, Harry Dent, Charles Colson and others.

"I honestly believe that government in Washington is too big and it is too expensive," Nixon told Garnett Horner of the *Star and Daily News.* Suspicious of bureaucracy since his own brief World War II stint as a bureaucrat, Nixon proclaimed a desire to prune away ineffective federal programs as well as superfluous employes. Actually, he had few alternatives if he wanted to redeem one of his most effective campaign pledges: to hold down spending and avoid a tax increase.

Congress balked at earlier Nixon efforts to reorganize and consolidate the federal machinery. Moreover, it appropriated in 1972 some $10 billion more than he wanted to spend. The result was a presidential decision to overrule the legislators through the exercise of executive powers.

A possible consequence could be a noisy row in 1973 between the President and the Democratic-controlled Congress. If 1972 offers a valid example, however, Nixon does very well at seeming to be above the battle. At year's end, in fact, the chief executive was hinting that the new year might find him above the fray both geographically and figuratively. Announcing that he would spend increasing amounts of time at Camp David, Nixon said:

". . . one constantly has the problem of either getting on top of the job or having the job get on top of you. I find that up here on top of a mountain, it is easier for me to get on top of the job . . ."

Above, kept on by the President was Secretary of State P. Rogers shown addressing U.N. General Assembly. The job of secretary of housing and urban development went to James T. Lynn, below, left, who had served as undersecretary of commerce. Surprise choice for the labor secretary post was Peter J. Brennan, below, center, veteran president of the New York State Building and Construction Trades Council. The key post of defense secretary went to Elliot L. Richardson, below, right, who had served Nixon as secretary of health, education and welfare

The Earth Heaved and Thousands Perished in Ravaged Managua

ALLEN POPE of Miami was relaxing in a Managua nightclub when the roof fell in. The time was 30 minutes past midnight on Saturday, Dec. 23.

"About the time the vocalist started to sing, there was a violent shake, and the ceiling came down," said the 44-year-old longshoreman. "It lasted about 5 to 10 seconds, but it seemed like an eternity."

Residents of Managua examining quake damage

The quake that shook Pope was the climax of a series that rolled over the Nicaraguan capital killing an estimated 7,000 persons and leaving nearly 200,000 of the city's 350,000 inhabitants homeless.

For more than two hours tremors rocked the city, setting buildings aflame and littering the streets with bodies and debris. At least 36 square blocks of the central business district were a jumble of rubble, as if smashed by a giant hand.

By dawn Saturday, the heart of the shattered city was bathed in an eerie orange light as the fires spread, finishing what the quakes had begun.

From piles of debris came the screams of trapped victims while in the ruined streets survivors sat stunned on the curbs or walked about in a daze.

"This is a terrible catastrophe," said Nicaragua's strongman, Gen. Anastasio Somoza, who declared that the number of dead and missing was "incalculable." Somoza and his junta quickly declared martial law to deal with the emergency and try to curb the looting.

Within hours, shaken survivors were giving stark accounts of the death and destruction they had witnessed.

"It was frightening, a terrible feeling," said airline stewardess Susan Goni. "We saw buildings fall, fires, people wandering around. . . ."

Juan Jose Barrios Taracena had left his Managua hotel to do an errand and was outside when the quake struck. It probably saved his life. There were only six survivors after the building in which he had been staying collapsed.

"I helped pull a beautiful young girl out of the debris, but she died as we were taking her to a first-aid station," Barrios Taracena said.

"The movement stopped, and I thought that if I was going to die, I should at least make a struggle first," said Vera Hernandez, of San Jose, Calif., who had been trapped in the wreckage of her hotel for six hours.

Uriel Gutierrez, an ambulance driver, described one of the death scenes. "There were about 80 persons dancing in the Plaza Cabaret," he said. "All of them were killed. Couples were found together, as if still dancing, and some musicians still had their instruments with them."

At the municipal jail in the heart of Managua, about 20 prisoners were killed. Some 450 others escaped from the shattered lockup. The dead prisoners were placed in the courtyard of the prison in hopes that friends or relatives would identify them.

Many of Managua's victims were said to be children from poor families who lived in the rickety buildings near the center of the city. In Oriente district, one of the poorest sectors in the capital, survivors huddled in the streets, crouched on battered chairs and dirty mattresses. On the second day, when a relief team brought in some fried chicken, the first food the people of Oriente had seen in nearly 48 hours, they grabbed the meat and wolfed it down.

Many bodies lay unclaimed in the streets. No medical facilities were functioning, until help began arriving Sunday from the United States and other countries.

By the third day thousands of relief workers were busy filling large common graves. Hundreds of bodies lay lined up along the banks of Lake Managua. With few coffins available, as many as three victims were crammed into a single casket. On one street, the body of a young child lay unclaimed and unidentified, but relief workers delayed burial in hopes the family would show up.

Police and national guardsmen patrolling Managua streets on the lookout for looters

There were Americans among the victims. U.S Ambassador Turner Shelton's secretary, Rose Marie Orlich, was one.

The quake caught Howard R. Hughes, the mysterious billionaire, in his tightly guarded half of the seventh floor of the Intercontinental Hotel where he had been staying in seclusion for four months.

The pyramid-shaped Intercontinental cracked and the ninth floor moved to one side and tilted. Power lines went out throughout the city and Hughes, said to have a fear of death by natural disaster, had to descend a darkened stairway to leave the building. Hughes was driven to the airport which was relatively undamaged and flew off in his private jet. Four days later, he surfaced in London where he went into seclusion in another hotel.

Two of Managua's three hospitals were destroyed by the quake, along with the headquarters building of the Red Cross. Many streets had buckled under the force of the tremors and public transport was virtually frozen. The roads were choked with pedestrians trying to get out of the burning capital.

By the fourth day the stench of death had become unbearable as thousands of bodies remained entombed in the rubble, but a few survivors refused to abandon the remains of their homes. Fearful that the thousands of decaying bodies might cause an epidemic, authorities ordered the Red Cross to stop serving food at emergency stations in the devastated areas. The hungry were told to seek food in stations outside the city.

"If we give them food they will stay," said Jorg Crojuc of the Mexican Red Cross. "It is against our mission not to give them food, but the government has ordered this."

Small tremors kept shaking the city several days after the quake, sending pieces of masonry from damaged structures crashing down into the street.

"It's like standing on jelly down here," radioed Ray Hash-berger, a U.S. communications satellite technician from a station two miles outside of Managua.

Some buildings inside the city had become so shaky that vibrations from passing trucks brought them down like piles of dominoes. The U.S. Army sent in a demolition team with a ton of explosives to blast dangerous structures.

The stricken city was now feeling the aftermath of the quakes. Water had to be brought in from Mexico because authorities feared any water available locally might be contaminated. Food supplies were running perilously low and stores began hiking their prices. Milk which usually sold for 27 cents a quart was going for $1 on Christmas Eve. Some families who had additional food stocks shared with the less fortunate.

Bulldozers droned through the streets trying to reach any survivors still buried underneath the debris. And orders went out to troops to shoot looters.

"Women and men ran in the streets with shoes, cloth and many other products from the remains of the destroyed stores," said Maria Elena de Gomez, a Colombian girl who had lived through the quake.

An airlift was set up to fly the injured out of Managua. In San Jose, the Costa Rican capital, 15 ambulances made successive runs from the airport to hospitals and back, carrying loads of unconscious and semiconscious people.

But some were too badly injured to be moved or were unable to get transport out of the capital.

At the Managua General Hospital, a U.S. Army medical team set up a treatment center. The patients had to be kept outside the half-shattered building which trembled dangerously with each aftershock. Patients wrapped in blood-stained sheets lay on the ground. Plasma bottles attached to their arms hung from tree branches.

"We are operating virtually under combat conditions," said

Capt. John Booth, a U.S. Army medical officer from Dayton, Ohio. As he spoke, a woman staggered in carrying a badly burned child. A sergeant yelled for a vehicle to rush the child to a nearby field hospital.

Nations of the Western Hemisphere and Europe responded quickly to Nicaragua's plight.

From his Florida White House, President Nixon ordered his Cabinet to make "an all-out effort" to provide all needed help.

On Christmas Eve, C141 planes began leaving at one-hour intervals from MacDill Air Force Base in Florida, carrying relief supplies and medical, water purification and communications equipment to Managua.

By the fourth day more than half a million tons of rolled oats and flour had been delivered to the Nicaraguan port of Corinto under the Food for Peace program. Six hundred tents were being flown from Miami by commercial aircraft and 900 more were airlifted from St. Louis aboard a military plane supplied by Canada.

Cuba's Communist government, a bitter foe of Somoza's regime, announced that it was sending medical supplies, plasma and teams of doctors and nurses. European governments and relief agencies mobilized their forces to help.

The American people emptied their wallets and cupboards on Christmas day to help the quake sufferers.

CARE reported in New York that it had 700 tons of food available for shipment to Managua. In Miami, the big Latin community turned out in force with their Christmas dinners, and with what money they could scrape up.

"They came with their turkeys and pigs and gave them to us for the people in Nicaragua," said a volunteer worker. "We are also collecting money, people are being very generous."

Right, mother and child sat, stunned by the disaster. Below, quake refugees preparing to leave battered Managua on Christmas Eve.

Final Shot of the Apollo Moon Series Paid Off Handsomely

Discovery of orange dust could cause major revision of man's lunar theories

T HE MONSTER ROCKET, stood on its launch pad, bathed in the glare of xenon spotlights. Finally, after a delay of 2 hours 40 minutes because of a computer problem, its mighty engines flashed to life.

It was 12:33 a.m. EST, on Dec. 7. Darkness suddenly became daylight as the Saturn 5 sent flames cascading over its launch pedestal.

Navy Capt. Eugene A. Cernan, 38; civilian geologist Harrison H. Schmitt, 37, and Navy Cmdr. Ronald E. Evans, 39, were on their way to the moon in the final shot in the historic Apollo series that already had landed 10 men on the lunar surface in 3½ years.

More than half a million visitors crowded vantage points in the Cape Kennedy area to bid farewell to Apollo and to observe the first after-dark launching of a U.S. man-in-space mission.

They were rewarded by the most dazzling liftoff in the history of the spaceport, where more than 3,000 rockets had been fired in 22 years.

With agonizing slowness, the 36-story-tall Saturn 5 rose, the thunder of its engines assaulting the ears and shaking the ground for miles around. The tail of flame expanded to 2,200 feet and filled the entire sky with an orange-pink glow.

As Apollo 17 climbed on its pillar of fire, the astronauts were busy monitoring systems and calling out gauge readings to Mission Control. But mission commander Cernan, veteran of two earlier space flights, remarked: "Let me tell you, this night launch is something to behold."

Apollo 17 soared smoothly into orbit more than 100 miles above the earth, and, after two circuits of the globe, ground controllers gave the okay to fire toward the moon. The spacemen reignited their third stage engine and they were on the way.

Apollo 17 lit up the dark sky as it blasted off the launching pad 2 hours and 40 minutes late on what was expected to be the final Apollo mission to the moon in this century

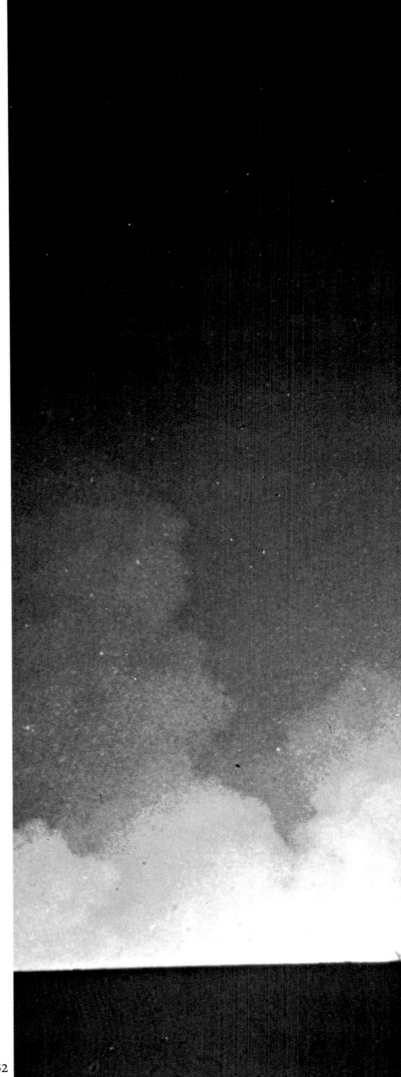

Command module pilot Ronald E. Evans far out in space as he retrieved film casettes from outside the vehicle

With Evans at the controls, command ship America separated, pivoted 180 degrees and linked with lunar ship Challenger, cradled in a compartment atop the third stage.

The astronauts discarded the third stage and America and Challenger sped on nose-to-nose toward the moon, 240,000 miles away. With only a few minor problems to occupy them during the three-day outward journey, Cernan, Schmitt and Evans were well rested when they shot into lunar orbit Dec. 10.

"Thumbs up! America has arrived on station for the challenge ahead," Cernan proclaimed in announcing the successful engine firing that settled them in orbit.

Evans described the excitement of reaching the moon when he remarked: "We're breathing so hard, the windows are fogging up on the inside."

Schmitt, realizing a geologist's dream rattled off descriptions of mountains, valleys, craters, rays and faults—with an expertise not available to earlier astronauts who had orbited the moon.

The next day, Monday, Cernan and Schmitt moved through a tunnel into the lunar ship Challenger and cast off for the descent to the moon, leaving Evans alone to conduct scientific and photographic experiments from orbit.

The target was a mountain-ringed valley named Taurus-Littrow in the northeast quadrant of the moon on the rim of the Sea of Serenity. The diving descent over 7,000-foot-high mountains was perfect, and after Cernan steered around several large boulders, Challenger touched down on the bull's-eye.

"The Challenger has landed," Cernan shouted as the spider-like craft settled in the black dust of the boulder-strewn valley. "We is here. Man, we is here."

Four hours later, Cernan backed down the nine-rung ladder from Challenger's cabin and planted his boot in the dust of Taurus-Littrow—the 11th man to walk on this alien world.

"I'd like to dedicate the first step of Apollo 17 to all those who made it possible," the commander said.

Minutes later, Schmitt became No. 12, and as he gazed around he commented: "It's a geologist's paradise if I've ever seen one."

The astronauts began their preliminary chores: familiarizing themselves with a lunar gravity one-sixth that of earth's; photographing the area; collecting contingency samples in case they had to make a quick departure from the moon; deploying and equipping their moon car, and setting up a nuclear-powered science station to relay data long after they left.

A television camera mounted on the battery-powered car relayed sharp color pictures to observers in Mission Control. Included was the traditional raising of the American flag on the moon. Then the men went about exploring the moon.

At one point on the TV screen, viewers saw Schmitt take a tumble as he reached for a rock.

"I still haven't learned how to pick up rocks, a very embarrassing thing for a geologist to admit," he quipped.

Cernan also had a reason to be embarrassed. With one swing of his geological hammer he accidentally clobbered the moon car, knocking off part of one of its rear fiberglass fenders.

Without this protective "mudguard," the astronauts were sprayed with dust later when they drove half a mile to a crater named Emory. Here they found rocks which Schmitt described as vesicular, and which provided one of the clues they sought: that Taurus-Littrow once had been the scene of volcanic activity.

Weary after the first of three seven-hour surface excursions, the astronauts headed back to Challenger for a long rest.

At the start of the second moon walk Tuesday, Cernan and Schmitt headed for the damaged taxi. Mission Control had worked out a solution to the fender problem—tape together four thin plastic lunar maps and attach them with clamps.

The scheme worked and even kept dust off the astronauts when Cernan opened the rover's throttle to more than 7 m.p.h. on the way to South Massif, a 7,000-foot-tall mountain 4.4 miles from the landing craft.

"Man is this mountain big," Schmitt exclaimed as they began sifting through the rubble of an ancient landslide that brought rocks down from several layers of the mountain, and thus from several periods in lunar history. Some of the boulders were the size of a house.

Schmitt described rock formations which indicated the astronauts had tapped a lode of very ancient material, perhaps dating back 4.6 billion years to the birth of the moon. These could fill in a missing chapter in science's understanding of the evolution of the moon.

En route back to Challenger, the explorers stopped at a crater nicknamed Shorty, and it was here that Schmitt made a discovery that electrified scientists watching at Mission Control.

"Hey, there is orange soil here. It's all over," he shouted. "That's incredible! It's really orange out here, Houston. It looks like oxidized desert soil."

"He's not going out of his wits," Cernan radioed. "It really is orange soil."

Color pictures snapped by the astronauts later showed the colored dust in striking contrast to the dark gray material that covers most of the rest of the moon.

On earth, the Manned Spacecraft Center's chief geochemist, Robin Brett, said: "We have witnessed one of the important finds in Apollo geology."

Dr. Christopher C. Kraft, director of the Manned Spacecraft Center, followed the custom of lighting up a cigar after a space crew had successfully completed their mission

There was good reason for the excitement. The orange color indicated the soil may have oxidized, or rusted. That, in turn, meant it probably had been exposed to water or oxygen. The only likely source for such vapors on the arid, airless moon would be volcanic vents that brought the gases from a molten interior.

Because the orange dust lay on top of other material, scientists speculated it was relatively young, perhaps only 100 million years old. That would make it the youngest material picked up on the moon. More important, it would suggest surprisingly recent volcanic activity on the moon—a body which most had theorized as having been largely dormant for about three billion years.

Cernan and Schmitt carefully collected samples of the mysterious soil, which was two to three inches deep and spread over 100-square-foot area. Then they headed back to the lunar ship.

The third excursion was perhaps man's last walk on the moon in the 20th century.

They drove their car two miles to another large mountain named North Massif where they chiseled at huge boulders which had tumbled down from different levels.

As he stood high up on a slope, Cernan glanced around and said: "When we finish tonight, we will have covered this whole valley from corner to corner."

There was even time for some hijinks as Schmitt kicked a

rock downhill and pretended to ski in the slippery dust with the comment "Whoosh! Whoosh! Whoosh! . . . It's a little hard to get hip rotation."

And Cernan hopped along with the declaration: "I can cover ground like a kangaroo."

Moving east to an area called the Sculptured Hills, which they described as resembling "the wrinkled skin of an old, old man," the astronauts sampled more rocks before driving back to Challenger for the last time.

They loaded aboard their rocks and soil samples and in their final moments outside the moonship, they unveiled a plaque attached to one of the craft's landing struts, which would remain on the surface after they departed.

It read: "Here man completed his first exploration of the moon, December, 1972 A.D. May the spirit of peace in which we came be reflected in the lives of all mankind."

Cernan also held up what he called "a very significant rock, composed of many fragments of all sizes and shapes and colors." Speaking to science-oriented youngsters of 79 nations who had been invited to Mission Control, Cernan said the rock would be divided among their countries "as a symbol that we can live in peace and harmony in the future."

Schmitt was first up the ladder into the cabin. As Cernan, the last man of Apollo to touch the moon, started up he said: "I take these last steps from the surface for some time into the future to come . . . I'd just like to record that America's challenge of today has forged man's destiny of tomorrow. And as we leave the moon and Taurus-Littrow we leave as we came,

Scientist Astronaut Harrison H. Schmitt photographed next to the U.S. flag at the Taurus-Littrow landing site

and, God willing, we shall return, with peace and hope for all mankind."

The next day, with a shout of "We're on our way," Cernan and Schmitt launched Challenger's cabin section from the surface and flew a rendezvous course that caught Evans and command ship America two hours later.

The two ships docked flawlessly and the moon adventurers transferred their precious cargo into America, then discarded Challenger to crash on the moon to excite seismic devices left on the surface.

Cernan, Schmitt and Evans spent two additional days in orbit to operate cameras and scientific instruments which measured the thin lunar atmosphere, studied subsurface characteristics with radar beams and drew a thermal map over the area which America passed.

During an orbit over the western edge of the Sea of Serenity, about 350 miles west of Taurus-Littrow, Schmitt spotted a large area of orange material.

"Man, we're seeing an orange moon now," he said, adding that the area appeared to have one or more volcanic cones. If so, the find, combined with the discovery at the landing site, would indicate more than one volcanoe was active in the recent evolutionary history of the moon.

On Saturday, Dec. 16, the astronauts ended their lunar exploration, firing out of orbit to start the long voyage back to earth.

"America has found fair winds and following seas and we're on the way home," Cernan reported after the successful engine burn.

En route, 180,000 miles from earth, Evans took a deep space walk, slipping through America's open hatch and moving to the rear to remove moon-mapping film canisters from an equipment bay. He was bundled in a stiff white suit and was attached to a 25-foot lifeline.

"Speaking of being a spaceman, this is it," he exclaimed as he floated like a feather in the weightless world.

On their last night in space, the astronauts held a televised news conference, answering reporters' questions relayed by Mission Control.

Schmitt said he and Cernan had sampled a "broad spectrum of lunar history" and had "increased the perspective for the future of mankind in the solar system."

Cernan predicted "now that we have begun we will continue into deep space. We may not return to the moon or go to Mars in this century, but I have faith it will happen."

On Tuesday, Dec. 19, the last men of Apollo came home, blazing back through earth's atmosphere to a pinpoint landing in the South Pacific, within view of hundreds of cheering sailors on the deck of the main recovery ship, the carrier USS Ticonderoga.

The astronauts were quickly hoisted aboard, and two days later flew home to Houston for Christmas reunions with their families.

The flight phase of Apollo was over. But scientists around the world will study the treasure of six moon landing flights for years as they attempt to unravel the history of how the moon, our earth and solar system evolved.

A preliminary science report called Apollo 17 the most "scientifically sophisticated" of the Apollos and said it could produce major revisions about man's theories of the moon. The report, compiled by lunar scientists observing the flight at Mission Control, called the orange dust a "remarkable discovery" because of its implication of a still active moon perhaps as recently as 100 million years ago.

CONGRESS PROBING U.S. NAVY RACIAL INCIDENTS

When the 80,000-ton aircraft carrier Kitty Hawk returned to its home port of San Diego at the end of December, the debarking crewmen were ordered not to discuss a race riot that had flared on the ship during its nine-month Vietnam tour of duty.

Capt. Marland W. Townsend Jr., commander of the big ship, said the riot which broke out at sea Oct. 12 and lasted for some 15 hours, was "small and incidental to the total mission," adding that since the trouble "we have seen a great quest for friendship and understanding among black and white sailors on the ship."

More than 45 men were injured in the incident which some sailors said stemmed from a fight in the ship's mess hall. According to several black crewmen, a white sailor accidentally spilled some milk and a black had to clean it up. The two argued, came to blows, and the fighting spread. The Navy said bands of blacks went on a rampage through the ship attacking whites.

The incident was one of several to surface in the Navy during the closing months of 1972.

On Nov. 26, 32 blacks and one white were locked up as the result of a riot at the Navy Correctional Center in Norfolk, Va. The Navy said the trouble apparently began when a white and a black fought, the white was knocked to the ground, and three other blacks joined in beating him. When Marine guards tried to confine the four, it said, other black inmates at the center reportedly burned mattresses and smashed a dormitory door.

The day before, at Naval Station Midway—a tiny island about 1,100 miles northwest of Honolulu—five sailors were injured in a clash involving some 130 men. The incident began with a confrontation between black and white sailors at a recreation area, but no specific cause for the altercation was determined.

The giant carrier Constellation broke off a training exercise and sailed to San Diego where 130 crewmen, most of them black, were ordered ashore Nov. 4 as a "landing party" by Capt. J. D. Ward, skipper of the big ship. The men had complained of discipline aboard the ship and racial discrimination in jobs.

They said Ward refused to listen to their problems. The captain said he put them off because of threats to the safety to his ship and apparent instances of sabotage.

When the 130 were ordered back aboard Nov. 9, only seven complied. Of the rest, 29 were discharged and the others were to be transferred to other ships after being fined or reduced in rank.

Four crewmen were hurt in an apparent racial clash Oct. 16 aboard the Navy oiler Hassayampa at Subic Bay in the Philippines. The Navy said 11 crewmen—five of them later released without charge—were placed in the base correctional center. All of those hurt were white and all detained were black.

As the year drew to a close, a Congressional group was investigating racial disorders aboard Navy ships.

Rear Adm. D. H. Bagley, chief of naval personnel, left, and Adm. Elmo R. Zumwalt, chief of naval operations, testifying before a House committee investigating alleged racial incidents aboard U.S. aircraft carriers

POP MUSIC FANS DIED IN FIRE

An overflow crowd—many of its members teen-agers—jammed a 3,000 seat theater in Seoul, Korea, Dec. 2, to enjoy a pop music festival.

The evening went well until, minutes after the entertainment ended and most of the rock fans were filing out, there was an explosion and then fire. Witnesses said the audience stampeded, fighting its way out of the building. Some jumped out of windows in the three-story building in an effort to escape the flames.

Firemen fought the blaze for more than three hours. When it ended there were 51 dead and more than 75 injured. Police blamed the fire on an overloaded power circuit.

United Mine Workers President Tony Boyle greeting newsmen before his defeat in union election

JET CRASH CLAIMED 155 LIVES

A jetliner taking holidaying tourists home to Europe had just taken off from the Canary Islands when it plunged to earth, killing all 155 persons aboard.

Witnesses said the Convair 990A was only 300 feet off the runway Dec. 3 when one of its four engines burst into flame and the plane crashed.

Those killed in Spanish aviation's worst disaster included 148 passengers, most of them Germans, and seven crew members.

Only one person was found alive after the crash. She was a young woman who kept crying, "Save me, save me." She died within minutes of reaching a hospital.

THE FALLING FORTUNES OF TONY BOYLE

The falling fortunes of United Mine Workers President W. A. "Tony" Boyle took another drop in December when union members voted him out of the post he had held for 10 years.

U.S. District Judge William B. Bryant ordered the election after finding evidence of widespread fraud in the balloting three years earlier when Boyle was reelected UMW president, defeating Joseph A. "Jock" Yablonski.

Several weeks after that election, Yablonski, his wife and daughter were murdered in their home (The World in 1970, 102). Later, several local and district officials of the union confessed or were indicted in connection with the case. The 70-year-old Boyle denied any knowledge of the slayings.

But the glare of publicity since 1969 resulted in federal actions that forced Boyle to step down as a director of the union-owned National Bank of Washington, to resign as one of three trustees of the union's multimillion-dollar welfare and pension fund, and the dissolution of trusteeships through which Boyle had directly run the affairs of most of the union's 22 districts.

It also led to Boyle's conviction in June and a five-year prison sentence plus $130,000 in fines for illegally contributing union money to candidates for political office. Boyle's attorneys appealed the sentence.

In January 1970, the day that Jock Yablonski was buried, his supporters agreed to form the nucleus of the Miners For Democracy, dedicated to ending the Boyle regime's control of the 200,000-member union and its $65 million in assets.

As the date for the new election drew near, Boyle denounced the Miners For Democracy's student volunteers as "outsiders" and "stinking hippies." Boyle's camp predicted that he would score a 55-to-60 per cent victory over his opponent, Arnold L. Miller, 49-year-old ideological heir of Yablonski.

But when the returns were in, Miller had defeated Boyle by a margin of more than 14,000 votes. Two days after the results became known, Boyle resigned the $50,000 a year presidency.

Miller held a victory news conference and vowed to increase the pensions of all miners to $200 per month and to cut the salaries of union officers by 20 per cent. He also promised to provide better health care for disabled miners. It was a subject in which he had a personal interest. The West Virginian had retired from the mines several years earlier because he had contracted "black lung" disease from breathing coal dust.

Lester B. Pearson

LESTER B. PEARSON, LED CANADA AND WON THE NOBEL PEACE PRIZE

They called him the "unhappy warrior" because he expressed distaste for the "hoopla and circus" aspects of politics. But once he entered the arena, Lester B. Pearson displayed a natural talent that boosted him to the post of Canada's prime minister.

Pearson, who died at the age of 75 on Dec. 27, was deeply interested in international affairs and emerged as a top diplomat on the world scene at the close of World War II.

With the United States and the Soviet Union locked in the first stages of The Cold War, Pearson, as a representative of a middle power was able to exert an influence for peace and world stability far beyond his country's actual stature.

Pearson's efforts in the United Nations were instrumental in stopping the 1956 battle over the Suez Canal and won him the Nobel Peace Prize for 1957. The award left Pearson "thunderstruck" and surprised many fellow Canadians who had never had a son so honored.

A scholar since his youth, Pearson received a fellowship in history at St. John's College of Oxford University. In the early 1920s, he taught history at the University of Toronto.

Pearson entered government service as a first secretary with Canada's new Department of External Affairs in 1928 and became an advisor at the London Naval Conference. This began his lifelong association with diplomacy and after a series of assignments, he was sent to Washington in 1942 as minister counsellor. Three years later, he was named ambassador to the United States.

The expanding activities of the infant United Nations fascinated Pearson and he served as senior advisor to the Canadian delegation at San Francisco when the world peace forum formally came into being in 1945.

For 11 General Assemblies until 1957, Pearson served as a potent force in the United Nations' top Political Committee. In 1952, he was elected president of the General Assembly and that same year presided over the North Atlantic Treaty Organization Council in Lisbon.

Pearson made his debut in politics in 1948 when he was tapped for the post of foreign secretary. To be a cabinet minister he had to occupy a seat in Canada's House of Commons and announced his candidacy to represent a rural Ontario district he had reportedly never visited.

As foreign secretary, Pearson shared responsibility for the partition of Palestine. He was also a leading architect of NATO in the 1950s. He played a key role in the Korean War truce.

The climax of Pearson's diplomatic career came in 1956 after Israel, backed by Britain and France, attacked Egypt and the Suez Canal. The action split the western alliance and threatened a new world conflict. Pearson took charge of the Canadian delegation at the United Nations and finally worked up a compromise formula that set up the U.N. Emergency Force to keep peace along the Gaza Strip.

The Liberal victory in 1963 made Pearson prime minister, but he had little liking for the infighting between partisan factions on the floor of Commons. His accomplishments during his five-year term were impressive, however. He brought in a national pension plan and a family assistance program. He also broadened Social Security benefits and laid the foundations for a National Free Medical Service.

Pearson regarded as one of his greatest achievements the adoption of Canada's first distinctive national flag—the red and white banner displaying a large maple leaf. He also inaugurated a sweeping study of French-English bilingualism, which had been a controversial issue, and biculturalism in Canada.

Pearson was never a politician in the conventional sense. Kissing babies other than his own grandchildren made him uneasy and when he campaigned in a cowboy hat, he still looked like a career diplomat. When he retired as prime minister in 1968 (*The World in 1968, 134*), Pearson said he was delighted to be out of the political arena. He returned to the academic grove and was named chancellor of Carleton University at Ottawa.

Pakistani President Zulfikar Ali Bhutto during his tour of the primitive Northwest Frontier areas bordering on Afghanistan

MARATHON PENTAGON PAPERS TRIAL STARTED UP AGAIN

With not a word of testimony yet spoken the Pentagon Papers trial of Daniel Ellsberg and Anthony Russo ended in Los Angeles and then began again.

By year's end Ellsberg had been under indictment for 18 months and pre-trial action had dragged more than a year.

Although the law forbids the trial of any defendant twice for the same crime, Ellsberg and Russo waived that right to protection from double jeopardy to get a new jury and a fresh start after months of legal complications.

U.S. District Court Judge Matt Byrne was still faced with decisions on disputes similar to others which had stalled the trial—disagreements over government practices of wiretapping telephones on which defense members' conversations were overheard.

The Ellsberg-Russo defense fund announced that the trial already had cost them $250,000 and they were $75,000 in debt. By the conclusion of the second trial they estimated their expenses would reach $750,000.

The case of Ellsberg and Russo, two former researchers on government projects, first surfaced in June 1971 *(The World in 1971, 182)* when newspapers printed contents of top secret government documents detailing origins of the Vietnam War. Days later Ellsberg acknowledged he had leaked the documents hoping their disclosure would end the war. He was immediately indicted.

That December, the government replaced Ellsberg's indictment with a new one which also named Russo and charged both men with espionage, conspiracy and theft.

Their impending trial was seen as a landmark and was expected to produce new interpretations of espionage and the constitutional guarantee of freedom of press.

It was the first time that Americans had been prosecuted for giving government secrets to a newspaper in their own country. Espionage laws previously were interpreted to apply only in cases in which a person intended harm to his country or aided a foreign power in doing such harm. The government alleged no such intent but said that didn't matter, it was espionage anyway.

From the start of pretrial court actions the trial ran into a series of delays.

At one point, the judge suffered an appendicitis attack causing a brief postponement. Then the defense presented a lengthy challenge of the jury selection system and argued numerous motions aimed at gaining a dismissal of the case.

When jury selection began in July there were vehement objections from the defense because the judge decided to question potential jurors himself rather than let attorneys do it. He said it would be speedier.

A jury was chosen within the month and the panelists swore to be impartial. But just after their swearing the government prosecutor prodded by the defense for months to say whether wiretaps were used in the case revealed that indeed a member of the defense team was overheard on a wiretap.

The defense demanded to know the contents of the wiretapped conversation, and the government refused. The judge said the tap was irrelevant to the case but defense attorneys decided to appeal to higher courts for permission to know what was overheard.

Daniel Ellsberg and his wife, Pat, rejoicing over mistrial decision

The trial recessed in August and did not resume until November when the U.S. Supreme Court said it would not hear the case.

The jurors, who had waited four months to serve, returned to court, but the defense asked for their removal. During the trial hiatus attorneys noted that President Nixon had been re-elected and said campaign rhetoric had covered many subjects at issue in the Pentagon Papers case. They claimed jurors had been prejudiced. The judge disagreed and allowed the jurors to stay when they swore they were still impartial.

Again, the defense appealed to a higher court. Just before opening statements were to start the 9th U.S. Circuit Court of Appeals declined to rule but issued a statement saying, "It ap-

pears to us as foolish to proceed to trial in the case with the jury selected four months ago."

The trial judge took the hint. He said the court seemed to be advising him that retention of the jury could lead to reversal if a conviction in the case were appealed. He called the jury to court and told them they were no longer involved in the case.

The jurors spoke out bitterly complaining that their lives had been "goofed up and messed up" for four months for no reason.

Pretrial motions began again and two weeks before jury selection was to begin the government submitted to the judge a secret report which said a member of the defense team again had been overheard on a government wiretap.

The defense demanded again to know who it was and what was overheard. The judge refused ruling the conversation had nothing to do with the trial.

But attorneys for the defense immediately accused the government of engaging in massive snooping into the private lives of defendants, their families, friends and associates.

They accused the government of illegally using grand jury subpoenas to get records of the defendants' telephone calls, of opening their mail and checking their bank records. They said the FBI had interrogated persons the defendants talked to on the phone or issued checks to. The judge ordered the government to answer the charges.

U.S. SUPREME COURT DRIFTED FARTHER TO RIGHT IN 1972

With four Nixon administration appointees performing up to expectations, the Supreme Court drifted even farther to the right in 1972.

But there were three important exceptions to the trend. The death penalty was nullified, a major administration wiretap policy was scuttled, and poor defendants were guaranteed a lawyer when they faced the prospect of a day in jail.

Chief Justice Warren E. Burger—whose legal philosophy was apart from that of the three remaining "Warren Court" liberals, William O. Douglas, William J. Brennan Jr. and Thurgood Marshall—seemed to have had more success shaping the Court to his liking during his third year. In his first year as chief justice, Burger was more or less isolated. But Harry A. Blackmun came aboard the second year, and they were later joined by two other administration nominees, William H. Rehnquist and Lewis F. Powell Jr. The four generally held together and were able to propel the Court to the right when they were joined by Justice Byron R. White.

And yet, it was Powell who delivered the opinion that the government no longer would be permitted to wiretap suspected domestic "subversives" without a warrant. Except for Rehnquist, who disqualified himself, the decision was unanimous. The Justice Department had argued that both the Constitution and the 1968 Safe Streets Act permitted bugging without judicial supervision to guard domestic security.

The death penalty decision June 29 and a school ruling a week earlier illustrated both the strength of the Burger bloc and the fact that 4 out of 9 still was not a numerical majority. The four administration appointees would have retained the death penalty. They considered the question one that should be left to "legislative judgment." Said Burger, expressing the overriding legal philosophy of the four, "The highest judicial duty is to recognize the limits on judicial power and to permit the democratic process to deal with matter falling outside of those limits." But the five other justices thought otherwise. They combined—some with reservations—to form a majority that probably ended capital punishment in the United States.

Similarly, the four administration appointees produced a significant division on the Court on the issue of school desegregation. They would have allowed Emporia, Va., a separate district apart from the more heavily black areas of Greensville county and would have limited the power of district judges to adjust geographic divisions as a means of speeding integration.

But here, too, the five other justices thought differently and prevailed. The ruling was important not so much for its effect upon a relatively small, Southern rural school system. What it could do was give a boost to judges—north and south—who were under pressure locally—and from the White House and Congress—to go slow in tinkering with school district lines.

These rulings were the exception, however. So was the almost unanimous judgment that defendants accused of even minor crimes were entitled to a free trial lawyer if a possible jail term hung over them. More typically, White and sometimes Potter Stewart swung over to join the Nixon appointees, leaving the three consistent liberals—Douglas, Brennan and Marshall—in a losing minority.

For example, White and the administration appointees produced 5-4 rulings that:

—A member of Congress may be called before a grand jury to tell how he acquired classified documents and arranged for their private publication.

—Newsmen have no right under the First Amendment to protect their sources when called before a grand jury.

—Cut off a test of the Army's surveillance of civilians.

—Unanimous jury verdicts were not required for convictions in state criminal trials.

Stewart and the four administration appointees also produced a 5-4 ruling that suspects generally were not entitled to a lawyer at lineup identifications.

And both White and Stewart combined with the Nixon appointees to produce 6-3 rulings that allowed private social clubs to bar blacks as guests even though the clubs operated with state liquor licenses, and broadened the powers of policemen to frisk suspicious persons.

In other decisions during 1972, baseball won an extension of its unique exemption from antitrust laws by a 5-3 vote, and ruled 6-0—with three justices not participating—that computer programing consisted basically of ideas and could not be patented. It held 6-3 Dec. 5 that the states may shut down saloons that feature bottomless dancers, sex films or other forms of "bacchanalian revelries," and two days later ruled 8-1 that labor unions could not fine workers who quit the union during a strike and returned to their jobs. It also held unanimously tenants in apartment complexes had a right under the 1968 federal civil rights law to sue landlords on charges of discriminating against black applicants.

American billionaire J. Paul Getty celebrating his 80th birthday in London received a helping hand from the Duchess of Argyll, left, while cutting his birthday cake. President Nixon's daughter, Tricia Cox, right, looked on

A BASEBALL SUPERSTAR KILLED ON MERCY MISSION

A baseball teammate's eyes filled with tears when he heard the news. Pittsburgh Pirate superstar Roberto Clemente had died in the crash of a plane taking relief supplies to survivors of quake-shattered Managua, Nicaragua.

"Clemente's work with the relief effort was typical," he said. "Roberto was always trying to help someone."

The 38-year-old Clemente, whose interest in Nicaragua may have been spurred by a visit to that country earlier in 1972 for an amateur baseball tournament, was heading Nicaraguan aid efforts in his native Puerto Rico. In a week his group had collected $160,000 and tons of supplies. The star outfielder apparently decided to go to Nicaragua personally, a friend said, to insure that the supplies got into the hands of the people they were meant for. According to Cristobal Colon, Clemente had "received reports that some of the food and clothing he had sent earlier had fallen into the hands of profiteers."

Late on Dec. 31, Clemente boarded a four-engined DC-7 piston-powered cargo plane loaded with relief supplies. The plane, carrying a crew of three and one other passenger besides Clemente, had just taken off from Puerto Rico's San Juan International Airport when it went down in heavy seas a mile and a half from shore. Searching aircraft later found wreckage of the downed plane in the water. There was no sign of survivors.

Clemente played baseball so well in high school that he was given a $500 bonus to join the Santurce team in the Puerto Rican League. It was not long before he moved up to the major leagues, starting the 1955 season with the Pittsburgh club when he was not quite 21. During his 18-season career, he won the National League batting championship four times, was named to the All-Star team 12 times, and was named the league's Most Valuable Player in 1966.

In addition, Clemente was the 11th man in more than 100 years of baseball history to get 3,000 hits; his career batting average was .317;

Pirates star Roberto Clemente

he was widely acknowledged as one of the great fielders of his time with a strong and accurate throwing arm, and he helped lead Pittsburgh to two world championships in 1960 and 1971.

"It was quite an honor to manage in the major leagues," said retired Pittsburgh manager Danny Murtaugh, "but it was a double honor to manage a superstar like Roberto . . . and he was a super-

star. I thought Roberto was the greatest player I've ever seen."

In Puerto Rico, where Clemente shone as the most popular sports figure in the island's history, Gov. Luis A. Ferre issued a proclamation ordering three days of official mourning because of "the death of the great Puerto Rican, Roberto Clemente."

FIRST FATAL CRASH OF JUMBO JETLINER

Two men were hunting frogs from an airboat in the dark Florida Everglades the night of Dec. 29 when "we saw the plane go over real low." Then, said Ray Dickens, "all of a sudden there was a bright flash that lasted 15 to 20 seconds."

Dickens and his companion sped to the spot, finding the wreckage of a jumbo jetliner that had crashed during an approach to Miami International Airport. The two began pulling victims from the water and soon were joined in the rescue effort by Coast Guard, Army and Air Force personnel.

"The first person I saw was still sitting in his seat, strapped in his safety belt, with nothing around him but knee-deep water," said Lt. Cmdr. B. G. Kingery, a Coast Guard helicopter pilot. "He was talking to a girl sitting in the water next to his seat. They didn't pay any attention to us. It was like they were in such deep shock they were oblivious to us and the bodies lying in the mud around them."

The man and girl were among the 77 persons

who survived the crash. Ninety-nine others died. Their plane, an Eastern Airlines L-1011 TriStar, was enroute from New York City to Miami and was on a routine approach pattern to Miami's airport when, investigators said, it vanished from the field's radar control scanners.

The TriStar was the first of the jumbo jets, such as the Boeing 747 and Douglas DC-10, to be involved in a fatal crash. The $19 million, three-engine jet can carry 226 passengers and a crew of 13.

FOR THE RECORD

PAROLED. The Rev. Philip F. Berrigan, after 39 months in prison. Berrigan, 49, was released Dec. 20. He had been granted parole Nov. 29 from concurrent sentences stemming from destruction of draft records and his conviction for smuggling letters in and out of a federal prison in the so-called Harrisburg Seven trial. On release, Berrigan, a Josephite priest, said he planned to work within the limits of his parole for an end to the war in Indochina.

KILLED. Forty-five persons, when a United Air Lines jet crashed into a row of houses in a crowded neighborhood on Chicago's southwest side Dec. 8. The plane was flying from Washington to Omaha with a stop at Chicago and crashed as it was descending to Midway Airport. Eighteen passengers survived the crash. Among the dead was Rep. George W. Collins, a Chicago Democrat.

CLOSED. Life magazine, which said it would publish its last issue Dec. 29, after 36 years of publication. Andrew Heiskell, Time Inc. board chairman, said there had been "emotional agony in the decision" to end publication of the magazine which had lost more than $30 million in the last four years. The end of Life left the nation without a major, general interest, text-and-picture magazine.

STABBED. Mrs. Ferdinand E. Marcos, wife of the Philippine president, by a man with a dagger during a public ceremony in Manila Dec. 7. The assailant was shot to death on the spot. Mrs. Marcos was not gravely injured, but wounds on her hands and arms required 75 stitches.

Project Supervisor: Keith Fuller

Editorial Director: Dan Perkes

Editor: Tom Hoge

Staff Writer: Phil Thomas

Writer-Researcher: Chris Conkling

Color Photos: Helen Seebach

Photo Production: Stanley Kohler

Promotion and Distribution: Jack Elcik

Photo Researchers: Aaron Klein, Robert White

Feature Narratives
Howard Benedict, Cocoa Beach, Fla.
  Apollo 16
  Apollo 17
Hal Bock, New York
  World Series
Chris Conkling, New York
  Drug traffic
Frank Cormier, Washington
  The President's year
Harry Dunphy, Beirut
  Middle East
Julie Flint, London
  World chess
Colin Frost, London
  Duke of Windsor
  Northern Ireland
Will Grimsley, New York
  Winter Olympics
Joe Hall, Washington
  Congress
Bruce Handler, Rio de Janeiro
  Brazil
Carl Hartman and Fred Coleman, London
  British economy
Vern Haugland, Washington
  Air hijacks
Howard C. Heyn, New York
  Crippling diseases
Tom Hoge, New York
  African growing pains
  Cyprus
  Munich terror
Harry Humphries, Washington
  Atomic weapons
John S. Lang, Washington
  The two-party system
Edith Lederer, San Francisco
  Angela Davis
Lee Linder, Philadelphia
  Harrisburg 7
Jules Loh, New York
  Presidential primaries
  National conventions
  National elections
Geoffrey Miller, London
  Wimbledon tennis
Betty Mills, Charleston, W.Va.
  West Virginia flood
Mike Rathet, New York
  Super Bowl
Terry Ryan, New York
  Howard Hughes
William L. Ryan, New York
  Nixon visits China, Russia
Larry Stuntz, New York
  Future car
Kay Tateishi, Tokyo
  Japan
Phil Thomas, New York
  Jackie Robinson
  Harry S Truman
William J. Waugh, Washington
  Education

John Wheeler, New York
  Bangladesh
  Vietnam
Stephen H. Wildstrom, Detroit
  Auto callbacks
Jeannine Yeomans, San Francisco
  Soledad brothers

Contributing Reporters
  Linda Deutsch, Los Angeles
  Sue Everly, New York
  Charles Layton, New Orleans
  William N. Oatis, United Nations
  Barry Schweid, Washington
  Bill Stockton, Los Angeles
Saigon Staff
  George Esper
  Richard H. Pyle
  Holger Jensen
  Hugh Mulligan
  Richard Blystone
  Edith Lederer
  Ann Blackman
  Dennis Neeld
  Michael Putzel

Photographs
(The illustrations in this volume
were selected for the most part
from the news photo reports of The
Associated Press and, except where
specifically credited, were taken
by staff photographers of The AP
and its member newspapers).

Staff Photographers
  Athens
    Aristotle Saricostas
  Beirut
    Harry Koundakjian
  Berlin
    Edwin Reichert
  Bonn
    Klaus Schlagman
  Buenos Aires
    Max Simon
    Domingo Zenteno Zeggara
  Copenhagen
    Henning Brink
    Mogens Holmberg
    Sigvard Holmer
    Poul Henrik Seifert
  Frankfurt
    Bernhard Frye
    Peter Hillebrecht
    Kurt Strumpf
  Hamburg
    Helmuth Lohmann
  Jakarta
    Cornelius Joost Katoppo
  Kuala Lumpur
    Tee Ee
  London
    Lawrence Harris
    Peter Kemp
    William F. Rider-Rider

  Sidney Smart
  Edward S. Worth
Madrid
  Leopoldo Gomez Gonzalez
Manila
  Alfonso del Mundo
Milan
  Raoul Fornezza
  Armando Trovati
Moscow
  Roger Leddington
Munich
  Dieter Endlicher
Oslo
  Tom Brauner Jensen
  Paul Oweson
Paris
  Phillipe Barbaud
  Spartaco Bodini
  Jean Pierre Etchegaray
  Pierre Godot
  Ernest Gacquere
  Michel Laurent
  Jean Jacques Levy
  Michel Claude Lipchitz
  Jacques Marqueton
  Michael Nash
  Georges Raulin Jr.
  Albert Roques
Rome
  Guiseppe Anastasi
  Giulio Broglio
  Giovanni Foggia
  Claudio Luffoli
  Massimo Sambucetti
  Mario Torrisi
Saigon
  Rick Merron
  Dang Van Phuoc
  Carl D. Robinson
  Neal Ulevich
  Huynh Cong "Nick" Ut
  Hubert Van Es
Seoul
  Kim Chon-Kil
Singapore
  Horst Faas
Tel Aviv
  Max Nash
Tokyo
  Yuichi Ishizori
  Max Desfor
  Mitsunori Chigita
  Akira Sekiguchi
  Keiichi Mori
Albany
  Robert Schutz
Atlanta
  Horace W. Cort
  Charles E. Kelly
  Joe Holloway
Austin
  Ted Powers
Baltimore
  William A. Smith
Boston
  William Chaplis
  Francis C. Curtin
  J. Walter Green
Chicago
  Frederick H. Jewell
  Edward S. Kitch
  Charles E. Knoblock
  Laurence E. Stoddard
Cincinnati
  Harvey E. Smith
Cleveland
  Julian C. Wilson
Columbia
  Louis Krasky
Columbus
  Steve Pyle
Dallas
  Charles Bennett
  Ferd Kaufman

  Dave Taylor
  Harold Waters
Denver
  Robert D. Scott
Detroit
  James McKnight
  Rich Sheinwald
  Preston Stroup
Hartford
  Robert Child
Harrisburg
  Paul Vathis
Houston
  Edward F. Kolenovsky
Indianapolis
  Charles Robinson
Kansas City
  William P. Straeter Jr.
Los Angeles
  George Brich
  Harold F. Filan
  Wallace H. Fong Jr.
  Jeff Robbins
  David F. Smith
Miami
  Mark Foley
  James P. Kerlin
  Steven Starr
  James Bourdier
Milwaukee
  Paul J. Shane
Minneapolis
  Jim Mone
New Orleans
  Jack R. Thornell
New York
  Anthony Camerano
  Ron Frehm
  Harry L. Harris
  Martin M. Lederhandler
  John J. Lent
  David Pickoff
  John P. Rooney
  Ray Stubblebine
  James Wells
Philadelphia
  Wilson G. Ingraham
  Ronald B. Kennedy
  Brian Horton
Pittsburgh
  Harry Cabluck
Raleigh
  Hal Valentino
San Francisco
  Richard Drew
  Robert H. Houston
  Robert K. Klein
  Sal Veder
Sacramento
  Walter Zeboski
Seattle
  Barry R. Sweet
Springfield
  John Filo
St. Louis
  Frederick O. Waters
Tallahassee
  William M. Hudson
Trenton
  Jack Kanthal
Washington
  Henry D. Burroughs Jr.
  Robert A. Daugherty
  John A. Duricka
  Harvey W. Georges
  Charles P. Gorry
  Henry Giffin
  Charles W. Harrity
  Byron H. Rollins
  John H. Rous
  Charles B. Tasnadi
  James Palmer

Almanac Editor
Dick Madden

264

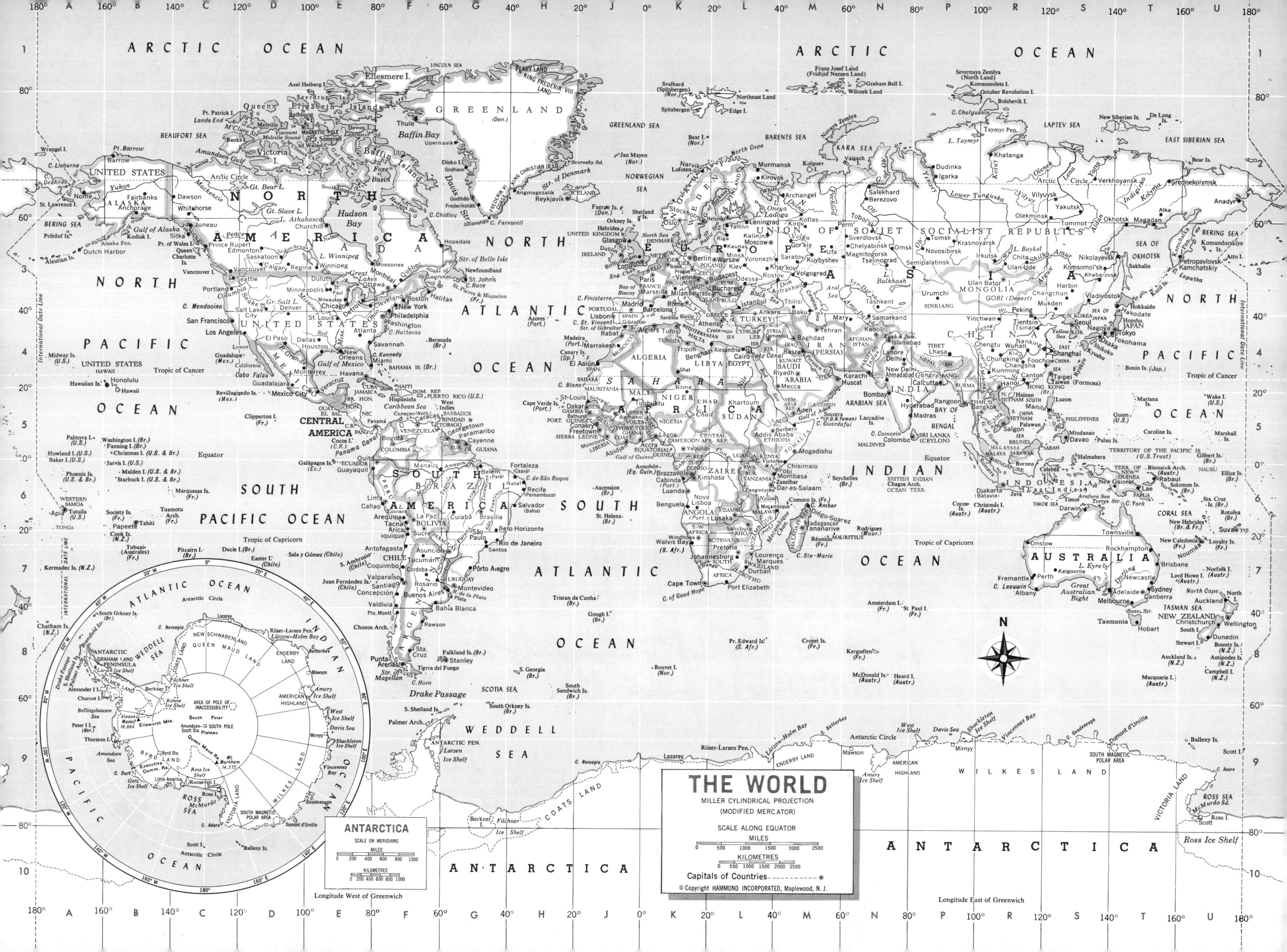

THE WORLD

MILLER CYLINDRICAL PROJECTION
(MODIFIED MERCATOR)

SCALE ALONG EQUATOR

MILES
500   1000   1500   2000   2500

KILOMETRES
500 1000 1500 2000 2500

Capitals of Countries ●

© Copyright HAMMOND INCORPORATED, Maplewood, N.J.

ANTARCTICA

SCALE ON MERIDIANS

MILES
200   400   600   800   1000

KILOMETRES
200 400 600 800 1000

Longitude East of Greenwich

Longitude West of Greenwich

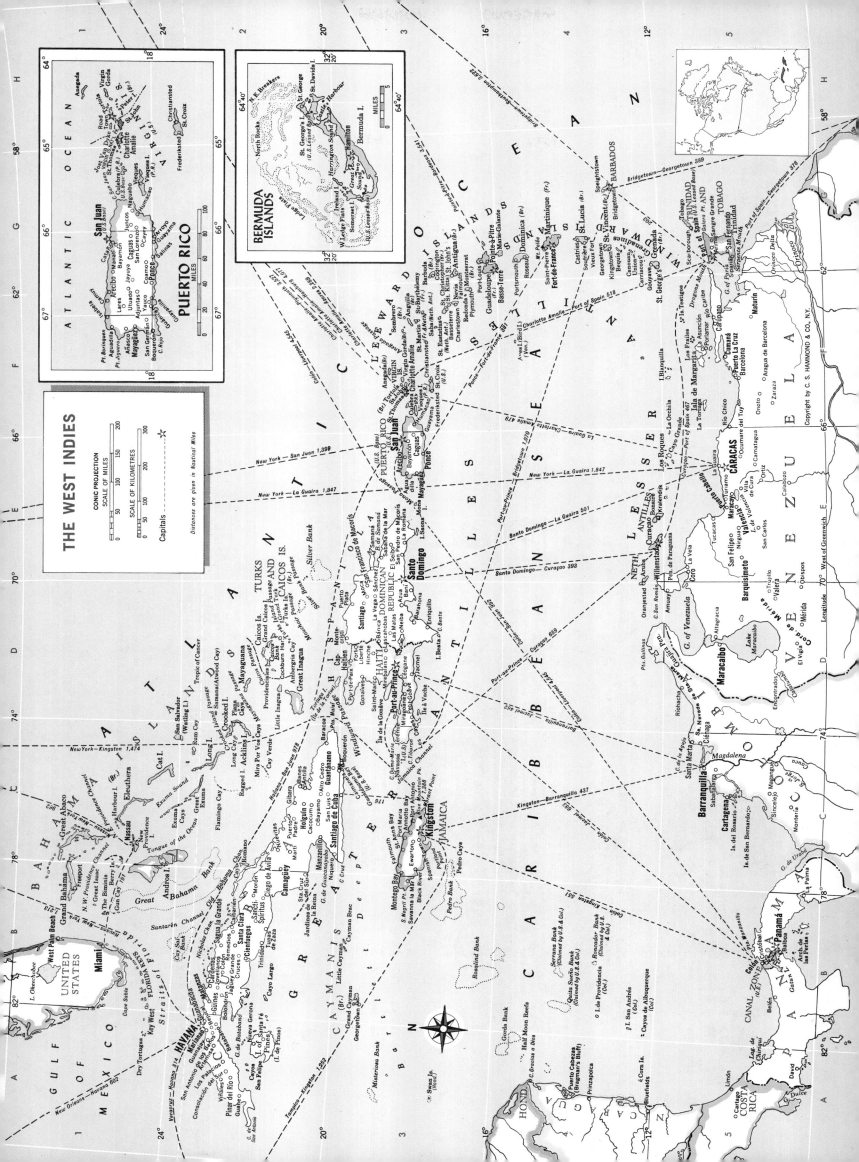

THE WEST INDIES

CONIC PROJECTION

SCALE OF MILES

SCALE OF KILOMETRES

★ Capitals

Distances are given in Nautical Miles

PUERTO RICO

ATLANTIC OCEAN

VIRGIN IS.

San Juan (U.S. Base)

Ponce

MILES

BERMUDA ISLANDS

N. E. Breakers

North Rocks

St. George I. St. David's I.

St. George

Castle Harbour

Harrington Sound

Hamilton

Ireland I.

Somerset I.

Bermuda I.

U.S. Leased Base

Little Flatts

Leper Point

MILES

Copyright by C. S. HAMMOND & CO., N.Y.

ATLANTIC OCEAN

GREATER ANTILLES

LESSER ANTILLES

LEEWARD ISLANDS

WINDWARD ISLANDS

CARIBBEAN SEA

VENEZUELA

COLOMBIA

PANAMA

COSTA RICA

NICARAGUA

HONDURAS

UNITED STATES

GULF OF MEXICO

BAHAMA ISLANDS

CUBA

JAMAICA

HAITI

DOMINICAN REPUBLIC

PUERTO RICO

HAVANA

Santiago de Cuba

Kingston

Port-au-Prince

Santo Domingo

San Juan

CARACAS

Maracaibo

Barranquilla

Cartagena

CANAL ZONE

TRINIDAD

TOBAGO

BARBADOS

Fort-de-France

CAYMAN IS.

TURKS AND CAICOS IS.

Miami

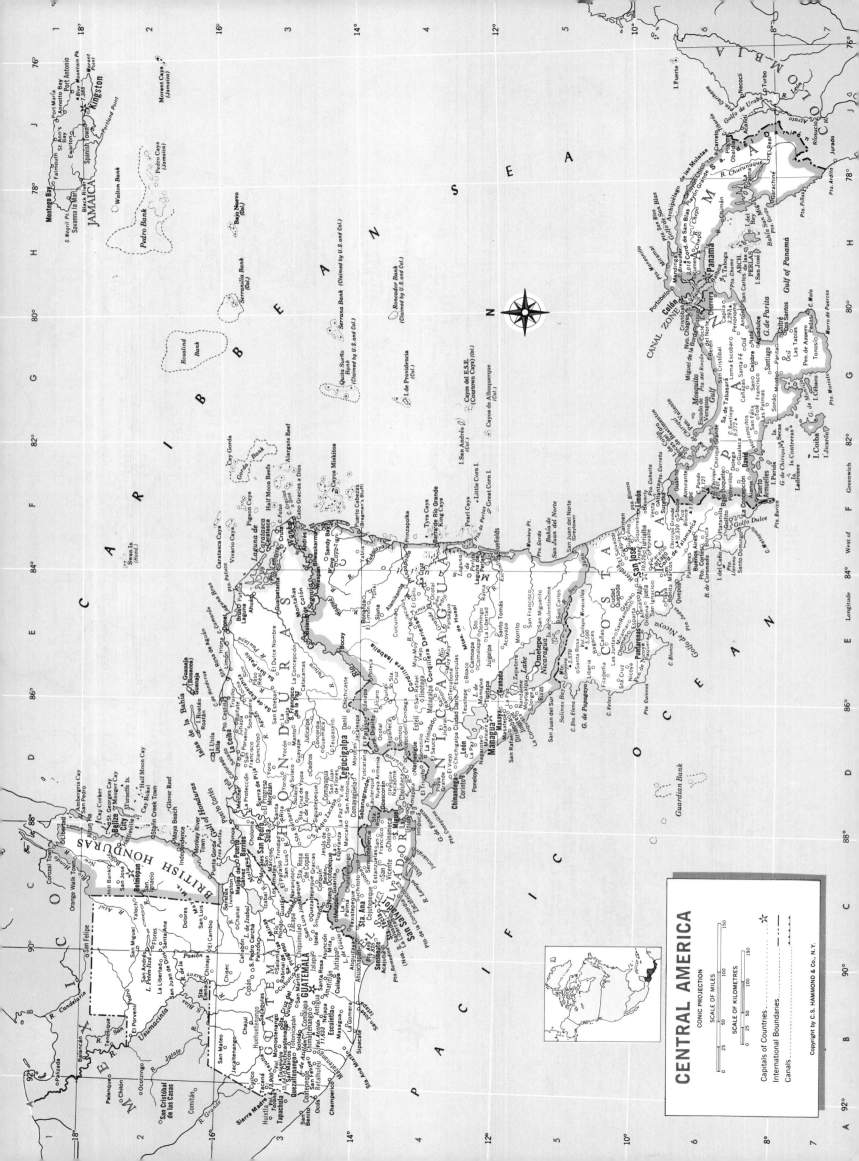

CENTRAL AMERICA

CONIC PROJECTION

SCALE OF MILES

SCALE OF KILOMETRES

Capitals of Countries..........
International Boundaries..........
Canals..........

Copyright by C.S. HAMMOND & Co., N.Y.

SOUTH AMERICA

LAMBERT AZIMUTHAL EQUAL-AREA PROJECTION

SCALE OF MILES
0   100   200   400   600

SCALE OF KILOMETRES
0   100 200   400   600

Capitals of Countries .... ☆
International Boundaries .... — - —
Canals ....

Copyright by C.S. HAMMOND & CO., N.Y.

EUROPE

LAMBERT AZIMUTHAL EQUAL AREA PROJECTION

SCALE OF MILES

SCALE OF KILOMETRES

Capitals of Countries ....☆
International Boundaries .....---
Canals ....

Copyright by C.S. HAMMOND & Co., N.Y

The government of the United States has
not recognized the incorporation of Estonia,
Latvia and Lithuania into the Soviet Union,
nor does it recognize as final the de facto
western limit of Polish administration in
Germany (the Oder-Neisse line).

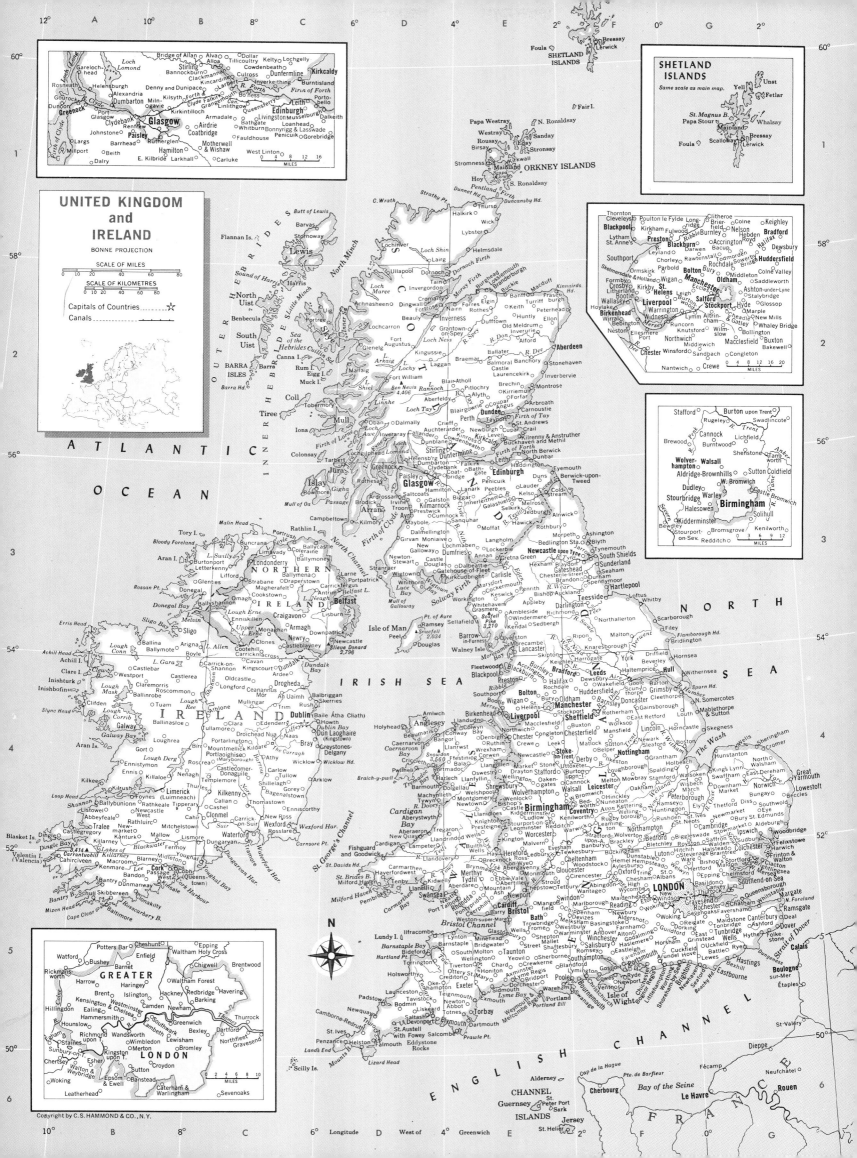

UNITED KINGDOM and IRELAND

BONNE PROJECTION

SCALE OF MILES

SCALE OF KILOMETRES

Capitals of Countries ⭐
Canals

SHETLAND ISLANDS

Same scale as main map.

GREATER LONDON

Copyright by C.S. HAMMOND & CO., N.Y.

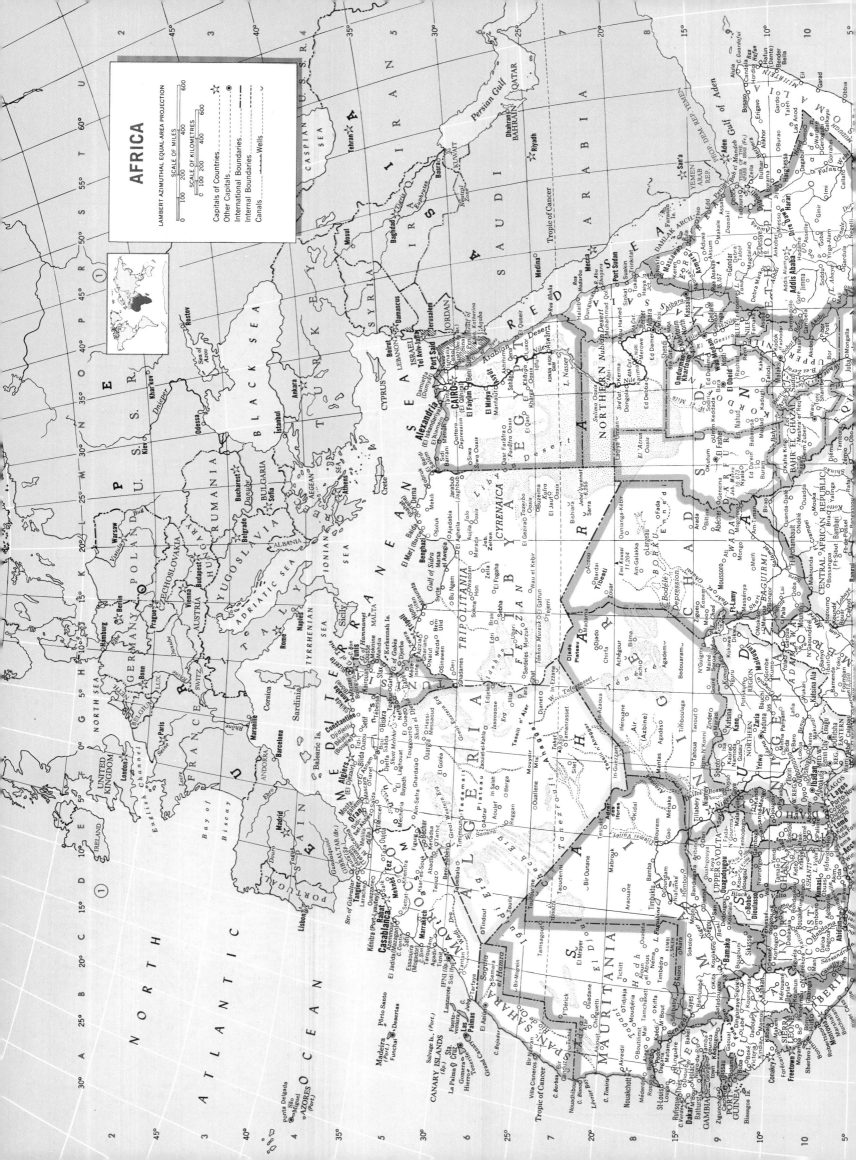

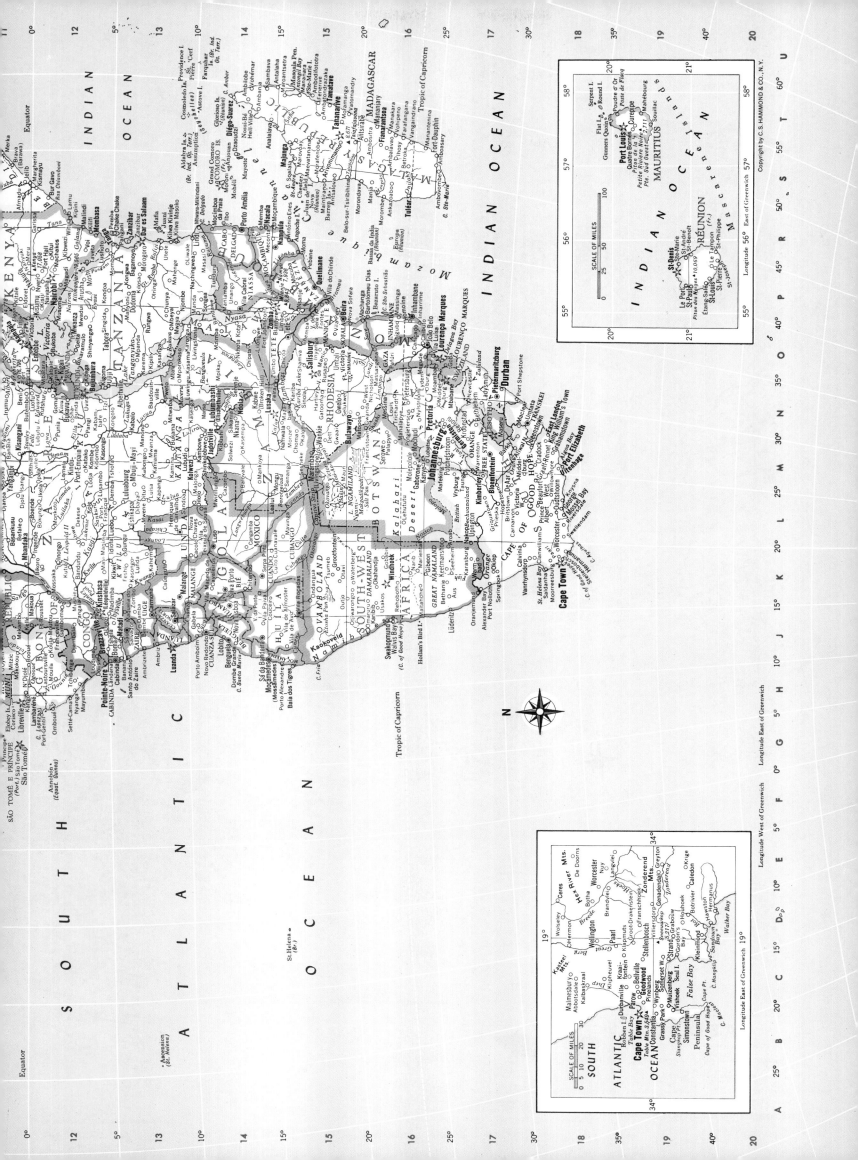

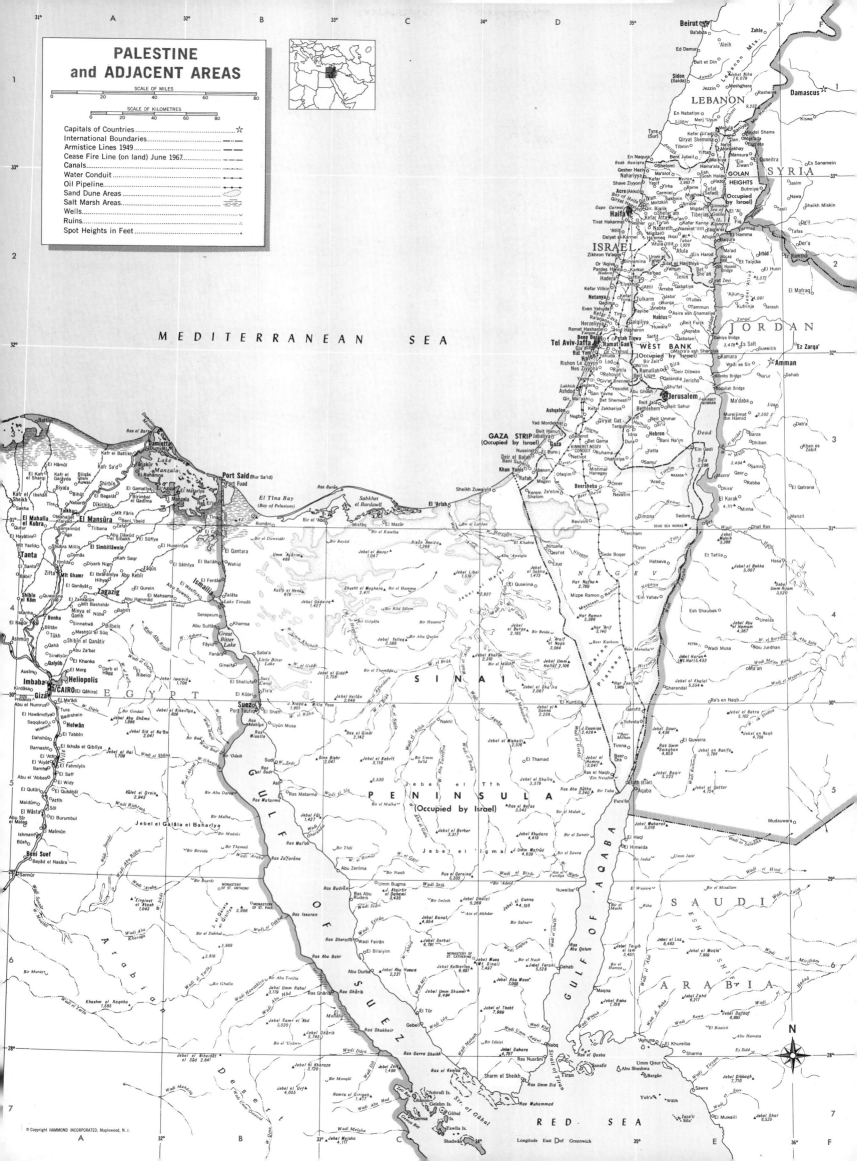

INDIAN SUBCONTINENT and AFGHANISTAN

CONIC PROJECTION

SCALE OF MILES

SCALE OF KILOMETRES

Capitals of Countries .... ☆
Provincial and State Capitals .... ◉
International Boundaries .... _____
Provincial and State Boundaries ... _._._.
Canals ....
Railroads ....

Copyright by C. S. HAMMOND & Co., N.Y.

CHINA and MONGOLIA

CONIC PROJECTION

SCALE OF MILES
100 · 200 · 300 · 400 · 500

SCALE OF KILOMETRES
100 · 200 · 300 · 400 · 500

Capitals of Countries........ ☆ International Boundaries....
Provincial Capitals........... ◉ Provincial Boundaries....
Canals............................ Walls....

Copyright by C. S. Hammond & Co., N.Y.

*Wuhan municipality consists of Hankow, Hanyang and Wuchang

BURMA, THAILAND, INDOCHINA and MALAYA

CONIC PROJECTION

SCALE OF MILES

SCALE OF KILOMETRES

International Boundaries ...._.._..
Provincial and State Boundaries ...._.._.
Capitals of Countries ....☆
Provincial and State Capitals...........◉

Copyright by C.S. Hammond & Co., N.Y.

Longitude East 96° of Greenwich

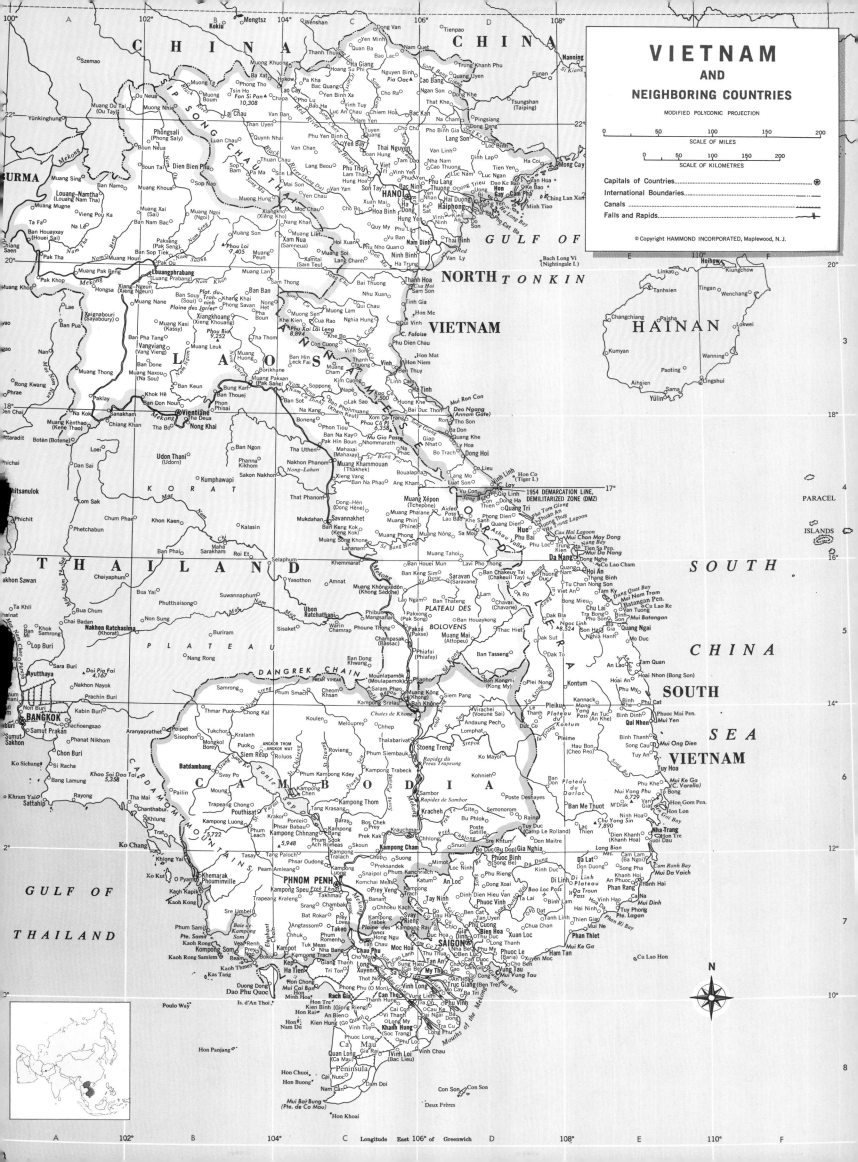

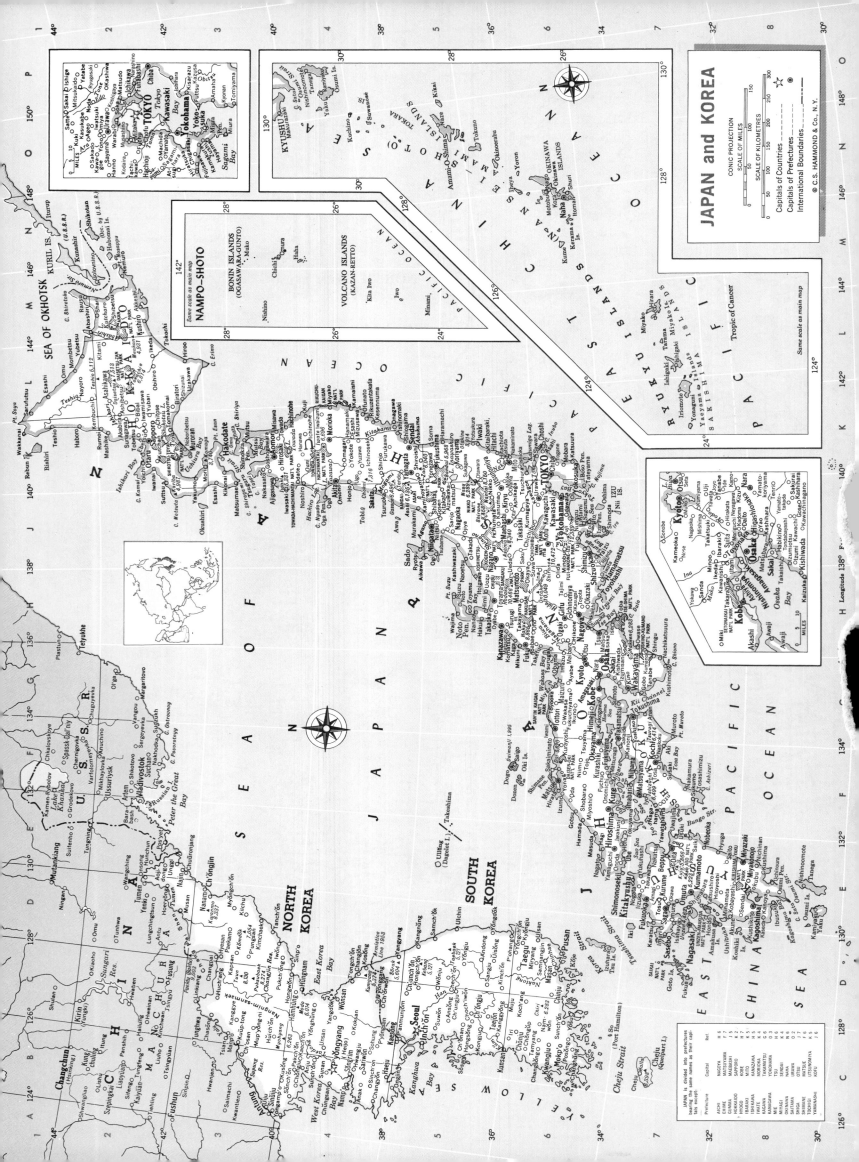

JAPAN and KOREA

CONIC PROJECTION

SCALE OF MILES

SCALE OF KILOMETRES

Capitals of Countries
Capitals of Prefectures
International Boundaries

© C.S. HAMMOND & Co., N.Y.

NAMPO-SHOTO

BONIN ISLANDS
(OGASAWARA-GUNTO)

VOLCANO ISLANDS
(KAZAN-RETTO)

Same scale as main map

SEA OF OKHOTSK

KURIL IS. (U.S.S.R.)

HOKKAIDO

SEA OF JAPAN

MANCHURIA

CHINA

NORTH KOREA

SOUTH KOREA

U.S.S.R.

TOKYO

KYUSHU

RYUKYU ISLANDS (NANSEI-SHOTO)

PACIFIC OCEAN

EAST CHINA SEA

YELLOW SEA

Tropic of Cancer

AP News Almanac

CHRONOLOGY—1972

2—President Nixon said in a nationally televised interview that 25,000 to 35,000 American troops would remain in South Vietnam until the North Vietnamese released all American prisoners of war.

5—President Nixon gave the go-ahead on development of a spaceship designed to shuttle from earth to planned space stations in earth orbit.

7—An Iberia Airlines jet crashed into a hill on the Mediterranean island of Ibiza, killing all 104 persons aboard.

8—Pakistan freed Sheik Mujibur Rahman, the eastern Pakistan leader, and flew him to London where he said at a news conference that an independent Bangladesh was "an unchallengeable reality."

10—An attempt by Baton Rouge, La., policemen to clear a street of an impromptu black militant rally erupted into a wild exchange of gunfire that left two policemen and two young blacks dead.

10—Sheik Mujibur Rahman received a tumultuous Bangladesh welcome from a crowd of half a million Bengalis in Dacca.

12—The automobile industry won the government's permission for a second round of price increases on 1972 models. The increase by General Motors of 0.9 per cent, by Ford Motor Co. of 1.07 per cent and by American Motors by 0.83 per cent was to pay for new safety equipment and improved antipollution devices.

13—President Nixon announced that, over a three-month period, 70,000 more American troops would be withdrawn from South Vietnam, reducing the number there to 69,000.

16—The Dallas Cowboys turned back the Miami Dolphins 24-3 in the Super Bowl championship in New Orleans.

18—A United States Coast Guard icebreaker obtained permission to fire warning shots to stop a Soviet vessel attempting to flee from an American boarding party after being accused of fishing inside the 12-mile limit off Alaska. The Coast Guard said later no firing was necessary.

20—President Nixon, in his State of the Union address, asked Congress to set aside partisanship in 1972 and to enact programs dealing "with the urgent priorities for the nation," specifically the legislation he had proposed in previous years.

20—A young man who hijacked a jetliner in Las Vegas, Nev., and parachuted from it with $50,000 in ransom over Colorado was captured a mile from where he landed near Akron, Colo.

22—Representatives of Great Britain, Denmark, Ireland and Norway signed the Treaty of Brussels, enlarging next Jan. 1 the European Common Market to 10 nations provided all four governments ratify the pact.

24—President Nixon sent Congress a budget of $246.3-billion for the 1973 fiscal year that contained an estimated deficit of $25.5-billion, higher than that of any other President since World War II.

24—Four food manufacturers were accused by the Federal Trade Commission of illegally monopolizing the breakfast cereal market and thus forcing consumers to pay inflated prices.

24—The U.S. Supreme Court unanimously upheld decisions of Federal District Courts that knocked down New York and Connecticut "emergency" laws barring state welfare aid to persons who had not lived in the states at least one year.

25—President Nixon made public a plan to end the war in Indochina that he said had been offered to the North Vietnamese in secret three months previously, but had been ignored. The plan included a general cease-fire, the withdrawal of all American and allied troops within six months and a political solution that included new elections and the resignation of President Nguyen Van Thieu. A day later Vietnamese Communists made it plain that President Nixon's peace proposals were un-acceptable and merely a scheme to maintain U.S. puppet regimes in Indochina.

30—British troops shot and killed 13 men in Londonderry, Northern Ireland, during a Roman Catholic civil rights rally held in defiance of a government ban.

30—Pakistan withdrew from the British Commonwealth after having been advised that Britain, Australia and New Zealand would recognize the Bengali government in Bangladesh.

31—North Vietnam made public the nine-point peace program it had secretly submitted to the United States in June 1971 and charged that Washington had not seriously considered it.

2—Demonstrators in Dublin, the Irish Republic capital, set the British Embassy on fire during a national day of mourning for the 13 civilians killed by British soldiers in Londonderry, Northern Ireland.

2—Egyptian President Anwar Sadat flew to Moscow to press Soviet leaders for more interceptor aircraft and antiaircraft missiles and for active support of Egypt's policy of preparing for a "zero hour" for an assault against Israel.

2—Heavy demand for gold, a barometer of monetary anxiety, pushed the price to nearly $50 an ounce in the currency markets of Europe.

2—The Israeli cabinet agreed to accept a three-month-old American proposal for indirect talks with Egypt aimed at the reopening of the Suez Canal.

6—North Vietnam said that American prisoners of war would not be released until the United States had withdrawn its support from the administration of President Nguyen Van Thieu in Saigon and had brought the war to an end.

7—President Nixon signed into law the Federal Election Campaign Act of 1971, which restricted a candidate's personal investment in his own campaign in Federal elections to $50,000 for President, $35,000 for the Senate and $25,000 for the House.

8—A tentative agreement was reached in the 123-day West Coast dock strike. Negotiators for the Warehousemen's Union and the Pacific Maritime Association said they had settled all economic issues and would arbitrate the rest.

9—In a foreign policy message to Congress, President Nixon said that the United States and the Soviet Union had reached an accord on the outline of an interim agreement on the limitation of strategic arms.

11—An agreement was announced by the United States and the Soviet Union to pool efforts in a fight against cancer, heart disease and environmental health problems.

15—Atty. Gen. John N. Mitchell resigned to direct the President's re-election campaign and President Nixon immediately nominated Deputy Atty. Gen. Richard G. Kleindienst to succeed him.

15—Juan M. Bordaberry, a wealthy 44-year-old conservative rancher, was officially proclaimed president-elect of Uruguay.

17—The British House of Commons approved by only eight votes, 309 to 301, British entrance into the European Common Market.

17—President and Mrs. Nixon, accompanied by a panel of Administration officials and advisers, departed for Communist China for a landmark conference on relations between the two nations.

17—The United States command announced that 125 American warplanes, flying through a barrage of surface-to-air missiles and antiaircraft fire, completed a 29-hour series of attacks on artillery and air defense sites in and just north of the demilitarized zone in Vietnam.

18—In a historic 6-to-1 vote, the California Supreme Court declared an end to capital punishment in that state.

21—President Nixon and his party arrived in Peking, where he was met by Premier Chou En-lai. Later in the day he attended a surprise one hour meeting with Chairman Mao Tse-tung.

22—In Aden, Southern Yemen, all 172 passengers, including Joseph P. Kennedy III, son of the late Robert F. Kennedy, were released by Arab hijackers who commandeered an Athens-bound jetliner from New Delhi.

22—Terrorists of the outlawed Irish Republican Army blew up an officers' mess at a military camp in Aldershot, England, killing seven persons.

23—Higher fringe benefits allowing wage increases of as much as 6.2 per cent, or more in some cases, were allowed by the Pay Board.

23—Angela Davis was released on $102,500 bail after Judge Richard E. Arnson ruled that last week's elimination of the death penalty in California invalidated a law prohibiting bail in capital cases such as hers; charges against her included that of murder.

26—A huge coal-slag heap serving as a dam burst under the pressure of three days of torrential rains, sending a wall of water through a narrow valley dotted with small mining towns in West Virginia, killing an estimated 70 persons.

28—President Nixon ended a week of talks with Premier Chou En-lai of Communist China and left Shanghai for home. The President and the premier issued a joint communique in which the United States pledged to reduce its forces gradually on Taiwan and in which both nations promised a gradual increase in contacts and exchanges.

28—President Nixon, on his return from Communist China, told a crowd of congressional leaders, Government officials and diplomats at Andrews Air Force base in Washington that his trip had established a basis for a structure of peace without sacrificing any of America's commitments to her allies.

1—Israeli and Syrian warplanes bombed their respective fronts in an aftermath of a four-day Israeli operation inside Lebanon, aimed at breaking up Palestinian commando encampments.

2—Pioneer 10, an American spacecraft, was launched on the first mission to explore the environs of the planet Jupiter.

3—The nation's unemployment rate declined to 5.7 per cent in February from 5.9 per cent in January.

3—Eighteen persons were killed when a Mohawk Airlines turboprop plane crashed in a residential section of Albany, N.Y.

7—Police using trained dogs found a bomb concealed in the cockpit of a jetliner less than an hour before it was set to explode. The Trans World Airlines plane had made an emergency landing at New York's Kennedy International Airport after a telephone caller had warned of the bomb.

7—Sen. Edmund S. Muskie won the New Hampshire Democratic Presidential primary with Senator George McGovern running a strong second.

8—A bomb placed in or near the cockpit of a Trans World Airlines jet exploded as the plane sat unoccupied at the Las Vegas, Nev., airport; the pilots' cabin was seriously damaged.

9—To prevent sabotage of American commercial aircraft, President Nixon ordered all airlines to adopt new and tighter security measures.

9—In New York, Clifford Irving's "autobiography" of Howard R. Hughes was officially discredited with the indictment of the expatriate author, his wife Edith and his researcher, Richard Suskind, on criminal charges.

9—Prince Norodom Sihanouk, the former Chief of State of Cambodia, said that Premier Chou En-lai of China had met North Vietnamese leaders since President Nixon's visit and had assured them of China's full support "until total victory."

10—The United States and China designated their ambassadors in Paris to serve as the diplomatic channel agreed upon by President Nixon and Premier Chou En-lai for continuing contacts between the two countries, the White House announced.

10—Government reports for February showed an advance in wholesale prices of seven-tenths of one per cent, after seasonal adjustment.

11—Cyprus and the United Nations agreed that the international peacekeeping force on the island should inspect and control a large cache of Czech-made weapons that President Makarios imported secretly in January.

12—Britain and China agreed to establish full diplomatic relations after months of negotiations aided in part by President Nixon's visit to Peking.

12—The world's major oil-producing countries accepted an offer by four United States petroleum concerns to give six nations a 20 per cent share in the companies and urged other international oil companies to follow suit.

12—Delegates to the first National Black Political Convention adopted a far-ranging political agenda calling for an "independent black political assembly" to strengthen the over-all effectiveness of some 7.5 million black voters in the United States.

13—Clifford and Edith Irving pleaded guilty in Federal District Court to charges of conspiracy in the $750,000 Howard Hughes autobiography case. Two hours later, joined by researcher Richard Suskind, they pleaded guilty to grand larceny and conspiracy charges in the New York State Supreme Court.

13—Britain and China formally agreed to establish full diplomatic relations after the British had acknowledged that Taiwan was "a province" of China and had announced that Britain's consulates in Taiwan would be closed.

14—After a face-to-face interview of an hour and 20 minutes with the American ambassador and President Luis Anastasio Somoza Debayle, Howard R. Hughes left Managua, Nicaragua.

14—Gov. George C. Wallace of Alabama won the Florida primary, capturing 75 of the state's 81 delegates to the Democratic National Convention and 42 per cent of the vote. Sen. Hubert H. Humphrey was second, and Sen. Henry M. Jackson was third.

14—Prime Minister Indira Gandhi's New Congress party gained control of 14 of the 16 states and one of the two union territories that elected new governments.

15—Harold S. Geneen, president of the International Telephone and Telegraph Corporation, testified that "there was absolutely no connection" between his company's pledge of up to $200,000 toward the expenses of the Republican National Convention and the Justice Department's settlement of three antitrust suits against the concern.

15—King Hussein of Jordan announced his plan to convert his kingdom into a federated state with two autonomous regions.

17—President Nixon asked Congress to place a moratorium on all court orders that would require busing to achieve school desegregation and to enact, during the moratorium, legislation that would place permanent restraints on the use of busing by the courts and the executive branch.

19—Prime Minister Indira Gandhi returned to India after signing a friendship treaty with Bangladesh and said that peace talks with Pakistan were planned.

20—In the heaviest attack against Phnom Penh since the Indochinese war spread into Cambodia two years ago, enemy troops fired 200 rockets and artillery shells into the city, killing 50 and wounding 120.

21—Lengthy residency requirements for voting in state and local elections were declared unconstitutional by the U.S. Supreme Court.

21—Generalissimo Chiang Kai-shek, receiving a record total of more than 99.9 per cent of the votes, was elected by the National Assembly for his fifth six-year term.

22—Led by George Meany, four A.F.L.-C.I.O. labor leaders on the Pay Board resigned from the 15-member board, saying there was "no fairness, no equity, no justice" in the economic program.

22—Sen. Edmund Muskie of Maine came out of the Illinois primary with 59 convention delegates committed to him and 63 per cent of the presidential preference vote over Eugene J. McCarthy, who polled 37 per cent.

22—The National Commission on Marijuana and Drug Abuse called for significant easing of criminal penalties for possession and use of the drug.

23—The Consumer Price Index for February rose by five-tenths of 1 per cent, the largest increase since last June.

23—President Nixon reconstructed the Pay Board as a seven-man body composed of five public members, one business member and the remaining labor member.

23—The United States broke off the Paris peace talks and said no further meetings would be held until the North Vietnamese showed a willingness for "serious discussions" on concrete issues spelled out in advance.

24—The provincial government and parliament of Northern Ireland was suspended by the British government, which ordered direct rule from London.

27—Two Soledad Brothers, black convicts accused of killing a prison guard, were acquitted by an all-white jury in San Francisco.

28—George Meany, president of the AFL-CIO, testified before the Price Commission that its controls had failed because the Administration had not provided the tools to enforce them.

30—In Turkey, police reported they stormed a house in a mountain village and killed 10 leftist terrorists after the terrorists had slain three foreign hostages, a Canadian and two Britons.

31—W. A. Boyle, 67, president of the United Mine Workers of America, was convicted on all 13 counts of conspiracy and making illegal political contributions with union funds. Two other officials of the union, John Owens and James Kmetz, were acquitted.

APRIL

2—The jury in the antiwar conspiracy trial in Harrisburg, Pa., convicted the Rev. Phillip Berrigan of smuggling a letter out of Lewisburg, Pa., federal prison; the jury deadlocked on charges against Father Berrigan and the other six defendants involving an alleged conspiracy to kidnap Henry A. Kissinger, an advisor to President Nixon.

2—North Vietnamese troops occupied the northern half of Quangtri Province, South Vietnam, as the South Vietnamese continued to fall back from the demilitarized zone.

3—After a 20-year absence from the United States, the 82-year-old master of silent comedy, Charles Chaplin, returned for a ten-day visit.

3—The United States accused Hanoi of launching an "invasion" of South Vietnam and said Washington was leaving open all retaliatory options, including renewed American bombing of North Vietnam.

4—The United States extended formal diplomatic recognition to Bangladesh, the nation of 70 million Bengalis that declared independence from Pakistan in December 1971.

4—South Vietnamese troops abandoned one of their remaining defense points on the north bank of the Cua Viet, and North Vietnamese tanks were reported moving south toward the embattled city of Quangtri, capital of South Vietnam's northernmost province.

4—The United States ordered the deployment of 10 or 20 more B52 bombers to Indochina to strengthen the American ability to respond to the new North Vietnamese offensive.

5—Complete returns from the Wisconsin Democratic Presidential primary showed that Sen. George McGovern had won 54 of the state's 67 delegates to the party's national convention. George Wallace came in second and Sen. Hubert Humphrey third.

5—The South Vietnamese military command reported that North Vietnamese troops opened a new drive in South Vietnam, striking in Binhlong Province, 75 miles north of Saigon.

6—Egypt broke relations with Jordan, charging that King Hussein's proposal for a federation of Jordanians and Palestinians would legitimize Israel's role in the Arab world.

7—Joseph Gallo, reputed by police to be a Mafia figure known as Crazy Joe, was assassinated in a lower Manhattan restaurant where he was celebrating his 43d birthday.

7—A jetliner carrying 89 passengers was hijacked to San Francisco and held captive while $500,000 ransom was delivered, along with parachutes; thereafter passengers were released and the plane was ordered to fly eastward. The hijacker parachuted over Provo, Utah, taking the money with him.

8—Secretary of Agriculture Earl L. Butz arrived in Moscow for talks opening negotiations for regular long-term sales of grain to the Soviet Union.

8—The Nixon Administration in Washington said word had been received that North Vietnam had committed its last "home division" to the invasion of South Vietnam; strategists in Washington said Hanoi's "one last throw of the dice" was meant to be the prelude to serious peace negotiations.

9—The Soviet Union and Iraq signed a 15-year treaty providing Iraq with help in strengthening its defenses.

10—Political extremists assassinated a powerful general, Juan Carlos Sanchez, and a kidnaped Italian industrialist, Oberdan Sallustro, in Argentina; Sallustro, a Fiat official, had been held captive 19 days.

10—A convention outlawing biological weapons was signed by 70 nations, including the United States, U.S.S.R. and Britain; the measure also required the destruction of any stocks of such weapons. Signing ceremonies took place in Washington, Moscow and London.

10—Unofficial reports from the ancient town of Shiraz said 2,000 to 4,000 persons were killed in an earthquake in Iran that struck an area about 600 miles south of Teheran and 100 miles southeast of Shiraz.

11—American officers and newsmen said North Vietnamese lost more than 1,000 soldiers and 30 tanks April 9 in attacks west of the city of Quangtri; American retaliatory bombings of North Vietnam were intensified.

11—Mrs. Paul Gilly, assured of a life sentence, pleaded guilty in the 1969 slayings of Joseph Yablonsky, Pennsylvania United Mine Workers Union official, and his wife and daughter; two others were found guilty earlier of first-degree murder and were given death sentences.

11—Former President Lyndon B. Johnson, who suffered a heart attack April 7, was transferred by plane from a hospital in Charlottesville, Va., to an Army hospital in San Antonio, Tex., nearer his home; doctors said he had shown steady improvement.

13—The first general strike in baseball history ended in its 13th day at meetings in New York and Chicago; negotiators agreed to start the season without making up any of the 86 games missed. The 600 players won increased pensions but lost nine days' pay.

14—Enemy reinforcements of infantry and tanks moved into the provincial South Vietnamese capital of Anloc, 60 miles north of Saigon, despite heavy American air strikes.

14—President Nixon and Prime Minister Pierre Elliott Trudeau of Canada signed in Ottawa a joint pact for a large-scale battle against pollution of the Great Lakes, world's largest fresh water reservoir.

15—The North Vietnamese port of Haiphong was struck by waves of U.S. bombers. It was the first time the port came under attack since air strikes south of the 20th parallel were curtailed at the end of March 1968.

16—Apollo 16 astronauts took off for the moon on the latest space mission, an exploration of an area of volcano-like mountains.

17—A protest note published in Moscow accused the United States of damaging four Soviet merchant ships during raids on Haiphong but officials in Washington rejected the note.

20—Two astronauts of Apollo 16 made a safe landing on the moon after a six-hour delay due to a defect in the command ship's rocket engine; the trouble proved to be not critical, Mission Control reported.

20—White House aide Peter M. Flanigan appeared before a Senate committee but declined to answer questions about contacts he might have had with Richard G. Kleindienst, President Nixon's nominee for attorney general, or with officials of the International Telephone and Telegraph Company regarding the settlement of three antitrust cases against the ITT.

20—Antiwar demonstrations brought National Guardsmen to the College Park campus of the University of Maryland and police to New York City's Columbia University, where student peace pickets invaded a closed meeting of the university senate.

20—North Vietnam's chief negotiator at the Paris peace talks formally proposed reopening the talks, suspended indefinitely by the United States in March.

21—The Labor Department in Washington reported that the consumer price index in March showed no increase at all, for the first time since late in 1966.

21—In Pakistan, Zulfikar Ali Bhutto was sworn in as president under an interim constitution that had been approved by that nation's national assembly.

23—After three days spent collecting rocks and exploring craters on the moon, two Apollo 16 astronauts rocketed back to their spaceship for another day in lunar orbit before starting the homeward trip.

23—The French electorate approved the treaty admitting Britain, Norway, Denmark and Ireland to the Common Market.

24—South Vietnamese suffered another setback as North Vietnamese troops, led by tanks, smashed the defenses of Kontum City, capital of Kontum, in the Central Highlands.

25—The White House announced that Henry A. Kissinger, President Nixon's national security adviser, had returned from a secret mission to Moscow and that the United States and South Vietnam were ready to resume peace talks in Paris with North Vietnam and the Viet Cong.

25—In the Central Highlands northwest of Kontum, North Vietnamese forces trapped 2,000 to 3,000 South Vietnamese troops at a border outpost and forced 5,000 others to retreat.

25—In Pennsylvania, Democratic Sen. Hubert Humphrey won the state preferential primary and Sen. George McGovern, D-So. Dak., ran second; in Massachusetts McGovern swept to victory in the Democratic presidential primary.

26—Despite the heavy offensive in South Vietnam, President Nixon in a nationwide address from Washington said that another 20,000 American troops would be withdrawn; air and naval attacks on North Vietnam, he said, would continue.

27—After a month's suspension, the Vietnam peace talks were resumed in Paris; each side accused the other of aggression.

27—Apollo 16 astronauts returned from the moon in a successful splashdown 215 miles southeast of Christmas Island, in the Pacific Ocean.

27—Following a series of defeats in the primaries, Maine Sen. Edmund S. Muskie withdrew from active campaigning in the race for the Democratic presidential nomination.

29—Amtrak, the taxpayer-financed corporation created by Congress to revitalize America's passenger trains, ended its first year deep in debt and without having reversed the national decline in rail travel that began 25 years earlier.

MAY

1—The Nixon Administration exempted local governments and thousands of small businesses from wage and price controls, freeing more than a quarter of the nation's work force and sales from complying with the economic stablization program. The Cost of Living Council said all businesses or government units with 60 or fewer employes need no longer comply with wage and price regulations.

1—U.S. District Court Judge William B. Bryant set aside the election of W. A. "Tony" Boyle as president of the United Mine Workers of America. The jurist found that evidence of wrongdoing by Boyle and other incumbents in the 1969 election was "too strong to resist."

1—The 1972 Pulitzer Prize for meritorious public service was awarded to the New York Times for publication of the Pentagon papers. Jack Anderson, syndicated columnist, won a Pulitzer award for reporting disclosures of Nixon Administration policymaking during the India-Pakistan war. Horst Faas and Michel Laurent of The Associated Press won the prize for their picture series showing vengeance against Pakistanis in Bangladesh. It was the second Pulitzer for Faas.

2—Sen. Hubert H. Humphrey won a narrow victory over Gov. George Wallace in the Indiana Presidential primary. Sen. Edmund S. Muskie, who had withdrawn from active campaigning in the primaries, trailed far behind.

3—President Nguyen Van Thieu of South Vietnam ordered a shakeup of the army following the loss of his country's northernmost Quang Tri Province to the North Vietnamese. Lt. Gen. Hoang Xuan Lam, commander of the northern military region, was replaced by Maj. Gen. Ngo Quang Truong who had been serving as commander in the Mekong Delta, south of Saigon.

3—President Nixon appointed Assistant Attorney General L. Patrick Gray 3rd as acting director of the Federal Bureau of Investigation, replacing the late J. Edgar Hoover.

4—The United States and South Vietnam declared an indefinite halt in the Paris peace conference; U.S. delegate William J. Porter said the decision resulted from "a complete lack of progress in every available channel."

4—The Vietcong announced establishment of a "provisional revolutionary administration" in Quang Tri City, Vietnam, three days after the capture of that South provincial capital by enemy forces.

5—The U.S. unemployment rate remained unchanged in April at 5.9 per cent, as it had for 18 months; wholesale prices continued to climb, despite a drop in food costs.

5—All 115 persons aboard an Alitalia DC8 jetliner were killed when the big plane slammed into a mountainside as it was about to land at Palermo's Punta Raisi Airport. The aircraft exploded in flames.

6—The hijacker who extorted $303,000 from Eastern Airlines parachuted into Central America. Authorities launched a search of an isolated mountain region in Honduras.

8—President Nixon announced that he had ordered the mining of all North Vietnamese ports and had taken other measures to prevent the flow of arms and other military supplies to the enemy. In his speech, the President appealed to the Soviet Union not to let its support of Hanoi lead it to a confrontation with the United States over his move.

8—Despite a tipoff and a security search, four armed Arabs hijacked an Israeli-bound Belgian Sabena jetliner carrying 101 persons. After landing in Tel Aviv, the hijackers threatened to blow up the plane and its passengers unless Israel freed 300 Palestinian guerrilla prisoners and flew them to Cairo.

8—The U.S. Pay Board directed East and Gulf Coast shippers and long shoremen to roll back their agreed wage boost from 70 cents an hour to 55 cents.

9—The Nixon Administration acknowledged that the President's decision to mine North Vietnam's harbors had posed a serious problem for Soviet policy makers and endangered the course of Soviet-American relations. Hanoi declared that "the Vietnamese people will never accept Mr. Nixon's ultimatum;" the Soviet press agency Tass accused the President of violating international law by sealing off the harbors.

10—Mrs. Nguyen Thi Binh, head of the Viet Cong delegation to the Paris peace talks, denounced President Nixon's address on Vietnam and categorically rejected his peace offers.

11—A long-awaited statement by the Soviet government assailed the U.S. blockade of North Vietnamese ports as "a gross violation of the generally recognized principle of freedom of navigation" and an "inadmissible" threat to Soviet and other shipping; the statement contained no ultimatum, however, and U.S. officials were known to consider it to be as mild a response as could be expected.

11—The Communist Chinese government blasted the new U.S. air and naval operations against North Vietnam as a "grave new step" which "grossly violates the freedom of international navigation and trade. . . ."

12—William Ruckelshaus, administrator of the Environmental Protection Agency, rejected the appeal of automobile manufacturers for a year's delay in equipping cars with anti-pollution equipment, scheduled for all 1975 cars.

12—The death toll in the Idaho silver mine disaster was fixed at 91 men, all of whom were trapped by a fire in a tunnel far below the surface.

13—Gov. Nelson Rockefeller vetoed the state legislature's repeal of New York's abortion law; the statute remained in effect at least until 1973.

14—The Okinawa Islands were formally transferred back to Japan by the United States, ending 27 years of American rule.

15—Gov. George C. Wallace of Alabama was shot and critically wounded after a Democratic primary campaign speech in Laurel, Md.; police immediately seized a suspect and later identified him as Arthur Herman Bremer, 21, of Milwaukee. Wallace, seeking the party's presidential nomination, later was reported in satisfactory condition by his doctors.

15—The Supreme Court, in a 7-0 decision, ruled that the Amish, a religious sect shunning the modern way of life, are not bound to comply with state laws requiring children to attend school beyond the eighth grade.

16—John B. Connally, Secretary of the Treasury, announced his resignation; President Nixon nominated Budget Director George P. Schultz to succeed Connally.

16—Gov. George C. Wallace of Alabama won in both the Michigan and Maryland Democratic presidential primaries by wide margins.

17—Dr. J. Garber Galbraith, a professor of neurosurgery at the University of Alabama Medical Center, said Alabama Governor George Wallace had less than a 50-50 chance of regaining the use of his paralyzed legs.

17—A House-Senate conference committee approved a massive higher education bill that included a provision that would delay, for up to 19 months, the implementation of any court-ordered desegregation that required the busing of children.

17—American officials in Saigon reported that South Vietnamese troops were transported to within two miles of the beleaguered provincial capital of An Loc; North Vietnamese officials said that they were clearing American mines as they were dropped by U.S. bombers into Haiphong Harbor, but administrative sources in Washington denied any minesweeping activity had taken place.

18—The Price Commission in Washington issued a regulation that limited rent increases on one-year leases to 8 per cent in cases where the older lease was longer than one year; the move was designed to restrict rent increases for long-term leases, the commission said.

19—An explosion that destroyed a restroom in the Pentagon in Washington spawned tighter security precautions around the country's military planning center; the Weathermen, a radical protest organization, claimed responsibility for the blast.

21—Proclaiming himself to be Jesus Christ, Laszlo Toth, a 33-year-old Australian, disfigured Michelangelo's sculpture, "Pietà," with a hammer in St. Peter's Basilica in Rome; the assailant broke off the left arm at the elbow and chipped the nose, the left eye and the veil of the figure of The Virgin Mary.

21—The Labor Department reported that the Consumer Price Index rose 0.2 per cent in April; food prices showed a decline of 1 per cent from March, and beef and veal prices showed their first decline since November.

22—President Nixon arrived in Moscow to begin summit talks with the Communist party chief, Leonid I. Brezhnev; they conferred for more than two hours after the President's arrival. Nixon was the first U.S. President to visit the Soviet capital.

22—In a 5-4 decision, the Supreme Court ruled that unanimous jury verdicts are not necessary for convictions in state criminal courts. In another decision, the court ruled 5-2 that witnesses may be compelled to testify before grand juries, even though they may later be convicted for the crimes they are forced to discuss. The decision also held that, as long as the prosecution is barred from using in court the compelled testimony and any leads developed from it, the witnesses' Fifth Amendment rights are not violated.

23—In Moscow, President Nixon met with Leonid I. Brezhnev, the Soviet Communist party leader, for five hours of intensive personal talks in the Kremlin; the two heads of state then signed two pacts providing for cooperative research on environmental problems and research on cancer, heart disease and environmental health.

23—Arthur Herman Bremer, 21, was indicted by federal and state grand juries in Baltimore for the May 15 shooting of Alabama Gov. George C. Wallace. Bremer was charged on four counts, including violating the civil rights of a presidential candidate and assaulting a federal officer.

23—South Dakota Sen. George McGovern won both Democratic presidential primaries in Oregon and Rhode Island by wide margins.

24—In Moscow, President Nixon and Soviet Premier Aleksei N. Kosygin signed a space cooperation pact that paved the way for a joint American-Soviet space flight in 1975.

26—In Moscow, President Nixon and Soviet Communist Party leader Leonid Brezhnev signed two agreements that put limits on the growth of American and Soviet nuclear arsenals; the first treaty dealt with defensive missile systems, while the second pact limited offensive missile launching sites.

27—Saigon officials acknowledged reports of a major defeat in the besieged capital of An Loc. Viet Cong mines and ambushes on Route 13, leading south from An Loc, destroyed 23 of 47 South Vietnamese armored personnel carriers that were trying to evacuate wounded troops from the area.

28—The Duke of Windsor died in Paris at age 77. The duke, formerly King Edward VIII, renounced the English throne in 1936 to marry Mrs. Wallis Warfield Simpson, a twice-divorced American.

29—President Nixon ended a week of negotiations with Soviet Communist party leader Leonid Brezhnev in Moscow. The two leaders issued a declaration of principles intended to mark a new, more stable and constructive era in Soviet-American relations.

30—Three gunmen identified by Israeli officials as Japanese fired at 250 passengers at the Lod International Airport in Tel Aviv, killing 26 persons and wounding at least 59; one attacker committed suicide, while another, captured by police, said he was a member of a left-wing Japanese group mobilized by Arab guerrillas.

31—President Nixon arrived in Warsaw, Poland, for a 24-hour visit, the last stop on his 13-day trip to four countries; the President conferred for more than an hour with Edward Gierek, Polish Communist party leader.

JUNE

1—Home from his 13-day trip to the Soviet Union, President Nixon told a joint session of Congress that his journey to Moscow had laid the basis for "a new relationship between the two most powerful nations on earth."

1—The government of Iraq nationalized the Iraq Petroleum Company after negotiations between the two parties collapsed; the company, jointly owned by U.S., British, French and Dutch oil concerns, produced 10 per cent of the Middle East's oil supply.

2—The Labor Department reported that wholesale food prices rose sharply in May and that the unemployment rate remained at 5.9 per cent, the level in the two preceeding months.

3—A black male hijacker and his female companion seized a Western Airline's jetliner during a flight from Los Angeles to Seattle and diverted it to San Francisco, where $500,000 ransom was paid and half of the 98 passengers were freed; remaining hostages were put aboard an intercontinental-range jet and flown to New York, where they were released before the plane proceeded to Algiers.

3—The U.S. Secretary of State and the foreign ministers of the Soviet Union, France and Britain signed an agreement opening the divided city of Berlin; the treaty also provided entry of both East and West Germany into the United Nations.

4—In San Jose, Calif., an all-white jury acquitted black militant Angela Davis of murder, kidnaping and criminal conspiracy charges arising from the slayings of a judge and three black prisoners abducted from a courtroom at San Rafael, Calif., in August 1970.

6—In Rhodesia, a coal mine explosion trapped 464 miners in the country's largest coal mine, the Wankie Colliery.

6—South Dakota Sen. George McGovern won the 271 delegates at stake in the California Democratic presidential primary; he also triumphed in the New Jersey, New Mexico and South Dakota Democratic primaries.

7—Reversing a 1967 decision of the Warren court, the Supreme Court ruled, 5-4, that criminal suspects do not have the right to have a lawyer present at police line-up identifications.

8—Voting 64-19, the Senate approved the nomination of former Deputy Attorney General Richard G. Kleindienst to be Attorney General, thus ending a four-month controversy that began with Senate Judiciary Committee hearings into charges that the Justice Department had shown political favoritism in the settlement of three anti-trust suits against the International Telephone and Telegraph Corporation.

9—The South Vietnamese army reported that one of its units, stalled for several weeks while trying to break through to the beseiged provincial capital of An Loc, had finally succeeded in reaching the town.

10—Congressional and military sources in Washington revealed that Gen. John D. Lavelle was relieved as commander of the U.S. Air Force units in Southeast Asia and retired after ordering repeated and unauthorized bombing attacks on military targets in North Vietnam.

10—Torrential rains and flash floods surged through Rapid City in South Dakota, bringing death and destruction over a wide area of the city and several smaller towns.

12—In a decision extending the Sixth Amendment's guarantee of counsel to misdemeanor trials, the Supreme Court ruled that no poor person could be jailed before trial for a petty offense unless he had been furnished with free legal counsel, or had waived his right to a lawyer. In another decision, the court ruled 6-3 that it was constitutional for states to grant liquor licenses to private clubs that practice racial discrimination.

13—American military officials in Saigon reported that large numbers of South Vietnamese troops were flown into An Loc as the 68-day battle seemed near an end.

13—President Nixon formally asked Congress to approve two strategic arms limitation agreements he signed in Moscow in May and to continue appropriating funds for weapon systems not covered by the treaties.

14—William D. Ruckelshaus, administrator of the Environmental Protection Agency in Washington, banned almost all uses of DDT in the United States, beginning Dec. 31, 1972; the Montrose Chemical Corporation, sole manufacturer of the toxic chemical pesticide in the country, immediately appealed the decision.

15—A civilian plane traveling from Bangkok to Hong Kong crashed in South Vietnam's Central Highlands, killing all 81 passengers aboard, including 17 Americans.

16—Clifford Irving, who collected more than $750,000 from McGraw-Hill, Inc. with a false autobiography of industrialist Howard Hughes, was sentenced in New York City to 2½ years in federal prison. His wife, Edith, was given a similar sentence but it was later reduced to two months. Each was fined $10,000.

16—The California Supreme Court upheld the 1st-degree murder conviction of Sirhan B. Sirhan in the assassination of Sen. Robert F. Kennedy, but reduced his sentence from death to life imprisonment to comply with the court's recent decision abolishing capital punishment in that state.

16—In Tel Aviv, Kozo Okamo of Japan was indicted before a military court on charges punishable by death in the massacre of 24 persons at the Lod International Airport on May 30.

17—A cave-in in a tunnel leading to the Vierzy train station in France caused the derailment and crash of a train from Paris. Minutes later a second train, headed for the French capital, entered the tunnel and collided with the first train. The crash killed 107 persons and injured more than 70 others.

18—In Britain's worst air disaster, all 118 persons aboard a British European Airways jet were killed when the plane crashed into a field minutes after leaving London's Heathrow airport.

19—A one-day international work stoppage by airline pilots, called to dramatize demands for more stringent measures against hijackings, shut down most airline travel in more than 30 countries.

19—The U.S. Supreme Court unanimously ruled unconstitutional the Federal government's practice of wiretapping domestic radicals without first obtaining court approval.

20—U.S. Defense Secretary Melvin Laird told the Senate Armed Services Committee in Washington that he would recommend scrapping the recently signed strategic arms limitation treaties between the United States and Russia if Congress failed to support the Nixon' Administration's proposal to modernize the country's offensive strategic forces.

20—A suit brought by the Securities and Exchange Commission in New York on June 16, charging that illegal sales of International Telephone and Telegraph Corporation stock had been made, was settled out of court by I.T.T. and the two New York investment banking firms that bought the stock, Lazard Freres & Company and Mediobanca. The settlement involved no penalties other than a permanent court injunction barring similar action by the defendants in the future.

20—Sen. George McGovern won a decisive victory in the New York State Democratic presidential primary after rolling up overwhelming margins in most districts across the state.

21—In New Orleans, a meeting of the United States Conference of Mayors reversed its policy and voted to support President Nixon's current strategy in Vietnam.

21—Six men were killed and 12 others were wounded when a 33-year-old gunman walked into an office building in the southern New Jersey suburban town of Cherry Hill and opened fire with two .22-caliber rifles. The slayer, identified by police as Edwin James Grace of New York City, a guard with the Pinkerton detective agency in Trenton, N.J., also fatally wounded himself.

23—The British Treasury announced that it would let the pound float in value for an indefinite period. The move was regarded as a de facto devaluation that would allow free market forces to set a new and lower international price for sterling.

23—President Nixon signed a bill making major innovations in federal aid to higher education but sharply criticized Congress for not providing the strict and uniform limits on school busing he had proposed. Among other things, the bill provided for the appropriation of $2 billion over the next two years to help communities that are in the process of desegregating their schools and the creation of a National Institute of Education to conduct educational research.

24—Back in Washington after four days of talks with Chinese Premier Chou En-lai in Peking, Presidential adviser Henry Kissenger said that they had discussed the Vietnam war at length but that he saw no indication of a break in the present diplomatic impasse at the Paris peace talks.

26—Flood waters caused by a week of nearly incessant rainfall in the northeastern region of the United States began to subside, leaving 122 persons dead, a half-million people homeless and $1.6 billion in damages. The damage caused by Hurricane Agnes prompted President Nixon to declare five states as disaster areas—Florida, Maryland, Pennsylvania, New York and Virginia—thus making them eligible for federal relief funds.

26—The United Nations Security Council voted to condemn "the repeated attacks of Israeli forces on Lebanese territory and population," and called on Israel to desist from any future assaults. The United States abstained from the vote, claiming that the resolution did not equally condemn Arab acts of terrorism.

26—The six member states of the Common Market voted to defend existing fixed currency relationships by buying more U.S. dollars in the exchange markets. The Market also agreed to further tightening of exchange controls in the wake of a monetary crisis touched off when the British treasury floated the pound on June 23.

26—The U.S. Supreme Court ruled 5 to 4 that the courts would not consider the constitutionality of the Army's surveillance of civilian political activities in suits claiming that such surveillance was discouraging criticism of the government. The majority held that the control of military surveillance must be left up to Congress and the executive branch of the government.

27—After three years of fighting between Irish Roman Catholics and Protestants in Northern Ireland, British and Irish combat forces began a cease-fire declared by the militant Provisional wing of the Irish Republican Army.

27—W.A. "Tony" Boyle, the 70-year-old president of the United Mine Workers of America convicted on March 31 of making illegal political contributions with union funds, was sentenced in Washington to five years in prison and fined $130,000 plus the $49,250 diverted from the union treasury to various political campaigns.

28—President Nixon ordered that no future military draftees be sent to Vietnam unless they volunteer for duty there. He also announced that 10,000 more American troops would be withdrawn from Vietnam by Sept. 1, thus reducing American military strength there to 39,000 men.

29—President Nixon disclosed during his first televised news conference in more than a year that the peace talks between the United States and North Vietnam would resume in Paris on July 13.

29—U.S. military officials in Saigon reported that 1,000 South Vietnamese troops were flown by U.S. helicopters into an area between the city of Quang Tri and the South China Sea in a drive to retake the Quang Tri Province from the North Vietnamese.

29—In Washington, the Democratic National Convention's Credentials Committee stripped Sen.

George McGovern of 151 convention delegates he had won in the California presidential primary. The committee voted 72 to 66 to divide the 271 delegates among all the candidates who competed in the June 6 primary, instead of following a California statute allotting all the delegates to whoever received the most votes.

29—The U.S. Supreme Court, in a vote of 5 to 4, ruled that capital punishment was unconstitutional "cruel and unusual" punishment. The decision saved 600 condemned men and women from execution, although it did not overturn their convictions. In another 5 to 4 decision the court held that journalists had no right under the First Amendment to refuse to divulge confidential names and information to federal and state grand juries.

30—Congress voted a 20 per cent boost in Social Security benefits after days of maneuvering. The pension increase for more than 27 million Americans cleared the Senate by a vote of 82–4 and the House by 302–35.

JULY

1—New violence struck Northern Ireland; thousands of Protestant youths, many wearing masks and gripping wooden clubs, set up barricades in Belfast to protest British policies. Two men were found shot to death in separate areas of Belfast.

1—John N. Mitchell, who as attorney-general had been one of the most powerful men in Washington, resigned as President Nixon's campaign manager to reenter private law practice.

1—Gen. Creighton W. Abrams slipped quietly out of Saigon after stepping down from his post as U.S. commander in Vietnam.

2—A South Vietnamese antiwar student was shot and killed in Saigon after trying to hijack a 747 airliner to Hanoi.

3—India and Pakistan agreed to pull back all troops from their common borders and freeze present troop positions in Kashmir pending further negotiations in that area; the accord was signed by Indian Prime Minister Indira Gandhi and Pakistani President Zulfikar Ali Bhutto.

4—A telephone hotline linking the capitals of North and South Korea was opened after the two Koreas signed a pact calling for termination of bitter antagonism since the end of the Korean War in 1953.

5—In Tokyo, Kakuei Tanaku, Japan's Minister of International Trade and Industry, was elected president of the governing Liberal-Democratic party; Tanaku automatically was designated as premier upon Eisaku Sato's retirement.

5—The U.S. Court of Appeals in Washington ruled that the Democratic Credentials Committee had been "arbitrary and unconstitutional" in stripping Sen. George McGovern of 151 California delegates to the party's national convention; the court upheld the committee's action in denying convention seats to Mayor Richard Daley and 58 other Chicago delegates.

5—At the San Francisco International Airport, two armed hijackers, demanding $800,000 in ransom for the 86 persons they held aboard a Boeing 737 jet, were shot and killed by federal agents. One passenger also died and two others were wounded in the gun battle.

7—Military officials in Saigon reported that North Vietnamese troops fought a South Vietnamese advance toward Quangtri City and forced one South Vietnamese unit to retreat under a strong tank attack.

7—The U.S. Supreme Court reversed a lower court's July 5 ruling and returned intact two rulings made by the Democratic Credentials Committee, one dividing the 271 California delegates among the nine Democratic presidential candidates and the other denying convention seats to Chicago Mayor Richard Daley and his 58-member delegation.

8—President Nixon announced a three-year trade pact between the United States and the Soviet Union providing for the sale of at least $750 mil-

lion worth of American wheat, corn and other grains to the Russians.

9—The Provisional wing of the Irish Republican Army ended its cease-fire in Northern Ireland after two weeks when shooting broke out in Belfast between I.R.A. and British troops.

10—British Army reinforcements numbering 1,200 men were ordered into Northern Ireland, raising the British forces there to 17,000, largest in three years of violence.

10—Prompted by a rash of airplane hijackings, the White House ordered detailed and time-consuming preflight screenings on all domestic short-haul, shuttle-type flights.

11—The opening session of the Democratic national convention in Miami Beach formally returned to Sen. George McGovern the 151 California delegate votes.

12—Sen. George McGovern of South Dakota was nominated as the 1972 Democratic presidential candidate at the party's national convention in Miami Beach.

12—Nearly 100,000 men marched throughout Northern Ireland in a vivid display of Protestant power during the annual Orange parade; three youths were killed and a series of explosions rocked downtown Londonderry.

13—Thomas F. Eagleton, Missouri's freshman senator, was nominated as Sen. George McGovern's vice-presidential running mate at the final session of the Democratic National Convention.

13—Two men accused of hijacking a National Airlines jet carrying 122 passengers from Philadelphia to New York on July 12 surrendered to federal agents at a small airport south of Houston. The $500,000 ransom was recovered.

13—In Dallas, Marvin Fisher, a 49-year-old Oklahoman suspected of hijacking an American Airlines 727 jet bound from Oklahoma City to Dallas on July 12, surrendered to police. The $200,000 paid by the airline was returned.

13—Vietnam peace talks in Paris resumed after a 10-week suspension.

15—Nearly 1,000 Catholic women and children fled Belfast for the Irish Republic; two soldiers and four civilians were killed, raising the death toll to 442 since the Catholic-Protestant violence in the province began in 1969.

16—Metropolitan Dimitrios, a progressive who had become Archbishop of the eastern Orthodox Church five months earlier, was elected by the Holy Synod in Istanbul to succeed Athenagoras I, who died July 7, as Patriarch of the world Orthodoxy.

17—In London financial leaders of the Common Market agreed on eight basic objectives for the reform of the world's monetary system; these included decisions that all currencies should be freely convertible into other currencies and that there should be effective international control of liquidity (money).

17—Kozo Okamoto, a 24-year-old Japanese revolutionary, was sentenced to life imprisonment by a military tribunal in Israel for his role in the slaying of 24 persons at the Tel Aviv airport on May 30.

18—Egyptian President Anwar Sadat announced in Cairo the immediate withdrawal of all Soviet military advisers and the placing of Soviet bases and weaponry in Egypt under exclusive control by the Sadat administration; in Moscow the Soviet press agency Tass acknowledged the withdrawal but said the action was taken by joint agreement of the two nations.

18—Britain's deputy Prime Minister and Home Secretary, Reginald Maulding, resigned following the disclosure of his past involvement with an international architectural company that had recently declared bankruptcy and that had been accused of attempting to bribe members of Parliament and other elected officials.

19—The U.S. government, in a change of policy, intervened in the foreign exchange markets to protect the value of the dollar by selling German marks at declining prices.

19—The White House announced that presidential adviser Henry Kissinger conferred secretly in Paris with North Vietnamese negotiators at the Vietnam peace talks.

19—The executive council of the A.F.L.-C.I.O. voted 27 to 3 to refrain from endorsing either President Nixon or Sen. George McGovern as presidential candidates.

20—Sen. George McGovern appointed former Democratic National Committee chairman Lawrence F. O'Brien as national chairman of his presidential campaign and assigned to him the task of promoting peace with labor and the party's old guard.

21—In Belfast, the Provisional wing of the I.R.A. claimed responsibility for detonating 22 bombs within 80 minutes, killing at least 13 persons and wounding 130.

21—The South Vietnamese government said its troops recaptured the district town of Bongson on the central coast without a fight after three months of enemy occupation.

22—President Nixon chose Vice President Spiro Agnew to be his running mate again in the November election.

22—Western Europe's two economic trading blocs, the Common Market and the Free Trade Association, were formally merged with the signing in Brussels of a joint treaty that produced a free trade zone of 300 million people.

24—By a vote of 50 to 45 the Senate adopted an amendment requiring the withdrawal of American troops from Vietnam in exchange for the release of prisoners of war, but then reversed its action by killing the overall bill proposing $1.8 billion in foreign aid.

25—The Cost of Living Council in Washington announced that 10 million more workers had been exempted from government wage controls; it said this was achieved by increasing—from $1.90 to $2.75 per hour—the wage level below which workers are not subject to the Pay Board's jurisdiction.

25—At a news conference in Custer, S.D., Democratic vice-presidential nominee Sen. Thomas Eagleton confirmed rumors that he had been hospitalized three times between 1960 and 1966 for "nervous exhaustion and fatigue" and that he had undergone psychiatric treatment, including shock treatments; his offer to step down was rejected by Sen. George McGovern, the party's presidential nominee.

26—U.S. Intelligence sources in Washington said there were "strong indications" that the Soviet Union was removing most of its warplanes assigned with Soviet flying crews to the Egyptian air force.

27—An additional 4,000 British Army troops were ordered into Northern Ireland by the British government to combat civil violence, bringing the total to 21,000.

27—Ralph Ginzburg, the former publisher of the quarterly magazine, Eros, was granted a parole after serving eight months of a three-year prison term; he was convicted in 1963 of sending obscene material through the mail.

28—Britain's 41,000 longshoremen went on strike for the second time in two years in support of their demands for greater job security in the face of increased use of containerization—a process by which cargo bulk in sealed containers can be loaded and unloaded wholly by crane.

31—Three bombs blasted the Belfast and Londonderry regions of Northern Ireland, killing six persons.

31—In Upper Marlboro, Md., a state trial opened for Arthur Herman Bremer, 21, accused of shooting Alabama Gov. George Wallace on May 15 in Laurel, Md.; the defense contended that Bremer was insane at the time he allegedly fired the shots that paralyzed Wallace from the waist down.

31—Sen. Thomas F. Eagleton, the Democratic vice-presidential nominee, bowed to a belated request from his running mate, Sen. George McGovern, and to pressure from party members, to withdraw from the Democratic presidential ticket; McGovern, on July 25, had declined to accept a similar offer by Eagleton.

AUGUST

1—Algerian officials confiscated $1 million extorted by three black American men who hijacked a Delta Airlines jet with 86 persons aboard over Miami, Fla., on July 31. Passengers had been released unharmed in Miami before the plane was flown to Algeria and the impounded money was turned over to U.S. diplomatic authorities in Algiers.

1—The U.S. Senate rejected, 59 to 33, an amendment, part of a military procurement bill, proposed by Sen. George McGovern that would have held defense appropriations to the $77.6 billion level set in 1971.

2—Monsoon rains, rising flood waters, increased disease and exhausted fuel supplies brought disaster to Manila, in the Philippines. Cholera claimed 362 lives and 96 died of typhoid after 26 days of rainfall.

2—The presidents of Egypt and Libya, Anwar Sadat and Muammar el Qaddafi, signed a joint agreement in Cairo to merge their respective countries within a year.

2—The U.S. Senate adopted, 49 to 47, an amendment for withdrawal of all American troops from Indochina within four months, subject to the reciprocal release of all U.S. prisoners of war by the North Vietnamese. The Senate then passed, 92 to 5, the $20.5 billion military procurement bill.

3—The Federal Power Commission in Washington adopted a new natural gas-pricing policy allowing producers to deliver additional gas to customers at prices above the present ceilings.

3—The U.S. Senate approved, 88 to 2, the anti-ballistic missile treaty signed with the Soviet Union in May during President Nixon's summit visit to Moscow. The treaty allowed for two defensive missile sites for both countries.

4—A jury of six men and six women in Upper Marlboro, Md., convicted Arthur Herman Bremer, 21, of shooting Alabama Gov. George Wallace and three other persons at a campaign rally in Laurel, Md., on May 15, and sentenced him to 63 years in prison.

4—The Justice Department in Washington dropped a perjury indictment against Leslie Ann Bacon in connection with a federal grand jury hearing in March 1971 concerning the bombing of the U.S. Capitol building on March 1, 1971; the department's action followed "the decision not to answer the defendant's motions for disclosure of electronic surveillance regarding the case."

4—In Washington the Labor Department reported the nation's unemployment level in July was at 5.5 per cent of the labor force, compared to 6.0 per cent in June, but another jump in farm and food prices raised the wholesale price index eight-tenths of one per cent.

6—Boris Spassky won the 11th game of the world championship chess match in Reykjavik, Iceland, on the 24th move and narrowed Bobby Fischer's lead to two points. Spassky's win made the score 6½ to 4½.

6—In New York City the Knapp Commission, a five-man panel appointed by Mayor John Lindsay in April 1970 to investigate sources of corruption in the city, recommended that Gov. Nelson Rockefeller appoint a special deputy attorney general to wage a five-year "war on corruption" among New York's policemen, prosecutors and judges.

7—In Washington the Council on Environmental Quality, appointed by President Nixon in 1969, reported that U.S. air quality improved between 1969 and 1970 but water quality deteriorated.

8—The Democratic National Committee in Washington nominated R. Sargent Shriver, the first director of the Peace Corps, to succeed Sen. Thomas Eagleton as the party's vice-presidential candidate.

10—The U.S. Defense Department disclosed that the renewal of heavy bombing and other military tactics in Vietnam since the North Vietnamese resumed their offensive in April had increased current fiscal year expenditures by $1.1 billion.

11—Mrs. Nguyen Thi Binh, the Viet Cong's chief delegate to the Paris peace talks, asserted in Paris that the issue of American withdrawal from Vietnam had been replaced by the issue of organizing power in Saigon.

11—American Bobby Fischer defeated his Russian opponent, Boris Spassky, in the 13th game of their world championship chess match in Reykjavik, Iceland, bringing the score to 8 to 5, in Fischer's favor.

12—In Danang, South Vietnam, the Third Battalion of the 21st Infantry Division was shipped back to the United States. With its departure the last American ground troops in Vietnam were gone, leaving 43,500 men serving as advisers to the South Vietnamese.

14—The East German press agency reported that an East German airliner crashed in a suburb of East Berlin minutes after taking off, killing all 156 East German tourists aboard.

14—In Sarafand, Israel, a military tribunal sentenced two 19-year-old female Arab guerrillas to life imprisonment for hijacking a Belgian airliner flying to Israel in May.

14—After a two-week visit to Hanoi, former U.S. Atty. Gen. Ramsey Clark retracted in San Francisco an earlier statement that the North Vietnamese would release American prisoners of war if the bombing of the North were halted, but added that he was convinced the POWs would be released upon "full settlement of the war."

15—The White House announced that presidential adviser Henry Kissinger met with South Vietnamese President Nguyen Van Thieu in Saigon in search of a settlement of the Vietnam conflict; a day earlier Kissinger was reported to have met in Paris with Le Duc Tho, the North Vietnamese government's chief negotiator to the peace talks, three times in a month.

15—In Washington, Federal District Judge George Hart, who issued an injunction in April 1970 blocking the construction of an oil pipeline across Alaska, dissolved the injunction after rejecting every legal argument by the environmentalists who had fought the pipeline.

16—President Nixon vetoed the $30.5 billion appropriations bill passed by Congress in early August for the Department of Health, Education and Welfare and the Department of Labor; the bill had allotted $1.8 billion more than Nixon had requested.

18—U.S. federal agents shot and captured a man in Vancouver, B.C., 13 hours after he allegedly hijacked a United Airlines jet in Reno, Nev., and forced it to fly to Vancouver; the $1 million ransom was returned to the airline.

18—President Nixon announced in Washington that the automobile industry would not be permitted to raise prices of its 1973 model passenger cars.

20—North Vietnamese troops overran the strategic Que Son Valley, 25 miles southwest of Danang, killing 22 South Vietnamese troops and threatening the safety of a 50-mile stretch of Highway I leading to Danang.

20—At the world championship chess match in Reykjavik, Iceland, Bobby Fischer and his Russian opponent Boris Spassky, agreed to a draw in the 16th game of their match. Fischer led Spassky 9.5 to 6.5.

22—In Miami Beach, Fla., Richard Milhous Nixon was formally renominated by the Republican National Convention for another term as President of the United States.

22—The Labor Department in Washington announced that the Consumer Price Index, spurred by higher food prices, rose 0.4 per cent in July, the biggest increase in five months.

23—President Nixon, accepting his renomination for another four years in the White House, called upon all citizens to "join our new majority;" Nixon's address during the closing session of the Republican National Convention in Miami Beach, Fla., followed the renomination of his chosen vice-presidential running mate, Spiro Agnew.

25—The Communist Chinese delegation to the

United Nations in New York City invoked its veto power for the first time since being admitted to the Security Council in October 1971; the veto barred Bangladesh from U.N. membership.

27—Maurice Stans, finance chairman of the Committee to Re-elect the President, demanded that the General Accounting office "begin immediately a full and comprehensive audit" of Democratic fund-raising records; Stans was responding to allegations by the G.A.O. on Aug. 26 of "apparent and possible violations" of the Federal Election Campaign Act by the Republican campaign organization.

28—In San Clemente, Calif., President Nixon declared that the national draft would end by July 1973 if Congress approved the Uniformed Services Special Pay Act of 1972, authorizing "bonus" payments to induce skilled specialists to join an all-volunteer military operation.

28—Democratic presidential candidate Sen. George McGovern said in Washington he would welcome an investigation of his presidential campaign funds by the congressional General Accounting Office.

29—The White House announced a reduction of 12,000 American troops in Vietnam, to be completed by Dec. 1, 1972. The reduction would bring total U.S. military strength there to 27,000 men.

29—President Nixon said in San Clemente, Calif., that he thought both the Democratic and Republican parties had committed "technical violations" of the new federal campaign spending and reporting laws. He declined to specify the nature of the violations but said he was confident they would be corrected.

30—The General Accounting Office announced in Washington that it had begun its examination of the campaign finance records of the Democratic presidential candidate, Sen. George McGovern.

31—Ugandan President Idi Amin ordered thousands of Asians holding British passports to leave Uganda by November, accusing them of being "economic parasites." Upon hearing of the order, the British government urged British citizens to show "traditional calm and resource" and called upon other nations to open their doors to those expelled.

31—President Nixon and Japanese Premier Kakuei Tanaka opened conferences in Honolulu in an attempt to revitalize the United States' troubled alliance with Japan.

SEPTEMBER

1—In Reykjavik, Iceland, American chess player Bobby Fischer won the international chess crown by defeating Boris Spassky in their final match.

1—President Nixon and Japanese Premier Kakuei Tanaka agreed during talks in Hawaii upon short-term measures to reduce the huge U.S. trade deficit with Japan.

1—A fire bomb hurled in a Montreal night club started a conflagration which took the lives of 37 patrons and injured at least 54; authorities arrested as suspects four persons who had been ejected earlier from the club.

4—The Museum of Fine Arts in Montreal reported that armed burglars stole paintings and other works of art which the museum valued at $2 million.

5—In Munich, West Germany, nine Israeli hostages, four of their Arab captors and a policeman died in gunfire at an airfield, ending a day of terror that began when Palestinian guerrillas killed two other members of the Israeli Olympic Games contingent in their quarters at Olympic Village.

5—Antiwar priest Philip Berrigan and Sister Elizabeth McAlister were sentenced in Harrisburg, Pa., to four concurrent two-year terms for smuggling letters in and out of prison.

5—President Nixon announced that extra security steps had been taken to insure the safety of Jews on the American Olympic team in Munich, where Arab guerrillas attacked Israeli athletes.

8—Scores of Israeli Air Force planes struck at 10 Arab guerrilla bases and naval installations in Syria and Lebanon in reprisal for the terror shooting of 11 Israelis in Munich. Israeli military officials said the planes hit at troop concentrations, training centers, supply depots and headquarters of Al Fatah, the Arab guerrilla organization.

9—Israeli air force jets intercepted four Syrian warplanes over the occupied Golan Heights, downing three, an Israeli military spokesman said.

9—Soviet authorities said the Russian spacecraft that reached Venus in July discovered that the planet's surface resembled the earth's granite rocks and that some sunlight did penetrate through the dense cloud cover.

10—The United States vetoed a resolution before the United Nations Security Council which would have called for an immediate halt to military operations in the Middle East but which failed to mention the terrorist attacks in Munich that had led to the Israeli air strikes against Syria and Lebanon. It was the second U.S. veto; the first came in March 1970 on a resolution concerning Rhodesia.

11—The West German government announced that it was granting about $1 million to relatives of the 11 Israelis killed in the commando raid in Munich.

11—Israel's highest court ruled that Meyer Lansky, American gambling figure, was not entitled to Israeli citizenship although he was a Jew. The Israeli government said it was offering Lansky a travel document letting him go to any country that would admit him. The U.S. government invalidated Lansky's passport except for return to the United States, where he was wanted in connection with tax-evasion charges and contempt of court.

14—The Senate, after more than a month of debate, approved the U.S.-Soviet agreement to freeze a major part of their offensive nuclear arsenals for five years. It stipulated, however, that there should be equality in the number of weapons in any future treaty governing strategic intercontinental arms.

15—Two former White House aides and five other men seized by police inside the Watergate complex on June 17 were indicted by a Federal grand jury on charges of conspiring to break into Democratic national headquarters at the complex in Washington. The indictment included charges of tapping telephones, planting electronic surveillance devices and stealing and photographing documents belonging to the Democratic National Committee.

16—South Vietnamese marines recaptured the Citadel in the heart of Quantri City, American and South Vietnamese officers reported. It was the most significant victory for the Saigon government since North Vietnam loosed its offensive March 30.

16—The White House made public a financial statement showing that President Nixon had a net worth of $765,118, an increase of $168,218 while he had been in the presidential office.

17—Israeli army units completed their withdrawal from southern Lebanon after encountering heavy resistance. An Israeli army spokesman said "at least 60" Arab guerrillas had been killed during the two-day sweep. Israeli casualties were placed at three dead and six wounded.

17—An American mother clasped her son and an American wife embraced her husband in Hanoi at a release cermony for three American war prisoners, pilots shot down over North Vietnam.

18—A small army that reportedly invaded Uganda from neighboring Tanzania in an attempt to unseat the president, Maj. Gen. Idi Amin, was apparently halted by Ugandan troops.

19—An Israeli diplomat, Dr. Ami Shachori, was killed when an envelope sent through the mail exploded in Israel's London embassy. A second Israeli diplomat, Theodor Kaddar, was slightly injured.

19—The United Nations General Assembly convened in New York for its 27th annual session and heard its new president, Stanislaw Trepczynski of Poland, declare that the war in Vietnam should be halted "once and for all." It was regarded as an exceptionally strong speech for such an occasion. The atmosphere on opening day was tense as extraordinary security precautions were taken for fear of a terrorist act. A stream of bomb threats had been received at U.N. headquarters and at individual missions around the city, most of them stemming from the unrest in the Middle East.

20—A move by the Soviet Union and Red China to place the question of reunification of Korea on the agenda of the U.N. General Assembly was defeated by the U.N. General Committee, which passed a British proposal to defer the question for another year. The governments of North and South Korea made direct contact in 1972 with the expressed aim of unifying their divided land. This bolstered the case of the West for not exposing these delicate negotiations to acrimonious U.N. debate.

20—Explosive devices concealed in envelopes and mailed from Amsterdam to Israeli officials were discovered in at least six cities abroad. Three of the envelopes addressed to officials of the Israeli Mission to the United Nations were spotted by U.S. Customs employes in New York.

21—Britain decreed an end to its controversial policy of interning, without trial, suspected terorists in Northern Ireland; a special tribunal was ordered to consider such cases.

21—For the first time since 1965, a week passed without American combat deaths in Indochina, the U.S. Command reported.

22—The Labor Department in Washington reported that U.S. consumer prices rose 0.2 per cent in August and 2.9 per cent in the first year of wage-price control, continuing what the Administration termed a relatively moderate rate of inflation.

23—In Manila, President Ferdinand E. Marcos declared martial law for the Philippines, ordering mass arrests of those he called communists seeking to overthrow the government.

24—Surveys showed President Nixon leading Senator McGovern 62 to 23 per cent in the race for the presidency.

26—The United States proposed a new world monetary system, permitting increased movement up and down in currency exchange rates and a reduced role for gold in the system.

28—In Peking, Chinese Premier Chou En-lai and Premier Kakuei Tanaka of Japan signed a joint communique resuming diplomatic relations, severed in 1949 upon formation of the Peoples Republic of China.

28—Three U.S. pilots freed by North Vietnam from war prison camps arrived in New York from Copenhagen after traveling from Hanoi through China and the Soviet Republic with an anti-war delegation as escort.

OCTOBER

1—An explosion ripped through a gun turret on the heavy cruiser *Newport News,* killing 19 sailors and injuring 10, the U.S. Navy announced. The 7th Fleet ship, the world's biggest gun cruiser, was operating just below the demilitarized zone, about 13 miles northeast of Quang Tri city, Vietnam.

1—Music and dancing marked festivities throughout Communist China as the nation celebrated the most momentous year since the Peoples Republic was founded 23 years earlier. Moscow congratulated the Chinese poeple on their anniversary.

1—Rabbi Meir Kahane, head of the Jewish Defense League, was arrested in Jerusalem by Israeli police in an alleged plot to smuggle arms out of Israel for use in a campaign against Arab terrorists abroad.

2—Danish citizens voted membership for Denmark in the European Common Market by a vote of 1,955,932 to 1,124,106. The vote would bring the nation of five million into economic union with the 240 million people of eight other West European nations.

2—The Philippine government decreed the death penalty for persons who kill with firearms not legally authorized. It decreed penalties of 20 years to life imprisonment for killings not covered by firearms restrictions.

3—China's Deputy Foreign Minister Chiao Kuan-hua told the United Nations General Assembly his nation would condone "just" wars, since "war is inevitable so long as society is divided into classes and the exploitation of man by man still exists;" he warned, however, that the world "must not be deluded by temporary and superficial phenomena of detente at the present time and develop a false sense of security."

3—In Washington, the House Banking and Currency Committee barred, 20 to 15, public hearings on certain aspects of the alleged bugging in Democratic party headquarters until after the Nov. 7 election.

3—President Nixon and Soviet Foreign Minister Andrei A. Gromyko signed documents implementing two pacts limiting the use of nuclear arms; the agreements were reached in Moscow in May.

4—Scientific academies of a dozen nations led by the United States and the Soviet Union set up a joint "think tank" to seek solutions to problems created by the increasing industrialization of societies. Problems to be examined included pollution control, urban growth, public health and over population.

4—Congress overrode President Nixon's veto of a bill to increase railroad retirement benefits by 20 per cent. The roll call in the House was 353-29 and the Senate followed up with a vote of 76-5.

5—Oil concerns reached accord with five Arab countries.

5—Legislation creating an independent consumer agency was blocked for the third time in the Senate, where a 52 to 30 vote failed to establish a two-thirds majority which would have limited debate; Senate leaders said there were no plans to renew consideration of the measure.

5—Near Saltillo, Mexico, a speeding train carrying about 1,600 passengers jumped the track, killing 149 and injuring 781.

6—Gen. Creighton W. Abrams was confirmed as Army Chief of Staff by the Senate Armed Services Committee.

8—North Vietnamese guerrillas moved as close as 10 miles from Saigon in a continuing drive along the Saigon River.

10—In London, Chancellor of the Exchequer Anthony Barber abolished Britain's bank rate, for 270 years the peg for monetary policy and interest rates, in favor of a fluctuating rate tied to the average discount rate for treasury bills; informed sources in Washington reported that, despite the British move, the U.S. Federal Reserve would not change its policy of setting a rigid discount rate.

10—The House of Representatives granted President Nixon the power to apply a $250 billion ceiling on federal spending in the current fiscal year; in praising this "responsible" action the President urged "quick and positive" compliance by the Senate in upholding this action.

11—In Hanoi, buildings of the French mission were wrecked during a U.S. bombing raid; a woman staff member at the mission and four North Vietnamese employes were killed. The injured included Pierre Susini, the mission's chief diplomat.

12—In the third consecutive day of debate, the Senate failed to achieve cloture and killed a bill to prevent cross-town busing and thus to desegregate schools; the anti-busing bill had been solidly supported by the Nixon Administration.

12—President Nixon's appointment of Gen. Creighton W. Abrams as Army chief of staff was confirmed by the Senate, 84 to 2.

12—The 1972 Nobel Prize for physiology or medicine was awarded jointly to an American and a Briton for their separate research in the chemical structure of antibodies; Dr. Gerald M. Edelman of Rockefeller University in New York and Dr. Rodney R. Porter of Oxford University shared the $101,000 prize.

13—Congress completed action on revenue-sharing legislation providing President Nixon with one of the chief domestic legislative proposals of his four years in office. The bill established a new system of Federal financial aid to states and local governments.

13—The leftist government of President Salvador Allende took over control of radio broadcasting in Chile as thousands of businessmen and shopkeepers went on strike defying a state of emergency.

13—Sen. Edward Kennedy, as chairman of a Senate judiciary committee, ordered a "preliminary inquiry" into the Watergate bugging incident, and charges of political espionage and sabotage in the Presidential campaign.

14—The United States and the Soviet Union signed a maritime agreement after Russian negotiators yielded to U.S. demands and agreed to pay premium rates to American ships carrying Soviet grain purchases.

14—A Soviet Aeroflot Ilyushin 62 airliner crashed while preparing to land in the rain in Moscow and more than 170 aboard were reported killed.

14—A mail clerk in a New York City Post Office had both hands mangled when an envelope similar to those which had been sent by Arab terrorists exploded. The envelope was addressed to a former officer of Hadassah, the women's Zionist organization. It bore a Malaysian postmark.

15—The U.S. Command reported that nearly 400 American fighter-bombers struck North Vietnam with the second heaviest bombardment of the year, carrying out more than 350 strikes. The heaviest raid occurred on Aug. 16, when more than 370 strikes were made.

15—Eight young men, identified as members of a black group called "De Mau Mau," were charged in Chicago in the slaying of nine white persons, including four members of one family and three of another.

16—President Nixon, in an emotional extemporaneous speech before a group of POW relatives, attacked "the so-called opinion leaders of this country" for not supporting him in May when he ordered the bombing of North Vietnam and the mining of its ports to deter the "specter of defeat."

16—Gen. Creighton W. Abrams was sworn in as U.S. Army Chief of Staff, and less than 12 hours later he was dispatched to Vietnam. Officially the trip was described as a routine on-the-scene assessment of growing South Vietnamese military capabilities.

16—Israeli Premier Golda Meir announced that three senior officials of her government's security service were ousted for failing to provide adequate protection for the Israeli Olympic team at Munich Germany.

16—A special force of 1,200 policemen swept through New York City and its suburbs serving grand jury subpoenas on hundreds of members of alleged Mafia families.

17—President Park Chung Hee proclaimed martial law throughout South Korea, suspended part of the Constitution, dissolved the National Assembly and suspended all political activities. U.S. State Department officials said the United States had conveyed its disapproval of the action "in the stiffest terms."

18—Congress adjourned after a final, defiant encounter with President Nixon on the spending issue. Both the Senate and House voted by wide margins to override a presidential veto of a $24-billion water pollution bill that Nixon had labeled "needless overspending."

18—The United States and Soviet Russia reached agreement on a sweeping trade package that included payment by the Russians of $722 million in World War II Lend-Lease debts.

18—Nineteen Jewish families in Moscow were unexpectedly given exit visas to emigrate to Israel without paying the heavy exit fees that Soviet authorities had been demanding since mid-August.

20—The Consumer Price Index rose four-tenths of one per cent in September, one of its largest increases of the year.

20—Henry A. Kissinger met again in Saigon with South Vietnam's President Nguyen Van Thieu. Their talks presumably centered around a peace formula to end the Vietnam War.

21—Henry A. Kissinger met with South Vietnamese Foreign Minister Tran Van Lam for a third day of private discussions. Usually well-informed American officials said the talks aimed at working out terms for a comprehensive settlement of the Indochina war. One diplomat said the talks were part of "the most important diplomatic negotiations of the last two decades."

21—North Vietnamese Premier Pham Van Dong said in an interview made public this date that his government was ready to accept a cease-fire as the first step in a settlement of the Vietnam War.

22—Henry A. Kissinger continued to seek South Vietnamese President Nguyen Van Thieu's support of a Vietnam War peace settlement that would be acceptable to Washington, Hanoi and Saigon.

22—The Oakland A's won the World Series by defeating the Cincinnati Reds, 3-2, in the seventh and last baseball game.

23—Four Turkish hijackers surrendered and freed more than 60 hostages they had held aboard a Turkish jetliner for 38 hours at the airport at Sofia, Bulgaria.

23—Henry A. Kissinger flew from Saigon to Washington after a five day effort toward a settlement of the Vietnam War. Neither American nor South Vietnamese officials would discuss the substance of the negotiations. A United States spokesman said, "We have made progress," adding that "talks will continue between us and the government of (South) Vietnam."

24—South Vietnamese President Nguyen Van Thieu said all peace proposals discussed by Henry A. Kissinger and the North Vietnamese in Paris so far were unacceptable. Thieu said there were great difficulties in the way of a cease-fire, but also said such a cease-fire could come "very soon."

24—Administration sources said the White House had ordered a temporary halt of all bombing north of the 20th parallel in North Vietnam. The sources said North Vietnam had made some concessions in recent secret negotiations.

25—A high-ranking French source said in Paris that a wide measure of understanding on a cease-fire and a subsequent political settlement in Vietnam had been reached between Henry A. Kissinger and the North Vietnamese negotiator, Le Duc Tho.

25—U.S. officials in Washington privately expressed belief that there would be a cease-fire in Indochina within a few weeks. But they warned that negotiations were still precarious and noted that Vietnamese President Nguyen Van Thieu did not authorize Henry A. Kissinger to arrange final details.

26—Henry A. Kissinger said "peace is at hand" in Indochina and added that a final agreement on a cease-fire and political arrangement could be reached in one more negotiating session with the North Vietnamese, "lasting not more than three or four days."

26—The South Vietnamese Foreign Ministry issued a statement in Saigon that South Vietnam is "ready to accept a cease-fire," but "would never accept a political settlement which goes against the interests of the 17 million South Vietnamese people."

27—President Nixon vetoed nine bills that he said would "breach the budget" by about $704 million in the current fiscal year and $1.9 billion in the next. His action seemed aimed mainly at backing up his pledge to hold down taxes in a second year.

27—President Nixon announced a second sale of grain to China and assured American farmers that he was committed to winning for them a "full fair share" of the nation's prosperity.

28—A high Administration official said in Washington that, even if North Vietnam agreed to President Nixon's request for an additional negotiating session between Henry A. Kissinger and Le Duc Tho in Paris, the United States would not sign the settlement until it had again consulted with South Vietnam.

28—In Saigon, South Vietnamese Foreign Minister Tran Van Lam said that acceptance of the proposal of a settlement of the war made public by Hanoi and Washington would amount to a "surrender" of South Vietnam and was "unacceptable."

28—President Nixon signed legislation creating an independent commission with authority to set and enforce safety standards on thousands of consumer products.

29—Arab hijackers seized a West German airliner over Turkey and won the release of three Arab guerrillas held in Munich for the slaying of 11 Israelis at the Olympic games on Sept. 5. The air pirates had threatened to blow up the airliner, if their demands were not met. The plane was flown to Tripoli with the air pirates, the guerrillas and 20 passengers.

29—In retaliation for the release of the Munich commandos, Israeli planes raided four Arab guerrilla bases outside Damascus and returned home safely.

29—Four hijackers armed with pistols and a shotgun killed an Eastern airlines agent and wounded another employe at Houston Intercontinental Airport before diverting a jet and its 29 passengers to Cuba. One of the air pirates was a former executive in the U.S. Department of Commerce.

30—At least 44 persons were killed and more than 320 were injured in the nation's worst train wreck in 14 years. An Illinois Central commuter train was crushed from behind by another in South Side Chicago.

30—President Nixon signed a $5 billion Social Security bill which contained 144 changes in welfare and health benefits.

31—Canadian Prime Minister Pierre Elliott Trudeau lost his majority in Parliament in a general election when his Liberal party lost 38 of the 147 seats they had held in the last Parliament. The Opposition Progressive Conservative party gained 34 seats.

31—The United States sought reassurances from Hanoi that, once the Indochina settlement took effect, North Vietnam would pull out many of the 35,000 troops it had stationed in the northern part of South Vietnam. The Communist Command was not required to do so under terms of the agreement worked out.

31—All 15 members of Chile's cabinet resigned to give President Salvador Allende a free hand in seeking means to end three weeks of strikes, street demonstrations, sabotage and political conflict.

NOVEMBER

1—President Nguyen Van Thieu denounced the draft peace agreement as "a surrender of the South Vietnamese people to the Communists." In a National Day Address Thieu said the draft accord was "only a cease-fire to sell out Vietnam."

1—More than 94.5 million Americans were registered to vote in the presidential election. It marked an increase of about 13 million over 1968.

2—President Nixon said the draft agreement for an Indochina settlement would not be signed until all remaining issues were resolved.

2—Canadian Prime Minister Elliot Trudeau said his government would carry on and face the next Parliament as a minority despite election setbacks.

3—Senior U.S. military analysts said additional North Vietnamese reinforcements were moving into South Vietnam, including some 100 tanks.

3—The nation's unemployment rate remained unchanged in October at 5.5 per cent of the labor force.

4—Xuan Thuy, leader of the North Vietnam delegation at Paris, indicated willingness to hold another cease-fire negotiating session provided the United States was "serious."

5—President Nixon said whoever was elected president should dedicate himself to 10 goals in the next four years, among them "a world at peace."

5—Sen. George McGovern said the war in Vietnam was "intensifying" rather than ending and that President Nixon had deliberately misled the nation into believing peace was near.

5—B52 bombers dropped some 2.5 million pounds of bombs over South Vietnam and North Vietnam.

5—Secretary of State William P. Rogers said he had "every reason to think" North Vietnam would agree to resume negotiations in the near future to conclude an agreement to end the Indochina war.

6—British Prime Minister Edward Heath announced a 90-day freeze on wages, prices, rents and dividends in a bid to curb inflation.

6—West Germany and East Germany finished negotiations on a treaty to establish formal relations between their two states.

7—President Nixon won re-election by a huge majority in defeating Sen. George McGovern, the Democratic candidate. Despite Nixon's sweep, the Democrats retained control of the House and Senate. Nixon called on the nation "to get on with the great tasks that lie before us."

8—President Nixon, after winning re-election by sweeping 49 states and getting a total of 521 electoral votes out of 538, said his first order of business would be a "significant" realignment of his staff and the executive departments.

9—President Nixon said he hoped to use his second term to lead the nation out of a crisis of the spirit. He said he would work to end "the whole era of permissiveness" as well as to work for "a new feeling of responsibility, a new feeling of self-discipline."

10—Adm. Elmo R. Zumwalt Jr., chief of naval operations, charged the Navy's senior commanders with failures in leadership and ignoring his directives on racial relations.

10—The first of 129 sailors who refused to return to duty aboard the aircraft carrier Constellation were brought before a captain's mast for punishment.

11—The U.S. Army turned over its big base at Longbinh to the South Vietnamese Army, symbolizing the end of direct U.S. Army participation in the war.

12—A Southern Airways jet landed at Miami, Fla., with 31 passengers and crew members who had been on a sister plane that was hijacked to Cuba by three gunmen in a 29 hour ordeal that began Nov. 10. The hijackers as well as the reported $2 million they extorted were reported in Cuban custody. During the long ordeal, the plane's tires were shot out at one point and at another the hijackers threatened to crash the plane into the Atomic Energy Commission's nuclear research plants in Oak Ridge, Tenn.

13—The Supreme Court cleared the way for resumption of the Pentagon Papers trial of Daniel Ellsberg and Anthony J. Russo Jr. In an unsigned order, the court refused to hear an appeal by the defendants of the trial judge's refusal to let them see the transcript of a defense lawyer's conversations that had been picked up by a government wiretap.

13—Sen. George McGovern, defeated Democratic presidential candidate, said he was determined "to keep the heat on" President Nixon to end the Vietnam war.

14—The Dow Jones Industrial Average closed at 1,003.16, finishing a trading session above 1,000 for the first time since it was begun in 1896.

15—Cuba and the United States expressed the desire to negotiate an agreement to curb the hijacking of airliners.

15—Canada, Hungary, Indonesia, and Poland, according to the State Department, had agreed in principle to take part in the international commission which would help supervise a cease-fire once it took effect in Vietnam.

16—The United States invited the Soviet Union to meet Jan. 31, 1973, to discuss reducing military forces in central Europe.

16—Secretary of State William P. Rogers asked the Swiss ambassador to tell Cuba the United States was willing to take any steps to work out an agreement to stop airplane hijacks.

16—Two blacks were killed and one wounded at Southern University in Baton Rouge, La., where students allegedly set fire to two buildings and exploded a bomb in a third.

17—Juan D. Peron returned to Argentina after a 17-year exile, with the declared intention of helping to pacify the country which had been divided since his rule ended.

19—West German Chancellor Willy Brandt's coalition government got a vote of confidence, taking 54 per cent of the total vote in the federal elections.

20—Cuba told the United States it would put on trial the three hijackers who forced a Southern Airways jet to land in Havana Nov. 12.

21—Israel and Syria fought an eight-hour series of battles in the heaviest fighting in more than two years along the cease-fire lines.

21—The U.S. Court of Appeals in Chicago reversed the convictions in the Chicago Seven conspiracy case. The decision freed five men convicted of crossing state lines with intent to incite a riot at the 1968 Democratic National Convention.

21—Samuel L. Popkin was ordered to start serving a jail sentence for having refused to answer questions of a grand jury investigating the release of the Pentagon Papers.

22—President Nixon, in a move to better relations with Peking, lifted a 22-year-old restriction on travel to Red China by American ships and planes.

22—The Federal Reserve Board announced an increase in the margin requirement for purchasing stock from 55 per cent to 65 per cent.

22—Military sources said a U.S. B52, which crashed after a bombing run over North Vietnam, was the first of the war to be lost to enemy fire.

23—President Hugo Banzer Suarez ordered a state of siege in Bolivia, declaring there was a conspiracy to topple his government. Suarez acted after La Paz factory workers called a 24-hour anti-government strike.

24—Air Force officials said a 39-day search for the missing plane that took Hale Boggs, House majority leader, and three others on a flight in Alaska had been suspended.

25—The Vietnam cease-fire talks ended in Paris, but it was announced they would resume Dec. 4.

26—The White House said President Nixon remained confident that an Indochina settlement would be achieved, but it was not clear how long this might take.

27—The State Department said negotiations had begun with Cuba Nov. 25 on an accord to halt air hijackings.

27—President Nixon said he had accepted the resignations of two cabinet members, Secretary of Housing and Urban Development George Romney and Secretary of Defense Melvin Laird.

28—Four persons died in Northern Ireland as IRA men staged their first rocket attacks in Ulster.

28—Samuel L. Popkin was released from jail after the federal government dismissed the grand jury investigating the public release of the Pentagon Papers.

30—President Nixon said William P. Rogers would remain as secretary of state to provide diplomatic "continuity" in the second Nixon Administration.

DECEMBER

1—The Irish Parliament approved legislation cracking down on the Irish Republican Army, soon after three explosions in Dublin killed two persons and injured 126.

2—The Australian Labor party ousted the conservative government of Prime Minister William McMahon in national elections.

2—A fire in a Seoul, South Korea, theater killed 50 persons and injured 76 others.

3—A Spanish jetliner crashed shortly after taking off from the Canary Islands, killing all 155 persons on board.

4—The Honduran Army overthrew President Ramon E. Cruz and installed Gen Oswaldo Lopez Arellano, commander of the armed forces, as president for the five remaining years of the presidential term.

5—The State Department said the United States and Cuba had agreed in principle that their proposed pact to curb hijackings should cover ships as well as airplanes.

5—The Australian government announced an end to the military draft and the freeing of all draft offenders.

5—The U.S. Supreme Court ruled a state could deprive a club of its liquor license for permitting acts of "gross sexuality" among its entertainers, waitresses and patrons.

5—The Administration ordered the nation's airlines by Jan. 5, 1973, to search all carry-on luggage and to search all passengers electronically for possession of weapons.

7—Apollo 17, after a 2 hour and 40 minute delay because of pressurization problems, blasted off for the moon on the United States' last planned lunar mission.

7—Mrs. Ferdinand E. Marcos, wife of the Philippine president, was wounded when a man stabbed her during a ceremony in Manila. Mrs. Marcos was not gravely injured. The man was shot dead on the spot.

8—Irish voters approved abolishing the "special position" of the Roman Catholic Church in the constitution.

8—Life magazine said it would cease publication with the Dec. 29 issue.

8—A United Air Lines jet crashed into a row of houses in Chicago. Forty-five persons were killed in the disaster.

9—Robert Strauss was elected chairman of the Democratic National Committee, following the resignation of Mrs. Jean Westwood.

10—Premier Kakuei Tanaka's Liberal-Democratic party was returned to power with a solid victory in nationwide elections in Japan.

11—The nations which wanted the United Nations to take strong action against terrorism, including air hijackings, were defeated in the General Assembly.

11—Apollo 17 astronauts Eugene Cernan and Harrison Schmitt landed in a valley of the moon and set up scientific instruments.

11—Treasury Secretary George P. Shultz said President Nixon had decided to continue wage and price controls in 1973.

11—Sen. Robert J. Dole of Kansas said he was resigning as Republican National Chairman and that George H. Bush, United States representative to the United Nations, had been picked to replace him.

12—South Vietnam President Nguyen Van Thieu proposed an indefinite truce between North and South Vietnam to begin before the Christmas holidays.

13—Apollo 17 astronauts found a patch of orange soil on the moon which a geochemist said possibly was "one of the most important finds in Apollo geology."

13—Henry Kissinger and Le Duc Tho suspended their secret peace talks in Paris, and the U.S. presidential adviser returned to Washington.

14—The White House disassociated itself from a cease-fire proposal made two days earlier by South Vietnam President Nguyen Van Thieu and said it would support only the plan Henry Kissinger had been negotiating with the North Vietnamese in Paris.

16—Henry Kissinger said the negotiations between the United States and North Vietnam had failed to reach what President Nixon regarded as "a just and fair agreement" to end the Vietnam War.

16—The Labor Department, based on unofficial final election returns, declared Arnold R. Miller the winner of the presidency of the United Mine Workers over W. A. Boyle.

17—Cmdr. Ronald E. Evans took a 47-minute floating walk outside the Apollo 17 spaceship as it returned from the moon to the earth.

18—The Nixon Administration announced a resumption of full-scale bombing and mining of North Vietnam. It said the raids "will continue until such time as a settlement is arrived at."

18—W. A. Boyle, defeated for re-election as United Mine Workers president, resigned at a meeting of the union executive board.

19—U.S. planes made the heaviest attack to date on the Hanoi-Haiphong area, but the U.S. command reported the loss of two B52 bombers and an F-111 fighter-bomber, making it the costliest day of the air war for the United States.

19—The Apollo exploration of the moon ended successfully with the landing of Apollo 17 and its three astronauts in the Pacific Ocean.

20—The Defense Department said intensive bombing of North Vietnam had caused "very significant damage" to a broad range of military targets.

21—A U.S. spokesman said four more B52 bombers had been shot down near Hanoi raising to eight the number lost in four days. Twenty-four crewmen were listed as missing.

21—The North Vietnamese and Viet Cong delegates walked out of the Paris peace talks to protest the intensive bombing of the North.

21—Leonid I. Brezhnev, Soviet Communist party leader, warned at a celebration marking the 50th anniversary of the Soviet Union that the future development of Soviet-American relations hinged largely on what happened on the issue ending the Vietnam war.

21—The two Germanys after negotiating for two years signed a treaty formally ending two decades of mutual enmity.

22—The Swedish Foreign ministry said in Stockholm that Hanoi's largest hospital, one mile west of the center of the city, had been damaged by American planes.

22—The White House said that the United States would continue its heavy bombing of North Vietnam and that the next step to end the Vietnam War was "totally" up to the North Vietnamese.

22—Pope Paul VI said the reasons for the break in the Vietnam peace talks were not "sufficiently apparent."

22—A series of strong quakes destroyed much of the Nicaraguan capital of Managua killing or injuring thousands of the 350,000 inhabitants.

23—The North Vietnamese vice minister of health said 25 doctors, pharmacists and male and female nurses were killed at Bach Mai hospital during an American bombing raid on Hanoi.

24—Xuan Thuy, North Vietnam's Paris peace negotiator, told an interviewer for the American Broadcasting Co. that Hanoi would not resume negotiations with the United States as long as the Nixon Administration continued bombing north of the 20th Parallel.

25—Informed U.S military officers in Saigon said the United States had at least temporarily halted the bombing of North Vietnam.

25—A Red Cross official in Managua said the Nicaraguan government had cut off food supplies to force survivors to leave the quake-shattered city before decaying bodies buried under the rubble caused an epidemic.

26—Harry S Truman, 33rd president of the United States, died in Kansas City's Research Hospital and Medical Center at the age of 88. President Nixon declared Dec. 27 a national day of mourning.

27—The 36-hour pause in the U.S. bombing of North Vietnam ended, and the U.S Command said planes once again were operating at the level preceding the suspension.

28—The U.S. Command in Saigon broke a nine-day silence on damage inflicted in the American air attacks against North Vietnam and listed nearly three dozen airfields, rail yards, power plants, supply depots and communications centers among facilities that had been bombed.

29—Four Palestinian guerrillas seized the Israeli Embassy in Bangkok and held six hostages for nearly 19 hours. They finally freed them and flew to Cairo after dropping their demands that 36 Palestinian prisoners in Israel be released on threat of death to the hostages.

29—The U.S. Military Command in Saigon reported the loss of two more B52 bombers as the attacks on North Vietnam continued.

29—Unrest grew in Congress among both Democrats and Republicans over the heavy bombing of North Vietnamese cities.

29—The United States, irritated by a statement by Swedish Premier Olof Palme comparing the bombing of North Vietnam to Nazi massacres of World War II, asked Stockholm not to send a new ambassador to Washington.

30—The loss of another B52 heavy bomber was announced by the U.S. Command bringing to 15 the number of the big planes the United States had reported shot down by the North Vietnamese since the start of the renewed heavy bombing.

30—The White House announced that President Nixon had ordered a halt to the bombing of North Vietnam above the 20th parallel and that Henry A. Kissinger would resume negotiations for a Vietnam settlement in Paris.

30—Hanoi sought to dispel the idea that it had yielded to military pressure in agreeing to resumption of the Paris peace talks.

31—The U.S. Command in Saigon reported that American planes were continuing their raids below the 20th parallel in North Vietnam where the halt in air strikes announced by the White House did not apply.

31—There were strong signs that President Nixon's halt in the bombing had brought him little respite from Congressional criticism over his Vietnam policies.

THE BIG STORIES OF 1972

(Selected by the news editors of Associated Press member newspapers and radio and television stations)

1. Nixon's China trip.
2. Assassination attempt against Gov. George Wallace.
3. Massacre at Munich Olympics.
4. Nixon election victory.
5. Kissinger's mission to end Indochina war.
6. Nixon's visit to Moscow.
7. The Eagleton affair.
8. The fighting in Vietnam.
9. Floods in America.
10. Supreme Court nullified death penalty.

DEATHS—1972

JANUARY

Maurice Chevalier, 83, actor and entertainer regarded by American fans as the number one Frenchman of screen and stage, charmed the world for over half a century with his jaunty, debonair and carefree manner. Born in an impoverished working class quarter of Paris, Chevalier's big break came in 1909 at the age of 21, when he was hired as a singer dancer for the Folies-Bergere. During World War I he was called for compulsory military duty, wounded in the lung and captured by the Germans. He was released after spending 26 months in a prison camp, where he learned English from a fellow prisoner. After overcoming his lung wound he began performing in various music halls in Paris. During that time he adopted the straw hat which remained his theatrical symbol throughout life. Chevalier made his first working visit to the United States in 1928, and in the following seven years appeared in 12 films. In 1958 he starred with Leslie Caron in the movie *Gigi*. Of his singing, Chevalier once said: "Thank God, it was my good luck not to have any voice. If I had, I would have tried to be a singer who sings ballads . . . but since I am barely able to half-talk and half-sing a song, it made me look for something to make me different from a hundred other crooners. Since I had no voice I had to find something that would hold the interest of the public." Much of Chevalier's popularity was due to the fact that he worked to bring joy to his audiences. "I believe in the rosy side of life. I believe in bringing to the people the encouragement of living," he said. Jan. 1 in Paris, of heart failure.

Padraic Colum, 90, author of numerous books of poetry, plays, children's stories, essays, travelogues and history during an Irish literary period when many critics felt that Colum was unjustly overshadowed by such writers as William Butler Yeats, James Joyce and Lady Gregory. He was a gentle, lyrical poet and a whimsical teller of tales. Born in Longford, in Ireland's County Longford, Colum recalled that as a child he spent long hours by the fire listening to his elders tell old folktales about their native land. This tradition, he once explained, was responsible for much of his own story telling ability. Colum and his wife moved to the United States in 1914 and lived there for the remainder of their lives. However, Colum continued writing about his old homeland. In Enfield, Conn., Jan. 11.

Mahalia Jackson, 60, rose from poverty in the Deep South to win world renown as a gospel singer. Closely linked in the last 10 years of her life with the black civil rights movement, Miss Jackson was chosen to sing at the Rev. Martin Luther King Jr.'s March On Washington rally at the Lincoln Memorial in 1963. The granddaughter of a slave, she had struggled for years for fulfilment and for unprejudiced recognition of her talent. Recognition finally came in 1950 with a debut at Carnegie Hall in New York. Her performances were so full of fire that she moved her audiences to shouting ecstasy. Many of Miss Jackson's songs were evocations of religious faith and were intended to be devotional in keeping with her own profound belief in God. Seeking to communicate her faith, which was nontheological, Miss Jackson did a great deal of her singing, especially in the early days, in storefront churches, revival tents and ballrooms. On Jan. 27 of a heart seizure, in Evergreen Park., Ill.

Ted Shawn, 80, who after the paralysis of both legs at 18, not only learned to walk again but became what many critics considered "the father of modern dance." As a young man he first saw Ruth St. Denis dance in a recital. He started dancing with her in 1914 and later married her. Together they founded the Denishawn School of Dancing in Los Angeles and built what experts termed the "foundation which was to support, in the years to come, the structure of a new American dance." After they went their separate ways in 1932, Shawn became the nation's most popular male dancer and formed the first exclusively male troupe. He also founded in 1932 a dance center tucked away in the woods at Jacob's Pillow in the Berkshire Hills near Lee, Mass., a commitment that he stayed with for most of the remainder of his life. He created such dances as *Kochitl* and *The Cosmic Dance of Siva*, and drew upon the dances of the Shinto cult in Japan and on the Palm Blossom dances of the Malays. Born in Kansas City, Mo., Shawn recalled once that in his childhood he saw theater constantly. When he was paralyzed from an overdose of antitoxin for diphtheria it was largely through ballet that he was rehabilitated. In Orlando, Fla., Jan. 9.

Betty Smith, 75, author of the best selling novel *A Tree Grows in Brooklyn*. Born in a slum area, Mrs. Smith based her novel largely on personal experiences. After her father died when she was 12, she quit school to go to work. Moving to Ann Arbor, Mich., the home of the University of Michigan, she began to take college courses although she had received only an eighth grade education. Eventually she was graduated and began writing plays. However, her impoverished life in Brooklyn remained in her mind. After writing a journal of the years of her youth she took it to Harper and Row in 1943 where it was cut in half before publication. The book was an instant success and thereafter has sold over six million copies. Mrs. Smith wrote three other novels but none reached the acclaim of *A Tree Grows in Brooklyn*. Mrs. Smith was married three times and had two daughters. Of pneumonia, Jan. 17 in Shelton, Conn.

Charles E. Wilson, 85, former president of the General Electric Company, served as industrial mobilizer for the government in both World War II and the Korean war. A man with a gift for solving complex industrial problems, he cleared the way for production of a record 93,369 military aircraft in 1944. Wilson exuded optimism about American productivity which he expounded as he ran General Electric. After World War II he directed the running of 115 factories that produced 200,000 items, from light bulbs to generator shafts. At that time the company's output was boosted by 385 per cent. Wilson, whose father died when he was 3, quit school at the age of 12 to go to work with the Sprague Electric Company, later absorbed by G.E. In 1939 he took over the presidency from which he resigned three years later to serve on the War Production Board. Between wars Wilson not only concentrated on making General Electric more productive but also on operating for the government the vast atomic energy plant at Hanford, Wash., which made plutonium for atomic bombs. In Jan. 3 at Lawrence Hospital, in Bronxville, N.Y.

FEBRUARY

Air Force Gen. Joseph T. McNarny, 78, succeeded Dwight D. Eisenhower as U.S. Commander in Europe after World War II. He became a pioneer in the air arm of the Army in France during the first world war. In 1941 he went to London as a special observer before the United States entered World War II. After the Japanese attack on Pearl Harbor McNarny was named to a commission which investigated U.S. military and naval activity at the time of the bombing. In March 1942 he was named deputy chief of staff of the Army. He was chosen to succeed Eisenhower as commander of American forces in Europe late in 1945. On Feb. 1, in La Jolla, Calif.

Marianne Moore, 84, famed poet, won the Pulitzer Prize in 1952 and many other awards in a long and extraordinarily busy life of writing. A writer of dazzling ability with a talent for describing things as if she were observing them for the first time, Miss Moore was not only one of America's most distinguished poets, she was one of its better known personalities. She was an inveterate frequenter of concerts, balls, parties, fashion shows and lecture platforms. Her poems utilized rhythms to create moods as well as to convey her admiration for such virtues as patience, firmness, courage, loyalty, modesty and independence. Much of her writing in this vein was a wry but gentle criticism of human conduct, literature and art. It was often presented in unusual typographical arrangements. She made her point obliquely as a rule, for animals and plants rather than people were usually the formal subjects of her verse. Miss Moore took pride in catching the reader's attention with the first lines of her poems. "I am very careful with my first lines," she once said. "I put it down. I scrutinize it. I test it. I evaluate it." Actually Miss Moore was not a prolific poet. Only 120 poems occupying 242 pages were in *The Complete Poems of Marianne Moore*, published for her 80th birthday. On Feb. 5, at her New York City home.

Edgar Snow, 66, an American journalist who had become friends with China's Communist leaders when he interviewed them in their cave redoubts in Yenan in 1936. In failing health in 1971, Premier Chou En-lai sent a medical team of three physicians and a nurse to attend him at his home in Switzerland. And, upon his death, Huang Hua, the Chinese ambassador to the United Nations, told Snow's wife in a telegram that Snow would forever be remembered as a true friend of the Chinese people for his unremitting efforts and important contributions to the promotion of the understanding and friendship between the Chinese and American peoples." Snow's two best-known books were *Red Star Over China*, published in 1937, the first in-depth report on the Communists and *The Other Side of the River: Red China Today*, published in 1962, which gave his impressions of the new society as he saw it. Snow was educated at the University of Missouri and Columbia School of Journalism. Having a strong yearning for travel, he first went to Central America, then to Hawaii, supporting himself by freelance writing. In 1928 he reached China and liked it so much that he stayed for 12 years. During his time there he wrote for the New York Herald Tribune, The Saturday Evening Post, Fortune and Look. After World War II Snow went back to the United States as a lecturer and writer. He visited China again in 1960, 1965 and 1970. On Feb. 15, of cancer, at his home in the village of Eysins, Switzerland.

Llewellyn Thompson, 67, former U.S. ambassador to the Soviet Union, had a diplomatic career that spanned four decades. For nearly 30 years, starting in the dark war days of 1940, he was involved with the Russians. He was twice ambassador to Moscow—from 1957 to 1962 and from 1967 to 1969. For 10 years ending in 1955 Thompson talked with the Russians about an Austrian state treaty. There were 379 meetings before an accord was finally worked out, a feat of endurance for which he received the United States Distinguished Service Award. The tall, slim envoy was a great practitioner of personal diplomacy. He was on cordial terms with Foreign Minister Andrei A. Gromyko and talked for hours on end with the then premier, Nikita S. Khrushchev. He began his career as a vice consul in Ceylon in 1929, shifting to Geneva in 1933 and moving up to consul in 1937. In 1941 he was sent to Moscow as second secretary and consul at the U.S. Embassy. That summer the Germans were at the gates of Moscow, and the foreign ministry with the diplomatic corps moved to Kuibyshev on the middle Volga. But Thompson was assigned to stay in Moscow to look after American interests. For having stuck it out in the embattled capital he was awarded the U.S. Medal of Freedom. On Feb. 6, at the National Institute of Health in Bethesda, Md.

Walter Winchell, 74, the glib song and dance man, became one of the most widely read newspaper columnists in the United States. From 1930 to 1950 he was one of the most influential journalists in this country. Millions read his nationally syndicated column *On Broadway* and millions more listened to his weekly newscast beamed at "Mr. and Mrs. America and all the ships at sea." Winchell not only created the modern gossip column, he also devised a language to go with it. A blessed event was a "bundle from heaven," movies were "moom pictures" and convivial individuals got bemused on "giggle water" along the "bulb belt." Winchell had friends in exalted places, including President Franklin D. Roosevelt and J. Edgar Hoover, director of the Federal Bureau of Investigation. In his heyday Winchell nightly made the rounds of Broadway in quest of news. He liked to respond to police and fire calls and had a police-band radio in his car. He made his name on the old New York Graphic and went on to national fame in the New York Daily Mirror. At one point his column appeared in 800 newspapers, but later slipped to 175. It virtually disappeared with the demise of the Mirror in 1963. On Feb. 20, in Los Angeles.

MARCH

Cristobal Balenciaga, 77, one of the world's leading couturiers due to his orginality of design. Balenciaga introduced, among other things, the semifitted suit, the chemise, the balloon-shaped dress, the pillbox hat, the high-waisted suit, wide shoulders and the evening dresses that were cut high in front and low in back. Balenciaga had designed for such women as Spain's last queen, Victoria Eugenie, Queen Fabiola of Belgium, Princess Grace of Monaco, the Duchess of Windsor, the Begum Aga Khan, Marlene Dietrich and Elizabeth Taylor. He chose never to mingle with his patrons, despised publicity and was completely dedicated to his work. He was envied and respected by many other leading couturiers, among them the late Christian Dior and the late Coco Chanel. Chanel said of him, "Balenciaga alone is a couturier. He is the only one who can design, cut, put together and sew a suit or a gown entirely alone." Raised by peasant parents in Spain, Balenciaga was encouraged by his mother, who was a seamstress. By 1937 he had left Spain to open a couture house in Paris. By 1960 his name was one that evoked reverence in the fashion world. He was often called the Leonardo da Vinci of the couture because he seemed to work as a sculptor. He retired in 1968 but did one last dress: the wedding gown for the granddaughter of Generalissimo Francisco Franco. Of a heart attack March 24, in Valencia, Spain.

Gabriel Heatter, 82, the radio commentator, found silver linings that soothed his listeners and annoyed his critics during a career that spanned the Depression, World War II, Korea and the East-West cold war. Heatter's utterances on any topic—from the attack on Pearl Harbor to the virtues of suntan lotion—were delivered in reassuring tones with a depth of feeling. A high point in his career came in 1936 when he spoke from Flemington, N.J., for nearly an hour without notes or script to a nationwide audience awaiting the execution of Bruno Richard Hauptmann, convicted kidnaper of the Lindbergh baby. His emotional broadcasts during World War II were carefully prepared, and the incidents were selected with much thought for their effect. On March 30, in Miami, Fla.

J. Arthur Rank, 83, founded the Rank Organization which financed many of the best-known British film productions and operated an extensive chain of theaters in which to show them. One of Britain's richest men, Lord Rank, who was created a baron in 1957, built an economic empire which was one of the most powerful in the world. He owned or controlled companies making cameras, radios, television sets, lenses, projection equipment, theater seats and cosmetics. He was also linked to other enterprises such as insurance, milk bars, publishing companies and newspapers. He was a director of about 100 companies and chairman of the board of 25. He dominated the British film industry by the end of World War II and controlled Britain's two largest theater chains—the Odeon and Gaumont British—which totaled 700 theaters. The J. Arthur Rank Organization put out such films as *Hamlet; In Which We Serve,* and *Colonel Blimp.* In 1937 Rank acquired a 25 per cent interest in Universal Pictures, giving him his first foothold in Hollywood, but reportedly sold his stock in the company. In 1944 he formed the now defunct Eagle-Lion Company with the late Robert R. Young, chairman of the New York Central Railroad. Rank also joined with the Xerox Corporation to distribute Xerox copying equipment in the United Kingdom. On March 29, in a hospital in Winchester, England.

APRIL

Hodding Carter Jr., 65, the outspoken publisher and editor, won the Pulitzer Prize in 1946 for his editorials against racial segregation in the South. As a small boy in Louisiana, two incidents made a lasting impression on Carter. When he was 6 he saw a gang of white youths chasing a Negro boy, and several years later he came upon the hanging body of a lynch victim. Carter embarked on a newspaper career in 1932 and three years later moved to Greenville, Miss., where he headed the Delta Star, a fledgling paper. Two years later he bought the Delta Democrat-Times and merged the two papers. Over the years his name became a synonym for the battle to improve race relations in a state often torn by racial strife. The Pulitzer award in 1946 cited especially an editorial he wrote appealing for fairness for Nisei (American-born individuals of Japanese extraction) soldiers returning from the war. On April 4 at his home in Greenville.

Brian Donlevy, 71, broad-shouldered actor, played tough-guy roles in motion pictures, and was a popular he-man in a variety of movie formats, including Westerns, World War II dramas and detective stories. He was nominated for an Academy Award for his supporting role in *Beau Geste* and he was also well known for his performances in *What Price Glory, The Great McGinty, I Wanted Wings* and *Wake Island.* Donlevy ran away from school at the age of 14, joined the Lafayette Escadrille in World War I and was wounded twice in three years of flying. After the first war he joined the Broadway cast of *What Price Glory* and began a successful stage career that was to lead eventually to Hollywood. He made a name in *The Milky Way* and his second film, *Barbary Coast,* marked Donlevy as star material. On April 5 in the Motion Picture Hospital in Hollywood.

Kwame Nkrumah, 62, the deposed president of Ghana, was the first man to lead an African colony to independence after World War II. He had been living in exile in Guinea since his overthrow in a military coup in 1966. After having brought Ghana to autonomy in 1957, with $400 million in foreign reserves, Nkrumah ran his country about $600 million into debt by 1966. He had his image placed on postage stamps in Ghana, put his name in lights all over the capital of Accra and dismissed the Ghanaian Supreme Court, making himself the final arbiter of appeal. He embarked on an ambitious Seven-Year Plan and as time went on secluded himself in his official residence which he converted into a virtual fortress. In his youth Nkrumah enrolled at Lincoln University in Pennsylvania and later at the University of Pennsyl-vania, accumulating three degrees over 10 years. In 1947 he returned to his homeland as general secretary of the United Gold Coast Convention, a political organization set up to win independence. In 1948 the British jailed Nkrumah for his attacks on the colonial administration and he became a living martyr. In 1951 he was released and assumed virtual control over the country. When Independence day came in 1957, he was named prime minister. In 1960 he was named president and a year later assumed absolute control. His drift to the left helped bring his downfall. On April 27 in Conakry, Guinea.

George Sanders, 65, delighted in playing the cynic and was typecast many times in motion pictures as a blase lover and man of the world. With the dissolute air of a cynic, the impeccable British diction of a fop and a sneer that marked him to millions of movie goers as a cad, Sanders became one of Hollywood's best-paid cinema villains. In at least 90 films, starting in the 1930s, he played the "heavy" in all but a handful. He won an Academy award in 1950 as the best supporting actor for his portrayal of a vicious drama critic in *All About Eve.* His last film was the *Kremlin Letter* in 1970 in which he played an ancient drag queen who became the center of a homosexual literary sect in Moscow. His autobiography, *Memories of a Professional Cad,* appeared in 1960. On April 25 in a hotel in Barcelona, Spain, of an overdose of sleeping pills.

MAY

Dan Blocker, 43, the amiable giant from Texas, created the role of Hoss Cartwright on the television series *Bonanza.* His 6-foot-4-inch, 280-pound frame enabled him to create the character which became the TV epic watched by millions of viewers in 70 nations. He blended humor, sensitivity and physical might, both on and off the screen. To the legions who watched him every Sunday night he was not Dan Blocker but Ole Hoss, the massive kindhearted middle son in the Cartwright family. He once observed that he had never lost a fistfight and that the local toughs in West Texas gave up trying to pick one when he was about 13. Blocker's interest in acting began while he was attending Sul Ross State College in Abilene, Tex. The drama teacher needed someone strong enough to carry bodies around in *Arsenic and Old Lace* and Blocker was the natural choice. With this taste of acting, he gave up a teaching career for show business. He was studying for a Ph.D at the University of California at Los Angeles when he landed a role in the TV show *Gunsmoke.* In 1959 he was cast as Hoss in the western series that made him rich. But even though he made $15,000 per show on the NBC series and another $15,000 per rerun, he missed teaching. "Let's face it," he once said. "I sold out for money." On May 13 in Inglewood, Calif., of a blood clot in the lung.

Cecil Day Lewis, 68, was Poet Laureate of Britain. He once wrote that he was a man who had been beguiled by the utopian promise of the Russian Revolution and then disillusioned by it. Although he quickly repudiated Communism, he was considered a revolutionary figure in the world of letters. But beneath the revolutionary gesture was a spirit nurtured by traditional schooling, an Oxford education and a strong pull to the old England, the rural landscape and the makeup of the past. As a craftsman steeped in traditional English forms, he was ill at ease in the sloganeering rhymes of the soap box. Instead he turned to parody, to lampoon, to the use of jazz rhythms. He was appointed Poet Laureate in 1968 to succeed John Masefield. In addition to being Poet Laureate he was professor of poetry at Oxford from 1951 to 1956, Norton Professor of Poetry at Harvard in 1964 and was made an honorary member of the American Academy of Arts and Letters in 1966.

To make money he wrote mystery stories and put out more than 20 under the name of Nicholas Blake. On May 22 in London.

Dame Margaret Rutherford, 80, delighted audiences for more than 40 years with her comedy roles. Portraying a wide range of film and stage eccentrics, she was a comedienne, with few peers, who attained stardom in middle age as a result of granite persistence and continued sharpening of her acting talents. Once established, she went from triumph to triumph, winning an Oscar in 1964 for her role as a Shakespeare-quoting impecunious British aristocrat in *The V.I.P.s.* Previously she had been Madame Arcati, the spiritualist in Noel Coward's *Blithe Spirit,* Miss Prism in *The Importance of Being Earnest,* the evil Mrs. Danvers in *Rebecca* and the tweedy Amateur detective, Miss Jane Marple, in four Agatha Christie films. In all she appeared in more than 100 plays and 30 films. On May 22 at her home in Chalfont St. Peter, Buckinghamshire.

JUNE

Jimmy Rushing, 68, portly blues singer who emerged from Kansas City with the Count Basie orchestra in 1936 and won fame as a male vocalist. He sang in an intense high pitched voice that in later years became somewhat husky. But it never lost the warmth and individuality that caused some critics to rate him the greatest of the male jazz singers. His career began in 1925 in California, where he played piano and sang in after-hours clubs. In 1927 he returned to Oklahoma City, where he was born, to join Walter Page's Blue Devils as a singer. In 1928 Count Basie became pianist for the band and in 1931, when Page broke up the band, he and Rushing and Basie all joined Bennie Moten's band in Kansas City. After Moten's death in 1935, the trio stayed together in a band under Basie's leadership. A year later they moved to New York and fame. Rushing remained with the Basie band until 1950, recording many songs, including *Good Morning Blues,* and *Goin' to Chicago.* On June 8 in a New York City hospital.

Edmund Wilson, 77, rated by many as the most erudite, most perceptive and the most finicky of American literary critics. For half a century he wrote elegant prose for the intellectual elite. Besides being a critic, he was a novelist, short-story writer, playwright, poet, historian, Bible authority, essayist and autobiographer. Four of Wilson's books represented attempts to apply his humanist and historical values to writers and the culture that nurtured them. They were *Axel's Castle* in 1931, *To the Finland Station* in 1940, *The Wound and the Bow* in 1941 and *Patriotic Gore* in 1962. In these and other books, Wilson gave his appraisal of many figures, from Charles Dickens to Ernest Hemingway. Wilson did not limit his comments to the kind of writers usually discussed in literary journals. He gave his views on Emily Post and her etiquette books and reported his conclusion that detective stories were a waste of an intelligent reader's time. His books of criticism brought Wilson renown. His significant work in later life was *Patriotic Gore,* on which he worked off and on for 15 years. Critics rated it a masterly study of the literature of the Civil War at once encyclopedic and profound. On June 12 in his 172-year-old home in Talcottville, N.Y.

JULY

Athenagoras I, was the Ecumenical Patriarch and leader of the world's 126 million Eastern Orthodox Christians. He was 86 years old. He was noted especially for his efforts to achieve Reunion of his Faith, with the Roman Catholic Church. Those efforts were symbolized in three dramatic meetings with Pope Paul VI, the first of which took place in the summer of 1967, when Paul journeyed to Istanbul, site of the Patriarchate. In 1967 Athenagoras returned Paul's visit by going to Rome. The Patriarch sought to heal the schism that was formalized in 1054 over matters of doctrine and church administration, among other things. The Patriarch had strong ties with the United States, stemming from his 18 years as Archbishop of North and South America. He became a U.S. citizen in 1938, but later resumed Turkish citizenship. Ordained a deacon in 1910, he was consecrated a bishop in 1922 and in 1930 was designated Archbishop of the Greek Orthodox Church in North and South America. Both Presidents Franklin D. Roosevelt and Harry S. Truman regarded him as a leading spokesman for the close-knit Greek community in the United States. After the election of Athenagoras as Patriarch in 1948, Truman loaned the religious leader his plane to fly to Istanbul. On July 6 in Istanbul.

Sen. Allen J. Ellender, D-La., was chairman of the Appropriations Committee and president pro tem of the Senate. He had served in the Senate 35 years. The peppery Dixie Democrat mingled Southern conservatism with some liberal attitudes that often surprised the Senate liberals. On civil rights, Ellender voted with the Southern bloc against desegregation bills, and his statements casting doubt on the capabilities of blacks in the United States and Africa roused considerable controversy. But on foreign policy matters the senator became an advocate in recent years of closer relations with the Soviet Union and a critic of defense spending. Ellender often traveled abroad and liberals appreciated his impressions of the Soviet Union. But they reacted with anger to the impressions the senator brought back from Africa. In 1962, while visiting in Rhodesia, he expressed doubt as to the ability of African blacks to govern themselves. As a result of that remark, the governments of Uganda and Tanganyika told him he was not welcome in those countries. On July 27 in the Bethesda Naval Hospital in Maryland.

Goeran Gentele, 54, the newly appointed director of the New York Metropolitan Opera, started attending opera at the age of eight. After studying for a degree in political science at the university in his native Stockholm, he decided on a career in the theater. He was accepted at the Royal Dramatic Acting School in the Swedish capital and was involved in some form of theatrical work thereafter. Acting failed to satiate his creative needs, however, and he turned to directing. His opera career began in 1951, when Sweden's Royal Opera commissioned him to direct a production of Gian Carlo Menotti's *The Consul.* The production won great critical acclaim and paved the way for Gentele to join the opera as a staff director. In 1963 he was named general manager of the Royal Opera, a post in which he served until 1971, earning renown as an efficient and innovative administrator. In November 1970 the president of the Metropolitan Opera announced the appointment of Gentele as director, succeeding Sir Rudolf Bing. Though he had full control for only a few weeks, he was responsible for many dramatic changes, including hiring the Met's first black conductor. In an automobile crash on the Italian island of Sardinia on July 18.

Ruth McKenney, 60, was best known for her humorous stories collected under the title *"My Sister Eileen."* The stories about Eileen first appeared in the New Yorker magazine in the 1930s. They were collected and published as a best selling book in 1938. Then they were made into a play and a movie of the same name and finally transformed into a musical called *Wonderful Town.* A sequel, *The McKenneys Carry On,* was published in 1940 and a third one, called *All About Eileen,* appeared in 1952. The Eileen stories told of the zany world of two sisters sharing a Greenwich Village apartment. One was brainy and hoped to make her way in the literary world. The other was beautiful and bubbling and given to spending money and falling in love. Although they gained her fame, Miss McKenney struggled against the reputation as a humorist and passed off her stories as a means of making money to allow her to do "serious" writing. This was invariably concerned with social causes and dealt with the industrial valleys of eastern Ohio and western Pennsylvania. Miss McKenney's sister, Eileen, died in an automobile accident with her husband, Nathaniel West, in December 1940, one night before the play about her opened on Broadway. On July 25 at Roosevelt Hospital in New York City.

Paul-Henri Spaak, 73, the Belgian statesman, was one of the chief architects of European unity after World War II. He helped write the charter of the United Nations and served as the first president of the General Assembly in 1946. He played a prominent role in the creation of the North Atlantic Treaty Organization (NATO) and served as its secretary-general from 1957 to 1961. Spaak was also one of the signers of the Treaties of Rome in March 1957 which set up the Common Market composed of France, West Germany, Italy, Belgium, Luxembourg and the Netherlands. Before that he had served as president of the European Coal and Steel Community, the first grouping of European nations. He had also been president of the Council of Europe and president of the Organization for European Cooperation. Upon his retirement in 1966, Spaak had served three times as Belgium's premier and six times as foreign minister. When Belgium was overrun by the German armies in World War II, Spaak fled to France where he was interned briefly. After France was attacked, he escaped to Spain, then to Lisbon and finally to London, where he and others set up a Belgian government in exile. After the liberation of Belgium in 1944, Spaak returned home and began the task of rebuilding a shattered Europe. He started as a firm supporter of the United Nations, but his faith in its effectiveness dwindled in later years. He became increasingly concerned with the establishment of a western Europe that was strong both militarily and economically. On July 30 in Brussels.

Joseph Fielding Smith, 95, was the 10th president of the Church of Jesus Christ Latter Day Saints and grand-nephew of Joseph Smith, founder of the Mormon faith. The spiritual leader of the world's three million Mormons assumed the presidency of the church in January 1970 when he was 93. Smith was born July 19, 1876, in Salt Lake City, at a time when polygamy was still a tenet of the Mormon faith and actively practiced. He was the fourth child of his father's second wife. Shortly before the turn of the century Smith worked in a church-owned department store in Salt Lake City, but since 1901 he had worked in branches of the church itself. He served two years as a Mormon missionary in Britain and became a church historian in 1906. In 1910 he was named one of the 12 Apostles. When David C. McKay, ninth president, died early in 1970, Smith was elected to succeed him. On July 2 in Salt Lake City.

Helen Traubel, 69, the Metropolitan Opera's illustrious Wagnerian soprano, left high school in her sophomore year to devote all her time to the study of voice. Under the auspices of her singing teacher, Mme. Vetta Karst, she made her professional debut a few years later with the St. Louis Symphony. In 1926, Rudolph Ganz, the symphony's conductor, was contracted as a guest conductor at the New York Philharmonic and he took Miss Traubel with him as soloist. Upon hearing her performance, Giulio Gatti-Casazza, then the director of the Metropolitan Opera, invited her to meet with him to discuss a contract. She declined the offer, feeling herself not yet ready for opera, and continued her vocal studies in St. Louis. She finally made her operatic debut with the Met in the spring of 1937, appearing as Mary Rutledge in Walter Damrosch's new opera, *The Man Without A Country.* Through the years she became a major figure in the world of opera, succeeding Kirsten Flagstad in 1941 as the leading singer of German opera at the Met. In 1953 she and Sir Rudolph Bing, then the Met's general manager, clashed over her work in nightclubs and films and on radio. He argued that the opera star lost dignity by such appearances, while she contended that "dignity is something a person maintains, whatever her surroundings." The dispute prompted Miss Traubel to leave the Met that same year and go work with Groucho Marx, Jimmy Durante and other popular comedians. On July 29 of a heart attack in Santa Monica, Calif.

AUGUST

Sir Francis Chichester, 70, became famous when he made a 28,500-mile solo voyage around the world at the age of 65. A pioneer of both sea and air, he once wrote "The only way to live life to the full is to do something that depends on both the brain and on physical sense and action." The urge to break out of the confinement of British middle class life surfaced early. At 17, he dropped out of Marlborough College and set off for New Zealand, where he tried mining coal, tending a sheep station, lumberjacking, boxing, gold prospecting and writing. Finally he made his fortune in real estate and returned to England in 1929. Earning a pilot's license, he set out with only a few months' training in a plane for Australia. His single-engine monoplane, Gypsy Moth, completed 12,600 miles in 180.5 hours. He made other such flights, finally crashing in Japan and winding up an invalid for five years. In the 1950s he turned to yachting and in 1960 won a solo race across the Atlantic. But the big adventure of Chichester's life began on Aug. 23, 1966, when he set out on a solo world girdling voyage in his 53-foot ketch Gypsy Moth IV. In recognition of the feat Chichester was knighted by Queen Elizabeth II. He tried another Atlantic crossing in July 1972, but was forced to drop out because of ill health. On Aug. 26 in Plymouth.

William Thomas Grant, 96, founder of the W. T. Grant department store chain, was a high school dropout who became a multimillionaire. The saga began in 1906 when, as a buyer for the Almy, Bigelow and Washburn bargain store in Salem, Mass., Grant noticed that the fastest selling merchandise was priced at 25 cents. "Gradually the idea dawned on me that 25 cents was the magic price," he wrote in his 1954 autobiography. He opened his first 25-cent department store in Lynn, Mass., in 1906, with 15 saleswomen and $8,000 in capital—$7,000 of which belonged to his three partners. In its first year the store earned $10,000 on sales of $99,000, despite poor business conditions at the time. Grant maintained his 25-cent limit on merchandise at a time when his competitors' prices began at 50 cents; his profits rocketed along with his sales. By the end of World War I there were more than 30 stores throughout the United States, and the 25-cent ceiling on goods was raised to $1. A no-limit policy was adopted in 1946, a move that enabled the store chain to sell such merchandise as refrigerators and television sets. Grant was president of the company until 1924, when he stepped down to become chairman of the board. Upon his retirement at the age of 90, he said about the retailing business, "I've loved every minute of it." At the time of his death his chain store organization was among the largest retailing outfits in the United States, with 1,176 units in the 50 states, 60,000 employes, and registered sales of $1.2 billion. On Aug. 6 of heart disease, in Greenwich, Conn.

Oscar Levant, 65, the pianist and radio and television wit who won accolades for serious music, hit tunes and movie scores. At times he was so engulfed in admiration for his hero and friend, George Gershwin, that he did little but play Gershwin's music. Until his retirement in the early 1960s, Levant appeared frequently on television talk

"In some situations I was difficult," he once said, "in odd moments impossible, in rare moments loathesome, but, at my best, unapproachably great." Levant first met Gershwin in 1929 when he was asked to stand in as a pianist for a recording of *Rhapsody in Blue.* The two became fast friends, and Levant played little else but Gershwin music for years after the composer's death in 1937. In 1945 Levant was cast as himself in a movie of Gershwin's life, also entitled *Rhapsody in Blue.* He recorded the title piece and *Concerto in F* for the movie and served as advisor on his friend's career. In later years Levant became a favorite guest on late night talk-shows, where he discussed his problems in public. Happiness to him was "not something you experience, but something you remember." Marriage was "a triumph over hate." On Aug. 14 at his home in Beverly Hills.

Jules Romains, 86, celebrated French author, was best known for *Men of Good Will,* one of the longest, most intricately designed and majestic of modern novels. Its English version ran to 14 volumes, totaling 3 million words. Romains was also noted as a playwright, mainly for his satirical comedy, *Dr. Knock,* and for his philosophic poetry. Romains was elected to the Academie Francaise in 1946 and was president of P.E.N., the international writers' organization, from 1933 to 1939, but fellow writers found him cold and aloof. From 1909 until shortly after the end of World War I he taught philosophy, first in the provinces and then in Paris. He then dropped his university career to devote his time to literature and to travel. Some of his poetry was pure lyricism, but much of it voiced the belief that one spirit pervades all matter. Turning to the theater in 1923, Romains wrote a number of plays including *Dr. Knock,* a satire on medical quackery and human credulity. As he wrote for the theater, Romains was also sketching the architecture for labyrinthine *Men of Good Will,* which described in clinical detail a world sent reeling by World War I and creeping toward its doom in the second world conflict. On Aug. 14 in Paris.

Adm. Harold R. Stark, 91, was chief of U.S. naval operations when the Japanese attacked Pearl Harbor on Dec. 7, 1941. He was credited with pushing the United States into a stepped-up shipbuilding program before America entered World War II. Shortly after his appointment in 1939, Stark urged Congress to construct a "two oceans navy" to stand guard against a possible attack by Axis forces. In the spring of 1940 Stark suggested a 25 per cent boost in the size of the U.S. fleet to maintain a 5-3 superiority over Japan. By June of 1940 he was urging a 70 per cent increase in U.S. naval power and a few months later warned about the "possibility of simultaneous attacks in either or both oceans." He also believed the Navy should operate its own air arm. Stark, who graduated from the U.S. Naval Academy in 1903, was awarded the Distinguished Service Medal in World War I for taking a flotilla of old destroyers from the Philippines to fight German submarines in the Mediterranean. President Franklin D. Roosevelt passed over 59 naval officers who were senior to Stark to select him as chief of naval operations, a post he held until a reorganization in 1942. Stark then commanded U.S. naval forces in Europe and won his second DSC for preparing naval operations leading to the liberation of Europe. He retired in 1946. On Aug. 20 in Washington.

Prince William of Gloucester, 30, was a cousin of Britain's Queen Elizabeth II and ninth in line of succession to the throne. A pilot with more than 700 hours of experience, he took up flying while a student in the early 1960s. "Flying is my relaxation," he said. "I use my plane as far as possible as others use their motor cars. It is a safer, more relaxing way to travel." In early 1972 he became the first member of the royal family to fly in a balloon,

logging a one-hour trip. He was killed on Aug. 28 when his light plane crashed in an air race near Wolverhampton.

SEPTEMBER

William Boyd, 74, had ridden to stardom as Hopalong Cassidy, a "good guy" who roamed the range on his horse Topper for a quarter of a century in movies and on television. Boyd went to Hollywood as a young man and became a romantic idol of the 1920s, appearing in such films as *The Volga Boatman* and *King of Kings.* The good life came to a halt in 1932, when his career began to plunge downhill. Then, in 1935, he made the first Hopalong Cassidy movie. The movies were popular, and he quietly bought up all the television rights. The first Hoppy show appeared in 1948 and it quickly became clear that Boyd had hit the jackpot. He soon became the hero of American kids and founded a club called Hoppy's Troopers, which rivaled the Boy Scouts in membership. He donated money to children's hospitals and homes, saying: "The way I figure it, if it weren't for the kids, I'd be a bum today. They're the ones who've made my success possible. They're the ones who should benefit from it." He retired in 1953 after making 106 Hoppy shows and moved to Palm Desert, Calif. On Sept. 12 in South Laguna Beach, Calif.

Charles J. Correll, 82, played the role of Andy in the popular radio show *Amos 'n' Andy* for more than 30 years, from 1928 to 1960. He was the deep-voiced half of the team whose radio serial in Negro dialect swept to enormous popularity in the 1930s. Correll and Freeman Gosden, who played the role of Amos, rose from $100 a week in 1927 to $100,000 a year by 1931. At the peak of their fame, restaurants turned up their radios so that patrons could listen to the show. Motion pictures were cut in midreel so that audiences could hear the nightly episodes. The show was a situation comedy. Andy played a lazy personality who always set himself up as the brains of whatever organization he and Amos got involved in. Amos was a good-natured, earnest character who was easily taken in. When the show moved to television in the 1950s, the roles were taken over by other actors. But times had changed. There were complaints that such racially stereotyped characters were not in good taste and the series was finally dropped from the air waves. On Sept. 26 of a heart attack at Wesley Memorial Hospital in Chicago.

Rep. William F. Ryan, 50, was a founder of the Democratic Reform Movement in New York and a liberal hero for more than a decade. In a primary campaign this spring, he defeated Rep. Bella S. Abzug, whose district was reapportioned into Ryan's by the state legislature. His progressive position was said to have cost him influence in Congress but won him the admiration and loyalty of his constituents. He was the first Congressman to vote against funds for the war in Vietnam and was one of the war's first critics. He was assailed for advocating the admission of Communist China into the United Nations and some regarded him as radical for marching in civil rights demonstrations throughout the South. He established the reform movement in New York as a force to be reckoned with as he moved from the city's reform district leader to become its first reform congressman in 1960. In recent years his major project was the establishment of a Gateway National Urban Recreation Area. On Sept. 17 in New York.

Akim Tamiroff, 72, came to the United States in 1923 as a member of a Russian repertory company and decided not to return, opting instead for an acting career in this country. Starting on the nightclub circuit, Tamiroff moved to Broadway and then to Hollywood, where he was to play hundreds of roles in a film career of more than 35 years. Because of his strong Russian accent, he often was cast in mad-Russian parts, but he also played serious roles. Tamiroff twice was nominated for an academy award, once for his portrayal of a Chinese general in *The General Died at Dawn* and again as a guerrilla leader in *For Whom the Bell Tolls*. In Palm Springs, Calif., Sept. 17.

OCTOBER

Richard Crooks, 72, the tenor, was for many years a star of the Metropolitan Opera and for 14 years the featured singer on the "Voice of Firestone." Crooks was already an established singer with a worldwide reputation when the management of the Met announced in 1932 that he would be one of eight new singers in the forthcoming season. His first appearance at the Met was in February 1933 in the role of Des Grieux in *Manon*. He also established a career on radio appearing frequently on the air in the 1930s and 1940s. His repertory included popular Irish ballads and similar pieces, a fact that led many to underrate his artistry. His voice was noted for its combined sweetness and virility. On the opera stage his strength often came as a surprise to listeners who had heard him only on records or on the radio. On Oct. 1 at his home in Portola Valley, Calif.

Dr. Louis S. B. Leakey, 69, archeologist and anthropologist, won world-wide fame by tracing man's history back nearly two million years. With his anthropologist wife, Mary, he made the fossil discoveries in the 350-mile-long Olduvai Gorge, on the Serengeti Plain in Tanzania, which led to his conclusion that mankind was far older than prior research had determined. Dr. Leakey spent most of his life exploring East Africa's dust-laden expanses, working alone at first, later with his wife and ultimately with his three sons as well. His survivors included Mrs. Leakey, the sons and a daughter. With dental tools the group meticulously examined rock and sediment in support of his belief man's origin widely predated any prior estimation. This evidence was not found until 28 years after their quest had begun. The day of triumph was July 17, 1959. Dr. Leakey had awakened with a fever and had stayed in camp when the others resumed their work. A few hours later Mrs. Leakey rushed in to announce: "I've found him—found our man!" Leakey's fever vanished. He hurried to the cliff site, where he found two large teeth. Weeks of meticulous work with tiny picks, brushes and sieves produced 400 fragments which, put together, formed a human skull, about 1.75 million years old. The Leakeys called him Dear Boy. In January 1967 Leakey announced that paleontological evidence gathered over 18 years indicated "the family of man is more than 19 million years old," originating in western Kenya. Leakey died Oct. 1, in a London hospital.

Dr. Harlow Shapley, 86, decided as a college freshman to make astronomy his life work and went on to become one of the world's best-known astronomers. After taking his Ph.D. from Princeton, Shapley went to California's Mount Wilson Observatory to work as a staff astronomer. His research there enabled him to use a newly discovered yardstick of astronomical distances to show that the earth and the sun are nowhere near the center of the Milky Way Galaxy, as had been supposed. Later, as director of the Harvard College Observatory, Shapley directed the activities of as many as 25 big telescopes in Massachusetts, Colorado, New Mexico, Peru, South Africa and temporary stations. His accomplishments in astronomy were described by scientists as "of Copernican importance." In Boulder, Col., Oct. 20.

Igor I. Sikorsky, 83, famed aviation pioneer, developed the world's first practical helicopter. The craft was a spindly contraption of steel tubing, gears and drive belts topped by a single three-blade rotor and a two-blade rotor at its tail. Sikorsky tried out the primitive craft in September 1939, bringing to reality a dream he had had since he had been a boy in Imperial Russia. It was the prototype of more than 5,000 such aircraft, many highly sophisticated, that were turned out by Sikorsky's plant in Stratford, Conn., before his death. The helicopter was not Sikorsky's invention, but his VS-300 was the first practical one to be exploited and the first with the single overhead rotor. His two other major aviation achievements were the building of a multiple-engine plane and the creation of a flying boat. Born in Kiev, in the Ukraine, Sikorsky came to the United States in 1920 where he eked out a living giving lectures to Russian immigrants on astronomy and aviation. In 1923 he formed the Sikorsky Aero Engineering Corp. His first plane built at Roosevelt Field, Long Island, crash-landed in April 1924. But he pursued his goal to build an all-metal, twin-engine passenger plane. The dream came true in September 1924, when Sikorsky produced a 14-passenger, twin-engine plane with a cruising speed of 100 miles an hour. On Oct. 26 at his home in Easton, Conn.

NOVEMBER

Martin Dies Sr., 71, was a burly, blond, cigar-smoking Texan who spent more than two decades in Congress, seven of the years as the first chairman of the House Un-American Activities Committee. Dies first went to Congress in 1931 and the following year he introduced a bill which would have expelled alien Communists from the United States. The measure failed to clear the Senate, although winning House approval. He was named to head the Un-American Activities Committee in 1938 and eventually shifted its focus from investigating Nazi subversives to probing Communism. Dies often stirred controversy. President Franklin D. Roosevelt and many Cabinet members openly disapproved of his tactics. Roosevelt pictured the committee's investigations as "flagrantly unfair and un-American." During its early years the committee developed information that was instrumental in the indictment of American Communist Party Secretary Earl Browder on a passport evasion charge and the conviction of Fritz Kuhn on charges of stealing money from the German-American Nazi Bund. Dies retired from Congress in 1945, but returned to politics in 1952 when he won election as a congressman-at-large from Texas. He retired again six years later. In Lufkin, Tex., Nov. 14.

Rudolf Friml, 92, composed more than 3 operettas, among them "Rose Marie," "The Vagabond King," and "The Firefly." Most were hits, with the last of these, "The Three Musketeers," presented in 1928. Friml moved to Hollywood in the 1930s—when musical theater tastes began to change—where several of his operettas were made into films, most notably "The Firefly." Friml dropped largely from sight in the 1940s to live quietly in Hollywood. But in 1969 he emerged at a gala concert held by the American Society of Composers, Authors and Publishers to mark his 90th birthday. In Hollywood, Nov. 12.

Margaret Webster, 67, the daughter of actors Dame May Whitty and Ben Webster, began her long theatrical career with walk-on parts as a child, moved on to drama school, and then toured Britain with provincial repertory companies. After joining the Old Vic Company in 1929, she was given a chance to direct when not acting and she soon concentrated on this aspect of the theater. Her direction of "Richard II" on Broadway in 1937 was a success, and in the following years she directed a number of other Shakespeare plays. The late critic George Jean Mathan called her "the best director of the plays of Shakespeare that we have." Miss Webster also was a lecturer on the theater and the author of several books, among them "Shakespeare Today." In London, Nov. 13.

Jennie Grossinger, 80, was co-owner and hostess for almost 60 years of the 1,200 acre Grossinger's resort in the Catskill Mountains. The resort began when her father, Selig Grumet, purchased a farmhouse in the Catskills and took in boarders. It became Grossinger's resort in 1914, two years after she married Harry Grossinger. The resort grew over the years by acquiring adjacent farmland and by attracting a steady stream of vacationers. By the mid-1960s, it had 36 buildings and could house 1,400 guests at one time. It was a showcase for entertainers like Milton Berle, Abe Lyman and Eddie Fisher. She became sole owner of the resort after the death of her husband in 1964. At Grossinger's, Nov. 20.

Harry Richman, 77, was a Broadway song and dance man who, in his peak years, was one of the highest paid performers in show business. Richman began by playing the piano in a Cincinnati, Ohio, saloon at the age of 10 and then worked one night stands as he grew older. He caught on as a radio entertainer, then connected in the theater—appearing in a number of Broadway musicals—and in the movies. Richman attained superstar status in 1936 when he and Henry T. Merrill, a veteran pilot, flew over the Atlantic in a monoplane which carried 50,000 ping-pong balls to keep it afloat if it crashed in the water. The plane made it from New York to Wales in 18 hours and 38 minutes and was the 29th crossing achieved until that time. In Los Angeles, Nov. 3.

Marie Wilson, 56, the buxom and dumb blonde of the television series "My Friend Irma," projected this image early in her career. She did it so successfully that she rarely was without employment in films, radio, nightclubs or television from the early 1930s to the middle 1960s. Her film credits included "Boy Meets Girl," "Never Wave at a Wac," and "Rookies on Parade." In June 1942 when impressario Ken Murray started his "Blackouts" show, he hired Miss Wilson to do a satirical striptease act. She did the act for five lucrative years. She began her long association in "My Friend Irma" on radio in 1947, and the show moved to television where it survived until the middle of the 1950s. On Nov. 23 at her home in Hollywood.

DECEMBER

Jose Arcadia Limon, 64, danced and studied with the Humphrey-Wedeman Company from 1930 to 1940 and worked as a dancer and choreographer in a number of Broadway shows. Limon taught his specialty at the Juilliard Institute and a number of colleges and universities. Limon formed his own company after World War II and the group toured the United States and Canada, and performed in Paris and Mexico City. His later tours took in Central and South America, Australia, the Far East and Southeast Asia. Limon was honored by Dance Magazine in 1950 for outstanding achievement in modern dance choreography. Clive Barnes, The New York Times critic, described him as "one of the giants of modern dance." At Flemington, N.J., Dec. 2.

Louella Parsons, 91, was a powerful figure in the motion picture industry for 40 years and reigned as queen of movie gossip columnists during Hollywood's golden years. Miss Parsons started with the old New York American in 1922 but became ill and went to California to recuperate. Upon returning to work a year later, she was told to remain in Hollywood and her column was syndicated. The column dealt with Hollywood's marriages, divorces, births and other movie news and was said to have had 20 million readers. During her years as arbiter of movieland society, Miss Parsons demanded from the principals themselves first tips about the stars' affairs. She gave up the column in 1969 when she was confined to a rest home. At Santa Monica, Calif., Dec. 9.

Chakravarti Rajagopalachari, governor general of India from 1948–50, was one of the foremost leaders in the nation's struggle for independence. Known publicly as Rajaji, he joined Mohandas K. Gandhi in the anti-British movement in 1919. An ardent supporter of the passive resistance approach, he was jailed five times in the years leading to independence. He split temporarily with the Congress party of Gandhi and Jawaharlal Nehru in 1942, saying it took unfair advantage with Britain's preoccupation with World War II. In 1959, he left the Congress party for good and formed his own Swatantra party which called for more free enterprise and less state control. In 1971 he formed a coalition which unsuccessfully opposed Prime Minister Indira Gandhi. He said he did not know his precise birth date, but it was generally assumed to be Dec. 8, 1878. On Dec. 25, in Madras.

Andrei N. Tupolev, 84, one of the world's leading aircraft designers, was identified with some of the Soviet Union's best-known military and civilian planes. In his half a century with the Soviet aviation industry, Tupolev and associates designed about 120 types of planes, including mainly heavy-duty, range aircraft like the TU104, a turbo-jet passenger plane, and the TU114, a turboprop airliner. Tupolev was regarded as a pioneer in the construction of all-metal planes which he first designed at the start of his career in the 1920s. In 1934, he built a huge, eight-engine plane with a wing span of 207 feet and weighing 40 tons. The plane flew, but crashed in May 1935 in an accident blamed on an accompanying fighter plane. One of the latest products of the Tupolev team was the supersonic TU144 scheduled to go into service in 1975. With the British-French Concorde, it was expected to dominate the world's supersonic market. On Dec. 23, in Moscow.

Mark Van Doren, 78, was a critic, teacher and Pulitzer prize-winning poet, taking that honor in 1939 with his *Collected Poems.* A prolific writer, Van Doren wrote more than 50 books of fiction, nonfiction and poetry, as well as a play, *The Last Days of Lincoln.* He taught English at Columbia University for 39 years before his retirement in 1959 and, according to one national magazine, became "a living legend" at the university and "one of the greatest teachers in Columbia's history," according to another. In his years of teaching, Van Doren saw literary success come to a number of his students. Among them were Thomas Merton, Clifton Fadiman, Mortimer Adler, Jacques Barzun and Lionel Trilling. At Torrington, Conn., Dec. 10.

PRIZES—AWARDS

PULITZER PRIZES

Meritorious Public Service in Journalism—The New York Times for "The Pentagon Papers." National Reporting—Jack Anderson for Exposes of Financial Affairs of Sen. Thomas J. Dodd of Conn.

General Local Reporting—Richard I. Cooper and John Machacek for coverage of Attica Prison Riots.

Special Local Reporting—Timothy Leland, Gerard M. O'Neill, Stephen A. Kurkjian and Ann De Santis for exposure of corruption in Somerville, Mass.

International Reporting—Peter R. Kann for coverage of the India-Pakistan War.

Editorial Writing—John Strohmeyer for an editorial campaign to reduce racial tensions in a situation of hostility encountered by Puerto Ricans amid charges of police brutality.

Editorial Cartooning—Jeffery K. MacNelly.

Spot News Photography—Horst Faas and Michel Laurent, for picture series on "Death in Dacca."

Feature Photography—Dave Kennerly for dramatic photos of Vietnam war.

Commentary—Mike Royko.

Criticism—Frank Peters Jr.

General nonfiction—Barbara W. Tuchman for "Stilwell and the American Experience in China, 1911-1945.

Biography—Joseph P. Lash for "Eleanor and Franklin."

Fiction—Wallace Stegner for "Angle of Repose."

History—Carl N. Degler for "Neither Black nor White."

Poetry—James Wright for "Collected Poems."

Music—Jacob Druckman for "Windows."

OSCARS

Best Actor—Gene Hackman in "The French Connection."

Best actress—Jane Fonda in "Klute."

Best movie—"The French Connection."

Best supporting performers—Ben Johnson in "The Last Picture Show," Cloris Leachman in "The Last Picture Show."

Best director—William Friedkin for "The French Connection."

Best song—Theme from "Shaft."

Best foreign-language film—"The Garden of the Finzi Continis."

Art direction—"Nicholas and Alexandra," John Box, Ernest Archer, Jack Maxsted and Gil Parrondo; set decoration, Vernon Dixon, "Nicholas and Alexandra."

Cinematography—"Fiddler on the Roof," Oswald Morris.

Costume Design—"Nicholas and Alexandra," Yvonne Blake and Antonio Castillo.

Film editing—"The French Connection," Jerry Greenberg.

Sound—"Fiddler on the Roof," Gordon K. McCallum and David Hildyard.

Best original song score—"Fiddler on the Roof," Adapted by John Williams.

Special visual effects—"Bedknobs and Broomsticks," Danny Lee, Eustace Lycett and Alan Maley.

Screen play based on material from another medium—"The French Connection," Ernest Tidyman.

Documentary short—"Sentinels of Silence."

Feature documentary—"The Hellstrom Chronicle."

Original dramatic score—Michel Legrand, "Summer of '42."

Story and screenplay, original—Paddy Chayefsky, "The Hospital."

NATIONAL BOOK AWARDS

Fiction—Flannery O'Connor for "Flannery O'Connor: The Complete Stories."

Biography—Joseph P. Lash For "Eleanor and Franklin."

History—Allan Nevins for "Ordeal of the Union Series."

Contemporary Affairs—Stewart Brand for "The Last Whole Earth Catalog: Access to Tools."

Arts and Letters—Charles Rosen for "The Classical Style: Haydn, Mozart, Beethoven."

Children's Book—Donald Barthelme for "The Slightly Irregular Fire Engine or The Hithering Thithering Djinn."

Philosophy and Religion—Martin E. Marty for "Righteous Empire: The Protestant Experience in America."

Science—George L. Small for "The Blue Whale."

Poetry—Howard Moss for "Selected Poems."

Translation—Austryn Wainhouse for his translation from the French of Jacques Monod's "Chance and Necessity: An Essay on the Natural Philosophy of Modern Biology."

NOBEL PRIZES

Peace—No award for 1972.

Literature—Heinrich Boell—W. Germany—for aiding postwar revival of German literature.

Physiology and Medicine—Dr. Gerald M. Edehlmen, USA, and Dr. Rodney R. Porter, Great Britain, for research on the chemical structure of antibodies.

Physics—Dr. John Bardeen—Dr. Leon N. Cooper, and Dr. John R. Schrieffer all USA, for research on super conductivity in ultra-cold metals.

Chemistry—Dr. Christian B. Anfinsen, Dr. Stanford Moore and Dr. William H. Stein all USA for research on ribonuclease.

Economics—Prof. John R. Hicks, Great Britain, and Prof. Kenneth J. Arrow, USA, for contribution of general economic equilibrium theory and welfare theory.

TONY AWARDS

Best Dramatic Play: "Sticks & Bones."

Best Musical Play: "Two Gentlemen of Verona."

Best Actor (Dramatic Play): Cliff Gorman—"Lenny."

Best Actress (Dramatic Play): Sada Thompson—"Twigs."

Best Actor (Musical): Phil Silvers—"A Funny Thing Happened on the Way to the Forum."

Best Actress (Musical): Alexis Smith—"Follies."

Best Actor (Dramatic Play, Featured or Supporting): Vincent Gardenia—"The Prisoner of Second Avenue."

Best Actress (Dramatic Play, Featured or Supporting): Elizabeth Wilson—"Sticks & Bones."

Best Actor (Musical Play, Featured or Supporting): Larry Blyden—"A Funny Thing Happened on the Way to the Forum."

Best Actress (Musical Play, Featured or Supporting): Linda Hopkins—"Inner City."

Best Director (Dramatic Play): Mike Nichols—"The Prisoner of Second Avenue."

Best Director (Musical Play): Harold Prince & Michael Bennett—"Follies."

Best Score: Stephen Sondheim—"Follies."

Best Book: John Guare & Mel Shapiro—"Two Gentlemen of Verona."

Best Scenic Designer: Boris Aronson—"Follies."

Best Costume Designer: Florence Klotz—"Follies."

Best Lighting Designer: Tharon Musser—"Follies."

Best Choreographer: Michael Bennett—"Follies."

Special Awards: Ethel Merman & Richard Rodgers.

THE COLLIER TROPHY

Col. David R. Scott
Lieut. Col. James B. Irwin
Maj. Alfred M. Worden
Dr. Robert R. Gilruth

NATIONAL ACADEMY OF RECORDING ARTS & SCIENCES (GRAMMYS)

Record of the Year: (Grammys to the Artist and A & R Producer) "It's Too Late"—Carole King. A & R Producer: Lou Adler (Ode).

Album of the Year: (Grammys to the Artist and A & R Producer) "Tapestry"—Carole King. A & R Producer: Lou Adler (Ode).

Song of the Year: (A Songwriter's Award) "You've Got A Friend". Songwriter: Carole King.

Best New Artist of the Year: Carly Simon (Elektra).

Best Instrumental Arrangement: (An Arranger's Award) "Theme from Shaft"—Isaac Hayes. Arrangers: Isaac Hayes and Johnny Allen (Enterprise).

Best Arrangement Accompanying Vocalist(s): (An Arranger's Award) "Uncle Albert/Admiral Halsey"—Paul & Linda McCartney. Arranger: Paul McCartney (Apple).

Best Engineered Recording: (Other than Classical) (An Engineer's Award) "Theme From Shaft"—Isaac Hayes. Engineer: Dave Purple (Enterprise).

Best Album Cover: (Awards to the Art Director, Photographer and/or Graphic Artist) "Pollution"—Pollution. Album Design: Dean O. Torrance/Kittyhawk. Art Direction & Photographer: Gene Brownell (Prophesy).

Best Album Notes: (Non-Classical Albums) (An Annotator's Award) "Sam, Hard and Heavy"—Sam Samudio. Annotator: Sam Samudio (Atlantic).

Best Pop Vocal Performance, Female: "Tapestry"—Carole King (Album) (Ode).

Best Pop Vocal Performance, Male: "You've Got A Friend"—James Taylor. (Single) (Warner Bros.).

Best Pop Vocal Performance by a Duo, Group or Chorus: "Carpenters" —Carpenters (A & M).

Best Pop Instrumental Performance: "Smackwater Jack"—Quincy Jones.

(Album) (A & M).

Best Rhythm & Blues Vocal Performance, Female: "Bridge Over Troubled Water"—Aretha Franklin (Single) (Atlantic).

Best Rhythm & Blues Vocal Performance, Male: "A Natural Man"— Lou Rawls (MGM).

Best Rhythm & Blues Vocal Performance by a Duo or Group, Vocal or Instrumental: "Proud Mary"— Ike and Tina Turner (United Artists).

Best Rhythm & Blues Song: (A Songwriter's Award) "Ain't No Sunshine". Songwriter; Bill Withers.

Best Soul Gospel Performance: "Put Your Hand In The Hand Of The Man From Galilee"—Shirley Caesar (Hob).

Best Country Vocal Performance, Female: "Help Me Make It Through The Night"—Sammi Smith (Mega).

Best Country Vocal Performance, Male: "When You're Hot, You're Hot"—Jerry Reed (RCA).

Best Country Vocal Performance by a Duo or Group: "After The Fire Is Gone"—Conway Twitty and Loretta Lynn (Decca).

Best Country Instrumental Performance: "Snowbird"—Chet Atkins (Single) (RCA).

Best Country Song (A Songwriter's Award) "Help Me Make It Through The Night". Songwriter: Kris Kristofferson.

Best Sacred Performance: (Musical) (Non-Classical) "Did You Think To Pray"—Charley Pride (RCA).

Best Gospel Performance (Other Than Soul Gospel): "Let Me Live" —Charley Pride (Single) (RCA).

Best Ethnic or Traditional Recording (Including Traditional Blues):

"They Call Me Muddy Waters"— Muddy Waters. (Album) (Chess).

Best Instrumental Composition: "Theme From Summer Of '42". Composer: Michel Legrand (Warner Bros.).

Best Original Score Written for a Motion Picture or a Television Special: (A Composer's Award) "Shaft". Composer: Isaac Hayes (MGM).

Best Score from an Original Cast Show Album: (Grammys to the Composer and A & R Producer) "Godspell". Composer: Stephen Schwartz. A & R Producer: Stephen Schwartz (Bell).

Best Recording for Children: "Bill Cosby Talks To Kids About Drugs"—Bill Cosby (Uni).

Best Comedy Recording: "This Is A Recording"—Lily Tomlin (Polydor).

Best Spoken Word Recording: "Desiderata"—Les Crane (Warner Bros.).

Best Jazz Performance by a Soloist: "The Bill Evans Album"—Bill Evans (Columbia).

Best Jazz Performance by a Group: "The Bill Evans Album"—Bill Evans Trio (Columbia).

Best Jazz Performance by a Big Band: "New Orleans Suite"—Duke Ellington (Atlantic).

Album of the Year, Classical: (Grammys to the Artist and A & R Producer). Horowitz Plays Rachmaninoff. (Etudes-Tableaux, Piano Music, Sonatas)—Vladimir Horowitz. A & R Producer: Richard Killough (Columbia).

Best Classical Performance—Orchestra: (A Conductor's Award) Mahler: "Sym. No. 1 in D Major". Carlo Maria Giulini conducting the Chicago

Symphony Orchestra (Angel).

Best Classical Performance—Instrumental Soloist or Soloists (with Orchestra): "Villa-Lobos: Concerto For Guitar"—Julian Bream (RCA).

Best Classical Performance—Instrumental Soloist or Soloists (without Orchestra): Horowitz Plays Rachmaninoff (Etudes-Tableaux, Piano Music, Sonatas)—Vladimir Horowitz (Columbia).

Best Chamber Music Performance: Debussy: "Quartet In G Min/Ravel: Quartet In F Major"—Juilliard Quartet (Columbia).

Best Opera Recording: (Grammys to the Conductor and A & R Producer) Verdi: "Aida". Erich Leinsdorf—conducting the London Symphony Orchestra. A & R Producer: Richard Mohr (RCA).

Best Classical Vocal Soloist Performance: Leontyne Price Sings Robert Schumann. Leontyne Price (RCA).

Best Choral Performance, Classical (other than Opera): (Grammys to the Conductor and Choral Director) Berlioz: "Requiem". Colin Davis conducting the London Symphony Orchestra. Russell Burgess conducting the Wandsworth School Boys Choir. Arthur Oldham conducting the London Symphony Chorus (Phillips).

Best Engineered Recording, Classical: (An Engineer's Award) Berlioz: "Requiem". Colin Davis conducting the London Symphony Orchestra. Russell Burgess conducting the Wandsworth School Boys Choir. Arthur Oldham conducting the London Symphony Chorus. Engineer: Vittorio Negri (Phillips).

UNITED STATES GOVERNMENT
EXECUTIVE DEPARTMENT

President: Richard M. Nixon
Vice President: Spiro T. Agnew

WHITE HOUSE STAFF

Counsellors to the President:
Robert H. Finch
Donald Rumsfeld

Assistants to the President:
John D. Ehrlichman—for Domestic Affairs
Peter M. Flanigan
H. R. Haldeman
Dr. Henry A. Kissinger—for National Security Affairs
William E. Timmons—for Congressional Relations

Science Adviser to the President:
Edward E. David, Jr.

Special Consultants to the President
Arthur S. Flemming—on Aging
Leonard Garment
Dr. Jerome H. Jaffe—for Narcotics and Dangerous Drugs
William M. Magruder
John A. Scali

Advisor to the President:
Gen. Lewis B. Hershey, USA—on Manpower Mobilization

Director of Communications:
Herbert G. Klein—for the Executive Branch

Press Secretary to the President:
Ronald L. Ziegler

Military Assistant to the President:
Brig. Gen. Brent Scowcroft, USAF

Deputy Assistants to the President:
Alexander P. Butterfield
Dwight L. Chapin

Special Counsels to the President:
Charles W. Colson
Harry S. Dent
Richard A. Moore

Counsel to the President:
John Wesley Dean III

Personal Secretary to the President:
Rose Mary Woods

Special Assistants to the President:
Desmond J. Barker, Jr.
George T. Bell
Patrick J. Buchanan
Michael J. Farrell
Max L. Friedersdorf
William L. Gifford
Mark I. Goode
Wallace H. Johnson
Daniel T. Kingsley
Virginia H. Knauer—for Consumer Affairs
Raymond K. Price, Jr.
Jonathan C. Rose
William L. Safire
Robert L. Schulz—for Liaison with Former Presidents
Ronald H. Walker

Deputy Press Secretaries:
Neal Ball
Gerald L. Warren

Deputy Assistants to the President:
Maj. Gen. Alexander Meigs Haig, Jr.,
USA—for National Security Affairs
Richard K. Cook—for Congressional
Relations
Tom C. Korologos—for Congressional
Relations
John C. Whitaker
Henry C. Cashen II

Deputy Director of Communications:
Ken W. Clawson—for the Executive Branch

Staff Director for Mrs. Nixon:
Constance Stuart

Social Secretary:
Lucy Alexander Winchester

Physician to the President:
Maj. Gen. Walter R. Tkach, USAF, MC

Chief Executive Clerk:
Noble M. Melencamp

Chief Usher:
Rex W. Scouten

EXECUTIVE OFFICES

Office of Management and Budget
Caspar W. Weinberger, *director*

Council of Economic Advisers
Herbert Stein, *chairman*

Central Intelligence Agency
Richard Helms, *director*

Domestic Council
John D. Ehrlichman, *executive director*

National Aeronautics and Space Council
Spiro T. Agnew, *chairman*

Office of Economic Opportunity
Phillip V. Sanchez, *director*

Office of Emergency Preparedness
George A. Lincoln, *director*

Office of Science and Technology
Edward E. David, Jr., *director*

Special Representative for Trade Negotiations
William D. Eberle

Office of Intergovernmental Relations
Spiro T. Agnew

Council on Environmental Quality
Russell E. Train, *chairman*

Office of Telecommunications Policy
Clay T. Whitehead, *director*

Office of Consumer Affairs
Virginia H. Knauer, *director*

Special Action Office for Drug Abuse Prevention
Dr. Jerome H. Jaffe, *director*

Council on International Economic Policy
Peter G. Peterson, *executive director*

CABINET

Department of State
SECRETARY
William P. Rogers

DEPUTY SECRETARY
John N. Irwin, II

MISSION TO THE UNITED NATIONS
George W. Bush, *ambassador*

ACTION CORPS
Joseph H. Blatchford, *director*

AGENCY FOR INTERNATIONAL DEVELOPMENT
Dr. John A. Hannah, *administrator*

Department of the Treasury
SECRETARY
George P. Shultz

UNDER SECRETARY
Edwin S. Cohen

UNDER SECRETARY FOR MONETARY AFFAIRS
Paul A. Volcker

INTERNAL REVENUE SERVICE
Johnnie M. Walters, *commissioner*

BUREAU OF CUSTOMS
Vernon D. Acree, *commissioner*

SECRET SERVICE
James J. Rowley, *director*

TREASURER OF THE UNITED STATES
Romana A. Banuelos

Department of Defense
SECRETARY
Melvin R. Laird

DEPUTY SECRETARY
Kenneth Rush

JOINT CHIEFS OF STAFF
Adm. Thomas H. Moorer, *chairman*
Gen. Creighton W. Abrams, *chief of staff, U.S. Army*
Adm. Elmo R. Zumwalt, Jr., *chief of Naval Operations*
Gen. R. E. Cushman, Jr., *commandant, Marine Corps*

DEPARTMENT OF THE ARMY
Robert F. Froehlke, secretary

DEPARTMENT OF THE NAVY
John W. Warner, *secretary*

DEPARTMENT OF THE AIR FORCE
Dr. Robert C. Seamans Jr., *secretary*

Department of Justice
ATTORNEY GENERAL
Richard G. Kleindienst

DEPUTY ATTORNEY GENERAL
Ralph E. Erickson

SOLICITOR GENERAL
Erwin N. Griswold

BUREAU OF NARCOTICS AND DANGEROUS DRUGS
John E. Ingersoll, *director*

FEDERAL BUREAU OF INVESTIGATION
J. Edgar Hoover, (Died May 2, 1972) *director*
L. Patrick Grey, *acting director*

U.S. Postal Service
POSTMASTER GENERAL
Elmer Theodore Klassen

DEPUTY POSTMASTER GENERAL
Merrill A. Hayden, resigned Aug. 1, 1972

Department of the Interior
SECRETARY
Rogers C. B. Morton

UNDER SECRETARY
Dr. William T. Pecora

Department of Agriculture
SECRETARY
Earl L. Butz

UNDER SECRETARY
J. Phil Campbell

Department of Commerce
SECRETARY
Maurice H. Stans, resigned Jan. 27, 1972
Peter G. Peterson

UNDER SECRETARY
James T. Lynn

BUREAU OF CENSUS
George H. Brown, *director*

Department of Labor
SECRETARY
James D. Hodgson

UNDER SECRETARY
Laurence H. Silberman

Department of Health, Education and Welfare
SECRETARY
Eliot L. Richardson

UNDER SECRETARY
John G. Veneman

PUBLIC HEALTH SERVICE
Dr. Jesse L. Steinfeld, *surgeon general*

SOCIAL SECURITY ADMINISTRATION
Robert M. Ball, *commissioner*

OFFICE OF EDUCATION
Dr. Sidney P. Marland, Jr.

FOOD AND DRUG ADMINISTRATION
Dr. Charles C. Edwards

Department of Housing and Urban Affairs
SECRETARY
George W. Romney

UNDER SECRETARY
Richard C. Van Dusen

Department of Transportation
SECRETARY
John A. Volpe

UNDER SECRETARY
James M. Beggs

FEDERAL AVIATION ADMINISTRATION
John H. Shaffer, *administrator*

NATIONAL TRANSPORTATION SAFETY BOARD
John H. Reed, *chairman*

UNITED STATES COAST GUARD
Adm. Chester R. Bender, *commandant*

MAJOR INDEPENDENT AGENCIES

ATOMIC ENERGY COMMISSION
James R. Schlesinger, *chairman*

FEDERAL RESERVE SYSTEM
Arthur S. Burns, *chairman*

CIVIL AERONAUTICS BOARD
Secor D. Browne, *chairman*

CIVIL SERVICE COMMISSION
Robert E. Hampton, *chairman*

FEDERAL COMMUNICATIONS COMMISSION
Dean Burch, *chairman*

FEDERAL POWER COMMISSION
John N. Nassikas, *chairman*

FEDERAL TRADE COMMISSION
Miles W. Kirkpatrick, *chairman*

GENERAL SERVICES ADMINISTRATION
Arthur F. Sampson, *acting administrator*

INTERSTATE COMMERCE COMMISSION
George M. Stafford, *chairman*

NATIONAL LABOR RELATIONS BOARD
Edward B. Miller, *chairman*

SECURITIES AND EXCHANGE COMMISSION
William J. Casey, *chairman*

SELECTIVE SERVICE SYSTEM
Byron V. Pepitone, *acting director*

NATIONAL AERONAUTICS AND SPACE
ADMINISTRATION
James C. Fletcher, *administrator*

SMALL BUSINESS ADMINISTRATION
Thomas S. Kleppe, *administrator*

UNITED STATES INFORMATION AGENCY
Frank J. Shakespeare, Jr., *director*

VETERANS ADMINISTRATION
Donald E. Johnson, *administrator*

ENVIRONMENTAL PROTECTION AGENCY
William D. Ruckelshaus, *administrator*

LEGISLATIVE

92nd Congress
Second Session

SENATE

PRESIDENT PRO TEMPORE: Allen J. Ellender (D.-La.)
Died July 27, 1972
James O. Eastland (D.-Miss.)
MAJORITY LEADER: Mike Mansfield (D.-Mont.)
MAJORITY WHIP: Robert C. Byrd (D.-W.Va.)
MINORITY LEADER: Hugh Scott (R.-Pa.)
MINORITY WHIP: Robert P. Griffin (R.-Mich.)
CHAPLAIN: Rev. Edward L. R. Elson

HOUSE OF REPRESENTATIVES

SPEAKER: Carl B. Albert (D.-Okla.)
MAJORITY LEADER: Hale Boggs (D.-La.)
MAJORITY WHIP: Thomas P. O'Neill (D.-Mass.)
MINORITY LEADER: Gerald R. Ford (R.-Mich.)
MINORITY WHIP: Leslie C. Arends (R.-Ill.)
CHAPLAIN: Rev. Edward G. Latch

STATE DELEGATIONS

Number which precedes name of Representative designates congressional district.

ALABAMA

Senators

John J. Sparkman   D   James B. Allen   D

Representatives

1. Jack Edwards   R
2. William L. Dickinson   R
3. George Andrews[1]   D
4. William Nichols   D
5. Walter Flowers   D
6. John Buchanan   R
7. Tom Bevill   D
8. Robert E. Jones   D

ALASKA

Senators

Ted Stevens   R   Mike Gravel   D

Representative
At large—Nick Begich[2]   D

ARIZONA

Senators

Paul J. Fannin   R   Barry Goldwater   R

Representatives

1. John J. Rhodes   R   2. Morris K. Udall   D
3. Sam Steiger   R

ARKANSAS

Senators

John L. McClellan   D   J. W. Fulbright   D

Representatives

1. Bill Alexander   D
2. Wilbur D. Mills   D
3. John P. Hammerschmidt   R
4. David H. Pryor   D

CALIFORNIA

Senators

Alan Cranston   D   John V. Tunney   D

Representatives

1. Don H. Clausen   R
2. Harold T. Johnson   D
3. John E. Moss   D
4. Robert L. Leggett   D
5. Phillip Burton   D
6. William S. Mailliard   R
7. Ronald V. Dellums   D
8. George P. Miller   D
9. Don Edwards   D
10. Charles S. Gubser   R
11. Paul N. (Pete) McCloskey, Jr.   R
12. Burt L. Talcott   R
13. Charles M. Teague   R
14. Jerome R. Waldie   D
15. John J. McFall   D
16. B. F. Sisk   D
17. Glenn M. Anderson   D
18. Robert B. (Bob) Mathias   R
19. Chet Holifield   D
20. H. Allen Smith   R
21. Augustus F. Hawkins   D
22. James C. Corman   D
23. Del Clawson   R
24. John H. Rousselot   R
25. Charles E. Wiggins   R
26. Thomas M. Rees   D
27. Barry Goldwater, Jr.   R
28. Alphonzo Bell   R
29. George E. Danielson   D
30. Edward R. Roybal   D
31. Charles H. Wilson   D
32. Craig Hosmer   R
33. Jerry L. Pettis   R
34. Richard T. Hanna   D
35. John G. Schmitz   R
36. Bob Wilson   R
37. Lionel Van Deerlin   D
38. Victor V. Veysey   R

COLORADO

Senators

Gordon Allott   R   Peter H. Dominick   R

Representatives

1. James D. (Mike) McKevitt   R
2. Donald G. Brotzman   R
3. Frank E. Evans   D
4. Wayne N. Aspinall   D

CONNECTICUT

Senators

Abraham A. Ribicoff   D   Lowell P. Weicker, Jr.   R

Representatives

1. William R. Cotter   D
2. Robert H. Steele   R
3. Robert N. Giaimo   D
4. Stewart B. McKinney   R
5. John S. Monagan   D
6. Ella T. Grasso   D

DELAWARE

Senators

J. Caleb Boggs   R   William V. Roth, Jr.   R

Representative

At large—Pierre S. du Pont 4th   R

FLORIDA

Senators

Edward J. Gurney   R   Lawton Chiles   D

Representatives

1. Robert L. F. Sikes   D
2. Don Fuqua   D
3. Charles E. Bennett   D
4. Bill Chappell, Jr.   D
5. Louis Frey, Jr.   R
6. Sam M. Gibbons   D
7. James A. Haley   D
8. C. W. Bill Young   R
9. Paul G. Rogers   D
10. J. Herbert Burke   R
11. Claude Pepper   D
12. Dante B. Fascell   D

GEORGIA

Senators

Herman E. Talmadge   D   David H. Gambrell[3]   D

Representatives

1. G. Elliott Hagan   D
2. Dawson Mathis   D
3. Jack Brinkley   D
4. Ben B. Blackburn   R
5. Fletcher Thompson   R
6. John J. Flynt, Jr.   D
7. John W. Davis   D
8. W. S. (Bill) Stuckey, Jr.   D
9. Phil M. Landrum   D
10. Robert G. Stephens, Jr.   D

HAWAII

Senators

Hiram L. Fong   R   Daniel K. Inouye   D

Representatives

1. Spark M. Matsunaga   D
2. Patsy T. Mink   D

IDAHO

Senators

Frank Church   D   Len B. Jordan   R

Representatives

1. James A. McClure   R
2. Orval Hansen   R

ILLINOIS

Senators

Charles H. Percy   R   Adlai E. Stevenson 3d   D

Representatives

1. Ralph H. Metcalfe   D
2. Abner J. Mikva   D
3. Morgan F. Murphy   D
4. Edward J. Derwinski   R
5. John C. Kluczynski   D
6. George W. Collins   D
7. Frank Annunzio   D
8. Dan Rostenkowski   D
9. Sidney R. Yates   D
10. Harold R. Collier   R
11. Roman C. Pucinski   D
12. Robert McClory   R
13. Philip M. Crane   R
14. John N. Erlenborn   R
15. [Vacant][4]
16. John B. Anderson   R
17. Leslie C. Arends   R
18. Robert H. Michel   R
19. Thomas F. Railsback   R
20. Paul Findley   R
21. Kenneth J. Gray   D
22. William L. Springer   R
23. George E. Shipley   D
24. Melvin Price   D

INDIANA

Senators

Vance Hartke   D   Birch Bayh   D

Representatives

1. Ray J. Madden   D
2. Earl F. Landgrebe   R
3. John Brademas   D
4. J. Edward Roush   D
5. Elwood Hillis   R
6. William G. Bray   R
7. John T. Myers   R
8. Roger H. Zion   R
9. Lee H. Hamilton   D
10. David W. Dennis   R
11. Andrew Jacobs, Jr.   D

IOWA

Senators

Jack Miller   R   Harold E. Hughes   D

Representatives

1. Fred Schwengel   R
2. John C. Culver   D
3. H. R. Gross   R
4. John H. Kyl   R
5. Neal Smith   D
6. Wiley Mayne   R
7. William J. Scherle   R

KANSAS

Senators

James B. Pearson   R   Bob Dole   R

Representatives

1. Keith G. Sebelius   R
2. William R. Roy   D
3. Larry Winn, Jr.   R
4. Garner E. Shriver   R
5. Joe Skubitz   R

KENTUCKY

Senators

John Sherman Cooper   R   Marlow W. Cook   R

Representatives

1. Frank A. Stubblefield   D
2. William H. Natcher   D
3. Romano L. Mazzoli   D
4. M. G. (Gene) Snyder   R
5. Tim Lee Carter   R
6. William P. Curlin, Jr.   D
7. Carl D. Perkins   D

LOUISIANA

Senators

Allen J. Ellender[5]   D   Russell B. Long   D

Representatives

1. F. Edward Hébert   D
2. Hale Boggs[6]   D
3. Patrick T. Caffery   D
4. Joe D. Waggonner, Jr.   D
5. Otto E. Passman   D
6. John R. Rarick   D
7. Edwin W. Edwards[7]   D
8. Speedy O. Long   D

MAINE

Senators

Margaret Chase Smith   R   Edmund S. Muskie   D

Representatives

1. Peter N. Kyros   D
2. William D. Hathaway   D

MARYLAND

Senators

Charles McC. Mathias, Jr.   R   J. Glenn Beall, Jr.   R

Representatives

1. William O. Mills   R
2. Clarence D. Long   D
3. Edward A. Garmatz   D
4. Paul S. Sarbanes   D
5. Lawrence J. Hogan   R
6. Goodloe E. Byron   D
7. Parren J. Mitchell   D
8. Gilbert Gude   R

MASSACHUSETTS

Senators

Edward M. Kennedy   D   Edward W. Brooke   R

Representatives

1. Silvio O. Conte   R
2. Edward P. Boland   D
3. Robert F. Drinan   D
4. Harold D. Donohue   D
5. F. Bradford Morse[8]   R
6. Michael J. Harrington   D
7. Torbert H. Macdonald   D
8. Thomas P. O'Neill, Jr.   D
9. Louise Day Hicks   D
10. Margaret M. Heckler   R
11. James A. Burke   D
12. Hastings Keith   R

MICHIGAN

Philip A. Hart   D   Robert P. Griffin   R

Representatives

1. John Conyers, Jr.   D
2. Marvin L. Esch   R
3. Garry E. Brown   R
4. Edward Hutchinson   R
5. Gerald R. Ford   R
6. Charles E. Chamberlain   R
7. Donald W. Riegle, Jr.   R
8. James Harvey   R
9. Guy Vander Jagt   R
10. Elford A. Cederberg   R
11. Philip E. Ruppe   R
12. James G. O'Hara   D
13. Charles C. Diggs, Jr.   D
14. Lucien N. Nedzi   D
15. William D. Ford   D
16. John D. Dingell   D
17. Martha W. Griffiths   D
18. William S. Broomfield   R
19. Jack H. McDonald   R

MINNESOTA

Senators

Walter F. Mondale   D   Hubert H. Humphrey   D

Representatives

1. Albert H. Quie   R
2. Ancher Nelsen   R
3. Bill Frenzel   R
4. Joseph E. Karth   D
5. Donald M. Fraser   D
6. John M. Zwach   R
7. Bob Bergland   D
8. John A. Blatnik   D

MISSISSIPPI

Senators

James O. Eastland   D   John C. Stennis   D

Representatives

1. Thomas G. Abernethy   D
2. Jamie L. Whitten   D
3. Charles H. Griffin   D
4. G. V. (Sonny) Montgomery   D
5. William M. Colmer   D

MISSOURI

Senators

Stuart Symington   D   Thomas F. Eagleton   D

Representatives

1. William (Bill) Clay   D
2. James W. Symington   D
3. Leonor K. (Mrs. John B.) Sullivan   D
4. Wm. J. Randall   D
5. Richard Bolling   D
6. W. R. Hull, Jr.   D
7. Durward G. Hall   R
8. Richard H. Ichord   D
9. William L. Hungate   D
10. Bill D. Burlison   D

MONTANA

Senators

Mike Mansfield   D   Lee Metcalf   D

Representatives

1. Richard G. (Dick) Shoup   R   2. John Melcher   D

NEBRASKA

Senators

Roman L. Hruska   R   Carl T. Curtis   R

Representatives

1. Charles Thone   R   2. John Y. McCollister   R
3. David T. Martin   R

NEVADA

Senators

Alan Bible   D   Howard W. Cannon   D

Representative

At large—Walter S. Baring   D

NEW HAMPSHIRE

Senators

Norris Cotton   R   Thomas J. McIntyre   D

Representatives

1. Louis C. Wyman   R   2. James C. Cleveland   R

NEW JERSEY

Senators

Clifford P. Case   R   Harrison A. Williams, Jr.   D

Representatives

1. John E. Hunt   R
2. Charles W. Sandman, Jr.   R
3. James J. Howard   D
4. Frank Thompson, Jr.   D
5. Peter H. B. Frelinghuysen   R
6. Edwin B. Forsythe   R
7. William B. Widnall   R
8. Robert A. Roe   D
9. Henry Helstoski   D
10. Peter W. Rodino, Jr.   D
11. Joseph G. Minish   D
12. Florence P. Dwyer   R
13. Cornelius E. Gallagher   D
14. Dominick V. Daniels   D
15. Edward J. Patten   D

NEW MEXICO

Senators

Clinton P. Anderson   D   Joseph M. Montoya   D

Representatives

1. Manuel Lujan, Jr.   R   2. Harold Runnels   D

NEW YORK

Senators

Jacob K. Javits   R   James L. Buckley   C-R

Representatives

1. Otis G. Pike   D
2. James R. Grover, Jr.   R
3. Lester L. Wolff   D
4. John W. Wydler   R
5. Norman F. Lent   R
6. Seymour Halpern   R
7. Joseph P. Addabbo   D
8. Benjamin S. Rosenthal   D
9. James J. Delaney   D
10. Emanuel Celler   D
11. Frank J. Brasco   D
12. Shirley Chisholm   D
13. Bertram L. Podell   D
14. John J. Rooney   D
15. Hugh L. Carey   D
16. John M. Murphy   D
17. Edward I. Koch   D
18. Charles B. Rangel   D
19. Bella S. Abzug   D
20. William F. Ryan[9]   D
21. Herman Badillo   D
22. James H. Scheuer   D
23. Jonathan B. Bingham   D
24. Mario Biaggi   D
25. Peter A. Peyser   R
26. Ogden R. Reid   R
27. John G. Dow   D
28. Hamilton Fish, Jr.   R
29. Samuel S. Stratton   D
30. Carleton J. King   R
31. Robert C. McEwen   R
32. Alexander Pirnie   R
33. Howard W. Robison   R
34. John H. Terry   R
35. James M. Hanley   D
36. Frank Horton   R
37. Barber B. Conable, Jr.   R
38. James F. Hastings   R
39. Jack F. Kemp   R
40. Henry P. Smith 3d   R
41. Thaddeus J. Dulski   D

NORTH CAROLINA

Senators

Sam J. Ervin, Jr.   D   B. Everett Jordan   D

Representatives

1. Walter B. Jones   D
2. L. H. Fountain   D
3. David N. Henderson   D
4. Nick Galifianakis   D
5. Wilmer (Vinegar Bend) Mizell   R
6. Richardson Preyer   D
7. Alton Lennon   D
8. Earl B. Ruth   R
9. Charles Raper Jonas   R
10. James T. Broyhill   R
11. Roy A. Taylor   D

NORTH DAKOTA

Senators

Milton R. Young   R   Quentin N. Burdick   D

Representatives

1. Mark Andrews   R   2. Arthur A. Link   D

OHIO

Senators

William B. Saxbe   R   Robert Taft, Jr.   R

286

Representatives

1. William J. Keating	R	13. Charles A. Mosher	R
2. Donald D. Clancy	R	14. John F. Seiberling	D
3. Charles W. Whalen, Jr.	R	15. Chalmers P. Wylie	R
4. William M. McCulloch	R	16. Frank T. Bow[10]	R
5. Delbert L. Latta	R	17. John M. Ashbrook	R
6. William H. Harsha	R	18. Wayne L. Hays	D
7. Clarence J. Brown	R	19. Charles J. Carney	D
8. Jackson E. Betts	R	20. James V. Stanton	D
9. Thomas L. Ashley	D	21. Louis Stokes	D
10. Clarence E. Miller	R	22. Charles A. Vanik	D
11. J. William Stanton	R	23. William E. Minshall	R
12. Samuel L. Devine	R	24. Walter E. Powell	R

OKLAHOMA

Senators

Fred R. Harris   D   Henry L. Bellmon   R

Representatives

1. Page Belcher	R	4. Tom Steed	D
2. Ed Edmondson	D	5. John Jarman	D
3. Carl Albert	D	6. John N. Happy Camp	R

OREGON

Senators

Mark O. Hatfield   R   Bob Packwood   R

Representatives

1. Wendell Wyatt	R	3. Edith Green	D
2. Al Ullman	D	4. John Dellenback	R

PENNSYLVANIA

Senators

Hugh Scott   R   Richard S. Schweiker   R

Representatives

1. William A. Barrett	D	14. William S. Moorhead	D
2. Robert N. C. Nix	D	15. Fred B. Rooney	D
3. James A. Byrne	D	16. Edwin D. Eshleman	R
4. Joshua Eilberg	D	17. Herman T. Schneebeli	R
5. William J. Green	D	18. H. John Heinz III	R
6. Gus Yatron	D	19. George A. Goodling	R
7. Lawrence G. Williams	R	20. Joseph M. Gaydos	D
8. Edward G. Biester, Jr.	R	21. John H. Dent	D
9. John Ware	R	22. John P. Saylor	R
10. Joseph M. McDade	R	23. Albert W. Johnson	R
11. Daniel J. Flood	D	24. Joseph P. Vigorito	D
12. J. Irving Whalley	R	25. Frank M. Clark	R
13. R. Lawrence Coughlin	R	26. Thomas E. Morgan	D
		27. [Vacant][11]	

RHODE ISLAND

Senators

John O. Pastore   D   Claiborne Pell   D

Representatives

1. Fernand J. St Germain	D	2. Robert O. Tiernan	D

SOUTH CAROLINA

Senators

Strom Thurmond   R   Ernest F. Hollings   D

Representatives

1. Mendel J. Davis	D	4. James R. Mann	D
2. Floyd Spence	R	5. Tom S. Gettys	D
3. Wm. J. Bryan Dorn	D	6. John L. McMillan	D

SOUTH DAKOTA

Senators

Karl E. Mundt   R   George McGovern   D

Representatives

1. Frank E. Denholm	D	2. James Abourezk	D

TENNESSEE

Senators

Howard H. Baker, Jr.   R   William E. Brock 3d   R

Representatives

1. James H. Quillen	R	5. Richard H. Fulton	D
2. John J. Duncan	R	6. William R. Anderson	D
3. LaMar Baker	R	7. Ray Blanton	D
4. Joe L. Evins	D	8. Ed Jones	D
		9. Dan H. Kuykendall	R

TEXAS

Senators

John G. Tower   R   Lloyd M. Bentsen   D

Representatives

1. Wright Patman	D	12. James C. Wright, Jr.	D
2. John Dowdy	D	13. Graham Purcell	D
3. James M. Collins	R	14. John Young	D
4. Ray Roberts	D	15. Eligio de la Garza	D
5. Earle Cabell	D	16. Richard C. White	D
6. Olin E. Teague	D	17. Omar Burleson	D
7. Bill Archer	R	18. Robert D. Price	R
8. Bob Eckhardt	D	19. George H. Mahon	D
9. Jack Brooks	D	20. Henry B. Gonzalez	D
10. J. J. (Jake) Pickle	D	21. O. C. Fisher	D
11. W. R. Poage	D	22. Bob Casey	D
		23. Abraham Kazon, Jr.	D

UTAH

Senators

Wallace F. Bennett   R   Frank E. Moss   D

Representatives

1. K. Gunn McKay	D	2. Sherman P. Lloyd	R

VERMONT

Senators

George D. Aiken   R   Robert T. Stafford   R

Representative

At large—[Vacant][12]

VIRGINIA

Senators

Harry F. Byrd, Jr.   I   William B. Spong, Jr.   D

Representatives

1. Thomas N. Downing	D	6. Richard H. Poff[13]	R
2. G. William Whitehurst	R	7. J. Kenneth Robinson	R
3. David E. Satterfield 3d	D	8. William L. Scott	R
4. Watkins M. Abbitt	D	9. William C. Wampler	R
5. W. C. (Dan) Daniel	D	10. Joel T. Broyhill	R

WASHINGTON

Senators

Warren G. Magnuson   D   Henry M. Jackson   D

Representatives

1. Thomas M. Pelly	R	4. Mike McCormack	D
2. Lloyd Meeds	D	5. Thomas S. Foley	D
3. Julia Butler Hansen	D	6. Floyd V. Hicks	D
		7. Brock Adams	D

WEST VIRGINIA

Senators

Jennings Randolph   D   Robert C. Byrd   D

Representatives

1. Robert H. Mollohan	D	3. John Slack	D
2. Harley O. Staggers	D	4. Ken Hechler	D
		5. James Kee	D

WISCONSIN

Senators

William Proxmire   D   Gaylord Nelson   D

Representatives

1. Les Aspin	D	6. William A. Steiger	R
2. Robert W. Kastenmeier	D	7. David R. Obey	D
3. Vernon W. Thomson	R	8. John W. Byrnes	R
4. Clement J. Zablocki	D	9. Glenn R. Davis	R
5. Henry S. Reuss	D	10. Alvin E. O'Konski	R

WYOMING

Senators

Gale W. McGee   D   Clifford P. Hansen   R

Representative

At large—Teno Roncalio   D

COMMONWEALTH OF PUERTO RICO

Resident Commissioner

Jorge L. Córdova   R

DISTRICT OF COLUMBIA

Delegate

Walter E. Fauntroy   D

CLASSIFICATION

Senate

Democrats	54
Republicans	44
Conservative-Republican	1
Independent	1
Total	100

House

Democrats	255
Republicans	177
Vacant	3
Total	435

Congress Footnotes

Alabama
[1] Died 12-25-71
Mrs. Elizabeth Andrews (wife) (D) 4-11-72

Alaska
[2] Missing in plane 10-16-72

Georgia
[3] Served till 11-7-72
Sam Nunn (D) 11-8-72

Illinois
[4] Clifford D. Carlson (R) 4-10-72

Louisiana
[5] Died 7-27-72
Elaine Edwards (D) 8-7-72
J. Bennett Johnston, Jr. (D) 11-14-72
[6] Missing in plane 10-16-72
[7] Resigned 5-9-72
John B. Breaux (D) 10-12-72

Massachusetts
[8] Resigned 5-1-72

New York
[9] Died 9-17-72

Ohio
[10] Died 11-13-72

Penna.
[11] William S. Conover III (R)
[11] 5-24-72

Vermont
[12] Richard W. Mallary (R)
[12] 1-18-72

Virginia
[13] Resigned 8-29-72
[13] M. Caldwell Butler (R) 11-7-72

JUDICIARY

SUPREME COURT

CHIEF JUSTICE OF THE UNITED STATES

	Home State	Date of Birth	Date took Court seat	Appointed By
Warren E. Burger	Minn.	Sept. 17, 1907	Oct. 6, 1969	Nixon

ASSOCIATE JUSTICES OF THE SUPREME COURT

	Home State	Date of Birth	Date took Court seat	Appointed By		Home State	Date of Birth	Date took Court seat	Appointed By
William O. Douglas	Wash.	Oct. 16, 1898	April 17, 1939	Roosevelt	Thurgood Marshall	Md.	July 2, 1908	Oct. 2, 1967	Johnson
William J. Brennan	N.J.	April 25, 1906	Oct. 16, 1956	Eisenhower	Harry A. Blackmun	Ill.	Nov. 12, 1908	June 9, 1970	Nixon
Potter Stewart	Ohio	Jan. 23, 1915	Oct. 14, 1958	Eisenhower	Lewis F. Powell, Jr.	Va.	Sept. 19, 1907	Jan. 7, 1972	Nixon
Byron R. White	Colo.	June 8, 1917	April 16, 1962	Kennedy	William Rehnquist	Ariz.	Oct. 1, 1924	Jan. 7, 1972	Nixon

UNITED NATIONS

THE SECRETARIAT

SECRETARY-GENERAL

Kurt Waldheim   Austria

UNDER-SECRETARIES-GENERAL

I. H. Abdel-Rahman   Egypt   Executive Director Industrial Development Organization.

Philippe de Seynes   France   Under-Secretary-General for Economic & Social Affairs.

Roberto E. Guyer   Argentina   Under-Secretary-General for Special Political Affairs.

Leonid N. Kutakov   U.S.S.R.   Under-Secretary-General for Political & Security Council Affairs.

Bohdan Lewandowski   Poland   Under-Secretary-General for Conference Services.

Name	Country	Title
C. V. Narasimhan	India	Chef de-Cabinet.
George F. Davidson	Canada	Under-Secretary-General for Administration & Management.
Vittorio Winspeare-Guicciardi	Italy	Director-General, U.N. Office at Geneva, Switzerland.
Constantin A. Stavropoulos	Greece	Under-Secretary-General for General Assembly Affairs & Legal Counsel.
Issoufous S. Djermakoye	Niger	Under-Secretary-General, Special Advisor on African Questions.
Bradford Morse	U.S.A.	Under-Secretary-General for Political & General Assembly Affairs.
Tang Ming-chao	China	Under-Secretary-General for Political Affairs & Decolonization.

GENERAL ASSEMBLY

Country	Year of Admission	Permanent Representative
Afghanistan	1946	Abdur-Rahman Pazhwak
Albania	1955	M. Rako Naço
Algeria	1962	Abdellatif Rahal
Argentina	1945	Dr. Carlos Ortiz de Rozas
Australia	1945	Sir Laurence McIntrye
Austria	1955	Dr. Peter Jankowitsch
Bahrain	1971	Dr. Salman Mahomed Al Saffar
Barbados	1966	Waldo E. Waldron-Ramsey
Belgium	1945	Edouard Longerstaey
Bhutan	1971	Sangye Penjor
Bolivia	1945	Dr. Walter Guevara Arze
Botswana	1966	Thebe David Mogami
Brazil	1945	Sergio Armando Frazão
Bulgaria	1955	Guero Grozev
Burma	1948	U Lwin
Burundi	1962	Nsanze Terence
Byelorussian, S.S.R.	1945	Vitaly Stepanovich Smirnov
Cameroon	1960	Michel Njine
Canada	1945	Dr. Saul Rae
Central African Republic	1960	Michel Adama-Tamboux
Chad	1960	Vacant
Chile	1945	Dr. Humberto Diaz Casanueva
China	1971	Huang Hua
Colombia	1945	Dr. Augusto Espinosa
Congo	1960	Nicolas Mondjo
Costa Rica	1945	José Luis Molina
Cuba	1945	Ricardo Alarcon Quesada
Cyprus	1960	Zenon Rossides
Czechoslovakia	1945	Dr. Zdeněk Cernik
Dahomey	1960	Wilfred de Souza
Democratic Yemen	1967	Abdul Malek Ismail
Denmark	1945	Otto R. Borch
Dominican Republic	1945	Dr. Porfirio Dominci
Ecuador	1945	Lepoldo Benites
Egypt	1945	Dr. Ahmed Esmat Abdel Meguid
El Salvador	1945	Reynaldo Galindo Pohl
Equatorial Guinea	1968	Primo José Esono Mica
Ethiopia	1945	Vacant
Fiji	1970	Semesa K. Sikivou, M.B.E.
Finland	1955	Aarno Karhilo
France	1945	Louis de Guiringaud
Gabon	1960	Jean Davin
Gambia	1965	Vacant
Ghana	1957	Vacant
Greece	1945	M. Stephane G. Stathatos
Guatemala	1945	Rafael E. Castillo-Valdés
Guinea	1958	Madame Jeanne Martin Cisse
Guyana	1966	Frederick H. Talbot
Haiti	1945	Jean Coradin
Honduras	1945	Roberto Martinez Ordoñez
Hungary	1955	Károly Szarka
Iceland	1946	Vacant
India	1945	Samar Sen
Indonesia	1950	Chaidir Anwar Sani
Iran	1945	Fereydoun Houeyda
Iraq	1945	Abdul Karim Al-Shaikhly
Ireland	1955	Cornelius C. Cremin
Israel	1949	Yosef Tekoah
Italy	1955	Piero Vinci
Ivory Coast	1960	Siméon Ake
Jamaica	1962	Keith Johnson, C.D.
Japan	1956	Toru Nakagawa
Jordan	1955	Sherif Abdul Hamid Sharaf
Kenya	1963	Joseph Odero-Jowi
Khmer Republic	1954	Truong Cang
Kuwait	1963	Abdalla Yaccoub Bishara
Laos	1955	Vacant
Lebanon	1945	Edouard Ghorra
Lesotho	1966	Mooki V. Molapo
Liberia	1945	Nathan Barnes
Libyan Arab Republic	1955	Vacant
Luxembourg	1945	Jean Rettel
Madagascar	1960	Blaise Rabetafika
Malawi	1964	Nyemba Wales Mbekeani
Malaysia	1957	H. M. A. Zakaria
Maldives	1965	Vacant
Mali	1960	Seydou Traore
Malta	1964	Joseph Attard Kingswell
Mauritania	1961	Moulaye El Hassen
Mauritius	1968	Radha Krishna Ramphul
Mexico	1945	Dr. Alfonso Garcia Robles
Mongolia	1961	Vacant
Morocco	1956	Mehdi Mrani Zentar
Nepal	1955	Shailendra Kumar Upadhyay
Netherlands	1945	Robbert Fack
New Zealand	1945	John Vivian Scott
Nicaragua	1945	Dr. Guillermo Sevilla-Sacasa
Niger	1960	Vacant
Nigeria	1960	Feyisara Adewebi
Norway	1945	Ole Algard
Oman	1971	Failsal Bin Ali Al-Said
Pakistan	1947	Iqbal Ahmad Akhund
Panama	1945	Aquilino E. Boyd
Paraguay	1945	Miguel Solano Lopez
Peru	1945	Dr. Javier Peréz de Cuellar
Philippines	1945	Narciso G. Reyes
Poland	1945	Eugeniusz Kulaga
Portugal	1955	Antonio A. de Medeiros Patricio
Qatar	1971	Jasim Yousif Jamal
Romania	1955	Ion Datcu
Rwanda	1962	Fidèle Nkundabagenzi
Saudi Arabia	1945	Vacant
Senegal	1960	Médoune Fall
Sierra Leone	1961	Ismael Byne Taylor-Kamara
Singapore	1965	Shunmugam Jayakumar
Somalia	1960	Abdulrahim Abby Farah
South Africa	1945	Carl F. G. von Hirschberg
Spain	1955	Don Jaime Alba
Sri Lanka (Ceylon)	1955	Hamilton Shirley Amerasinghe
Sudan	1956	Rahmatalla Abdulla
Swaziland	1968	N. M. Malinga
Sweden	1946	Olof Rydbeck
Syrian Arab Republic	1945	Haissam Kelani
Thailand	1946	Vacant
Togo	1960	Jacques D. Togbe
Trinidad and Tobago	1962	Eustace E. Seignoret
Tunisia	1956	Rachid Driss
Turkey	1945	Osman Olcay
Uganda	1962	Grace S. Ibingira
Ukrainian S.S.R.	1945	Mikhail Deonisovich Polyanichko
Union of Soviet Socialist Republics	1945	Yakov Aleksandrovich Malik
United Arab Emirates	1971	Dr. Ali Humaidan
United Kingdom of Great Britain and Northern Ireland	1945	Sir Colin Crowe
United Republic of Tanzania	1964	Salim Ahmed Salim
United States	1945	George Bush
Upper Volta	1960	Vacant
Uruguay	1945	Vacant
Venezuela	1945	Vacant
Yemen	1947	Yahya H. Geghman
Yugoslavia	1945	Lazar Mojsov
Zaire	1960	Vacant
Zambia	1964	Paul J. F. Lusaka

ECONOMICS

EMPLOYMENT

Year	Civilian Labor Force	Un-employed	Percent-age Unem-ployed
1929	49,180,000	1,550,000	3.2
1933	51,590,000	12,830,000	24.9
1940	55,640,000	8,120,000	14.6
1944	54,630,000	670,000	1.2
1960	70,612,000	3,931,000	5.6
1961	71,603,000	4,806,000	6.7
1962	71,854,000	4,007,000	5.6
1963	72,975,000	4,166,000	5.7
1964	74,233,000	3,876,000	5.2
1965	75,635,000	3,456,000	4.6
1966	75,770,000	2,875,000	3.8
1967	77,348,000	2,975,000	3.8
1968	78,737,000	2,816,000	3.6
1969	80,733,000	2,831,000	3.5
1970	82,715,000	4,088,000	4.9
1971	84,113,000	4,994,000	5.9

1972 by month (seasonally adjusted)

January	85,707,000	5,071,000	5.9
February	85,535,000	4,912,000	5.7
March	86,313,000	5,072,000	5.9
April	86,284,000	5,079,000	5.9
May	86,486,000	5,092,000	5.9
June	86,395,000	4,728,000	5.5
July	86,467,000	4,785,000	5.5
August	86,860,000	4,887,000	5.6
September	87,049,000	4,827,000	5.5
October	87,276,000	4,794,000	5.5
November	87,037,000	4,506,000	5.2

(Source: Bureau of Labor Statistics, Dept. of Labor)

GROSS NATIONAL PRODUCT

(The total output of goods and services in the United States measured in terms of expenditures by which they were acquired)

Year	GNP
1929	$103,100,000,000
1933	55,600,000,000
1940	99,700,000,000
1945	211,900,000,000
1950	284,800,000,000
1960	503,700,000,000
1961	520,100,000,000
1962	560,300,000,000
1963	590,500,000,000
1964	632,400,000,000
1965	683,900,000,000
1966	743,300,000,000
1967	789,663,000,000
1968	865,700,000,000
1969	931,400,000,000
1970	974,100,000,000
1971	1,050,400,000,000
1972 (est.)	1,152,100,000,000

(Source: Department of Commerce)

U.S. TOTAL GROSS PUBLIC DEBT

Year	Total	Per capita
1860	$65,000,000	$2
1900	1,263,000,000	17
1920	24,299,000,000	228
1930	16,185,000,000	132
1940	42,968,000,000	325
1945	258,682,000,000	1,849
1960	286,331,000,000	1,585
1961	288,971,000,000	1,573
1962	298,201,000,000	1,598
1963	305,860,000,000	1,615
1964	311,713,000,000	1,622
1965	317,274,000,000	1,631
1966	319,907,000,000	1,625
1967	326,221,000,000	1,638
1968	347,578,000,000	1,727
1969	353,720,000,000	1,741
1970	370,919,000,000	1,811
1971	398,129,000,000	1,922
1972	427,260,000,000 (preliminary)	2,045

(Source: Department of the Treasury)

PER CAPITA PERSONAL INCOME

Year	Income	Year	Income
1950	$1,496	1967	3,159
1960	2,215	1968	3,421
1961	2,264	1969	3,687
1962	2,368	1970	3,921
1963	2,455	1971	4,156
1964	2,586	1972 (est.)	4,474
1965	2,765		
1966	2,978	(Source: Department of Commerce)	

STATES OF

State	Rank in Population*	Population*	Capital	Population of Capital*
Alabama	21	3,444,165	Montgomery	133,386
Alaska	50	302,173	Juneau	6,050
Arizona	33	1,772,482	Phoenix	581,562
Arkansas	32	1,923,295	Little Rock	132,483
California	1	19,953,134	Sacramento	256,127
Colorado	30	2,207,259	Denver	514,678
Connecticut	24	3,032,217	Hartford	158,017
Delaware	46	548,104	Dover	17,488
Florida	9	6,789,443	Tallahassee	71,763
Georgia	15	4,589,575	Atlanta	496,973
Hawaii	40	769,913	Honolulu	324,871
Idaho	42	713,008	Boise	74,990
Illinois	5	11,113,976	Springfield	91,753
Indiana	11	5,193,669	Indianapolis	744,624
Iowa	25	2,825,041	Des Moines	200,587
Kansas	28	2,249,071	Topeka	125,011
Kentucky	23	3,219,311	Frankfort	20,054
Louisiana	20	3,643,180	Baton Rouge	165,963
Maine	38	993,663	Augusta	22,104
Maryland	18	3,922,399	Annapolis	28,042
Massachusetts	10	5,689,170	Boston	641,071
Michigan	7	8,875,083	Lansing	131,546
Minnesota	19	3,805,069	St. Paul	309,980
Mississippi	29	2,216,012	Jackson	153,968
Missouri	13	4,677,399	Jefferson City	51,921
Montana	43	694,409	Helena	22,730

CONSUMER PRICE INDEX (Living Costs)

Year	All Items	Food	Apparel	Housing	Rent	Medical Care	Transportation
1913	34.5	33.6	33.8	--	55.7	--	--
1920	69.8	70.8	98.0	--	72.9	--	--
1929	59.7	55.6	56.2	--	85.4	--	--
1933	45.1	35.3	42.8	--	60.8	--	--
1940	48.8	40.5	49.6	--	63.2	--	--
1945	62.7	58.4	71.2	--	66.1	--	--
1950	83.8	85.8	91.5	83.2	79.1	73.4	79.0
1960	103.1	101.4	102.1	103.1	103.1	108.1	103.8
1961	104.2	102.6	102.8	103.9	104.4	111.3	105.0
1962	105.4	103.6	103.2	104.8	105.7	114.2	107.2
1963	106.7	105.1	104.2	106.0	106.8	117.0	107.8
1964	108.1	106.4	105.7	107.2	107.8	119.4	109.3
1965	109.9	108.8	106.8	108.5	109.8	122.3	111.6
1966	113.1	114.2	109.6	111.1	110.4	127.7	112.7
1967	116.3	115.2	114.0	114.3	112.4	136.7	115.9
1968	121.2	119.3	120.1	119.1	115.1	145.0	119.6
1969	127.7	125.5	127.1	126.7	118.8	155.0	124.2
1970	135.3	132.4	132.2	135.9	123.7	164.9	130.6
1971	121.3	118.4	119.8	124.3	115.2	128.4	118.6

1972 by month	All Items	Food	Apparel	Housing	Rent	Medical Care	Transportation
January	123.2	120.3	120.2	127.3	117.5	130.5	119.0
February	123.8	122.2	120.7	127.6	117.8	131.0	118.3
March	124.0	122.4	121.3	127.9	118.0	131.4	118.4
April	124.3	122.4	121.8	128.2	118.4	131.7	118.6
May	124.7	122.3	122.5	128.5	118.6	132.0	119.5
June	125.0	123.0	122.1	129.0	119.0	132.4	119.8
July	125.5	124.2	121.1	129.5	119.2	132.7	120.3
August	125.7	124.6	120.8	129.9	119.6	132.9	120.5
September	126.2	124.8	123.1	130.1	119.9	133.1	121.0
October	126.6	124.9	124.3	130.4	120.3	133.9	121.2
November	126.9	125.4	125.0	130.8	120.5	134.1	121.4

Source: BLS—Dept. of Labor

THE UNION

Largest City	Population of Largest City*	Governor	Party	Term Expires
Birmingham	300,910	George C. Wallace	D	1975
Anchorage	48,029	William A. Egan	D	1974
Phoenix	581,562	John R. Williams	R	1975
Little Rock	132,483	Dale Bumpers	D	1975
Los Angeles	2,816,061	Ronald Reagan	R	1975
Denver	514,678	John A. Love	R	1975
Hartford	158,017	Thomas J. Meskill	R	1975
Wilmington	80,386	Sherman W. Tribbitt	D	1977
Jacksonville	528,865	Reubin Askew	D	1975
Atlanta	496,973	Jimmy Carter	D	1975
Honolulu	324,871	John A. Burns	D	1974
Boise	74,990	Cecil D. Andrus	D	1975
Chicago	3,366,957	Daniel Walker	D	1977
Indianapolis	744,624	Otis R. Bowen	R	1977
Des Moines	200,587	Robert R. Day	R	1975
Wichita	276,554	Robert B. Docking	D	1975
Louisville	361,472	Wendell H. Ford	D	1975
New Orleans	593,471	Edwin W. Edwards	D	1976
Portland	65,116	Kenneth M. Curtis	D	1975
Baltimore	905,759	Marvin Mandel	D	1975
Boston	641,071	Francis W. Sargent	R	1975
Detroit	1,511,482	William G. Milliken	R	1975
Minneapolis	434,400	Wendell R. Anderson	D	1975
Jackson	153,968	William L. Waller	D	1976
St. Louis	622,236	Christopher S. Bond	R	1977
Billings	61,581	Thomas L. Judge	D	1977

State	Rank in Population*	Population*	Capital	Population of Capital*
Nebraska	35	1,483,791	Lincoln	149,418
Nevada	47	488,738	Carson City	15,264
New Hampshire	41	737,681	Concord	30,022
New Jersey	8	7,168,164	Trenton	104,638
New Mexico	37	1,016,000	Santa Fe	41,167
New York	2	18,190,740	Albany	113,988
North Carolina	12	5,082,059	Raleigh	121,577
North Dakota	45	617,761	Bismarck	34,703
Ohio	6	10,652,017	Columbus	539,677
Oklahoma	27	2,559,253	Oklahoma City	366,481
Oregon	31	2,091,385	Salem	68,296
Pennsylvania	3	11,793,909	Harrisburg	65,828
Rhode Island	39	949,723	Providence	179,213
South Carolina	26	2,590,516	Columbia	113,542
South Dakota	40	680,514	Pierre	9,732
Tennessee	17	3,924,164	Nashville	447,877
Texas	4	11,196,730	Austin	246,904
Utah	36	1,059,273	Salt Lake City	175,885
Vermont	48	444,732	Montpelier	9,102
Virginia	14	4,648,494	Richmond	249,621
Washington	22	3,409,169	Olympia	22,143
West Virginia	30	1,744,237	Charleston	71,505
Wisconsin	16	4,417,933	Madison	173,258
Wyoming	49	332,416	Cheyenne	40,914
District Of Columbia		756,510		
Commonwealth Of Puerto Rico		2,712,033	San Juan	440,952

* Source of population totals: 1970 Estimate Bureau of the Census

SPORTS

BASEBALL

FINAL MAJOR LEAGUE STANDINGS

AMERICAN LEAGUE

EASTERN DIVISION

	W.	L.	Pct.	G.B.
Detroit	86	70	.551	—
Boston	85	70	.548	½
Baltimore	80	74	.519	5
New York	79	76	.510	6½
Cleveland	72	84	.462	14
Milwaukee	65	91	.417	21

WESTERN DIVISION

	W.	L.	Pct.	G.B.
Oakland	93	62	.600	—
Chicago	87	67	.565	5½
Minnesota	77	77	.500	15½
Kansas City	76	78	.494	16½
California	75	80	.484	18
Texas	54	100	.351	38½

NATIONAL LEAGUE

EASTERN DIVISION

	W.	L.	Pct.	G.B.
Pittsburgh	96	59	.619	—
Chicago	85	70	.548	11
New York	83	73	.532	13½
St. Louis	75	81	.481	21½
Montreal	70	86	.449	26½
Philadelphia	59	97	.378	37½

WESTERN DIVISION

	W.	L.	Pct.	G.B.
Cincinnati	95	59	.617	—
Houston	84	69	.549	10½
Los Angeles	85	70	.548	10½
Atlanta	70	84	.455	25
San Francisco	69	86	.445	26½
San Diego	58	95	.379	36½

Oakland defeated Detroit 3 games to 2 to win American League Championship.

Cincinnati defeated Pittsburgh 3 games to 2 to win National League Championship.

Oakland defeated Cincinnati 4 games to 3 to win World Series.

PRO FOOTBALL

Final Standings

NATIONAL CONFERENCE

Eastern

	W	L	T	Pct.	PF	PA
Washington	11	3	0	.786	336	218
*Dallas	10	4	0	.714	319	240
N.Y. Giants	8	6	0	.571	331	247
St. Louis	4	9	1	.321	193	303
Philadelphia	2	11	1	.179	145	352

Central

	W	L	T	Pct.	PF	PA
Green Bay	10	4	0	.714	304	226
Detroit	8	5	1	.607	339	290
Minnesota	7	7	0	.500	301	252
Chicago	4	9	1	.321	225	275

Western

	W	L	T	Pct.	PF	PA
San Francisco	8	5	1	.607	353	249
Atlanta	7	7	0	.500	269	274
Los Angeles	6	7	1	.464	291	286
New Orleans	2	11	1	.179	215	361

*Qualified for playoffs.

AMERICAN CONFERENCE

Eastern

	W	L	T	Pct.	PF	PA
Miami	14	0	0	1.000	385	171
N.Y. Jets	7	7	0	.500	367	324
Baltimore	5	9	0	.357	235	252
Buffalo	4	9	1	.321	257	377
New England	3	11	0	.214	192	446

Central

	W	L	T	Pct.	PF	PA
Pittsburgh	11	3	0	.786	343	175
*Cleveland	10	4	0	.714	268	249
Cincinnati	8	6	0	.571	299	229
Houston	1	13	0	.071	164	380

Western

	W	L	T	Pct.	PF	PA
Oakland	10	3	1	.750	365	248
Kansas City	8	6	0	.571	287	254
Denver	5	9	0	.357	325	350
San Diego	4	9	1	.321	264	344

N.F.L. Playoffs

Semifinal Round

NFC—San Francisco 28, Dallas 30
Washington 16, Green Bay 3

AFC—Pittsburgh 13, Oakland 7
Miami 20, Cleveland 14

Final

NFC—Washington 26, Dallas 3
AFC—Miami 21, Pittsburgh 17

Washington wins NFC championship.
Miami wins AFC championship.

Washington and Miami
meet in the Super Bowl in
Los Angeles, Jan. 14.

Largest City	Population of Largest City*	Governor	Party	Term Expires
Omaha	347,328	J. James Exon	D	1975
Las Vegas	125,787	D. N. O'Callaghan	D	1975
Manchester	87,754	Meldrim Thompson Jr.	R	1975
Newark	382,417	William T. Cahill	R	1974
Albuquerque	243,751	Bruce King	D	1975
New York	7,895,563	Nelson A. Rockefeller	R	1975
Charlotte	241,178	James E. Holshouser Jr.	R	1977
Fargo	53,365	Arthur A. Link	D	1977
Cleveland	750,903	John J. Gilligan	D	1975
Oklahoma City	366,481	David Hall	D	1975
Portland	382,619	Tom McCall	R	1975
Philadelphia	1,948,609	Milton J. Shapp	D	1975
Providence	179,213	Phillip W. Noel	D	1975
Columbia	113,542	John C. West	D	1975
Sioux Falls	72,488	Richard F. Kneip	D	1975
Memphis	623,530	Winfield Dunn	R	1975
Houston	1,232,802	Dolph Briscoe	D	1975
Salt Lake City	175,885	Calvin L. Rampton	D	1977
Burlington	38,633	Thomas P. Salmon	D	1975
Norfolk	307,951	Linwood Holton	R	1974
Seattle	530,831	Daniel J. Evans	R	1977
Huntington	74,315	Arch A. Moore Jr.	R	1977
Milwaukee	717,099	Patrick J. Lucey	D	1975
Cheyenne	40,914	Stanley K. Hathaway	R	1975
San Juan	440,952	Rafael Hernandez Colon		1977

COLLEGE FOOTBALL

Ratings

The top teams, with points figured on a 10-9-8-7-6-5-4-3-2-1 basis for first through 10th places (first-place votes in parentheses) and won-lost records:

	W.	L.	T.	Pts.
1—Southern California (35)	11	0	0	350
2—Oklahoma	10	1	0	302
3—Ohio State	9	1	0	237
4—Alabama	10	1	0	209
5—Texas	9	1	0	172
6—Michigan	10	1	0	150
7—Auburn	9	1	0	144
8—Penn State	10	1	0	131
9—Nebraska	8	2	1	66
10—Louisiana State	9	1	1	59

ALL-AMERICANS

Offense

Pos.	Player	College			
E	Steve Holden, Ariz. St.	Sr	6-2	202	
T	Jerry Sisemore, Texas	Sr	6-4	255	
G	Geary Murdock, Iowa St.	Sr	6-2	255	
C	Tom Brahaney, Okla.	Sr	6-2	231	
G	John Hannah, Alabama	Sr	6-3½	262	
T	John Dampeer, ND	Sr	6-2	235	
E	Charles Young, USC	Sr	6-4	255	
QB	Bert Jones, LSU	Sr	6-3	205	
RB	Greg Pruitt, Okla.	Sr.	5-9	176	
RB	Johnny Rodgers, Neb.	Sr	5-9	173	
RB	Otis Armstrong Purdue	Sr	5-11	197	

Defense

Pos.	Player	College			
E	Bruce Bannon, Penn St.	Sr	6-3	244	
T	Greg Marx, ND	Sr	6-5	265	
G	Rich Glover, Neb.	Sr	6-1	234	
T	George Hasenohrl, OSU	Sr	6-2	262	
E	Willie Harper, Neb.	Sr	6-2	207	
LB	Jamie Rotella, Tenn.	Sr	6-2	220	
LB	Rich Wood, USC	So	6-2	218	
LB	Randy Gradishar, OSU	Jr	6-3	224	
DB	Randy Logan, Mich.	Sr	6-2	192	
DB	Conrad Graham, Tenn.	Sr	6-1	184	
DB	Frank Dowsing, Miss St.	Sr.	5-10	185	

Intercollegiate Champions

National—Southern California.
Eastern (Lambert Trophy)—Penn State.
Eastern (Lambert Cup)—Delaware.
Eastern (Lambert Bowl)—Franklin and Marshall.
Ivy League—Dartmouth.
Big Ten—Ohio State-Michigan (tie).
Yankee Conference—Massachusetts.
Southeastern Conference—Alabama.
Atlantic Coast Conference—North Carolina.
Southern Conference—East Carolina.
Mid-American Conference—Kent State.
Big Eight—Oklahoma.
Missouri Valley—Louisville-West Texas-Drake.
Pacific Eight—Southern California.
Ohio Valley—Tennessee Tech.
Southwest Conference—Texas.
Big Sky—Montana State.
Pacific Coast A. A.—San Diego.
Western Athletic—Arizona State.

Bowl Games

Sugar Bowl—Oklahoma 14, Penn St. 0.
Cotton Bowl—Alabama 13, Texas 17.
Orange Bowl—Nebraska 40, Notre Dame 6.
Rose Bowl—USC 42, Ohio State 17.

TENNIS

International Team Champions

Davis Cup—United States.
Wightman Cup (Women) United States.
Federation Cup (Women) South Africa.

Wimbledon Champions

Singles, Men—Stan Smith—USA.
Singles, Women—Billie Jean King—USA.
Men's Doubles—Bob Hewitt—Frew McMillan—South Africa.
Women's Doubles—Billie Jean King, USA & Betty Stove—Netherlands.

U.S. Open Champions

Singles, Men—Lua Nastase—Rumania.
Singles, Women—Billie Jean King—USA.
Men's Doubles—Cliff Drysdale, South Africa & Roger Taylor, Britain.
Women's Doubles—Francoise Durr, France & Betty Stove, Netherlands.

U.S. Indoor Champions

Men—Stan Smith—USA.
Women—Virginia Wade—Britain.
Men's Doubles—Andres Gimeno & Manuel Orantes.
Women's Doubles—Rosemary Casals & Virginia Wade.

U.S. Clay Court Champions

Men—Bob Hewitt—South Africa.
Women—Chris Evert—USA.
Doubles—Hewitt—McMillan—South Africa.

BOXING

World Professional Champions

Flyweight—Masao Ohba, Japan.
Bantamweight—Enrique Pinder, Panama.
Featherweight—Ernesto Marcel, Panama.
Junior Lightweight—Ben Villaflor, Philippines.
Lightweight—Roberto Duran, Panama.
Junior Welterweight—Alfonso Frazer, Panama.
Welterweight—Jose Napoles, Mexico.
Middleweight—Carlos Monzon, Argentina.
Light-heavyweight—Bob Foster, Washington.
Heavyweight—Joe Frazier, Philadelphia.

GOLF

US OPEN—Jack Nicklaus.
PGA—Gary Player.
MASTERS—Jack Nicklaus.
US AMATEUR—Vinny Giles.
BRITISH OPEN—Lee Trevino.
BRITISH AMATEUR—Trevor Homes.
NCAA TEAM—Texas.
NCAA INDIVIDUAL—Ben Crenshaw—Tom Kite Texas (Tie).
WOMEN'S OPEN—Sue M. Berning.
WOMEN'S PGA—Kathy Ahern.
WOMEN'S AMATEUR—Mary Anne Dudke.
RYDER CUP—U.S.A.

TRACK & FIELD

NCAA CHAMPIONS
100 Meters—Warren Edmonson—UCLA.
110 Meter High Hurdles—Jerry Wilson—So. Calif.
200 Meters—Larry Burton—Purdue.
400 Meters—John Smith—UCLA.
400 Meter Intermediate Hurdles—Bruce Collins—Penn.
800 Meters—Willie Thomas—Tennessee.
1,500 Meters—Dave Wottle—Bowling Green.
5,000 Meters—Steve Prefontaine—Oregon.
10,000 Meters—Johan Halberstadt—Oklahoma.
3,000 Meter Steeplechase—Joe Lucas—Georgetown.
440 Yd. Relay—So. California.
One Mile Relay—UCLA.
Decathlon—Ron Evans—Conn.
Shot Put—Fred DeBernardi—Texas at El Paso.
Javelin—Rick Dowswell—Ohio.
Pole Vault—Dave Roberts—Rice.
High Jump—Tom Woods—Oregon St.
Discus—Fred DeBernardi—Texas at El Paso.
Triple Jump—James Butts—UCLA.
Long Jump—Randy Williams—So. Calif.
Hammer Throw—Al Schoterman—Kent State.
Team Champion—UCLA.

AAU CHAMPIONS
110 Meter High Hurdles—Rod Milburn—Southern Univ.
200 Meters—Chuck Smith—So. Calif. Striders.
400 Meters—Lee Evans—Bay Area Striders.
400 Meter Hurdles—Richard Bruggeman—Ohio Tc.
800 Meters—Dave Wottle—Bowling Green.
1,500 Meters—Jerome Howe—Mid American Tc.
5,000 Meters—Mike Keogh—N.Y. A.C.
5,000 Meter Walk—Larry Young—Mid American Tc.
10,000 Meters—Greg Fredericks—Penn State.
3,000 Meter Steeplechase—James Dare—Navy.
Shot Put—Randy Matson—Texas Striders.
Long Jump—Arnie Robinson—U.S. Army.
Hammer Throw—Al Schoterman—N.Y. A.C.
Discus—Jay Silvester.
Triple Jump—John Craft—Chicago Tc.
Pole Vault—Dave Roberts—Rice.
Javelin—Fred Luke—Husky Spike Club.
High Jump—Barry Schur—Mid American Tc.

PRO BASKETBALL

NATIONAL BASKETBALL ASSOCIATION

Final Standings
Eastern Conference
Atlantic Division

	W	L	PCT.	GB.
Boston	56	26	.683	—
New York	48	34	.585	8
Philadelphia	30	52	.366	26
Buffalo	22	60	.268	34

Central Division

	W	L	PCT.	GB.
Baltimore	38	44	.463	—
Atlanta	36	46	.439	2
Cincinnati	30	52	.366	8
Cleveland	23	59	.280	15

Western Conference
Midwest Division

	W	L	PCT.	GB.
Milwaukee	63	19	.768	—
Chicago	57	25	.695	6
Phoenix	49	33	.598	14
Detroit	26	56	.317	37

Pacific Division

	W	L	PCT.	GB.
Los Angeles	69	13	.841	—
Golden St.	51	31	.622	18
Seattle	47	35	.573	22
Houston	34	48	.415	35
Portland	18	64	.220	51

All-Star Game
Jan. 18, at Los Angeles
West 112, East 110.

Playoffs
Eastern Division—Boston defeated Atlanta 4 games to 2.
N.Y. defeated Baltimore 4 games to 2.
N.Y. defeated Boston 4 games to 1.
Western Division—Los Angeles defeated Chicago 4 games to 0.
Milwaukee defeated San Francisco 4 games to 1.
Los Angeles defeated Milwaukee 4 games to 2.
Championship—Los Angeles defeated N.Y. 4 games to 1.

INDIVIDUAL SCORING

	FG.	FT.	PTS.	AVG.
Jabbar, Milwaukee	1,159	504	2,822	34.8
Archibald, Cincinnati	734	677	2,145	28.2
Havlicek, Boston	897	458	2,252	27.5
Haywood, Seattle	717	480	1,914	26.2
Goodrich, Los Angeles	826	475	2,127	25.9
Love, Chicago	819	399	2,037	25.8
West, Los Angeles	735	515	1,985	25.8
Lanier, Detroit	834	388	2,056	25.7
Clark, Baltimore	712	514	1,938	25.2
Hayes, Houston	832	399	2,063	25.2

MOST VALUABLE PLAYER
Kareem Abdul-Jabbar, Milwaukee.

ROOKIE OF THE YEAR
Sidney Wicks, Portland.

AMERICAN BASKETBALL ASSOCIATION
Final Standings

Eastern Division

	W	L	PCT.	GB.
Kentucky	68	16	.810	—
Virginia	45	39	.536	23
New York	44	40	.524	24
Floridians	36	48	.429	32
Carolina	35	49	.417	33
Pittsburgh	25	59	.298	43

Western Division

	W	L	PCT.	GB.
Utah	60	24	.714	—
Indiana	47	37	.560	13
Dallas	42	42	.500	18
Denver	34	50	.406	26
Memphis	26	58	.310	34

All-Star Game
Jan. 29, at Louisville, Ky.
East 142, West 115

Playoffs
Eastern Division—N.Y. defeated Kentucky 4 games to 2.
Virginia defeated Florida 4 games to 0.
N.Y. defeated Virginia 4 games to 3.
Western Division—Utah defeated Dallas 4 games to 0.
Indiana defeated Denver 4 games to 3.
Indiana defeated Utah 4 games to 3.
Championship—Indiana defeated N.Y. 4 games to 2.

INDIVIDUAL SCORING

	FG.	FT.	PTS.	AVG.
Scott, Virginia	956	525	2,524	34.6
Barry, N.Y.	829	641	2,518	31.5
Issel, Kentucky	969	591	2,538	30.6
Brisker, Pittsburgh	520	248	1,417	28.9
Simpson, Denver	917	457	2,300	27.4
Erving, Virginia	907	467	2,290	27.3
Jabali, Floridians	467	375	1,615	19.9
Carter, Carolina	538	388	1,464	19.5
Daniels, Indiana	598	317	1,513	19.2
Brown, Indiana	475	323	1,444	18.5

MOST VALUABLE PLAYER
Artis Gilmore, Ky.

ROOKIE OF THE YEAR
Artis Gilmore, Ky.

COLLEGE BASKETBALL

MAJOR CONFERENCE CHAMPIONS
IVY LEAGUE—Penn.
MIDDLE ATLANTIC—Temple.
YANKEE—Rhode Island.
ATLANTIC COAST—No. Carolina.
SOUTHERN—Davidson.
SOUTHEASTERN—Kentucky.
BIG TEN—Minnesota.
OHIO VALLEY—East Kentucky.
MID-AMERICAN—Ohio U.
OHIO—Wittenberg.
MISSOURI VALLEY—Louisville.
BIG EIGHT—Kansas St.
SOUTHWEST—Texas.
WESTERN ATHLETIC—Brigham Young.
BIG SKY—Weber St.
PACIFIC COAST CONF.—UCLA.
WEST COAST ATHLETIC—San Francisco.
FAR WESTERN—San Francisco St.
SOUTHWESTERN—Grambling.
PACIFIC COAST ATHLETIC—Long Beach St.

NCAA CHAMPION—UCLA.

NIT CHAMPION—Maryland.

Final Ratings

The top teams with votes figured on a 10-9-8-7-6-5-4-3-2-1 basis for first through 10th places (first-place votes in parentheses) and won-lost records:

	W.	L.	Pts.
1—U.C.L.A. (34)	26	0	340
2—North Carolina	23	4	279
3—Penn	23	2	247
4—Louisville	24	3	197
5—South Carolina	22	4	193
6—Long Beach State	23	3	187
7—Marquette	24	2	127
8—Southwestern Louisiana . . .	23	3	67
9—Brigham Young	21	4	50
10—Florida State	24	5	35

LEADING SCORERS

Player, College	G	FG	FT	Pts.	Avg.
Lamar—SW Louisiana	29	429	196	1054	36.3
Fuqua—Oral Roberts	28	423	160	1066	35.9
Collins—Illinois St.	26	352	143	847	32.6
Robinson—W. Virginia	24	265	176	706	29.4
Averitt—Pepperdine	24	263	167	693	28.9
Williamson—N. M. St.	25	276	126	678	27.1
Kohls—Syracuse	28	263	222	748	26.7
Miller—Florida	19	195	117	507	26.7
Taylor—Murray St.	21	200	138	538	25.6
Martiniuk—St. Peter's	24	233	145	611	25.5

All-American

Player	College
Bill Walton	UCLA
Dwight Lamar	Southwestern Louisiana
Ed Ratleff	Long Beach State
Jim Chones	Marquette
Tim Riker	South Carolina

HOCKEY

NATIONAL HOCKEY LEAGUE
Final Standings

East Division

	W	L	T	PTS
Boston	54	13	11	119
New York	48	17	13	109
Montreal	46	16	16	108
Toronto	33	31	14	80
Detroit	33	35	10	76
Buffalo	16	43	19	51
Vancouver	20	50	8	48

West Division

	W	L	T	PTS
Chicago	46	17	15	107
Minnesota	37	29	12	86
St. Louis	28	39	11	67
Pittsburgh	26	38	14	66
Philadelphia	26	38	14	66
California	21	39	18	60
Los Angeles	20	49	9	49

STANLEY CUP PLAYOFFS

East Preliminaries—
Boston defeated Toronto 4 games to 1. N.Y. defeated Montreal 4 games to 2.
West Preliminaries—
Chicago defeated Pittsburgh 4 games to 0. St. Louis defeated Minnesota 4 games to 3.
Semi-Finals
N.Y. Defeated Chicago 4 games to 0. Boston defeated St. Louis 4 games to 0.
Championship Final
Boston defeated N.Y. 4 games to 2.

TROPHY WINNERS

Ross Trophy (Leading Scorer) P. Esposito—Boston.
Norris Trophy (Best Defenseman) B. Orr—Boston.
Calder Trophy (Best Rookie) K. Dryden—Montreal.
Hart Trophy (M.V.P.) B. Orr—Boston.
Vezina Trophy (Leading Goalie) T. Esposito—Chicago.
Lady Byng Trophy (Sportsmanship) J. Ratelle—N.Y.

ALL STAR TEAM

First Team
Goal—T. Esposito, Chicago—Defense—B. Orr, Boston—Defense—B. Park, N.Y.—Center—P. Esposito, Boston—Right Wing—R. Gilbert, N.Y.—Left Wing—B. Hull, Chicago.

Second Team
Goal—K. Dryden, Montreal—Defense—B. White, Chicago—Defense—P. Stapleton, Chicago—Center—J. Ratelle, N.Y.—Right Wing—Y. Cournoyer, Montreal—Left Wing—V. Hadfield, N.Y.

SCORING LEADERS

	G	A	PTS
P. Esposito, Boston	66	67	133
Orr, Boston	37	80	117
Ratelle, N.Y.	46	63	109
Hadfield, N.Y.	50	56	106
Gilbert, N.Y.	43	54	97
F. Mahoulich, Montreal	43	53	96
B. Hull, Chicago	50	43	93
Cournoyer, Montreal	47	36	83
Bucyk, Boston	32	51	83

HORSE RACING

Kentucky Derby
Churchill Downs, Ky.

HORSE	JOCKEY	
1—Riva Ridge	R. Turcotte	$140,300
2—No Le Hace	Rubbicco	MARGIN
3—Hold Your Peace	C. Marquez	3¼ Lengths

Preakness
Pimlico, Md.

HORSE	JOCKEY	
1—Bee Bee Bee	Nelson	$135,300
2—No Le Hace	Rubbicco	MARGIN
3—Key To The Mint	Baeza	1¼ Lengths

Belmont Stakes
Belmont Park, N.Y.

HORSE	JOCKEY	
1—Riva Ridge	R. Turcotte	$93,540
2—Ruritania	Venezia	MARGIN
3—Cloudy Dawn	Hartack	7 Lengths

Awards

Horse of the Year—Secretariat.
Two-Year-Old Colt—Secretariat.
Two-Year-Old Filly—La Prevoyante.
Three-Year-Old Colt—Key to the Mint.
Three-Year-Old Filly—Susan's Girl.
Older Horses—Autobiography.
Older Fillies and Mares—Typecast.
Grass Horse—Cougar II.
Sprinter—Chou Croute.
Steeplechaser—Soothsayer.

WINTER OLYMPICS
Sapporo, Japan

Biathlon—Magnar Solberg—Norway.
Biathlon Relay—USSR.
Bobsledding—4 Man Bob—Switzerland, 2 Man Bob—W. Germany.
Figure Skating—Men's Singles—Ondrej Nepela—Czechoslovakia.
Women's Singles—Beatrix Schuba—Austria.
Pairs—Irna Rodnina & Alexei Ulanov—USSR.
Alpine Skiing—Men's Downhill—Bernhard Russi—Switzerland.
Men's Giant Slalom—Gustavo Thoeni—Italy.
Men's Slalom—Francisco Fernandez Ochoa—Spain.
Women's Downhill—Marie Therese Nadig—Switzerland.
Women's Slalom—Barbara Cochran—USA.

Women's Giant Slalom—Marie Therese Nadig—Switzerland.
Nordic Skiing—Men's Cross County—15 Kilometers—Sven-Ake Lundback—Sweden.
30 Kilometers—Vyacheslav Vedenin—USSR.
50 Kilometers—Paal Tyldum—Norway.
40 Kilometer Cross-County Relay—USSR.
15 Kilometers Cross County & Jumping—Ulrich Wealing, E. Germany.
Ski Jumping (90 Meters) Woziech Fortuna, Poland.
Ski Jumping (70 Meters) Yukio Kasaya, Japan.
Women's Events—5 Kilometers—Galina Koulacova—USSR.
10 Kilometers—Galina Koulacova—USSR.
15 Kilometer Cross County Relay—USSR.

Ice Hockey—USSR.
Luge—Men's Singles—Wolfgang Scheidel—E. Germany.
Men's Doubles—Italy, E. Germany (Tie).
Women's Singles—Anna M. Muller—E. Germany.
Speed Skating—Men's Events—500 Meters—Erhard Keller—W. Germany.
1,500 Meters—Ard Schenk—Netherlands.
5,000 Meters—Ard Schenk—Netherlands.
10,000 Meters—Ard Schenk—Netherlands.
Women's Events—500 Meters—Anne Henning—USA.
1,000 Meters—Monika Pflug—W. Germany.
1,500 Meters—Dianne Holum—USA.
3,000 Meters—Stien Kaiser Baas—Netherlands.

SUMMER OLYMPICS
Munich, W. Germany

Men's Archery
Individual Championship—John Williams, USA.

Womens Archery
Individual Championship—Doreen Wilbert—USA.

Boxing
Light Flyweight—Gyoergy Gedo—Hungary.
Flyweight—Gheorghi Kostadinov—Bulgaria.
Bantamweight—Orlando Martinez—Cuba.
Featherweight—Boris Kousnetson—Soviet Union.
Lightweight—Jan Szcepanski—Poland.
Light Welterweight—Ray Seales—USA.

Welterweight—Emilio Correa, Cuba
Light Middleweight—Dieter Kottysch, W. Germany.
Middleweight—Viatcheslav Lemechev—Soviet Union.
Light Heavyweight—Mate Pavlov—Yugoslavia.
Heavyweight—Teofilo Stevenson—Cuba.

Basketball
Team Championship—Soviet Union.

Cycling
1,000 Meter Time Trial—Niels Fredborg—Denmark.
Individual Pursuit—Knut Knudsen—Norway.
Team Pursuit—W. Germany.
Tandem—Soviet Union.
Road Race—Hennie Kuiper—Netherlands.
100 Kilometer-Time Trial—Soviet Union.

Equestrian
Individual Three Day Event—Richard Meade—England.
Team Three Day Event—England.
Individual Jumping—Graziano Mancinelli—Italy.
Dressage Grand Prix Team—Soviet Union.
Individual Dressage—Liselott Linsenhoff— W. Germany.
Team Jumping—W. Germany.

Men's Fencing
Foil—Witold Woyda—Poland.
Saber—Viktor Sidiak—Soviet Union.
Saber Team—Italy.
Individual Epee—Csaba Fenyvesi—Hungary.

Women's Fencing
Individual Foils—Antonella Lonzo Rango—Italy.
Team Foils—Soviet Union.

Men's Gymnastics
Parallel Bars—Sawao Kato—Japan.
Floor Exercises—Nikolai Andrianov—Soviet Union.
All Around—Sawao Kato—Japan.
Side Horse—Viktor Klimenko—Soviet Union.
Horse Vault—Klaus Koeste—E. Germany.
Horizontal Bar—Mitsuo Tsukahara—Japan.
Team Competition—Japan.

Women's Gymnastics
Individual—Ludmila Tourischeva—Soviet Union.
Floor Exercises—Olga Korbut—Soviet Union.
Balance Beam—Olga Korbut—Soviet Union.
Uneven Bars—Karin Janz—E. Germany.
Team Competition—Soviet Union.

Handball
Team Championship—Yugoslavia.

Field Hockey
Team Championship—W. Germany.

Judo
Light Heavyweight—Shoto Schochoshuili—Soviet Union.
Heavyweight—Willem Ruska—Netherlands.
Welterweight—Toyokazu Nomura—Japan.
Lightweight—Takao Kawaguchi—Japan.
Open Class—Willem Ruska—Netherlands.

Pentathlon
Individual—Andras Balczo—Hungary.
Team—Soviet Union.

Rowing
Coxed Fours—W. Germany.
Coxless Pairs—E. Germany.
Singles Sculls—Yuri Malishev—Soviet Union.
Coxed Pairs—E. Germany.
Coxless Fours—E. Germany.
Doubles—Soviet Union.
Eights—New Zealand.

Shooting
Small Bore Rifle Prone—Ho Junli—N. Korea.
Trap—Angelo Scalzone—Italy.
Small Bore Rifle, Three Positions—John Writer—USA.
Rapid Fire Pistol—Jozef Zapedzki—Poland.
Moving Target—Lakov Zhelezniak—Soviet Union.
Free Rifle—Lones Wigger—USA.

Men's Swimming
100 Meter Butterfly—Mark Spitz—USA.
200 Meter Butterfly—Mark Spitz—USA.
100 Meter Backstroke—Roland Matthes—E. Germany.
100 Meter Breast Stroke—Nobutaka Tagushi—Japan.
200 Meter Free Style—Mark Spitz—USA.
400 Meter Free Style—Brad Cooper—Australia.
400 Meter Free Style Relay—Dave Edgar, John Murphy, Jerry Heidenreich, Mark Spitz—USA.
800 Meter Free Style Relay—John Kinsella, Fred Tyler, Steve Genter, Mark Spitz—USA.
400 Meter Individual Medley—Gunnar Larsson, Sweden.
200 Meter Breaststroke—John Hencken—USA.
200 Meter Backstroke—Roland Matthes—E. Germany.
200 Meter Individual Medley—Gunnar Larsson—Sweden.
100 Meter Free Style—Mark Spitz—USA.
1,500 Meter Free Style—Mike Burton—USA.
400 Meter Medley Relay—Mike Stamm, Tom Bruce, Mark Spitz, Jerry Heidenreich—USA.

Women's Swimming
100 Meter Free Style—Sandra Neilson—USA.
200 Meter Free Style—Shane Gould—Australia.
400 Meter Free Style—Shane Gould—Australia.
100 Meter Butterfly—Mayumi Aoki—Japan.
200 Meter Breaststroke—Beverly Whitfield—Australia.
200 Meter Medley—Shane Gould—Australia.
400 Meter Medley—Gail Neall—Australia.
400 Meter Free Style Relay—USA.
100 Meter Breaststroke—Cathy Carr—USA.
100 Meter Backstroke—Melissa Belote—USA.
800 Meter Free Style—Keena Rothammer—USA.
400 Meter Medley Relay—USA.
200 Meter Butterfly—Karen Moe—USA.
200 Meter Backstroke—Melissa Belote—USA.

Women's Diving
Three Meter Springboard—Micki King—USA.
Platform—Ulrika Knape—Sweden.

Men's Diving
Springboard—Vladimir Vasin—Soviet Union.
Platform—Klaus DiBiasi—Italy.

Men's Track & Field
20-Kilometer Walk—Peter Frenkel—E. Germany.
100-Meter Dash—Valery Borzov—Soviet Union.
400-Meter Hurdles—John Akiibua—Uganda.
800 Meter Run—Dave Wottle—Canton Ohio—USA.
Discus Throw—Ludwik Danek—Czechoslovakia.
Pole Vault—Wolfgang Nordwig—E. Germany.
Javelin Throw—Klaus Wolfermann—W. Germany.
10,000 Meter Run—Lasse Viren—Finland.
50 Kilometer Walk—Bernd Kannenberg—W. Germany.
3,000 Meter Steeplechase—Kipchoge Keino—Kenya.
Triple Jump—Victor Sanev—Soviet Union.
200—Meter Dash—Valery Borzov—Soviet Union.
100 Meter Hurdles—Rod Milburn—USA.
400 Meter Run—Vince Matthews—USA.
Hammer Throw—Anatol Bondarchuk—Soviet Union.
Decathlon—Nikolai Avilov—Soviet Union.
Long Jump—Randy Williams—USA.
Shot Put—Wladyslaw Komar—Poland.
1,500 Meter Run—Pekka Vasala—Finland.
High Jump—Juri Tarmak—Soviet Union.
5,000 Meter Run—Lasse Viren—Finland.
400 Meter Relay—USA.
1,600 Meter Relay—Kenya.
Marathon—Frank Shorter—USA.

Women's Track & Field
Long Jump—Heide Rosendahl—W. Germany.
Javelin—Ruth Fuchs—E. Germany.
100 Meter Dash—Renate Stecher—E. Germany.
Pentathlon—Mary Peters—England.
800 Meter Run—Hildegard Falck—W. Germany.
High Jump—Ulrika Meyfarth—W. Germany.
200 Meter Dash—Renate Stecher—E. Germany.
Shot Put—Nadezhda Chizhova—Soviet Union.
400 Meter Dash—Monika Zehrt—E. Germany.
100 Meter Hurdles—Annelie Ehrhardt—E. Germany.
1,500 Meter Run—Ludmila Bragina—Soviet Union.
400 Meter Relay—W. Germany.
Discus Throw—Faina Melnik—Soviet Union.
1,600 Meter Relay—E. Germany.

Men's Canoeing
Canadian Two Man Slalom—Walter Hofmann & Rolf Dieter Amend—E. Germany.
Kayak Slalom—Siegbert Horn—E. Germany.
Canadian Slalom—Reinhard Eiben—E. Germany.
Kayak Singles—Aleksandr Shaparenko—Soviet Union.
Canadian Singles—Ivan Patzaichin—Rumania.
Kayak Pairs—Nikolai Gorbachev & Viktor Kratassyuk—Soviet Union.
Canadian Pairs—Vladas Chessyunas & Yuri Lobanov—Soviet Union.
Kayak Fours—Soviet Union.

Women's Canoeing
Single Kayak Slalom—Angelike Bahmann—E. Germany.
Kayak Singles—Yulia Ryabchinskaya—Soviet Union.
Kayak Pairs—Ludmila Pinayeva & Ekaterina Kuryshko—Soviet Union.

Women's Volleyball
Team Championship—Soviet Union.

Men's Volleyball
Team Championship—Japan.

Water Polo
Team Championship—Soviet Union.

Soccer
Championship—Poland.

Weight Lifting
Flyweight—Zygmun Smalcerz—Poland.
Bantamweight—Imre Foeldi—Hungary.
Featherweight—Norair Nurikyan—Bulgaria.
Lightweight—Mukharbi Kirshinov—Soviet Union.
Middleweight—Yordan Bikov—Bulgaria.
Heavyweight—Van Talts—Soviet Union.
Super Heavyweight—Vassili Alaxayev—Soviet Union.

Greco-Roman Wrestling
105.5 Pounds—Gheorghe Berceanu—Rumania.
114.5 Pounds—Petar Kirov—Bulgaria.
125.5 Pounds—Rustem Kazakov—Soviet Union.
136.5 Pounds—Gheorghi Markov—Bulgaria.
149.5 Pounds—Shamil Khisamutdinov—Soviet Union.
163.5 Pounds—Vietzlav Macha—Czechoslovakia.
180.0 Pounds—Csaba Hegedus—Hungary.
198.0 Pounds—Valery Rezantsev—Soviet Union.
220.0 Pounds—Nicolae Martinescu—Rumania.
Over 220 Pounds—Anataoly Roshin—Soviet Union.

Yachting
Soling—Harry Melges—USA.
Dragon—John Bruce—Australia.
Star—David Forbes—Australia.[9]
Flying Dutchman—Rodney Pattison—Britain.
Tempest—Valentin Mankin—Soviet Union.
Finn—Serge Maury—France.

THE WORLD IN 1972—INDEX